JESUS IN Q

JESUS IN Q

The Sabbath and Theology of the Bible and Extracanonical Texts

KY-CHUN SO

Foreword by Dennis R. MacDonald

WIPF & STOCK · Eugene, Oregon

JESUS IN Q
The Sabbath and Theology of the Bible and Extracanonical Texts

Copyright © 2017 Ky-Chun So. All rights reserved. Except for brief quotations in critical publications or reviews, no part of this book may be reproduced in any manner without prior written permission from the publisher. Write: Permissions, Wipf and Stock Publishers, 199 W. 8th Ave., Suite 3, Eugene, OR 97401.

Wipf & Stock
An Imprint of Wipf and Stock Publishers
199 W. 8th Ave., Suite 3
Eugene, OR 97401

www.wipfandstock.com

PAPERBACK ISBN: 978-1-4982-8211-6
HARDCOVER ISBN: 978-1-4982-8213-0

Manufactured in the U.S.A.   MARCH 24, 2017

This book is dedicated with love to James M. Robinson
(June 30, 1924–March 22, 2016)
who variously shared, endured, satirized, but encouraged my efforts since 1978.

Contents

Foreword by Dennis R. MacDonald | ix
Introduction | xi

Part 1: Sabbath and the Gentile Mission

    I   Jewish Sabbath | 3
    II   Sabbath Institutions and Observances | 14
    III   Q 14:5 and a Jewish Christian Community | 23
    IV   Jesus and Jewish Law | 34
    V   The Sabbath in the Synoptics | 52
    VI   Between Jewish Law and the Gentile Mission | 70
    VII   The Gentiles in the Synoptics | 87
    VIII Euanggelion and the Gentile Mission | 112

Part 2: Theology of Q and the Gospels

    IX   Predating the Sayings Gospel Q | 125
    X   The God of Jesus | 137
    XI   Jesus' Understanding of Spirit | 146
    XII   The Eschatology of the Q Community | 157
    XIII A Tradition-History Development of the Meals | 166
    XIV The Narrative of the Raising of the Widow's Son from Nain | 174
    XV   Korean Recent Trends in the Study of the Gospels | 186

Part 3: Jewish Influences and Christological Insights

    XVI   A Theological and Anthropological Understanding of Creation | 205
    XVII A Rhetorical Aspect in the Wisdom of Solomon | 213
    XVIII Thomas Christianity | 220
    XIX   Jewish Gnosticism in the Apocalypse of Adam | 233

XX   PssSol and Q in the Christological Insights | 244
XXI   Religion and Science | 276
XXII Robinson's Impacts on the Scholarship of the New Testament and Q | 289

Conclusion | *301*
Bibliography | *307*

Foreword

WHAT A PRIVILEGE TO write this preface for *Jesus in Q: The Sabbath and Theology of the Bible and Extraconanical Texts*! As this title suggests, Ky-Chun (James) So offers here a far-reaching assessment of Jewish influences on early Christian theology (especially with respect to Sabbath observance and the Gentile mission), how the lost Gospel Q looked back to the teachings of Jesus and informed the Synoptic Gospels, and the importance of apocryphal Jewish texts in shaping emerging Christologies. One also will find here chapters on "Religion and Science" and "Korean Recent Trends in the Study of the Gospels." This volume thus represents the culmination of three decades of research and teaching by a pillar of New Testament studies in Korea and beyond.

So's most important scholarly contribution may have been his consistent advocacy for the study of the lost Gospel Q in Korea, where few scholars have been skeptical of the Two-Document Hypothesis and the existence of Q. His facility with the Synoptic Gospels and Q scholarship was apparent as early as his 1998 doctoral dissertation at the Claremont Graduate University under the direction of Professor James M. Robinson, to whom he graciously dedicates the book and its final chapter. Throughout his career So encouraged students and younger colleagues to investigate Q for its own sake but also for its contributions to Matthew and Luke, not to mention modern appreciation of the growth of early reflections on traditions about Jesus. Parts 1 and 2 of this book represent his mature and distinctive views on these issues, including their enduring significance for religious life.

The author of Q could not have chosen a better interpreter of his writing than he insofar as he painstakingly assesses the ambiguities and tensions in the text as advocates of the Two-Document Hypothesis generally reconstruct it, as in *The Critical Edition of Q* (edited by James M. Robinson, Paul Hoffmann, and John S. Kloppenborg [Fortress, 2000]). This reconstruction is not the only one available, and I, of course, prefer the one I published in *Two Shipwrecked Gospels* (Society of Biblical Literature, 2012). These two reconstructions are significantly different from each other and often differ precisely on the central issue So discusses in this book, namely, Jesus' attitude toward Jewish Torah. Simply stated, the more conventional textual reconstruction views Q as a rather loose collection of Jesus' sayings that later was given a modest narrative. My reconstruction suggests that is was a polemical substitution for the book of Deuteronomy in which Jesus is depicted as the promised prophet like Moses. Its attitude toward Jewish law thus is more hostile than most commentators, including So, have held.

This preface is not intended to be an advertisement of my own book but a celebration of So and his exemplary career. I mention my work because I think it assists the reader in appreciating the book at hand in two ways. First, it reminds the reader that research on Q is not stagnant but vital; much more work needs to be done. After all, any reconstruction of the lost gospel is conjectural and hypothetical.

Second, even though my reconstruction differs from the one this book largely endorses, it confirms the essential correctness of So's major conclusions as follows:

- Jesus did not overturn Jewish law but humanized it, placing human welfare above torah purity, what So calls Jesus' commitment to God's love.
- Although Jesus' attitude to the law was evolutionary it also was revolutionary.
- The author of Q struggled with the demands of the law on one hand and the love of God on the other, which accounts for apparent paradoxes and ambiguities throughout So's work.
- The Q community welcomed the Gentile mission but was not actively engaged in it. Jesus' immediate followers were to missionize other Jews.
- The community responsible for Q seems to have merged into the Matthean community, where attitudes toward torah changed and commitments to the Gentile mission expanded.
- After the failure of Q to survive intact and the absorption of its community into other early Christian groups, according to So, the distinctive voice of Jesus was variously and creatively transformed.

My own work confirms each of these conclusions and suggests that So's fair, extensive, and nuanced treatment of Gospel texts and mountains of scholarly literature is an enduring contribution to New Testament scholarship. I thus applaud the publication of this work and encourage its readers to relish its breadth, erudition, and provocative insights.

Dennis R. MacDonald

Introduction

THIS BOOK, *JESUS IN Q*, looks like an electric plug because the true bulb lights on when we plug into Jesus, i.e., the Gospel. The Gospel does not simply express a Jesus tradition that exists only in the memories of an evangelist and his reader. The Gospel texts take place in the context of special social events and draw together the past and the present, reaffirm traditional social values and understandings, and connect a community in its present with its traditions or its past. The Jesus tradition's textual shape arises in the Gospel texts, but the tradition itself exists prior to and outside of texts. Hence there are the source texts and the receptor texts in the Gospels.

The case of the source texts and the receptor texts is explained in the relationship between the Q text, which is the source text, and the Gospel of Matthew or the Gospel of Luke, which are the receptor texts in the Synoptics. The Gospel of Matthew and the Gospel of Luke used, and from their point of view improved, a very archaic written Greek sayings gospel and its existence was postulated through a careful study from the sources of Matthew and Luke, which has a nickname, "Q," from the German word for source, *Quelle*. This was no longer copied by Christian scribes, who preferred to copy Matthew and Luke, for this reason, no manuscripts of this lost gospel have survived. Scholars in Claremont of the United States, Toronto of Canada, and Bamberg of Germany have worked in reconstituting this lost gospel, word by word. By observing how Matthew and Luke edited their other main source, the Gospel of Mark, which has survived, one can establish and understand their editing policies. Then, when these are detected in Matthew or Luke, they can be discounted in Q sayings. The text of the Sayings Gospel Q,[1] which is the earliest gospel or the closest known account on the history of Jesus, behind Matthew and Luke could thus be reconstructed.

1. The International Q Project (IQP), sponsored by the Society of Biblical Literature (SBL) and the Institute for Antiquity and Christianity (IAC), has assembled a massive database of opinions by scholars over the past 180 years about the Sayings Gospel Q. After sorting English, German, and French excerpts from scholarly works in chronological order, the IQP has begun publishing the enormous database under the title *Documenta Q: Reconstructions of Q through Two Centuries of Gospel Research Excerpted, Sorted and Evaluated* at Peeters in Leuven since 1996. The IQP also published a one-volume critical edition of Q, which is already being edited in eight columns under the title *The Critical Edition of Q: A Synopsis Including the Gospels of Matthew and Luke, Mark and Thomas with English, German*

Introduction

Jesus tradition is the story in the texts of the historical Jesus; Q tradition is the memory in the texts of the sayings of Jesus. The tradition's stability and variability in texts are rooted in the early memory of Jesus as well as in the memory of various texts, i.e., retellings that were exerted on the Q community itself. The particular text of Jesus tradition transmits the same form that the earliest Sayings Gospel Q transmitted, even if the verbal and sequential structure of the latter texts did not, and could not have, reproduced exactly the verbal and sequential structure of earlier texts of Jesus. When Jesus tradition is composed in texts, the performative environment forms the textual shape of the Jesus tradition. But this textual shape is one embodiment of Jesus tradition; Jesus tradition itself, i.e., its essence, transcends the textual shape. Thus Q text actualizes the Jesus tradition, and the Q community enters into it and perceives the Q text in reference to their ambient tradition of the historical Jesus.

My focus of interest in this book is not the exegesis of biblical texts, nor is it to reconstruct the primitive text of the Sayings Gospel Q. My attention focuses on the presence of sayings of Jesus in the early literatures. This is why I have chosen to limit the examination to the Sabbath controversy and the theology of Jesus in Q, and to the texts of the Hebrew Bible and the Gospels and Apocrypha in which literary influence of the sayings of Jesus is manifested. In the course of my study, I shall often speak of literary contact.

Historical approaches are based on the application of logical rules and deductive reasoning to the available evidence in texts, but the proper application of these rules requires an understanding of the cultural and historical context of the evidence in texts. The essential starting point in studying ancient texts is the effort to understand the perspectives, motives, and biases of the author that underlie the words of the texts. However, the literary sources provide a useful perspective to our subject if understood in their proper context. A proper understanding of basic historical methodology and its application to written materials will, therefore, greatly enhance our appreciations of literary sources. I mean to use the term "literary" in a rather strict sense, when speaking of contact, sufficiently striking verbal concurrence puts the discussion in a context that already points toward the sayings of Jesus. These literary contacts do not exhaust the literary influence of the sayings: one can expect, without a properly so-called literary contact, the use of typical vocabulary, themes, and ideas of the sayings of Jesus.

James M. Robinson, referring to the problem of the Sayings Gospel Q and the Torah, has suggested that "Q refrains from presenting Jesus violating Torah."[2] Robinson argued that the Q community did not portray Jesus as "consciously repudiating parts of Torah," but neither did it invoke torah as a source of "proof-texts," because the

---

and French Translations of Q and Thomas at Fortress in Philadelphia and Peeters in Leuven, 2000, and *The Sayings Gospel Q in Greek and English with Parallels from the Gospels of Mark and Thomas* at Fortress in Minneapolis, 2002.

2. Robinson, "Sayings of Jesus," 32.

INTRODUCTION

Q community was not "a rabbinic school." Rather, the Q text is "an interpretation of Torah." Q represents Jesus as the representative of a "radicalized or idealized Torah." Indeed, Q is interested in an "interpretation rather than a violation of Torah." Then in Robinson's view, the Q community stood somewhere between those who accepted the law and its traditional interpretation and those who rejected it completely such as the ones in favor of a Gentile mission.

This book builds on Robinson's observations by seeking to locate Q's attitude toward the law and Gentiles more precisely. An important text in this regard is Q 14:5 reconstructed from verbal agreements among Matt 12:11 and Luke 14:5. Though often regarded as isolated sayings, a closer examination suggests they derive from a common source that is form-critically and redaction-critically close to the block material in Q 13:24—14:35. This book regards Q 14:5 as a historical saying of Jesus, rather than an eschatological and christological saying engendered by the early church.

The point of this discussion is that the Q community was not merely a passive onlooker as the Gentile mission unfolded, but by creatively using the Jewish tradition it helped create the rationale for a Gentile mission and thus was instrumental for its ultimate success. It is likely that the Q community contributed in some way to the early Christian missionary activity from the Jewish mission to the Gentile mission. Even though the Q community did not carry out a strong Gentile mission, it must have affected the missionary activity of the early Christian communities as they wrestled with the tension between the Jewish law and the Gentile mission. They were a true Christian community because of their fidelity in practicing God's love as a Christian missionary principle.

In order to determine exactly and define the extent of the influence of the sayings of Jesus, this book is divided into several chapters. Each corresponding to a stage of the influence, the attitude of authors toward other Hebrew and New Testament writings ought to be examination as a basis for comparison. I consider the early Fathers, who have generally used in a free way, the sayings of Jesus drawn from the Gospels or/and oral tradition. I look to the later writings, which manifest a wider usage and contain citations not only of the legislative sayings of Jesus but also of the biblical texts in the parables, narratives, paraenesis, and controversies of Jesus. I also examine the Apologists, whose writings constitute a well-defined literary genre and give witness progressively to a more bookish use of the sayings of Jesus. I also take the Wisdom of Solomon and the Psalms of Solomon for rooting the announcement of Jesus in early Judaism because I understand the two extracanonical documents in early Judaism as a prerequisite for understanding the appearances of Jesus. And I try to observe the Apocalypse of Adam under Jewish influences to show that Jewish influences in the Apocalypse of Adam are not only with regard to images which are derived from the Hebrew Bible, but also with regard to traditional Jewish themes. These apocryphal studies would help explore the place of Jesus within early Judaism.

Introduction

The usage of the sayings of Jesus from the Synoptics to second-century Christian literatures is not identical to the history of the canon or to the extracanonical status of individual books. However, the sayings of Jesus were both known and used by the late first or the early second century furthermore increased frequency as time passed. Nevertheless, I argue that biblical texts in first- and second-century literatures were primarily dependent not only on the written gospels, but also on the oral tradition of the church. Whether the earliest Fathers of the church knew the written Synoptic or if they were dependent primarily on the same pre-Synoptic oral tradition, a study of the influence of the sayings of Jesus on Christian literatures up to the time of the second century is critical for an understanding of both the development of the canon and the rich diversity of second-century Christianity. Later on it is viewed as both orthodox and heterodox manifestations.

Overall there studies look at the links between early Christian literatures and the New Testament. Nevertheless, a detailed and exhaustive study considering the place and influence of the sayings of Jesus in the first centuries would still have its usefulness. Moreover, biblical texts of these general works propose the most diverse and contradictory opinions. These reasons have led me to examine in detail and in a systematic fashion how and in what measure the influence of the sayings of Jesus has exerted itself from early times to second-century Christian literatures.

This book constitutes a revised version of my doctoral dissertation, "The Sabbath Controversy of Jesus: Between Jewish Law and the Gentile Mission," which was publicly finished at the Claremont Graduate University, Claremont, California, in August 1998. It is one of several studies within the multidisciplinary project of the International Q Project at the Claremont Graduate University, sponsored by the Society of Biblical Literature, to which I am especially gratefully, since their sponsorship has enabled me to do this research.

I am also grateful to various minor or major funds of the president Allen Moore scholarships at the Claremont School of Theology, of the full fellows and scholarships at the Claremont Graduate University, and of the several sabbatical permissions at the Presbyterian University and Theological Seminary. I wish to express my thanks to my adviser James M. Robinson for inviting me to participate as an acting member in the International Q Project, for giving me doctoral student scholarships at the School of Religion at the Claremont Graduate University and for allowing me the intellectual freedom to develop new perspectives and experiment in matters of methodology. I wish to express my deepest thanks to him for their numerous and lively discussions, which have been of enormous help in defining my position, and for his indefatigable work of reading and commenting on the manifold versions of this book. James M. Robinson gave me the topic for this book, helped me to ask questions, encouraged me for what turned out to be a long haul, and spent his time with me while I was working on Q in the International Q Project. I now dedicate this book to him.

INTRODUCTION

There are numerous people to whom thanks are due. Thanks are due to Dennis MacDonald, who visited me at the Presbyterian University and Theological Seminary to present his paper on Q+,[3] to Gregory J. Riley, who pushed me to formulate my own ideas and made many helpful suggestions on this book, and to William A. Beardslee, who brought the academic realities into focus and made this book a stronger, more clearly argued presentation.

Thanks are due to James Sanders, who challenged me to understand a methodology of midrash interpretation as well as intertextuality and canonical criticism. His profound knowledge of Jewish studies in general and rabbinic Judaism in particular, as well as his interest in Jewish-Christian relations, made him the perfect teacher for thorough and stimulating discussions.

For additional financial support involving the Society of Biblical Literature, I wish to thank Kilian P. McDonnell, OSB, who gave me hospitality during my sabbatical stay in the spring and summer of 2005 and is the founder of the Institute for Ecumenical Cultural Research at Saint John's University, Collegeville, Minnesota.

Gratias agimus tibi propter magnam gloriam tuam.
(We give thanks to you for your great glory.)

---

3. His paper was published by the Society of Korean Q. Cf. MacDonald, "Alternative Q," 62–77.

PART 1

Sabbath and the Gentile Mission

I

Jewish Sabbath

PROLOGUE

THIS CHAPTER EXAMINES MEANINGS and regulations of the Sabbath from the Hebrew Bible in order to investigate the background of Jesus' attitude to the Sabbath. Moreover, this chapter constructs Jesus' overall understanding of the Jewish law in relation to the range of the law. Hence, this chapter examines punishment in the prophetic writings where most of the Sabbath accounts seem to be seen in relation to the sign of the covenant between God and Israel. For this reason, this chapter investigates the Sabbath and its meaning in relation to the Jews from the Hebrew Bible.

The aim of primary study is to prepare the Sabbath controversy of Jesus because this chapter presupposes that Jesus was influenced by the background of such a Jewish tradition on the Sabbath in the Hebrew Bible. This book turns to Sabbath and its regulation in order to investigate how the Jewish Sabbath developed as a social institution.

The question of Jesus' relation to Jewish law is not only one of the important issues to the Christian origin in the Synoptic Gospels, but one of the difficult ones to the reconstruction of early Christianity. It is therefore of vital importance to ask the more basic question: What was Jesus' attitude to the Jewish law? Was the conflict with the Pharisees the cause of his woes in Q? What was Jesus' attitude to the Sabbath in relation to the Jewish law and the Gentile mission? The traditional way of handling these questions is to proceed exegetically. R. Banks has correctly stressed the need to distinguish among the written law, the oral law and customs is assessing Jesus' relationship to the Judaism of his day.[1] With respect to the Jewish law, Jesus kept the Sabbath and wished his followers to observe it faithfully. Jesus' personal observance of the Sabbath is undoubtedly rooted in the Hebrew Bible.

Hence, this chapter begins to investigate meanings and regulations of the Sabbath within the Hebrew Bible so that the background of Jesus' attitude to the Sabbath

---

1. Banks, *Jesus and the Law*, 90–91.

can be revealed. Moreover, it will form Jesus' overall understanding of the Jewish law relating to the scope of the law.

The Holy Sabbath Day

The most important of all Israelite holy days is the Sabbath,[2] which is the longest commandment in the Decalogue. Ahad Ha-'Am, a Hebrew essayist, points out the significance of the Sabbath for the Jewish people in the history of Israel and says, "More than Israel has kept the Sabbath, it is the Sabbath that has kept Israel."[3] Thus all the Jews are told to "remember the Sabbath and to keep it holy" (Exod 20:8) because the Sabbath is described as the sign of the covenant between God and the Israelites.[4] From this perspective, this chapter shall describe the Sabbath not only as a memorial of holy festival based on the creation (Gen 2:2–3; Exod 20:11) and the exodus (Deut 5:15), but as the sign of the covenant in Israel's understanding of her covenant relationship with God (Exod 31:13–17).[5] R. J. Rushdoony also applies this implication and understands the Sabbath as a sign of the Mosaic covenant.[6]

The greatest interest of the Sabbath among Hebrew Bible scholars relate to finding the meaning of rest on the basis of the creation. The passage in Gen 2:1–4a; Exod 20:8–11; 31:13–17 mention the "divine rest motif"[7] of the Sabbath which is established by God's creation activity. These passages can be compared with the old Babylonian creation epic *Enuma Elish*,[8] which surely existed prior to the three passages in the Priestly writings. Of course, there are other passages (2 Chron 6:41; Ps 95:11; 132:8; Isa 40:27–28; 66:1) about the divine rest. However, here in the creation Sabbath, God rests on the seventh day after the creation activity of the previous six days. Why does God rest on the seventh day? These passages answer that God created the entire creation during the six days and rested on the seventh day right after his act of creating humanity. This answer firmly establishes the Sabbath and the divine rest on the basis of the creation alone: The seventh day is called the Sabbath; therefore, the Jews keep it holy as a day of rest because

---

2. Moore, *Judaism*, 21.

3. I quote this from Milgram, *Sabbath*, 1.

4. Moore, *Judaism*, 21: "The Sabbath is called 'an eternal covenant,' 'an eternal sign' (cf. Ezek 20:12) between God and Israel (Exod 31:16–17; cf. 31:13)."

5. McCarthy, *Old Testament Covenant*, 57–58. He investigates the relationship between the cult and the covenant or the "covenant feast," i.e., "there was surely a ceremony which instituted covenant and repaired or renewed it when it was broken."

6. For more information, see his *Institutes of Biblical Law*, 128.

7. Andreasen, *Old Testament Sabbath*, 185. He concludes that the "divine rest motif" is also in other Near Eastern creation myths and there the creative deities rested after their creative works, especially "immediately after the creation of man." Cf. Von Rad, "There Remains," 96: "This notion of 'rest' now comes to occupy an important place in the religious thought of Israel. It is thought of as a rest found by the weary nation through the grace of God in the land he has promised them."

8. *Enuma Elish* is regarded as a creation epic written in the period of the first part of the second millennium, the old Babylonian period BCE. Cf. Heidel, *Babylonian Genesis*, 13–14.

God rested after his creative works. Andreasen argues that "the seven-day scheme was attached to the creation account prior to the association between the seventh day and the creation Sabbath" (ibid., 186) and that "the special role of the seventh day is merely a by-product, under the influence of the Sabbath institution, of the seven-day scheme by which the creation account is framed" (ibid., 187).

It is generally perceived that a "rest" is a "divine rest" in the Hebrew Bible.[9] Gen 2:1–4a states God's creation activity in the description of the divine rest[10] on the seventh day (2–3)[11] and an epilogue (1, 4a) to the whole creation activity[12] in Gen 1. On the one hand, it is worthwhile to note that vv. 2–3 do not mention the noun שַׁבָּת[13] but instead the verb שָׁבַת (2b, 3b)[14] and the phrase "the seventh day" (2a, 2b, 3a).[15] In the Hebrew Bible שַׁבָּת is usually addressed with יוֹם (Exod 20:8, 11; 31:15; Num 15:23; 28:9; Deut 5:12; Neh 10:31; 13:5, 17, 19, 22; Jer 17:21–22, 24; Ezek 46:1, 4) and with בְּשַׁבַּתּוֹ (Num 28:10; Is 66:23). שַׁבָּת is also used for certain festivals, such as the day of atonement (Lev 16:31; 23:32), the day of trumpets (Lev 23:24), and the days of the festival (Lev 23:39). Moreover, שַׁבָּת is associated with new moon and other festivals (Isa 1:13; Hos 2:11; Amos 8:5; 2 Kgs 4:26). At the same time, שָׁבַת is used for the Sabbatical year (Exod 21:2–6; 23:10–11; Deut 15:1–8).[16] In the exilic and postexilic literature the phrase "the seventh day" is identified with the noun "שַׁבָּת."[17] This seems to mean that the initial purpose of the priestly writer was related to the divine rest after God's creative work, not to the "recognition of the Sabbath institution."[18] Sabbath's association with the noun שַׁבָּת is a "post-exilic development" and the basic meaning of the root שָׁבַת is "coming to an end or completion." Hence the seventh day brings the work of the preceding days to completion. From this perspective, it is likely that "rest from work" is not a central issue in the Hebrew Bible, at least, in the preexilic writings.[19]

---

9. Von Rad, "There Remains," 96.

10. Robinson, "Idea of Rest," 32–42; Braulik, "Menuchah," 75–78.

11. Clause Westermann argues that 2a and 3a include the key motif of the creation in Gen 1 and that 2b and 3a. See his *Genesis 1–11*, 232.

12. Von Rad, "There Remains," 113.

13. For this sort of argument regarding the relationship between the Sabbath and new moon, see McKay, *Sabbath*, 11–42.

14. Andreasen proposes that this verb means "cease," "stop," "come to an end" and that it is frequently translated as "rest" (Gen 2:2, 3; Exod 5:5; 16:30; 23:12; 31:17; 34:21; Lev 23:34–35) and "keep Sabbath" (Lev 23:32; 25:2; 2 Chron 36:21). For more information, see ibid., 104–7.

15. For more information, see Andreasen, *Old Testament Sabbath*, 108, 113–16.

16. For more information, see ibid., 108–11.

17. However, the attempts to relate "שַׁבָּת" to the seventh day date back to "premonarchical and undoubtedly to Mosaic times" (ibid., 8, 117–21).

18. Ibid., 193.

19. Bloch, *Biblical and Historical Background*, 1: "Semitic tradition, prior to the Torah did not prescribe and official day of rest. The verse in Genesis proclaiming the Sabbath a holy day (2:3) was not followed by a provision for enforced rest, nor did it prescribe a ritual observance"; Robinson, "Idea of Rest," 42.

Here we can assume that the Sabbath could not have been a rest institution originally. Thus the Sabbath is released from its religious and cultic attachment and put to new use in the structure of the Priestly account of creation.[20] Therefore, the Sabbath does not seem to be conceived of as a socio-religious or cultic phenomenon. On the other hand, the Sabbath here cannot be seen as "creation ordinance,"[21] which is not a useful term to understand the creation Sabbath.[22] The term "creation ordinances" is said to "originate with an inescapable necessity and thus must be considered as implied in the divine plan of creation."[23] Gen 2:2–3 does not state a religious and cultic festival or any Sabbath institution. Rather the passage mentions that God accomplished his creative work during the six days and that he rested on the seventh day. This explanation is further supported by the terms in Exod 20:11 (34:21; cf. Deut 5:14) and 31:17 (23:12): "וַיָּ֫נַח" (rested) and "וַיִּנָּפַשׁ" (refreshed). This may explain that the divine rest after the six days of creation activity provides an "etiology of the Sabbath."[24] This may be closer to the real explanation, which the priestly writer was capable of giving for the seventh day. On the Sabbath,[25] God stopped working, but he had "completed"[26] his work, therefore he "rested" and was "refreshed." Thus the Hebrew Bible understands the reason for the Sabbath rest as a divine command.

Exod 20:8–11 states the creation Sabbath motif in the description of the fourth commandment and spells out the objective of the Sabbath as "the proclamation of monotheism, stressing man's obligation to God."[27] The passage constitutes the general introduction to the fourth commandment (8) as well as the specific regulations on the Sabbath law (9–10). Moreover, the reason for the Sabbath regulations referring to God's creation and rest (11a) is seen within the passage. Finally, the conclusion on the Sabbath in its blessing (11b) is illustrated. Unlike Gen 2:2–3,[28] here in Exod 20:9 the seventh day is specifically applied to the "Sabbath." Andreasen also proposes that in the creation Sabbath theme in Gen 2:2–3 provided a specific conclusion to the creation

---

20. Andreasen, *Old Testament Sabbath*, 194.

21. The concept of God's ordinances (originally, "my ordinances") is found is Ezekiel 20 (11, 13, 16, 19, 21, 24–25) in relation to the Sabbath as a sign of the covenant between God and Israel. For this sort of argument, see Piper, *Christian Ethic*, 159.

22. The argument of "creation ordinances" could theoretically carry force; however, its advocates exegetically have great difficulty in making the case that the priestly writer treated the Sabbath in this way.

23. Beckwith and Stott, *This Is the Day*, 6–7.

24. In fact, scholars often speak of an "etiology" of the Sabbath. For a discussion of some of these features, see Long, *Problem of Etiological Narrative*, 6–7, 87; Childs, *Book of Exodus*, 415.

25. Gen 2:2–3 does not state the term "Sabbath." Rather it speaks of the "seventh day." Unless the reader identifies the "seventh day" with the "Sabbath," there is no reference to the Sabbath here.

26. Von Rad, *Genesis*, 62; Lincoln, "From Sabbath to Lord's Day," 348: "The seventh day is to be seen as representing the completion of the whole creation."

27. Bloch, *Biblical and Historical Background*, 4.

28. Andreasen argues both similarities and dissimilarities between Gen 2:2–3 and Exod 20:8–11. Cf. ibid., 198–99.

account and Exod 20:9–10 brought a reason for the Sabbath regulation.[29] Therefore, one can also regard v. 11 as "a further feature typical of an etiology."[30] Lincoln pays attention to the word play between the terms "the seventh day" and the "Sabbath." He also argues that the presence of these features in v. 11 can be seen as providing an explanation of a present institution, which is the mosaic Sabbath, by reference to a past event, God's rest on the seventh day after the creation, utilizing the terminology of Gen 2:3.[31] Exod 20:8 commands "remembering" or "thinking about" the Sabbath.[32]

Exodus 31:13–17 mentions a "sign (אוֹת)" (31:13a) of the covenant between God and Israel in the description of sanctifying Israel (13b), of the holiness of the Sabbath (14a, 15a), and of "solemn rest" (15a). Above all, here in Exod 31:13a the Sabbath itself is called a "sign" of the whole relationship between God and Israel (cf. Ezek 20:12, 20). Then the Sabbath is called a "perpetual covenant" (16b). The sign, which is further described as a sign of God's creation works during the six days and rest on the seventh, is also a "sign forever" (17). M. G. Kline points out similarities in this perspective between ancient Near Eastern treaties and the biblical covenants. He argues that the biblical covenants were purposes in accomplishing redemption in the midst of the historical process.[33] For this reason, the Sabbath is described as a sign of the permanent relationship between God and Israel (13, 16–17). Therefore, it is not strange at all that the mosaic Sabbath functions as a sign and memorial of God's creative activity and its consummation in God's rest. On the other hand, "the seventh day is a Sabbath to the Lord *your* God" in 20:10 and "you shall keep *my* Sabbaths" in 31:13 seem to show the nature of the Sabbath.[34] God's ownership of the Sabbath[35] attributes the Sabbath to the divine creation activity and commands Israel to keep it holy. Thus the holiness of the Sabbath commands Israel to rest from working on the seventh day.

The Sabbath Accounts in the Prophetic Writings

Now this chapter shall move to examine punishment in the prophetic writings where most of the Sabbath accounts seem to be seen in relation to the sign of the covenant between God and Israel. In Exod 31:13 the Sabbath is designated as "a sign between me [God] and you [Israel]," which is fitted not only into the immediate context (Exod

---

29. Ibid., 199.
30. Lincoln, "From Sabbath to Lord's Day," 349.
31. Ibid.
32. Avemarie and Lichtenberger, *Bund und Tora*, 121.
33. Kline, *Structure of Biblical Authority*, 94–96.
34. Here the affinity of the Sabbath to holiness is expressed. Cf. Bloch, *Biblical and Historical Background*, 7.
35. To the Jews the Sabbath was an institution peculiar to their religion; it belongs to their God (Exod 16:25), and is sacred unto him (Exod 16:23); he calls them "my Sabbaths" (Ezek 20:12, 16, 20; Isa 56:4).

19:5–7; 24:7–8; 34:10, 27–28).[36] But also as a sign of the covenant, the Sabbath is also found in Ezekiel (20:12–24; 22:8, 26; 23:38).

First, Ezek 20:12–24 declares one of the most prominent references to the Sabbath in terms of Israel's covenant relationship with God: "Moreover I gave them my Sabbaths, as a sign between me and them so that they might know that I the Lord sanctify them" (12; cf. 20:20). W. Eichrodt denies that in Ezekiel the Sabbath materials are original, because he argues that the priestly writer inserted them into Ezekiel in order to declare the universal Sabbath institution.[37] Why did God want to sanctify his Sabbath? The reason is that Israel rebelled against God in the wilderness (13a, 13b, 17, 21b, 23) and profaned his Sabbath (13a, 16, 21a, 24), which God acted for the sake of his name (14, 22; cf. 20:9), and that Israel rejected his ordinances (13, 16) and did not observe them (19, 21, 24). In the characteristic manner of Ezekiel 20, the Sabbath materials fit well to the threats of judgment (15, 23, and 25).[38] Ezek 22:8, on the one hand, declares directly a threat of punishment in the description of a judgment oracle against Jerusalem (1–16), which fits consistently with the whole book of Ezekiel.[39] For this reason, Ezekiel contains "accusations directed against the general lack of respect for the sanctuary, holy items, and the Sabbath."[40] On the other hand, Ezek 22:26 is close to a threat of judgment oracle in the description of a punishment against all "the people in the land" (23–31). There are five different groups in the land: "its princes" (25), "its priests" (26), "its officers" (27), "its prophets" (28), "the people of the land" (29). The last seems to be the lay community (Ezek 46:3).[41] However, after the exile, the "people of the land" are often named "people of the land" and refer to "non-Jewish" or "faithless Jewish inhabitants of Judah." Ezek 23:38 also mentions profaned Sabbath in the description of a judgment against the two sisters, who represent the divided kingdoms of Judah and Israel (36–39).[42]

These passages (Ezek 20:12–24; 22:8, 26; 23:38) show that profaning the Sabbath was an act of breaking a sign of the covenant between God and Israel, and that judgment took place in the exile of Judah. In Ezek 22:31 the description of punishment seems to refer to a past event, probably the fall of Jerusalem in 587 BCE. In comparison with the judgment against breaking the Sabbath profanely, it is likely that keeping

---

36. Dressler, "Sabbath in the Old Testament," 30. For this sort of argument, see Cassuto, *Commentary on the Book of Exodus*, 404.

37. For more information, see Eichrodt, "Sabbat bei Hesekiel," 65–74. However, scholars refute Eichrodt's conclusion on the Sabbath materials in Ezekiel and suggest that Ezekiel 20 was written after 587 BCE at the exile in Babylonia (Eissfeldt, *Old Testament*, 376); Fohrer, *Hauptprobleme des Buches Ezechiel*, 83; Zimmerli, *Ezechiel*, 440; Andreasen, *Old Testament Sabbath*, 40–43.

38. Allen, *Ezekiel* 20–48, 11.

39. Zimmerli, *Ezechiel*, 509–10.

40. Andreasen, *Old Testament Sabbath*, 44.

41. For more information, see Andreasen, *Old Testament Sabbath*, 47. He argues that the "people of the land" refer to the "whole body of citizens."

42. Allen, *Ezekiel* 20–48, 48.

the Sabbath holy promised blessings for Israel in Ezekiel and Isaiah. The passages in Ezek 44:24; 45:17; 46:1–4 reflect keeping the Sabbath holy. Ezek 44:24 replaces the problem in Ezek 22:26, where the priests profaned the holy Sabbath of God. Ezek 45:17 assigns the duty of providing the Sabbath offerings to the prince. Ezek 46:1–4 reflects the roles of the prince (3, 4) and the people of the land (3). It seems that in Ezek 46:4 the six lambs and one ram correspond to the six days for work and the one day for keeping the Sabbath, although nothing reflects the actual practices.[43]

In relation to these passages in Ezekiel, the passages in Isa 56:2, 4, 6; 66:23; 58:13–14 also introduce a situation originated in "Jerusalem after the exile."[44]

Isa 56:2, 4, 6 mentions that all the members of community have to keep from profaning the Sabbath in the description of the status of foreigners and eunuchs in the community (1–7). Here scholars assume that the Sabbath may become a unique institution after the exile.[45] There is a reference to the new moon and the Sabbath in Isa 66:23, where the holy days are part of the delights of the future (cf. Ezek 46:3) as part of the vision of New Jerusalem given there.[46] J. D. Smart sees Isa 66:23 as describing a glorification of worship at the temple, with the climax of the new creation represented by renewed Sabbath worship.[47] From this perspective, Isa 66:23 does not mean that the Sabbath and the new moon should be used in "that way in this single place."[48] Rather, this reference seems to state that there should be worship on the Sabbath after the exile, referring to a future glorious age. After the exile, keeping the Sabbath holy seems to be recognized by the Israelites as the most conspicuous sign of their true covenant relationship with God.[49] The seventh day is consecrated to God as a sign of the sacred covenant between God and his people. An "unexpected promise"[50] given to the Israelites who keep the Sabbath holy: They will dwell in God's house and will be given an everlasting name (Isa 56:5). Andreasen says, "This promise strongly implies that God's covenant relationship no longer depends on one's national (or social) identity but on one's individual decision and devotion to YHWH, which is to be demonstrated by one keeping the Sabbath." In Isa 58:14 a stronger promise is also made, which is in comparison with the conditional clause in Isa 58:13. In Isaiah 58 the reference to the Sabbath in v. 14 climaxes in the situation after the exile. Here the unexpected promise is made: They will delight in the Lord. A kind of reward to the Israelites is

43. Andreasen, *Old Testament Sabbath*, 47; cf. Fohrer and Galling, *Ezechiel*, 254.

44. Andreasen, *Old Testament Sabbath*, 36, 39. However, Isa 66:23 can be dated later. Cf. Fohrer, *Introduction to the Old Testament*, 388.

45. Muilenburg, "Introduction and Exegesis," 248; Andreasen, *Old Testament Sabbath*, 38.

46. Watts, *Isaiah 1–33*, 21; McKay, *Sabbath and Synagogue*, 17–18: In order to understand Isa 66:23, she proposes that "the reader has to envisage all of a future humanity converging on Jerusalem, in some amicable and co-operative way, to given a concerted offering of worship to God."

47. Smart, *History and Theology*, 291–92.

48. Andreasen, *Old Testament Sabbath*, 40.

49. Sanders and Kent, "Messages of the Bible," 361.

50. Andreasen, *Old Testament Sabbath*, 44–45.

accompanied by keeping the Sabbath and joyfully honoring the holy day of the Lord (13). In relation to the heritage of Jacob, a promise as a reward for keeping the Sabbath holy is also seen in v. 14.

The Sabbath and Other Writings

This chapter moves to the book of Jubilees. Jubilees (οἱ Ἰωβηλαι) is sometimes called the Little Genesis (λεπτὴ Γένεσις). Jubilees relates the history of the Jews from the creation to the revelation of the law by God to Moses through the medium of the angel of the presence.[51] In Jubilees 2, we are told that there was a long passage on "the significance of the Sabbath as a sign"[52] (Jub 2:17–33). In the description of the significance of the Sabbath as sign, McKay observes: "day of rest and day on which the people are to eat and drink and bless the Creator." In the description of the divine creation activity, Jubilees 2 states the significance of the Sabbath (17–24) as a sign of God's election of "the seed of Jacob" as his people and the Sabbath regulations keeps it holy (25–33). First of all, Jubilees 2 declares that the sun has been created as a sign for days, Sabbath, months, feasts and years (Jub 2:9) and describes that the "angel of the presence and all the angels of holiness . . . keep the Sabbath day with Him in heaven and on earth" (18).[53] Jub 2:25 states that the Sabbath is holy due to divine creative work. Hence, those who profane the Sabbath should be put to death (25–27). In Jubilees 1:12, making war on the Sabbath is forbidden under penalty of death. This idea can be compared with the passage in Exod 31:15; 35:2; Num 15:35.[54] J. C. VanderKam argues that Jubilee 2 wanted "his fellows Jews to observe carefully the divine laws about sacrifice, festivals, Sabbath and the cultic calendar in order to advent the sort of punishments that God had meted out to their ancestors." However, Jub 2:28 contains a promise for those who keep the Sabbath holy and blessed like the angels.[55] Thus VanderKam argues that Jubilees 2 draws parallels between Israel and the Sabbath in terms of "an alternating induced harmony," which God had blessed and sanctified both Israel and the Sabbath. Therefore, "keeping the Sabbath holy means Israel's holiness is marked and through which it finds expression." Thus the Israelites are keeping the Sabbath holy as a sign in the relationship between God and Israel (Jub 2:25–33). Here the Sabbath has power to influence the relationship between God and Israel (Jub 2:25–33). Moreover, the Sabbath has power to influence the cosmic harmony on behalf of Israel.[56] Scholars

---

51. Zeitlin, "Book of Jubilees," 1. He dates Jubilees back to the fifth century BCE (ibid., 8–16). However, J. C. VanderKam prefers to date Jubilees around the first century BCE. See his *Textual and Historical Studies*, 283–84.

52. McKay, *Sabbath and Synagogue*, 56.

53. Wintermute, "Jubilees," 56.

54. Cf. VanderKam, "Book of Jubilees," 113.

55. Ibid., 119.

56. Cf. Jaubert, "Calendrier des Jubilé," 60; Jaubert, "Jésus et le calendrier de Qumrân," 27–28; Van Goudoever, *Biblical Worship*, 190.

have also proposed that the Christian Sunday observance is viewed to be rooted in an ancient Jewish sacerdotal calendar similar to or identical with what is known from Jubilees and the Qumran literature. For this reason, the Sabbath is given to Israel to be kept (31–32) because the Sabbath is eternal (33). By doing so, Jubilees 2 declares the Sabbath as a sign of Israel's unique covenant relationship with God, as does Exod 31:12–17. In order to keep the Sabbath as a sign between God and Israel, Jub 50:6–13 recommends staying indoors on the Sabbath and forbids long journeys.

In the Dead Sea Scrolls, CD[57] X.14–XI.18; XII.3–6 presents some specific regulations on the Sabbath. Kimbrough has proposed that there are similarities between CD and rabbinic literature on the Sabbath law.[58] However, Dupont-Sommer outlines differences between CD and rabbinic literature.[59] Scholars suggest that the Essenes[60] divided into two groups: one group lived near the Dead Sea, did not marry, and preserved the so-called "Community Rule" (1QS); the other group lived in a town in Palestine, married,[61] and preserved the so-called "Damascus Document" (CD). CD X.14–XI.18 describes a manual of various Sabbath regulations,[62] whereas CD XII.3–6 describes a specific regulation to punish profane activity breaking the Sabbath. CD X.14 begins to state specific regulations that the Essenes were interested in the Sabbath observance. The Essenes were "stricter than all Jews abstaining from work on the seventh day, not only do they prepare their food on the day before in order to avoid kindling a fire, but they do not venture to remove any vessel or even to go to stool thereon."[63] Thus their specific character of the enumeration of these prohibitions shows: the Essenes were specifically concerned at guarding against doing business on the Sabbath and the Sabbath regulations prohibited all commercial activities. In CD XI.14–15 the Essenes were forbidden to "spend the Sabbath in a place near Gentiles." Even helping an animal give birth on the Sabbath was forbidden and taking the newborn animal out of a wall or a pit was also forbidden (CD X.13–14). CD XII.3–6 clearly prohibits profaning the Sabbath to avoid death penalty (esp. vv. 3–4; Num 15:35; Jub 6). This shows that in CD the Sabbath laws were quite strict.

---

57. The Damascus Document (CD) of the Dead Sea Scrolls can be dated between 100 BCE and 70 CE. Cf. Kimbrough, "Concept of Sabbath," 483.

58. Ibid., 487–98.

59. Cf. Dupont-Sommer, *Essene Writings*, 145.

60. The Essenes were the Qumran dwellers. However, according to Josephus they must have been well acquainted with city life, although they were not aristocrats of society by any means. Cf. Josephus, *Bellum Judaicum*, II.8: "They have no certain city, but many of them dwell in every city; and if any of their sects come from other places, what they have lies upon for them, just as it were their own."

61. Josephus, *Bellum Judaicum*, II.8: Many of the Qumran dwellers did not marry, although some may have married. If we trust Josephus' record, there is a group of marrying Essenes.

62. Zahavy, "Sabbath Code of Damascus Document," 589–91. He concludes that "internal formal characteristics of the Sabbath Code of *Dam. Doc.* suggest that it is a composite rather than unitary text" (ibid., 591).

63. Josephus, *Bellum Judaicum*, II.8.

EPILOGUE

So far this chapter has investigated the Sabbath and its meaning in relation to the Jews from the Hebrew Bible. The aim of primary study is to prepare the Sabbath controversy of Jesus because this chapter presupposes that Jesus was influenced by the background of such a Jewish tradition on the Sabbath. This chapter has turned to Sabbath and its regulation in order to investigate how the Jewish Sabbath developed as a social institution.

Moreover, this chapter has shown bases of the Sabbath such as the creation activity and the divine rest in Gen 2:2–3; Exod 20:8–11; 31:13–17. However, the Sabbath is also described by the theme of "the deliverance from Egypt and the rest which Israel must enter"[64] and developed into a theological concern in the lawgiving context.[65] This perspective is seen in another version of the fourth commandment in Deut 5:12–15. The relationship between the Sabbath and labor is described in the Sabbath regulations (13–14) on the basis of the deliverance from Egypt (15a). The opening commandment to keep the Sabbath holy (12a) is connected with the Deuteronomistic formula (12b): "as the Lord your God commanded you" (Deut 5:12; 6:1; 13:15; 20:17), which is referring the conclusion (15b) to the Sabbath. Scholars argue that Deut 5:12–15 shows a theological orientation more than a simple humanitarian concern[66] because the reason given for the Sabbath is that God delivered Israel from Egypt. "The Sabbath command is enjoined in one case (Exod 20:11) with reference to creation and in the other (Deut 5:14–15) on humanitarian grounds to provide respite for servants with specific reference to the tradition of Israel in Egypt."[67] Therefore, Deut 5:12–15 can be called the exodus Sabbath in comparison with the creation Sabbath. For this reason, in Deuteronomy one can frequently find exodus images (Deut 5:15; 6:12; 7:18–19; 15:15; 16:3, 12; 24:18, 22), with the implication that Israel must remember her past experience on the Sabbath.[68] In this concern, the exodus Sabbath commands Israel to remember that God has delivered them from "the house of bondage" (Exod 20:2). Therefore, the concern to obtain rest (Deut 5:14) recalls the deliverance of Israel when they were servants in Egypt. A memorial[69] fact is that God brought Israel out of slavery into rest. Hence in Deuteronomy the term "rest" was to be seen in relation to the

---

64. Andreasen, *Old Testament Sabbath*, 134.

65. Dressler, "Sabbath in the Old Testament," 30: Arguing that "this reiteration of the Sabbath commandment concludes the lawgiving event on Sinai." Cf. Andreasen, *Old Testament Sabbath*, 158–59, 226–27; Lincoln, "From Sabbath to Lord's Day," 355–58.

66. Jenni, *Die theologische Begründung*, 15–19; Andreasen, *Old Testament Sabbath*, 123, 133.

67. Blenkinsopp, *Wisdom and Law*, 106.

68. Andreasen, *Old Testament Sabbath*, 133.

69. In fact, in Deut 5:12–15 the Sabbath commandment begins with "observe" rather than "remember." Although A. R. Hulst shows that these words are used synonymously, one must distinguish this from the Decalogue of Deuteronomy. For more information, see Hulst, "Bemerkungen zum Sabbatgebot," 159.

land into which God will bring his people (Deut 12:9).⁷⁰ Here I would carefully like to suggest that the Sabbath has an eschatological aspect. It is likely that the Sabbath can be interpreted as a memorial of the great acts accomplished by God for the Israelites in both creation and redemption (Exod 31:17; 20:11). With this interpretation, in Exod 35:2, we can find a Sabbath command with the punishment. A more extensive formulation of command and punishment appears in Exod 31:14–15.⁷¹ In relation to the Sabbath, there are references expressing punishment against those who fail to fulfill the law or those who profane the sign of the covenant between God and his people.

---

70. Lincoln, "From Sabbath to Lord's Day," 353.
71. Brin, *Studies in Biblical Law*, 54.

II

Sabbath Institutions and Observances

PROLOGUE

THIS CHAPTER WILL SURVEY the Sabbath institutions and observances in the Torah and prophetic writings. In order to investigate further, this chapter shall turn to the specific regulations toward the Sabbath institutions which were taken as important parts of the Sabbath observances. Therefore, not only will this chapter investigate the Sabbath and its meaning in connection to the Jews from the Hebrew Bible, but also investigate the connection with Greco-Roman literature by examining some writings of the Greco-Roman period. Through this process, the study of the origins and influences of Jewish Sabbath and its affects on Greco-Roman society will be dealt with in this chapter.

Sabbath Institutions

From its primitive form, Sabbath regulations have applied a strict attitude toward the Sabbath institution. For example, Exod 23:12; 34:21 is in "the oldest stratum of the Pentateuch" and the Sabbath in the passages is "to be understood as a social institution."[1] Thus these passages have a function in "premonarchical times"[2] or "premonarchical settlement."[3] From this perspective, it is likely that the Sabbath has been designed for the institution as the seventh day rest. In Exod 23:12, the Sabbath institution is linked with relief for the "ox and donkey" along with the "slaves and resident alien."[4] In Exod 34:21, the Sabbath institution is linked to "plowing time and in harvest time," reflecting the busiest seasons in the agricultural year.[5] Thus it is likely that the concern for

---

1. Rordorf, *Sunday*, 12.
2. Andreasen, *Old Testament Sabbath*, 89; Morgerstern, "Oldest Document of the Hexateuch," 63.
3. Andreasen, *Old Testament Sabbath*, 91.
4. Sanders and Kent, *Messages of the Bible*, 134.
5. Noth, *Exodus*, 264.

the humanitarian care in Exod 23:12 and the rest within the busiest agricultural time in Exod 34:21 assert the vitality of the Sabbath institution from its primitive form. Now this chapter shall briefly attempt to investigate the Sabbath institution through possible passages from the Hebrew Bible to the Dead Sea Scrolls.

First of all, one can find that the Sabbath institution is clearly connected to cultic regulations. Although scholars assert that מִקְרָא־קֹדֶשׁ[6] in Levi 23:3 is secondary,[7] the cultic regulations in v. 3 generally remind us that "a traditional Sabbath law lies behind it in its present form."[8] This implication is strongly supported by the phrase, "you shall do no work," which occurs identically in the Decalogue (Exod 20:9; Deut 5:14)[9] and by the phrase, "Six days shall work be done; but the seventh day is a Sabbath of complete rest," which occurs in Exod 23:12; 34:21; 35:2.[10] That cultic regulation in the Sabbath institution is joined with the phrase מִקְרָא־קֹדֶשׁ is unusual. The phrase means a "holy festival" or a "holy feast day," not simply a "holy assembly."[11] Thus the מִקְרָא־קֹדֶשׁ is perhaps a national festival at "the temple or at least Jerusalem."[12] Wenham proposes that the מִקְרָא־קֹדֶשׁ should be "a national gathering for public worship."

For this reason, one can easily imagine that the Sabbath should be a festival assembly held at the sacred place, as 2 Kgs 11:4-12; 16:18; 2 Chron 23:4, 8 describes it. In 2 Kgs 11:4-8, 9-12; 2 Chron 23:4, 8, the Chronicler shows that there were old accounts[13] of the Sabbath cultic regulations, which concern the "provenance of that part of the story which refers to the Sabbath."[14] It is likely that in the present accounts "the military maneuvers at the temple on the Sabbath were no longer practiced."[15] It is very difficult to reconstruct what really did take place on that day. Andreasen proposes that "it is likely that the event was recorded in the official archives of Judah, undoubtedly shortly after it took place."[16] However, the accounts show that the changing of guard happened on the Sabbath when the people gathered together at the temple.[17] In 2 Kgs 16:18, King Ahaz removed "the outer entrance for the king" from the temple, that is,

---

6. This phrase is characteristic in Lev 23:3; Exod 12:16; Num 28-29. Cf. Wenham, *Book of Leviticus*, 301.

7. Kilian, *Literarkritische und formgeschichtliche Untersuchung*, 53, 63-64; Andreasen, *Old Testament Sabbath*, 58-59, 141-42.

8. Andreasen, *Old Testament Sabbath*, 77.

9. Sanders and Kent, *Messages of the Bible*, 134.

10. Ibid., 210, 355.

11. Andreasen, *Old Testament Sabbath*, 59. Cf. *New Oxford Annotated Bible*, which translates it a "holy convocation."

12. Ibid., 147.

13. Fohrer, *Hauptprobleme des Buches Ezechiel*, 236-37; Childs, *Introduction to the Old Testament*, 288-90; Jones, *1 and 2 Kings*, 76.

14. Andreasen, *Old Testament Sabbath*, 51.

15. Ibid.

16. Ibid.

17. Ibid., 52.

Part 1: Sabbath and the Gentile Mission

"the house of the Lord." This account reminds us that in order to observe the Sabbath the king visited a holy temple as the people did and that in doing this the Sabbath practices were regularly observed.[18]

Through the passages discussed above one can know that the people and the king gathered together in a holy place to celebrate the Sabbath by offering sacrifices.

In the prophetic books, Isa 1:13: Hos 2:11 also describe the cultic characteristics of the Sabbath institution in offering sacrifices. In these passages the association of the Sabbath and the new moon is well known (cf. 2 Kgs 4:23; Isa 66:23; Ezek 46:1, 3; Amos 8:5).[19] The phrase in Isa 66:23 is literally translated "from Sabbath to Sabbath" and compared with the phrase "from new moon to new moon." Like Lev 23:3, on the one hand, the expression מִקְרָא in Isa 1:13 can be translated as "festival," and not simply "assembly" or "convocation." Moore says that "the Sabbath is frequently joined with the annual festivals, and is like the high days of those festivals, new years, and the Day of Atonement, a day of 'holy convocation.'" On the other hand, Hos 2:11 implies that the people did not recognizes God's Sabbath by observing "*her* [Israel's] mirth," "*her* festivals," "*her* moons," and "*her* Sabbaths." From these expressions it appears that the people did not regard the Sabbath as God's Sabbath in his ownership.

In relation to cultic regulations, one must now pay attention to Sabbath sacrifices. A number of passages mention the Sabbath sacrifices. In the historical books, 1 Chron 9:32; 23:31, 2 Chron 2:4; 13:11 (cf. 2 Chron 8:13; Neh 10:32–33) the characteristics of the Sabbath institution appear in description of the sacrifice offerings. Here the term לֶחֶם הַמַּעֲרֶכֶת[20] is interpreted as "the rows of bread" by the NRSV. Although this term is assigned to the Kohathites by the Chronicler to date back to very ancient times, it is possibly dated in the post-exile time. It is likely that the bread was usually prepared by the Levites for the Sabbath sacrifices. 2 Chron 8:13 describes the offerings for "the Sabbaths, the new moons, and the three annual festivals,"[21] required the commandment of Moses (cf. Num 28–29). The expression "the commandment of Moses" is compared with the term "the law of the lord" in 2 Chron 31:3. Paul Giem sees that there are references to the series of "new moons seasons, and Sabbaths" (Jub 1:14; 6:34–38; 23:19; IQM 2:4–6; 1 Enoch 82:7). The law here does not refer to Solomon's duty to provide the offerings, but only to the offerings themselves.[22] Andreasen says, "Rather, the law referred only to the prescribed types of sacrifices for the daily, weekly, and monthly feast days, as well as for the annual festivals." Neh 10:32–33 asserts that the expenses of the Sabbath at the temple were regulated: "yearly one-third of a shekel" (32) and "rows of bread" for the "regular grain offerings, the regular burnt offerings" (33). According to the Sabbath sacrifices described by the Chronicler, the Sabbath offerings

---

18. Gray, *1 and 2 Kings*, 572.
19. Moore, *Judaism*, 23. For annual festivals, see ibid., 40–54.
20. Albright, "Date and Personality," 104–24.
21. Giem, "Sabbaton," 202–6.
22. Andreasen, *Old Testament Sabbath*, 56–57.

dated back to as early as Solomon's time. The presentation of holy bread described by the Chronicler may have been performed on the Sabbath "in much earlier times."[23] Sabbath practices were carried out by the Levites. However, the burnt offerings (Num 28:9–10; Ezek 46:4–5) should be dated back to the exile or the post-exile period.[24]

Sabbath Observances

Now this chapter shall turn to the specific regulations toward the Sabbath institutions which are taken as important among the Sabbath observances. The Sabbath regulations in the Pentateuch are very rare but they mainly require rest from work. Exod 16:22–30; 35:2–3; Num 15:32–35 neither explicitly define buying merchandise or grain as work, nor exceedingly explain casuistic regulations in detail. Exod 16:22–30, first of all, describes a double portion of manna on the sixth day and the absence of manna on the seventh day shows the description of the foundation of the Sabbath rest. This is a specific application of the Sabbath for the Israelites to recognize a work regulation forced upon them by the Sabbath institution.[25] Here scholars suggest that the Sabbath had already existed before the giving of manna[26] but "the Sabbath is not commonly known to the people."[27] Andreasen proposes that the Israelites "now have to learn to regulate their work according to its regulation." However, Exod 16:22–30 reflects the general principles of the Sabbath regulations:[28] preparing for the Sabbath (22), the holiness of the Sabbath (23), work during the six days (26a), the distinctiveness of the Sabbath (25, 26b–27), and rest on the Sabbath (30). Exod 35:2–3; Num 15:32–36 describe a more specific regulation in comparison with Exod 16:22–30.[29] Exod 35:3 provides that the Israelites could conceive of casuistic Sabbath laws at one stage, and Andreasen argues that this passage demonstrates "the passage form apodictic to casuistic law."[30] Therefore, Exod 35:2 looks like a standard Sabbath prohibition and Exod 35:3 and seems to be intended to make v. 2 applicable to the context.[31] It is likely that in v. 3 the prohibition against kindling a fire on the Sabbath actually means prohibition of work to keep the Sabbath holy. Although Num 15:32–36 is often related to Exod 35:3,[32] the issue in Num 15:32–36 is not with fire making. Rather, Num

---

23. Ibid., 144.
24. Ibid., 142–43; Sanders and Kent, *Messages of the Bible*, 358–60, 360–63.
25. Moore, *Judaism in the First Centuries*, 32.
26. Childs, *Book of Exodus*, 290.
27. Andreasen, *Old Testament Sabbath*, 130.
28. Childs, *Book of Exodus*, 290.
29. Sanderd and Kent, *Messages of the Bible*, 366.
30. Andreasen, *Old Testament Sabbath*, 153.
31. Ibid., 137; cf. Sanders and Kent, *Messages of the Bible*, 81.
32. Moore, *Judaism in the First Centuries*, 25; Noth, *Numbers*, 117; Andreasen, *Old Testament Sabbath*, 136–38, 153.

15:32–36 is concerned that the man who picked up sticks on the Sabbath (presumably, to make a fire; cf. 1 Kgs 17:12) "shall be put to death" and "the entire congregation shall stone him outside the camp" (35).

In the prophetic books, Isa 58:13–14; Jer 17:19–27; Amos 8:5 are based on the covenant relationship in the description of the special regulations on the Sabbath. Isa 58:13–14, first of all, describes restrictions on traveling on the Sabbath (cf. Exod 16:29) and restrictions in pursuing interests (cf. Neh 13:15–22; Amos 8:5). These are very specific to Sabbath regulations. From Isa 58:13 it was deduced that the Sabbath observance approved and required by God not only showed peculiar honors to the day, but the indulgence in some unusual luxury on it, especially in the way of food and drink.[33] On the one hand, scholars argue that Jer 17:19–27 is based on the Deuteronomistic style,[34] but its main content seems to come from Jeremiah's own comments[35] to keep the Sabbath holy, which is "operated within the Jeremiah tradition."[36] Jer 17:21–22 describes specific regulations to "not bear a burden on the Sabbath day or bring it in by the gates of Jerusalem" and to not do any work "but keep the Sabbath day holy." this regulation of the Sabbath may be brought about by the *Sitz im Leben* in a particular context in which the commercial activities on the Sabbath may be a key issue. Those who keep the Sabbath holy shall be blessed (25–26). Here are the promises for them: the restoration of the throne of David, the restoration of Jerusalem, the restoration of the towns of Judah, the restoration of the rituals by "bringing burnt offering and sacrifices, grain offerings and frankincense, and bringing thank offerings." These should be the "blessings of the covenant bestowed by Yahweh on his obedient people."[37] The covenant blessings should be "forever" (25). However, those who profane the Sabbath shall be brought into the destruction of Jerusalem (27, cf. Neh 13:18; Ezek 20:23). This negative warning has a sense of an eschatological perspective which is to encourage the Israelites to keep the Sabbath.[38] Amos 8:5, on the other hand, does not allow any commercial activity on the Sabbath[39] and shows that the Israelites before the exile already understood the Sabbath law as forbidding trade. This implication seems that "general trade or commerce was not approved on the Sabbath, although we cannot conclude that strict inactivity was called for." Thus it is implied that merchants should devote themselves to keep the Sabbath holy.[40]

---

33. Moore, *Judaism in the First Centuries*, 24–25, 33, 35, 37–38.

34. Mowinckel, *Zur Komposition des Buches Jeremia*, 47; Leslie, *Jeremiah*, 316; Bright, *Jeremiah*, 120; McKane, *Critical and Exegetical Commentary*, 416–19; Carroll, *Jeremiah 1–25*, 368–69.

35. Rudolph, *Jeremiah*, 109: Thompson, *Book of Jeremiah*, 427–28; Andreasen, *Old Testament Sabbath*, 32–34.

36. Jones, *Jeremiah*, 248–49.

37. Thompson, *Book of Jeremiah*, 430.

38. McKane, *Critical and Exegetical Commentary*, 419.

39. Andreasen, *Old Testament Sabbath*, 62.

40. Mays, *Amos*, 144.

In the historical book, Neh 10:31:13:14–22 relates to general trade or commercial activities. Neh 10:31, first of all, prohibits any commercial trade or any grain from sale on the Sabbath. Neh 13:14–22 then belongs to the Nehemiah-Memoirs.[41] In the time of Nehemiah, the Gentiles, the tyrants (presumably, "tradesmen,"[42] v. 16), brought fish and all kinds of merchandise and sold them to the Israelites on the Sabbath. Thus the Israelites felt that keeping the Sabbath holy imposed "an unfair commercial disadvantage."[43] Hence, Nehemiah warns them that buying on the Sabbath was a profane act of breaking the Sabbath. Finally, he suggests some practical measures (19–22) taken from Jer 17:19–27.[44] Clines evaluates that Nehemiah's measure is an excellent example of the Jewish tendency to make "a hedge about the Torah." The reason is that the marketing in Jerusalem on the Sabbath was one of the major causes of the destruction of Jerusalem in the past and could cause even greater disasters in the future (18).[45]

The Sabbath and Other Writings

This chapter moves to the Gospel of Thomas (GTh). In GTh 27:1–2 the Sabbath is obviously connected to "fasting," although it is unclear how one could "keep the Sabbath a Sabbath."[46] In relation to fasting, this saying is connected to GTh 6:1–4; 14:1–3. These three passages may point in the same direction. The saying in GTh 27:1–2 is seen as an "ascetic reinterpretation of the obligation to fast and keep the Sabbath" and could be read as a "call for more dedicated Sabbath observance."[47] Sabbath's association with fasting is often found in the Sabbath observance in early Christianity.[48] In essence, the Jews themselves appeared to have made the Sabbath anything but a day of fasting (Judith 8:6; Jub 50:10, 12–13; CD XI.4–5). In Panarion 42.3.4, Epiphanius quotes a reason for fasting on the Sabbath from Marcion: "Since of the rest of the God who made the world on the seventh day, let us fast on this day, to a nothing appropriate to the God of Jews."[49] The early Christian church seems to have this Jewish tradition of the Sabbath fast. One of the widespread practices of Coptic Christianity was observing both the Sabbath and the Lord's Day.[50] The Apostolic Constitutions, however,

---

41. Cf. Neh 5:19; 6:14; 13:14, 22, 29, 31.
42. Andreasen, *Old Testament Sabbath*, 29, 127.
43. Williamson, *Ezra, Nehemiah*, 395.
44. Clines, *Ezra, Nehemiah, Esther*, 244–45.
45. Andreasen, *Old Testament Sabbath*, 127.
46. Patterson, *Gospel of Thomas*, 86.
47. Wilson, *Related Strangers*, 90.
48. Strand, "Some Notes on the Sabbath Fast," 167–74.
49. Williams, *Panarion of Epiphanius*, 274.
50. Bishai, "Sabbath Observance," 25–43.

propose clearly that one did not fast on the Sabbath, except at Passover/Easter time in memory of the Lord's death (Ap. Const. V. 14:20; 18:1–2; 20:19; VII.23:3–4).[51]

In the time of Maccabeus, there were serious problems regarding the Sabbath. 1 and 2 Maccabeus regard the Sabbath as a "sacred institution"[52] and treat the problems decisively by extending the attitudes of war on the Sabbath. 1 Maccabeus 2:32–38 describes how the Gentile troops[53] attacked the Jews in the wilderness on the Sabbath but the Jews refused to fight against them to keep the Sabbath strictly. In the time of Mattathias, Antiochus Epiphanes undertook by force of arms to compel the Jews to obey his edict of conformity. As a result, a thousand Jews[54] were killed.[55] After the event, Mattathias and his friends determined to fight against the Gentile troops for the defense of the Jews. 1 Macc 2:39–41 describes how the Jews attacked them. 1 Macc 9:43–49 describes that when Bacchides attacked the Jews on the Sabbath the Jews defended themselves against Bacchides and killed "one thousand of Bacchides' men." At that time Mattathias said, "We will not come out, nor will we do what the king commands and so profane the Sabbath day" (34). This shows that there was a strict observance of one particular Sabbath regulation at the time of Mattathias. After learning of the massacre, in their extreme need 1 Macc 5:24–27 describes another attack of Apollonius who was sent by Antiochus (24). He attacked them on the Sabbath (25) and killed a "great numbers of people" (26b) because Judas Maccabeus withdrew himself into the wilderness without fighting against them (27). In 2 Macc 5:25–26 one can find the holiness of the Sabbath strictly observed by the Jews. These passages show that we can find a specific Sabbath regulation to keep the Sabbath holy in the time of Maccabeus. Only the regulation of the Sabbath in relation to war was "massacre rather than fight on the Sabbath," even though the Jews took up the "sword for defend[s]e."[56] It is likely that the Jews were obliged to defend themselves on the Sabbath and they refrained from making war offensively on the Sabbath, and even from defending themselves (2 Macc 6:11). In 2 Macc 8:25–28, the Jews are told to have given up the attack on the army of Nicanor, because of approaching of the Sabbath.

This chapter now finally moves to some references concerning the Sabbath found in the Greco-Roman writings. In this chapter some writings of the Greco-Roman period will be examined for the study of the origins and influences of Jewish Sabbath. Thus this chapter shall pay attention how Jewish Sabbath affairs affect the Greco-Roman society.

---

51. Kraft, "Some Notes on Sabbath Observance," 24.

52. Marcus, *Law in the Apocrypha*, 76.

53. Cf. Moore, *Judaism in the First Centuries*, 26.

54. ". . . with their wives and children and livestock, to the number of a thousand persons" (1 Macc 2:38b).

55. Cf. Josephus, *Antiquitates Judaicae*, XII.274–75.

56. Schurer, *History of the Jewish People*, 474.

A historian, Pompeius Trogus, in the first century BCE describes Moses as an important figure for Jewish Sabbath in consecrating the Sabbath as a "custom of the nation" in *Epitoma* 36, II.14–16.[57] This evidence shows that Pompeius Trogus conceived of the Sabbath as a sacred day for the Greco-Roman Gentiles, too. Ovid (43 BCE–18 CE) recognizes the Jewish Sabbath as a foreign Sabbath in *Remedia Amoris* 217–20. He also regards the Sabbath as a "sacred" day preserved by the Jews[58] (*Ars Amatoria* I.75–78) and a day "less fit for business" (*Ars Amatoria* I.413–17). Stern argues that the term "Jews" is synonymous with the Palestine Syrians or the Syrian Jews at that time. This evidence shows that Ovid viewed the Jewish Sabbath as a day, leisure, or idleness[59] which may affect the Greco-Roman Gentiles as a day of rest. In *De Superstitione*, a Philosopher Seneca (?–65 CE) "censures the sacred institutions of the Jews, especially the Sabbath." He describes that the Sabbath practice are inexpedient, "because by introducing one day of rest in every seven they lose in idleness almost a seventh of their life, and by failing to act in times of urgency, they often suffer loss."[60] Here one knows that Seneca also blames the Jews for wasting a seventh day of their lives in the Sabbath rest. But this is also evidence that the Jewish Sabbath spread out through the time of Seneca as a day of rest, though he criticizes the Sabbath rest in "idleness in almost a seventh of their life." In the *Historiae* V.4.3–5.5,[61] the "rest on the seventh day because that day ended their toils" (4.3) was also addressed by Tacitus at the end of first century CE. Frontinus describes a religious understanding of Sabbath observance at the late first century CE. In Strategemata II.1.17,[62] he regards the Sabbath as the day of rest, "Saturn's day is a day which is sinful for the Roman people to do any business." McKay interprets this Sabbath observance "as a moral or religious obligation is a more sympathetic view of Jewish abstention from work than the common accusation of idleness."[63]

EPILOGUE

So far this chapter has investigated the Sabbath and its institutions in relation to cultic regulations, Sabbath sacrifices, special regulations on travel and commercial activities on the Sabbath, the attitudes to war, and the Sabbath prohibitions. This primary study is to understand that the Sabbath regulations had developed in the various situations as social institutions and such a Jewish law had necessarily been related to the Gentiles in its social relationship. This study with no doubt has prepared a background of Jesus'

---

57. Justinus, *Historiae Philippicae*.
58. Cf. Stern, *Jewish Identity*, 348–49; Goldenberg, "Jewish Sabbath," 436.
59. Michael, "Jewish Sabbath," 120.
60. Augustine, *City of God*.
61. Tacitus, *Historiae*.
62. Frotinus, *Strategemata*.
63. McKay, *Sabbath and Synagogue*, 109.

attitude to law in Q. Thus this book later on shall help to move to Jesus and the Jewish law in Q in order to investigate how Jesus and the Q community understood the Mosaic law, especially for divorce, remarriage, tithe, purity, and the Sabbath.

Through the various writings above, it shows that the Jewish Sabbath spread out in the Greco-Roman world and was recognized as a Jewish custom by the Gentiles. Few Greco-Roman writings on the Jewish Sabbath regard it as a day of rest, although some non-Jews misunderstanding may support the widespread situation of the Jewish Sabbath in the Greco-Roman world.

III

Q 14:5 and a Jewish Christian Community

PROLOGUE

SINCE LUKE 14:5 PORTRAYS Jesus violating tradition about what is acceptable on the Sabbath and justifying his actions based on an appeal to common sense, many scholars have focused on this text and its parallel (Matt 12:11) in order to understand the early Christians' view of Jewish law. But the nature of the controversy in Q 14:5 is still unclear. I posit that one way to understand the Sabbath controversy in Q is to study it in the context of the tension between Jewish law and the Gentile mission. That is to say, we must understand how Jewish law and the Gentile mission were seen in the Q context in order to understand the Sabbath controversy. Of particular interest is Jesus' emphasis on compassion as a basis for violating tradition, which places Jesus' attitude toward the Sabbath somewhere between strict observances of the law on the one hand, and the Gentile mission, with its (nearly) complete abrogation of the law on the other. To put it another way, Q 14:5 represents a step away from Jewish tradition and toward the Gentiles by suggesting compassion as the true basis for God's dealing with humanity.

To develop this thesis, I first concentrate on the understanding of the Jewish law in Q. I suggest that the Q community as a Jewish Christian community was essentially conservative in its attitude toward the law. Jesus in Q does not directly reject observance of Jewish law,[1] representing, no doubt, the community's practice (Q 11:42; 16:17). In Q 16:16a, for instance, the law is regarded as still valid for the community and as the basis of the preaching of the kingdom of God. Q's missionary activity thus seems to have been "confined to Judaism."[2]

---

1. Sanders, *Jewish Law*, 1.
2. Tuckett, *Q and the History of Early Christianity*, 425–26. In spite of Q's confinement to Judaism, he argues that "Q seems to show awareness of the existence of a Gentile mission, or at least of the presence of (perhaps isolated) Gentiles within the sphere of salvation offered by the Christian message."

Part 1: Sabbath and the Gentile Mission

Nevertheless, there also seems to be an awareness of breaking the law in Q,[3] as in Q 14:5, where Jesus violates the rules for Sabbath keeping in favor of obeying the divine intention to do well on the Sabbath.[4] Thus although Q generally maintains a conservative attitude toward Jewish law, Q 14:5 appears to relax the standard. Since one could rescue an ox from a pit on the Sabbath, why could not one save a human? Of course, the point was not simply to violate Jewish law but to replace it with the higher standard of God's compassion.

On the other hand, I also discuss evidence for the existence of the Gentile mission in Q. Unlike the Jewish mission, which began in the lifetime of Jesus, the Gentile mission began only after the death and resurrection of Jesus (Matt 28:19–20; Luke 24:47). But it is clear that the Gentile mission was progressing successfully possibly before 50 CE and certainly before 70 CE, that is to say, during the time when Q was being written. It is reasonable to assume, then, the Q community knew about the Gentile mission and possibly regarded it as a challenge to its own missionary activity. It may be that originally the Q community recognized that the Gentiles were entering the kingdom along with the Jews, but it continued to evangelize only Jews. Tension developed within the community over the issue: the Q redactor came to see the Gentiles' conversion as part of God's eschatological scheme; Judaizers,[5] conversely, only allowed the conversion of Gentiles who would be circumcised. The Sabbath saying may represent a middle position. Hence, before the Q community grew at a later date into the Matthean community,[6] the Q redactor understood the Gentiles in an eschatological perspective, despite the Judaizers who were also active within the Q community.

The Sabbath controversy in Q 14:5, meanwhile, seems to have created an awareness of breaking Jewish law in the Q community, or at least the Sabbath law. This poses the question of how far the Q community was expected to obey Jewish law. The existence of the Sabbath controversy in Q seems to have persuaded the Jewish Christians[7] within the Q community to respond positively to the missionary activity for

---

3. Riley, *One Jesus, Many Christs*, 88.

4. Sigal, *Halakah of Jesus of Nazareth*, 158.

5. Robinson, "Down-to-Earth Jesus," xvi: "The Judaizers: 'those of circumcision' who would 'Judaize' the Gentiles if they could."

6. Robinson, "Q Trajectory," 193: "The Q community ... merged into the Matthean community"; Robinson, "Real Jesus," 148–49: "So it has become a new scholarly task to supplement the standard version of church history, based on Paul and Acts, with the church history that leads from Jesus via the Sayings Gospel to Matthew, that is to say, from Galilee directly to Antioch without the detour via the Damascus road. For the Gospel of Matthew probably comes from the region of Antioch, from a small community that had begun in Galilee and continued there for some time, since one was told not to go on the roads of the gentiles or into the towns of the Samaritans but only to the lost sheep of Israel (Matt 10:6–7)."

7. Robinson and Koester, *Trajectories*, 115: Koester argues that "everyone in the first generation of Christianity was a Jewish-Christian"; Segal, "Jewish Christianity," 326–51; Riegel, "Jewish Christianity," 410–15; Wilson, *Related Strangers*, 157: Wilson argues that Jewish Christianity has "a profound concern with the meaning of scripture, a tendency to favor the Gospel of Matthew, and the observance of the Jewish Law."

the Gentile Christian community. Such a persuasion in Q may have also been inevitably confronted with the success of the Gentile mission, which was widely developed in the era of the early Christian church after the death and resurrection of Jesus. In this context, when the Q community was struggling to affirm the Jewish law on the one hand and to respond to the Gentile mission on the other, the Sabbath saying of Jesus helped it to decide the proper course: God's love, not literal adherence to the law, was to be the basis for missionary activity.

I propose to reconstruct early Christianity's trajectory from Jewish law to the Gentile mission on the basis of the Sabbath controversy in Q 14:5. Such a shift did not occur all at once, but over time and on the basis of new ideas about God's will.

I survey the Q community's conservative attitude toward the Jewish law (Q 11:42; 16:17). Q did not represent Jesus as living contrary to Jewish law,[8] nor did Jesus abrogate Jewish law. Rather he rejected Jewish traditions and customs. Schulz, for example, argues that in Q 11 the conflict with the Pharisees was based on the Q community's strict interpretation of the law. In Q 16:16–18, though some scholars argue that Q 16:16 originally announces the end of the law, Q 16:17 corrects that view by depicting the eternal validity of the law.[9] Similarly, while Q 16:18, the saying on divorce and adultery, looks like a radical attack on Deut 24:1–4, the prohibition of divorce and remarriage is not an attack on the law itself. Hence, one can argue that Q "appears to exhibit a strongly 'conservative' attitude to the law. It shows a deep concern that the law should be maintained; it is aware that Jesus could be seen as antinomian, and Q appears to represent a strong movement to 'rejudaize' Jesus. Further, there is a concern to uphold the pharisaic interpretation of the law."[10] Hence, it is likely that Q was the product of a "Torah-observant Jewish community."[11] This conservative attitude toward the Jewish law served to build the inner solidarity of the Q community. The conflict between the Q community and the Pharisees was thus not that of Jews and non-(or former) Jews, but between two Torah-observant communities.

I examine the missionary activity of the Q community. In contrast to other scholars, I argue that the Q community ignored the Gentile mission in favor of the Jewish mission, even though the Q community knew of Jesus' positive attitude toward the Gentiles. The persecution faced by the Q community (Q 6:22–23; 11:49–50) is evidence of the community's Jewish orientation. Persecution arose because the community regarded itself as a Jewish movement, but the larger Jewish society did not accept the Q community as a Jewish movement because they had rejected Jesus. Much of the polemic in Q arose precisely as a result of this persecution and it is directed against the perpetrators (i.e., Pharisees). Nevertheless, Q saw the Gentile mission as valid, but

---

8. Loader, *Jesus' Attitude*, 429.
9. Hübner, *Gesetz*, 31; Bultmann, "What the Saying Source," 30.
10. Tuckett, "Q, the Law and Judaism," 98.
11. Kloppenborg, "Nomos and Ethos in Q," 47.

only in the future.¹² Jesus' view of the Gentiles was thus retained but not as a present reality for Q. Later, of course, as evidenced by the Gospel of Matthew, Q engaged in a full-blown mission to the Gentiles.

Persecution and Exhortation

In relation to the circumstances of persecution in the Q community, it is important to investigate the exhortation imperatives of the community rules. In Q 6:27–42, one can note that the community rules were unconditionally imperative, giving the sense of warning or exhortation.¹³ It is no surprise that Q presents Jesus' ethical teaching in the forms of paraenetic characteristics, namely exhortations and admonitions, as such forms was often presented in antiquity.¹⁴

John G. Gammie argues, however, that admonitions are distinct from exhortations.¹⁵ Objecting to the argumentation of Leo G. Perdue,¹⁶ Gammie prefers to distinguish between the two. For Gammie, the term "prohibition" is close to "admonition," and "admonition" to "exhortation." Gammie regards "prohibition" as "a form or sub-type of admonition."¹⁷ Following the suggestion of Richter, Gammie thinks that "legal formulations in Israel do favor the prohibitive form," distinguishing admonitions from exhortations. "The exhortation invites, encourages, directs or commands that the addressee pursue a given course of action or adopt a given attitude." Furthermore, he argues that "most (but not all) usages of the imperatives would best be classified as exhortations."¹⁸

I agree with the suggestion of Gammie. Admonitions, as prohibitions, warn (negatively) the addressee against taking a given course of action or attitude; however, admonitions distinguished from exhortations invite (positively) the addressee to a

---

12. Jeremias, *Jesus' Promise*, 46–47.

13. In Q there are a number of exhortations. They begin with Q 6:23, but they are dominated by the community rules in Q 6:27–42.

14. Baumgartner, "Literarischen Gattungen," 161–98; Kitchen, "Basic Literary Forms," 235–82.

15. John G. Gammie's article points out exhortations and admonitions which are recognizable as subtypes of paraenetic literature; see "Paraenetic Literature," 58–61. He defines "admonitions" as follows: "Sub-genres or species aimed at discussion" (ibid., 67). And he also defines "exhortations" as follows: "Sub-genres of each of the three main branches of rhetoric, as well as of Paraenetic Rhetoric and Literature, in which the addressee is invited, encouraged, directed or commanded to pursue a given course of action or to adopt a given attitude. The counterpart of exhortations is admonitions in which addressees are warned against a given course of action or attitude" (ibid., 69).

16. See the paper of Perdue, "Wisdom Sayings of Jesus," 18–19.

17. According to him, "My chief objection to Perdue's understanding of admonition is that the term more readily, in my judgment, carries with it the idea of warning (compare German *Mahnung* and *Mahnwort*) and thus does not readily suggest the notion of the pursuit of a positive course of action." Cf. Gammie, "Paraenetic Literature," 67n1.

18. Gammie, "Paraenetic Literature," 59–60. For more details, see Richter, *Recht und Ethos*, 68–146.

given course of action.[19] For this reason, it is noticeable that in the study of Q 6:27–42 the community rules are based on correct exhortations. Such community rules encouraged the Q community to complete a given course of action or practice a given such as attitude. In this regard, I would like to return to Jesus' inaugural sermon in Q to examine the community rules with the paraenetic characteristics, namely exhortations. The community rules would be better classified as exhortations because the usage of the imperative should be classified as exhortative. Even if Q 6:42a is accompanied by the vocative, the statement could also be considered exhortative because it surely has the imperative form as well.

The community rules as exhortations are also employed in the form of direct statements by Jesus. Throughout the entire community rules, Jesus encourages, commands, or directs the Q community to be disciples who follow or imitate Jesus. In the community rules, therefore, exhortations are always mingled with concrete ethical teachings of Jesus which challenge the daily life of the Q community. As Leif E. Vaage mentions, however, "Before the exhortation is an ethical ideal, it is a practical strategy."[20] For example, the exhortation, "love your enemies" in the community rules is a practical strategy for the Q community, by which Q explains how to handle inimical opposition. We must consider why the exhortations are typically employed in the imperative statements. The reason is that the imperative forms can offer strong positive encouragement for the Q community under the circumstances of persecution. Burton L. Mack also points out that such a predominance of the imperative forms in Jesus' sayings is attributed to "a strong authority to the speaker (ethos)."[21] In Q, the imperatives show the authority in the character of the speaker, Jesus. On Luke 12:22–31, Mack argues that the imperatives reveal "a heightened concern" so that the Q community could accept such strong maxims as "rule (pathos)."[22] Likewise, by collecting such community rules from Jesus' inaugural sermon, the redactor of the first layer of Q (Q¹) attributes a strong attitude to Jesus in order to let the Q community practice the rules in their life even under the circumstances of persecution. An indicative or infinitive clause in the community rule, without an imperative form, would not have encouraged such a strong Q movement to last. Jesus' disciples themselves would have needed such community rules to build their own community, to maintain their unity continuously, and to prohibit retaliation against the attacks raised from the outside or within their community.

---

19. Gammie, "Paraenetic Literature," 58–60, 69.

20. Vaage, "Q: Ethos and Ethic," 408–9.

21. Mack, *Rhetoric*, 51. Especially in 50–52 Mack deals with the issue of the exhortation in Jesus' teaching on anxiety (Luke 12:22–31), showing "the major premise of a rhetorical syllogism."

22. Ibid., 50–52. In addition, in a rhetorical trait Mack suggests a remarkable argumentation on Luke 12:22–31, "an exhortation not to worry."

Christological or Eschatological Implications

I consider the reason why the Sabbath controversy in Q 14:5 cannot be understood in the christological and eschatological perspective. Both pericopes in Matt 12:9–14 and Luke 14:1–6 focus not on the healing, but on the saying about the Sabbath (Matt 12:11 // Luke 14:5). Both mention that Jesus entered into a synagogue on the Sabbath. It is likely that Jesus wanted to teach the meaning of the Sabbath in the synagogue.[23] In spite of the same climax of the pericopes in relation to the question of the Sabbath, however, the parallel sayings (Matt 12:11 // Luke 14:5) are in rather different contexts.

Matt 12:9–14, on the one hand, contains several traits of Matthean redaction. Matthew adds *metabas ekeithen* (12:9)[24] and *exestin* (12:2, 4, 10, 12)[25] in order to connect Matt 12:1–8 and 12:9–14 in a sequence. This redaction seems to be created by Matthew in order to represent the messianic authority[26] of Jesus as the "Lord of the Sabbath" (12:8) as "eschatological expectations" that anticipated salvation.[27] In Matt 12:9, the addition of *auton* to *ten sunagogen* presents the fact that in Matthew the synagogue might be a place of conflict or confrontation among Jews,[28] and that the Matthean community might have already been distinguished from the Pharisaic community.[29] In Matt 12:11 and 12:12, Matthew adds his favorite term *probaton* (Matt 9:36; 10:6, 16; 15:24; 18:12; 25:32, 33; 26:31) to draw some aspects in relation to the parable of the lost sheep (Matt 18:12–13).[30] Luke 14:1–6, on the other hand, comes from the Lukan *Sondergut*, and there are Lukan redactions. Luke uses frequently *kai egeneto* (11:1; 14:1; 17:11) and *apokritheis* (22 times).[31] In Luke 14:5, scholars point out some redactions: *pros autous*,[32] *en hemera tou sabbatou*,[33] and *frear*.[34] It is likely that Luke stylistically improves the

---

23. Rordorf, *Sunday*, 67. "Jesus used the opportunity to deliver his message in the synagogue where people were assembled on the Sabbath."

24. The phrase *metabas ekeithen* is characteristically Matthean, and makes the tie between the previous and present stories more apparent. Cf. Davies and Allison, *Critical and Exegetical Commentary*, 317.

25. Ibid.: "This strengthens the link between 12.1–8 and 12.9–14 (cf. 12.2,4)."

26. In Matt 12:12, Jesus' answer is based on messianic authority and is understood christologically.

27. Riesenfeld, *Gospel Tradition*, 118. "Therefore deeds of healing on Sabbath days must be interpreted as signs that in the person of Jesus was being realized something of what the Sabbath had pointed forward to in the eschatological expectations of the Jewish people; the message of the dawn of the time of salvation, of the fullness of life, of the new creation, received its expression in glimpses of none the less concrete manifestations and in symbolic acts where ordinary people weighed down by illnesses and infirmities could experience release from the shackles of their deformity and suffering."

28. Davies and Allison, *Critical and Exegetical Commentary*, 317.

29. Doyle, "Concern of the Evangelist," 18.

30. Gundry, *Matthew*, 226; Davies and Allison, *Critical and Exegetical Commentary*, 319, 321.

31. Braun, *Feasting and Social Rhetoric*, 13, 23. For *apokritheis*, he mentions several passages in Lukan *Sondergut* (Luke 7:40; 10:41; 13:2, 15; 14:3; 17:17, 20; 19:40).

32. Jeremias, *Sprache des Lukasevangeliums*, 33.

33. Kilpatrick, *Origins of the Gospel*, 27; Neirynck, "Luke 14,1–6," 258.

34. Busse, *Wunder des Propheten Jesus*, 309. He regards fršar as Lukan redaction because of its parallel with Luke 6:39.

eschatological perspective, adding the term *en hemera* to the original Q text. Yang, regarding this eschatological view, argues that in Luke 14:1–6 Jesus' healing can be seen "in terms of the urgency of experiencing Jesus' own eschatological power of healing, and thus has (though implicitly) an eschatological character."[35] This application further supports his conclusion that the eschatological healing power on the Sabbath brings a christological character to the heart of our discussion because Jesus is the Lord of the Sabbath (Luke 6:5 // Matt 12:8; compare Mark 2:28).

However, the eschatological and christological application to the Sabbath controversy is by no means self-evident from the text of Q in Q 14:5. For the conclusion that there are no christological implications in the Sabbath controversy of Q, one should consider that the saying in Q 14:5 does not have the framework of the healing in Matt 12:9–14 and Luke 14:1–6. It is likely that Q 14:5 existed without the framework of the Matthean and Lukan redaction. Rather Q 14:5 is form-critically in a wider context with the sayings part of Q 13:24—14:35 which are prophetic sayings in Q. I would argue that Q 14:5 is rather placed in Jesus' public ministry, in spite of the christological and eschatological interpretation of the Sabbath in Matthew and Luke. The Q redactor may understand Q 14:5 to refer to Jesus' prophetic ministry in Galilee. Thus it is possible that Q 14:5 is an earlier form of Matt 12:11 // Luke 14:5, and was uttered by Jesus as a statement about his prophetic ministry.

The Audience of the Sabbath Saying

Regarding the prophetic ministry of Jesus in Q 14:5 one may infer with some confidence what the Q redactor refers to in the phrase *kai eipen autous*. This phrase appears three times in Q (7:22; 14:5, 16). In Q 7:22, the dative pronoun obviously refers to the disciples of John, but in Q 14:5, 16 it is not easy to distinguish who the audience was. In Matt 12:2; Luke 6:2, they are the Pharisees on the basis of the saying of Mark 2:24.[36] However, it is not easy to determine the audience to whom Jesus referred in the Sabbath controversy in Q 14:5. Did Jesus originally speak the Sabbath saying to the Pharisees? The audience in a smaller chapter of Q 11:39–48, 52 is designated as "Pharisees." However, Kloppenborg has distinguished the "actual audience," the Q community itself, from the "projected audience," the impenitent and the opponents

---

35. Yang, *Jesus*, 266: The Sabbath controversy after the christological healing activity of Jesus is "effective enough to show the eschatological significance of his Sabbath healing ministry."

36. Doyle, "Concern of the Evangelist," 18. He summarizes why there is a focus upon Pharisees in Matthew in a negative sense: (1) Matthew received such references from both Q and Mark; (2) Pharisaic Judaism was the dominant form of Judaism at the time of the writing of Matthew; (3) the separation of Matthew's community from Judaism was complete (Matt 10:17–18; cf. John 9:22; 12:42; 16:2); (4) the Pharisees were considered the wise ones, and Matthew is showing that their wisdom was superseded by Jesus' wisdom; (5) there remains the possibility that converted Pharisees within Matthew's own community were causing trouble.

of the Q community.[37] For the projected audience, according to this distinction, in Q 3:7–8 the Q redactor projects the audience to be the crowds who came to John the Baptist without repentance, in Q 6:20–49; 10:2–10, 16–24 to be the disciples who follow the teaching of Jesus, in Q 11:49–51 to be the descendants of the murderers of the prophets, in Q 12:54–56 to be the people who are oblivious to the imminent catastrophe, and in Q 16:16 to be the people who violently oppose the kingdom of God. However, in a larger group of Q 7:31–35; 11:29–32, 49–51 the Q redactor projects the audience as "this generation," all impenitent Israel. Kloppenborg further argues that "this generation" was the "ostensible audience," i.e., "impenitent Israel."[38] From this perspective, he argues that impenitent Israel is also addressed in Q 12:8–10; 13:26–27, 29, 28, 30, 34–35; 14:16–24. Therefore, in reference to Lewis A. Coser,[39] Kloppenborg implies that in Q's redaction the sayings articulated "the conflict between the Q group and their Jewish contemporaries over the preaching of the kingdom."[40] This implication means that in the larger group Q's sayings are addressed to all the people of Israel including the members themselves of the Q community, but primarily to the outsiders or opponents like the Pharisees. From this perspective, one may infer that the audience for Q 14:5 was "this generation" or all of Israel including the members of the Q community. Because Q 14:5 coheres with the sayings of Q 13:24—14:35, Q 14:5 seems to refer to "this generation" as Israel. Even though in the saying of Q 13:28 there is no phrase "this generation," one may infer the people who were "thrown out" were "this generation" or Israel in general.[41] In a similar way, Israel is generally implied in the phrase *kai eipen autous* of Q 14:5. The saying of Q 14:5 is buttressed by the rhetorical question regarding the practice of the Sabbath law. The tone of the Sabbath saying here is rhetorical and paraenetic, rather than polemical or threatening. In Q 14:5 all of Israel, Pharisees, opponents, even the members of the Q community, are told that they must practice a new teaching of Jesus about God's will of love on the Sabbath. Thus the implied audience or the ostensible audience as all of Israel is told as an "exhortation"[42] to the mission of the kingdom.

---

37. Kloppenborg, *Formation of Q*, 167.
38. Ibid., 238: "The tone is hortatory and instructional, not polemical or threatening."
39. Coser, *Function of Social Conflict*, 38, 87–95.
40. Kloppenborg, *Formation of Q*, 167.
41. Jacobson, *First Gospel*, 208. In Q 13:28–29 "it is addressed more widely to Israel in general or more precisely to 'this generation.'"
42. Kloppenborg, *Formation of Q*, 238. He argues that the hortatory or instructional sayings in Q were quite different from the sharp rebukes and threats, and that the sayings thus were originally intended as exhortations to the community. Rather he suggests that "mild warnings are found (Q 6:47–49; 9:61–62; 12:33–34; 14:34–35) and the speaker chastises his audience for not observing his words (6:46) and for their little faith (12:28, *holigopistoi*)—but not for their lack of faith or rejection of the kingdom!"

EPILOGUE

I discuss what role the Sabbath saying played from its form-critical and redaction-critical perspectives, and how the other Sabbath sayings in the Gospels are related to Q 14:5. According to the traditional view based on the two-source hypothesis, the Sabbath controversies in Matt 12:11 and Luke 14:5 belong to the Matthean *Sondergut* and the Lukan *Sondergut*. On the basis of linguistic reminiscences[43] between Matthew and Luke, however, the original historical situation of Jesus is probably preserved in the Sabbath controversy.[44] That is to say, in spite of the different contexts for the sayings in Matthew and Luke, Q 14:5 can be regarded as an older tradition.[45] Some scholars have also suggested that Q 14:5 was probably in Q because it seems well placed in the sequence of the prophetic sayings[46] of Q 13–14. Matt 12:9–14 contains the same tradition as that transmitted in Luke 14:1–6, hence Matt 12:9–14 may be a conflation of Mark 3:1–6 with Q 14:5. Matt 12:11 and Luke 14:5 may have been in Q because it represents an authentic saying during Jesus' public ministry.[47] I show that while many scholars view Jesus' statement as the result of later Christian christological speculation (perhaps too high a Christology for Q?), Jesus' words make perfect sense when set into the context of Jewish sectarian debates and hence could stem from Jesus himself. Since Luke 14:5, then, appears to stem from the same source, was known to Matthew, is consistent with its Q context and represents a primitive tradition, it very well could be in Q. While this is assumed in the rest of this book, that it is correct will be reinforced by the main argument. The Q community moved incrementally from a Jewish to a Gentile mission; Q represents an (otherwise missing) intermediate step in the process.

I narrow the focus from the broader context of the Q community to the Sabbath controversy of Jesus in Q. I argue that the Sabbath controversy is the intermediate step between Jewish law and the Gentile mission. I focus on Sabbath observance and practice in Judaism and Jewish Christianity as the environment of Jesus' policy. Here the references in Epiphanius and earlier documentation for Jewish Christianity[48] help us to see in relative terms how fluid the Q community was. This examination shows that the Q community, consistent with its observance of the Torah, relegated the Gentile mission to God at the end of time. The Sabbath controversy served to move the community beyond such a narrow focus to the point where it could accept the missionary activity of the Gentile Christian community. Of course, Q was influenced in this direction by the

---

43. Schürmann, "Sprachliche Reminiszenzen," 193–210.
44. Lohse, "Jesu Worte über den Sabbat," 79–89.
45. Tuckett, *Revival*, 98.
46. Schulz, *Q*, 153, 163; Hengel, *Charismatic Leader*, 18–24; Theissen, *Biblical Faith*, 89–104; Esler, *Community and Gospel*, 117.
47. Banks, *Jesus and the Law*, 128–29.
48. Epiphanius, *Panarion of Epiphanius of Salamis*.

success of the Gentile mission. Hence, this chapter also illustrates the tension between the Jewish mission and the Gentile mission in the Synoptics and Paul.

This chapter is an attempt to draw together the threads of the preceding arguments and reflect upon their consequences. The scope of my inquiry has been rather modest and I have restricted myself to a single focus in order to remain effective and responsible. Therefore, I examine an issue found in Q 14:5, specifically the impact of the Sabbath controversy of Jesus for the early Christian missionary activity. I suggest the love of God as the foundational missionary principle for early Christianity. In the Sabbath saying, we understand the relation between the deeper meaning of the Jewish law and the Gentile mission. I now consider why it is so and how Jesus' view of a particular aspect of the Sabbath concurs with his views of Jewish law and the Gentiles as a whole.

I argue that the two elements of the Q context, Jewish law and the Gentile mission, display God's love as a missionary principle for the Q community in the Sabbath controversy of Jesus. Unlike the Synoptics, the Sabbath saying in Q appears only in a single verse of Q 14:5; nevertheless, Jewish law and the Gentile mission help interpret the Sabbath controversy of Jesus. In the Sabbath saying, the Q community sees that there was both a concrete remark about the observance of Jewish law, and, underlying that, a spur to missionary effort which would expand a Jewish mission to a Gentile mission. God's love which is attentive to the needs of the person is a basic missionary principle for the Q community. I demonstrate that the love of God which the Q community understood through the true meaning of the law is a certain missionary principle for early Christianity.

I see the Sabbath controversy of Jesus as reflecting the potential tension between Jewish law and the Gentile mission, because Jewish law tends to focus on the Jewish mission for the Q community, while the Sabbath controversy of Jesus heightens the needs of every person and highlights the Gentile mission. The Sabbath controversy even more significantly displays a distinct awareness, nowhere to be found in Jewish law, of breaking the law because of a newly meaningful interpretation of Jesus on the basis of God's love. This attention to a deeper concern is most characteristic of the Christian missionary principle, placing the Sabbath controversy of Q between Jewish law and the Gentile mission.

The understanding of the Sabbath controversy between Jewish law and the Gentile mission foreshadows the Q community in a long transition from Q to Matthew. I discuss that the Matthean community is influenced by Q, and that the Q community will become the Matthean community. Both Q and Matthew show themselves to be the communities with full observance of Jewish law. Jewish law is an internal context for the Q community as a conservative Jewish group. The Q community, therefore, confines itself to Judaism and preaches the gospel only to the Jews. In this perspective, the Matthean community follows the Q community in retaining elements of Judaism and the responsibility for the Jewish mission. The Gentile mission nevertheless is also an external context for the Q community as a Jewish Christian group. The Q community is confronted with the circumstances of the Gentile mission which was progressing successfully before the 50s CE. Here we can find the different understanding of relations to the Gentiles between the Q community and the Matthean community. The Q community relates their understanding of the Gentiles in the eschatological perspective on the basis of the public ministry of Jesus. However, the Matthean community positively accepts the Gentile mission because Matthew knows well the fact that the Gentile mission has flourished since the death and resurrection of Jesus.

In the time between their background in the Jewish law and their observance of the Gentile mission, the Q community remembers the Sabbath controversy of Jesus which depicts him aware of a reason for breaking Jewish law. Maintaining the Jewish traditions of Jesus, Q transforms its missionary activity on the basis of God's love that surpasses the law. Ultimately, God's love gives the Q community a logical development into the Matthean community, which leads to a Christian interest in the mission for the Gentiles. The Q community, though, still does not practice a Gentile mission in their contemporary life.

This study's importance, therefore, is threefold. First, it articulates the Sabbath controversy of Jesus in Q 14:5, which can be placed between Jewish law and the Gentile mission for their community life. Put simply, this single issue of the Sabbath controversy must be examined between Jewish law and the Gentile mission prior to our examination of the law itself in Q. Second, in examining the relationship between Q and Matthew, this study suggests possible evidence that the Q community merged into the Matthean community on the basis of similar views toward Judaism and Jewish Christianity. Third, in terms of Q scholarship, this study rules out a description of Q 14:5 isolated from Q 13:24—14:35. Rather, this study suggests Q 14:5 did not exist in isolation and was a prophetic saying in a wider context of Q.

We learn and try to show the readers that Jesus' recognition that one must love, as applied to the Sabbath controversy, suggests one should love toward Gentiles and toward all. God's love is the basic missionary principle. In terms of early Christianity's missionary activity, therefore, future descriptions of God's love in Q 14:5 must take into account Jesus' frequent and close contact with the needs of the people in the Q text.[49] We find that Q, therefore, is in basic agreement with the missionary thrust of the New Testament.

---

49. Q 7:1–9, 18–23, 24–28, 31–35; 10:2–16, 21–24; 11:14–23, 24–26; 12:2–12, 22–31, 32–34; 13:18–21, 24–30; 14:5, 16–23, 26–27; 17:33; 14:34–35; 15:4–7; 16:13; 17:1–6, 23–35; 19:12–26.

IV

Jesus and Jewish Law

PROLOGUE

THE QUESTION OF THE Q community's relation to Jewish law is not only one of the important issues in the study of the Synoptic Gospels, but one of the difficult issues in the reconstruction of early Christianity. There is by no means one answer to the question. Some have argued that Q was conservative toward Jewish law and others that Q abrogated it. Much of the confusion arises from Q itself: according to Q 16:16, the law ended with John; according to Q 16:17, it is eternal and valid; according to Q 16:18, it is either abrogated or intensified. This chapter tries to sort out the confusion of Q 16:16–18 first by looking at the Synoptic witness to Q's conservative attitude toward the law, second, by considering Matthew's special relationship to Q and third, by a careful exegesis of Q 16:16–18 and Q 11:42; 39b–40 as well.

Jewish Law in the Synoptics

This chapter investigates the attitude toward Jewish law in Mark, Luke, and Matthew. Of course, it is difficult to talk about only one attitude toward Jewish law in the Synoptics because the view of the law varies somewhat on the basis of each evangelist's theological concerns. Moreover, since Matthew and Luke used Mark and Q as their sources, it is reasonable to conclude that their theology was influenced by Mark and Q, and hence that their understanding of Jewish law must also be dependent on Mark and Q. Some differences arise based on the degree of dependence on one source or the other. Additionally, the evangelists are writing primarily about Jesus, not about the law itself. That is to say, for the Synoptic authors the issue of the law is secondary to Jesus' identity and their understanding of the law is based on their beliefs about Jesus.

Let us begin with Mark. Mark presents a rather startling portrayal of Jesus. It is common among biblical scholars to portray Jesus as a law-abiding Jew. For instance, Vermes, noting that Jesus did not always follow Jewish customs and traditions, nevertheless finds that in the Synoptics there are no examples in which Jesus abrogated Jewish law.[1] Hence he sees Jesus as a law-abiding Jew.[2] Vermes's characterization works because he makes a distinction between Jewish law, traditions and customs. Banks concurs, stressing the need to distinguish between the written law, the oral law, and traditions and customs in assessing Jesus' relationship to the Judaism of his day.[3] He believes that Jesus respected the law and wished his followers to observe it faithfully. A closer reading of Mark, however, challenges this view. While Mark 7:1–23 (esp. 7:10–13) suggests that Jesus upheld the law, in Mark 7:19, Jesus abrogates the dietary restrictions of Leviticus. In the Sabbath controversies of Mark 2:23—3:6, Jesus violates at least Pharisaic interpretations of the law, and suggests that that law is subordinate to other larger concerns. In brief, Mark's Jesus has a liberal view of the law.

Luke and Matthew, in contrast, portray Jesus with a more conservative attitude toward the law. For instance, while the term *nomos* is used eight times in Matthew (Matt 5:17, 18; 7:12; 11:13; 12:5; 22:36, 40; 23:23) and nine in Luke (Luke 2:22, 23, 24, 27, 39; 10:26; 16:16, 17; 24:44), and their use of the term is characterized as "conservative and Jewish,"[4] it is not found in Mark at all. Wilson has argued that while Luke tends to emphasize Moses' role as a prophetic figure (Acts 3:22; 7:37), a variety of phrases in Luke-Acts suggest a "connection between Moses and the law,"[5] highlighting his role as a "lawgiver"[6] or a "mediator of the Law."[7] Luke 16:16–18 is sometimes not seen as Lukan interest in the law itself, but the result of his faithfulness in preserving the tradition (compare 14:2–5) even when it does not yield to his particular concerns. For instance, Banks makes the point that Luke 16:16–18 implies a fundamentally conservative attitude toward the law.[8] In his interpretation, therefore, Banks handles Luke 16:16–18 as at first sight "an anomaly in the gospel, for nowhere else has we found Lucan interest in the Law itself."[9] Other scholars argue that Luke's use of this cluster of sayings is intended to show that Jesus rejected the law, since Luke 16:18 would have been understood as an abrogation of the law on divorce.[10] Others suggest, however, a more moderate aim on Luke's part: Wilson argues that Luke 16:17 implies that the law is valid and that keeping the law is the way to salvation,[11] thus maintaining "the

---

1. Vermes, *Jesus the Jew*, 35; Sanders, *Jewish Law*, 2; Segal, "Matthew's Jewish Voice," 7, 22; Snodgrass, "Matthew and the Law," 118–23.

2. Vermes, *Religion of Jesus*, 13–16.

3. Banks, *Jesus and the Law*, 90–91.

4. Jervell, *Luke and the People of God*, 136–37.

5. Wilson, *Luke and the Law*, 1–2.

6. Jervell, *Luke and the People of God*, 137.

7. Wilson, *Luke and the Law*, 3.

8. Banks, *Jesus and the Law*, 247.

9. Ibid., 219. Further, the "retention of vv. 17–18 probably results from his faithfulness in preserving the tradition (cf. 14:2–4) even when it does not yield to his particular concerns" (ibid., 220).

10. Blomberg, "Law in Luke-Acts," 61–62. He sees that Jesus abrogates the custom in Luke 16:18.

11. Wilson, *Luke and the Law*, 13–18. He sees that Luke does not condemn Pharisaic mistreatment,

eternal validity of the whole law."[12] Conzelmann sees the law functioning primarily within the framework of Luke's salvation history.[13] Luke integrates the law issue within his salvation historical scheme of promise and fulfillment[14] and portrays Jesus fulfilling the law in the sense of fulfilling what it predicts.[15] Hence, Luke includes the conservative statement in Luke 16:17. In any case, that Luke includes 16:17 at all, and his evident interest in Moses as lawgiver, at least suggest his Jesus is more conservative toward the law than is Mark's Jesus.

Matthew's version of Jesus is much more straightforward. In contrast to Mark, Jesus does not violate food laws (Matt 15) and does not accept the Gentiles until his resurrection (Matt 10; Matt 28).[16] Hummel points out that Matt 5:17–20, a chapter created by Matthew, is directed against antinomists, and is designed to underline the validity of the law.[17] Of course, this is not to say that Matthew is simply advocating Judaism. According to Hübner, for instance, Matthew's Jesus is not in favor of the law for its sake, but interprets it on the basis of promise and fulfillment. Hence, Jesus stands over the law.[18] McConnell notes that Matt 5:17 is central to Matthew's position: "This position is that Jesus is the divinely authoritative teacher who sets forth the true meaning and intention of the law, expressed in the love for God and for one's neighbor."[19] McConnell also suggests that in Matt 5:17, the expression "the Law and the prophets," can designate the whole Old Testament as the revelation of the will of God.[20] Thus, he argues that Matthew's Jesus' primary interest in the law is to "reveal the true will of God that the disciples might strive to fulfill this will."[21] One can conclude that while Jesus' mission

---

but only the neglect of essentials (ibid., 18).

12. Ibid., 13. Wilson regards Luke's statement in Luke 16:17 as "a confirmation of the absolute validity of the Law."

13. Conzelmann, *Theology of St. Luke*.

14. Hübner, *Gesetz*, 208.

15. Ibid., 209–11. Here is the reason: "Jesus ist von der Autorität des Gesetzes getragen, nicht aber steht er autoritär über dem Gesetz" (ibid., 211).

16. Barth argues that Matthew implies the validity of the Torah. See ibid., 58–88, 149–54. He argues that Matthew does not show Jesus entirely rejecting rabbinic tradition, but rather differing concerning the basis for interpretation of the law (ibid., 83–86).

17. Hummel, *Auseinandersetzung*, 69.

18. Hübner, *Gesetz*, 206. He concludes: "Mt von Mt 5, 18 aus zu interpretieren sollte eigentlich der Vergangenheit angehören! Demgegenüber ist es aber völlig überspitzt und widerspricht der ausgleichenden Tendenz des ersten Evanglisten, diesen als 'radikalen Antinomisten' zu bezeichnen" (ibid.).

19. McConnell, *Law and Prophecy*, 9.

20. Ibid., 13, 49–54.

21. Ibid., 50. "In the antitheses Jesus does not aim at giving new laws to replace the old; nor does he oppose certain Mosaic decrees for the sake of a sharp attack on the old laws" (ibid., 54).

takes priority over Jewish law, in Matthew Jesus is also regarded as a new Moses[22] and as the messianic interpreter,[23] who maintains the validity of the law.[24]

By comparison with Mark, Matthew's more conservative attitude toward the law can be found in his interpretation of Sabbath laws in Matt 12:1–8, 9–14. In his version of these stories, Jesus and his followers do not break Sabbath laws, but criticize Pharisaic interpretations of the law.[25] Compared with Mark 3:23–28, Matt 12:1–8 adds that Jesus' disciples were hungry on the Sabbath, emphasizes that the priests could do as the disciples had done without blame, and, citing Hosea 6:6, suggests that the disciples themselves are guiltless since they fulfill the scripture (see 1 Sam 21:1–6). Matt 12:9–14 adds a saying from Q (Matt 12:11) to Mark 3:1–6[26] in order to emphasize that the purpose of the Sabbath law is to save life. While Mark's version is ambiguous—does Jesus violate the Sabbath or not?—Matthew's version shows that Jesus fulfills the law by healing on the Sabbath. Matthew's position, summarized by the saying of Jesus, is this: the fulfillment of the command is love (Matt 5:43–48; 7:12; 12:1–8, 9–14; 18:12–35; 22:34–40). This means for Matthew that the entire body of the law is still in effect, but that it must be evaluated through the principles of love which Jesus preached. Applying the dominant principles of love and compassion, therefore, the Matthean community is seen as fulfilling the law and enacting the will of God (Matt 7:12; 12:50; 21:31).

It appears, then, that, when compared to Mark, Jesus in Matthew is consistently Torah observant and enjoins Torah observance. Both Matthew and Luke, therefore, portray Jesus keeping and advocating the law. Why do Matthew and Luke portray Jesus with a conservative attitude toward the law? A likely reason is that they used Q as their source and that Q maintained such a conservative view of Jesus. At this point, it will be helpful to pursue Matthew's special relationship to Q and "Jewish Christianity."[27]

---

22. Allison, *New Moses*, 185–90, 320–23.

23. Schäfer, "Torah der messianischen Zeit," 198–213.

24. Barth, "Matthew's Understanding of the Law," 58–164.

25. Segal, "Matthew's Jewish Voice," 7: "This is quite different from Paul's position that all observances are equally irrelevant. Here the primacy of the Law is affirmed, but the Pharisaic authority to interpret [it] is disputed."

26. As a framework of Matt 12:11, Matt 12:9–10, 12–14 contains Matthean redaction. The phrase *metabas ekeithen* in the beginning of Matt 12:9 makes a connection between Matt 12:1–8 and Matt 12:9–14. In Matt 12:10 *exestin* also has a function to connect Matt 12:1–8 and Matt 12:9–14 in a sequence (cf. Matt 12:2, 4, 12). In Matt 12:9 the phrase *ten sunagogen auton* is seen as a characteristic of Matthean redaction. The addition of *auton* to *ten sunagogen* seems to represent the fact that the synagogue was a place of conflict or confrontation among Jews, and that the Matthean community was already distinguished from the Pharisaic community. In Matt 12:11 and Matt 12:12, Matthew adds his favorite term, *probaton*. Such an interpolation seems to draw some aspects in relation to the parable of the lost sheep in Matthew. From this view, it is likely that Matt 12:11 fits well in the context of Matt 12:9–10, 12–14 as its framework.

27. Stanley K. Riegel points out that there are four different forms of the term: Jewish Christianity, Judaeo-Christianity, Judaistic Christianity and Judaic Christianity. For more information, see his "Jewish Christianity," 410–15.

Matthew and Q

In order to reinforce the conclusion that Q keeps the law, this chapter argues that Matthew is a prime example of Jewish Christianity and that the Q community either founded or developed into the Matthean community. Since Q would then be an earlier stage of the Matthean community's development and Matthew's community kept the law, Q must have kept the law as well.

To identify Matthew as a Jewish Christian text poses difficulties from the outset, because scholars cannot agree on much except that the term "Jewish Christianity" refers to first-generation Christians.[28] Daniélou's definition may be the most helpful: Jewish Christianity is that type of Christianity that manifested itself in a type of thought that was expressed in forms borrowed from Judaism.[29] We may apply it to Matthew, since Matthew shows a consistent tendency to favor Judaism. As noted above, in Matt 5:17–19, Matthew's conservative attitude toward Jewish law comes to clearest expression. Wilson notes that for Matthew, "the law itself remains intact; Jesus' aim is to interpret it, to expose the true intention obscured by the current experts."[30] Käsemann agrees: "While this passage is the subject of lively controversy, it is essentially unambiguous, and commands obedience to the whole Torah."[31] Likewise, Matthew applies the term *anomia* to someone who deviates from the will of God: both the enthusiastic prophets in Matt 7:15–17 and the scribes and Pharisees in Matt 7:23; 23:28 can be called *anomia* because of their corruption of the law and the will of God.[32]

While the evidence that Matthew is a Jewish Christian community is strong, the claim that the Q community can be considered as an earlier stage of Matthean community is more tentative. Nevertheless, there are important clues. For instance, Q plays a prominent role in Matthew: Matt 3–11 appears to be based on Q since it follows Q's order,[33] not Mark's, in its presentation. How the order of Matt 3–11 is influenced by the order of Q? Let us look at the order of Matthew and Q, comparing with Mark as follows:

---

28. Koester, "*Gnomai Diaphoroi*," 115; Segal, "Jewish Christianity," 326.
29. Daniélou, *Théologie du judéo-christianisme*.
30. Wilson, *Related Strangers*, 49.
31. Käsemann, "Beginnings of Christian Theology," 85.
32. Overmann, *Matthew's Gospel and Formative Judaism*, 88–89. He argues that *anomia* does not refer to "a specific group within the Matthean community," but to "anyone who does not accurately understand God's law and will or corrupts it" (ibid., 99).
33. Robinson, "Real Jesus," 149. "The first major part of the body of the Gospel of Matthew, chapters 3–11, into which the text of Q is largely compressed, was composed as a kind of rationale or justification for the Q community's having held out so long in its exclusively Jewish orientation"; Robinson, "Matthean Trajectory": "Matthew began this redactional procedure by imbedding Mark into his Q, not Q into Mark.... It is the intrusion of Mark into the Q-Matthew trajectory already in Matt 3–11 that suggests one should not speak of a late draft of QMatt, but rather of a first installment of Matthew, now involving (to a limited extent) Mark and so deserving already the designation Matthew"; Silberling, "Text and Tradition in Matthew," 73–115. Referring to Matt 3–11, Silberling also concludes, "Q is the primary source. The Q structure is generally followed, Q material predominates, and Markan material is used only to support or enhance Q structural and theological concerns" (ibid., 209).

Jesus and Jewish Law

Subject	Order of Q	Order of Matthew	Order of Mark
1. John	3:2b	3:1	1:4a
2. Jordan	3:3a	3:5a	+
3. The prophesy of Isaiah	3:3b–4	3:5b	1:2a–3
4. Brood of vipers	3:7	3:7	1:5
5. Announcement of judgment	3:8–9	3:8–9	+
6. The Coming One	3:16b	3:11	1:8a, 7b, 8b
7. The fire	3:17	3:12	+
8. The baptism of Jesus	3:21	3:13, 16a	1:5, 9
9. The Beloved Son	3:22	3:16b–17	9:7b–c
10. The temptation story	4:1–13	4:1–11	1:12–13a
11. Nazara	4:16	4:13a	6:1–2a
12. Capernaum	4:31	4:13b	1:21
13. The Sermon on the Mount (1)	6:20–23	5:3–12	+
14. The Sermon on the Mount (2)	6:27–28, 35c–d	5:43–5	+
15. The Sermon on the Mount (3)	6:29–31	5:38–42, 7:12	+
16. The Sermon on the Mount (4)	6:32, 34, 36	5:46–48	+
17. The Sermon on the Mount (5)	6:37–38	7:1–2	4:24
18. The Sermon on the Mount (6)	6:39	15:14	+
19. The Sermon on the Mount (7)	6:40	10:24–25a	+
20. The Sermon on the Mount (8)	6:41–44a	7:3–5, 18–19; 12:33b	+
21. The Sermon on the Mount (9)	6:44b–c	+	+
22. The Sermon on the Mount (10)	6:45	12:34–35	+
23. The Sermon on the Mount (11)	6:46–49	7:21, 24–27	+
24. The Sermon on the Mount (12)	7:1a	7:28a	+
25. Capernaum	7:1b–	8:5a	2:1a
26. The Centurion's faith (1)	7:3	8:5b–7	5:22–23
27. The Centurion's faith (2)	7:6b–9	8:8–10	+
28. The Centurion's faith (3)	7:10	8:13	7:30
29. John's question	7:18–19, 22–23	11:2–3, 4–6	+
30. About John (1)	7:24–26	11:7–9	+
31. About John (2)	7:27	11:10	1:2
32. About John (3)	7:28	11:11	+
33. For and against John	7:29–30	21:32	+
34. The Children of Wisdom	7:31–35	11:16–19	+
35. Discipleship	9:57–60	8:18–22	+
36. The Lord of harvest	10:2	9:37–38	+
37. Sheep among wolves	10:3	10:16	+

Subject	Order of Q	Order of Matthew	Order of Mark
38. No provisions	10:4	10:9–10a	6:8–9
39. What to do in house	10:5	10:12	6:10a–b
40. A son of peace	10:6	10:13	+
41. Eating and drinking	10:7–8	10:10b–11	6:10b–c
42. Cure the sick there	10:9	10:7–8	6:12–13
43. Shake off the dust	10:10–11	10:14	6:11
44. Sodom	10:12	10:15	+
45. Three Galilean towns	10:13–15	11:21–24	+
46. Whoever takes you	10:16	10:40	9:37
47. Thanksgiving prayer	10:21–22	11:25–27	+
48. The Lord's Prayer	11:2b–4	6:9–13	+
49. The answer of prayer	11:9–13	7:7–11	+
50. The Beelzebul accusation (1)	11:14	9:32–33	+
51. The Beelzebul accusation (2)	11:15	9:34	3:22

As noted above comparing the order of Matt 3–11 and Q with Mark, Q 3–11 is mainly divided into five sections which all are corresponding to Matt 3–11. In the order of the first section, nos. 1–12, the order of Matt 3–4 is followed by Q without any single exception. In contrast to this, the order of Mark is distorted and differs somewhat from Matthew. In the second section, nos. 13–24, the Sermon on the Mount in Matt 5–7 is also influence by the order of Q except Matt 10:24–25a. In addition, the sayings of Matt 15:14; 12:33b; 12:34–35 corresponding to Q 6:39; 6:4–44a; 6:45 cannot be considered as a main concern of counting the order due to surpass the limitation within Matt 3–11. In the third section, nos. 25–34, and the fourth section, nos. 35–45, the order of Matthew is also exactly identified with the order of Q except the saying of Matt 21:32 which also surpass the limitation of Matt 3–11. The remaining section, nos. 46–51, looks like a problem. This final section looks outwardly to break the order of Q, but it is not true. Let us divide this section with three subsections: nos. 46–47, nos. 48–49, and nos. 50–51. After dividing to do so, the final section is also corresponding to the order of Q on the basis of its subject that Matthew divided.

What is the result of this comparison? In a word, the Matthean community thoroughly depends on Q to preserve his theological characteristics. As a result, this comparison definitely shows us how the sayings of Jesus in Q affect to the Matthean community. It is also to be noted that much of the material peculiar to Matthew overlaps with Q,[34] as "conspicuously Jewish" and "distinctly anti-Gentile."[35] For instance, Matt 10:5-6, 23 show strong pro-Jewish tendencies. A final clue is that from a sociological standpoint, Matthew's community looks like the Q community. In this sense the Gospel of Matthew comes from a Jewish Christian community like Q.[36]

Jesus' Attitude toward Jewish Law in the Sayings Gospel Q

After having shown that Q was most likely a Torah-observant Jewish Christian community by looking at Q's interpreters and successors, this chapter considers more carefully Q's explicit statements about the law and Jewish practices: Q16:16-18; 11:42; 11:39b-40.[37] In each case, a reconstruction of the Q wording of the verse will be suggested, followed by a discussion of its meaning for the Q community.

The reconstruction of Q 16:16 poses several difficulties: differences between Matthean[38] and Lukan readings,[39] the precise meaning of the words *arpazein* and *biastes*,[40] and the position of Q 16:16 in Q.[41] Q 16:16a is parallel to Luke 16:16a and Matt 11:13.[42] The formula "*ho nomos kai hos prophetai*" refers to the Hebrew Bible.[43] Matthew's version of Q 16:16a (Matt 11:13) implies that the law as well as the prophets have a prophetic function. Nevertheless, Matt 11:11-13 probably reflects Matthew's redactional concerns based on the catchwords "*ioannes*" and "*basileia*."[44] Likewise, in

---

34. Brown and Meier, *Antioch and Rome*, 55. "Particularly in the case of Q, there is a strong possibility that a certain amount of M material was conflated with Q in written form. Hence, Matthew would have been working with this conflated, pre-Matthean form of Q." Schweizer, *Good News according to Matthew*, 12-14; Lührmann, *Redaktion der Logienquelle*, 11-23, esp. 18 and 21n2.

35. Streeter, *Four Gospels*, 232.

36. Luz, *Matthew 1-7*, 83: "Therefore we argue that the Gospel of Matthew comes from a community which was founded by the wandering messengers and prophets of the Son of man of the Sayings Source and remains in close contact with them. The traditions of Q thus reflect, for the community, experiences from its own history."

37. The reconstruction of Q texts is mainly indebted to the International Q Project. The *Critical Text of Q: Journal of Biblical Literature Format* (5 May 1995) is especially useful. Though unpublished, it is now available from the Institute of Antiquity and Christianity at the Claremont Graduate University.

38. Schulz, *Q*, 261-62; Kloppenborg, *Formation of Q*, 28.

39. Barth, "Matthew's Understanding," 63-64; Polag, *Fragmenta Q*, 74; Marshall, *Gospel of Luke*, 628; Catchpole, *Quest for Q*, 234-35; Kloppenborg, *Formation of Q*, 113.

40. Jacobson, *First Gospel*, 117-18; Schrenk, "biazomai, biastes," 609-14; Hoffmann, *Studien zur Theologie*, 50-79; Sand, *Gesetz und die Propheten*, 179-81.

41. Lührmann, *Die Redaktion*, 27-28; Schenk, *Synopse zur Redenquelle*, 44; Hoffmann, *Studien zur Theologie*, 51; Jacobson, *First Gospel*, 118-19; Kloppenborg, *Formation of Q*, 115-17; Polag, *Christologie der Logienquelle*, 47-48.

42. Hübner, *Gesetz in der synoptischen Tradition*, 28. He verifies that Luke 16:16 belongs to Q.

43. Barth, "Matthew's Understanding," 92. The formula in older times simply meant the Hebrew Bible, and there are several passages referring to the whole Hebrew Bible by using it (2 Macc 15:9; 4 Macc 18:10; Matt 7:12; Luke 24:44; John 1:45; Acts 24:14; Rom 3:21).

44. Likewise, in Matt 21:31b-32 the catchwords "John" and "kingdom" appear as the Matthean redaction.

Matt 11:13 the verb *propheteuein* is probably a Matthean insertion.[45] For this reason, the IQP does not retain the verb in Q 16:16 and the reconstruction are as follows:

> The law and [[ ]] the prophets ... until John. From [[then]] the Kingdom of God has suffered violence and the violent take it by force.[46]

What then is the meaning of Q 16:16? That Q 16:16a connects the formula *ho nomos kai hoi prophetai* to the phrase *he basileia tou theou* in Q 16:16 probably points to the fact that the law is to be fulfilled by the kingdom, not abrogated by it. Both Matthew and Luke interpret it this way. Matthew 5:18 refers to Jesus' fulfillment of the law[47] and Luke 16:16b connects the proclamation of Jesus to the Hebrew Bible ("the Law and the prophets"—that is, God's message in the Hebrew Bible) and shows his missionary concern by using the verb *euanggelizesthai*. The proclamation of the new age by the verb becomes "a thematic statement for the rest of Luke and Acts."[48] But apart from the Matthean and Lukan settings of the saying, the saying appears at first to end the law. So Streeter, in an earlier study, regarded Q 16:16 as a Gentile saying that implied abrogation of the law.[49] Bultmann asserts that "the old Law no longer plays a role"[50] and that "the saying that concerns the eternal validity of the Law (Matt 5:18 // Luke 16:17) displays crass disregard of the spirit of the new restructured view of the Law."[51] From this starting point, Hübner concurs with Bultmann and concludes that Q 16:16 depicts the end of the law, while Q 16:17 affirms the abiding validity of the law.[52]

However, this is not Q's intention. In discussing the problem of Q and the law, Kloppenborg, regarding the validity of the law in Q 16:16–18,[53] points out that "Q 16:17 appears to be one attempt on the part of an editor of Q to obviate the possibility of an antinomian interpretation of Q's paraenesis."[54] Here he sees Q 16:17 as the Q redactor's interpretation to obviate a potentially false understanding of Q 16:16. The saying in Q 16:16 imply that the era of the kingdom continues what was begun in the era of the law and prophets. Thus, Jesus does not reject the validity of the law in Q

---

45. The aspect of the law's operations is explicitly insisted upon by Matt 11:13, which speaks not only of the prophets but also of the law as "prophesying." Banks, *Jesus and the Law*, 210.

46. Moreland and Robinson, "International Q Project," 499.

47. France, *Gospel according to Matthew*, 114; Hübner, *Gesetz in der synoptischen Tradition*, 15–16.

48. Robinson, "Way of the Lord," 101.

49. Streeter, *Four Gospels*, 233.

50. Bultmann, "What the Saying Source," 29.

51. Ibid., 30.

52. Hübner, *Gesetz in der synoptischen Tradition*, 31. Kosch also argues that Q assumes the validity of Torah. See Kosch, *Eschatologische Tora*, 210–11, 451–52.

53. Kloppenborg, "Nomos and Ethos," 43. For more information, see ibid., 46.

54. Ibid., 45.

16:17, rather, he asserts "the converse, the affirmation of its permanent validity."[55] Q does not represent Jesus as living contrary to Jewish law.[56]

Q 16:17

But it is easier for heaven and earth to pass away than for [[ ]] one stroke of the law to <<lose its force>>.[57]

There is no scholarly consensus regarding the history of the tradition lying behind Q 16:17,[58] but there is widespread agreement that the saying comes from Q. Q here maintains an extremely conservative view of the law.[59] In Q 16:17, Jesus explicitly affirms the eternal validity of the law. The saying about permanence of the law in Q 16:17 is secondary in its Matthean format, because Matt 5:17–20 is composite[60] and betrays strong Matthean redactional concerns.[61] This indicates that the Lukan setting is more likely to be original. For example, the term *eukopoteron* in Luke 16:17 is not a typical Lukan term.[62] This suggests the Lukan position (after Q 16:16) may also be original.[63] Meyer points out correctly that in this position (after Q 16:16) and following Luke's wording, "Q's saying, in contrast to Matthew's revision, is not concerned with the future possibility of the Law becoming void but with the present impossibility of its being void."[64] Turner adds: "The law's eternal validity is certainly maintained, despite the dawning of the new age, but it has been transcended and changed by being sucked up into the powerful vortex of Jesus' messianic teaching and demands."[65] Regarding Luke 16:17, Blomberg sees that "the Law is valid in the age of this world. But with the end of this 'Weltzeit' and the arrival of the kingdom of God and the Son of man, the Mosaic Law loses its validity and becomes superfluous."[66] In this sense, Blomberg concurs with Banks that the demands of the law should be seen as fulfilled in part by Jesus' ministry and sacrifice, while others are fulfilled in Christ's ethical

---

55. Robinson, "Sequence of Q," 231.

56. Loader, *Jesus' Attitude*, 429.

57. The IQP reconstructs this saying on the basis of Lukan wording which is more likely to be original than Matthew's.

58. Mohrlang, *Matthew and Paul*, 137; Snodgrass, "Matthew's Understanding," 372.

59. However, Philip Esler has shown that a conservative view of the law in general does not prevent a more relaxed approach to the food laws in particular. For more information, see his *Community and Gospel*, 71–109.

60. Barth, "Matthew's Understanding," 65–71; Vouga, *Jésus et la loi*, 191–92.

61. Hübner, *Gesetz in der synoptischen Tradition*, 18; Meier, *Law and History*, 58; Davies and Allison, *Gospel according to Saint Matthew*, 494; Luz, *Matthew 1-7*, 258.

62. Catchpole argues that the form *eukopoteron estin* is used by Luke "in dependence on tradition," but it is used in Luke 5:23 and 18:25. See Catchpole, *Quest for Q*, 236.

63. Laufen, *Doppelüberlieferungen*, 588n84.

64. Meyer, *Community of Q*, 67.

65. Turner, "Sabbath," 110.

66. Blomberg, "Law in Luke-Acts," 61.

demands.⁶⁷ Esler also finds in Luke 16:17 a strong affirmation of the law's validity. He sees in the juxtaposition of Luke 16:17 and Jesus' divorce logion in Luke 16:18 a play by Luke to argue that Jesus' words intensify rather than abrogate Torah.⁶⁸ This is supported by Fitzmyer, who also finds the law's validity affirmed in Luke 16:17.⁶⁹ In brief, Q 16:17 affirm the present validity of the law in the Q community and establish that Q was indeed a law affirming Jewish Christian group.⁷⁰

Q 16:18

Everyone who divorces his wife [[ ]] commit [[s]] adultery, and the one who marries a divorcée, [[ ]] commits adultery.⁷¹

Q 16:18 may be regarded as an example of how Q 16:17 was put into practice by the Q community. Since it forbids divorce, it enjoins a stricter observance of the law on divorce than Jewish law was generally understood to demand.⁷² But such strict practice need not be read in anti-Mosaic terms:⁷³ the theme of adultery is introduced only in a subordinate way to emphasize Q's strict attitude toward the law.⁷⁴ While Deut 24:1–4 permits divorce, focusing particularly on the remarriage of the divorced wife, and Q 16:18 regards both divorce and remarriage as adultery,⁷⁵ Q 16:18 seems to have Gen 2:24 in view, which requires a man and woman to unite and not be separated.⁷⁶ Jesus in Q thus bases his teaching about marriage on God's purpose in creation, and

---

67. Ibid., 62.

68. Esler, *Community and Gospel*, 118–20.

69. Fitzmyer, "Jewish People and the Mosaic Law," 180–81.

70. The present validity in Q 16:17 can be compared with an eschatological horizon in Matt 5:18. For more information, see Henderson, *Jesus, Rhetoric and Law*, 313.

71. The IQP reconstruction is mainly based on the Lukan wording in Luke 16:18.

72. Deut 24:1–4 on divorce and remarriage; Deut 22:22 on adultery.

73. Q's stricter observance of the law shows that the Q community maintained a conservative attitude toward Jewish law because the Q community regarded itself as a Jewish Christian group. Q 16:18 shows the prohibition of divorce and remarriage would be kept by the Q community more rigorously than by some Jews. Tuckett, *Q*, 408; Stephen G. Wilson argues that Q 16:18 could be seen as a radical attack on the written law of Moses. For more information, see his book, *Luke and the Law*, 46–47.

74. Strecker, *Weg der Gerechtigkeit*, 133–35.

75. Banks argues that "no rabbi would have regarded a re-marriage of the divorced wife as adultery, though certainly he would have objected less to that idea than the ascription of adultery to the man when he re-married" (ibid., 193). Tomson argues that "a fundamental rejection of polygamy is included." However, this interpretation cannot be supported, because this saying just focuses on Jewish law on divorce. See Tomson, *Paul and the Jewish Law*, 113. He argues that Q 16:18 not only includes divorce but presupposes monogamy.

76. It is likely that in the Q community the dissolution of the first marriage would be unacceptable. In Q, adultery is committed in the divorce of the marriage and at the same time in the remarriage of the divorcée. The union of male and female corresponds to the divine will; consequently, the dissolution of the unity must violate the will of God, relating to the story in Genesis 2 (male and female become one flesh). Derrett, *Law in the New Testament*, 370.

hence remarriage after divorce is not allowed. Q 16:18 can thus be seen as a radical affirmation of Gen 2:24, not as an attack on the law in Deut 24:1–4.[77]

Tuckett, following Klinghardt,[78] appeals to the Dead Sea Scrolls (CD 4:20—5:1; 11Qtemple 57:17–19) for such a conservative reading of Q 16:18. The Qumran texts, interpreting the purity regulations of the law, require that priests should not marry or remarry anyone other than a virgin or a widow who is the widow of a priest (Lev 21:7, 13–14; Ezek 44:22). This requirement is not an exact parallel to the Q prohibition, since only the priests are in view, but it does show that a stricter interpretation of the law is consistent with the affirmation of the law.[79]

We may conclude, therefore, that for the Q community divorce proper, which was allowed by the Mosaic law, is absolutely prohibited[80] and at the same time that, no attack on the law is intended. The Q community observed the law more rigorously than most Jews and as a result chose the strictest possible interpretations of its demands. The Q community criticized the Jews, not for keeping the law, but for not keeping it strictly enough.

This criticism is also found with respect to tithing. Biblical tithes are imposed on grain, wine, oil, fruit, and animals (Deut 14:22–23; Num 18:12; Lev 27:30), but the precise amount to be given is not fixed (Lev 6–7; Num 18; Deut 18).[81] The *Mishnah* testifies to an expansion of tithing on the part of the Pharisees to include all things, including vegetables and herbs (*m. Ma'as* 1:1; 4:5), such as mint, dill and cummin.[82] According to Neusner, the Pharisees in Greco-Roman times made scrupulous tithing of their food a distinctive characteristic of their program for reform, thus indirectly testifying to general laxity in the payment of tithes.[83]

Q 11:42

But woe to you Pharisees, for you tithe mint and [[dill]] and [[cummin]], and neglect justice and the love of God; but these things you ought to have done, without neglecting the others.

77. Tuckett, "Q, the Law and Judaism," 93.

78. Klinghardt, *Gesetz und Volk Gottes*, 83–96.

79. Fitzmyer, *Gospel according to Luke I-IX*, 256.

80. This may be close to the saying of the Shammaites, who permitted divorce only for adultery (*Mishnah Gittin* 9:10). Watson, *Jesus and the Law*, 72.

81. Sanders, *Jewish Law*, 43–51. He gave us a review of the evidence for tithing.

82. Saldarini, *Matthew's Christian-Jewish Community*, 142 and 276n81. "Dill and cummin were also used for medicinal purposes. Tithing of dill is mentioned specifically in *m. Ma'as* 4:5. Cummin is transliterated into Greek from Hebrew (Isa. 28:25)." Neusner, *From Politics to Piety*, 80: "Tithing was a dietary law." According to Neusner, tithing was as much concerned with table-fellowship as ritual purity (cf. ibid., 83); Catchpole, *Quest for Q*, 264. According to *Mishnah Ma'aserot* 4:5; *Mishnah Demai* 2:1, dill and cummin are required to be tithed but mint is not mentioned in this context. Westerholm, *Jesus and Scribal Authority*: "Mint, dill, and cummin were all used at food and thus subject to tithing."

83. Neusner, *Rabbinic Traditions*, 180–238. Paying tithes had not been pictured merely as a religious practice. Tithes were a tax used to support the central religious and political institutions of Israel, the temple and its priests.

Q 11:42, one of the woes against the Pharisees,[84] charges the Pharisees with doing things "not required by the Law in order to gain a reputation for great piety,"[85] by criticizing them for their scrupulous tithing while neglecting human compassion.[86] This is clearly a disagreement between law-observant groups. Both groups agreed that the law required careful observance of all God commanded, but from Q's standpoint the Pharisees had too narrow a focus. The Pharisees are accused of tithing "mint, dill and cummin"[87] but neglecting "justice[88] and the love of God." Q 11:42c attacks Pharisaic inaction: "these things you ought to have done, without neglecting the others."[89] This final clause does not allow an either/or approach to the law, since, as Tuckett observes, tithing "must still be undertaken and any appeals to great principles such as justice," the love of God, etc., "must not undermine in any way the actual practice of tithing."[90] Q 11:42c thus not only criticizes the Pharisees for their practice of tithing but affirms the necessity of tithing (along with just and the love of God) for the Q community.[91] As in Q 16:18, therefore, Q 11:42 do not abrogate the law but intensifies it.

Before moving on to Q 11:39b–40, I suggest here why the Q community rejected and attacked the Pharisaic circle in Judaism. In Q, the hostility and animosity between

---

84. Q 11:42 is probably the "kernel" of the woes against the Pharisees in Q 11:39–52. David Kosch argues that Q 11:39–52 is divided into two sayings: one directed against *nomikos* or *grammateos*, the other against *pharisaioi*. For more information, see his *Eschatologische Tora*, 92. However, the IQP reconstructs the sayings in Q 11:39–52 has woes against Pharisees, because in Matt 23:23 "*grammateos* and *pharisaioi*" may be Matthean redaction. The general editors favor a position more like that of Kosch.

85. Manson, *Sayings of Jesus*, 236; Matthew's concern with the interpretation of the law is stronger than Luke's. The Matthean reference to "*ta barytera tou nomou*" is probably his redaction. Barth, "Matthew's Understanding," 80; Schulz, *Q*, 100; Kosch, *Die eschatologische Tora des Menschensohnes*, 113–14; Tuckett, *Q and the History*, 409. Here it is worthy to note the evidence of the history-of-tradition analysis of Matthew, which seems to indicate that an earlier reshaping of the Jesus-tradition took place in a conservative direction vis-à-vis the law and Israel; Dunn, *Jesus, Paul, and the Law*, 134.

86. Schürmann, "Zeugnis der Redenquelle," 174.

87. Rabbinic literature proposed a tithing law: "Whatever is used for food and is watched over (i.e., cultivated on one's property) and grows from the soil is liable to tithes" (*Mishnah Maʾas* 1:1). Westerholm, *Jesus and Scribal Authority*, 57; Safrai and Stern, *Jewish People*, 825: They see that tithes were levied on grain, wine and oil, according to the written Torah (Lev 27:30; Num 18:27; Deut 12:17; 14:13), a law which is echoed in other parts of the Bible (Neh 10:38; 13:5; 2 Chron 31:5) and in the Apocrypha (Tob 1:1; Judith 11:13). According to them, however, in rabbinic literature tithing was extended to take in "anything used as food, anything stored, and anything that grows from the soil" (*Mishnah Maaseroth* 1:1). They also propose that the custom of tithing non-agricultural products was already known in the temple era, and can be detected with some certainty behind Jubilees 32:2, and the CD 14:11–15.

88. The IQP here regards *krisis* as "justice," not as "judgment." Jolliffe, "Woes on the Pharisees," 117.

89. Scholars regard this final clause as a redaction in Q. Kloppenborg, "Nomos and Ethos," 42–43; Catchpole, *Quest for Q*, 272.

90. Tuckett, *Q and the History*, 410.

91. Q 11:42 may lie in Jesus' polemic context because it fits well with Jesus' polemic against the Pharisees. Westerholm, *Jesus and Scribal Authority*, 59.

the Q community and the Pharisaic community come to fullest expression. In Q, the Pharisees are described as hypocrites (Q 6:42; 11:43–45), bigots (Q 7:32), persecutors (Q 6:23; 11:49), murderers (Q 11:47–51), and faithless leaders who misguide and corrupt the crowd (Q 11:46). The hostility toward the Pharisaic leadership and the harsh terms of denunciation and rejection are employed by Q help to locate the Jewish community before 70 CE. For Q, the Pharisaic community is hypocritical, obstinate, and corrupt, while the Q community is faithful, conservative, and the true children of Abraham. Q tries to condemn the Pharisaic circle in association with the evil generation (Q 11:29–32). Q seeks to legitimate the position of its community by associating and implicating the current Pharisaic leadership with the widely accepted sins and errors of past leaders. The persecution of the Q community at the hands of the Pharisaic leadership parallels the persecution and rejection of the prophets by the false leaders of Israel's past history. Q 6:23; 11:49 claim that the contemporary Jewish leaders rejected the prophets God had sent, and that they killed and persecuted them. These contemporary leaders indeed are implicated in the murder of all righteous blood in the history of Israel (Q 11:50–51). According to the Deuteronomistic understanding of history, Israel rejected the prophets and wise men. For this reason, God punished Israel with the destruction of Jerusalem (Q 13:34–35).[92] Hence, the Pharisaic leadership is an evil generation (Q 11:29). Q's depiction of the Pharisaic leadership, culminating as it does in Q 11, serves as a warning to the Pharisaic community. However, despite all of the criticism and rejection of the Pharisaic leadership in Q 11, the Q redactor ascribes a position of authority and power to the Pharisees by saying that "this generation is an evil generation; it seeks a sign." Moreover, Jesus in Q said, "no sign shall be given to it" (Q 11:29). In this sense, the Q community sets its values over against the values and behavior of the Pharisaic leadership. The Q redactor would reject the Pharisaic leadership on the basis of Jesus' interpretation of the law. That is to say, the Pharisees are interested in their practice of legal traditions and customs, but Jesus' teaching leads the Q community to a newly meaningful interpretation of the law itself. At this point, one may consider the possibility that the Q redactor builds a firm Christian community based on the teaching of Jesus on the law.

Q 11:39b–40

Woes to you Pharisees, for you cleanse the outside of the cup and the dish, but the inside is full from grasping and lack of self-control. (40) . . . Did not he who made the outside make the inside also?

Q 11:39b–40 is next to the saying about tithing in the series of woes against the Pharisees. The sequence of the woes is different in Matthew and Luke. Luke may have inverted the order of Q 11:42 (cf. Matt 23:23), 39b–40 (Matt 23:25–26) in order to insert the saying about not washing (Luke 11:38) before Q 11:39. Thus Matthew

92. Steck, *Israel*, 227–39.

23:25–26 may preserve here the Q order of the woes better than Luke 11:39–42.[93] Q 11:39b–40 implies that the Pharisees cleansed "the outside of the cup and the dish" but not "the inside."

In Q 11:39b, by contrast, Jesus maintains that cleansing[94] "the outside of the cup and the dish" occurs at the same time as cleansing "the inside." In this view, cleansing only the outside of the cup would have been impossible because, according to the Hebrew Bible, vessels must be totally immersed in water, then left until evening when they became clean (Lev 11:32–33).[95] The Pharisees were following biblical practice,[96] but Q 11:39b could not be criticized of their actual cleansing procedure. Rather, according to Kloppenborg, it was "an absurd caricature" and "ridicule."[97] But if Pharisaic ritual was not being ridiculed, what was? Q 11:39b suggests that the cup and dish are metaphors for "the whole person"[98] since "the inside is full of grasping and lack of self-control."

The metaphor continues in Q 11:40: "Did not he who made the outside make the inside also?"[99] Q's point is that the Pharisaic practice of purity is based on external

---

93. Westerholm, *Jesus and Scribal Authorit*, 87. He argues that Matthew is "certainly more appropriate and probably original" and Luke can "scarcely be original."

94. With reference to E. P. Sanders, however, Watson's suggestion is that disputes about purity are probably not authentic to Jesus. Watson, *Jesus and the Law*, 55.

95. Maccaby, "Washing of Cups," 3–15. He thus ignores the implication of the saying that the practice of cleansing cups and plates has particular reference to the Pharisees (Matt 23:16–26, "you say . . . you tithe . . . you cleanse").

96. Sanders, *Jewish Law*, 39. According to *Tosefta Berakoth* 5:26, the Pharisees thought that the outside of the cup would be kept clean due to the outside could be washed by hands. This account implies that Pharisees were not worried about the inside of the cup. Rather Mishnaic tradition focuses on hand-washing, not on washing the cup. *Tosefta Berakoth* 8:2–3 states that the Shammaite Pharisees' concern was primarily to wash their hands before touching the cup. For more information, see Sanders, *Jewish Law*, 203–4. He proposes that "the hands may have touched a dead insect, and if there is liquid on the outside of the cup, the impurity would be mediated to the cup via the liquid" (Sanders, *Jewish Law*, 39). Jacob Neusner also verifies that such a practice of the Shammaite Pharisees was true. See his article, "First Cleanse the Inside." *Mishnah Kelim* 25:1 asserts that the outside of the cup and the inside are separate for the purposes of purity. Neusner, "First Cleanse the Inside," 494–95. He sees in Matt 23:25–26 evidence of a stage in Pharisaic thinking at which the purity of the inside of a cup was not determinative for cleanness ("the Shammaite rule").

97. Kloppenborg, "Nomos and Ethos," 39.

98. Culpepper, *Gospel of Luke*, 247: "The Pharisees should realize that God made the whole person, inside and out."

99. The Luke 11:40 seems to receive the saying from Q, but the Gospel of Thomas 89:2 does not seem to depend on Q and Luke. See Patterson, *Gospel of Thomas and Jesus*, 62. "Q probably had something corresponding to Luke 11:41 // Matt 23:26; this too does not appear in the Thomas version" (ibid., 63). He here thinks Thomas did not know Q and Luke. Wolfgang Schrage has also argued in detail for Thomas' independence upon Q and Luke. For more information, see his book, *Verhältnis des Thomas-Evangeliums*, 170–71. Q 11:40 occurs as part of a block of material that is highly rhetorical. Thus this saying ends with the polemical question and is organized around the theme of the conflict between Jesus and the Pharisees. See Bultmann, *Geschichte der synoptischen Tradition*, 139.

rituals,[100] not on the purity of the whole heart.[101] But according to Q's Jesus, external purity is guaranteed by purity of heart. The Pharisees are just interested in cleansing the outside because they do not realize that the cleanness of the inside itself guarantees the cleanness of the outside.[102] As in the tithing woe, the point is not to abrogate the law (in this case purity laws) but to offer a new way to fulfill it.[103]

This chapter has investigated Jesus' statements about Jewish law in Q (Q 16:16–18; 11:42; 11:39b–40). This investigation has shown that according to Q, the law is not changed or abrogated, but newly interpreted by Jesus. It is to be fulfilled, as promised in "the law and the prophets" (Q 16:16). The Q community is expected to observe the demands of the law, but to do so as they are understood through Jesus' teaching.[104] As we saw, in most cases this means fulfilling the intent of the law from pure motives. But Q 16:17 points out, in this context, that Jesus teaching does not allow for even the details of the law to be abrogated. Q 16:18 gives an example of this principle in action: the concerns for divorce in Deut 24:1–4 are best addressed. Q 16:18, therefore, cannot be interpreted as an abrogation of the law. Rather, the Q community seems to have stricter demands than the divorce law requires. Q 11:42 shows that it is clear, then, that the Q community was a torah-observant Jewish Christian community. Q has a polemic against Pharisaic practices (Q 3:8; 7:9; 11:42–52; 13:29; 22:28–30), but the Jesus of Q does not directly reject the observance of Jewish law.

EPILOGUE

The purpose of this chapter has investigated the Synoptics' understanding of Jewish law, and the conflict revealed between the Q community and the Pharisees interpreting and practicing Jewish law in Q. This chapter has described the range of the law

---

100. That the Pharisees cleanse the outside of the vessel may refer specifically to the Shammaite practice, since they would pay attention to the outside of a vessel. Neusner, "First Cleanse the Inside," 494.

101. Culpepper, *Johannine School*, 247. "God is not just concerned with the observance of rituals of purity but with the purity of one's heart."

102. In general, the Pharisees quite simply sought to apply the purity laws governing the temple ritual to their everyday lives. Jacob Neusner concludes that the purity laws referred only to the priest when performing their temple service and to themselves only when they went to the temple; outside the temple the laws of ritual purity need not be observed. Neusner, *From Politics to Piety*, 83. "But the Pharisees held that even outside the temple, in one's own home, the laws of ritual purity were to be followed in the only circumstances in which they might apply, namely, at the table. Therefore, one must eat secular food (ordinary, everyday meals) in a state of ritual purity as if one were a temple priest."

103. Catchpole, *Quest for Q*, 267. He argues that in Q 11:39b *arpage* is used in Jewish literature as a vivid metaphor for the predatory activities of wolves and lions (Gen 49:27; Pss 7:2; 22:13; 104:21; Ezek 19:3, 6; 22:25, 27; Hos 5:14; Mic 5:8; Matt 7:15; John 10:12), and in an indirect sense for injustice done by the rich and powerful to the poor and vulnerable (Job 20:19; 24:9; Pss 10:9; Isa 3:14–15; 10:2; 61:8; Ezek 18:7, 12, 16; Mic 3:2).

104. Käsemann, *New Testament Questions*, 85. In the case of Matthew, he sees that Matt 5:17–20 demands obedience to the law.

in Q and scholarly debates about it. In doing this, we have suggested that Jesus in Q has a conservative attitude toward Jewish law; that one of the major interests of the Q community was the observance of Jewish law; and that the conflict between the Jewish Christian community and the Pharisaic circle was transformed in the woes addressed by Jesus. Jesus seems to uphold the validity of the law. Hence, legal disputes can be read as a debate about their true meaning of the law. As a result of this investigation, this chapter concludes the following:

Although Mark abrogates Jewish law (Mark 2:18–22; 2:23—3:6; 7:1–23), the Lukan and Matthean understanding of the law is central to the deepest religious focus of Jesus because they are based on Jesus' conservative Jewish attitude toward it and see it as eternally valid. Luke often identifies the law and custom (Luke 2:27; Acts 6:11–14; 15:1, 5; 21:21), but Jesus in Luke seems to abrogate some of the custom, not the law itself (Luke 16:18). Luke and Matthew strongly maintain the validity of the law (Luke 16:17; Matt 5:17–20). This understanding of Jewish law should be identified with Jesus' attitude toward the law in Q because Q understands Jesus as a Torah-observant Jew (Q 11:42; 16:16–17).

Matthew's Jewish Christian tendency seems to be in harmony with Q because Q is in an earlier stage of Jewish Christianity which is first-generation Christianity. Therefore, Q exhibits distinct Jewish Christian tendencies on the basis of a Torah-observant Christian community. Matthew's Jewish Christian attitude toward Jewish law is found in his legal interpretation regarding the law (Matt 5:17–20; 12:1–14), but he criticizes *anomia* of scribes and Pharisees (Matt 7:23; 23:28) because of their corruption of the law. Matthew's polemic fights against the Pharisaic interpretation of the law (Matt 5:20; 16:12; 23:1–36). This polemic comes from Q. Q's polemic against the Pharisaic circle (Q 3:8; 7:9; 11:42–52; 13:29) seems to derive from Jesus who condemned the Jewish leadership (Q 11:29–32). Q criticizes the Pharisaic leadership because the Pharisees' concern is in legal traditions and customs, not in practicing the will of God through a new interpretation of the law itself.

Jesus' understanding of Jewish law in Q is conservative because Q's attitude toward the law comes from the background of Jewish Christianity. Q 16:16 presents that Jesus' overall understanding of Jewish law for the Q community. The saying states that the kingdom of God was begun in the era of the law. Q 16:17 shows that the Q community as a Jewish Christian group upheld an extremely conservative interpretation of the law, and that they considered themselves as a community with full observance of the law. In Q 16:17, Jesus has a conservative attitude toward the law. Q 16:17 represents the Q community as a Jewish religious group that builds on its Jewishness. Q 16:18 can be regarded as an example of how Q 16:17 was put into practice by the Q community. The Mosaic law generally permits divorce according to a valid procedure. However, Q 16:18 prohibits divorce because the Q community regards divorce as adultery and remarriage as adultery. From this perspective, Q 16:18 states a stricter observance of the law on divorce and adultery. Q's special attitude toward the law is stronger than the Jewish law in Deut 24:1–4. However, Q's Jewishness cannot be interpreted as a radical attack on the Mosaic law. Rather it encourages the Q community to observe more rigorously the present validity of the law than other Jews. The Sabbath has a meaning of an eschatological nature, unlike the prophetic writings of the Hebrew Bible. The law in Q is obviously related to the present validity.

There are two sayings relating to Jewish law in a series of woes against the Pharisees in Q. First, Q 11:42 criticize the Pharisaic attitude of tithing on the basis of their interpretation of the law and the Pharisaic practice of the law: tithing mint, dill and cummin, but neglect justice and the love of God. Q 11:42 emphasizes that true observance of the tithing law is completed by practicing "justice and the love of God" as well as tithing "mint and dill and cummin." From this perspective, the Pharisaic interpretation and practice of tithing are rejected, but Q's practice of the tithing law is preserved. The criticism against the Pharisees here is that God commanded the practice of "justice and the love of God" as well as tithing "mint and dill and cummin." The Pharisaic understanding of the commandment of God requires a careful observance of the tithing law. The Pharisees are criticized due to neglecting "justice and the love of God" that may be identified with the will of God. Second, Q 11:39b–40 criticizes Pharisees cleansing the outside of the cup and the dish but not the inside on the basis of their practice of purity. The saying implies that Pharisees cleansed "the outside of the cup and the dish" but not "the inside," following the conventional practice of the Shammaites. The saying of Q 11:40 is rhetorical in tone. The polemical question represents a theme of the conflict between the Q community and the Pharisees. This Pharisaic purity is criticized by the Q community because the Pharisees' practice is based on the rituals of the outside, not on the purity of the whole heart. The two woes in Q 11 related to Jewish law show that there was a conflict between the Q community as a Jewish Christian group and the Pharisaic circle as a Jewish religious group, but Jesus encouraged the Q community to stand firmly upon his teaching.

Another Q tradition that concerns the law is the saying about rescuing an ox from a pit on the Sabbath in Q 14:5. Since Sabbath law is part of the Decalogue, it is a more fundamental issue than is seen elsewhere in Q's discussion of the law. The Sabbath saying in Q 14:5 shall be further investigated.

V

The Sabbath in the Synoptics

PROLOGUE

THE GOSPELS FREQUENTLY REPORT that Jesus violated the Sabbath law.[1] While there is a broad consensus that such controversies are one of the features of the Gospel tradition that goes back to Jesus himself, there is as yet no agreement that Q contains such a controversy in Luke 14:5 // Matt 12:11. This chapter (1) reviews scholars' opinions regarding placing the Sabbath controversy of Luke 14:5 // Matt 12:11 into Q; (2) examines Q 14:5 form-critically and redaction-critically to show that it is consistent with other Q materials and appropriate to its Q context; and (3) considers its possible derivation by comparing it to other Sabbath controversy stories (Mark 3:1-6; Luke 6:6-11; Matt 12:9-14; Luke 14:1-6; Luke 13:10-17). On the basis of this analysis, this chapter shows that Luke 14:5 par. indeed derives from Q; it considers the love of God as a missionary principle for the Q community in relation to Jewish law and the Gentile mission. The International Q Project voted Luke 14:5 par. into Q but with a C grade (i.e., doubtful). Its reconstruction is as follows:[2]

[[Q 14:5]]

And he said to them, which [[ ]] [[will there be]] among you who will have [[ ]] an ox, and if it fall on the Sabbath into a [[pit]], «will» not «extricate» it?

---

1. Mark 2:23-28; Matt 12:1-8; Luke 6:1-5; Mark 3:1-6; Matt 12:9-14; Luke 6:6-11; Luke 13:10-17; Luke 14:1-6; John 5:1-18; John 9:1-41.

2. The reconstruction of Q texts in this chapter is mainly indebted to the International Q Project databases and evaluations. Especially, the *Critical Text of Q: Journal of Biblical Literature Format* (5 May 1995) is useful. Though unpublished, this is now available from the Institute for Antiquity and Christianity at the Claremont Graduate University. A first draft of a critical edition of the Sayings Gospel Q of Jesus had already been published by the *Journal of Biblical Literature* since 1991.

The Sabbath and the Synoptic Problem

A brief review of biblical Sabbath observances will help place the Sabbath controversy in the Gospels in context. The Sabbath is one of the most important Israelite festivals[3] and there was a great deal of speculation about it. In the Decalogue, for instance, two reasons are given for observing the Sabbath: the creation and the exodus. The Sabbath, on the one hand, was related to the meaning of "rest"[4] which came from creation (Exod 20:11). In Exod 20:8–11, the fourth commandment is based on God's rest after creating the world. According to Genesis 1–2, God created the heavens and the earth during six days, but he rested on the seventh day. The seventh day is called "Sabbath" and the Israelites observed the day in imitation of God. Deut 5:15, on the other hand, bases the command to rest on the deliverance[5] from Egypt. Since they had been freed from working for the Egyptians by God, they were to give their servants a day off. The Sabbath was also seen as the sign of the covenant between God and Israel (Exod 31:13).[6] Specifically, in the prophetic writings, "punishment" is pronounced on those who fail to keep the Sabbath holy as the sign of the covenant between God and his people. In Ezek 20:12–14, for example, God commands his exiled people to sanctify the Sabbath, because their ancestors had profaned it in their rebellion against God. On the other hand, Isa 58:13–14 describes a new more hopeful situation after the exile.[7] An "unexpected promise"[8] is made here: The reward for the returning exiles is that they will be able to keep the Sabbath holy and honor the day of the Lord joyfully.

The Sabbath commandment was expanded by numerous practical (Exod 23:12; 34:21)[9] and cultic regulations (Lev 23:3; 35:2) including sacrifices (1 Chron 9:32; 23:31; 2 Chron 2:4; 13:11; Isa 1:13; Hos 2:11). The Pentateuch focused on the prohibition of work and on sacrifices to be offered on the Sabbath (Exod 16:22–30; 35:2–3; Num 15:32–36); the prophetic books highlighted the covenant dimension of the Sabbath (Isa 58:13–14; Jer 17:19–27; Amos 8:5); and the historical books detailed the implications for trade and commerce (Neh 10:31; 13:14–22). In the time of the Maccabees: the issue of the Sabbath and war emerged (1 Macc 2:32–38). When Gentile

---

3. Moore, *Judaism*, 21.

4. Andreasen, *Old Testament Sabbath*, 185. He concludes that the "divine rest motif" is also in other Near Eastern creation myths. There the creative deities rested after their creative works, especially "immediately after the creation of man." See von Rad, "There Remains Still a Rest," 96. "This notion of 'rest' now comes to occupy an important place in the religious thought of Israel. It is thought of as a rest found by the weary nation through the grace of God in the land he has promised them."

5. Dressler, "Sabbath in the Old Testament," 30.

6. Moore, *Judaism in the First Centuries*, 21: "It [the Sabbath] is called 'an eternal covenant,' 'an eternal sign' (compare Ezek 20:12) between God and Israel (Exod 31:16–17; cf. 31:13)."

7. Muilenburg, "Introduction and Exegesis," 653–54; Andreasen, *Old Testament Sabbath*, 38.

8. Andreasen, *Old Testament Sabbath*, 44–45. He says, "This promise strongly implies that God's covenant relationship no longer depends on one's national (or social) identity but on one's individual decision and devotion to YHWH, which is to be demonstrated by one's keeping the Sabbath."

9. Rordorf, *Sunday*, 12.

troops attacked the Jews on the Sabbath, Mattathias and his followers, out of respect for the Sabbath, refused to fight. As a result, a thousand Jews were killed.

The Sabbath is obviously connected to "fasting" in the *Gospel of Thomas* 27:1–2, although it is unclear how one could "keep the Sabbath a Sabbath."[10] Sabbath's association with fasting is often found in the Sabbath observance in early Christianity.[11] In essence, the Jews themselves appeared to have made the Sabbath a day of fasting (Judith 8:6; Jub 50:10, 12–13; CD XI.4–5). The early Christian church seems to have followed this Jewish tradition of the Sabbath fast. In this sense observing both the Sabbath and the Lord's Day was the widespread practice of Coptic Christianity.[12] The *Apostolic Constitutions*, by contrast, propose clearly that one did not fast on the Sabbath, except at Passover/Easter time in memory of the Lord's death (*Apostolic Constitutions* V. 14:20; 18:1–2; 20:19; VII. 23:3–4).[13]

Jesus' statement about the Sabbath can be better understood against this background. As shown in chapter 4, since Sabbath observance was one of the distinctive marks of Israel's covenant with God, it became one of the reasons by which Jews separated themselves from Gentiles in the Greco-Roman world. Accordingly, when Jesus taught the Sabbath, he created the possibility for a different relationship between Jews and Gentiles.

This chapter begins by surveying the opinion of scholars who think that Luke 14:5 par. is not derived from Q. Rudolf Bultmann understood Luke 14:1–6 as a variant of Mark 3:1–6. According to him, Luke 14:5 is simply an isolated saying interpolated into the story. Likewise, he saw Luke 13:10–17 as a further variant on the theme of Sabbath healing, composed on the basis of an originally isolated saying (v. 15). The sayings in Luke 14:5 // Luke 13:15 // Matt 12:11 were for Bultmann typical of "ein traditionelles Argument in den Sabbatdebatten der Urgemeinde."[14] For Bultmann the Gospels were declarations of the faith of the primitive church, not records of the historical Jesus. Hence his focus was not whether these sayings belong to Q, but whether the controversies in them are historically reliable. For him, Matthew and Luke have just added an isolated saying about the Sabbath (Luke 14:5 // Luke 13:15 // Matt 12:11) into the framework of the early church with the story of Mark 3:1–6. The saying had developed in the course of tradition in the primitive church. This means that the *Sitz im Leben* of the saying was the Sabbath controversy which took place in the early

---

10. Patterson, *Gospel of Thomas and Jesus*, 86; this saying is connected to fasting in the *Gospel of Thomas* 6:1–4; 14:1–3. The saying in the *Gospel of Thomas* 27:1–2 is seen as an "ascetic reinterpretation of the obligation to fast and keep the Sabbath" and could be read as a "call for more dedicated Sabbath observance." Wilson, *Related Strangers*, 90.

11. Strand, "Some Notes on the Sabbath Fast," 167–74.

12. Bishai, "Sabbath Observance," 25–43.

13. Kraft, "Some Notes on Sabbath Observance," 24.

14. Bultmann, *Geschichte der synoptischen Tradition*, 10.

church. His conclusion here seems to be applicable to the interpretation of the situations of the Gospel of John, not to the situations of Jesus' saying in Q.[15]

Berger and Klumbies[16] agree with Bultmann. They consider the Sabbath saying in Matt 12:11 // Luke 14:5 to be part of a christological interpretation that is in harmony with the frame story. Neirynck has evaluated that the christological interpretation along the lines investigated by Klumbies is "a more correct understanding of the Sabbath healings in Luke [14:1–6]."[17] According to this line of thought, the sayings could not be authentic since the implied Christology is too high. Yang simply argues that Matthew's two Sabbath stories (Matt 12:1–8, 9–14) go together with a further Matthean Sabbath (Matt 24:20).[18] Employing socio-historical and literary criticism, Yang concludes that for Matthew the Sabbath is fulfilled by Jesus[19] in that "Jesus' redemption" provides "the true meaning and significance of Jesus' fulfillment of the Sabbath."[20] Considering the christological and eschatological character of the two Sabbath controversy pericopes,[21] Yang suggests that such an emphasis stands over against the Pharisees' casuistic concerns and betrays Matthew's awareness of the danger of a legalistic tendency in Sabbath observance in the Matthean community. It is, however, possible that the Sabbath saying in Q 14:5 has "no Christological implications."[22] While the conflict stories derived from Mark (Matt 12:1–8; Mark 2:23–28; Luke 6:1–6) clearly have this sense—the statement that the Son of Man is the Lord of the Sabbath is the christological perspective of early Christianity—Luke 14:5 par. only takes on this meaning when read in that context. However, the saying in Q 14:5 is quite apart from the christological point. In fact, in Q 14:5 the focus is not on the Sabbath laws, but on the practice of God's love. If this Sabbath controversy indeed does not contain christological implications, it is more likely to have been in Q.

Neirynck, in a study of the minor agreements of Matthew and Luke against Mark, concludes that "the influence of Q in a limited number of passages and the coincidences of the independent editing of Matthew and Luke for the bulk of the

---

15. Lohse also observes that the Sabbath pericopes in John 5 and 9 are created by the Evangelist of the Gospel of John and are thus formations of the Christian community. The reason is because in John 5 and 9 there are some additions relating to the Sabbath matter. For example, the Evangelist added the phrase "at the Sabbath" (John 5:9b; 9:14a) into his pericopes and thus transformed the narrative into a Sabbath controversy. Such an addition and transformation reflect the situation of the church and synagogue at the end of the first century when Christianity was already definitely separate from Judaism (compare John 5:18). Lohse, "Jesu Worte über den Sabbat," 79–80.

16. Berger, *Gesetzesauslegung Jesu*, 583; Klumbies, "Sabbatheilungen Jesu," 173–74 and 176–78.

17. Neirynck, "Luke 14,1–6," 260.

18. Yang, *Jesus*, 16–17, 230–41.

19. Ibid., 205, 213, 224–29, 307–8.

20. Yang, *Jesus*, 228–29; Sigal has already regarded "the very purpose of the Sabbath as a redemptive-healing day." See *Halakah of Jesus*, 158.

21. Yang, *Jesus*, 18–19, 205–6, 213–14, 266–68, 272.

22. Banks, *Jesus and the Law*, 129.

instances can explain the minor agreements."[23] Neirynck thus assigns some of the minor agreements to Q.[24] Though Matt 12:11 // Luke 14:5 appear to be such an agreement, however, Neirynck does not assign it to Q.[25]

In 1975, Neirynck recognized the difficulties in studying the Sabbath controversy of Q.[26] He confirmed that the term "Sabbath" cannot be found in Q and that the primary source of the Sabbath controversy is only found in Mark 2:23–28 and Mark 3:1–6. Therefore, he concluded that "there should be no doubt about the secondary character of the two healing stories in Luke 13 and 14. In my view they are almost completely due to Lukan redaction. The dependence of Luke 14 upon Mark 3,1–6 is especially relevant and attempts to reconstruct a Q passage are based on a false evaluation of the similarities with the Matthean redaction of the pericope of the man with the withered hand (12,9–14)."[27] Neirynck thus totally rejected the possibility of the reconstruction of a Q text in Luke 14:5 par. due to the dependence of Luke 14:1–6 upon Mark 3:1–6. In 1991, Neirynck reexamined the question of whether or not the saying of Jesus about the Sabbath in Matt 12:11 // Luke 14:5 can be ascribed to Q. Neirynck focused on *nomikoi* in Luke 14:3, *tinos hymon* in Luke 14:5 and *tis estai ex hymon* in Matt 12:11, since they are typical of Matthean and Lukan redaction, but as to whether they attest a Q-saying, he concluded that they cannot be determined to belong to Q.[28]

Braun regards Luke as "a master of narrative evocation of the Greco-Roman social dining scene, of adjusting older Jesus traditions towards his narrative aims, and of characterizing Jesus as a kind of *deipvosophistes* (dinner sage)."[29] From this presupposition, he argues that Luke 14:1–24 stands out in its "setting (an upper-class dinner party)," and the scene consists of "*quaestiones convivales*, topics related to banquets and proper dinner behavior."[30] For this reason, he concludes that the narratives recorded in Luke 14:1–24 can be defined form-critically as pronouncement stories or *chreiae*.[31] "Luke 14,1–6 belongs to this form-critical class." However, Braun does not

---

23. Neirynck, *Minor Agreements*, 37.

24. See ibid., 42n137. Here he suggests that some passages are commonly accepted as overlapping with Q.

25. Ibid., 78. Helmut Koester also argues that the attribution of the saying of Luke 14:5 // Matt 12:11 to Q is doubtful because Matthew attached the sayings of 12:11–12 to the sayings of "Matt 12:9–14 = Mark 3:1–6." Koester, however, does not explain how the sayings in Matt 12:9–14 are the same as the ones in Mark 3:1–6 and why Matthew attached Matt 12:11 to the sayings of Matt 12:9–14. According to him, "it is more likely that this was a favorite and well-known argument against Sabbath observation which circulated in the oral tradition." See Koester, *Ancient Christian Gospels*, 147n3.

26. Neirynck, "Jesus and the Sabbath," 227–70.

27. Ibid., 230.

28. Neirynck, "Luke 14,1–6," 249–57.

29. Braun, *Feasting and Social Rhetoric*, 1. He argues that such dining scenes and dinner sages are recognizable and credible figures to first-century Mediterranean readers. Ibid., 6, 30–38, 47–54.

30. Ibid., 2.

31. Ibid., 6. "Luke 14,1–24 consists . . . a *chreia* (cre . . . a)." For more information, see ibid., 41, 132, 145–75. He explains the *chreia* pattern in Luke 14.

regard Luke 14:5 as a Q text because he thinks that "the evidence for a pre-Lukan existence of 14,1–6 is scarce and indecisive" and that the significant differences between Luke 14:5 and Matt 12:11 are hardly "explained with an appeal to different redactions of a common Q saying."[32] However, his conclusion is weak because he does not pay attention to the verbal agreements between Luke 14:5 and Matt 12:11.

Yang has attempted to show that Jesus' attitude to the Sabbath is only one aspect of his attitude to the Hebrew Bible in Matthew. He argues that Jesus' attitude toward the Sabbath in Matthew has been placed "in the context of Matthew's more general presentation of Jesus' view of the law in Matthew." Yang acknowledges Matt 12:11 is traditional (i.e., not a Matthean creation) but suggests that Matt 12:11 // Luke 14:5 is based on "Q material (rather than Q)." The difficulty for Yang is the distinction between Q material and Q ("a written document").[33] In addition, he does not succeed in explaining what the significant differences are in form and content between Q material and Q, making me wonders what a distinction between them might look like. In line with various scholars' comments, Yang doubts that Luke 14:1–6 came from Q, rather than from L *Sondergut*. Thus he doubts that the sayings in Luke 14:5 and Matt 12:11 came from exactly the same source, Q.[34]

By contrast, a number of scholars believe that Luke 14:5 and Matt 12:11 is in Q. Schürmann suggests a method for determining the existence of Q materials omitted or changed by Matthew and Luke, and for recognizing Q material in *Sondergut* passages. The method is "Sprachliche Reminiszenzen." When Matthew and Luke drew material from *Sonderverse*, some linguistic reminiscences remained.[35] Similarly, where Matthew and Luke omitted or completely changed Markan material, linguistic reminiscences can be seen. This method is useful for discovering an omitted Q text when verbal reminiscences of Q can still be detected.[36] He thus argues that all of Luke 14:1–6 is from Q, and that Matt 12:9–14 is a combination of Mark 3:1–6 with Q (Matt 12:11 = Luke 14:5). Besides the verbal agreements (reminiscences) of Matt 12:11 // Luke 14:5, for evidence, he points to νομικος in Luke 14:3 which is characteristic of Q.[37]

Lohse proceeds on a different tack, arguing that Luke 14:5 par. is in Q by first tracing it back to the historical Jesus. He raises a question neglected by Bultmann concerning the historical context of Luke 14:5. Noting that the practice in Matt 12:11 // Luke 14:5 is unusual in the situation of Pharisaic Judaism in Jerusalem, he points out it corresponds well to the rural situation in Galilee. The practice of rescuing an

---

32. Ibid., 23–25. "This plain evidence is that the story is an item of exclusively Lukan material which contains one saying (14,5) that may have had a prior life (cf. Matthew 12,11)" (ibid., 25).

33. Yang, *Jesus*, 140, 196 and n238.

34. Ibid., 258 and 264n83. He argues that Matt 12:11 also came from M *Sondergut* (ibid., 196).

35. Schürmann, "Sprachliche Reminiszenzen," 193–210.

36. Ibid., 194–96, 199–200, 210.

37. Schürmann, "ProtoLukanische," 266–86. Specifically, see 270n22 and 276.

ox from a pit on the Sabbath is closer to the countryside situation of Galilee[38] Hence, the original historical situation of Jesus probably has been preserved in the Sabbath saying: "Ihr ältester Bestand kann auf den historischen Jesus zurückgeführt werden: Mc 2:27; 3:4 par und Mt 12:11–12 par Lc 14:5."[39] Since, then, the sayings are old and fit well the Galilean milieu, Lohse, following Crum, argues Matt 12:11 // Luke 14:5 // Luke 13:15 were all in Q. Apparently, an authentic saying of Jesus has come down in several versions, of which Matt 12:11–12 is the oldest. Lohse then argues that the pericope of Luke 14:1–6 is based on the saying in v. 5, for which the story forms a suitable frame.[40] In this sense Max M. B. Turner simply argues that the Evangelist Luke has taken the incident from the saying in Q.[41]

Banks recognizes that the central problem for the Sabbath is that the parallel sayings (Luke 14:5 // Matt 12:11) are in rather different contexts. Luke 14:5 is the account of the healing of a man suffering from dropsy, a healing that took place on the Sabbath. Matt 12:11 is from an account of the Sabbath healing of a man with a withered hand (cf. 12:9–14), a pericope which itself has very obvious parallels in Mark 3:1–6 and Luke 6:6–11. With the reference to the different context, Banks concludes that the context of the logion in Matt 12:11 is perhaps original.[42]

---

38. Adolf von Harnack once noted that its rural themes implied an exclusively Galilean horizon, devoid of any urban, Hellenistic or Gentile elements. See his book, *Sayings of Jesus*, 121. Such a practice like rescuing an ox on the Sabbath is probably closer to the countryside situation of Galilee than the one of Jerusalem. There are frequent references to the language of "country life" in Q. See Vassiliadis, "Nature and Extent," 63. His explanation of "the use of language of the countryside of Q" was indebted to Crum, *Original Jerusalem Gospel*, 49–63 (IV, "Q and Country Life."). Crum's attempt was to discover more ancient evidence within and behind the evidence of the Gospels of Luke and Matthew: "an evidence which goes back to Galilee behind the evidence which knows the great Mediterranean world outside" (ibid., 49). He has confirmed that those passages which fulfill some of the following conditions seem *likely* to stem from Q: "They accord with the country life language of Q" (ibid., 67); "Village life in Galilee, the open sky, the work in the fields, is here in Q. There is as good internal evidence of the country origin of Q as any you will find" (ibid., 62); Robinson, "Down-to-Earth Jesus," xvi: "Q apparently does not reflect the Jesus movement's headquarters in Jerusalem, but rather its remnants in Galilee."

39. Lohse, "Jesu Worte über den Sabbat," 84. For this reason, Lohse argues that the pericope of Mark 3:1–5 also can be understood in "eine Situation im Wirken des historischen Jesus" (ibid.).

40. Lohse, "*Sabbaton*"; specifically, see 24n197.

41. Turner, "Sabbath, Sunday," 100. "There is some evidence that the Sabbath incident in Luke 14 is derived from Q." With reference to Luke's Q material, he argues that "the Q origin of the story of the healing of the man with dropsy on the Sabbath is inferred from the nature of the contacts between verses 3b, 5 and Matthew 12:11, and from Luke's use of Q in the immediately previous section (13:18–35; especially vv. 34–35). It must immediately be admitted that a number of difficulties face this hypothesis and the majority of scholars are of the opinion that 14:1–6 is either to be derived from L or is a Lukan creation based on a pre-Lukan logion (v. 5). If the Q origin *is* sound then the passage probably provides further evidence for the hypothesis that Matthew and Luke used different recessions of that material; it is almost impossible to account for the divergences between Matthew and Luke simply in terms of different redactional activities."

42. Banks, *Jesus and the Law*, 128–29. "Since it has been demonstrated that the differences between the Matthean and Lucan versions of the saying can largely be resolved in terms of redactional activity, it is possible that the story is the original context of the logion in Matt 12:11" (ibid., 129).

Tuckett argues that the Sabbath saying of Luke 14:5 is not a completely isolated saying and hence the saying needs a narrative framework to make sense. Luke 14:5 for him "must have been part of a story which involved some breach of the Sabbath law." Luke 14:3 may also derive from Q because it contains some un-Lukan features. He suggests as evidence that the three verbs *apokritheis . . . eipen . . . legon* overload the sentence.[43] He agrees with Cadbury's observation that the use of *apokritheis*, in a context where there is no real answer (because there is no explicit prior question), is less common in Luke.[44] Tuckett also suggests that the use of *nomikos* is attested for Q, whereas Luke generally uses *grammateos*. The use of *nomikos* for him appears to be an un-Lukan word and hence pre-Lukan, i.e., Q.[45] Tuckett concludes through this investigation that "there are still traces of an earlier tradition in the question in verse 3, as well as in the answer in verse 5."[46] Tuckett argues concerning the law in Luke that "the Law was not regarded as permanently valid for the Christian."[47] The Q tradition which is relevant for this argument is the saying about rescuing an "ox"[48] from a pit on the Sabbath in Q 14:5. Tuckett here points out that the force of the saying is clear: "Jesus is shown as not acting wantonly. If he does break the Sabbath Law, he does so by appealing to accepted and legally defined exceptions to the Law."[49]

This chapter has discussed whether Luke 14:5 and Matt 12:11 can be placed into Q or not. Scholarly opinion is fairly divided. In the next two chapters, therefore, I will study the form-critical and redaction-critical understanding of Q 14:5 and its relationships with Mark 3:1–6; Matt 12:9–14; Luke 6:6–11; 13:10–17; 14:1–6, in order to confirm that Jesus' Sabbath controversy is in Q.

Genre and the Q Redactor

This chapter considers the form-critical understanding of the Sabbath saying in Q 14:5. Bultmann identifies Luke 14:5 is an "aphophthegm" because he regards the pericope of

---

43. Tuckett, *Revival*, 98.

44. Cadbury, *Style and Literary Method*, 170–71. In Luke 14:3, the word comes at the beginning of a new speech with little or no reference to the situation and thus it is perhaps a Semitic idiom.

45. This view differs from the opinion of Rehkopf, who claims that *nomikos* is characteristic of proto-Luke. Tuckett, *Revival*, 98–99; Rehkopf, *Lukanische Sonderquelle*, 95. He points out that *nomokos* is found in Matt 22:35; Tit 3:9, 13; and specifically Luke 7:30; 10:25 (= Matt); 11:45, 46, 52 (= Matt), 53; cf. 14:3 in the pre-Lukan sayings.

46. Tuckett, *Revival*, 99.

47. Tuckett, *Q and the History*, 405. "The issue of whether the Christian should obey the detailed commands of the Law does not seem to have been a varying one for Luke."

48. Various manuscripts support "son," "ox," "ass" or almost any combination of these three. Tuckett has examined them and concluded that the primitive form is probably a "son" who had fallen into a pit on the Sabbath. See Tuckett, *Q and the History*, 414. However, an ox in Q may be preferred on the basis of the assimilation with original tradition between Luke 14:5 and Luke 13:15.

49. Tuckett, *Q and the History*, 416. "The Jesus of Q thus operates on the Sabbath within the Law as defined by later tradition to a far greater extent than the Jews of Mark or the Jesus of Matthew."

Luke 14:1–6 as a variant of Mark 3:1–6. As an aphophthegm, it is distinguished from "Streitgespräche," "Schulgespräche," and "Biographische Apophthemgmata."⁵⁰ Apophthegms are isolated, free-floating sayings of Jesus. He then subdivides the isolated sayings into "Logien (Jesus als Weisheitslehrer)," "Prophetische und apokalyptische Worte," "Gesetzesworte und Gemeinderegeln," "Ich-Worte," and "Gleichnisse und Verwandtes."⁵¹ The purpose of this classification is to address the question of authenticity: at first, the isolated sayings of Jesus were widely scattered; later, the pericope settings were created. Hence, Bultmann believes that Luke 14:5 as an isolated saying is preserved by the narrative setting of Luke 14:1–6. Mark 3:1–6 par. and Luke 13:10–17 // Luke 14:1–6⁵² thus are not miracle stories, according to him, for the miracle has been completely subordinated to the "apophthegm."⁵³ This apophthegm is excluded from Q, though he does not explain the reason.⁵⁴ Many apophthegms can be reduced to bare *dominical* sayings by determining the secondary character of their frame.

Taylor has a similar assessment. He calls these "pronouncement stories." The cornfields story in Mark 2:27–28 serves as an illustration: "It may be that the saying was current as an isolated word of Jesus, and was simply appended to the cornfields story; but it is also possible that it formed the climax of a lost Pronouncement-Story."⁵⁵ Taylor emphasizes here that the saying is the climax of the story while the story is essential to the way in which the saying is taken. Mark 3:1–6 is similar. It is to be distinguished from a miracle story by the fact that the healing is not related for itself, but almost incidentally and for its bearing on the principal point of interest, the question of the observance of the Sabbath. Other scholars treat these pericopes in much the same way, though with different terminology.⁵⁶

50. Bultmann, *Geschichte der synoptischen Tradition*, 39–63.

51. Ibid., 73–222. He regards Matt 12:11 // Luke 14:5 as a "Gesetzeswort" (ibid., 138).

52. The sayings of Luke 14:1–6 and 13:10–17 do not seem to be in the same framework as the saying of Mark 3:1–6, even though Bultmann argues that the scene of Jesus' healing was composed as a framework for the Sabbath controversies in Mark and Luke.

53. Ibid., 223; Martin Dibelius classified this narrative type as "paradigm." See his *Formgeschichte des Evangeliums*, 37–69. He considered "the paradigm as a type in the form in which it may have existed in the earliest stories" (Dibelius, *Die Formgeschichte des Evangeliums*, 42). He regarded Luke 14:1–6 as "a less pure type" of the paradigms (Dibelius, *Die Formgeschichte des Evangeliums*, 43). Due to the characteristic of the isolated and independent existence of the paradigms, he noted in them "*an external rounding-off*." Hence the paradigms were "not a connected biography of Jesus. In fact, we see that the majority of these stories end with a complete rounding-off of the event" (ibid., 44).

54. I think we can find the reason why the apophthegms are excluded from Q in one of the principles for reconstruction of the Q-Document suggested by P. Vassiliadis. "Short apophthegms or sayings of a proverbial character, especially those found in a different context in Matthew and Luke, should be excluded as possibly due to the oral tradition (ibid., 66)." See "Nature and Extent," 49–73.

55. Taylor, *Formation of the Gospel Tradition*, 63, 81.

56. Two sayings in Mark 2:23–28 and 3:1–6 are called by Lohse independent "Predigtsprüche." Lohse, "Jesu Worte über den Sabbat," 81–82. The term "Predigtspruch" at first is used by Dibelius with reference to Mark 2:27–28 only. In comparison with these two sayings in Mark, Lohse also calls the two sayings in Luke 13:10–17 and Luke 14:1–6 short "Streitgespräche." Dibelius, *Die Formgeschichte des Evangeliums*, 64–65; Lohse, "Jesu Worte über den Sabbat," 80–81.

Form critical scholars, then, following Bultmann, see Q 14:5 as an isolated saying. However, Tuckett pervasively argues that Q 14:5 cannot have existed in isolation; that the saying must have been "part of a wider context" in the rhetorical intention; and that the saying has clearly acted as part an *a minori ad maius* argument.[57]

If Q 14:5 was originally an independent saying, how and why did the Q redactor use it? John S. Kloppenborg has analyzed the redactional intention and composition-history of the Q blocks 13:24—14:35.[58] He notes that the contents of Q 13:24—14:35[59] are very diverse: "It begins with a 'two ways' motif (13:24), moves to threats of exclusion from the Kingdom (13:25-27, 28-30), a lament (13:34-35), the parable of the great supper (14:16-24) and concludes with discipleship sayings (14:26-27; 17:33; 14:34-35)."[60] Underlying this diversity he identifies two basic types of materials: the first or earliest layer of Q (Q¹) contains sapiential admonitions and discipleship sayings (Q 13:24; 14:26-27; 17:33; 14:34-35), and the second or later layer of Q (Q²) prophetic pronouncements and threats against impenitent Israel (Q 13:25-27, 29, 28, 30, 34-35; [];[61] 14:16-21, 23). Q 13:24; 14:26-27; 17:33; 14:34-35 are attributed to Q¹ by Kloppenborg. However, I would argue that they correspond well to Q². Kloppenborg argues that their sayings fit much better the theme of discipleship which he situates in Q¹.[62] However, I would contend that it is not necessary to regard these sayings as sapiential sayings in Q¹ because the theme of discipleship also appears as an important theme in prophetic sayings in Q², as Kloppenborg argues that Q 12:42-46; 19:12-26; 22:28 pertain to the theme of discipleship and that they belong to Q².

Though Kloppenborg does not consider Luke 14:5 par. part of Q since it is "integral to Luke 14:1-6,"[63] in fact it fits well with the prophetic or judgment sayings of Q².[64]

---

57. Tuckett, *Q and the History*, 415; Complicating the discussion of the Sabbath controversy in Q is not simply the parallel of Matt 12:11 to Luke 14:5, but there also exists a saying in Luke 13:15 that has striking similarities to Luke 14:5 and Matt 12:11. Luke 13:10-17 is the Sabbath day healing of a woman crippled for eighteen years where Jesus uses the following saying in a "minor to major" form of argument (from the lesser to the greater), as Matthew did in the dispute. "Of how much more value is a human being than a sheep?" (Matt 12:12a).

58. Kloppenborg, *Formation of Q*, 223-37.

59. This block is divided into various independent sections as follows: Q 13:24, 25-27, 28-29, 30, 34-35; 14:16-24, 26, 27; 17:33; 14:34-35.

60. Ibid., 223.

61. If Kloppenborg wished to regard Luke 14:5 as Q, he would have placed Q 14:5 here in [] between Q 13:34-35 and Q 14:16-21 because he agrees here that the order of Q is preserved by Luke. Hence, I put Q 14:5 between Q 13:34-35 and Q 14:16-21 according to the sequence of Luke. Kloppenborg, *Q Parallels*, 160. However, Kloppenborg has precisely determined that Luke 13:31-33; 14:1-6, 7-14, 28-33 belong to "Lukan *Sondergut*" (Kloppenborg, *Formation of Q*, 223).

62. Ibid., 237.

63. Kloppenborg, *Q Parallels*, 160. He asserts that there is no proof whether Luke 14:5 belonged to Q.

64. Kloppenborg argues the nature of Q² as follows: "The call to repentance, the threat of apocalyptic judgment and the censure of 'this generation' for its recalcitrance are prominent in several clusters of Q sayings" (Kloppenborg, *Formation of Q*, 102). Agreeing with Koester and Kloppenborg, Burton

Q 13:25–27 is better preserved by Luke than Matthew (compare Matt 7:22–23), and may have circulated as an independent cluster of sayings. The sayings are prophetic in nature. The following sayings of Q 13:29, 28, 30 are independent prophetic pronouncements that warn of exclusion from the kingdom of God. Following that, the Lament of Q 13:34–35 "coheres with some of the characteristic emphases of 13:24–30."[65] As a lament, Q 13:34–35 is close to the context of prophetic sayings in Q 13:25–27, 28–29, 30. A little later Q 14:16–21, 23 offers a similar prophetic condemnation of Israel. The guests are invited to a great banquet (the kingdom of God), but they refuse to go. This theme is quite in keeping with the point of view developed in the preceding sayings "which concern the invitation to repent and respond to preaching, the threat of the exclusion of Israel and the eschatological reversal of the respective fates of Israel and the Gentiles."[66] Q 14:5 coheres redaction-critically with the sayings of Q 13:25—14:23, both in that in it Jesus exhorts his hearers to respond to God's love which stands behind the Mosaic law (compare Q 11:42, "do not neglect justice and the love of God") and in that it implies a new attitude toward the Gentiles.

It may be helpful to elaborate briefly on the prophetic character in Jesus' sayings in Q and the corresponding prophetic nature of Q 14:5.[67] Q 13:34–35 reflects the motif of the violent fate of the prophets (Q 6:22–23; 11:49–51) and indicates that Jesus regards his own fate as linked with them. Jesus stands within and appeals to the tradition of Israel (Q 14:5; 16:17). Jesus quotes Scripture (Q 4:4, 12, 8; 7:27). Jesus receives divine revelation through intimate communion with God and he understands his mission to proclaim God's will (Q 10:22). Jesus is conscious of a mission to all Israel (Q 22:30). Jesus also has a broader vision; his vision anticipates the eschatological defeat of Satan and emphasizes the preliminary presence of the kingdom of God through him (Q 11:20). From this perspective, one can understand Jesus in Q 14:5

L. Mack suggests the language of judgment entered the Q tradition at the second layer. "Heady promises about divine providence for those who turned their backs on social constraints and labors (such as family ties) turned into calls for repentance, then, finally, pronouncements of judgment and doom upon 'this evil generation.' . . . It was then that the language of the kingdom became apocalyptic and the figure of Jesus at the beginning was matched by the figure of the Son of Man to come at the end." Mack, *Myth of Innocence*, 85.

65. Kloppenborg, *Formation of Q*, 227.

66. Ibid., 230.

67. One can find some prophetic characters in Q as follows: (1) *tis ex humon* (Q 11:11–12; 12:25; 14:5; 15:4); (2) *lego humin* (Q 3:8; 7:9, 26, 28; 10:21, 24; 11:9, 51; 12:22, 27, 44; 15:7; 17:34); (3) *ouai* (Q 10:13 twice; 11:42, 39b, 43, 44, 46, 47, 52; 17:1); (4) *plen* (Q 10:14; 17:1). For *plen*, see Dawsey, *Lukan Voice*, 161–63: He lists 51 particles in Luke with narrational occurrences. Among them, *plen* is only used by Jesus 15 times. Cadbury verifies that *plen* is probably in Q, even if *plen* is a favorite conjunction of Luke. See ibid., 147. For *ouai*, see Moulton and Milligan, *Vocabulary*, 464. This word—which is not found in classical Greek, but is common in the LXX and NT—occurs in a date rather earlier than the Roman period.

as a prophet[68] who expresses his view that the Sabbath law must be practiced in the context of love of one's neighbor.[69]

The formula *tis ex humon* in Q 14:5 may be understood as further evidence of the prophetic nature of the saying. Kloppenborg argues that the formula appears in "real questions," and is not "prophetic." The formula is to be understood as a sapiential reflection on "ordinary human experience."[70] However, the formula *tis ex humon* is better regarded as prophetic in character. Schulz points out that the formula is a "typische prophetische Einleitungsformel"[71] used to introduce prophetic sayings of the Hebrew Bible (Isa 42:23; 50:10; Hag 2:3 [LXX 2:4]; Mal 1:10).[72] In view of this tradition, the formula *ti ex humon* probably introduces prophetic sayings in Q as well.

Tis ex humon of Q 14:5 can also be understood as a prophetic pronouncement according to its syntactical patterns. Beyer[73] states: *tis* introduces an interrogative noun-clause, a relative clause sets out the presupposition (the protasis), and a rhetorical question is the apodosis. Luke 14:5 // Matt 12:11 is one such sayings. Others are found in Matthew and Luke: Matt 6:27; 7:9–10; 12:11; 24:45–46; Luke 11:5–7, 11–12; 12:25, 42–43; 14:5, 28, 31; 15:4, 8; 17:7–9. Jeremias argues that Jesus used this formula in disputes with opponents or in addressing the crowds[74] because it required a common answer: "Of course!" or "No one!"[75] It is therefore not an invitation to dialogue but an introduction to a pronouncement.

When or under what circumstances does Jesus use this rhetorical interrogative formula? In Q 11:11–12, after the teaching of the Lord's Prayer, Jesus gives instructions on attitudes in prayer. The rhetorical question *tis ex humon* is used as an introductory formula in order to emphasize God's care. In Q 12:25, Jesus encourages those who are anxious about their life-span. In Q 14:5, Jesus tells his hearers to extricate an ox that has fallen into a pit, even though it is on the Sabbath. Here the Q redactor makes clear the seriousness of the Sabbath controversy with the opponents by embedding the controversy in a context where Jesus' and his own teaching authority is defended against

---

68. Scholars often characterize Jesus as prophet, and there is certainly evidence that the members of the Q community also understood themselves as prophets (Q 6:23). See Sanders, *Jesus and Judaism*, 237–40. Sanders prefers Hengel's term, "eschatological charismatic"; Hengel, *Charismatic Leader*, 18–24; Theissen, *Biblical Faith*, 89–104.

69. Marshall, *Gospel of Luke*, 235. "Jesus relates the institution of the Sabbath to the good purpose of God for men which lay behind it and hence to the principle of love for each other which ought to characterize their use of it"; Patterson, *God of Jesus*, 101, "The law itself was created for humanity's sake. If the law is a gift from God whose fundamental nature is compassionate love, it would simply not make sense to place observance of the law before human need."

70. Kloppenborg, *Formation of Q*, 205, 219.

71. Schulz, *Q*, 153, 163.

72. Greeven, "Wer unter Euch," 255 and 255n14; Jeremias, *Die Gleichnisse Jesu*, 103.

73. Beyer, *Semitische Syntax*, 287.

74. Jeremias, *Die Gleichnisse Jesu*, 103–4, 158, 171.

75. For Jeremias, as evidence for a prophetic saying, the formula in the Gospels introduces questions which expect the "emphatic answer 'No one, Impossible' or 'everyone, of course!'" See ibid., 158.

that of his opponents.[76] In Q 15:4, Jesus gives them instructions to go and find the lost sheep. In all these cases, Jesus uses the rhetorical question *tis ex humon* to present his own teachings[77] which differ from those of his contemporaries.

Therefore, Luke 14:5 par., though originally an isolated saying, due to its prophetic nature and themes, fits well in the context of Q 13:25—14:24. In this sense Q 14:5 can be placed between Q 13:34–35 and Q 14:16–21.

Jesus and the Sabbath in the Sayings Gospel Q

This chapter now raises the question of the origin of Luke 14:1–6. In the Synoptics, the Sabbath sayings may be grouped into three basic blocks of material. The first block is the sayings in Mark 2:23–28; Matt 12:1–8; Luke 6:1–5 which are based on the statement that the Son of Man is the Lord of the Sabbath. The second block is the sayings in Mark 3:1–6; Matt 12:9–14; Luke 6:6–11 based on the healing of a man with a withered hand. The third block is the sayings in Luke 13:10–17; 14:1–6 which both concern helping animals on the Sabbath.

In the first block, Mark 2:23–28 is the primary source for Matt 12:1–8 and Luke 6:1–5. Jesus' disciples were plucking grain as they walked through the fields on the Sabbath. The Pharisees complained to Jesus because they thought that his disciples were breaking the law. Jesus then cited 1 Sam 21:1–6, justifying the disciples' actions. He concluded: the Son of Man is the Lord of the Sabbath (Mark 2:28). This conclusion is limited to the christological assertion of the Son of Man's Lordship[78] over the Sabbath in the Synoptics. Mark finishes his allusive arguments from Scripture when he alluded to Lev 23:3, which says that the seventh day is a "Sabbath to the Lord." The implication is that Jesus is the Lord of the Sabbath, a role which is accepted by Mark. It is likely thus that Jesus was remembered as expressing the principle which governed his attitude toward the Sabbath law: The Sabbath was given for human benefit, not as an end in itself.

In the second block, Mark 3:1–6 was the primary source for Matt 12:9–14 and Luke 6:6–11. In the Synoptic context the story serves as a test case, when Jesus

---

76. Neyrey, "Thematic Use," 460–61.

77. Rordorf, *Sunday*, 71: "We are really standing face to face with Jesus' own self-proclamation."

78. Jesus' usages of the Son of Man in Q 6:22; 7:34; 11:30; 12:10, 40; 17:24, 26, 30 say nothing to us about the development of Christology because Jesus does not use the term as a christological title with a theological content. There is no use of the Son of Man as a title in connection with Christology in Jesus' usage. Even in Rev 1:13 and 14:14, there is no hint that the Son of Man might be a title for Jesus. There can be clearly seen that the Danielic terminology as "one like a son of man" in a descriptive meaning without any suggestion of a title. Although in Dan 7:13 the phrase is identified with an apocalyptic figure, in Jesus it is used as a self-designation of himself without any stress on identification with the apocalyptic messianic figure. However, the christological connotative usage of the Son of Man seems to be attested by the development of Christianity in the post-resurrection period. The christological connotation of the Son of Man is based on the church's proclamation of the heavenly lordship of Jesus which reflects the resurrection experience. This development was the result of the activity of the evangelists themselves.

performs an unnecessary healing on the Sabbath. Thus Jesus was remembered as approaching the whole question of the Sabbath law from quite a different angle than the Pharisees. This story therefore emphasizes that there was a higher responsibility to help the sick man than to keep the Sabbath law itself. Jesus' attitude toward the law was based on his own principle, "love your neighbor."

In the third block, Luke 13:10–17 is peculiar to Luke. Jesus attended the service in a synagogue on the Sabbath. As Jesus was teaching, he noticed a woman. Jesus called her and healed her. Luke 14:1–6, also peculiar to Luke, is the account of the healing of a man suffering from dropsy. Luke 14:1–6 is unusual in that Jesus asked a question before performing the healing. The two stories are similar, but the differences should be noticed. Luke 14:5 is not simply another version of Luke 13:15. The point however is the same: The Sabbath is an appropriate day for healing in view of God's love. Jesus' attitude toward the law is conservative, but is motivated by God's love. Luke 13:10–17 and 14:1–6 thus appear to derive from the same source.

The anomaly is the parallel between Luke 14:5 and Matt 12:11. The context of one derives from an unknown source, the other from Mark. James M. Robinson[79] raises a question concerning whether Matt 12:9–14 contains other parts of the same tradition transmitted in Luke 14:1–6, on the basis that Matt 12:9–14 is conflated with Mark 3:1–6 and Luke 6:6–11, but Luke 14:5 occurred in the independent narrative framework of Luke 14:1–6 which does not occur as an independent stratum in Matthew. This question deserves further consideration.

Bultmann believes they are from the same source, but only because he thought Luke 14:1–6 was derived from Mark 3:1–6. Many other scholars have adopted this view.[80] According to Braun, however, "Luke 14:1–6 evinces too many differences in structure and detail to be a demonstrable derivation of the Markan Sabbath conflict story."[81] While there are thematic relationships between Luke 14:1–6 and Mark 3:1–6 on the basis of form-critical presuppositions,[82] we cannot prove a literary relationship between the two passages. Thus Luke 14:1–6 is not conflated with Mark 3:1–6; rather, Luke 6:6–11 is conflated with it.[83]

---

79. Robinson, "Enlarged Database Q 14:5," 2.

80. Trautmann, *Zeichenhafte Handlungen Jesu*, 286. "Lk 14,1–6 zeigt auch auffällige Ähnlichkeit mit Mk 3,1–6 bzw. par Lk 6,6–11"; ibid., 288. "Die Frage Jesu, ob es am Sabbat erlaubt ist zu heilen, ist in den Worten *exestin to sabbato* [Luke 14:3] mit Lk 6,[9]/Mk 3,4 (*tois sabbasin*) identisch; sie bezieht sich konkreter als in Mk 3,4 direkt auf die Heilung... Die Reaktion der Gegner in v. [6] [Luke 14] entspricht Mk 3,4c"; Tuckett, *Revival*, 98–99. He argues that Luke 14:1–6 is designed to act as a framework for the saying of v. 5 based on the story of Mark 3:1–6; Neirynck, "Luke 14,1–6," 259. "Luke appended the saying to the healing story he composed in dependence on Mk 3,1–6."

81. Braun, *Feasting and Social Rhetoric*, 24.

82. Sanders, *Jewish Law*, 20. "These [Luke 13:10–17 and 14:1–6] seem to be dependent on Mark 3:1–6—or, more precisely, they are variants of the sort of tradition which resulted in the Markan passage." Thus Sanders concludes that the sayings of the Sabbath in the Lukan passages are probably not "authentic."

83. Derrett, "Positive Perspective," 174. He argues that Luke knew Mark 3:1–6. Ibid., 284n12,

Part 1: Sabbath and the Gentile Mission

Other scholars say there is simply no connection between Matt 12:9–14 and Luke 14:1–6: both derive their parallel material from *Sondergut*. Even though Luke 14:1–4, 6 and Matt 12:9–10, 12–14 are not from Q, Luke 14:5 and Matt 12:11 belong to a common source, because there are several almost verbal agreements between them.[84] The close agreements in the wording of the sayings between Luke 14:5 and Matt 12:11 argue that those two passages, at least, derive from a common source, which is probably Q. That these sayings come from Q is proven by the fact that they are almost identical, though there are exceptions like *huios e bous // probaton; phrear // bothunon*. The sayings in Luke 14:5 // Matt 12:11 can also be understood as Q's terminology.[85] The terminology in Q lets us recognize that Luke 14:5 and Matt 12:11 could have been part of a context in Q and did not exist in isolation of Q.

That is not to say that Luke 14:1–6 as a whole derives from Q, though many scholars have thought that it might have.[86] Rather Luke 14:1–6 is to be ascribed to a source peculiar to Luke, i.e., to the Lukan *Sondergut*. In 1907, Bernhard Weiss argued that Luke 14:1–6 is derived from the Lukan *Sondergut*.[87] But he changed his position in 1908, arguing that the saying in Matt 12:11b, 12 is parallel to Luke 14:5, and is derived from Jesus' oral tradition.[88] Later, Creed argued that the saying in Luke 14:1–6 is peculiar to Luke, but Luke 14:5 was interpolated by Matthew into his version of the Markan sayings (12:11).[89] The narrative framework of Luke 14:1–6 does not seem to be original. The

---

"Luke's own version (6,6–11) differs from Mark chiefly in the allegation that Jesus' opponents were scribes and Pharisees. . . . By this device Luke sews 6,6–11; 13,10–17; and 14,1–6 together." Braun, however, just verifies that Luke 6:6–11 is "generated" by Mark 3:1–6 (Braun, *Feasting*, 24).

84. *Pros autous eipen// eipen autois; tinon humon // tis estai ex humon; peseitai // empese; ouk // ouxi; auton // auto; en hemera tou sabbatou // tois sabbasin*.

85. *Kai eipen autois* (Q 7:22; 14:5, 16) // *kai eipen auto* (Q 4:3, 6; 19:17, 19) // *kai eipen* (Q 13:20) // *eipen tois* (Q 3:7) // *eipen* (Q 10:21; 11:29, 39a); *tis ex humon anthropos* (Q 11:11–12; 15:4) // *tsi ex humon* (Q 12:25; 14:5); *estai* (Q 10:12, 14; 12:34; 13:28; 14:5; 17:24, 26, 30); *ouxi* (Q 6:32, 39; 12:6; 14:5); *bothunos* (Q 6:39; 14:5); *hupokrita* (Q 6:42).

86. Streeter, "Original Extent of Q," 193. "The account of a healing on the Sabbath, which immediately follows, 14,1–6, is also probably Q, for Mt 12,9–10 seems to conflate this story with that which he derives from Mk 3,1f. Mt 12,11('the ox or ass in a pit', not in Mark) = Lk 14,5, and the form of the questions is influenced from the same source. It is told, not for the sake of the miracle but of the moral, which it is lawful to heal on the Sabbath. It would indeed have been strange if Q had not a word to say on Christ's teaching as to the Sabbath, a point which must have been so important in the primitive controversy with Pharisees. Thus St. Luke has three stories of Sabbath cures, all told to bring out the same lesson, 6,6–11, 13,10–17, and 14,1–6. The first is from Mark; the second from some special source, the third from Q"; Schürmann, *Traditionsgeschichtliche Untersuchungen*, 218; Marshall, *Gospel of Luke*, 578; Derrett, "Positive Perspective," 285n27. "Luke 14,1–6 is an example of Q material omitted by Matthew (the latter combining Mark 3,1–6 with Q)."

87. Weiss, *Quellen des Lukasevangeliums*, 206. "Von den beiden *Sabbatheilungen* in L [Lukan *Sondergut*] spielt die eine (14,1–6), wie die Salbungsgeschichte, im Hause eines Pharisäers; wo er zum Sabbatmahl geladen."

88. Weiss, *Quellen der Synoptischen Überlieferung*, 74–74. "Aussprüche Jesu, deren Stelle in Q nicht mehr nachweisbar, oder die von Matth. aus der mündlichen Überlieferung geschöpft sind: . . . Mt 12,11b, 12."

89. Creed, *Gospel according to St. Luke*, 188.

pericope may be "a doublet of Luke 13:10–17"⁹⁰ to which there has been added a piece of Q tradition by Luke (14:5 // Matt 12:11).⁹¹ That is to say, Luke may have created 14:1–6 based on the saying in v. 5, for which the story forms a suitable frame.

But if both Matt 12:11 and Luke 14:5 derive from Q,⁹² how are the differences in wording to be explained? A case can be made that the differences are attributed to the redactional work of the two evangelists.⁹³ Luke transmitted the saying of Q 14:5 in the framework of the miracle story of a healing in Luke 14:1–6. In Luke 14:1–6, Jesus is in the house of a ruler of the Pharisees at the table for a meal and takes the initiative to raise a question for his opponents. Luke uses a question here which is transmitted by Q (14:5). This question shows an original argument of Jesus about Sabbath law observance: a rescuing of an ox from a pit on the Sabbath is an action of love which actualizes the will of God. This behavior on the Sabbath is commonly determined by an awareness of need and a feeling for the sufferings of others. Matthew seems to conflate Mark 3:1–6 with Q 14:5.⁹⁴ A question is raised here whether Matthew knew a similar story to that in Luke 14:1–6. But it is difficult to explain, then, why Matthew omitted the story. It is easier to believe that Matthew knew only Q 14:5 and interpolated it into the Markan story. If so, this solution would explain all differences in Matt 12:11 as the result of Matthew's editorial reworking of Q 14:5. In Matt 12:9–14, Matthew would use an independent saying (Q 14:5) which has also been transmitted by Luke 14:1–6.

It is likely that the saying in Matt 12:11 // Luke 14:5 originated from Q. On the basis of this conclusion, this chapter has examined the fact that it is likely that Luke 14:1–6 is not conflated with Mark 3:1–6, but rather Matthew conflated Mark 3:1–6 with Q 14:5 (Matt 12:9–14, compare Luke 6:6–11); and that Q 14:5 existed without the suitable frameworks (Matt 12:9–10, 12–14 and Luke 14:1–4, 6).

EPILOGUE

In sum, the purpose of this chapter has investigated the question of whether the saying of Luke 14:5 par. belongs to Q. More specifically, this chapter has examined (1) scholarly arguments which place Luke 14:5 // Matt 12:11 into Q; (2) the form-critical

---

90. Schmithals, *Evangelium nach Lukas*, 157.

91. Rordorf, *Sunday*, 59. Unlike Schmithals, he argues that Luke 14:1–6 may well be a doublet of Luke 6:6–11.

92. Vouga, *Jésus et la loi*, 60–61.

93. For example, the introductory phrase of Matt 12:11 is even more like Matt 7:9 than Luke 11:11 (Q), whereas the beginning in Luke 14:5 differs from the one in Matthew. This shows that the wording of Luke 14:5 has been changed on the basis of Lukan redactional work.

94. Schürmann, *Traditionsgeschichtliche Untersuchungen*, 23 and 23n25; Ernst, *Das Evangelium nach Lukas*, 421, 435; Yang, *Jesus and the Sabbath*, 196. He summaries that the two-source hypothesis regards Mark and Q as the main sources of Matt 12:9–14: "vv. 9–10, 12b–14 from Mark; v. 11 from Q; v. 12a probably from Matthew himself." However, Yang doubts that Matt 12:11 came from Q. Rather, he suggests that Matt 12:11 came "either from M *Sondergut* or from Q material" ("rather than Q").

and redaction-critical investigation of prophetic aspects of Q 14:5 and the milieu of the Q community; (3) and the close relationships among the sayings of Mark 3:1–6; Luke 6:6–11; Matt 12:9–14; Luke 13:10–17; Luke 14:1–6 and the audience of the Sabbath controversy of Jesus. The result of the examination is that one can conclude as follows:

As widely investigated, Q 14:5 cannot be integral to Luke 14:1–6, Lukan *Sondergut*, because of its close parallel with Matt 12:11 and the close context in the construction of Q 13:25—14:24. The fact that the wordings between Luke 14:5 and Matt 12:11 are similar shows that the sayings are originally derived from Q. Hence, the saying of Q 14:5 cannot be classified with the Sabbath sayings giving expression to the faith of the primitive church. Rather, it is likely that the Sabbath controversy in Q 14:5 is spoken by the historical Jesus during his public ministry.

It is worthwhile to note a prophetic element in the saying of Luke 14:5 // Matt 12:11 as an example. The investigation of the form-critical and redaction-critical backgrounds supports the possibility of Q 14:5 being a prophetic saying. A close context of prophetic sayings in Q 13:25—14:24 shows Q 14:5 can be understood within the immediate prophetic context. On the other hand, the interrogative formula (*tis ex humin*) may be understood as a historical aspect of Jesus' saying in prophetic sayings because the interrogative formula is introducing a typical prophetic saying in Q. The formula originally comes from prophetic sayings of the Hebrew Bible (Isa 42:53; 50:10; Hag 2:3 [LXX 2:4]; Mal 1:10). I have argued that the formula can also be understood as a prophetic saying derived from Jesus' saying during his public ministry. This would mean that the interrogative formula can be regarded as *ipsissima verba*. In Q Jesus preferred to use the prophetic formula in disputes with his opponents. On the lips of Jesus this formula question requires a common answer "No one! Impossible!" In Q, Jesus seems to use this rhetorical interrogative formula in order to give quite new teaching to his hearers (Q 11:11–12; 12:25; 14:5; 15:4). In the saying of Matt 12:11 // Luke 14:5, Jesus asks his hearers to extricate an ox that has fallen into a pit, even if it is on the Sabbath. It is likely here that the rhetorical formula is used as a signal for preaching his idea when it differs completely from the idea of Jewish leaders.

It is most convincing that Luke 14:1–4, 6 cannot be understood as a framework for Q 14:5. It is also wrong to raise an alternative view that Luke 14:1–6 has conflated Q 14:5 with Mark 3:1–6. Rather Matt 12:9–14 conflated Mark 3:1–6 with Q 14:5. This wording can be understood as Q's terminology, because it is likely that Matt 12:11 is close to Luke 14:5, even though Luke 14:1–4, 6; Luke 13:10–14, 16–17 is attested as Lukan *Sondergut* and Matt 12:9–10, 12–14 as Matthew conflating Mark 3:1–6 with Q 14:5 interpolated into Matt 12:9–14.

Matt 12:9–14 has a different context in comparison with Luke 14:1–6 and Luke 13:10–17. The central problem here is that Luke 14:5 is paralleled with Matt 12:11, but not with Luke 13:15; and that the parallel sayings (Luke 14:5 // Matt 12:11) are in different contexts. Matt 12:11 is in the story of the healing of a man with a withered hand, which is paralleled with the sayings in Luke 6:6–11 and Mark 3:1–6, but Luke

14:5 is in the story of the healing of a man suffering from dropsy. In addition, Matt 12:9–14 is surely paralleled with the sayings in Mark 3:1–6 and Luke 6:1–6. It is likely that Matthew conflated Mark 3:1–6 with Q 14:5. In other words, Matthew seems to be influenced by a common source, which has been interpolated into Matt 12:9–14, and then he edited it with Mark 3:1–6. It is unlikely therefore that Matt 12:11 is assigned to Matthean *Sondergut*, because Matt 12:11 came from Q as an original saying distinguished from the Matthean framework (Matt 12:9–10, 12–14). The close agreement in wording of the sayings between Matt 12:11 and Luke 14:5 show that the sayings came from the common source, Q.

Matt 12:11 originally comes from Q before it was interpolated into the framework of Matt 12:9–10, 12–14. The Sabbath saying in Q does not have the framework of the miracle story like a healing story in Matt 12:9–14. It is likely therefore that the Sabbath saying in Q existed without the framework of the Matthean redaction. However, Q 14:5 is form-critically in a wider context within the sayings of 13:24—14:35 which are prophetic sayings in Q. Q 14:5 cannot exist in isolation and seems to be part of a wider context in Q, although many scholars since Rudolf Bultmann have argued that the saying in Q 14:5 is a kind of isolated saying. I think that the saying in Q 14:5 may be placed among the prophetic sayings in Q from the perspective of Q's compositional presuppositions and that the saying in Q 14:5 is in the close context of the composition of Q 13:24—14:35 as prophetic sayings, because the theme of discipleship certainly appears too as an important one in prophetic sayings (Q 12:42-46; 19:12-26; 22:18). Thus the saying in Q 14:5 seems to correspond well to the prophetic sayings in Q 13:24—14:35. I have argued that the Sabbath controversy in Q 14:5 should be placed in Jesus' public ministry. The Q redactor understands the Sabbath controversy to refer to Jesus' public ministry in Galilee. It is likely that the Sabbath saying in Q 14:5, which is an earlier form of Matt 12:11 // Luke 14:5, was given by Jesus as one of his statements about his prophetic ministry.

VI

Between Jewish Law and the Gentile Mission

PROLOGUE

MANY THEOLOGICAL CATEGORIES FIND their basis in the Bible.[1] The Sitz im Leben in the Bible forms theology, and theology is formed by critical reflection on religious praxis. This chapter therefore presupposes the fact that all religious reflection is determined by social situations. In relation to the Gentiles that were present in the Jewish world, Jewish Sabbaths had been socialized. Many Gentiles, on the one hand, knew of the Jewish Sabbath, though they did not follow it. The Sabbath sayings in Q 14:5 are based on the relationship between the Jewish history of the law and the interpretation of the law in the first century CE. The Q community, on the other hand, knew full well the Gentile mission that was practiced by Paul before the 50s CE (Gal 2). To this point we have seen how the Q community, though living in a world in which the Gentile mission was succeeding, nevertheless refused to reach out to the Gentiles. That Q eventually evolved into Matthean Christianity, however, suggests that the community ultimately changed its thinking. We have also seen that Luke 14:5 // Matt 12:11 was probably in Q. The purpose of this chapter is to explain how Q made the transition from anti-Gentile to pro-Gentile by means of the theology found in Q 14:5.

It is difficult to date Q because "its traditions and the document itself went through various phases of development and redaction." Ivan Havener simply suggests that Q predates Matthew and Luke, as well as the event of Jerusalem in 70 CE which follows the dating of Mark. If Mark is dated "either during the Jewish War (66–70 CE) or shortly after it," Q must be dated to "sometime before the year 70 CE."[2] Dating Q to sometime before 70 CE has been the general consensus among New Testament scholars.[3] Vincent Taylor in 1930 dated Q before 60 CE because he regarded the date

---

1. Schnackenburg says that theology looks back to the Bible, especially to Jesus, namely his message and his behavior. For more information, see his "Befreiung in der Blickweise," 11.

2. Havener, Q, 42, 45.

3. There are exceptions. Burton L. Mack dates the latest layer of Q in 75 CE. See his *Lost Gospel*, 177; a Finish scholar, Risto Uro, also dates the latest layer of Q in 75 CE.

of Mark as during the period 65–70 CE.[4] Recalling Streeter's dating of Q to 50 CE[5] without any comment, Taylor says that the date of Q is comparatively early. It is impossible for him to conclude that the dating of Q is later than 60 CE; however, it may be considerably earlier.[6] In 1969, Dieter Lührmann asserted that "all these observations indicate that the redaction of Q should not be placed too early but rather in the Hellenistic community of about the 50s or 60s."[7] Kloppenborg, in a summary of the opinions about Q's date, observed that "Q is normally dated sometime in the period between 50 CE and 70 CE."[8]

If indeed Q is to be dated between 50 CE and 70 CE, it follows that the Q community must have known the fact that the Gentile mission was progressing successfully, since according to Gal 2:11–14 Peter was in Antioch eating with the Gentiles and had met with Paul before 50 CE.[9] The Q community may also have known of the success of the Gentile mission led by Paul. The Q community may also have known of the division of the Christian mission into the Jewish mission and the Gentile mission, agreed on by the Council of Jerusalem (Acts 15). That they did not have their own Gentile mission, but preached the gospel only to the Jews, may reflect their conformity to this division.

At the very least the Q community knew some of the rationale for the Gentile mission before 50 CE: (1) pharisaic persecution, (2) the early Christian church's use of the prophecies of the Hebrew Bible, and (3) Paul's Damascus experience.

Q was aware of how Jesus' followers were persecuted by the Pharisees. Among the Jewish social groups in Q, the Pharisees are the only group subjected to an obvious polemic. In Q 11:39–52, the "this generation" sayings against the Pharisees are connected with the persecution of contemporary Christian prophets like the Q leaders. This persecution image gives us assistance in understanding the relationship between Q and the Pharisees. Such a persecution of Q by the Pharisees may have originated between 50 CE and 70 CE. In Q 11:42, 39b–41, 43–44, 46–52, it is suggested that the Q community was separated from the Jewish community, as evinced by the imagery

4. Taylor, *Gospels*, 8.

5. Streeter, *Four Gospels*, 150: Streeter dates Q in 50 CE, Mark in 60 CE, Luke in 80 CE and Matthew in 85 CE.

6. Taylor, *Gospels*, 23.

7. Lührmann, "Q in der Geschichte des Urchristentums," 88; Lührmann, "Q in the History of Early Christianity," 62.

8. Kloppenborg, introduction to *Q-Thomas Reader*, 5. Here Kloppenborg mainly summarizes the work on the dating of Q by Ivan Havener; more recently, however, Gerd Theissen wished to date the Sayings Gospel Q "between 40 and 70 CE." See Theissen, *Gospels in Context*, 221. To investigate the dating of Q between 40 and 70 CE, Theissen deals with the description of three social groups in Q: Israel, Gentiles and Pharisees. However, Theissen's weak point is that he does not give an appropriate picture of the social world in Q because he argues for such social groups on the basis of a number of traditions in the New Testament, not in Q. For more detail, see 221–34. I feel that his social reconstruction is not quite fitting to the picture of Q.

9. Riley, *One Jesus*, 105. "There Paul rebukes Peter for refusing to eat with gentile Christians, as he had been doing previously, because a group of Jewish-Christian rigorists had come up from Jerusalem and somehow influenced him to withdraw from meals with the Gentiles."

of the Pharisees having persecuted the prophets, the predecessors of the Q leaders.[10] Expelled by the Pharisees, the Q community was probably in the same situation as "churches" in 1 Thess 2:14–16. But Pharisaic persecution of Jesus and his followers had begun long before Q reflects it. In the early 30s CE, Paul was active in the persecution before his Damascus experience (Acts 7:54–60; 12:2–3; Gal 1:13, 23; 2 Cor 11:23–27; 1 Thess 2:14–16).[11] One common response among Christians to Pharisaic persecution was for them to turn to Gentiles.[12] Following Stephen's martyrdom circa 37 CE,[13] Christian Hellenists fled from Jerusalem to the Gentile areas in Judea and Samaria (Acts 8:1). In the south, Philip preached the gospel around Gaza (Acts 8:26); in the north, Christians traveled as far as Phoenicia, Cyprus and Antioch (Acts 11:19). The Gentile mission was thus partly the result of the scattering of early Christians caused by the persecution in Jerusalem.

Q was also aware that early Christians used the prophecies of the Hebrew Bible to justify the Gentile mission.[14] For example, Terence L. Donaldson observes that Paul used four arguments from the Hebrew Bible to connect the Gentiles with their salvation.[15] First, Paul states that God promised salvation beforehand through his prophets (Rom 1:2). He claimed that his gospel about the "righteousness of God for all who believe" was "attested by the law and the prophets" (Rom 3:21). Second, Paul refers to the Genesis account of Abraham in Rom 4:17–18 (compare Gen 17:5) and Gal 3:8 (compare Gen 12:3), as a declaration of the gospel to Abraham "beforehand." Third, in Rom 15:9–12, Paul ties together four texts (Deut 32:43; Pss 18:49; 117:1; Isa 11:10) to establish that "Christ became a servant of the circumcised . . . in order that the Gentiles might glorify God for his mercy" (Rom 15:8–9). Fourth, there are five occasions in Rom 9 and 10 where Paul argues for the legitimacy of the Gentile mission, citing the Hebrew Bible prophecies: Rom 9:25–26 (Hos 1:10; 2:23); Rom 10:11 (Isa 28:16); Rom 10:13 (Joel 2:32); Rom 10:20 (Isa 65:1); and Rom 10:19 (Deut 32:21). Paul was convinced from this perspective that the Hebrew Bible promised salvation

---

10. Q 11:39–52 stems from an "anti-synagogue 'ecclesiastical' redaction." Schürmann, "Zeugnis der Redenquelle," 174–75. This suggestion challenges the very existence of the Pharisees in relation to the Wisdom oracle in Q 11:49–51 which is connected to the woes (Q 11:47–48) on the basis of the catchwords "prophets" and "kill" and at the same time the deuteronomistic theme of the killing of God's prophets. See Steck, *Israel*, 222–27, 282–83, 286; Kloppenborg nicely summarizes the function between the woe oracle and the Wisdom oracle: "whereas the woes offer reproaches, the Sophia oracle is a threat of retribution on this generation." Kloppenborg, *Formation of Q*, 144.

11. Theissen, *Gospels in Context*, 229–32; Wilson, *Related Strangers*, 175. "There is some evidence for Jewish harassment of Christians in both Judea and the Diaspora."

12. Some scholars have dismissed the evidence for Jewish hostility toward Christians, suggesting that it is based on facile assumption and an "anti-Jewish bias": Parkes, *Conflict of the Church*, 75–78.

13. Frend, *Martyrdom*, 152.

14. Riley, *One Jesus*, 102. He asserts that "the prophet did not control the prophecy; that was of divine origin and its meaning was of divine, not human content. . . . The prophecy had originated with God and meant what God intended, not what the prophet or the audience thought was intended."

15. Donaldson, *Paul and the Gentiles*, 100–101.

for the Gentiles. Luke also used Hebrew Bible prophecies to try to explain the Gentile mission. Stephen G. Wilson has argued that the theme of promise and fulfillment is a central theme of Luke-Acts in "Luke 2:30–32, 3:6, 4:21, 25–27 and, above all, in 24:45–46."[16] In these verses Luke connects the Gentile mission with the fulfillment of prophecy in the Hebrew Bible. Wilson has asserted that the fulfillment of prophecy was one of the most prevalent themes in Luke, and that Luke used quotations[17] and allusions to the Hebrew Bible[18] to "prophesy, explain and justify the proclamation to the Gentiles."[19] Wilson is certainly right. Luke indicates that turning to the Gentiles in the early Christian mission was a fulfillment of the prophecies of the Hebrew Bible, and thus truly the will of God.[20] That Q is aware of such arguments is seen in Q 13:29, 28, which anticipates that in the end the Gentiles will share in the blessings of the kingdom (see also Q 7:29, compare Matt 8:11 // Luke 7:29). These sayings seem to be an echo of the prophetic expectation that all nations would eventually be brought into the kingdom (Isa 49:12; 56:6; Mal 1:11).

Q may have known, moreover, that some Christians embraced the Gentile mission as a result of divine revelation. Paul, for instance, following his Damascus experience, abandoned the conviction that observing the law was necessary for salvation. Since salvation could not be obtained through the law, a law-based distinction between Jews and Gentiles became irrelevant to Paul.[21] Before his Damascus experience, Paul was a zealot for the law and a "persecutor of the church" (Gal 1:13–14; Phil 3:5–6). After his experience, however, Paul was called to "proclaim God's Son among the Gentiles" (Gal 1:15–16). From this perspective, the Damascus experience of Paul can be described as a turning point, a call to the Gentile mission.

---

16. Wilson, *Gentile*, 53. "In this manner Luke makes it clear that the inclusion of the Gentiles is not the result of a mere quirk of history or a whim of God; rather, it is grounded in the eternal will of God and is an integral part of his promises to Israel."

17. Luke 3:6; Acts 2:27; 3:25; 13:47; 15:17.

18. Luke 2:32; 4:25–27; Acts 1:8; 2:39; 10:35; 15:14; 26:17; 28:26–27.

19. Wilson, *Gentile*, 243: He argues that the passages from the Bible were used to justify the Gentile mission *post eventum*.

20. Ps 98:2; Isa 42:6; 43:7, 21; 49:6; 57:19; Jer 14:9.

21. Cerfaux, *Christ in the Theology*, 69. "The principle by which Israel had lived is done away with. *The abolition of the Law and the call to the pagans are correlated*, since in the divine plan revealed to Paul the heathens do not enter the Church through the intermediary of Judaism, but through the wide-open door of mercy"; Donaldson, *Paul and the Gentiles*, 16. Paul's Damascus experience was essentially a "conversion from Torah to Christ and . . . a conversion from Judaism to [a] universal religion in which ethnic distinctions between Jew and Gentile have been eradicated." For Paul, therefore, the Gentile mission must be regarded as an outcome of his Damascus experience; E. P. Sanders remarks about Paul and the law in relation to the Gentile mission: "God revealed his Son to Paul and called him to be an apostle to the Gentiles. Christ is not only the Jewish Messiah; he is also Savior and Lord of the universe. If salvation is by Christ and is intended for Gentile as well as Jew, it does not come by the Jewish law." Sanders, *Paul, the Law*, 152; Hurtado, "Convert," 277. He argues a similar conclusion that "some sort of prophet-like sense of being divinely commissioned to the gentiles came to him and that subsequently and as a consequence and corollary of that eschatological commission, Paul developed his emphasis on salvation through Christ without observance of Torah."

In spite of such awareness, it is interesting that Q never embraces the Gentiles but refers frequently to them only in the eschatological perspective (Q 10:13–15; 11:31–32; 13:29, 28; 14:21, 23). Thus Q 11:31–32 refers to the Gentiles judging Jews (compare 1 Cor 1:18–31), while the invitation to the Gentiles (Q 14:21, 23) to feast at a great banquet (Q 14:16) was a part of Q's eschatology, but not Q's practice. The Q community thus did not have a Gentile mission, even though there were sound reasons for undertaking such an effort. As noted above, one of the elements that prevented them from going to Gentiles as other Jesus groups had done was Q's strict adherence to the law. It is equally interesting, in this context, that Q, in the form of the Matthean community, eventually did embrace Gentiles. How did the Q community evolve in this way? If the above mentioned rationales for the Gentile mission did not persuade Q to go to the Gentiles, what did?

The Jewish War

One of the primary factors in Q's change of heart must have been the Jewish War. While there is no direct evidence about the influence of the war in Q (as noted above, Q was probably written before the war), we can deduce its effect by noting how the war affected other groups. It has quite often been suggested that the war was the crucial turning point in relation between Jews and Christians.[22] In general, it appears that the war led to a complete separation between the two groups.[23] Wilson also argues that two events of the war are related to Christian development: "the destruction of the Temple and the banishment from Jerusalem." These two significant events drew two main responses from the earliest Christian writers: "a redefinition of their eschatological timetable" by the Synoptics and "a focus on superior heavenly counterparts of the earthly city and Temple" by John, Hebrews, and Revelation.[24]

For Christians in Palestine, the war was, obviously, the most traumatic. According to the *Panarion* 29.7,7–8; 30.2,7–8 of Epiphanius, Christians left Jerusalem and settled in Pella. Eusebius also speaks of the flight of the Christians to Pella (*Historia ecclesiastica* 3.5,3).[25] The mention of "those who are in Judea flee to the mountains" in Luke 21:20–22 probably also reflects knowledge of this Pella tradition.[26] Such

---

22. Wilson, *Related Strangers*, 8; Samuel George F. Brandon and Gosta Lindeskog have developed almost the same arguments in various ways. For more information, see Brandon, *Fall of Jerusalem*, 12–14; Lindeskog, *Jüdische-christliche Problem*, 43–44.

23. Harnack, *Mission and Expansion*, 63.

24. Wilson, *Related Strangers*, 10. For more information, see Han, *Jerusalem*.

25. Stowers, "Circumstances and Recollection," 305–20; Gunther, "Fate of the Jerusalem Church," 81–94; Gray, "Movement of the Jerusalem Church, 1–7; Koester, "Origin and Significance," 90–106; Epiphanius, *Panarion*.

26. Koester, "Origin and Significance," 103–5. However, he argues that Luke 21:20–22 differs significantly from the Pella tradition (esp. 104); Gunther, "Fate of the Jerusalem Church," 84.

upheaval apparently pushed Palestine Christians into different groups.[27] Epiphanius, for instance, made a connection between the early Jewish Christians and refugees from Jerusalem after the Jewish War. In Pella, according to Epiphanius, the heresy of the Nazoraeans and the Ebionites had its beginning.[28] He says that the Nazoraeans and Ebionites influenced each other (*Panarion* 30.2,9). In *Panarion* 30.26,1–2; 33.4,7, Epiphanius states that the Ebionites observed Jewish customs in their attempt to imitate Christ. Epiphanius also said of the Nazoraeans that they were descended from a group who left Jerusalem and went to Pella (*Panarion* 29.7,7; 30.2,7) and that they maintained Jewish practice in keeping the Sabbath (*Panarion* 29.7,5; 29.8,4; 30.17,5; 30.32,1–3). Thus, the Jewish War seems to have cemented some Jewish Christian groups in a rigidly conservative view of the law.

For Judaism, of course, the effects of the war were also profound. In terms of geography, the Jewish population of Judea declined after the Jewish War.[29] They were scattered in the Diaspora areas of Palestine, Syria, Egypt, and Asia Minor.

In terms of cult, Jewish life is centered on synagogues after the Jewish War to an even greater degree than before.[30] It appears too that synagogue life itself was affected in that Jewish Christians became disaffected with Judaism and joined the early Christian house churches.

The Jewish War therefore caused significant changes for Jews and Gentiles both in Palestine and in the Diaspora. Since it is likely that the Q community lived in Palestine or Syria, the war must have had a profound impact on them as well. This conclusion is confirmed when we consider that Q did indeed experience a radical reorientation in its attitude to the Gentiles after the war. We must conclude that in part at least the war facilitated this change of heart. But was this the only factor? The reports of the Ebionites and Nazoraeans show that the war itself did not necessarily drive previously conservative Jewish Christians to a more liberal attitude. The next chapter will consider an important factor in the Q community's reorientation.

27. Quispel, "Discussion of Judaic Christianity," 81–93; Schoeps, *Jewish Christianity*; Klijn and Reinink, *Patristic Evidence*; Berger and Wyschogrod, *Jews*; Vallée, *Study in Anti-Gnostic Polemics*; Callan, *Forgetting the Root*; Taylor, "Phenomenon of Early Jewish-Christianity," 313–34.

28. Lüdemann, "Successors of pre-70 Jerusalem Christianity," 161–73. He has found the origins of the tradition in the foundation story of the Pella community. For the Ebionites, see Daniélou, *Theology of Jewish Christianity*, 55–63. The term "Ebionites," however, became a term that the church fathers used to refer to Jewish Christian sects in whom Jewish customs were practiced. Strecker, "Problem of Jewish Christianity," 241–85; *Rechtgläubigkeit und Ketzerei*, 272–83. He sees that "Ebionites" were originally applied to a specific Jewish Christian group who tried to uphold the Jewish ideal of poverty, but that it was later transformed by the heresiologists into a general designation for sectarian Jewish Christianity. Origen, for example, makes a clear connection between the words "Jews" and "Ebionites" (*In Lucam* 14,18–20; *Contra Celsum* 5,61).

29. Avi-Yonah, *Jews under Roman*, 19. He estimates that the Jewish population declined one quarter in Judea and three quarters in Galilee after the Jewish War.

30. The synagogues for Jews seem to have become increasingly a substitute for the temple. Brown and Meier, *Antioch and Rome*, 49: "Christian Jews and non-Christian Jews could sometimes find themselves in the same synagogue." Wilson, *Related Strangers*, 22. He proposes that there was "the most dramatic example of the association of Diaspora Jews with Gentiles" in the period.

PART 1: SABBATH AND THE GENTILE MISSION

The Sabbath Controversy and Breaking the Law

If the Jewish war represents an externalure that pushed the Q community toward the Gentiles, there nevertheless must have been an internal cause as well. Since other Jewish Christian groups responded to the war by becoming more conservative, there must already have existed within the Q community an ideology that allowed them to turn outward when the opportunity arose. Q 16:16 indeed could have been read in antinomian terms. Presumably since it was the law that stood in the way of the Gentile mission, the abrogation of the law would open the door to the Gentiles. Only the juxtaposition of Q 16:17 prevented this. This chapter makes explicit the tension between opposing factions within Q, a tension implicit in the tension of Q 16:16 and 16:17.

Klinghardt uses Luke to suggest that within the Jewish Christian community precisely such divisions were possible. He infers that Jewish Christianity was in the process of separating from Judaism, drawing a direct parallel between groups in Luke's narrative and the groups in Luke's community: scribes are equivalent to non-Christian Jews, Pharisees are equivalent to strict Jewish Christians, the crowds are related to other Jewish Christians, and the God-fearers would be the Gentiles.[31] Q may reflect a similar division. Q 7:1–10, for example, uses the image of the centurion as a Gentile to illustrate the point that Gentiles put Israel to shame (Q 7:9). This seems to stand in tension with the fact that the Q community observed the Torah and did not accept Gentiles converted through the Gentile mission.

Thus we see evidence of factions in Q. One faction we might label "Judaizers." Scholars have focused in recent years on "Judaizers" who adopted, in varying degrees, the lifestyle of the Jews.[32] Wilson, however, has called them "Christian Gentiles."[33] Because of the confusion of the term "Judaizers" among the scholars, it requires a brief definition. Marcel Simon uses it for Jewish Christians who tried to impose their practices on Gentile Christians.[34] James M. Robinson also uses the term "Judaizers" of Jewish Christians ("those of circumcision," Gal 2:12b) "who would 'Judaize' the Gentiles if they could" (Gal 2:14b).[35] The Judaizers thus were a Judaizing group living in Christian communities.[36] But in this context it refers to a group within a Jewish community which is trying to keep the community Jewish.

---

31. Klinghardt, *Gesetz und Volk Gottes*, 310–13. See more on almsgiving (41–68), on divorce (85–96), on the Sabbath (238–40), and on the temple (303–5).

32. Gaston, "Judaism of the Uncircumcised," 33–44; Gager, *Origins of Anti-Semitism*.

33. Wilson, *Related Strangers*, 161. He also proposes calling them "Gentile Judaizers" or "Judaizers" (ibid., 159 and 167).

34. Simon, *Verus Israel*, 306–7.

35. Robinson, "Down-to-Earth Jesus," xvi. He here defines Judaizers as Jewish Christians; Gaston, "Judaism of the Uncircumcised," 35–36: He proposes that the Judaizers were forced converts to Judaism in its ancient and technical sense, Esther 8:17 LXX and Josephus, *Bellum Judaicum* II.454, and that they adopted certain Jewish customs in Josephus, *Bellum Judaicum* II.463, Plutarch, *Cicero* 7:6, *Acts of Pilate* 2:1, and Ignatius, *Letter to the Magnesians* 10:3.

36. Murray, *Playing a Jewish Game*, 1–9.

It is likely that the Judaizers were active within the Q community and may have been the leaders in the Q community, as evidenced by the distinctively conservative attitude toward Jewish law we have seen in Q. But there must have been an opposition as well. As noted, Q 16:16 may have been from a more liberal Q group. Q 7:1–10, in its praise of a centurion, raises the possibility of a pro-Gentile group within the Q community as well. In the previous chapter, I argued that Luke 14:5 par. is in Q. If so, it represents the best evidence for a pro-Gentile ideology in Q.

If indeed Q was a divided community, Q 14:5 favored the more liberal side. The text suggests, at the least, that the law can be stretched, and, at the most, that the law can be broken for a good cause. In any case, it suggests that the law is subservient to a greater principle than merely the slavish obedience to its prescriptions. Human life was more important than adherence to the letter of the law.

Such a saying must have caused tension within the community. Q's conservative attitude toward Jewish law as applied to Judaism would make the Q community a Sabbath observant group. By contrast, an awareness of breaking the law in the saying about rescuing an ox from a pit on the Sabbath would encourage the Q community to practice God's love in Christian missionary activity. The meaning of the Sabbath controversy in Q 14:5 for the Q community, therefore, is to practice the love of God rather than to observe the Sabbath law itself strictly.

This awareness of the need for breaking the law is first to be raised by Jesus in Q.[37] One can see here an abrogation of the law in the Sabbath sayings in which Jesus justifies transgression of the law on the basis of his authority. Abrogation of specific precepts of the written Torah might be usual in Jesus' milieu[38] even though Jesus argues that his concern might not be for violating what the Scripture taught about the Sabbath, but about the divine intention to do well on the Sabbath.[39] Although the Q community had a conservative attitude toward the law, in the Sabbath saying of Q 14:5 they might have been challenged to loosen their attitude toward the law because Jesus asked them to practice God's love expressed in the law.

Part of the controversy over the law may have arisen precisely in response to the success of the Gentile mission. While that mission prospered in the years 50–70 CE, the Q community's efforts among Jews met with repeated resistance. Thus some may have advocated a more liberal policy toward the Gentiles in order to replenish the diminishing ranks of the Q community. But unlike other Jewish Christians, the rationale was not that God had rejected the Jews, but that God loved all humankind. Q 14:5 would have served this group well. Not only does it emphasize God's care for

---

37. Riley, *One Jesus*, 88. "One of the most difficult issues raised by Jesus was his willfulness in breaking traditional rules connected with observance of Mosaic Law—he is perceived as a breaker of the Sabbath and other traditions."

38. Sigal, *Halakah of Jesus*, 23.

39. Ibid., 158. He argues that Matt 12:12b proclaimed "the very purpose of the Sabbath as a redemptive-healing day."

people, but as a reevaluation of the Sabbath it has specific application to the Gentile mission as well. The following chapter elaborates on this point.

Sabbath Practice

Q 14:5 was an appropriate text to serve as a basis for a new attitude toward the Gentiles because in Jewish tradition Sabbath speculation was frequently linked to attitudes toward the Gentiles. Several texts make this clear.

The most striking fact relating to our topic is that in both Decalogue's *ger* is mentioned in the phrase, the list of people are required not to work on the Sabbath: "you, your son or your daughter, your male or your female slave, your livestock, or the alien in your towns." The *New Oxford Annotated Bible* translates "the alien resident in your towns" more literally as "the alien in your gates."[40] This translation suggests what the Decalogue originally meant by the term. The alien (Gentile) in the gates was waiting for hospitality or a job: Gen 19:1–2 (Lot meets the two angels who come to Sodom) and Judges 19:15–21 (the Levite and his concubine wait in Gibeah). Thus, the Gentiles in the town are those taken in as guests[41] of an Israelite household. As such they must observe the Sabbath with the rest of the household. According to the fourth commandment, then, in pre-monarchic Israel, Gentiles could only be accepted into the Israelite community if they were subordinate members of the community and if they observed the Sabbath.[42]

Philo of Alexandria (ca. 30 BCE–45 CE) and Flavius Josephus (ca. 38–100 CE) both discuss Sabbath practices in relation to the Gentiles.

Philo uses the allegorical method to fulfill "a two-fold mission"[43] to make Greek philosophy understandable to the Jews and at the same time to transmit the Mosaic

---

40. George Foot Moore gives a brief description of the Gentiles in the course of his presentation of Jewish conversion. However, his main interest was in describing those aspects of Judaism, such as its monotheism, which predisposed it to an acceptance of converts. For more information, see his *Judaism in the First Centuries*, 323–53. T. J. Meek's article on the translation of *ger* and its bearing on the documentary hypothesis is a major step forward. He traces the meaning of the term through the documents of the Hexateuch. He concludes: (1) in J and E, *ger* denotes a Hebrew living in a foreign land and is best translated as "immigrant"; (2) in Deuteronomy, the Covenant Code and the Priestly writings, *ger* refers to the native population of Israel who have been conquered and are now in a subordinate position to the Israelites. This is best translated as "alien resident"; (3) in the Holiness Code and the Priestly source, the status of the *ger* has become equal with that of the native-born. See his article, "Translation of *Ger*," 172–80. Christina van Houton argues that the LXX generally translates *ger* as *proselytos* and the translation indicates that the phenomenon of conversion existed. For more information, see her *Alien in Israelite Law*, 179–83.

41. The second person singular suffix attached to the word "*ger*" also indicates that he is in a dependent position. Thus in some sense, the alien belongs to the patriarch.

42. Nielsen, *Ten Commandments*, 38. Exodus uses "recall" or "remember," and Deuteronomy "observe." In the deuteronomistic work, the word "observe" is the preferred word for obeying the law.

43. Schürer, *History of the Jewish People*, 878. "These two tendencies are clearly identifiable as the mainsprings of Philo's comprehensive literary undertaking. . . . Since he [Philo] united both strains of

law to the Greeks. Philo emphasizes in his allegorical interpretations that the Sabbath law was the most conspicuous Jewish observance in the ancient world (*De Vita Mosis* II.17–23).[44] Philo's main concern is how Jewish law and tradition relate to the Gentiles. In endeavoring to show the divine origin of the Mosaic law, he compares Jewish and Gentile concepts of the Sabbath, for he regards the Sabbath as evidence that Jewish law has universal value.[45] Philo himself takes pride in the fact that the Sabbath is observed by some Gentiles.[46] He also notes that others criticized the Jewish Sabbath since it seems that the Jews were idle or wasting time by keeping the Sabbath. Philo responds to their criticisms[47] by showing the actual purpose and practice of the Sabbath.[48] The Jews do not waste time but rather study their holy law, the true philosophy.[49] Philo also mentions physical benefits of keeping the Sabbath and offers a humanitarian justification for the Sabbath rest.

As part of this apologetic,[50] Philo adopts an allegorical interpretation of the Sabbath, especially in relation to the number seven.[51] Accordingly, he prefers the term the "seventh day" instead of the word "Sabbath." He uses this allegory to describe the physical benefits of observing the Sabbath law (*De Specialibus Legibus* II.60). Philo indicates that the Sabbath has been given the name of rest because the number seven is the most peaceful (*De Abrahamo* 28). For Philo, "peace" and "seven" are identical because on the seventh day of creation God ceased his activity and took a rest (*De Fuga et Inventione* 173). However, the rest does not signify "inactivity," for God never

---

thought in his own background and outlook, this harmonization of Greek and Jewish elements does not need to be interpreted as the product of a conscious [program]; little of his extant oeuvre could be described as overtly apologetic or propagandist." According to Borgen, this allegorical interpretation of the Sabbath is based on a "dual purpose." Borgen, "Philo of Alexandria," 235. Borgen argues that this dual purpose fits well the situation of the Jewish community of Alexandria, for at the time of Philo the Jews were actively penetrating the Greek community.

44. Goldenberg, "Jewish Sabbath in the Roman World," 429; Sevenster, *Roots of Pagan*, 124–26.

45. Drummod, *Philo Judaeus*, 315. He argues that in Philo there are two supreme reasons for the Sabbath: the one is relating to God; the other to man. Duty to God is expressed through piety and holiness, that to man through philanthropy and justice.

46. Belkin, *Philo and the Oral Law*, 193–94.

47. Distinguishing sharply Jews and non-Jews and condemning bitterly apostate Jews, Philo even criticizes prosperous Jews (*De Vita Mosis* I.131). See Borgen, "Philo of Alexandria," 257.

48. *De Vita Mosis* II.211–12; *De Specialibus Legibus* II.60–70; *Hypothetica* VII.11–16. Cohn, "Einteilung und Chronologie," 387–435 (esp. 415–16); Goodenough, "Philo's Exposition," 109–25 (esp. 110–11). They regard *De Vita Mosis* as an introduction to Judaism, written for the Gentiles.

49. Drummond, *Philo Judaeus*, 287. He argues that on this ground rests the commandment to observe the seventh day, ceasing from work, and giving it to philosophy, contemplation, and the improvement of human characters.

50. Mendelson, *Philo's Jewish Identity*, 77–113.

51. Philo recognizes that the sacred number seven was in popular understandings and argues that the distinctiveness of the number seven was recognized by his contemporaries, especially by the Pythagoreans. See Borgen, "Philo of Alexandria," 256. "From the Phythagoreans come speculations on numbers"; ibid., 270–72. Philo elaborates in Pythagorean fashion on the number seven, as did his predecessor Aristobulus; ibid., 276–77. For Philo the number seven is spread out over all the human knowledge.

stops working (*De Cherubim* 26). It is a part of the divine happiness to enjoy perfect rest and peace. Rather, God's rest is a working with absolute ease, without toil and without suffering (*De Cherubim* 87). Philo, therefore, insists that the people who observe the Sabbath law can take a rest on the Sabbath day for their body. Philo carefully points out, however, that on the Sabbath day their soul does not take a rest.[52] Philo also states that the Decalogue (*De Decalogo* 154–58 on the fourth commandment regarding the Sabbath) was given by God directly, while the other laws were given by Moses.[53] For Philo, Moses recognized in the seventh day the creation of the world, and celebrated it in heaven and on earth, as all things rejoice in the full harmony of the "sacred number"[54] seven. Hence, the Jews, and the Gentiles, who follow the laws of Moses, must celebrate the Sabbath (*De Vita Mosis* II.210–11).[55] He also expects that a new era will come when the Gentiles (Greeks) cast aside their ancestral customs and honor the laws of Moses alone (*De Vita Mosis* II.43–44), during which there will be an eschatological Sabbath celebration in which the Jews and the Gentiles will participate. He points to the fact that some Gentiles had accepted the Sabbath already in his time as proof of a future universal acceptance.

A similar picture of Sabbath practices in relation to Gentiles is found in the works of Josephus. Josephus' main concern is also how Jewish law relates to the Gentiles.[56] His focus is on Gentile attitudes to resting on the Sabbath. In *Antiquitates Judaicae*, he systematizes the material in the laws concerning the sacrifices (III.224–36), the festivals (III.237–54), and ritual cleanliness (III.258–73)[57] and makes several references to Jewish rest or inactivity on the Sabbath, explaining the biblical Sabbath to his readers (*Antiquitates Judaicae* III.237–38; *Contra Apionem* II.175–83). Regarding the Essenes, Josephus reports that they "are stricter than all Jews in abstaining from work on the seventh day" (*Bellum Judaicum* II.147). In describing the Jewish attitudes to war on the Sabbath, he says that it is "a day on which from religious scruples Jews abstain from even the most innocent acts" (*Bellum Judaicum* II.456).[58] For Jo-

---

52. *De Specialibus Legibus* II.64; *De Vita Mosis* II.215; *De Opificio Mundi* 128; *De Vita Comtemplativa* 30–36; *De Decalogo* 96–105.

53. *De Vita Mosis* II.188–200; *De Decalogo* 18, 175; *De Praemiis et Poenis* 2. Borgen, *Philo, John and Paul*, 26.

54. Philo regards the number seven as a "sacred number" belonging to God in holiness and dignity (*De Specialibus Legibus* II.41, 86, 224; *De Opificio Mundi* 128; *De Decalogo* 98–100; *De Vita Mosis* II.218–19, 263–64).

55. The celebration of the Sabbath is thus founded on creation (Gen 2:2–3). Philo is well familiar with this celebration of the Sabbath and its cosmic role. Basically, these celebrations, feasts, and joy belong to God alone, for God alone is entirely blessed (*De Specialibus Legibus* II.53–55; *De Cherubim* 86); Wolfson, *Philo*, 2:265–66.

56. References to the Gentiles in relation to Jewish law are widely distributed within the writings of Josephus (*Antiquitates Judaicae* XVI.225; XVIII.82; XX.34–53; *Contra Apionem* II.123, 210; *Bellum Judaicum* II.454, 463, 560; VII.45).

57. Bilde, *Flavius Josephus*, 81.

58. Attridge, "Josephus and His Works," 196.

sephus, inactivity on the Sabbath is a key. Hence he often describes the refusal of the Jews to fight with enemies on the Sabbath (*Bellum Judaicum* II.517, 634; VII.520) and makes many references to the Sabbath rest (*Antiquitates Judaicae* XIII.252-53; XIV.63-64, 226-46).[59] Noting, however, that Jews sometimes did fight on the Sabbath, he explained how Mattathias, when Antiochus Epiphanes attacked the Jews on the Sabbath (*Antiquitates Judaicae* XII.274-75, cf. 1 Macc 2:32-38), abrogated the law: "With these words he [Mattathias] did persuade them, and even to this very day endures the practice among us of fighting even on the Sabbath, were it ever necessary" (*Antiquitates Judaicae* XII.277, compare 1 Macc 2:40-41).

According to Josephus, the Jewish concept of rest or inactivity on the Sabbath was widespread throughout the Gentile world. *Antiquitates Judaicae* XIV.241-43, 244-46, 256-58, 262-64;[60] XVI.162-65, 167-68 shows the Jews observed their Sabbath within the context of the Roman world. *Bellum Judaicum* IV.97-105; VII.96-99 shows that when Titus attacked Gischala in 67 CE he respected the Jewish Sabbath. The Romans were acquainted with this custom so that they spent their time in the preparation of the war-machines. Josephus thus describes that "there is not one city, Greek or barbarian, nor a single nation, to which our custom of abstaining from work on the seventh day has not spread" (*Contra Apionem* II.282, also 123). Josephus also recognizes that not all Gentiles respected the Sabbath.[61] The Gentiles' hostile attitude to the Jewish Sabbath, for example, is mentioned in *Contra Apionem* II.21-27. In spite of this hostility, however, the Jews observed the Sabbath in the Roman world in honor of God's providence and guidance, and did not try to force non-Jewish people to observe it with them (*Contra Apionem* II.160, 165-67, 180-81).[62]

The rabbinic literature (*Mishnah, Tosefta*, the early *Midrash*, and *Talmuds*[63]) also connects the Sabbath and Gentiles. The rabbis saw the Sabbath as a practice that separated Jews and Gentiles.

There are a relatively small number of passages which discuss the Sabbath and the Gentiles in *Mishna-Tosefta*. It is likely that Sabbath observance had developed originally in Israel as a means of marking the differences between the Israelites and

---

59. Unfortunately, however, Josephus does not give direct accounts of what he considers to be proper observance of the Sabbath within the context of the Roman Empire.

60. *Antiquitates Judaicae* XIV is influenced by the numerous official documents which mention various forms of honors and privileges bestowed on the Jewish community throughout the world as it was known at the time. See Bilde, *Flavius Josephus*, 85-86.

61. *Antiquitates Judaicae* XII.5-6; XIV.244-46, 256-58, 262-64; XVI.27-30; *Contra Apionem* I.209.

62. It is likely that Josephus uses special terminology for fate and providence, drawn from the Greek historiographical tradition to express his belief in the divine governance of history. Attridge, "Jewish Historiography," 327.

63. Within these documents, various strands of Jewish thought, cultural views, and intellectual situations, have been joined together. For a discussion of diversity within early Judaism, see Overmann and Green, "Judaism in the Greco-Roman Period," 1037-54.

the Gentiles.⁶⁴ If there were Gentile converts,⁶⁵ they were considered to be equal to native Israelites with respect to their obligation to observe the Sabbath. From this perspective, according to the rabbinic literature, the Sabbath was an ethnic holiday.⁶⁶ *Mishna-Tosefta* follows Deuteronomy (5:12–15) concerning Sabbath observance, rejecting the views of Genesis (2:1–4) and Exodus (20:8–12). The rabbis accepted Deuteronomy's claim that only the Israelites needed to rest on the Sabbath because only they acted in commemoration of the exodus. This motive for observing the Sabbath was a uniquely Israelite phenomenon.⁶⁷ Converts, however, like native-born Israelites, had to observe the Sabbath completely (Exod 20:10; Deut 5:14).⁶⁸ The converts also must follow the travel restrictions placed upon native-born Israelites during the Sabbath. If the converts were immersed on the Sabbath after sunrise, the place of immersion was regarded as the converts' primary residence, so they could not move more than 2,000 cubits⁶⁹ in any direction from the spot (*Palestinian Talmud 'Eruvin* 4:5; 5:3). *Mishnah Shabbat* 16:6, 8 provides a specific example which follows the general rule that on the Sabbath an Israelite may benefit from something the Gentiles had provided, but not from something the Gentiles did with the intention of benefiting the Israelite. Thus, an Israelite may use a lamp provided by a Gentile, water his animals from a well which a Gentile had filled with water for his own animals, and use a gangplank which a Gentile had erected.⁷⁰

Christians also saw the Sabbath as significant in their relationship with Jews. The *Epistle of Barnabas'* Sabbath teaching reflects anti-Judaism.⁷¹ In *Barnabas* 4:6–7; 16:1–

64. Porton, *Goyim*, 205: "The marking out of sacred time thus becomes a way of distinguishing between Israelites and Gentiles. Israelites observe the restrictions connected with the sacred days, while Gentiles do not."

65. In the passages quoted by the *Babylonian Talmud Bekhorot* 30b, Tosefta states that only the Gentiles who agree to follow the law should be accepted as converts (*Tosefta Demai* 2:5). But, once the Gentiles have become Israelites, even if they are suspected of violating all of the Torah's requirements, they still are classified as Israelites (*Tosefta Demai* 2:4; *Babylonian Talmud Bekhorot* 30b; *Tosefta Demai* 2:3–7). These passages points to the fact that some rabbis believed that the converts underwent a radical transformation, for once the Gentiles freely became Israelites, they were Israelites forever. For more information, see Porton, *Stranger*, 177–92.

66. Stern, *Jewish Identity*, 76–77. Stern argues that Israel was distinct from all the nations due to the observance of the Sabbath (*Genesis Rosh HaShanah* 11:8; *Pesahim Rosh HaShanah* 23:6). Moreover, the Sabbath was presented as constitutive of Israel, for it increased their holiness.

67. Porton, *Goyim*, 206–11; Jacob Neusner, *Rabbinic Traditions*, 143–79.

68. The converts were expected to observe the Sabbath, therefore, for example, they could not profit from a bath-house which they inherited from their Gentile father which operated on the Sabbath (*Tosefta Demai* 6:13; *Jerusalem Talmud Shabbat* 3:3). Goldenberg, *Sabbath-Law*, 138–40.

69. Goldenberg, *Sabbath-Law*, 62. He states that the 2,000 cubits to the Sabbath-limit must be measured on an absolutely horizontal line.

70. In *Mishinah Shabbt* 16:8, Rabban Gamaliel II permits the Jews to use a gangplank in order to come down from a ship made by the Gentiles (and also a lamp lighted by the Gentiles).

71. *Barnabas* can be dated between 70 CE (the destruction of Jerusalem) and 132–135 CE (the second destruction of Jerusalem) on the basis of the internal evidence from *Barnabas* 16. It is likely that *Barnabas* was written in Alexandria because of "the author's extensive use of allegory, which was

2, for example, the author discusses the covenant and the temple. The author rejects the Jews because their covenant with God had been broken by idolatry (*Barnabas* 4:13–14). The destruction of the Jerusalem temple was a sign of this. Conversely, the true temple is the Christian in whom God dwells (*Barnabas* 16). Similarly, the Sabbath was one of the main features of his anti-Judaism. In *Barnabas* 15 the Sabbath is not a weekly holy day but a "future seventh millennium."[72] Therefore, the Sabbath, while valid, was something to be observed only in the future. It is likely that the purpose of *Barnabas* 15 was to abrogate the Old Testament Sabbath laws in order to justify Christian worship on Sundays.[73] The author's opposition to the Sabbath was thus one of the main features of his overall anti-Judaism.

Justin Martyr also attacked the Jews on the basis of Sabbath observance. To him, the Sabbath was legislated on account of the sinfulness of the Jews (21:1–3; 43:1; 46:2, compare Ezek 20:21–22).[74] In 19:6—20:1, Justin also indicates that the Sabbath was commanded so that the Jews would nurture remembrance of God. Like circumcision, therefore, Sabbath observance seems to be known widely among the Gentiles as the most conspicuous custom of the Jews (16:2–3; 92:2–3. compare 10:3). Sunday existed apparently at first in a Jewish environment side by side with the social observance of the Sabbath.

Discussion of Sabbath practices was thus a main topic in the ongoing encounters between Jews and Gentiles. That Jesus should have abrogated the law precisely with regard to Sabbath regulations is therefore not fortuitous. To change one's thinking about Sabbath inevitably meant to change one's thinking about the relationship

---

so typical of Alexandrian thought . . . at least under considerable Gnostic influence." Shea, "Sabbath in the *Epistle of Barnabas*," 150. For the evidence of allegory, he refers to *Barnabas* 13:1–4, 7 in comparison with Gal 4:22–31. For the evidence of Gnostic influence, he proposes frequent references to and respect for "knowledge" (Gnosis): *Barnabas* 1:5; 2:1–3, 9, 10; 4:1, 6; 5:3; 6:5, 10; 7:1; 9:7; 10:11–12. Cf. Shea, 150–51.

72. Shea, "Sabbath in the *Epistle of Barnabas*," 156. He argues that the author of *Barnabas* allegorized the Sabbath into a "future millennium." The millennialism with 6,000 years appears in Christian writings for the first time here in Barnabas. The millennial ages system in *Barnabas* 15 makes the future symbolic seventh and eighth days identical in respect to commencement and duration; Kromminga, *Millennium in the Church*, 35: "He [the author of *Barnabas*] seems to be of the opinion that there will be a seventh world period all right, but that period will be identical with the perfection of the eternal state. There can be no doubt about the identity of his seventh and his eight day." Barrett argues that the author of *Barnabas* did not clearly state whether the eighth day starts at the beginning, during, or at the end of the future seventh day (*Barnabas* 15:8). Barrett, "Eschatology of the Epistle to the Hebrews," 370. "But this leads him [the author of *Barnabas*] to include the explicit statement that the eighth day is the beginning of a new world, and if by this he means the eighth millennium what he says here is inconsistent with what he says in xv. 5–7, where the Sabbatical millennium in which sin is overcome is the seventh."

73. The institution of Sunday goes back to early Christianity; hence, Sunday is a purely Christian creation. It is attested by the *Didache* as follows: "And on the Lord's own Day gather yourselves together and break bread and give thanks" (*Didache* 14:1).

74. For Justin the Sabbath constitutes a sign of the transgressions and sins of the Jews. Thus Ezekiel's complaints against the breaking of the rule of the Sabbath are cited as the reason for the giving of the Sabbath.

between Jews and Gentiles. Q 14:5, then, provides the foundation for a new attitude toward the Gentiles in the Q community. If the specific regulations for rest could be abrogated in favor of humanitarian concern, then so could the wall dividing Jews and Gentiles be broken down in favor of God's love for all people?

EPILOGUE

This chapter has been modest in its scope and restricted in its focus, in order to remain methodologically effective and responsible. I have discussed that God's love, as a Christian missionary principle, is revealed through the Sabbath controversy of Jesus in Q 14:5. The Sabbath saying must be understood as related to both the Jewish law and the Gentile mission. As a result of the discussion, this chapter can conclude as follows:

The Greco-Roman religions were already active in its missionary field when Christianity began its mission toward the Gentiles. Pagan beliefs in the Greco-Roman world had an influence on Christianity. Missionary activity, therefore, would be natural to a Christian missionary like Paul. However, Paul has taken over some Greco-Roman beliefs, and woven them into his new Christian ideas. The Q community must have known the Gentile mission established by Paul before the 50s CE. Q's missionary activity, nevertheless, seems to be confined to the Jews because the Q community would have been limited to the Jewish mission during the public ministry of Jesus. We have learned that the Gentile mission was a result of the scattering of Jewish Christianity caused by the persecution by the Pharisees in Jerusalem. Early Christianity also found the foundation of the Gentile mission in the Hebrew Bible prophecies and in Paul's Damascus experience.

The Jewish War sharpened the tensions between Jewish Christians and other Jews. In Jewish-Christian interaction, one can imagine the precise milieu of Christian hostility toward Judaism. The Q community did not think of themselves as a separate group apart from the Jewish community. There is no indication that they were encouraged to separate themselves from the social and religious life of their Jewish neighbors. On the basis of this presupposition, it is likely that the Q community was obviously a Jewish movement that kept the law, but interpreted it through the Jesus tradition. Q emphasizes that Jesus had a conservative attitude toward the law; therefore, Q portrays Jesus as the one who was thoroughly obedient to Jewish law. This can be verified in relation to tithing practices (Q 11:42) and the law-observance (Q 16:17) of the Q community.

Our discussion concludes that the Q community did not regard themselves as a sectarian group apart from Judaism. This Christian group reflected in Q, however, we see as an independent movement, strongly influenced by Jesus' Jewishness. But Jesus' Jewishness is a very different thing from the Jewishness of Judaism. The Q community was a reformed movement warning the Jewish people. One can understand here the milieu of persecution in the Q community in relation to the Jewish characteristics of

Q. The persecution in Q can be understood in that the Q community regarded themselves as a movement within Judaism. But the Jewish people did not regard them as a Jewish movement because Israel rejected Jesus. Under the milieu of the persecution, Christian hostility toward Judaism seems to have grown within the Q community.

In the relationship between Jews and Christians, it is more important to me to consider that the Q community still has a conservative attitude toward Jewish law (Q 16:16–18; 11:42, 39b–40), in spite of the persecution by the Pharisees. The Sabbath controversy of Jesus in Q 14:5 seems to break the old law. The Sabbath controversy in Q would create an awareness of breaking the law in the Q community, and make them a deviant Jewish group. Even if the Q community maintained a conservative attitude to Jewish law (Q 11:42; 16:17), the existence of the Sabbath controversy might persuade them to respond positively to the Christian mission in order to practice the love of God. In the Sabbath controversy, Jesus did not undermine Jewish law, but he had challenged and superseded it. Jesus did not allow the Q community nevertheless positively to preach the gospel to the Gentiles. Rather, Jesus clearly commanded them to preach the gospel to the Jews and to keep Jewish law conservatively. But here I have argued that the Sabbath controversy in Q 14:5 can be placed between Jewish law and the Gentile mission in order to support a general principle for the early Christian missionary activity. The love of God was a basic missionary principle for the early Christian community.

We have surveyed the Jewish attitude toward the Gentiles who lived with the Jewish people at that time. Philo emphasized that the Jewish law concerning the Sabbath is the most conspicuous observance followed in the ancient Jewish world. He had a general interest in exploring the relationship between Gentile conceptions of the Jewish Sabbath and certain Jewish apologetic remarks made to the Gentiles. His main concern was in how the Jewish law relates to the Gentiles. Philo cited the divine origin of the Mosaic law, and related the Jewish concern and Gentile concern for the Sabbath. Although he regarded the Jewish Sabbath as evidence that the Jewish law had a universal value, scholars thought that the Gentiles did not seem to have been universally in favor of the Jewish Sabbath. Some Gentiles would not accept the Jewish customs.

A similar picture of Sabbath practice in agreement with Philo is found in Josephus. Josephus' main concern is also on how the Jewish law relates to the Gentiles. Josephus therefore quite often states that the Jewish concept of rest or inactivity on the Sabbath was widely valued in the Gentile world. He states that the Jews faithfully observed their Sabbath within the context of the Roman world and that the Romans were well acquainted with this Jewish custom. Josephus, however, shows that there were some mistreatments by the Gentiles for those observing the Jewish custom of the Sabbath.

In rabbinic literature, Sabbath observance had grown in the Jews' eyes as a means of marking the difference between the Israelites and the Gentiles. The Jews followed the Sabbath regulations which were strictly applicable to the Jews as well as the Gentiles (*Mishnah Shabbat* 1:5–9). The Gentiles were affected by the Jewish tradition, because the Jews were coming into contact with the Gentiles (*Tosefta Demai* 2:5). Some passages discuss however that certain Gentiles were seen as dangerous people to the Jews (*Mishnah Shabbat* 6:10; 16:6). Although the Jews and the Gentiles lived together, the Jews regarded some Gentiles as different populations because they were threatening to the Jews (*Mishnah Makshirim* 2:3–10; *Tosefta Tohorot* 5:2). Nevertheless, that situation could be helpful for the Jews because the threatening by the Gentiles would encourage the Jews to follow even more closely their own tradition.

Early Christianity seems to have received these Jewish traditions of the Sabbath. In fact, the Jews made the Sabbath anything but a day of fasting. But Sabbath association with fasting is often found in the Sabbath observance in early Christianity. In the *Gospel of Thomas* 27:1–2 the Sabbath is connected to fasting. Epiphanius quotes a reason for fasting on the Sabbath in *Panarion* 42.3,4. In the *Epistle of Barnabas*, the author uses the Sabbath in relation to keeping Sunday ("the eighth day"). In *Barnabas* 15 the Sabbath does not apply to a weekly holy day, but rather to a future seventh millennium. It is likely that the purpose of *Barnabas* 15 was to avoid the Sabbath, because the author believed that Jews with their Sabbath were wrong, but Christians with their Sunday were right. Justin Martyr's *Dialogue with Trypho* is one of the most comprehensive early Christian writings. In the dialogue between Justin and Trypho, Justin frequently refers to the Gentiles and the Sabbath. From this dialogue, one may infer that Sabbath observance seems to be known widely among the Gentiles. Many Gentiles, however, knew of the Jewish Sabbath but did not allow it.

VII

The Gentiles in the Synoptics

PROLOGUE

ONE CAN ASK WHETHER the Gentile mission was permitted within the Q community. Q scholars are divided into two groups in the efforts to explain whether Q knew of the Gentile mission.[1] In investigating the passages Q 7:1–10; 10:2, 5–6, 13–15; 11:31–32; 13:18–19, 28, 29; 14:21–23, some scholars assert that these passages show that the Gentile mission originated in the Q community. Yet, there is no clear evidence of a Gentile mission in Q like the one of Matt 28:19.[2] Nevertheless, some scholars argue that the Gentile mission originated in the Q community, or was conceived by Jesus during his public ministry. Others argue, however, that there is no direct reference to the Gentile mission. The Q redactor, unlike Mark (Mark 13:10), deliberately eliminated the traits which characterize the Q community as favorable toward anything but the Jewish mission. The Q community like Matthew's community experienced no tension between the Jewish mission (Matt 10:5b–6) and the Gentile mission (Matt 28:19). The members of the Q community wanted to remain Jewish Christians. I argue that Q itself did not have a Gentile mission and that the Q community understood the mission to the Gentiles mainly in an eschatological perspective. Still, Q knew the circumstances of Paul's Gentile mission and the efforts of others as well. Nevertheless, the Q community confined itself to the Jewish mission.

---

1. The question of whether Q accepts the Gentile mission is not easy to answer. Stanton, without determining whether the mission was sent to the Gentiles or not, touches the issue in that "both Mark and Q record that Jesus sent out his disciples on a mission (Mark 6:6b–13; Matt 9:37–38; 10:7–16; 11:20–24; 10:40 = Luke 10:1–20)." See his *Gospels and Jesus*, 188.

2. The expression *panta ta ethne* appears four times in Matthew (24:9, 14; 25:32; 28:19) and certainly comes from the redaction of Matthew. For more information, see Kingsbury, "Composition and Christology," 577. Some argue that the phrase *panta ta ethne* can be translated "all the Gentiles," i.e., only non-Jews: Hare and Harrington, "Make Disciples," 363; Levine, *Social and Ethnic Dimensions*, 186–92, 278. But Meier argues that the phrase can be translated "all (the) peoples" or "all (the) nations": see "Nations or Gentiles," 94; "Two Disputed Questions," 411.

The Gentile Mission and the Synoptic Problem

Thomas Walter Manson insists that there is a Gentile mission in Q. He regards Q as "a book of instruction for converts from Gentile paganism." Q, for him, thus has "a friendly attitude towards Gentiles" "more than any other of the Synoptic sources."[3] He does not give, however, a reasonable explanation for this position.[4] He repeats, when arguing later on Luke 14:21–23, that the Gentile mission was "characteristic of Q" and that "this is doubtless meant to suggest a mission beyond the borders of Israel to the Gentiles."[5] For Manson Matt 8:5–13, 11:21–24, and Matt 12:38–42 assume "a tacit invitation to the Gentiles" in Q and keeps "an invitation to Gentiles to share in the good things of the Kingdom" in Q.[6]

Ferdinand Hahn, in examining Matt 8:11–12 // Luke 13:28–29, considers Matthean order and his wording to be more original.[7] He argues that the Semitic nature of the sayings of Matt 8:11–12 is clear. Hahn states that Matt 8:11–12 explains the attitude of Jesus to the Gentiles. "The earliest church therefore maintained the claim to the whole of God's people, but at the same time observed and followed out the line already drawn by Jesus' own acceptance of individual Gentiles and by his words in Matt 8.11f."[8] Hahn argues that a reference to the Gentiles is also evident in the marriage feast (Matt 22:1–10; Luke 14:16–24). Here he notes that, whereas there is no direct reference to the Gentile mission, nevertheless, "the Church has with good

---

3. Manson, *Sayings of Jesus*, 20. Manson infers from this conclusion that Q is connected with "Antioch, the first headquarters of the Gentile mission" and Q can be dated about "the middle of the first century, probably rather before than after AD 50."

4. For him the story of the centurion, the people of Tyre and Sidon, the men of Nineveh, the Queen of the South, and the people from the west and east are all Q characters for the Gentile mission.

5. Manson, *Sayings of Jesus*, 130. Manson stands here on the position of the Pauline motto: "To the Jews first, and also to the Greek" (Rom 1:16; 2:9–10). The Gentile mission did not originate with Jesus during his public ministry; Harnack, *Mission und Ausbreitung*, 48. Harnack argues that for Paul it is not quite clear how the Gentile mission arose. For Harnack Paul certainly was not the first missionary to the Gentiles: "Paul never claims in his letters to have been absolutely the pioneer of the Gentile mission. Gal 1.16 merely says that the apostle understood already that his conversion meant a commission to the Gentiles; it does not say that his commission was something entirely new.... All we are to understand is that after his conversion he needed no further conflict of the inner man in order to undertake the Gentile mission. Nevertheless, it is certain that Paul remains *the* Gentile missionary. It was he who really established the duty and the right of Gentile missions; it was he who raised the movement out of its tentative beginnings into a mission that embraced all the world"; Bultmann recognizes that the final invitation (Luke 14:23) which refers clearly to the Gentile mission is from Luke, not from Q. Bultmann, *Geschichte der synoptischen Tradition*, 189. The IQP, however, regards Luke 14:23 as Q.

6. Manson, *Teaching of Jesus*, 28n2 and 34.

7. Hahn, *Verständnis der Mission*, 34n1. "In Luke the transposition is explained by the composition of 13:22–24. Probably, too, Matthew usually keeps the oldest form of words, only Luke is to be preferred in 13:28 *fin* to Matt 8:12a. The statement in Matt 8:12b could be a later addition."

8. Ibid., 35: "For where Gentiles put their trust unconditionally in Jesus they accept the offer that Israel rejects, and therefore Jesus' acceptance of such Gentiles is simply a matter of course." Here Hahn obviously sees the future acceptance of the Gentiles. Compare ibid., 51.

reason related the text to the mission." For him, the promises to all nations and the narratives of the acceptance of individual Gentiles must not be considered in isolation. Though Jesus did not perform a mission to the Gentiles, his mission and work "in Israel became a witness among the Gentiles, and still more: as the eschatological event began to be realized, salvation came within reach of the Gentiles."[9] Hahn states that there is no sign in the New Testament of a "particularistic Jewish Christianity of Palestine" which would have rejected the Gentile mission in general.[10] Matt 10:23 does not reveal a rejection of the Gentile mission for him; Matt 25:31–46 and Rev 14:6–7 cannot be interpreted as being opposed to the Gentile mission.[11]

Dieter Lührmann concludes that it is not accidental that a Gentile is shown as a model for following Jesus in the story of the centurion's servant (Luke 7:1–10).[12] But Lührmann also finds a problem in arguing for the Gentile mission. The centurion's faith is praised in Q, but Jesus does not enter his house. More surprisingly, the centurion is not said to follow Jesus, and Jesus does not suggest the Gentile mission to his disciples in the story. Nevertheless, the image of the harvest in Q 10:2 may refer to the judgment of the Gentiles;[13] hence the call to send laborers to the harvest may imply the existence of a Gentile mission.[14] Lührmann also interprets the parable of the banquet (Q 14:16–24) as a warning after the Jewish failure to respond to Jesus, and that the mission was sent out to the Gentiles. Thus Lührmann refers to the polemic against Israel in Q as evidence that the Gentile mission was embraced by the Q community. All hope for Israel was abandoned and the mission turned to the Gentiles.[15]

---

9. Ibid., 36. Even Hahn thinks that the banquet in Luke 14:16–24 must not be described as the mission to the Gentiles. Compare ibid., 39.

10. Ibid., 54–59. In this section, Hahn deals with Matt 10:23; 25:31–46; Rev 14:6–7 to support his view of the "particularist Jewish Christianity of Palestine."

11. Hahn consistently asserts that there is a Gentile mission of Jesus in Q, without distinguishing the sayings of Jesus from Matthean sayings or others.

12. Lührmann, *Redaktion der Logienquelle*, 58.

13. The use of the harvest here is characteristic because it is applied to the missionary activity which is found in the context of apocalyptic judgment: Isa 18:5–7; 24:13; Jer 51:33; Hos 6:11. Harvest time is an eschatological metaphor. It is used for God's judgment upon the nations of the earth (Joel 3:13 [4:13 LXX]; Mic 4:12–13) or for the final gathering of the scattered Israelites (Isa 27:12). The image of harvest time also comes to signify the final division between the righteous and unrighteous in Israel (2 *Apoc. Bar.* 70:2; 4 Ezra 4:28–32).

14. Lührmann, *Redaktion der Logienquelle*, 60. For the judgment of the Gentiles, see Isa 27:11; Hos 6:11; Joel 3:13–14. Lührmann argues that the harvest in Q 10:2 seems to include the Gentiles, since the harvest is regularly used as an image for God's judgment of the Gentiles (Joel 4:1–21; Isa 24:13; Mic 4:11–13; Rev 14:15). Bornkamm, "End-Expectation and Church," 18.

15. Lührmann, *Redaktion der Logienquelle*, 47. "Weiter setzt Q, wie die Geschichte von 'Hauptmann von Kapernaum' (Lk 7,1–10/Mt 8,5–13), die betonte Gegenüberstellung von Heiden und Israel in den für Q typischen Drohworten (sc Lk 10, 13–15; 11,31f und 13,28 par Mt) und vor allem die mit einem solchen Drohwort schließende, aber mit einer Verheißung für die Heiden beginnende Aussendungsrede (sc Lk 10,2 par Mt) zeigen, m. E. die Heidenmission voraus. Mindestens findet sich in Q eine positive Haltung gegenüber den Heiden . . . Diese Haltung lediglich als 'Heidenfreundlichkeit' zu bezeichnen, ist wohl doch zu wenig, auch der Verweis auf die alttestamentlichen Propheten reicht

Paul D. Meyer asserts: "The Q-Community was at least profoundly aware of the Gentile mission."[16] Meyer examines the negative statements about Gentiles in Q and acknowledges that "it cannot be said that the community was particularly sympathetic with that [the Gentile] mission."[17] Nevertheless, Meyer later argues that "the Gentile mission and the subsequent inclusion of Gentiles in Christian communities [were] widely recognized as having been a traumatic experience for the primitive church... and several passages in Q reveal that community's particular response to this challenge."[18] In Luke 11:29–32 // Matt 12:38–42; Matt 8:11–12 // Luke 13:28–29; Luke 14:15–24 // Matt 22:1–10, the Q community recognized the Gentile mission as legitimate and as the activity of God, but explained it as God's response to Israel's impenitence.[19] Throughout his article, Meyer indicates that the Q community regarded the Gentile mission as "a *fait accompli.*" For him, the Gentiles' faith was used by the Q community to shame Israel into repentance, and the mission was understood to be God's response to Israel's past impenitence. But Meyer's interpretation seems to be influenced by Paul. Meyer interprets the Gentile mission in Q on the basis of the Pauline motto: "God had offered the kingdom to Israel, but it had been rejected; God has turned to the nations since the Jews spurned their opportunity." He concludes that Israel's stubbornness reflected in Q provides an explanation for the "unanticipated influx of Gentiles into the church through the Gentile mission."[20] Meyer thus claims that Q presupposed the Gentile mission, but that Q's primary concern was to address the Jewish people and that it used the success of Christian appeals to Gentiles as part of its message to the Jews.

Rudolf Laufen understands the Gentile mission as the beginning of the eschatological fulfillment of the kingdom of God. He endorses the opinion of Lührmann against Schulz, and affirms that the Q community pursued the Gentile mission.[21] Laufen argues that Luke 10:8b is in Q and that this instruction seems to make sense in the context of a Gentile missionary situation where Jewish food laws were not presupposed.[22] The woes in Luke 10:13–15 point neither to the life of Jesus nor to problems of Christian

---

nicht, mindestens wird man wie Manson von diesen Stellen sagen müssen: 'all contain a tacit invitation to the Gentiles'. Doch dürften vor allem Lk 7,1–10/Mt 8,5–13 und Lk 10,2/Mt 9,37f darauf hinweisen, daß die Gemeinde, in der Q überliefert worden ist, diese Einladung auch ausgesprochen hat" (ibid., 86–87).

16. Meyer, "Community of Q," 85. "The Q-community was found to be acutely aware of the Gentile mission" (ibid., 86).

17. Ibid., 85. "No joy is evident over the Gentile mission" (ibid., 86). "Its [the Q community] attitude toward the Gentile mission was quite chauvinistic..." (ibid., 87).

18. Meyer, "Gentile Mission in Q," 405.

19. Ibid. For him in those passages the success of the Gentile mission is therefore being used by the community to address the Jews.

20. Ibid., 417.

21. Laufen, *Doppelüberlieferung*, 192–94, 247–43.

22. Ibid., 219–20, 288, 292.

missionaries in Galilee. The address is more general.[23] Laufen believes that the parable of the mustard seed is an allusion to the influx of Gentiles into the kingdom of God.[24]

Dieter Zeller argues that the saying of Matt 8:11-12 // Luke 13:28-29 has the motif of the people's pilgrimage and, at the same time, that of the Gentile mission. He stresses the traditions of the pilgrimage of the people to Zion.[25] Even though the Gentiles were not literally streaming into Zion, it was only natural that the success of the Gentile mission was seen in the light of biblical predictions. In comparison with the pilgrimage of the people, Zeller regards the saying in Matt 8:11-12 // Luke 13:28-29 as the text of the Gentile mission of Q. Zeller argues that Q's attitude toward the Gentiles had been developed in the course of time.[26] Later, Wolfgang Schenk also used the term "Völkermission"[27] for Matt 8:11-12 // Luke 13:28-29 to show the Gentile mission was in Q.

Risto Uro sees in Q a clear pro-Gentile attitude and thinks that the Q community was active in the mission to the Gentiles and accepted them into the community. Of course, Uro agrees that there is no strong Gentile mission in Q like Matt 28:18-20 and that there is no direct instruction toward the Gentile mission. Uro asserts, nevertheless, that the Gentile mission appears in a very positive light in Q. He doubts that the Q community was set in a strictly Jewish milieu.[28] Uro insists that the Q community did not reject the Gentile mission, and "Luke 13.28-29 and the whole section 13.24-30 . . . appear to presuppose the Gentile mission and the acceptance of it by the 'Q communities.'" Accepting Manson's statement, Uro argues for the presence in Q of further indications of the Gentile mission: "Throughout Q, the contrast between Israel's failure and the Gentiles' willingness appears as a recurring theme (Luke 7.1-10; 10.13-15, 21-22; 11.31-32; 13.28-29; 14.15-24)." He concludes that Q's interest in the Gentile mission is "so vivid"; "Q accepts the Gentile mission and sees in it a realization of God's eschatological act and the turning point in the salvation history."[29]

Christopher M. Tuckett, although recognizing the evidence of the Gentile mission in Q as "inconclusive and ambiguous,"[30] agrees with Meyer and concludes that "Q is aware of a Gentile mission, but not actively engaged in it."[31] Tuckett agrees that the story in Q [Q 7:1-10] functions as a "warrant for a full-blown Gentile mission," and that the way in which the centurion functions in the story is similar to the way

---

23. Ibid., 275-76. Lührmann, *Redaktion der Logienquelle*, 63; Ernst, *Evangelium nach Lukas*, 336.

24. Laufen, *Die Doppelüberlieferung der Logienquelle*, 192-93.

25. Zeller, "Logion Mt 8,11f/Lk 13,28f," esp. 226-31.

26. Ibid., 91-93.

27. Schenk, *Synopse zur Redenquelle*, 105.

28. Uro, *Sheep among the Wolves*, 210.

29. Ibid., 217, 221-22. Uro's conclusion is much stronger than any other scholars before him. He also infers that Q not only accepted the Gentile mission, but also encouraged it (ibid., 222).

30. Tuckett, *Q*, 394.

31. Ibid., 403. His conclusion is still ambiguous; Meyer, "Gentile Mission," 405-17.

in which other Gentiles function elsewhere in Q 10:13–15; 11:31–32.³² For him "any references to the Gentile conversions, or the Gentile participation in the blessings of the Kingdom of God, are not so much a reflection of the missionary activity of Q Christians but are used as part of Q's polemical arsenal to address a Jewish audience by intensifying the appeal to other Jews."³³

By contrast, other scholars claim that Q rejected the idea of the Gentile mission and was not concerned with the issue. Adolf von Harnack argues that the Gentile mission was entirely outside Jesus' concern because Jesus' sayings are directed to the Jews. Harnack does not regard Matt 8:11–12 // Luke 13:28–29 as a saying of Jesus. He concludes that the evangelist Matthew inserted "any allusion to the Gentile mission into the framework of the public preaching of Jesus." For Harnack, Jesus gives no instructions for a Gentile mission. Thus Harnack reminds us that "the gospel was at first preached to the Jews exclusively."³⁴ In order to reinforce Jesus' concern for the Jews, however, Harnack wrongly states that "it [the gospel] says nothing about the Gentile mission either in Mark's version (12:1–2), or in Matthew's (21:33–34)."³⁵ Even the word "a nation" in Matt 21:43 does not refer to the Gentiles because Harnack regards the "nation" as being opposed to official Israel.

John M. C. Crum asks "was Q 'Judaistic?'" He answers that Q was the document "given by Jewish Christians living [in] Jerusalem [in] 30, 40, 50 CE." He describes the Q community as "Judaistic Christianity."³⁶ Crum believed that all debatable verses in Matt 10:5, 6, 23–26 belong to Q. The wonder is that these Gentile-ignoring verses should have survived in Q. Crum's explanation is that the Q community lived in Jerusalem as Jewish Christians,³⁷ and expected the immediate return of the Son of Man.

---

32. Tuckett, *Q*, 397. Though Tuckett disagrees with Jacobson that Q does not have the Gentile mission, he seems to agree with him that Q uses the fact of the success of Christian appeals to the Gentiles against the Jews (Tuckett, 394); Jacobson, *First Gospel*, 110, 256.

33. Tuckett, *Q*, 403–4.

34. Harnack, *Mission and Expansion*, 40, 45.

35. Ibid., 39n3. Harnack criticized Wellhausen's Markan priority against Q, but he agreed with him on the Gentile mission. Julius Wellhausen addressed indirectly the theme "Jesus and the Gentiles in Q." Now we can understand what his background of that issue was: "In Q erhebt sich Jesus über den jüdischen Horizont, in dessen Grenzen er sich bei Markus hält. Er nimmt die Verwerfung der Juden und die Bekehrung der Heiden in Aussicht. Er macht es dem Täufer zum Vorwurf, dass er in der alten Ära stecken geblieben und zu der neuen, die schon da ist, nicht durchgedrungen sei. Er selber hat das Christentum eröffnet und setzt dessen Ablösung vom Judentum als schon eingetreten voraus." See his *Einleitung in drei ersten Evangelien*, 165.

36. Crum, *Original Jerusalem Gospel*, 84. In fact, Crum supposes that Q was written by Jewish Christians in Jerusalem about 40 CE. He says this is "to suppose an Apocalyptic atmosphere in the church there: a church of Jews over whom is imminent the return of their Lord: Christian Jews persecuted by un-Christian Jews and still devoting themselves to the conversion of their Jewish neighbors only" (ibid., 93).

37. Ibid., 92–93, 95. "The people among whom Q was first received were Jews, but they were Christian Jews. They lived in Jerusalem. But it was in Jerusalem that they found their dearest enemies, yea, their own familiar friends in whom they had trusted. It was the next-door neighbor who interested them, the Jews who had rejected their Christ" (ibid., 90).

Johannes Munck recognizes that the early church favored the priority of the mission to the Jews: "Jewish Christianity does not carry on a mission to the Gentiles." For him the sayings of Jesus indicate that "the message is to be taken only to Israel."[38] But he concludes that Paul wanted to reverse the order and missionize first among the Gentiles; and this view was explicitly approved at the Apostolic Council at Jerusalem.[39] Matthew similarly concludes his Gospel by telling how the risen Christ commanded his disciples to leave the Jews, and to go and make disciples of all the Gentiles (Matt 28:19–20). When Joachim Jeremias discusses the final fate of the Gentiles, he maintains that the Gentiles will have a part in the resurrection. He thinks that the Gentiles are included in Jesus' declaration of the eschatological expectation.[40] Jeremias insists that in Matt 8:11 // Luke 13:29 we have "a succinct summary of the Old Testament utterances concerning the eschatological pilgrimage of the Gentiles to the Mount of God at the time of the Last Judgment: Isa 49:12 and 25:6–7." Returning to the original message of Jesus, Jeremias concludes that "the Gentile mission is the beginning of God's final act in the gathering of the Gentiles. The Gentile mission is God's own activity."[41] Jeremias recognizes that, in the sayings of Jesus, one can view the Gentile mission eschatologically, rather than historically.

David Bosch analyzes the details of the parable of the banquet (Luke 14:16–24; Matt 22:1–10) in terms of Jesus' prediction of the exact development of the mission of the early church.[42] If one accepts his interpretation, however, one would have to conclude that the church's experience has so colored the narrative that Jesus' original meaning has been lost. If Jesus referred to the Gentiles, it was probably along the lines of Matt 8:11–12, namely as part of his teaching about the Messianic banquet. Unfortunately, in Q there is no term "Messiah" and no Messianic banquet, as in the other Gospels. Explaining the relationship between Matt 10:23 and Mark 13:10, however, Bosch says, "We must therefore regard Matt 10:23 as an independent word of Jesus which, by analogy with the saying about the Gentile mission [in] Mark 13:10, expects a Jewish mission during the whole time between (der ganzen Zwischenzeit) the Resurrection and the Parousia." The fact, which Bosch himself notes, is that "according to Mark 13:10 the Gentile mission appears as an *opus perfectum*, while according to Matt 10:23 the Jewish mission would not yet have come to an end." This is only one of the difficulties of his interpretation.[43] Later, Bosch goes further and confirms that the

---

38. Munck, *Paul and the Salvation of Mankind*, 255–56.

39. Ibid., 275–81. Arguing that this is a superseded construction of the Tübingen school, Munck denies that there was any opposition between the Jewish Christians and Paul in their view of the missionary work after the Jerusalem council (ibid., 69–71).

40. Jeremias, *Jesus' Promise*, 46–47.

41. Ibid., 62, 74.

42. Bosch, *Heidenmission*, 124–25.

43. Ibid., 157.

question about the earthly Jesus' attitude to the Gentiles is important but secondary.[44] Thus he concludes that Jesus' mission was to "*all* Israel,"[45] agreeing with the opinion that "all Israel" would be saved.[46] Bosch rightly recognizes that the Gentiles appear in Q, but mainly within the framework of judgment sayings or as a warning to Israel. Hence for Bosch it is not surprising that the Gentiles can sometimes be portrayed as substitute guests at the eschatological banquet.[47]

Odil Hannes Steck points out that there are some positive descriptions of the Gentiles in Q (Matt 8:5–10, 13; Luke 10:13; Matt 12:41–42), but argues that those sayings do not refer to the Gentile mission at all. The purpose of those sayings in Q for him is "nicht das Verhalten dieser Heiden, sondern die so unterstrichene Halsstarrigkeit der Israeliten."[48] By this explanation, Steck shows that in Q, Jesus sent out his disciples to enable the Jews to repent for the stubbornness of Israel, not to save the Gentiles. Siegfried Schulz agrees with Steck[49] and confirms that Q originally had to do with the Jewish mission, not with the Gentile mission.[50] For example, Schulz argues that Q 10:13–15 differs from the early "mission code." He refers to this and also lists several other reasons for labeling Luke 10:13–15 the Hellenistic Jewish Christian stratum of Q. In his interpretation, the saying is a "Rückblick auf die Vergangheit des Heils"[51] and shows the awakening of the interest in the miracles of Jesus in the earlier stratum of Q.[52] Schulz refers in the context to Q's attitude toward Jewish law, arguing that Q's conservative position in relation to the law must exclude the possibility of Q's acknowledging positive elements in the Gentile mission. Schulz also argues that the saying of Matt 8:11–12 // Luke 13:28–29 does not presuppose the Gentile mission, but rather shows the eschatological proclamation to accept the Gentiles in the future.[53] For him the presence of mission activity in Israel is already an apocalyptic end-time event.[54] It may be recalled that A. Schweitzer, who held that eschatology and ethics were mutually exclusive, turned to the mission charge as evidence that ethical

---

44. Bosch, *Transforming Mission*, 26.

45. Ibid. Here he is interested in the salvation of only a *remnant* of Israel.

46. Goppelt, *Theology of the New Testament*, 207–13; Meyer, *Early Christians*, 62.

47. Bosch, *Transforming Mission*, 30: He suggests that "scholars are today far more ready to credit Jesus himself with laying the foundations for the Gentile mission."

48. Steck, *Israel*, 287n2.

49. Schulz, Q, 244n461.

50. Ibid., 244–45, 305–6, 402, 410–11.

51. Ibid., 363–64.

52. Although Schulz's criteria simply go in a vicious circle and perhaps are not conclusive for the provenance of Q 10:13–15, I agree with Schulz in that this saying reveals features which belong to a later stage in the Q tradition of Jesus.

53. Ibid., 244, 306. "Diese Q-Gemeinde kannte keine Völkermission vor dem nahen Ende, weil nirgendwo in Q die Kulttora grundsätzlich und bewußt abrogiert wird" (ibid., 401–2).

54. Ibid., 410.

teaching played no role in Jesus' mission, or more precisely that ethical teaching must be subsumed under the call to repentance.[55]

Paul Hoffmann criticizes Lührmann's opinion that the Q community already pursued the Gentile mission.[56] Hoffmann argues that the Q group can be understood as Jewish "Volksgenossen."[57] Thus he argues that the sayings of Q have a Jewish Christian character.[58] He maintains that Matt 8:11–12 // Luke 13:28–29 contain the prophetic picture of the eschatological people's pilgrimage. Hoffmann disagrees that the Gentile mission is focused in Luke 10:13–15 and suggests that the judgment was pronounced only against the opponents of Q, since the Q community was still working among fellow Jews. The mission and judgment do not, however, exclude each other, if the disciples' task was understood in prophetic terms as a proclamation of judgment.[59] Thus Hoffmann concludes that, in Q, the situation of the messengers can be described as "eschatological."[60] He remarks, "Die 'Mission' ist also für Q nicht von der Erntezeit unterschieden, sondern ist selbst endzeitliches Geschehen." As Hoffmann observes, the Gentiles mentioned generally were not people present for Q; rather, the reference was to the past (Q 11:31–32) or to the future (Q 10:13–15; 13:28–29).[61] Moreover, the Q missionaries appear in a role elsewhere reserved to the angels, namely, the gathering of the eschatological harvest (Mark 13:27; Matt 13:39–41; Rev 14:15).

Stephen G. Wilson claims that Jesus did not foresee a Gentile mission because there is no evidence that Jesus preached to the Gentiles. Rather, Wilson argues, "the only reference to the Gentiles, therefore, is in the statement that they will judge the Jews—another startling, direct reversal of Jewish expectation."[62] Wilson believes that Jesus limited his task to Israel and that the main thrust of his teaching was that the Gentiles would come into the kingdom of God in the future. For Wilson, Jesus himself could have seen this and yet still have maintained a basically futuristic hope for

---

55. Schweitzer, *Mystery of the Kingdom*, 87, 89–97.

56. Hoffmann, *Studien zur Theologie*, 289–93.

57. Ibid., 293.

58. Hoffmann, "Jesusverkündigung in der Logienquelle," 53–54. "Dem judenchristlichen Charakter der Sammlung entspricht es, wenn in der Frage des Gesetzes ein dem Judentum entgegenkommender Standpunkt eingenommen wird. Der Vers Mt 5,18 par. Lk 16,17 betont nachdrücklich die Gültigkeit des Gesetzes (vgl. auch Lk 13,25f); die Gesetzeskritik Jesu am Verhalten der Pharisäer und Schriftgelehrten [scheint] eingeschränkt zu sein (Mt 23,25f; Lk 11,44.46; Mt 23,13). Die Antithesen der Bergpredigt (Mt 5,21–48), die Streitgespräche über Rein und Unrein (Mk 7,1–23) oder über den Sabbat (Mk 3,1–6) fehlen bezeichenderweise in Q."

59. Hoffmann, *Studien zur Theologie*, 169–71, 293.

60. Ibid., 292. He thus argues that even the harvest saying does not have any relationship to the Gentile mission.

61. Ibid., 290, 293.

62. Wilson, *Gentiles and the Gentile Mission*, 5. Wilson concludes that the original form of the saying about the sign of Jonah (Mark 8:11–12; Matt 12:38–42; Luke 11:29–32) can probably be found in Matt 12:39 (ibid., 4).

the Gentiles which would be fulfilled in the future.⁶³ Thus he concludes that "Jesus did not expect there to be a historical Gentile mission" and that "his teaching on the Gentiles is inseparably linked with his teaching on eschatology."⁶⁴

Uwe Wegner, examining whether Q rejected the Gentile mission or not, concludes that Q did not presuppose the Gentile mission.⁶⁵ Wegner selected several passages for examining the relationship between Q and the Gentiles (though not the Gentile mission).⁶⁶ But Wegner speaks of a "gesetzfreie Heidenmission."⁶⁷ No Gentile mission in Q was entirely "gesetzfrei" for him, not even Paul's. An appeal to Q's rigorous attitude to the law cannot necessarily determine Q's attitude to any missionary activity directed to the Gentiles.

Arland D. Jacobson also claims that Q did not presuppose the existence of the Gentile mission. He states that the mission charges in Q 10:2–16 are "no longer a mission but an errand of judgment, in which 'laborers' who went out to Israel were the instruments of judgment." In the mission charge, Jacobson recognizes a combination of several traditions, including prophetic, sapiential, eschatological, apocalyptic, and charismatic.⁶⁸ It was the failure of the mission which led to a reconceptualization of the community's situation which was made possible by the use of deuteronomistic language. For example, in Q 7:1–10 Jacobson interprets the purpose of the Gentile mission to be to put Israel to shame: "Behind the story in its present form stand Israel's rejection of Jesus and his followers and the reflection of the Q community upon these experiences." For him, one cannot understand Q 7:1–10 as evidence that Q was engaged in a mission to the Gentiles. Rather, the stories put Israel to shame. Jacobson even concludes that the Q community did not contain "gentile members,"⁶⁹ suggesting that the Q community did not have a mission to the Gentiles in Q 7:1–10. Thus eschatology is clearly present in the mission view of Q. It is likely that in Q God is abandoning the present generation (13:34–35) and will replace it (13:29, 28; 14:16–18). In the eschatological perspective, Q gives a final warning to Israel to repent, welcoming the Gentiles into the kingdom of God.

David Catchpole disagrees with the presuppositions of Meyer and Uro, and states that the *Sitz im Leben* of Q 10:13–15 must surely be "that of a mission, not to

---

63. Ibid., 13–14. Here Wilson stresses that we cannot use the Gentile healing miracles as evidence that Jesus either inaugurated or intended there to be a historical Gentile mission.

64. Ibid., 28. For him Jesus believed that the Parousia was imminent, so that there was no room for a historical Gentile mission.

65. Wegner, *Der Hauptmann*, 334.

66. Ibid., 305. Here are the passages: Matt 5:47 // Luke 6:33; Matt 6:32 // Luke 12:30; Matt 8:5–10, 13 // Luke 7:1–10; Matt 8:11–12 // Luke 13:18–19; Matt 11:20–24 // Luke 10:12–15; Matt 12:38–42 // Luke 11:16, 29–32; Matt 13:31–32 // Luke 13:18–19; Matt 22:1–10 // Luke 14:16–24; Matt 7:6 and Matt 10:5–6, 23; Matt 4:25–27.

67. Ibid., 332.

68. Jacobson, "Divided Families," 256. For more information, see ibid., 137–49.

69. Ibid., 110.

Gentiles but to Israel."⁷⁰ Catchpole concludes that the Q mission charge contained the instruction neither to go into the way of the Gentiles nor to enter into the town of the Samaritans. In Q, there is a preoccupation with a mission to Israel. Finding authentic Jesus material in Q 10:13–15 and 16, however, he sees that "there is a sense of the eschatological ultimacy of that mission which is carried out in anticipation of the imminent kingdom." Catchpole argues that the Gentiles mentioned in Q 10:13–15; 11:31–32 are used to rebuke those who have not responded to the preaching.⁷¹

I have discussed Q's rejection of the Gentile mission in favor of concern for the Jews, even though the Q community had a positive attitude toward the Gentiles. From the deuteronomistic view, though, the Q community recognized that they were sent out to enable the Jews to repent of their stubbornness. I have also examined the eschatological perspective of Q and have it relate to the Jews and the Gentiles.

The Milieu of the Q Community

Before determining whether the Q community carried on the Gentile mission or not, it is helpful to remember that the Q community was a Jewish religious movement.⁷² James M. Robinson has suggested that "the Q community . . . merged into the Matthean community."⁷³ This suggestion deserves further consideration. His suggestion can be answered in relation to the Jewishness of both the Q community and the Matthean community on the basis of their Jewish mission. If it is correct, it may corroborate the claim that Q did not carry out a Gentile mission.

Arland D. Jacobson argues that Q is not "Christian" because Q does not have "Christology" in the sense of the Messiah or the redeemer. Q was, rather, "pre-Christian."⁷⁴ If Q itself is pre-Christian, it stands within Jewish traditions, including the deuteronomistic tradition, just as much as any other Jewish document. Jacobson has rightly suggested that, "despite very sharp tension with other Jewish groups, the community reflected in

---

70. Catchpole, *Quest for Q*, 173.

71. Ibid., 188. "The Gentiles mentioned in Q 13:13–15 are not models of actual response but simply means to an end of rebuking the presumed audience in Israel" (ibid., 283).

72. Some scholars have investigated the Jewishness of Jesus, and the Jewish roots and background of Christianity: Lee, *Galilean Jewishness of Jesus*; Cwiekowski, *Beginnings of the Church*, 205. "Overall, Jesus' life and ministry are unintelligible apart from his Jewishness and the Jewish milieu in which he lived. Jesus conducted his mission as one who proclaimed the dawning of God's kingdom and who sought to bring Israel to the core, as he saw it, of its religious faith. Even if very soon after the resurrection some of his followers pushed to new frontiers and began a mission to the Gentiles, the early church can only be seen correctly if we see its Jewish roots"; Charlesworth, *Jesus' Jewishness*.

73. Robinson, "Q Trajectory," 193. Here Robinson quotes Luz: "Therefore we support the thesis that the Gospel of Matthew comes from a community which was founded by the wandering messengers and prophets of the Son of man of the Sayings Source and remains in close contact with them. The traditions of Q thus reflect, for the community, experiences from its own history. They are 'its own' tradition"; Luz, *Evangelium nach Matthäus*, 66.

74. Jacobson, "Divided Families," 376.

Q could not conceive of itself as anything but Jewish."[75] Tuckett accepts this suggestion, but believes that the members of the Q community were "Christians." Tuckett argues that the Q Christians regarded themselves as "Jewish and (at least of) Israel."[76] In this discussion of the relationship between the Q community and the Jewish people, one can imagine the precise milieu of the Q community in terms of the *Sitz im Leben*, as the group of people who preserved Q. In Jewish-Christian interaction, the precise milieu of Christian hostility toward Judaism seems to have been growing within the Q community. Tuckett rightly argues that "the Q Christians had not given up hope for Israel; and they did not think of themselves as a separate community."[77] There is thus no indication that the Q community separated itself from the social and religious life of their Jewish neighbors. On the basis of this investigation, we can regard the Q community as a Jewish movement that keeps the law, interpreted through the Jesus tradition. Q emphasizes "Jesus as advocate of strict Torah observance."[78] Q portrays Jesus as the one who is thoroughly obedient to the law. This can be illustrated in relation to the tithing practices (Q 11:42) and law-observance (Q 16:17) of the Q community. In the discussion of Q and the law, Q's Jesus displays an extremely conservative attitude toward the law.

Perhaps the Q community did not regard themselves as a sectarian group apart from Judaism. To put Israel to shame, Q needed to remind its community that they were not a sectarian group within Judaism, but were an independent movement founded on Jesus' life and teachings. Riley asserts that "the Jewishness of Jesus was a very different thing from the Jewishness of Moses or David or the prophets of Israel,"[79] arguing that the issue is whether Q was like first-century Judaism. Tuckett argues that "the Christian group reflected in Q may have been more of a 'reform movement' working within Israel than a 'sect' separated from its Jewish contemporaries by a rigid line of demarcation."[80] Tuckett is indebted here for the terms, i.e., "sect" vs. "reform movement," to Watson.[81] Tuckett identifies a distinction between a "reform movement," working within a parent group, and a "sect," with its own defined boundaries which distinguish it from the parent. Tuckett claims that the Q community does not seem to have reached a state of self-conscious "sectarian" differentiation from its neighbors.

---

75. Jacobson, *First Gospel*, 32. James M. Robinson examines the distinction between two stages in the tradition of Q: "the kerygma of the Jewish-Christian Q community" and "the kerygma of the younger Q community of Syria" drawn by Siegfried Schulz; Robinson, "Q Trajectory," 187.

76. Tuckett, Q, 426. In comparison with Q, Quispel insists that many of the Jesus traditions in the Gospel of Thomas come from a Jewish Christian environment. Quispel, "Gospel of Thomas," 218–66. The list of Logia containing Jewish Christian influences can be found on pp. 242–44: Logia 2, 6, 12, 16, 23, 27, 31, 39, 44, 62, 64, 65, 68, 69, 71, 81, 84, 88, 90, 93, 95, 99, 104, 107, 109, and 113.

77. Tuckett, Q, 434.

78. Robinson, "Q Trajectory," 193.

79. Riley, *One Jesus*, 63–64. "Jesus was heir, as were his disciples, to centuries of pervasive and influential new ideas and cultures. Their worldview was very different from that of the Israelite tribal religion of the Old Testament."

80. Tuckett, Q, 436.

81. Watson, *Paul, Judaism and the Gentiles*, 19–20, 38–41.

That Q was a persecuted community also supports the contention that Q was Jewish. The persecution can be explained by the fact that the Q community regarded itself as a movement within Judaism, but other Jews did not accept them just as they had not accepted Jesus. Q 10:3 has been taken as an example of persecution. Schulz argues: "Mörderische Konflikte bis hin zum Martyrium werden das tägliche Brot für die Endzeitboten sein."[82] The saying in Q 10:3 is harsh in that the disciples are to work like helpless sheep among wolves. More striking than Q 10:3, Q 6:22 presuppose the special circumstances by which Jesus' followers would be confronted. John S. Kloppenborg considers Q 6:22–23 as "oriented toward the specific situation of persecution of the Christian community."[83] William David Davies also argues that "it is possible that the reference to persecution [in Luke 6:22] may have a catechetical interest."[84] Such argumentation would allow the community rules[85] in Jesus' Inaugural Sermon (Q 6:20–49) to be connected to the persecution that probably was directed against the Q community. In order to prove the circumstances of persecution for the Q community, we can compare Q 6:22 with Matt 5:11. The main difference is in the choice of the verb: *oneidizo* or *dioko*. In Matt 5:11, *dioko* appears to be the product of Matthean redaction, because Matthew adds it already as part of the eighth Beatitude (5:10). In spite of this, the IQP accepts *dioko* as the Q terminology in Q 6:22.[86] But it also generally considered *oneidizo* Q-terminology because it is shared by Matthew and Luke.

Oneidizo is connected to the title "the Son of Man," and may thus reflect the situation of Jesus' first followers, since the title was used by Jesus to refer to himself during his public ministry.[87] However, Q 6:22–23 also reflects the situation of the members of the Q community, likening them to prophets in the Old Testament tradition (compare Q 11:49–50; 13:34–35). Steck asserts that Q 11:49–50 belongs to the "jüdische[s] Traditionsstück."[88] The use of the verb *dioko* is probably connected with this group. It is

82. Schulz, *Q*, 413. Many scholars insist on the milieu of persecution in Q relating to Q 10:3: Manson, *Sayings of Jesus*, 75; Hoffmann, *Studien zur Theologie*, 295; Haenchen, *Weg Jesu*, 224.

83. Kloppenborg, *Formation of Q*, 173.

84. Davies, *Setting of the Sermon*, 382.

85. The Q community probably contained the community rules in Jesus' Inaugural Sermon (Q 6:20–49) as a disciples' community following the teaching of, as well as imitating, their master (Q 6:27a, 28b, 29a, 29b, 30a, 30b, 31, 36, 37a, 42a). The seventh, eighth and ninth exhortations, among others, in the community rules, are accompanied by motive clauses. In some instances, these motive clauses may be altered, but here in the community rules the Q community is encouraged by the motive clauses to treat others as they want people to treat them (Q 6:31), to be merciful like their Father (Q 6:36), and not to be judged or be measured (Q 6:37a, 38b). These three exhortations all are addressed in the second person plural. Those seem to encourage the Q community to establish an ethically strong community as Jesus' community which must be distinguished from other communities at that time.

86. The general editors of the IQP voted *dioko* is in Q 6:22 with a grade of C, as well as *oneidizo*.

87. Robinson, "Son of Man," 318; as James M. Robinson points out, in the oldest layer the designation "the Son of man" is rare (Q 6:22; 9:58), but in the redactional layer it is frequent (Q 7:34; 11:30; 12:8, 10, 40; 17:24, 26, 30). Here our concern is based on the persecution related to the designation "the Son of man."

88. Steck, *Israel*, 223, 226.

used elsewhere, in Q 11:49–50, in a passage commonly thought to be in the redactional layer of Q. Several scholars thus insist that Q 6:23c is part of the second layer as well.[89] According to Kloppenborg, "Verse 23c is a further expansion of vv. 22–23b, introducing the deuteronomistic motif of Israel's persecution of the prophets."[90] In Q 6:23c, according to Steck, the saying of the prophets is connected to the "Vorstellungstradition vom Leiden des Gerechten."[91] Because of the fact that there is no term *dikaios* in Q, I will rather discuss further the persecution of the prophets, following Steck's analysis of the deuteronomistic idea of the persecution of the prophets. Q 6:23c thus reflects the image of the prophets in the deuteronomistic view of history and seems to be directed to the Q community who stood in the succession to the prophets.[92] Like prophets, the Q community was abused and rejected according to the second layer of Q (Q²). Jacobson suggests that it may have been the onset of persecution which led to the redaction of Q. This has provided the deuteronomistic-prophetic stratum that he postulates was a major stage in the compositional history of Q.[93]

The Q community thus suffered persecution. Q revealed a lot of the polemic and hostility directed against the perpetrators of such persecutions. Q's polemic against "this generation" must be understood in this context. Tuckett interprets Q's positive references to Gentiles coupled with a negative attitude toward "this generation"[94] in this way. In Q 11:31–32, for example, the queen of the south and the people of Nineveh are held up as examples of people who responded positively to the wisdom of Solomon and the kerygma of Jonah, in contrast to this generation which failed to repent even though "something greater" was present. This hardly can be contrasted as affirming the Gentile mission. Q 7:1–10 likewise holds the centurion up as an example of one who has shown "faith," and whose faith apparently exceeds anything that Q's Jesus found in Israel. But again, as noted above this story cannot be considered evidence for a Gentile mission. Therefore, though Q's negative assessment of Judaism coupled with its positive assessment of Gentiles is consistent with a Gentile mission, it is not proof that such a mission was undertaken. The date is also consistent with a milieu of persecution. Indeed this second alternative is more likely since, as shown above, Q followed the law and regarded itself as a Jewish community.

It is the Jewishness of Q and avoidance of Gentiles that makes it a good candidate for being the founder of the Matthean community. The Jewish identity of the

---

89. Jacobson, *First Gospel*, 127; Kloppenborg, *Formation of Q*, 173; Schulz, Q, 452–57.

90. Kloppenborg, *Formation of Q*, 173.

91. Steck, *Israel*, 283. For more information on "the suffering of the righteous," see ibid., 254–63.

92. Schulz, Q, 257–60, 456–57, esp. n404; Steck, *Israel*, 259.

93. Jacobson, "Literary Unity of Q," 189.

94. Tuckett, Q, 201–7, 284–96. He argues that Q is almost exclusively concerned with the negative side of the polemic against "this generation." Following the opinions of Coser and Elliott, however, Kloppenborg argues that the conflict with outsiders serves "a positive and constructive purpose" in social terms "as a means to define more clearly group boundaries, to enhance internal cohesion and to reinforce group identity" (Kloppenborg, *Formation of Q*, 167–68).

Q redactor is a factor which helped to enable the Q community develop into the Matthean community. Meier treats the Matthean community as the "second Christian generation"[95] in Antioch. Matthew regards Jesus as the one who gave the Mosaic law a new interpretation, but Matthew expected the church to remain faithful to the law. Moreover, in Matthew Jesus restricts himself to the land and people of Israel during his public ministry (Matt 10:5–6 and 15:24).[96] Jesus himself was sent only to the lost sheep of the house of Israel (Matt 15:24) and his missionary charge to the disciples during the Galilean ministry instructs them not to go to the Gentiles or Samaritans, but only to the lost sheep of the house of Israel. Matthew thus remembers a time when followers of Jesus rejected a Gentile mission and confined themselves to the boundary of Judaism, both geographically and religiously. It is possible that Matthew is recalling the history of his own community and thus, if Q became Matthew, he is acknowledging that Q originally had no Gentile mission.

But if the Q community grew into the Matthean community, then Matthew is also evidence that Q (in the form of the Matthean community) eventually accepted Gentiles (Matt 28:19–20). How did this change come about? Q 14:5 provided the rationale for a Gentile mission.

The Gentiles in the Eschatology of the Sayings Gospel Q

This chapter addresses the fact that Q's positive statements about the Gentiles are to be interpreted from an eschatological perspective, if the Q community did not carry out a Gentile mission due to its Jewishness and conservative attitude toward the law. The question of the Gentiles in the eschatology of Q has received a good deal of attention from Edwards.[97] In order to investigate the place of the Gentiles in the eschatology in Q, this chapter considers the data in Q 10:13–15; 11:31–32; 13:29, 28; 14:21, 23.[98]

> Q 10:13–15
>
> (13) Woe to you, Chorazin! Woe to you, Bethsaïda! For if the mighty works done in you had been done in Tyre and Sidon, they would have repented long ago, [[ ]] in sackcloth and ashes. (14) But it shall be more tolerable in the judgment for Tyre and Sidon than for you. (15) And you, Capharnaum, will you be exalted to heaven? You shall be brought down to Hades.

---

95. Brown and Meier, *Antioch and Rome*, 51, 57.

96. These passages are in different parts of Matthew: Matt 10:5–6 in "MR¹" and Matt 15:24 in "MR²." One thus can infer that Matt 15:24 opens the ministry to non-Jews, showing a chance in Jesus' limited mission. Silberling, "Text and Tradition."

97. Edwards, *Sign of Jonah*, 47. "Q preserves the eschatological teaching more than any other stratum of tradition."

98. The texts discussed are as follows: *Journal of Biblical Literature* 114/3 (1995) on Q 10:13–15; *Journal of Biblical Literature* 111/3 (1992) on Q 11:31–32; *Journal of Biblical Literature* 110/3 (1991) on Q 13:29, 28; *Journal of Biblical Literature* 111/3 (1992) on Q 14:21, 23.

Part 1: Sabbath and the Gentile Mission

The woes pronounced on Galilean cities in Q are linked together with the mission charge (Q 10:1–12) according to the original Lukan order. Matthew places the woes (Matt 11:20–23) after the sayings of John and Jesus in Matt 11:2–19 // Luke 7:18–35. Matthew's wording is in all probability more original than Luke's.[99] However, the woes in Q 10:13–16 originally do not seem to have belonged to the context of the mission charge in Q. In Luke 10:2–15, the formal discrepancy between the threat against Galilean cities and the rest of the discourse shows the secondary character of the connection.[100] Hence it is likely that Q 10:13–15 is an isolated saying which was secondary to the speech. This saying bases its condemnation of the Jewish cities on the predicted repentance of the Gentiles.[101] As with Q 7:1–10 and 11:31–32, in Q 10:13–15 Gentile faith is interpreted as a condemnatory sign for Israel: the probability of the repentance of Tyre and Sidon is contrasted with the refusal of Bethsaida and Chorazin. This idea is somewhat radical, because it is given as an example of how the Gentiles are regarded more positively than the Jews in Q.

Q 10:13–15 is classified as a saying of prophetic judgment[102] upon "this generation" (Israel)[103] and is directed not at the community, but at its opponents, and reflects

---

99. Uro, *Sheep*, 84–86. Examining the originality of the Lukan order for Q 10:13–15, Uro argues that the Matthean text is the composition of the evangelist of Matthew. His evaluation seems to be based on the conclusion by Streeter. For more information, see Streeter, *Four Gospels*, 273–74. "We infer that Luke's order is original." "Matthew also expands the discourse with Q material found elsewhere in Luke." In spite of the originality of Lukan order, Bultmann argues that Matthew's text is closer to Q than Luke's.

100. Bultmann regarded the woes in Luke 10:13–15 as a community formulation, since they look back on Jesus' activity as something already completed and presuppose the failure of Christian preaching in Capernaum. Bultmann, *Die Geschichte*, 117–18. Käsemann agreed with Bultmann on the inauthenticity of Luke 10:13–15 and took the sayings as an indication of a prophetic-enthusiastic movement in early Palestinian Christianity. See Käsemann, *New Testament Questions*, 100. For Käsemann's thesis of the enthusiastic Palestinian Christianity, see 66–80 ("Sentences of Holy Law") and 82–107 ("Beginning of Christian Theology"). Sanders has claimed that Jesus was not a preacher of a national repentance in the style of John the Baptist; consequently, he does not regard Luke 10:13–15 as authentic. For more information, see Sanders, *Jesus and Judaism*, 106–19.

101. This saying resembles many prophetic woes or lamentations over Israel in the OT (Isa 5; Jer 13:23–27; Amos 6:1–7), but has its special character in the contrast between the Israelite towns and the pagan examples.

102. Kloppenborg, *Formation of Q*, 193. Kloppenborg argues that this saying is found in the context of apocalyptic judgment. He seems to agree with Bultmann in classifying Luke 10:13–15 into the group of *Drohworte* under the category of "prophetic and apocalyptic sayings." Bultmann, *Die Geschichte*, 117–18. For related information, see Dibelius, *Formgeschichte des Evangeliums*, 259; Schulz, *Q*, 361–62; Käsemann, *New Testament Questions*, 100. Here, on the one hand, Käsemann mentions some prophetic traits of Luke 10:13–15. Cures and blessings are to be counted among the forms of prophetic proclamation. On the other hand, he argues that the exaltation of Capernaum to heaven and its casting down to the Hades are genuinely apocalyptic; Jacobson, *First Gospel*, 64 and n13. Jacobson argues that in Q most of the sayings announce judgment in view of impenitence or failure to respond to a divine appeal: Q 3:7–9; 6:46; 10:13–15; 11:31–32, (39), 42–44, 46–47, 52, 49–51; 12:8–9, 54–56; 13:26–27, 28–29, 34–35; 17:26–27, 34–35. In addition, he infers that Q 11:47–51 takes the form of a prophecy of disaster; Steck, *Israel*, 51–53.

103. Lührmann, *Die Redaktion*, 24–48, 63. As Lührmann has shown, a polemic tone is present in

Q's experience of rejection. Here the Q redactor makes an unfavorable comparison of Israel's fate with that of the Gentiles.[104] This saying concludes for the mission charge with an antithetic saying concerning acceptance and rejection of the people. The threat of rejection for those who reject the call to return is attested in Q 10:13–15 (compare Q 12:10) and is also considered an element in pre-Christian deuteronomistic preaching.[105] Uro argues that the fate of the historical Jesus was interpreted in the light of the deuteronomistic pattern, and that the earthly Jesus was seen as a preacher of repentance in the style of the deuteronomistic tradition. We can understand, thus, that in place of promises to Israel, Q offers a redefinition of Israel (Q 3:7–9; 7:35; 10:13–15; 11:19, 31–32; 13:29, 28; 14:16–21, 23; 16:16; 22:28, 30). In Q 10:13–15, we can see the combination of arrogance and refusal to repent. Steck argues that the motif of the eschatological separation of the righteous from the sinners is often found in Q: Q 3:17; 10:13–15; 13:24, 27, 29, 28; 17:34–35.[106] *En te krisei* in Q 10:14 are characteristic of the eschatological view. Here the saying not only implies that any reward to be accorded to the Gentiles is reserved for the judgment, but recalls the restriction of Jesus' mission by stating that no miracles were performed in at least these two Gentile cities.

Q 11:31–32

(31) The queen of the south will be raised at the judgment with this generation and will condemn it; for she came from the ends of the earth to listen to the wisdom of Solomon, and behold, something greater than Solomon is here. (32) The men of Nineveh will arise at the judgment with this generation and condemn it; for they repented at the preaching of Jonah, and behold something greater than Jonah is here.

We can find here a strong polemic. Agreeing with A. Fredrichsen, Bultmann shows that the structure is the same in Matt 12:41: *kai idou pleion . . . hode* and Matt 11:22, 24: *plen lego humin . . . anektoteron estai*. For him, this is a strongly polemic accent.[107] The double saying in Q 11:31–32 is connected to the saying of asking for

---

this saying. He sees in the attachment of Luke 10:12, 13–15 an activity of the Q redactor, paralleling the additions of Luke 7:31–35 (the children in the market place), 11:30, 31–32 (the sign of Jonah), and 11:49–51 (the wisdom sayings). In his analysis, all these passages reflect a sharp contrast between "this generation" (Israel) and the Q community.

104. Actually, in the OT, Tyre and Sidon were represented as enemies of Israel (Ps 83:8; Isa 23; Jer 47; Ezek 26–28:11–12, 22–23; Joel 4:4–8; Amos 1:9–10; 3:11 LXX; Zech 9:2–4; 1 Macc 5:15). To the Jews, Tyre and Sidon represented especially sinful places and were often subject to divine judgment.

105. Steck, *Israel*, 217–18; Tödt, *Son of Man*, 114–25, 217.

106. Uro, *Sheep*, 184, 187, 286n5.

107. Bultmann, *Die Geschichte*, 118. Bultmann quotes an accent for a "scheme of early Christian polemic" from Fredrichsen, *Problem of Miracle*, 49. See Bultmann 118n1. This is also stressed by Edwards, *Sign of Jonah*, 83. He argues that this was on the basis of Q's anti-Jewish polemic with a "strong emphasis on judgment." See also Lührmann, *Die Redaktion*, 42.

Jonah's sign in Q 11:29–30[108] because both consist of judgment on this generation.[109] In both references the Gentiles are contrasted with unbelieving Israel, which has refused to have faith in the *kerygma* (Q 11:32). "This generation" in Q 11:31–32, in contrast to the queen of the south and the people of Nineveh, will witness "something greater than" Solomon and Jonah. This means that the teaching of Jesus is the "something greater than" the Wisdom of Solomon and Jonah's preaching that is rejected by Israel. In Q 11:31 the queen of the south is the queen of Sheba, a Gentile (compare 1 Kgs 10:1–13). In Q 11:32 the people of Nineveh are convinced by the preaching of Jonah (compare Jonah 3–4). This is a *tertium comparationis* between Jesus and Jonah, which can be understood as the preaching of repentance before the judgment.[110] "Such a failure to grasp the presence of the *pleion iona*[] can only be interpreted as abject moral blindness, worthy of judgment and condemnation."[111] Whereas the people of Nineveh responded positively to Jonah's preaching, this generation fails to repent, though something greater than Jonah is here now.[112] The Gentiles are thus portrayed in a positive light in Q. Nevertheless, regardless of the implications of the verb tenses in Q 11:31–32, the phrases *en te krisei meta tes geneas tautes* seems to indicate that the Gentiles will only be accepted by God in the future.

Here it must be added that in Q 11:31–32 wisdom and kerygma are not only juxtaposed but functionally identified. The Wisdom of Solomon in Q 11:31 and the preaching of Jonah in Q 11:32 are a kind of juxtaposition and imply a "*communicatio idiomatum*" between wisdom and kerygma. Agreeing with Lührmann, Jacobson argues that wisdom takes the place of God as the sender of prophets (Q 11:49–51; cf. Prob 1–9; Sir 51:13–30).[113] Wisdom as well as the kerygma are regarded as calls to repentance, because the response of the queen of the south to the wisdom and the repentance of the people of Nineveh after the kerygma were introduced as factors in condemning this generation in the eschatological view. The later sequence of Q is ordered to make this eschatological point. Q 11:34–36 "concerns the eschatological

---

108. The saying in Luke 11:29 comes from Q and Mark, but it is impossible to decide whether the form of Q or that of Mark is original. In Mark, the saying is in the apophthegm (Mark 8:11–12); it has no reference to Jonah's sign but a denial of any sign which can be understood in the pre-Markan tradition. In Q the saying of 11:30 functions as a link between the asking for the sign and 11:31–32. The saying in Q 11:31–32 may have been attached to 11:29 by the catchword, "Jonah." Q 11:30 may have been the last saying added. Many scholars have adopted the view that the preaching of judgment is meant in 11:30. See Harnack, *Mission and Expansion*, 23; Edwards, *Sign of Jonah*, 80–89; Schulz, *Q*, 255–56 and n545; Lührmann, *Die Redaktion*, 41; Uro, *Sheep*, 171. "The sign of Jonah was already interpreted in a polemic way described above before the attachment to Luke 11:14–23 (24–26) . . . the double saying was already linked to Luke 11:29 (30) before the formation of the whole section."

109. Uro, *Sheep*, 169 and n34. Uro points out that "this generation" was a stereotype expression used in the polemical context.

110. Edwards, *Sign of Jonah*, 86.

111. Kloppenborg, *Formation of Q*, 138.

112. Here Edwards argues that "the eschatological correlative" correlates Jonah and Jesus (Edwards, *Sign of Jonah*, 47–58, 85–87).

113. Jacobson, *First Gospel*, 168; Lührmann, *Die Redaktion*, 39.

'either-or' of radical obedience with respect to Jesus' intensified Mosaic Torah and uncompromising discipleship,"[114] even though nothing indicates that a radical Torah is an issue here. The immediate Q context, moreover, suggests the same interpretation. The double saying in Q 11:31–32 announces judgment upon the people who refuse to respond to the present reality of something greater than Jonah or Solomon. This saying was understood by the Q community as an eschatological sign. In the evangelistic activity of the Q community, God's plan at the judgment was being realized and the eschatological events were rolling toward the final consummation. In Q 10:2, the mission is also to be carried out through men, not by angels, but it is still in God's plan: workers must be prayed for from God who sends them into the field.[115] Jesus calls his disciples to pray for more workers for the eschatological reaping going on in his ministry.

Q 13:29, 28

(29) [[Many]] shall come from the east and the west and recline (28) with Abraham and Isaac and Jacob in the kingdom of God, but [[you]] «will be» thrown out; there people will weep and gnash their teeth.

The saying of Q 13:29, 28 in the Matthean order and wording (8:11–12) are taken to be original.[116] This saying can be called a prophetic "announcement," which is amply attested in Q (cf. Q 3:16; 10:9b, 15; 11:20; 12:10; 17:34–35; 7:22).[117] The saying in Q appears to speak apparently about the coming of the Gentiles into the kingdom of God. The kingdom of God here is easily interpreted as the heavenly banquet where the Gentiles can share the meal. The reference to the people who come "from the east and the west" is certainly to the Gentiles. Thus some scholars believe that this saying can be taken as evidence of the Gentile mission.[118] However, this saying also can be

---

114. Schulz, Q, 470.

115. Loader, *Jesus' Attitude*, 410–11. "Nothing indicates a mission to the Gentiles is in view, although Q may well have envisaged the harvest as also including Gentiles. The assumption in 10:2 is that Jesus addresses disciples, but in doing so asks them to pray that God will send harvesters into the harvest. Q apparently envisages that Jesus is addressing a group out of which, from among whom, God will send the harvesters, rather than addressing one group about people outside of it."

116. Kloppenborg, *Formation of Q*, 227; Jeremias, *Jesus' Promises*, 55–56; Hahn, *Das Verständnis der Mission*, 34n1. "Matthew's word order may well be the earlier." Matthew gives the saying in connection with the story of the centurion's servant (8:5–13). This location is widely regarded as being due to Matthean redaction. See Lührmann, *Die Redaktion*, 57; Walter Grundmann, *Das Evangelium nach Matthäus*, 250; Wegner, *Der Hauptmann*, 3–5. In Luke, the saying is part of the section in 13:22–30. The Lukan saying is more redactional than the Matthean since Luke has the phrase "from the north and south" in addition to the phrase "from the east and the west." Robinson, "Sequence of Q," 228. "Q 13:28–29 does not belong in this Lukan sequence, but rather uses the sequence Q 13:29, 28bca, that is to say, follows the Matthean sequence: Mt 8,11–12."

117. Sato, Q, 116–46. It is to Sato's credit that he also investigates the subsequent history of these genres in intertestamental literature; in this case, he shows that the "announcement" is very rare in apocalyptic literature.

118. Hahn, *Das Verständnis der Mission*, 35, 57; Meyer, "Gentile Mission," 405; Zeller, "Logion Mt

used as evidence for the argument that the Q community rejected the Gentile mission, and that they also accepted this saying in view of eschatology[119] in order to condemn and warn the Jewish people. In this saying there is no phrase "this generation," but we may regard the people who were thrown ([[you]] in v. 28) as "this generation." The saying of Q 13:29, 28 here predict the culpability of this generation by speaking of the inclusion of the Gentiles. Hence, Q 13:29, 28 is usually read as referring to future judgment and the entry of the Gentiles into the kingdom of God. The Q community here presupposes that Jewish people have lost their privilege for the heavenly banquet, and they will be thrown out and will weep and gnash their teeth.[120] It is more likely that Q 13:29, 28 implies Gentile participation in the kingdom as a result of Israel's refusal. However, this interpretation cannot be used as evidence for the assumption that "both Paul and Q agree that Israel has lost its prerogative in the salvation history." This interpretation by Uro seems much too close to Pauline theology (Rom 1:16; 2:9-10). Uro argues that this interpretation fits well "in terms of [] salvation history: the last (that is, the Gentiles) will be first and the first (Israel) will be last."[121] I would rather conclude that this is typical salvation history for Paul, not for Q. The Q community may have known the salvation history of Paul, but they give little evidence of accepting it within their community. The initial problem is whether Q was mainly interested in the Gentile mission in the structure of Pauline theology. However, the saying in Q 13:29, 28 was addressed more widely to Jewish people in order to warn them. The saying focuses on the eschatological view of the entry of the Gentiles to the banquet which is seen as applying to the failure of Israel to respond to Jesus in Q.[122] This interpretation is also based on deuteronomistic theology: if Israel does not listen, God will destroy them. The fact that Israel will be excluded from the banquet in the kingdom of God may warn Israel to obey God.

Q 13:29, 28 are paralleled with 5 Ezra [2 Esdras] 1:30b, 38-40 in the same eschatological sense.[123] Hence, scholars question the relationship between Q and 5 Ezra. Jacobson argues that because 5 Ezra 1:38-40 is independent of Q, both 5 Ezra and Q stand in a common tradition. The independence of 5 Ezra from Q however cannot be addressed conclusively. John Dominic Crossan argues that Q and 5 Ezra depend upon

---

8,11-12/Lk 13, 28-29," 222-37; Uro, 211.

119. Schulz, Q, 326; Zeller, 16 (1972), 92-93; Kloppenborg, *Formation of Q*, 236. "Q 13:29 implies only an eschatological pilgrimage of Gentiles, not an active Gentile mission."

120. Kloppenborg, *Formation of Q*, 237. "Israel's lack of faith will indeed provoke a drastic eschatological reversal: the formerly privileged will lose their special status to newcomers."

121. Uro, *Sheep*, 217; Grundmann, *Das Evangelium nach Matthäus*, 286-87; Marshall, *Gospel of Luke*, 568.

122. Wegner, *Der Hauptmann*, 265-67. "Uns scheint daher die Intention, die Mt mit dem Einschub dieser Vv verfolgt, darin zu liegen, Glaube und Unglaube gegenüber Jesus—in ihrer eschatologischen Relevanz für Heiden und Juden zugleich—der Gemeinde seiner Zeit transparent zu machen (ibid., 267)."

123. Crossan, *In Fragments*, 137-45.

"Christianized Deuteronomic traditions."[124] Graham N. Stanton believes that 5 Ezra has a "continuation into the second century of Matthean Christianity."[125] K. Berger and C. Colpe, however, regard 5 Ezra as Jewish, not Christian.[126] I prefer to conclude that 5 Ezra may know the Jesus tradition including Q sayings, and also the deuteronomistic traditions on which Q also stands. Thus, we can conclude that 5 Ezra was heir to both traditions, Jewish and Christian.[127] The motifs assembled in one manner by 5 Ezra into 1:30b, 38–40 are also assembled by Q into 13:29, 28. Both passages address the same motif (the Gentiles welcomed and the Jews excluded) in an eschatological sense.

[[Q 14:21, 23]]

(21) And [[upon returning]] the servant announced these things to his master. Then the householder [[,]] enraged [[,]] said to his servant, Go out [[quickly]] into the [[streets]] and [[whomever you may find]], invite «to the occasion.» (23) And after going out into the streets the servant <> [[gathered all whom he found]] [[ ]]; [[and]] the house was filled. <..>

This pericope focuses on the invitation of the sinners and religious outsiders to the kingdom of God. The parable in Q 14:16–23 may originally have contrasted the sinners and the pious,[128] but in the light of passages such as Q 10:13–15; 11:31–32; 13:29, 28 the contrast between the Jews and the Gentiles[129] is also intended (Q 14:21, 23). After the failure of Israel to come to a great banquet, the people on the streets are invited. One can interpret this event as having the same characteristic as that of Q 13:29, 28. After Israel failed to come, the Gentiles are filed into the kingdom of God. Thus this parable can also be understood in the light of eschatology.

The eschatological characteristics of the parable in Q may be compared with the *Gospel of Thomas* 64. Even though the parable in the *Gospel of Thomas* is a tradition independent of Q, many scholars have examined it in comparison with intracanonical traditions, especially for Q.[130] The anger of the householder is not addressed in *Thomas*, but in Q 14:21 it is. In addition, in Q the exclusion of the original guests is emphasized at the end. This also justifies the anger of the householder in having to

---

124. Ibid., 141, 143.

125. Stanton, "5 Ezra and Matthean Christianity," 80. Jean Daniélou sees themes in 5 Ezra well situated in an apocalyptic Christianity of the second century. See his "Le Ve Esdras," 162–71.

126. Berger and Colpe, *Religionsgeschichtliches Textbuch*, 111.

127. Kraft, "Ezra's Materialsm," 119–36.

128. Jeremias, *Parable of Jesus*, 176–80; Steck, *Israel*, 187.

129. Wegner, *Der Hauptmann*, 370; Vögtle, "Einladung zum grossen Gastmahl," 171–218. See also Ernst, *Das Evangelium*, 238. "Das Droh-und Verheißungswort, das Mt an den Schluß der Perikope gestellt hat (8, 11–12), mußte Lk fallenlassen (er bringt es statt dessen in dem eschatologischen Zusammenhang 13, 28–30), weil er ja gerade an der Überwindung des Gegensatzes zwischen Juden und Heiden interessert ist."

130. Layton, *Gnostic Scriptures*; Crossan, *Four Other Gospels*; Jacobson, *First Gospel*, 218; Patterson, *Gospel of Thomas*, 77–78.

invite substitute guests. When the original guests fail to come to the great banquet, the householder quickly arranges for substitute guests. This would explain why this story should be interpreted in the light of eschatology, not in the light of allegory. The primary focus of this parable is placed upon the exclusion of the original guests. The focus fits very well into the deuteronomistic view.[131] The fact that the original guests failed to come and the substitute guests were invited to the banquet functions in Q as a warning for the Jews: If Israel rejects the invitation to the banquet; they may be excluded from the kingdom of God at the end. This parable is interpreted in light of the eschatological banquet as a message of shame and warning to Israel.[132]

Jewish attitudes toward the Gentiles in relation to Sabbath practice began to be known as an eschatological expectation, starting in the post-exile period.[133] Jews expected Gentiles to keep the Sabbath at the eschaton. Hence, the Gentiles were included in Jewish expectations of future salvation. The eschatological expectation for Q anticipated the Gentiles' share in salvation based on their response to God's saving vindication of Israel in the eschatological future, not on any activity in the present.

Through the whole examination of such passages as Q 10:13–15; 11:31–32; 13:29, 28; and 14:21, 23, it seems unlikely that the Q community was actively engaged in any mission to the Gentiles. Instead, they devoted themselves to calling Israel to repent.[134]

---

131. Jacobson, *First Gospel*, 255–56. "At the compositional level of Q the deuteronomistic tradition was used to interpret the meaning for Israel of John, Jesus, and the Q community itself. John and Jesus are placed in the context of a series of prophets whom God sent to call Israel to repentance and renewal but whom Israel rejected. The persecution suffered by the Q community was interpreted as the continued resistance of Israel, now directed against the 'prophet' of the Q group."

132. Jacobson sees that the rejection of Jesus (and of John) brings with it an eschatological condemnation (ibid., 258).

133. The passages in Isa 56:2, 4, 6; 66:23; and 58:13–14 introduce a situation originated in Jerusalem after the exile. Fohrer, *Introduction to the Old Testament*, 388. Here the blessings for keeping the Sabbath holy are made to the Israelites. Isa 56:2, 4, 6 mentions all members of the community have to keep from profaning the Sabbath in description of the status of foreigners and eunuchs in community (1–7). Here scholars assume that the Sabbath may become a unique institution after the exile; Muilenburg, "Introduction and Exegesis," 653–54. There is a reference to new moon and the Sabbath in Isa 66:23, where the holy days are part of the delights of the future (compare Ezek 46:3) as part of the vision of the New Jerusalem given there. Smart sees Isa 66:23 as describing a glorification of worship at the temple, with the climax of the new creation represented by renewed Sabbath worship. Smart, *History and Theology*, 291–92. This reference seems to state that there should be worship on the Sabbath after the exile, referring to a future glorious age. After the exile, keeping the Sabbath holy seems to be recognized by the Israelites as the most conspicuous sign of their true covenant relationship with God. An unexpected promise given to the Israelites who keep the Sabbath holy: They will dwell in God's house and be given an everlasting name (Isa 56:5). In Isa 58:14 a stronger promise is also made, in comparison with the conditional clause in Isa 58:13. In Isaiah 58 the reference to the Sabbath in v. 14 climaxes in the situation after the exile. Here the unexpected promise is made: They will delight in the Lord. A kind of reward to the Israelites is accompanied by keeping the Sabbath and joyfully honoring the holy day of the Lord (13). In relation to the heritage of Jacob, a promise as a reward for keeping the Sabbath holy is also seen in v. 14.

134. Jacobson, *First Gospel*, 256. He argues that the call to Israel was not a call to believe in Jesus, but a call to holiness, to the piety described in Jesus' teaching: "The response of the Q group to this seems to have been an intensification of their call to Israel. For an understanding of this development,

Moreover, they looked for the turning of the Gentiles toward the God of Israel in good time, but they did not work toward this. In Q, the community located in Galilee did not practice the Gentile mission like Matt 28:19-20, but they focused on putting Israel to shame and warning it that the Gentiles cities in Tyre and Sidon would have repented long ago (Q 10:13); that the queen of the south and the people of Nineveh will be raised at the judgment with this generation (Q 11:31-32); that many people shall come from the east and the west (Q 11:29); and that the substitute guests would fill the kingdom of God (Q 14:23) in the eschatological perspective. In all these sayings, Jesus discussed only the eschatological fate of the Gentiles, while he was warning the Jews. What would happen to the Jews and the Gentiles at the end? "Mercy will be extended to the Gentiles, and Israel will be excluded."[135] Thus one can conclude that Q assured the Gentiles of acceptance and warned the Jews about exclusion at the end. This picture is part of the eschatological future, not a feature of present reality. Thus the Q community probably gave a warning to Israel with accompanying threats that the Gentiles would replace the Jews in the kingdom of God in the eschatological sense.

EPILOGUE

The purpose of this chapter was to investigate the question of whether Q undertook a Gentile mission. Specifically, this chapter has discussed (1) the two viewpoints about Q's mission, and (2) the milieu of persecution that clarifies Q's attitude toward Jews and Gentiles, and (3) the evidence from Matthew that Q did not originally accept Gentiles, and (4) the eschatological perspective of Q with respect to the Gentiles. This chapter, as a result of the examination, concludes as follows:

The Gentile mission could not be integral to Q because of Q's close relation to a Jewish religious movement, even if the Gentile mission could be regarded as an external context for the Q community. This is proven in Q 11:42 and 16:17, where the Q community is shown to be in full observance of the law. Because the Q community was conservative in observing the law, one would assume that the Q community naturally grew into becoming the Matthean community on the basis of the Jewishness of both communities.

The Q community's closeness to Judaism resulted in persecution by the Jews because the Jews wanted to separate them from the Jewish social and religious life. Even though the Q community had a conservative attitude toward Jewish law, they followed the teaching of Jesus, whom the Jews rejected. Thus the Q community was persecuted by the Jews. The sayings in Q 6:22-23; 11:49-50; 13:34-35 were oriented toward the specific milieu of persecution in the Q community. In this milieu of persecution, the Q community wanted to preserve the community rules as exhortations in imperative forms to build the inner solidarity of their community. They developed the polemic

---

too, the deuteronomistic perspective proved useful."

135. Jeremias, *Jesus' Promises*, 51.

directed against their persecutors by referring to the Gentiles in a very positive way, not by referring to the Jews in a negative way.

It is most convincing that support for the Gentile mission was not a concern of the Q community because Q first preached to the Jews exclusively. The Q community was certainly a Jewish Christian group; however, Q knew well the practice of the Gentile mission that was already progressing successfully before 50 CE. In Q there is no evidence that Jesus actually preached to the Gentiles. The purpose of such references to the Gentiles in Q was to put Israel to shame. The Q community devoted itself to Israel's repentance from her stubbornness. There are no direct references to the Gentile mission in Q. The Gentile mission was not seen as Jesus' concern, because Jesus' sayings were directed to the Jewish people and the gospel was first preached to them exclusively. The composition of Q was originated by Jewish Christians between 50 CE and 70 CE. This means that Q must have known well the circumstances of the Gentile mission. Nevertheless, the Q community, as Jewish Christians, did not carry out a mission to the Gentiles because the sayings of Jesus indicated that the gospel should be taken only to Israel. Q nevertheless contains many references to the Gentiles and a positive attitude toward the Gentiles in the eschatological perspective.

The woes against the Galilean cities in Q 10:13–15 are given together with the mission charge in Q 10. It is likely that the woe sayings in Q 10:13–15 are secondary to the mission charge. One can see here the refusal to repent. The probability of repentance by Tyre and Sidon is contrasted with the arrogance of Bethsaida and Chorazin. This statement implies that any reward accorded to the Gentiles is reserved for the judgment. Here one finds a motif of the eschatological separation of the righteous from the sinners. At this point, the saying about the queen of the south and the people of Nineveh in Q 11:31–32 can also be interpreted as an eschatological saying. One can find that Q refers to the Gentiles in a positive way, in contrast with the negative attitude to "this generation." This is an eschatological view, not a view of the Gentile mission. The Gentiles will be raised to condemn this generation at the judgment, in other words, because the Gentiles believed God's messengers and repented as they responded to the preaching of Jonah. Thus in the saying the sign can be understood as an eschatological warning to this generation. The saying about the people from the east and the west in Q 13:29, 28 speak of the coming of the Gentiles into the kingdom of God. The kingdom of God is interpreted here as the heavenly banquet where the Gentiles can share the meal. The reference to the people, who came from the east and the west, certainly means the Gentiles here. We see this saying as speaking about the future judgment and entry of the Gentiles into the kingdom of God. This saying should not be taken as evidence of the Gentile mission in Q. It is addressed more widely to Jewish people in order to warn them. This saying focuses then on the eschatological view of the entry of the Gentiles to the banquet. This is seen as applying to the failure of Israel to respond to Jesus in Q. The saying about the invitation of the people on the streets in Q 14:21, 23 focus on the invitation of sinners and religious outsiders to the kingdom of God. The people on the streets are invited immediately after the failure of Israel to come to a great banquet. This saying can also be understood in the light of eschatological view, that the original guests failed to come and the substitute guests were invited to the banquet. This was a warning for the Jews.

It seems unlikely that the Q community was engaged in the Gentile mission, in light of the examination of those sayings in Q 10:13–15; 11:31–32; 13:29, 28; and 14:21, 23. The Q community devoted itself to calling on Israel to repent. The Q text in all those sayings discusses only the eschatological fate of the Gentiles, and words of warning to the Jews. Jesus in Q assures the acceptance of the Gentiles, and warns the exclusion of the Jews. This presentation is part of the eschatological future, not a feature of present reality. The Q text thus gives a warning to Israel with accompanying threats that the Gentiles will replace the Jews in the kingdom of God in the eschatological sense.

We know that the Jewish mission was given by the historical Jesus during his public ministry, and also that the Gentile mission was spoken by the risen Lord as in Matt 28:19–20. The references to the Gentiles in Q are certainly a part of the element in preaching which uses a Christian deuteronomistic perspective focusing on the preaching of repentance before the judgment. In spite of a history of Israel's persistent rejection of God's preachers, at the judgment the Gentiles will be raised to lead this generation (Israel) to repent. Q asserts, in comparison with the deuteronomistic view, that the Gentiles will replace Israel in the kingdom of God in the eschatological perspective.

VIII

Euanggelion and the Gentile Mission

PROLOGUE

How did the gospel, i.e., *euanggelion*, appear to the Gentiles in discussing the tension between the Jewish mission and the Gentile mission? The Synoptics do not easily let Jesus make open predictions of the Gentile mission before his death and resurrection. Jesus, during his public ministry in Matthew, on the one hand, sends his disciples to the lost sheep among Israel (15:24) and prohibits the disciples from a Gentile mission (10:5–6).[1] After the death and resurrection of Jesus,[2] however, the risen Lord[3] commands the disciples to go all over the world (28:18–20).[4] It is likely here that there was a "two-fold representation"[5] of the mission in Matthew. Scholars have questioned the tension between the Jewish mission (Matt 10:5–6, 23) and the Gentile mission (Matt 28:19–20).[6] The tension between Matt 10:5–6, 23 and Matt 28:19–20 may be caused by a difference between the viewpoint of the evangelist in Matthew's Gospel and the situation of his community. This does not mean that Matthew was the only evangelist to include

---

1. Matt 10:5–6 designates the command to restrict the missionary scope to the mission to the Jews.

2. The death and resurrection are recognized as a single one event, an eschatological turning point for the Gentile mission in the case of Matthew.

3. Barth, "Exegetical Study in Matthew 28:16–20," 63. "This [Matt 28:19–20a] is the crucial affirmation of the whole text [Matt 28:16–20]. It is the charge and commission of the risen Jesus, the authority for which was asserted in verse 18." This suggestion is based on the "identity of the risen Lord with the crucified (Matt 18:1–6 and 9)" (ibid., 57).

4. The sayings of the risen Lord in Matt 28:18–20 consist of three parts: the declaration of authority (18b), the Gentile mission (19–20a), and the promise of the abiding presence of the Lord (20b). Barth, "Matthew's Understanding of the Law," 133–35; Matthey, "Great Commission," 160–61, 166–70.

5. Brown, "Two-Fold Representation," 21–32.

6. Feuillet, "Origines et la signification," 182–98; Beare, "Mission of the Disciples," 1–13; Meier, "Salvation-History," 203–15; LaVerdiere and Thompson, "New Testament Communities," 567–97; Brown, "Mission to Israel," 73–90; Brown, "Matthean Community," 193–221; Bosch, *Transforming Mission*, 59–60, 82.

the Gentiles in his community. Matthew mentions two contradictory missions toward both the Jews, and later, the Gentiles, which might be advocated within the community of Matthew.[7] Those missions toward the Jews and the Gentiles in Matthew seem to be correlated with each other between the evangelist and the situation of his community, because the mission to "the lost sheep of the house of Israel" (10:5–6) would extend to all the Gentiles (28:19–20) after the death and resurrection of Jesus in the Matthean church's missionary effort.[8]

Although the Gospel of Matthew was written at the end of first century CE, the Matthean community would find the foundation of the Gentile mission from the situation after the resurrection of Jesus. Thus continuity with the past is assured, since the same disciples are now sent to baptize all Gentiles and to teach everything that Jesus has taught them. As a result, the disciples preach the gospel to the Gentiles and welcome them into their community after the death and resurrection.[9]

In the Matthean redactional concern for the Sabbath law, Jesus did not abrogate it; rather, he is seen as a new or authoritative interpreter of it.[10] Matthew is invoking the authority of the risen Lord, whom first Christian disciples recognized as judge and ruler. Jesus goes beyond a surface level to the intention of the will of God in expressing the Sabbath law. Jesus was challenging them to practice acts of love for human benefit as a primary concern of the Sabbath, not to conflict with the Sabbath law.

Luke-Acts

The "paradigm shift"[11] of the mission from the Jews to the Gentiles[12] has been seen more clearly in Luke's writings, because the Jewish mission is not an issue by the time of the author of Luke-Acts.[13] The milieu of Luke is similar to in several aspects that of

---

7. Käsemann, "Anfänge christlicher Theologie," 167. Käsemann argues how Matthew may have reconciled the two contradictory viewpoints and states that "Das bedeutet, daß eine verschiedene Eschatologie die beiden ins Auge gefaßten Gruppen der ältesten Christenheit voneinander trennt."

8. Meier, "Salvation-History," 207. He argues that the death and resurrection of Jesus was "*die Wende der Zeit*," which is grounded in Matthew's own depiction.

9. However, Schniewind argues that there was a Gentile mission before the death and resurrection in Matthew. In Matthew, for example, he sees a reference to the theme of salvation from the Jews to the Gentiles. Hence, he argues that the theme is found elsewhere in Matthew (3:9; 8:11–12; 21:43; 22:1–4; 23:38–39). See Schniewind, *Evangelium nach Mattäus*, 127–28. However, the Gentile mission does not seem to be self-evident before the death and resurrection of Jesus in Matthew. Moreover, even in Matt 10:23 there is nothing in the command to flee from "one town" to "the next" which would suggest that the disciples are to go to a Gentile city.

10. Snodgrass, "Matthew and the Law," 118–27.

11. Küng and Tracy, *Paradigm Change*, 3–33, 212–19, 439–52. Küng submits that the entire history of Christianity can be subdivided into six major paradigms: primitive Christianity; the patristic period; the Middle Ages; the Reformation; the Enlightenment; and the ecumenical era.

12. Bosch, *Die Heidenmission*, 91–96, esp. 94–95. "The Gentile mission only became possible after the Jews had rejected the gospel" (95).

13. Gagnon, "Luke's Motives," 131.

Matthew. As in the case of Matthew, Luke addresses the mission in Judea and Galilee during the public ministry of Jesus. After narrating the ascension of the risen Lord (Luke 24:50–51), Luke states that the disciples returned to Jerusalem. It is likely that the actual carrying out of the missionary command had to wait until Pentecost (cf. Luke 24:49). Hence, the Gentile mission would be the task of the church,[14] not of the historical Jesus.[15] In Luke 24:47 the risen Lord has encouraged his disciples to preach the gospel to "all nations." This saying presupposes that after the resurrection the disciples have been called to carry the gospel to the Gentile world through an encounter with the risen Lord.[16] It is likely that Luke has already regarded Jesus' mission as universal in intent, but was yet incomplete in execution before Pentecost. In Luke the Gentile mission is mentioned only once in 24:46–47, in comparison with Matt 28:19–20 on the basis of the sayings of the risen Lord.[17] Luke expects the era of the church to be a distinct phase of redemptive history not beginning until Pentecost. Luke's concerns with the predominantly Gentile churches in Acts can be seen from his presentation[18] of Christianity's movement from its Judean or Galilean cradle into the Gentile world through the work of the Spirit. In Luke, the Spirit is promised at the time of the commissioning (Luke 24:49). He is received at Pentecost (Acts 2:1–4). In Matthew the risen Lord reassures the disciples that He will remain always with them, but the Spirit is mentioned in the baptismal formula (Matt 28:19–20). We can infer from this that the Spirit has bridged the saying of the risen Lord to the mission of the church in order to preach the gospel to the Gentiles.

In Acts the progress of the Gentile mission is indicated by the scattering of Hellenistic Jewish Christians[19] from Jerusalem after persecution (8:1; 11:19–20), and

14. Bultmann, *History of the Synoptic Tradition*, 289. He argues that the motif of a missionary charge of the risen Lord (Matt 28:16–20; Luke 24:44–49; Acts 1:4–8) is a "quite late achievement of Hellenistic Christianity (if not also in part of Hellenistic Jewish-Christianity)." I agree with Bultmann that the Gentile mission is hardly *ipsissima verba Jesu*. However, I disagree with his opinion that the universal missionary command is based on a late achievement of Hellenistic Christianity, since the Apostolic Council in Acts 15 and Gal 2 has approved the Gentile mission that Hellenistic Jewish Christians might bring; Kümmel, *Introduction to the New Testament*, 180.

15. Hahn, *Mission in the New Testament*, 129; Wilson, *Gentiles*, 52–53.

16. Hubbard, *Matthean Redaction*, 124, 126–27. Turning to the reference on Paul (Gal 1:16), he argues that Paul began to preach the gospel to the Gentiles.

17. Hubbard, *Matthean Redaction*, 102–22. He argues the thesis of a common tradition which lies behind Matt 28:16–20 in comparison with the sayings in Mark 16:14–18; Luke 24:36–49; John 20:19–23.

18. Luke's separation of the destruction of Jerusalem and the dispersal of the Jews (Luke 21:5–24) from his account of the end of the world (Luke 17:22–37; 21:25–28) presupposes that a number of years have passed since the Jewish war and that this event is no longer viewed apocalyptically (Luke 17:20–21). In Acts 1:8 Luke designates the nature of his enterprise. Hence, in 9:31 a universal church has a somewhat broader extension when Luke refers to the church in Judea, Galilee, and Samaria.

19. The term "Hellenists" is introduced in contrast to the corresponding term "Hebrews" (Acts 6:1) and is clearly a linguistic designation. S. Brown argues that the term "Hellenists" seems to have meant both the "Greek-speaking Jews, whether Christians (Acts 6:1) or not (9:29)," and the "Gentiles (11:20), who were obviously Greek-speaking." For more information, see Brown, "Matthean Community," 74–79.

their gradual expulsion from the synagogues of the Diaspora. Peter was credited with a primordial role in opening the gospel to the Gentiles by Acts 10:1—11:18;[20] 15:7, but he was not the apostle for the Gentile mission. Rather, Paul was regarded as the apostle for the Gentile mission in Acts 9:15; 15:3, 12; 22:21. This chapter will turn to the Lukan understanding of Paul the Apostle for the Gentile mission in Acts because one of the most important themes in Acts is that of the Gentile mission.[21]

In Acts 13:46–48 Luke states that Paul and Barnabas "turn to the Gentiles" in Asia Minor because the Jews have rejected the gospel (cf. Acts 3:26; 8:25). In v. 47, Luke quotes Isa 49:6 to verify that the Gentile mission was advocated by Old Testament prophesy.[22] This evidence for the Gentile mission here replaces the fact that the motivation for it was the rejection of the gospel by the Jews.[23] Jervell argues, however, that Paul and Barnabas turn to the Gentiles as a result of their acceptance of the gospel, not of the Jews' rejection,[24] even though the plain meaning of Acts 13:46–48 is the exact opposite of this explanation. The citation from Amos 9:11–12 in Acts 15:16–17 also gives Luke's understanding of the Gentile mission and Paul's relation to the Jews and the Gentiles. E. Haenchen regards this as a reference to the resurrection, the event which causes the Gentiles to seek the Lord.[25] Most scholars regard this as a reference to the reconstitution or salvation of Israel which would precede the influx of the Gentiles.[26] From this view, Luke understands that the quotation from Amos advocates the inclusion of the Gentiles into the salvation history of God. In Acts 28:26–28, according to Luke, Paul turning to the Gentiles in Rome is the result of the Jews' refusal. It is the generally accepted opinion of scholars that Luke saw the reception of the Gentiles and the Gentile mission as being a result of the Jews' rejection of the gospel.

In Acts 15, the apostolic council shows Luke's attitude toward the Gentile mission. Stephen G. Wilson proposes that "the problem of the Gentiles and the Gentile mission is once and for all decided at a meeting in Jerusalem of all the main figures in the early

---

20. The emphatic repetition of the vision to Peter (Acts 10:9–16; 11:5–10) and to Cornelius (Acts 10:3–8, 30–33) serves to stress the divine direction behind the Gentile mission. See Fitzmyer and Dillon, *Acts of the Apostles*, 187–88.

21. Tyson, "Gentile Mission," 621.

22. Ibid., 623. "This is probably the most explicit place in Luke-Acts where a prophetic scripture is used to legitimate the Gentile mission."

23. After the report of Luke in Acts 13:46–48, Paul still goes to the Jews (14:11; 17:1, 10, 17; 18:4; 19:8, 26; 28:28), since not all of the Jews reject the gospel.

24. Jacob Jervell's evidence can be summarized as follows: In Acts we can find references to the success of the mission to the Jews (2:41, 47; 4:4; 5:14; 6:1, 7; 9:42; 12:24; 13:43; 14:1; 17:10–11; 21:20). On the basis of this observation Jervell asserts that Luke shows that the mission to the Jews was successful, particularly in Jerusalem. However, Luke thinks that the majority of the Jews rejected the gospel and that this was the primary cause of the Gentile mission for Paul in Acts. See Jervell, "Gespaltene Israel," 76–77, 83.

25. Haenchen, *Apostelgeschichte*, 389.

26. Munck, *Paul and the Salvation*, 235; Jervell, "Gespaltene Israel," 79–82.

Church."²⁷ This "once and for all" view, however, misrepresents the basic nature of Acts 15. Earl Richard correctly states that the main theme of Acts 15 is a "law-free" mission to the Gentiles,²⁸ because the solution of the problem is depicted as a "spirit-given compromise" (15:28).²⁹ In Gal 2:1–10, Paul outlines the historical development of his relationship to the Jewish church. Summarizing the apostolic council in Acts 15, Paul sees the Gentile mission justified: "We [Paul and Barnabas] should go to the Gentiles, but they to the circumcised" (9c). This phrase does not mean that a strictly geographical division of mission territory is projected. It shows rather that the council confirmed to Paul "the independent legitimacy of the mission among the Gentiles."³⁰ In reporting to Peter, James and John what God had done in the Gentile mission, Paul tells them that he has been entrusted with the gospel to the "uncircumcised" just as Peter has been entrusted with the gospel to the "circumcised" (Gal 2:2, 7–9). It is obvious that there was a close link between Jewish law and the Gentile mission in the mind of Paul.

Paul

It is likely that Paul's conviction for the Gentile mission results from his Damascus experience during his "former life in Judaism" (Gal 1:13). The experience is a "call"³¹ where God asked him to bring the gospel to the Gentiles.³² His mission is "to proclaim God's Son among the Gentiles" (Gal 1:15–16). E. P. Sanders does not distinguish "conversion" from "call," but he goes further to illustrate the point of the Gentile mission for Paul: "God revealed his son to Paul and called him to be apostle to the Gentiles."³³ Edward P. Blair argues that Paul's experience at Antioch also seems to form a decisive turning point in his career for the Gentile mission, and that the success of the Antioch Gentile mission makes necessary the Apostolic council to settle the basis of the Gentile mission (Gal 2:1–10).³⁴

At the early stage of his mission, Paul was content to preach the gospel to Jews. In Rome 11:12–13, however, scholars assert that Paul also recognized his mission for the Gentiles coming after Israel's rejection,³⁵ connecting the "stumbling of Israel" and the

---

27. Wilson, *Gentiles*, 178.
28. Richard, "Divine Purpose," 267.
29. Kurz, *Reading Luke-Acts*, 93.
30. Verseput, "Paul's Mission," 51.
31. Donaldson, *Paul and the Gentiles*, 249. He argues that Paul's Damascus experience is to be understood as a "call," not as a "conversion"; Beker, *Paul the Apostle*, 144; Gaventa, *From Darkness to Light*, 18.
32. Stendahl, *Paul among Jews*, 7. "Paul receives a new and special calling in God's service."
33. Sanders, *Paul, the Law*, 152.
34. Blair, "Paul's Call," 26–32.
35. Significant scholarly reappraisals have been undergoing on this issue: Dunn, "New Perspective on Paul," 97, 100; Jewett, "Law and the Coexistence," 341; Watson, *Paul, Judaism*, 168–69; Getty, "Paul and the Salvation," 456; Donaldson, "Riches," 82–92, 97; Donaldson, *Paul and the Gentiles*, 215–30, 241.

"riches of the Gentiles." Paul indicates here that the salvation of the Gentiles is grounded in Israel's failure or rejection (Gal 1:11, 12 and 15): "Israel's loss is the Gentiles' gain; because Israel has rejected the gospel, God offers it instead to the Gentiles."[36] Thus the Gentile mission seems to be developed from the mission to Jews. In Romans 9–11, nevertheless, Paul shows that the final goal of the Gentile mission will also be the salvation of the Jews (11:1–16, 25–27). As 11:11 puts it, salvation for the Gentiles makes Israel jealous and recipients of salvation: Paul preaches to the Gentiles "in order to make my fellow-Jews jealous, and thus save some of them" (11:13–14). Paul's mission to the Gentiles seems to affect Jews indirectly. Romans 9–11 shows us the dialectical interrelationship between Jews and Gentiles in Paul's thinking. In Rom 1:1, 5 Paul briefly states his aims of the apostolate: "set apart for the service of the gospel" by Jesus Christ, through whom he has "received the privilege of a commission in his name to lead to faith and obedience men in all nations."

The Early Christian Literatures

It is important to include some early church fathers' works on the Gentile mission in discussing the issue of the gospel and the Gentiles. *Euanggelion* means originally the "good news" in the Synoptics and Paul. In Q, however, the word is absent[37] and Matthew uses the word *euanggelizontai* only once in Matt 11:5 // Luke 7:22, where he reproduces Q.[38] In the *First Apology* 66:3, for example, Justin Martyr regards the word "*euanggelia*" as the "good news,"[39] while the Didache uses the word "*euanggelion*" four times (8:2; 11:3; 15:3, 4) and does not regard it as references to the "good news."[40] The four passages in the Didache rather seem to refer to the sayings of the risen Lord. This chapter calls attention to the fact that the Gentile mission belonged to the time of the evangelists of the Gospels. It did not start until Acts 10.[41] This means that the question of whether a hint of the Gentile mission is considered possible in the sayings of Jesus during his public ministry cannot be proven, as our study has already concluded in the previous chapter.

---

36. Donaldson, "Riches," 216.

37. In Q 7:22, *euanggelizontai* is only used in the phraseology of Isa 61:1.

38. Harnack, *Constitution & Law*, 277.

39. Justin frequently refers to certain books that he calls "Memoirs" (*First Apology* 67; *Dialogue with Trypho* 100–104; 106; 115; 117). He refers it in his favorite term—the Memoirs called Gospels. See Barnard, *St. Justin Martyr*, 181–82.

40. Massaux, *Influence of the Gospel of Saint Matthew*, vol. III, 145.

41. Hubbard, *Matthean Redaction*, 127. "The Cornelius episode (Acts 10) had made clear God's will regarding the Gentile mission"; Tyson, "Gentile Mission," 629. Tyson argues that the Cornelius episode shows that for Luke scripture provides a justification for the Gentile mission. He states: "The fact is that scripture seems to stand in the way of the Gentile mission at this point and that Luke is aware of this barrier" (ibid., 629). Michael Green regards Antioch as a gateway to the Gentile mission. See Green, *Evangelism*, 112–14. Christopher Francis Evans also states that Luke was "aware that a similar question about eating with the unclean (Gentiles) was a grave issue in the churches," referring to Acts 10:1–11, 18; 15; Gal 2:11–16; 1 Cor 8–10. For more information, see Evans, *Saint Luke*, 307.

Part 1: Sabbath and the Gentile Mission

Mark 13:10 states that "the gospel must first be preached to all the Gentiles," but F. C. Burkitt interprets that "the subject is not missionary instruction, but warning that the *parousia* may [be] delayed."[42] The communities of Matthew and Luke do not have Jesus make open predictions of the Gentile mission before his death and resurrection. The Gentile mission has first been addressed by the risen Lord later in Matthew and Luke (Matt 28:19–20; Luke 24:46–47).

It is important to examine the relation of the gospel and the Gentiles in the Greco-Roman world and to investigate the influence of the Gentile mission on second- and third-century Christian literature.[43] Just as the discovery of the Dead Sea Scrolls[44] reopened the question of the canon of the Hebrew Bible, so too has the discovery of the Nag Hammadi Library[45] stimulated interest in the study of the development of the New Testament, especially the question of the status of Christian literature in the second and third century.

We can start such a discussion by examining some passages about the Gentile mission after the resurrection of the risen Lord. Christian writings of interest to us can be loosely clustered according to their content. The rise of Christianity to dominance in the Roman Empire during the first three centuries is the pivotal development in world history. Yet for all that has been written on the early history of Christianity, the sources of this history are widely scattered, difficult to find, and generally unknown beyond those specifically trained in the field. Hence, most of the ancient texts addressed in this following are taken from literary sources. This is not meant to denigrate the importance of the extant archaeological materials, which are often essential to supplement or correct the conclusion one would draw solely from the literary sources. However, the literary sources do provide a most convenient and useful introduction to our subject if understood in their proper context.

It is likely that the Didache intends to call attention to the Gospel of Matthew.[46] Therefore, in relation to Matthew, the title of the Didache also seems to be connected to Matt 28:19–20 in that the risen Lord sent his disciples to the Gentiles. In fact, *didaxe* corresponds well to *didasxontes* in Matthew, and *ethnesin* to *ethne*; moreover, the Didache speaks of the teaching of the Lord, which may be equivalent to *panta hosa eneteilamen humin* in Matthew. The expressions *matheteusai panta ta ethne kai baptisai eis ton autou thanaton* in Oxyrhynchus 65 (Re L 14; Ro 8): *Apostolic Constitutions* 5.7 recalls *poreuthentes oun matheteusate panta ta ethne* in Matt 28:19.

---

42. Burkitt, *Christian Beginnings*, 137.

43. For more information, see Keresztes, *Imperial Rome*.

44. For the history, see LaSor, *Dead Sea Scroll*; Shanks, *Understanding the Dead Sea*; Charlesworth, *Jesus and the Dead Sea*; Martínez, *Dead Sea*; Wise, *Dead Sea*.

45. For more information, see Robinson, "Discovery of the Nag Hammadi," 206–24; Brown, *Nag Hammadi Library in English*; Tuckett, *Nag Hammadi*; Robinson, "Nag Hammadi," 3–33; Hedrick, *Nag Hammadi*.

46. Jefford, *Sayings of Jesus*, 138n142.

Justin Martyr's *Dialogue with Trypho* is one of the most comprehensive Christian writings prior to the literature of Irenaeus. The *Dialogue* is a document for the Gentiles in the second century and a product of the Jewish Christian controversy in handling the problem of the Mosaic law.[47] In the *Dialogue*, Justin refers frequently to specific Gentiles (17:1; 23:3; 24:1-3; 26:1; 29:1; 32:1, 5; 64:2; 95:1-2 119:4)[48] in the dialogue between Justin and Trypho and addresses specifically a Roman, Marcus Pompeius, who is clearly a Gentile, rather than either a Christian or Jew (8:3; 141:5). In the *Dialogue*, however, the Gentile characteristics of the law are not the starting point; rather, Christian characteristics are mostly found in it.[49] Justin's main concern to handle the issue of the law is the problem of why the law was rejected by Christians, a question of the basis of the Christian rejection of the cultic and ceremonial law with which Justin time and again deals with theologically and exegetically (10:3-4; 12:3; 15:1; 16:1). Why did Christians reject the law? The answer is that the law is invalid because its purpose was specific and limited, not eternal and universal. In the *Dialogue* 32:2, Justin indicates the purpose and intent of the *Dialogue*. The purpose of it is to demonstrate the truth of the Christian claims on the basis of the authority of Scripture; therefore, the intent of it is to convince some of the Jews as to the truth of these claims.

The Ascension of Isaiah[50] 3:17b-18 states that the Beloved One will send his disciples who would teach "all nations and every tongue" his resurrection. This passage seems to constitute reminiscence for the Gentile mission of the sayings of the risen Lord.[51] The main motif of the Ascension of Isaiah is related to Matt 28:19-20: the risen Lord sends his disciples to teach the Gentiles. It is likely that the writer of the Epistle of Barnabas and his/her readers were Gentiles,[52] and they were told that Jesus had saved them from error, darkness, and death and that the universal promises associated with Abraham or the Isaiah servant were fulfilled in him (Barnabas 14:5-8). In the Odes of Solomon, it is likely that the themes, the descent of Christ into Hades[53] and the resurrection of Christ,[54] are connected to the sayings of the risen Lord. The Odes of Solomon 23:17 and 42:6 seem to recall apocalyptically the saying of Christ in Matt

---

47. For the history of the *Dialogue with Trypho*, see Hulen, "Dialogue with the Jews," 58-70; Barnard, *Justin Martyr*; Bellinzoni, *Sayings of Jesus*; Stylianopoulos, *Justin Martyr*.

48. Scholars have claimed that the *Dialogue* was written for Christians and Gentiles, not for Jews: Harnack, "Judentum und Judenchristentum," 51-52 and n2; Goodenough, *Theology of Justin*, 96-100; Hyldahl, *Philosophie und Christentum*, 16-22; Voss, *Dialog in der frühchristlichen Literatur*, 169-95.

49. For "the Christian Gentiles," see 11:3-4; 26:2-3; 28:5-6, and for "the believing Gentiles," see 26:1; 52:4; 91:3.

50. For the history of this book, see Perrone, "Introduzione," 2-43; Tisserant, *Ascension d'Isaie*, 3-77; Charlesworth, "Christian and Jewish Self-Definition," 2:41-46.

51. Knight, *Ascension of Isaiah*, 56. He argues that the author of the *Ascension of Isaiah* probably knew Matthew's Gospel and that the author probably took the material about Jesus from oral sources.

52. Wilson, *Related Strangers*, 161. He argues that Barnabas 3:6; 16:7 points decisively to their Gentile origin.

53. Harris, *Odes and Palms of Solomon*, 140.

54. Charlesworth, *Odes of Solomon*, 147.

28:19–20. In those two passages the motifs, they are sent and gathered, are echoed in the sayings of the Gospel of Matthew. The Odes of Solomon 10:6 speaks of the Gentiles[55] who have "become my people." Jews are not mentioned, and the intent might be polemical. In the case of Clement of Alexandria, the Stromateis[56] quotes a saying of Jesus from a writing Kerygma petrou.[57] This writing may have appeared in the second century[58] among Egyptian Christians. In the Stromateis VI.5.43[59] Peter transmits the saying that the risen Lord spoke to his disciples and sent them to proclaim in the entire world the joyous message. This saying is compared with that of Luke 24:46–47 because both sayings are considered as the final instruction of Christ to the apostles after the resurrection.[60]

When the gospel is introduced to pagans in the Greco-Roman world, three types of worship—civic cults,[61] the Emperor Cult,[62] and Mystery-Religions[63]—were widely spread in the Hellenistic world. These made up the public religions of the Greco-Roman world. These Greco-Roman religions were quite open to other cults. Thus these public religions were quite syncretistic.[64] These Greco-Roman religions were already in the field when Christianity began its mission. The Christian missionary leaders could not underestimate these public religions in the Hellenistic world. But Gentiles realized that there was something new and different in Christian faith.[65] The converts to Christianity had to learn what was to them surprising because "Christianity presented ideas that demanded a choice."[66] Exorcisms may be specified as one major cause of conversion.[67] The gospel represented "Jesus as attracting attention primarily as a miracle worker."[68]

55. Wilson, *Related Strangers*, 91. He argues that the Gentiles were "presumably Christian[s]."

56. For more information, see Faye, *Clément d'Alexandrie*, 96–108; Ferguson, *Clement of Alexandria*, 107; Tollinton, *Clement of Alexandria*, 1:186–94, 202, 205; 2:322, 325–31.

57. Schneemelcher, *New Testament Apocrypha*, 2:94–102; Grand and Quispel, "Note on the Petrine Apocrypha," 31–32; Altaner, *Précis de Patrologie*; Wilson, *Related Strangers*, 92–94.

58. It is clear that the Gnostic *Heracleon* used it in the *Commentary on John* of Origin in the middle of the second century. See Schneemelcher, *New Testament Apocrypha*, 2:95, 97.

59. Klostermann, *Apocrypha I*, 15; Resch, *Agrapha*, 275. I follow the Greek text printed by Klostermann and Resch.

60. Schneemelcher, *New Testament Apocrypha*, 97. "It must therefore be said that the surviving fragments of the KP [*Kerugma Petrou*] have only given currency in a particularly distinctive way to certain tendencies in early Christian missionary preaching."

61. Oliver, *Civic Tradition and Roman Athens*.

62. Sweet, *Roman Emperor Worship*; Herron, *Caesar and Jesus*; Durant, *Caesar and Christ*; Taeger, *Charisma*; Taylor, *Divinity of the Roman Emperor*; Wlosok, *Römischer Kaiserkult*.

63. Cumont, *Mysteries of Mithra*; Angus, *Mystery-Religions*; Hinnells, *Mithraic Studies*, 2 vols; Schütze, *Mithras-Mysterien*; Godwin, *Mystery Religions*; Burkert, *Ancient Mystery Cults*.

64. Grant, *Hellenistic Religions*, xiii–xx.

65. MacMullen, *Christianizing the Roman Empire*, 10–13.

66. Ibid., 17. "To the possibility of a new deity and new cult, no opposition arose."

67. Ibid., 28–29. "In religious usage, a miracle is an event in which one knows one is dealing with God."

68. Ibid., 22. He argues that divine, miraculous powers might be "points of contact" between

The Christian gospel, therefore, was consistent with a positive attitude toward the public religion in the Greco-Roman world (Acts 17:22), even though the Romans called Christianity a "superstition"[69] with a negative attitude. The Synoptic certainly had little in common with the public religions, since Jesus' work was confined to Palestine. Missionary activity, however, was inevitable to a Christian missionary like Paul. Paul had been a Pharisee, and the Pharisees were noted for proselytism. The Judaizing Christians of Jerusalem wished to make converts, who would fulfill the obligations of Judaism. Paul, however, began a real offensive against them.[70] This was a turning point in history. Paul must convince the church why the Gentile converts were to be free from the law and not treated like Jewish proselytes. His polemic was long and fierce on this subject. There was a threat in the Judaizing view limiting the universality of the new faith. The same purpose was served by his theory of justification. In Paul's belief, Jews needed justification (these people whom God has chosen he has justified—that is, he has *made them just*[71]) as much as Gentiles. No one had a right to make distinctions when all were alike justified. This accounts for Paul's indignation with Peter for refusing to eat with the Gentile converts (Gal 2:12). The culmination of this is that Christianity passed from what was apparently a sect of Judaism into an independent world religion which stood alone in its relation to the pagan background. This chapter has to ask, therefore, what inspiration Gentile Christianity drew from this background and what points of contact rendered it intelligible in relation to it.[72]

In the relation to this issue, this chapter should touch upon the question of pagan influences on the Gentile mission. Reitzenstein[73] and Dietrich[74] have found strong influences of the mystery religions in Paul's terminology and conceptions, whereas it is more likely that Paul took over Hellenistic practices and ideas, and wove them into his new faith.[75] It is easier to derive technical terms, names, and ideas from the common Hellenistic milieu. Paul used the term "mystery" with reference to the Gentile mission (Rom 11:25–26; 16:25–27). One can say nevertheless that the broader interpretation of Paul became the basis of orthodox Christianity. Paul himself confessed that he had been called by God "to reveal his Son in me, that I might preach him

---

Christianity and pagans (cf. Acts 8:11). For more information on the points of contact between them, see ibid., 25–42.

69. Riley, *One Jesus*, 2, 181–83. He has read various texts of "superstition." "Tacitus calls it a 'deadly superstition' (*Annals* 15.44), Suetonius 'a new and injurious superstition' (*Nero* 16), and the accuser in the dialogue *Octavius* a 'vain and demented superstition' (Minucius Felix *Octavius* 9.1)" (ibid., 181).

70. MacMullen, *Christianizing the Roman Empire*, 19. "Paul is said to serve and to preach to a non-Christian audience."

71. Justification is originally a Jewish idea, and the divine choice is the calling of a new Israel. The word dikaiow normally means "make just."

72. Murray, *Playing a Jewish Game*, 29–41.

73. Reitzenstein, *Poimandres*; Reitzenstein, *Hellenistic Mystery-Religions*.

74. Dietrich, *Eine Mithrasliturgie*.

75. Goodenough, *By Light, Light*, 10.

among the Gentiles" (Gal 1:16). This confession led to great events, the real beginning of universal Christianity and its mission to the Gentiles of the Greco-Roman world. Paul defined its universality for all time in these words: "There is one body, one spirit, one Lord, one faith, one baptism, and one God" (Rom 3:30; 1 Cor 8:4, 6; 11:12; 15:28; 2 Cor 5:18; Gal 3:20; 1 Thess 1:9; compare Eph 4:4–6).

When the Christian gospel first appeared to pagans, they might have regarded it as a mystery cult because of its characteristics. There were some positive attitudes. The process of Christian baptism could be understood as "enlightenment" in relation to the Mysteries in the Greco-Roman world.[76] The Christian Eucharist also could be seen as "a mystery that guaranteed immortality."[77] As time passed, however, the Romans persecuted Christians because Christianity could not avoid some negative considerations. Christianity was seen, as a result, as a religion of "superstition" to the Romans.[78] Romans killed many Christians because they believed that Christianity was an immoral religion. Romans regarded Christianity as a kind of "cannibalism," with directions to eat flesh and drink blood, so that they persecuted Christians. In this milieu of persecution, Justin would write his treatise in order to declare the true meaning of the Christian Eucharist (1 *Apologia* 66).[79]

EPILOGUE

Conflict with the persecutors actually may have served a constructive purpose as a means of defining the boundary of the Christian community, and to enhance its identity.[80] The fact that the Christian group realized themselves as facing some kind of situation of persecution, one can infer that a lot of the polemic and hostility was directed against the perpetrators of such persecutions. In the process of this polemic, Christianity would defend its essence to the pagans. Evangelizing efforts began in the Hellenistic cities; missionary efforts were soon taking place among the pagans along the trade routes of the Greco-Roman world.[81] In the course of this process, Christianity moved from its Jewish Christian beginnings to become a new religion for the pagans, seeking to find a place in the Greco-Roman world. Christianity because a faith for the entire world with the passing of the Roman Empire.

---

76. Lampe, *From Paul to Vallentinus*; Crossan and Reed, *In Search of Paul*.

77. Riley, *One Jesus*, 147–49.

78. Wilken, *Christians as the Romans*, xii. "The first mention of the Christian movement by a Roman writer, Pliny, governor in the province of Bithynia (modern Turkey), was at the beginning of the second century. He called Christianity a 'superstition.'"

79. Riley, *One Jesus*, 147–49, 150.

80. Lieu, *Christian Identity*, 98–146.

81. Novak, *Christianity and the Roman Empire*.

PART 2

Theology of Q and the Gospels

IX

Predating the Sayings Gospel Q

PROLOGUE

SCHOLARS INSIST THAT THE inaugural sermon (Q 6:20-49)[1] in Q shows significant evidence of the main concerns of the Q redactor and the Q community.[2] Among other things, in Q 6:27-42 the community rules disclose the identity of the Q community. The Q community would probably contain such community rules to place themselves as a disciples' community who follows the teachings of their master and imitates his actions. The Q redactor would transmit the community rules to firmly build the inner solidarity of the Q community under the persecution circumstances in early Christianity between 30 and 70 CE. All these observations indicate that the earliest redaction of Q is probably dated between 30 and 40 CE and the secondary redaction of Q is sometime before 50.

---

1. The reconstruction of Jesus' inaugural sermon is mainly indebted to the IQP Databases and Evaluations. Especially, useful is the *Critical Text of Q: JBL Format* (5 May 1995), originally unpublished but now available from the Institute of Antiquity and Christianity at the Claremont Graduate University. A first draft of a critical edition of Jesus' inaugural sermon of the Sayings Gospel Q has already been published by *JBL* since 1991. The texts discussed and those who prepared the Databases with Evaluations and Respondents are as follows: *JBL* 110.3 (1991) 494-98 on 6:41-42 (Reed; Carruth; Robinson) and 6:46-49 (Daniels; Carruth; Robinson); *JBL* 111.3 (1992) 500-508 on 6:20-21 (Carruth; Kloppenborg; Robinson), 6:39-40 (Carruth; Douglas; Robinson) and 6:43-45 (Carruth; Piper; Kloppenborg); *JBL* 112.3 (1993) 500-506 on 6:23 (Kloppenborg; Boring; Hartin); *JBL* 113.3 (1994) 495-99 on 6:22 (Kloppenborg; Boring; Hartin; Hoffmann; Robinson), 6:27-35 (Douglas; Carruth; Piper; Hoffmann; Hoffmann), 6:37-38 (Carruth; Yieh; Douglas; Robinson) and 6:36 (Douglas; Carruth; Piper; Hoffmann; Robinson); *JBL* 114.3 (1995) 475-85 on 6:24-26 (Hoffmann; Kloppenborg; Johnson); Robinson, *Documenta Q*; Robinson, *Critical Edition of Q*.

2. Carruth, "Persuasion in Q"; Catchpole, "Jesus and the Community," 296-316; Catchpole, "Inaugural Discourse," in *Quest for Q*, 79-134; Davies, *Setting of the Sermon on the Mount*; Lührmann, "Liebet euer Feinde," 412-38; Vaage, "Composite Texts," 424-39; Vaage, "Ethics," 40-54.

Part 2: Theology of Q and the Gospels

Turning toward the Tasks

The inaugural sermon in Q 6:20–49 is attributed to Jesus early in his public ministry. The reconstructed inaugural sermon begins with the section commanding "the love of enemies" follows directly after the Beatitudes in Q 6:20b–23. Matthean and Lucan wording order of Q 6:27–35 is different from each other in a way that "Matthew's hand is visible in the creation of the introductory formulae in 5:38 (39a?) and 5:43 (44a?)" and "Luke 5:34, 35a,b—which recalls this interpolation—is Lucan."[3] In Q 6:36 and 37–38, Matthew and Luke share the original order of Q, "while Luke uses 6:36 as a transitional saying introducing 6:37–38, Matthew employs it as a conclusion for his sixth antithesis."[4] In Q 6:39–45, Matthew and Luke disagree in the rearrangement of these sayings because this section of Q is composed from several of the originally independent sayings: 6:39, 40, 41–42, 43–44, and 45.

The community rules in Jesus' inaugural sermon of Q 6:27–42 are expressed in the imperative. The imperative forms represented are addressed directly by Jesus. Even in the commandment that begins with a vocative,[5] all the rules evidently employed imperatives within the community rules for the Q people. In Jesus' inaugural sermon there are twelve imperative forms uttered by Jesus.[6] I, however, would like to exclude the double imperatives "*kairete kai agalliasthe*" in Q 6:23 from the community rules. The reason is that this concluding phrase to the Beatitudes in Q is preserved in the redactional words in both Matthew and Luke, even though they are based from Q's vocabulary. The imperatives here can be understood in the reflection of the former Beatitudes of Q. The members of the Q community are like those who are poor, in hunger, weeping and are hated and excluded may be rewarded in heaven; thus, the Q community should rejoice and be glad for compensation is awaiting them. The Q redactor would create such double imperatives in Q 6:23 to connect them to the former Beatitudes.

Regarding Q 6:23 as *exordium*,[7] Shawn Carruth argues that "the section Q 6:20b–23 fits the characterization and requirements of the *exordium* of a speech in ancient rhetorical theory."[8] Carruth suggests that *exordium* has the function of the introductory section of the speech. The purpose of *exordium* is to gain the attention and favor of the audience to one's position, to establish the credibility of the speaker, and

---

3. Kloppenborg, *Formation of Q*, 174.
4. Ibid., 180.
5. The commandment in Q 6:42a is accompanied by the vocative of "hypocrite!"
6. Q 6:23(2x), 27a, 28b, 29(2x), 30(2x), 31, 36, 37a, and 42a.
7. See for more information, Mack, "Elaboration of the Chreia," 31–67. Mack quite well summarizes the function of exordium as follows: It is "to acknowledge the speech-situation in such a way as to establish his right to address the audience about the matter at hand." Thus the persuasion introduction, according to him, is connected with "the credibility of the speaker to the nature of the theme" (ibid., 53).
8. Carruth, "Persuasion in Q," 239.

to prepare the audience to follow. Thus this function of the introductory section of the speech was generally recognized by the ancient rhetorical theorists. *Exordium* gains the attention of the audience through self-esteem and self-interest and by introducing the content and the type of argument which will be continued in the remainder of the discourse. In the earliest layer of Q, the Q redactor would set such an *exordium*, which is related to the Beatitudes, into the introductory section of Jesus' inaugural sermon.

For these reasons, while excluding two imperatives in Q 6:23 from the community rules, I am considering the imperatives in Q 6:27–42 as the community rules for the Q people.

In the reconstruction of Q 6:27–35, among the imperative forms, Q 6:29–30 which is in second person singular is placed in the middle between Q 6:27–28 and Q 6:31–35 but in second person plural. In Q 6:36–38 and Q 6:41–42, the inaugural sermon shows the change from second person plural to second person singular. It is likely that the Lukan version is identical with, and therefore reflects Q.

Rudolf Bultmann subdivides the sayings of Jesus as a teacher of wisdom into "logia," "prophetic and apocalyptic sayings," "commandments and rules of the community," "I-sayings," and "parables and the relative."[9] Actually, these categories are characteristic of the content of the Gospel. According to him, Q 6:27–42 belongs to the words of "*Wiedervergeltung und Feindesliebe mit den Worten vom Richten.*"[10] As the result, he points out that it is followed by the sayings of the fruit-bearing and of the builders (Q 6:46–49). These commandments are based on ethical teaching. So to speak, in the *Sitz im Leben* of persecution, not only are these community rules given for catechetical teaching, but they are given for encouragement to set the inner solidarity of the Q community. Here we need to understand the background of these commandments under the circumstances of persecution in the Q community.

Characterizing the Context of the Community Rules

Q 6:22 presupposes special circumstances in which Jesus' followers can be confronted. John S. Kloppenborg regards that Q 6:22–23 is "oriented toward the specific situation of persecution within the Christian community."[11] W. D. Davies also argues that "it is possible that the reference to persecution may have a catechetical interest"[12] in Luke 6:22. Such argumentation would allow the community rules to be connected to the persecution that probably existed in the Q community. In order to prove the persecution circumstances for the Q community, it is meaningful that we examine Q 6:22 in comparison with Matt 5:11. Here two phrases involve two verbs: *oneidizo* and *dioko*. In Matt 5:11, *oneidizo* is expressed in the context of Matthean redaction because Mat-

---

9. Bultmann, *Geschichte der synoptischen Tradition*, 73–222.
10. Ibid., 349.
11. Kloppenborg, *Formation of Q*, 173.
12. Davies, *Setting of the Sermon on the Mount*, 382.

thew adds the eighth Beatitude in 5:10 in addition to the older sermon tradition. For this reason, IQP did not take *dioko* as the Q terminology in Q 6:22. Even if *oneidizo* occurred in the Lucan version, the verb is generally considered as Q-terminology because it is shared by Matthew and Luke. Hence, *oneidizo* is certainly ascribed to Q. This may serve to confirm that the usage of the verb has indicated the following: in Jesus' inaugural sermon Q is unaware of *dioko*, but *oneidizo* seems to preserve the persecuted circumstances of the Q community. I recognize that the *Sitz im Leben* of persecution in Q is generally presumed by the verb *oneidizo*. Therefore, this reveals that the the Q community can be understood in the context of persecution.

In Q 6:22, *oneidizo* related to "the Son of man" designation, discloses the redactional purpose of Q in order to establish firmly the Q community as Jesus' followers, in spite of such a persecution like *oneidizo* which existed at that time for the Q people. In the earliest layer of Q, Q 6:22 shows that Jesus refers to himself as "the Son of man" during his public ministry.[13] As James M. Robinson points out, in the oldest layer of the designation "the Son of Man" is rare (Q 6:22; 9:58), but in the redactional layer it is frequent (Q 7:34; 11:30; 12:8, 10, 40; 17:24, 26, 30). Here our concern is based on the persecution related to the designation "the Son of man."

Q 6:22–23 is connected with the saying toward the Q people making them similar to prophets in the Old Testament tradition (cf. Q 11:49–50; 13:34–35). According to O. H. Steck, Q 11:49–50 belongs to the "*jüdischen Traditionsstück*,"[14] which is appropriate to the "*Konvergenzpunkt zwischen Weisheits-und dtr Tradition*."[15] In the second redaction of Q, it is no surprise that in Q 11:49 the verb *dioko* is shown. By using the verb *dioko*, this is important evidence to represent that the persecution has existed in the Q community. Connected to Q 11:49–50, Q 6:23c is derived from the Q redactional work in the secondary redaction.[16] According to Kloppenborg, "verse 23c is a further expansion of vv. 22–23b, introducing the deuteronomistic motif of Israel's persecution of the prophets."[17] When Steck repeatedly emphasizes the persecution circumstances of the saying of deuteronomistic prophets to the *Sitz im Leben* of Q, he is obviously concerned with countering the opinion that Q sayings are based on the deuteronomistic tradition; Q and deuteronomistic history are both concerned with obedience toward God's will.[18] In Q 6:23c, according to Steck, the saying of the prophets is connected to the "*Vorstellungstradition vom Leiden des Gerechten*."[19] But interested in the fact that there is no term *dikaos* in Q, I would rather discuss further

---

13. Robinson, "Son of Man," 318.

14. Steck, *Israel*, 223.

15. Ibid., 226.

16. Several scholars insist that Q 6:23c is a secondary redaction. Cf. Jacobson, *First Gospel*, 127; Kloppenborg, *Formation of Q*, 173; Schulz, *Q*, 452–57.

17. Kloppenborg, *Formation of Q*, 173.

18. Steck, *Israel*, 286–88.

19. Ibid., 283. For more information, see "the suffering of the righteous," 254–63.

the persecution of the prophets, following Steck's analysis of the deuteronomistic idea of the persecution of the prophets. Q 6:23c reflects the figure of the prophets in the deuteronomistic view of history and seems to be directed to the Q community who stand in the succession of the prophets. Like the prophets, the Q community are abused and rejected at the stage of the second layer of Q.

More important to me is to consider why the Q community contains such community rules under the persecution circumstances. Following E. G. Selwyn, W. D. Davies argues that in times of persecution, Christians especially needed exhortation and support.[20] In the process of the trajectory to find the fundamental ethical rules of Christian behavior, the Q redactor would collect these community rules under the persecution circumstances that certainly present something of the Q community. Encouraging the formation of a firm Christian community, the Q redactor would face transmitting such rules in the imperative forms as the community rules existing under the persecution circumstances, aiming at setting the inner solidarity of the Q community. There is no doubt that to practice concretely these community rules is a way of becoming true disciples who follow Jesus.

Discerning a Disciples' Community or a School?

This chapter may begin with Stendahl's argumentation, which is focused on the quotations of Matthew from the Hebrew Bible.[21] Stendahl claims that Matthew derived from a school of scribes in which emerged methods of interpretation very similar to those followed by the sect at Qumran. With such a thought, Stendahl evaluates that "the synagogue was an undefined combination of a house of worship and a school."[22] For him the synagogue was a place where teaching was carried on. In the Gospels of the New Testament, "synagogue" and "teaching" are constantly used in the same breath, as the passages have shown.[23] By such an argumentation, Stendahl intends that the Matthean church, as one of the early Christian groups, can be regarded as the Matthean School, a scholastic community. Therefore, Stendahl finally concludes that "thus the Matthean School must be understood as a school for teachers and church

---

20. Davies, *Setting of the Sermon on the Mount*, 376n1. Davies argues that such an exhortation was "intertwined with the eschatological hope" in early Christianity. As one expects to approve it, he suggests the eschatological hope in 1 Peter and 1, 2 Thessalonians. According to him, "The inevitability of persecution was a regular part of the Apostolic teaching from the beginning and a pattern for this existed which was largely based on verba Christi" (ibid.).

21. Stendahl, *School of St. Matthew*. Stendahl's main purposes of the study of the quotations in Matthew are two: "to throw light upon the relations between the sources and their development and to see how the form of the quotations helps to explain the milieu of the gospel" (ibid., 42).

22. Ibid., 33.

23. Matt 4:23; Mark 1:21; Luke 4:15, 31–33; 6:6; 13:10; John 6:59; 18:20.

leaders, and for this reason the literary work of a school assumes the form of a manual for teaching and administration within the church."[24]

Following the investigation of Stendahl, R. Alan Culpepper argues that "Jesus and his disciples constituted a school. Jesus the teacher gathered disciples, taught, and was regarded as the founder of a religious tradition who transmitted his teachings and later wrote gospels about his words and deeds."[25] His argumentation is based on the study which a number of the ancient schools regarded themselves as the community who considered themselves to be disciples of the same master. Thus like Stendahl, Culpepper claims that a school stands behind Matthew. Dealing with Matt 23:8–10, Culpepper insists that the terms "rabbi," "teacher," "brothers," "father," and "instructor" all suggest that the community was a school. Culpepper develops further his idea to show that "the Gospels firmly attest that Jesus was regarded as a teacher and that teaching was an integral part of his ministry."[26] Therefore, he insists that a school is shown through many evidences of the Gospels: references to the disciples,[27] their personal commitment to their teacher Jesus,[28] references to "rabbi,"[29] practices of Jesus' teaching,[30] Jesus' private teachings,[31] and finally the demands of discipleship.[32] In the Gospels Jesus was regularly addressed as "rabbi." And a group of disciples gathered around Jesus. Following B. S. Easton,[33] Stendahl agrees that "the social pattern of the rabbi and his disciples made a deep impression on early church life."[34]

However, the text of Q shows us a different picture of the argumentation of "a school." The quotation formulae like those in Matthew do not appear in Q except those in Q 7:27 and Q 4:10–13, namely, the temptation story (Q³): *houtos estin peri ou gegraptai* (Matt 10:11) in Q 7:27 and *gegraptai* (Matt 4:4, 10, 6, 7) in Q 4:4, 8, 10, 12. In Q 7:27 and the temptation story, the quotation formulae are identical to those in Matthew and Luke. Though these formulae in Q show clear examples under "the influence of the Hebrew text,"[35] such formulae do not mean that Matthew and Luke quoted those directly from the Hebrew text. Rather Matthew and Luke probably quoted those formulae from Q. In Q those quotation formulae are ascribed to the sayings of Jesus. Stendahl also says that the quotations in Matt 10:11 and Luke 7:27 are "included in the

---

24. Ibid., 35.

25. Culpepper, *Johannine School*, 215.

26. Ibid., 222.

27. Matt 8:21, 23–26; 10:1, 24–25; 11:1; Mark 10:23–31; 15:41; Luke 6:17, 9:59–62; 12:21; 14:26–27; 19:37; John 6:60, 66.

28. Luke 14:26–27. Cf. Matt 10:37; Mark 10:29; John 12:25.

29. Especially, John 1:38, 49; 3:2; 4:31; 6:25; 9:2; 11:8; 20:16.

30. Matt 5:1; Mark 2:1–2; 9:33; Luke 4:20–21.

31. Matt 17:19; 20:17; Mark 4:34; 6:31, 35; 8:31; 9:28, 31; Luke 10:23; 11:1.

32. Matt 8:22; 10:37; 18:3; Mark 10:15; Luke 9:60, 62; 14:26–27; 18:17; John 3:3, 5.

33. Easton, "First Evangelic Tradition," 148.

34. Stendahl, *School of St. Matthew*, 34.

35. Ibid., 53.

Q material," but he argues that the longer forms in the temptation story (Matt 4:4 par. Luke 4:4; Luke 4:10 // Matt 4:6) were "LXX."[36] However, because of Q's independence from both Matthew and Luke, the quotations in the temptation story must also be ascribed to Q. In this case, it is true that Q was indebted to LXX. Thus those quotation formulae in Q are also different from the cases of those in Matthew in that Q has those as part of the sayings on the lips of Jesus.

According to James M. Robinson, Q is the collection of "the sayings of the sages" or "the words of the wise,"[37] fitting into the sayings genre. At the earliest stage of collecting those sayings, the Q redactor would not need to work in the same way as the school of scribes in Matthew in order to transmit the sayings of Jesus in Q. For this reason, I agree with Kloppenborg's evaluation, in that "Robinson implies that the genre had its main function within an oral context of remembering Jesus' sayings."[38] But here the oral remembrance of Jesus' sayings does not mean that Q was a "random collection of sayings."[39] Rather Q added Jesus' sayings by "a secondary redaction."[40] But, even if Q has a secondary edition, nevertheless Q is unlike the work of Matthew which was produced by a scribal school.

It is impossible that in the earliest stage of a Jesus movement like the Q community, Jesus and his people constituted a school, even if in the inaugural sermon, the members of the Q community consider themselves to be Jesus' disciples. Carruth also argues that "the members of the Q community consider themselves to be disciples."[41] But, she concludes that the Q community has the "self-understanding as a community of disciples."[42] It does not mean that the Q community constituted a school. Rather the Q people see themselves as a community of Jesus disciples. Even if the Q community is not considered as a school, however, it is important that the Q people considered themselves as the disciples who follow and imitate the same master, Jesus. How was such a fact possible? In Q 6:33 and 41–42, the relation of individual disciples to Jesus appears to make them brothers and sisters to each other. Often the concept of discipleship includes the expectation of imitation of the master.

Carruth suggests that there are three functions of disciples of Jesus in Q 6:20–49. So to speak, disciples can be recognized simultaneously as listeners, actors, and imitators in Jesus' inaugural sermon.

In Q, Jesus' disciples would not intend to constitute a school in order to collect, interpret and transmit the sayings of Jesus. The Q community would only want their community following and practicing the teaching of Jesus. In Q, collecting,

36. Ibid., 88–89 and 149.
37. Robinson, "Logio Sophon," 73 and 111–12.
38. Kloppenborg, *Formation of Q*, 29.
39. Koester, "Apocryphal and Canonical Gospels," 112.
40. Ibid., 113.
41. Carruth, "Persuasion in Q," 227.
42. Ibid., 228.

interpreting or transmitting the traditions about Jesus is not ascribead to the result of a school, but to the Q community itself. The purpose is that the Q community's concern was not about establishing a school, but about building their firm community on the basis of the teaching of Jesus.

Here I feel it is necessary to defend or explain the use of the term "the Q community." Q would contain "this generation (*te genea taute*)" sayings (Q 7:31; 11:29, 30, 31, 32, 51) in order to distinguish the Q community from other groups who belong to this world. In Q 11:39a, 42, 39b, 40–41, 43–44, 46–52, the community of Pharisees was woed by Jesus due to their attitudes and behaviors. Those "woe" sayings may indicate differences between the attitudes of the Q community, as distinguished from the Pharisaic community. The fact that the second person singular or plural is frequently uttered in Jesus' sayings in Q should present that "there was an effort to shape the beliefs and praxis of a community."[43] The mission instructions in Q 10:2–12 would also indicate other indirect evidence that there was a community in Galilee.[44]

Among others, fortunately, to me the more important evidence is the fact that Jesus' inaugural sermon shall indicate the existence of the Q community as a disciples' community in the most obvious way. In Jesus' inaugural sermon, Q would transmit such community rules in order to build a community that follows or imitates Jesus. The community rules in Q 6:27–42 may be aimed firmly setting the Q community by the Q community themselves, who were trained through Jesus' practical sayings related to human relationship. The fact that the Q community was built by Jesus' followers is well approved by their community rules in Jesus' inaugural sermon.

Specifically, let's move on to the people in the Q community. First of all, who are the "they" or the "you" in the community rules? In the inaugural sermon, according to Carruth, the "they" are the people "who would have considered themselves to be part of Israel who claimed the prophets to be people who articulated the true tradition of Israel." In Q 6:20b–23, the "they" are the people who "have betrayed the prophetic traditions and are aligned with those who reviled and rejected the prophets." In comparison with the "they," therefore, Carruth considers the "you" in the community rules as "the Q people who are truly loyal to the traditions of the prophets."[45]

All these observations indicate that the Q community can especially be specified as a disciples' community. The term "disciples" presents the people who "follow" or "imitate" Jesus. The concept of such a discipleship really comes from the community rules in Jesus' inaugural sermon in Q^1. The community rules instruct the concept of

---

43. Reed, "Places in Early Christianity," 99.

44. For more information, see ibid., 47–94 and 143–45. Referring the "mental map" of the community behind Q, Reed regards the mental map as "all the places, both imaginative and real, that the Q community shares" (ibid.). His mental map is understood as the concept to "locate the Q community in Galilee" (ibid.). Reed's goal is to clue to the actual location of the Q people in Galilee. After investigating the archaeological evidence, Reed is eager to conclude that "many members of the Q community lived in Sepphoris and Tiberias" (ibid.) among the Galilean cities.

45. Carruth, "Persuasion in Q," 237.

discipleship for the Q people to let them be a disciples' community. In the process, the community rules acquire new accents: discipleship is carried out by loving one's enemies (Q 6:27a), by praying for the abuser (Q 6:28b), by prohibiting of retaliation (Q 6:29–30), by practicing the Golden Rule (Q 6:31), by imitating God (Q 6:36), and by abstaining from judgment (Q 6:37a, 42a). These applications of Jesus' sayings in the community rules explain why I regard the Q community as a disciples' community.

Jesus, as a teacher, would intend to train his disciples to be like their master as much as possible. Not only would Jesus train his disciples to be able to repeat his most important sayings accurately, but also to be able to teach others also. The Q community would require such rules to keep the unity of their community going continuously. The main concern of the Q redactor is to suggest the practical attitudes for setting the firm unity of the Q community. All these community rules are based on the prohibition of retaliation either toward the outside world, or within the Q community.

Turning toward Dating Jesus' Inaugural Sermon in Q

It is very difficult to date the Sayings Gospel Q because it is true that "its traditions and the document itself went through various phases of development and redaction."[46] Ivan Havener simply suggests that Q predates Matthew and Luke, as well as the event of Jerusalem in 70 CE which operates the dating of Mark. If Mark is probably dated "either during the Jewish War (66–70 CE) or shortly after it," Q may be dated to "sometime before the year 70 CE."[47] Dating Q to sometime before 70 CE has a general consensus among New Testament scholars.[48] This is also my opinion upon which I base my own predating of Q to sometime before the destruction of Jerusalem. In 1930, Vincent Taylor predated Q before 60 CE because he regarded the date of Mark as during the period 65–70 CE.[49] Just recalling Streeter's dating of Q to 50 CE[50] without any comment; Taylor says that the date of Q is comparatively early. For him it is impossible that the dating of Q is later than 60 CE; it may be considerably earlier than 60 CE.[51] In 1969, considering all these argumentations on the predating of Q, Dieter Lührmann summarized that "all these observations indicate that the redaction of Q should not be placed too early but rather in the Hellenistic community in around the 50s or 60s."[52] Recently, John S. Kloppenborg advocated a compromise of all estimations of Q's dat-

---

46. Havener, Q, 42.

47. Ibid., 45.

48. Except Mack. He dates Q^3 in 75 CE. Cf. Mack, *Lost Gospel*, 177.

49. Taylor, *Gospels*, 8.

50. Streeter, *Four Gospels*, 150. Streeter dates Q in 50 CE, Mark in 60 CE, Luke in 80 CE and Matthew in 85 CE.

51. Taylor, *Gospels*, 23.

52. Lührmann, "Q in der Geschichte des Urchristentums," 88; Lührmann, "Q in the History of Early Christianity," 62.

ing as "early" or "late," therefore he summarized that "Q is normally dated sometime in the period between 50 CE and 70 CE."[53]

Most recently, however, Gerd Theissen wished to predate the Sayings Gospel Q "between 40 and 70 CE."[54] To investigate the predating of Q between 40 and 70 CE, Theissen deals with the description of three social groups in Q: Israel, Gentiles and Pharisees. However, Theissen's weak point is that he does not give an appropriate picture of the social world in Q because he argues for such social groups on the basis of a number of traditions in the New Testament, not in Q. For this reason, I feel that his social reconstruction is not quite fitting to the picture of Q. Among three social groups in Q recognized by Theissen, nevertheless, the Pharisees are "the only group subjected to an obvious polemic in Q."[55] Theissen quite recognizes that "this generation" sayings against the Pharisees "are traditional, but their collection into a 'chain' of accusations betrays a redactional interest." He also finds that Q differentiates into two overlapping groups: "the Pharisees" (Q 11:39–44) and "the lawyers" or "the scribes" (Q 11:46–52). According to Theissen, this differentiation of the addressees corresponds to differences in the content of the polemic.[56] The most important thing to me is that in the chain of woes, "this generation" sayings against Pharisees and scribes are connected with "the persecution of contemporary Christian prophets"[57] like the Q community. It should be noted that the persecution image helps understand the relationship between the Q community and Pharisees or scribes. This persecution image of the social world in Q can offer an important time reference for predating Q because it is apt to the development of the attack of Pharisees and scribes against Christians between 40 and 70 CE.[58]

Such a persecution image by the Pharisees, according to Theissen, may have originated between about 30 and 70 CE. For example, one Pharisee testified to his part in the persecution of Christians—namely, Paul who was active in the persecution in the early 30s. The image of persecution by the Pharisees in Q² is probably appropriate to the *Sitz im Leben* of between 30 and 50 CE. In Q 11:42, 39b–41, 43–44, 46–52, it is alluded that the Q community were kicked out from the Jewish community, as evinced by the imagery of the Pharisees having persecuted the prophets, who are the representative of the Q community. Expelled by Pharisees and scribes, the Q community was probably in the same background as Paul has written in 1 Thess 2:14–16.

---

53. Kloppenborg, "Sayings Gospel Q," 5. Here Kloppenborg mainly summarizes the work on the dating of Q by Ivan Havener.

54. Theissen, *Gospels in Context*, 221.

55. Ibid., 227.

56. Theissen recognizes that some of "this generation" sayings are added by a latest redaction.

57. Ibid., 229.

58. Ibid., 229–32. Specifically, there are some evidences of persecutions by the Pharisees during the 30s and 40s in the New Testament: Acts 7:54–60; 12:2–3; Gal 1:13, 23; 1 Thess 2:14–16.

The period of Agrippa I began in 41 CE.[59] When Paul refers to the deuteronomistic tradition of the killing of prophets in 1 Thess 2:14–16, he is experiencing the same circumstance as the Q redactor. Therefore, if 1 Thessalonians was written in 50 CE,[60] Q² should certainly be dated sometime before 50 CE.

However, Jesus' inaugural sermon in Q¹ shows an earlier picture of the persecution than the one of Q². Generally speaking, the term *oneidizo* in Q¹ refers to earlier circumstances than those of Q² which are operated by the term *dioko*. The persecution circumstances like *oneidizo* certainly seem to be getting worse than the ones represented by *dioko*. Thus Q¹ is dated earlier than Q². Most importantly to me is that the exhortations in the imperatives offered a stronger practical strategy before the time of struggling with Pharisees recorded in the prophets' sayings in terms of "woe" sayings. Before launching the debates with Pharisees and scribes, the Q community would require such community rules because their primary concern was setting the firm Q community. After the death of Jesus who was their teacher, the Q community would face persecution by Pharisees after 30 CE, as Paul was active in doing. When the Q community was faced with such persecution, they would require such community rules to firmly set their inner solidarity of the Q community as a disciples' community. To prohibit retaliation against attack, which is raised from the outside, the best way may be protecting the Q community. In the earliest stage of Q, thus, the Q redactor would transmit the community rules to encourage the Q community as a disciples' community under the persecution circumstances. If Q² is dated in sometime before 50 CE, Q¹ should be dated earlier than Q². To date Q¹ earlier than Q², it is useful that I can compare the community rules in Jesus' inaugural sermon with the imperative exhortations in 1 Thess 5:16–22. As Phil 2:6–11 has been transmitted by early Christianity, Paul could have transmitted such imperative forms in Thessalonians which were taken from the early Christian tradition. When Paul wrote the letter to Thessalonians in 50 CE, he probably knew already that such imperative exhortations existed which were transmitted by early Christianity before the time of the writing of 1 Thessalonians in 50 CE. Paul would transmit such exhortations in 1 Thess 5:16–22 to encourage their practical strategy for the Thessalonians, as the Q redactor really wanted to do. When I compare the community rules in Q with the imperatives in Thessalonians, however, it can be testified that the imperative paraenesis in Thessalonians were colored by the early Christian traditional history. Contrary to this, it is sure that the community rules in Q were part of Jesus' original sayings. This observation may be helpful to date that the community rules in Q are earlier than the imperative exhortations in Thessalonians. Through all these observations, therefore, I presume

---

59. Ibid., 231 and n56. For more historical of the persecution by the Pharisees, Theissen argues that "For the persecution under Agrippa I between 41 and 44 CE we have to rely on indirect references. Josephus regarded Agrippa I as an indulgent ruler who gladly forgave his opponents, for he considered mildness a more royal trait than passion (Ant. 19.334)." See for more information on Agrippa I, cf. Schürer, *Geschichte des Jüdischen Volkes*; Schürer, *History of the Jewish*, I:442–54.

60. Kümmel, *Introduction to the New Testament*, 257.

that the earliest redaction of Q is probably dated before 40 CE, in the standard of 41 CE when Agrippa I began his reign over all Palestine and after 30 CE, in the standard of the event of Paul's conversion. In short again, Q^1 is predated to sometime between 30 and 40 CE.

EPILOGUE

This chapter has been restricted to one focus in order to remain really effective. I have examined a single issue in Jesus' inaugural sermon, the community rules, specifically in order to disclose the identity of the Q community as a disciples' community, rather than a school. Thus I have traced the community rules for the Q community in persecution circumstances. Without any doubt, the community rules in the imperatives revealed the fact that the Q people established inner solidarity in spite of the period of the persecution prior to 40 CE.

John M. C. Crum had already asked "was Q 'Judaistic?'" in 1924. He answered that Q was the document "given by Jewish Christians living [in] Jerusalem [in] 30, 40, 50 CE" and described the Q community as a "Judaistic Christianity."[61] In fact, Crum supposed that Q was written by Jewish Christians in Jerusalem in about 40 CE and said this is "to suppose an Apocalyptic atmosphere in the church there: a church of Jews over whom the return of their Lord is imminent: Christian Jews persecuted by non-Christian Jews and still devoting themselves to the conversion of their Jewish neighbors only."[62]

Thus it is no surprise that the Q community presented Jesus' ethical teaching as their practical strategy in forms of paraenetic imperative and characteristic exhortations. Having set the *Sitz im Leben* of the Q community rules, I then resumed the predating of Q^1 to sometime between 30 and 40 CE and that of Q^2 to sometime before 50 CE in order to newly launch the issue of the predating of Q, even if these suggestions should be forwarded to the hot discussion among the scholars.

---

61. Crum, *Original Jerusalem Gospel*, 84.
62. Ibid., 93.

X

The God of Jesus

PROLOGUE

THIS CHAPTER WILL ANALYZE the theology of Jesus as evidenced by the Q community, which was founded by the followers of Jesus after his death and resurrection. We can identify the God of Jesus as we trace the trajectory back through Matthew and Luke to the Q community in Galilee, which was influenced by the Hebrew Bible, and reflecting the thought of Jesus has critically affected the Matthean and Lukan concept of God.[1] This chapter argues that the theology of Jesus and the Q community conceives of God as the God of compassionate love (Q 12:24, 28), the God of the heavens and earth (Q 10:21; 16:13; cf. 10:2), and the father (Q 10:21–22; 11:2, 13; 12:30) in order to show the portrayal of God in the Lukan use of Q.

Human Circumstances

The story of the temptation of Jesus is the starting point for understanding the theology of the Q community. Before beginning his public ministry, Jesus is led by the Spirit into the wilderness where, after eating nothing for forty days, he is hungry (Q 4:1–2) as he is tempted by the devil (Q 4:2a). The temptation story raises the problem of the self-identity of Jesus, "Is Jesus really the son of God?" (Q 4:3, 9). It is a question about God as well as about Jesus himself. Jesus replies to the devil by quoting Deuteronomy as follows:

> It is written, you shall not test the Lord your God (Q 4:12, cf. Deut 6:16 LXX).
>
> It is written, worship the Lord your God, and only serve him (Q 4:8, cf. Deut 6:13 LXX).

---

1. Heil, "Beobachtungen zur theologischen Dimension," 649: "Die Auffassung ist weitverbreitet, das frühe Christentum entwickele kein eigenes Gottesverständnis, sondern übernehme den Gottesgedanken des Judentums. Als sein Proprium füge es daran sein Bekenntnis zu Jesus als dem Messias, das Verständnis seines Todes als Heilsgeschehen und den Glauben an seine Auferweckung lediglich an."

Here we learn that the God of Jesus is also the God of the devil (*ton theon sou*). Hence we cannot deny that "the God of Q is not, then, a 'new' God but a God who has revealed himself and his reign in a new way, namely, through Jesus."[2]

Jesus also says that the kingdom of God is for the poor (Q 6:20) and the least in the kingdom of God is greater than John the Baptist (Q 7:28). This emphasis on the needy and humble is reinforced in Q 11:20 and 16:16. Thus, for the Q community, the kingdom of God is already present: *ēggiken basileia tou theou* (Q 10:9). On the other hand, for outsiders (the Jews opposing Jesus), God is the eschatological Judge (Q 13:28) and the Lord of justice (Q 11:42a) who is able to raise children to Abraham from stones (Q 3:8b).

R. Bultmann regards the biblical God as "*der ferne und nahe Gott.*" In Q, however, God is not distant from human experience, but he is near. According to Stephen J. Patterson, "God is not remote, but directly involved in lives of ordinary people, a part of human history."[3] Jesus in Q experiences God as close to the concrete situations of human life through God's love and mercy. In Q 11:4, for example, Jesus prays, "Pardon us our debts as we too have pardoned those in debt to us."[4] Why does Jesus mention *opheiletes* or *pheliema* instead of *hamartia*? It is because Jesus expects God to assist people in pain. Just as Jesus himself had experienced hunger and need (Q 4:2), he reached out to the poor (Q 6:20) and hungry (Q 6:21). Because he suffered temptation by the devil (Q 4:1–13), Jesus understood the persecution of his followers (Q 6:22–23; 11:47–51) and was prepared to take his own cross (Q 14:27).

Next, we see that Jesus experiences God in his daily life. The God of the Q community understands human experience and cares of even little things in the world of nature. God in Q also feeds the ravens (Q 12:24) and clothes the grass of the field (Q 12:28, cf. Gen 3:21). The Gospel of Matthew, which is colored by Jewish Christian tradition, prefers the expression of the birds of the heaven (Matt 6:26) instead of the ravens, which, according the Hebrew Bible, are unclean (Lev 11:15; Deut 14:14. cf. *Epistle of Barnabas* 10:1, 11).[5] The phrase, birds of the heaven, also stands in contrast to the expression, the grass of the field (Matt 6:30). The birds of the heaven and the grass of the field are thus part of a parallel structure that betrays Matthean redaction. Therefore, we can conclude that the ravens in Luke 12:24 represents Q. The point is

---

2. Havener, *Q*, 49–50.

3. Patterson, *God of Jesus*, 114.

4. The Matthean version of the prayer is preferred here. One reason is that Matthew and Q appear to have a genetic relationship: the Q community eventually merged with the Matthean community. For more information, see So, "Sabbath Controversy of Jesus," 16–18, 170–71; Urlich Luz, *Matthew*, 83. Robinson argues that the content of Matt 3–11 is expanded broadly on the basis of the sequence of the Q text in his article, "Real Jesus," 149. Such an argumentation can be considered as great evidence which the Matthean Community is based on the Q community. Cf. Robinson, "Matthean Trajectory from Q to Mark"; Silbering, "Text and Tradition in Matthew."

5. Davies and Allison, *Critical and Exegetical Commentary*, 648.

that in spite of uncleanness of the birds, God takes care of them (Pss 147:9; Job 38:41).[6] God also clothes the grass of the field, even though it is of little value (Q 12:28).[7] This figure of a merciful God who takes care of weeds that is only useful as kindling may be compared to the portrayal of God clothing Adam and Eve in leather.[8] Jesus thus expresses God's overwhelming love for human beings: Will God not much more clothe you? (Q 12:28). The answer, of course, is "yes."[9]

As stated above, the God of the Q community is ordinarily expressed as the natural God who can be experienced in the world of nature and human circumstances. This fact proves the regional characteristics of Galilee where the Q community takes its foundation of life. In relation to Galilean circumstances, the Q texts often suggest passages that the Q community is based on the rural area (Q 3:9, 16–17; 6:42, 43–44; 47–49; 7:24; 10:2, 7–8; 11:24, 42; 12:6, 24, 27–28, 54–56; 13:19–21; 14:5; 15:4–7; 17:2, 35; 19:20–21).[10]

The Lord of Heaven and Earth

The God of the Q community is addressed again in the expression, "the Lord of heaven and earth" (Q 10:21), which is found in both Matthew's and Luke's version of the saying. Marcion omits the word "earth" in Matt 11:25, probably in order to exaggerate the idea of "heaven" in the Gospel of Matthew. Nevertheless, it must be acknowledged, consistent with Marcion's reading of Matthew, that the expression, "God of heaven" rather than "God of heaven and earth" is much more common both in the Hebrew Bible and the Christian tradition.[11] In fact, "the Lord of heaven and earth" is found only three times in the New Testament (Matt 11:25; Luke 10:21; Acts 7:24). But we should also keep in mind that the expression is an important one in texts based on the Hebrew Bible. It is found in the *Testament of Benjamin* 3:1, and is similar to *Jubilees* 32:18, which identify God as "the Lord who created heaven and earth." James M. Robinson observes that although the phrase of "heaven and earth" is not in the Qumran formula, but is added in Q, the phrase is part of the *hodayot* formula that

---

6. Jeremias, *Sprache des Lukasevangeliums*, 17.

7. Here the verb "clothe" is a semantic expression of *amphiennumi* in Matthew and *amphiejo* in Luke. Although Michael Steinhauser regards *amphiennumi* as a language of the Q texts in his book, *Doppelbildworte*, 219, IQP disagrees with him and regards *amphiejo* as the reconstructed Q text, so I am sure that we can reconstruct the text of Q 12:28 as *amphiejo*.

8. Davies and Allison, *Gospel of Matthew*, 1:655.

9. Likewise with Q 12:28, Q 12:23 also contains a rhetorical question of Q, requesting a positive answer like "yes." Such rhetoric of Q is contained within the passages in Matthew 6:25b, 26b, 27, 30b; Luke 12:25. Luke 12:23 not longer has a rhetorical question. Luke 12:24b and Luke 12:28b are often expressed as an exclamation (!) rather than as a question (?). Cf. Carr, *From D to Q*, 10.

10. Crum, *Original Jerusalem Gospel*, 9–63; Vassiliadis, "Nature and Extent of the Q-Document," 63; Robinson, "Down-to-Earth Jesus," xvi. These scholars insist that the background of the Q community is not the city like Jerusalem but the region of Galilee in the rural atmosphere.

11. Simon, *Heaven in the Christian Tradition*, 52–125.

crops up often in the prayers and songs of early Christian tradition and has that it has been transmitted in the Qumran texts as well.[12] The phrase thus predates Jesus and it is conceivable Q's use of it reflects Jesus' own usage.[13]

On the basis of this evidence, we can understand Jesus praising[14] God in Q as "Lord of heaven and earth" as an allusion to the creator of Gen 1:1. This God, however, is also identified to the devil as "the Lord your God" (Q 4:12, 8). According to the second temptation, the devil takes Jesus to Jerusalem, places him on the pinnacle of the temple and says to him, "If you are the son of God, throw yourself down" (Q 4:9). Then Jesus answers him, "You shall not test the Lord your God" (Q 4:12). According to the third temptation, the devil takes Jesus to a very high mountain and shows him all the kingdoms of the world and their splendor, and says to him, "All these I will give you, if you worship me" (Q 4:5–7). Then Jesus answers him, "Worship the Lord your God, and only serve him" (Q 4:8). Who is God in Q? He is the Lord of everything, including the devil, heaven and earth. He is the creator.

Belief in God the creator in Q comes to fullest expression when it is connected to the concept of the kingdom of God. According to Q, God the creator is the ruler of the kingdom. The Gospel of Matthew prefers the phrase "the kingdom of heaven" (32 times) to "the kingdom of God,"[15] while Q only uses the expressions "the kingdom of God," "your kingdom," "his kingdom," or "the kingdom" (Q 6:20; 7:28; 10:9; 11:2, 20; 13:20, 28; 14:16; 16:16; 22:30). Norman Perrin understands the concept of the kingdom of God as a symbol.[16] Hence, we can distinguish between different meanings of the term "the kingdom of God."

First, the concept of the kingdom of God has a possessive meaning in Q. Q 6:20 says that the kingdom that God possesses will be given to the poor. This does not mean that the poor possess the kingdom of God or that it is established by them.[17] Rather the kingdom belongs only to God.[18] Therefore, if one seeks his kingdom, God will give all things needed for life as well (Q 12:31). Unfortunately, since they do not know this mystery, the Gentiles only seek the things they need for life (Q 12:30).

---

12. Robinson, "Hodajot-Formel in Gebet," 197. His argumentation is very important for current New Testament scholarship.

13. Jeremias, *New Testament Theology*, 187.

14. The idiom *exomologeo* + *soi, kurie* often appeared in the texts of the *septuaginta* (*LXX*): Gen 29:35; 1 Chr 16:34; 23:30; 29:13; 2 Chr 5:13; 30:22; Pss 7:17; 9:2; 17:49; 21:25; 32:2; 34:18; 70:22; 137:1. In those texts, the meaning of *exomologeo* is "praise" or "thank." Hence, the verb *exomologeo* in Q 10:21 is not the meaning of "confess" (Matt 3:6) but "praise" or "thank."

15. The Gospel of Thomas also prefers the expression of "the kingdom of heaven" or "the kingdom of the father" to "the kingdom of God." Cf. Patterson, *Gospel of Thomas*, 43.

16. Perrin, *Jesus and the Language of the Kingdom*, 1–14, 15–88. He regards the kingdom of God as the most symbolic title in biblical scholarship.

17. Davies and Allison, *Gospel of Matthew*, 1:445.

18. *Humetera* (plural second pronoun) in Q 6:20 well fit to the context of the entire Q texts.

Second, the kingdom of God is described as present or at hand in Q 10:9; 11:20; 16:16. Jesus considers the kingdom of God as present during his public ministry and says that his people also already experienced its presence.[19] The expression "*eph humas hē basileia tou theou*" in Q 10:9 and 11:20 may be compared to "*hē basileia tou theou entos humon*" in Luke 17:21. "*Entos humon*" can mean (1) dwelling in you; (2) in your midst; or (3) is in your hand (when the kingdom of God comes),[20] but the meaning of "*eph humas*" can be (1) above you; (2) before you; (3) toward you (when the kingdom of God comes). Hence, Q 16:16 regards the kingdom of God as suffering violence as the violent take it by force.

Third, in contrast to the present meaning, the kingdom of God has a future meaning in Q 11:2 (cf. 13:29, 28). Since the wording of Matt 6:10 and Luke 11:2b is identical, the IQP reconstructs the Q text as: *eltheto hē basileia sou*.[21] Here Jesus instructs his disciples to ask for a future when God reigns with power.

Fourth, Q 7:28 says that in the kingdom of God the least is greater than John the Baptist. This suggests that in the kingdom of God, there will be a new order, which is not structured according to human standards or the views of this generation. The parables of the kingdom of God, Q 13:20–21 and 14:16–23, also reflect this perspective: the kingdom is like leaven that a woman puts in three measures of flour until it leavens the whole (Q 13:21), and like a great banquet which is filled with the uninvited guests (Q 14:23).

Finally, Q 13:29, 28 refers to the kingdom of God as imminent.[22] Israel will be relegated to the place where there is weeping and gnashing of teeth, while the Gentiles will come from the east and the west to participate in the messianic banquet. In this short pericope Jesus warns Israel to repent, foretelling their fate if they do not. Though the Q community has a conservative view of the law (Q 11:42; 16:17–18) and aims to preserve Jewish traditions as it carries out a Jewish mission, we discover here a pericope that encourages the Gentiles (Q 7:1–9). The point, however, is not that Q has a positive view of the Gentiles, but that Jews should be shamed by the potentially positive response of the Gentiles. Q 11:31–32 adds that the Queen of the South and the men of Nineveh will judge "this generation." The relationship between Jews and Gentiles is thus clarified, for, as Q 22:30 suggests, the eschatological reversal in the kingdom of God means that the followers of Jesus will sit on thrones judging the twelve tribes of Israel.

---

19. Stanton, *Gospels and Jesus*, 192–93.

20. Conzelmann, *Outline of the Theology*, 112.

21. Anderson, *Documenta Q*, 4–10, 18. It is much more likely, as numerous scholars have suggested that the passages in Q 11:2b comes from Jesus. Hence IQP grades them in {A}.

22. Borg, "Temperate Case," 81–102. His chapter seems to argue superficially that we do not understand Jesus or the kingdom of God in the eschatological perspective, but rejects that we can understand them in an apocalyptic view. For this reason, Jesus does not teach, as apocalyptic literatures have stated, the kingdom of God in the catastrophe of human history or the great reversal of human order, but both instructs to give hope and comfort for the Q community and warns to lead the Jews to repent in the eschatological sense.

Jesus' teaching about God as creator and Judge also serves to challenge the Q community itself. Jesus observes that no one can serve two masters and must choose between God and mammon (Q 16:13). His followers must choose one or the other: God or money.

The God of Jesus is also presented as the Lord of the harvest who sends out laborers. The followers of Jesus are called to work in the harvest, carrying neither money, nor bags, nor sandals, nor staffs, nor even greeting anyone (Q 10:4).

Father

That Jesus addresses God as the father has provoked discussion. It is the characteristic idea of God in Q. Jesus calling God "father" could reflect Jesus' special awareness of himself as the son and could go back to the historical Jesus. It is a new way of speaking to God. Against this interpretation, in the first place, the word does not have the connotation of familiarity. Second, even if it was certain that Jesus spoke in this way, the main question is whether Jesus alone used this form of address (or did his disciples also use it?) and thus whether it evidenced his unique consciousness of being son.[23] The answer is clear: In Q 3:8, Abraham is also a "father" to the Jews. If the address "father" goes back to Jesus himself, then it is clear that he did not use it for God alone. In the parable of the rich man and Lazarus (Luke 16:19–31), Abraham is called "father" three times (Luke 16:24, 27, 30). Why is Abraham so often called "father?" Probably his role in Israel's history is more important than that of any other person. As the epitome of fatherhood in Jewish tradition, he affected Christian theology.[24]

Q 10:21–22 is a thanksgiving prayer in which Jesus praises God, calling him "father." According to Robinson, the more common address is *kurie*, a standard part of the *hodajot* formula shared with the Qumran texts. Hence he argues that *pater* is secondary; it is a Christianizing of the *hodayot* formula.[25] There is no other instance of Jesus using the *hodayot* formula. In Q 11:2, Jesus also addresses God as "father" in prayer. Matthew's "who is in heaven" is to be rejected as redactional. Thus the vocative *pater* in Q 10:21 confirms *pater* as the form of address in Q 11:2. The fact that Jesus calls God father offers us not only an existential understanding of the co-relationship between father and son, but also points to the need for humans to treat each other as brothers and sisters.[26]

God as father gives "good things to those who ask him" (Q 11:13). This verse draws an analogy with parents loving their children in human circumstances: "If you, then, though you are evil, know how to give good gifts to your children, how much more will the father from heaven give good things to those who ask him!" It is an

---

23. Conzelmann, *Outline of the Theology*, 103a.

24. Vermes, *Religion of Jesus the Jew*, 152. He argues that the fatherhood of God would affect the liturgical prayer in the Hebrew Bible, the inter-testament writings, and the rabbinic literatures.

25. Cf. Anderson, *Documenta Q*, 105.

26. Vermes, *Religion*, 153, 165–66.

expression of trust in the God of love and acceptance and praise for the God of heaven. Hence Q 12:30 raises the problem of the one-dimensional attitude of the Gentiles toward materialistic concerns as contrasted to God the father who knows everything that the humans need. Q criticizes the lack of insight of the Gentiles, reflecting the Jewish orientation of the Q community. Although some Gentiles are amazed by Jesus (cf. Q 7:9), most do not know the law and Jesus' teaching that God will provide all that humans need if they seek the kingdom of God (Q 12:31). Q tells the community that the father knows everything that it needs (Q 12:30), confirming the close relationship between God and the Q community. Here we can find again the expression "your father." The God of Jesus has become the God of the Q community. In Q 10:22, Jesus asserts that "everything has been handed over to me by my father." This means that all the wisdom sayings of Jesus himself have been given to him by God.

The expression "my father" in Q 10:22 and "your father" in Q 12:30 are interchangeable because they are identified by each other. The expression "my father" is found only once in Q (10:22), though Matt 10:32–33 uses it again, adding it to Q 12:8–9. Luke 12:8–9, however, reads "the angels of God." Hence it is difficult to reconstruct the Q text.[27] Q 12:30, at any rate, make clear that God is the father of the Q community and they are God's children.

Jeremias regards Jesus calling God "father" as the most innovative and unique of all the expressions of Jesus.[28] According to him, "father" reflects "*abba*"[29] in Aramaic, a term used by children when addressing their father.[30] He regards the expression as *ipsissima verba* of Jesus.[31]

Based on the fact that Jesus called God "father," early Christianity adopted the term to express its basic idea of God. Its confession of God was one of "loving kindness and fatherhood."[32] Early Christians calling God "father" (Q 10:21; 11:2) or "my father" (Q 10:22) was a privilege and blessing to them. In our contemporary situation, as the role of the father is gradually collapsing, the recovery of a theology of God as the father is useful for the recovery of the relationship between fathers and children. The merciful God who is the father wants us to practice love and justice in our daily life (Q 11:42).

---

27. IQP recognizes many difficulties reconstructing the expression of "my father" in Q 12:8–9 so that the reconstructed Q texts have a blank like " . . . " In my opinion, however, the expression of "my father" in Matt 10:32–33 seems to have a somewhat original tradition.

28. Jeremias, *New Testament Theology*, 36, 63–68.

29. For "*abba*," many scholars like Perrot (1979), Rowland (1985), Zeitlin (1988), Meier (1991) agree with the opinion of Jeremias. To this opinion, however, Vermes argues that *abba* is already been used in the Jewish traditions before the time of Jesus, remembering James Barr's chapter, "Abba Isn't Daddy!," 28–47. Cf. Vermes, *Religion*, 152–83.

30. Jeremias, *New Testament Theology*, 67.

31. Ibid., 37, 67.

32. Hagner, *Jewish Reclamation of Jesus*, 209. Referring to the chapters of Montefiore, "Spirit of Judaism," 35–81, "Synoptic Gospels," 649–67, and "Jewish Conceptions," 246–60, Hagner argues that Jesus calls God as the father, based on the Jewish traditions from the Hebrew Bible. Hence Hagner concludes that the idea of God as the father is thoroughly Jewish and rabbinic.

The Portrayal of God in the Lukan Use of Q

In Matt 12:8–12, Jesus heals the man with a shriveled hand on the Sabbath, in Matt 12:15 Jesus heals all the sick, and in Matt 12:16–21 Jesus approves his activity of the healing quoting the passages of Isa 42:1–3 and Isa 61:1. After that, he heals the dumb demon (Matt 12:22), and then there is the controversy of Beelzebul (Matt 12:23–29). Here we must explain the relationship between "my spirit" in Matt 12:18 and "the spirit of God" in Matt 12:28. Quoting the passages of Isaiah, Matthew seems to be persuaded by "my spirit," "the spirit of God" in Matt 12:16–21. When Matthew quotes the story of a dumb demon in Q 11:14 and the Beelzebul controversy in Q 11:15–22, it is likely that Matthew distinguishes the power of God from that of the demon on the basis of the theme of "power" and he alters "the finger of God" in Q 11:20 to "the spirit of God" in Matt 12:28, in order to harmonize in the theme of "spirit" compared to Matt 12:18.

In contrast, Luke is using the Q text to depict God's nature. Luke faithfully preserves "the finger of God" from the original Q text. Luke provides a good example in the way Luke reads and uses Q. Accepting the Q tradition of the story of the dumb demon in Luke 11:14 and the Beelzebul controversy in Luke 11:15–22, Luke uses a typically redactional expression, "the Holy Spirit" in Luke 11:13. Hence in this context "the finger of God" in Luke 11:20 might be altered to "the spirit of God." Nevertheless, it is quite possible that Luke accepts the tradition of "the finger of God" without alteration and preserves it on the basis of the Q text.

The most important thing, however, is a question whether there is any difference in meaning between "the finger of God" in Q (Luke faithfully uses it) and "the spirit of God" in Matthew. When we consider the tradition of the Hebrew Bible, we are sure that the expression of "the finger of God" means primarily "the hand of God" (Exod 3:20; 8:19). According to James D. G. Dunn, it is likely that all the expressions can be understood as "the power of God," when disregarding the problem of whether Matthew alters "the finger of God" in Q to "the spirit of God" with the basis of the Matthean context, and whether Luke preserves the expression of Q without any Lukan context.[33] In the Old Testament, "the spirit" and "the hand of the Lord" (or "the hand of God") are synonyms (Ezek 3:14; 8:1–3; 37:1; Pss 8:3; 33:6; 1 Kgs 18:12; 2 Kgs 2:16; 1 Chron 28:12, 19; Isa 8:11).[34] In the case of these passages, "the spirit of God" or "the hand of God" connotes activities of the power of God. In other words, the spirit of God has been understood in the miracle power of God or the miracle itself.[35] Hence the spirit of God, the finger of God, the hand of God, and the power of God is the

---

33. Dunn, *Jesus and the Spirit*, 46, 374.

34. Conzelmann, *Outline of the Theology*, 38. He argues that "in the connection with Judaism, the first mention is of the spirit of *God*, but then there follows mention of the spirit of *Christ*, or of the *Lord*." Cf. Dunn, *Jesus*, 46, 373.

35. Conzelmann, *Outline of the Theology*, 182–84.

same as the expression of the Hebrews which wanted to portray the great activity of God.[36] Q, Matthew, and Luke show that the exorcism is due to the great power of God. That God stood at the back of the exorcism, therefore, is a basic point of faith in Q.

It is likely that in the Q community, the spirit is the spirit of God, the finger of God is a synonym of the spirit of God, and all the expressions are concepts representing the power of God. When we regard the spirit as the spirit of God, we can understand that the spirit announced Jesus as the son of God and descended from heaven at the time of Jesus' baptism. The Q community also describes that when Jesus is tempted by the devil in the wilderness, God is with him in the background of the event. In other words, the Q community regards the baptism and the temptations of Jesus as connected to the mission of the kingdom of God prepared thoroughly by the spirit of God.

Hence, we can understand that the Q community is based on the mission of the kingdom of God provided by the spirit, which is the spirit of God. In other words, that the teaching of Jesus is that when the demons with the unclean spirits are cast out, the kingdom of God has come upon them, and that the earthly Jesus begins his public mission after the baptism and the temptation led by the spirit, all this would encourage the Q community in being devoted to the kingdom of God and that it all is designed by the spirit of God.

EPILOGUE

In conclusion, the God of Jesus in Q is the basis for the idea of God in the Gospel of Luke. Luke uses Q's concept of God to maintain the portrayal of God of the Lukan community. Hence the God of Jesus becomes the God of the Lukan community and the members of the community call each other brothers and sisters because God is their father.

The twofold understandings of God in Q, as the Judge of the Jews and as the comforting father in the Q community's daily life, is to be explained on the basis of Jesus' understanding of God. To Jesus, God is the Lord of heaven and earth, the creator and, above all, the father (Q 10:21–22; 11:2, 13; 12:30). The idea of God as father is unique in Q. This perspective on God would later inform Lukan theology as well.

God the father in Luke is also the God of heaven and earth. Hence faith in the God of Luke is faith in God the creator (Luke 10:21). This concept of God shows that Jesus' ideas are based on ancient concepts of the Hebrew Bible. On the other hand, Jesus often speaks of the kingdom of God; hence God is conceived by early Christians as their sovereign. As a Jewish community in Galilee, the Q community would readily accept the traditions of the Hebrew Bible that God is creator, and, as followers of Jesus, they would also embrace his practice of calling God "father."

---

36. For this understanding, Alan Richardson suggests that Christ is not identified with the spirit of God as he is with the wisdom of God, the word of God, and the power of God, although in the Old Testament the spirit is a personification of the divine activity of the same order as the wisdom, the word, and the power. Cf. Richardson, *Introduction to the Theology*, 121.

XI

Jesus' Understanding of Spirit

PROLOGUE

THIS CHAPTER WILL EXAMINE the Synoptic passages to come to know Jesus' understanding of spirit. The Synoptic Gospels, Matthew, Mark, and Luke, who include sayings and descriptions of the life of Jesus, offer us a lot of material on Jesus' understanding of spirit. New Testament scholars have been able to identify and study as a common source known as the Sayings Gospel Q which was used by Matthew and Luke in many passages of the Synoptics. Q is the sayings collection transmitted by the earliest Christian community which resided in or near the upper Galilee, and is the basic source of Matthew and Luke. It is evaluated as being especially important as a document of the historical Jesus' sayings by some modern scholars. The Q Community in Galilee consisted of the disciples of Jesus and his followers, thus they are the first tradents of the sayings of Jesus. The purpose of this study is to examine the characteristic view of Jesus' understanding of spirit as a main topic in Q, to investigate how Matthew and Luke are affected Jesus' view of spirit based on Q, and to study further how the Q community overcome the constraints of their particular milieu including persecution and other matters on the basis of Jesus' understanding of spirit.

The Spirit and the Earthly Jesus

The fundamental problem in connection with knowledge of the teaching of Jesus is the problem of reconstructing the reality of Jesus' understanding of spirit from small passages in Q available to us (Q 3:16, 22; 4:1; 11:24; 12:10), and the truth of the matter is that the more we learn about those passages the more difficult our task seems to become. Many modern scholars say that those passages contain a great deal of teaching material ascribed to Jesus, and yet it turns out to be precisely that the teachings of those passages ascribed to Jesus, in fact, stem from the early church. Referring to this problem, for example, Hans Conzelmann and Andreas Lindemann say, "Probably neither John nor Jesus speaks about the 'Spirit'; it is the Christian community that speaks of the Spirit on the basis of its own experience of the Spirit."[1] Hence they do not say anything further about Jesus' view of spirit or that of the Q community.

In contrast, Norman Perrin disagrees with their opinions from the beginning. According to him, although we distinguish between the kerygma spoken by the risen Lord in the early church, and the facts and words of the earthly Jesus, when we consider that the early church absolutely knew the literary form of the gospel stemming from the earthly Jesus and conceived all its traditions (oral traditions and written traditions) we can conclude that "the early Church absolutely and completely identified the risen Lord of her experience with the earthly Jesus of Nazareth"[2] and that the sayings and facts ascribed in the consciousness of the early church to both the earthly Jesus and the risen Lord were originally set down in terms of the literary form of the gospel.

These conclusions can be recognized by the New Testament scholars as a turning point. We now cannot say anymore that there is no relationship between the earthly Jesus and the risen Lord, as Rudolf Bultmann said. Rather the early church confesses the risen Lord as the earthly Jesus in her thorough and complete experience. In other words, the early church does not hesitate to confess that the historical Jesus of Nazareth and the kerygmatic Christ after the resurrection is one.

In spite of these conclusions, it is true that there is a difference between the spirit in the teaching and experience of Jesus and the spiritual experience in Acts and the early church. According to the spirituality of the early church, the spiritual experience is described as charismatic types: the apostles all filled with the Spirit began to speak in other tongues (Acts 2:4; cf. 2:11); they taught and preached the word, healed the sick, carried out miracles, made prophecies, distinguished between spirits, and interpreted tongues (1 Cor 12:4–10). In contrast to these charismatic types, the spirit experience in Q can be understood in the limited works and words of the earthly Jesus and John the Baptist. In Q, when Jesus is baptized by John the Baptist, the spirit descended upon him from heaven (Q 3:21–22). Before launching his public ministry, "Jesus was led by the spirit into the wilderness to be tempted by the devil" (Q 4:1–2). And among the teachings of Jesus we can find some passages addressed to the spirit as follows: the saying that "whoever blasphemes against the Holy Spirit will not be forgiven" (Q 12:10); the saying "When a clean spirit has gone out of a person, it passes through waterless places seeking rest and finds none. . . . Then it goes and brings with it seven spirits more evil than itself" (Q 11:24–26). Finally, referring to the ministry of Jesus in his preaching, John the Baptist says, "He will baptize you with the Holy Spirit and fire" (Q 3:16). These passages related to the spiritual experience in Q are limited and speak of different experiences in comparison with the charismatic types of the early church.

---

1. Conzelmann and Lindemann, *Interpreting the New Testament*, 299.

2. Perrin, *Rediscovering the Teaching of Jesus*, 15. Although he distinguishes between the teaching of Jesus and the kerugma of the early church, he does say that "when we say that 'the teaching of Jesus' we mean the teaching of the earthly Jesus, as the early Church did not" (ibid., 15).

Although Q's understanding of spirit is different from the spirit experience or the gifts of the spirit, we can find some similarities in relating the ministries of Jesus with the ministries of the early church: He teaches (Q 7:22; 14:5), preaches (Q 6:20–49), heals (Q 7:1–9), works miracles (Q 10:13), casts out demons (Q 11:14, 18–20), and distinguishes spirits (Q 4:1–13; 11:24–26). Like the charismatic ministries of the church, we can also consider the words and works of Jesus as ministries empowered by the spirit. At this point Ivan Havener's opinion of the following is corrective: "But this does not mean that these are not spiritual gifts, for Jesus does all these things after having received the heavenly Spirit. His entire ministry must be understood as a manifestation of the Spirit."[3]

Nonetheless, I cannot agree with the opinion of James D. G. Dunn that regards Jesus as a charismatic figure in the Pauline charismata[4] and I cannot find charismatic gifts from Jesus, for unlike the gifts of the spirit in 1 Corinthians and Acts Q is interested in the reality and acts of the spirit, or more correctly speaking, the ministry of the spirit working together with the public ministry of the earthly Jesus. Paul does not show an interest in the ministry of the spirit in the earthly Jesus but is interested in the concrete gifts of the spirit or the charismatic works. Likewise, Luke on the one hand presents Jesus' understanding of spirit through the sayings tradition and introduces the ministry of Jesus beginning with the withdraw of the devil (Luke 4:13) and with the spirit-filled acts in Galilee (Luke 4:14), and he on the other hand focuses on the successful ministry of the spirit and the spiritual experience after the resurrection and Pentecost (Acts 2:1–4).

Unlike Luke, however, Matthew does not consider the ministry of Jesus as the direct ministry of the spirit, for Matthew can be understood in relation to the Q community. In the process of the emergence of the Q community into the Matthean community, the spirit-view of the Q community is adopted through that of the Matthean community. Hence, we must examine here the milieu of the Q community as it basically affects to the Matthean community.

The Milieu of the Q Community

Although the Q community does not preach the word of God in the spirit-filled way as the early church in the Acts does, its preaching ministry in Galilee is practiced by obeying the teachings of Jesus (Q 10:2–16). We can evaluate that its mission is a kind of preaching practice and charismatic ministry. Hence we can find traces in Q that the Q community blesses peace (Q 10:5–6), heals the sick (Q 10:9a), preaches the kingdom of God (Q 10:9b), and speaks of the gospel of repentance (Q 10:12–15), even though the disciples of Jesus are faced by the milieu of persecution (Q 10:3).

---

3. Havener, *Q*, 91. Hence, he concludes that "despite the relatively few references to the Spirit in Q, the Spirit plays a decisive role in Q theology."

4. Dunn, *Jesus and the Spirit*, 41–92.

Jesus' Understanding of Spirit

The preaching activity of the Q community does not concur with the activity which was in fashion among stoic philosophers and Cynics,[5] for it is unlike Hellenistic philosophers in every respect. It does not practice the teaching style of the professional begging charismatics, though it practices its gospel mission as wandering charismatics. Rather the Q community tries to find its model case from the prophets in the Old Testament.[6] It is applied to the early Christian traditions (1 Thess 2:15; Rom 11:3; Acts 7:52; Mark 12:1–12) that the activity of the prophets in the Old Testament was to keep going in the milieu of rejection even if they were killed (1 Kgs 18:4, 13; 19:10; 1 Chron 16:22; 2 Chron 24:19–22; Neh 9:26; Ps 105:15; Jer 26:20–23). It is sure that the Q community was affected by these traditions (Q 6:22–23; 11:47–51; 13:34–35).[7]

For this prophetic tradition on the sufferings, Odil Hannes Steck concludes that this perspective originated in the deuteronomistic view of history in Israel (2 Kgs 17:7–20).[8] This reconstruction of the Israelite history on the basis of the deuteronomistic view is basically characterized by the following elements: (1) The disobedience or sins of Israelites; (2) God with patience sends prophets and calls Israel to repent; (3) Israel always rejects the prophets and kills them. Hence, (4) God destroys Israel (the destruction of the northern kingdom: 722 BCE; the destruction of the southern kingdom: 587 BCE). Steck concludes that the tradents of this deuteronomistic view of history were Levitical members and later the Hasidian circles[9] and that this view was being circulated in the Jesus movement and affected in the forming of the Christian community in Galilee.[10]

It can be found in the internal evidence of Q that the Q community suffered preaching the gospel. The saying of Q 14:27, "He who does not take his cross and follow me cannot be my disciple," means clearly that to become the disciple of Jesus means to take his cross and that there is no true discipleship without suffering. At the time of the early church, the way of the disciples was followed by many persecutions. Q 6:22–23 and Q 11:47–51 attest that even the Q community overcame the fact of martyrdom beyond persecution and stood firm in testifying to the gospel. The Q community identifies the lives of the prophets in the Old Testament as its real lives and commits itself to preaching the gospel. The deuteronomistic view of history gives the discovery of self-identification to the Q community and is present later in the Matthean community (Matt 5:11–12; 23:29–32, 34–36). We can find the same self-identification of both the Q community

---

5. For more information on the stoic-cynic relationship with the Q community, see Mack, *Lost Gospel*. His cynic hypothesis was accepted by some minor scholars; however, main Q scholars like Robinson, Kloppenborg, Koester, and Hoffmann do not agree with him.

6. Robinson, "Building Block," 104–5.

7. Uro, "Sheep among the Wolves," 175–76.

8. For more information, see Steck, *Israel*, 60–80. As to the persecution of the prophets in the Old Testament, Steck is deeply affected by Fischel, "Martyr and Prophet," 265–80, 363–86.

9. Ibid., 197–205.

10. Ibid., 212. For Steck's application to the death of Jesus, see 278–79; for Steck's interpretation of Q, see ibid., 286–88.

and the Matthean community, by identifying with the former prophets of the Old Testament in the midst of suffering, persecution, and martyrdom.

Spirit

Now let us discuss Jesus' understanding of spirit in Q. There are two kinds of spirit in Q: spirit (Q 3:22; 4:1) and unclean spirit (Q 11:24–26). These are distinguished by the Holy Spirit and related to a real phenomenon and its characteristics in Q. Hence we must pay attention to Q in that both the spirit of God and the spirit of evil exist on earth, and they are expressed in terms of representing real phenomena in Q. It is true that the Q community as a Christian group lives in a *Sitz im Leben* of the spirit or the unclean spirit. This view is quite different from Pauline and Lukan pneumatology which regards the works of the spirit as charismatic. Before collecting Q, however, referring to the works of the spirit, Paul also mentions "the mind of the spirit" (Rom 8:27) or "the spirit of God" and "the spirit of the world" (1 Cor 2:11–12). We can evaluate this phenomenon in the fact that the church faced with the struggle of the spirit before the time when Q appeared in the world. Hence, dealing with Q, we can learn how Jesus takes this topic and how the Q community accepts the teaching of Jesus about the spirit. It seems that the Q community understands it in relation to the mission of the kingdom of God.

Unclean Spirit

Q 11:24–26 shows us an interesting story as follows: An unclean spirit has gone out of a person; it passes through waterless places seeking rest and finds none. And comes into a place where it is well swept and in order. Then it goes and brings with seven other spirits eviler than itself, and they enter and dwell there; and the last situation of that person becomes worse than the first. Referring to this passage, Dale C. Allison interprets it from the view of the kerygma of the kingdom of God.[11] If these passages are intended to preach the kingdom of God, who is the audience for this text? When we remember that on the basis of its genre Q 11 refers to the judgment and woe against this age, it seems that the audience is the Pharisees (Q 11:42, 39, 43, 46, 52). Matt 12:43–45 regards that the Matthean community gave the Pharisees this saying based on Q on the one hand, expands the possibility of the audience inserting scribes on the other (Matt 12:38).[12] The common content between Q and Matthew, however, is that the clean spirit means this age, the characteristic of the Pharisees and the false religious phenomena of Jewish leaders is shown in a parable. Here Jesus severely criticizes the Jewish leaders as the evil doers who load people with unbearable burdens

---

11. Allison, *Jesus Tradition*, 130.
12. Gundry, *Matthew*, 246.

Jesus' Understanding of Spirit

and themselves not moving their finger (Q 11:46) and as false leaders who are under the supervision of an unclean spirit and seven other spirits as well.

The "waterless places" means primarily wilderness and desert, but they can be compared to the wilderness where Jesus is led to be tempted by the devil in Q 4. Jesus eats nothing for forty days, he is hungry, and furthermore he is tempted three times by the devil. The unclean spirit is wandering in the wilderness and seeking a rest area, but it does not find any place and goes back to the person from which it came with the seven other spirits eviler than itself. If Jesus surrendered to the evil in the wilderness, if the unclean spirit found its resting place in Jesus, consequently it might be praised by the seven other spirits. John the Baptist preaches to an audience the gospel of repentance in the very same wilderness (Q 3:1–17; 7:18–24). Although many people come to be baptized, he says to the crowds, "Brood of vipers" and warns them, preaching the message of judgment. Hence the wilderness is "the place of spiritual combat."[13]

It seems likely that in Q Beelzebul is almost identified as Satan (Q 11:18–19). One of Satan's various names is Beelzebul, along with Asmodeus (Tob 3:8; T. Sol 5), Belial (Jub 1:20; 2 Cor 6:15), and Mastemah (Jub 10:8; 11:5; 48:15). That in Q 11:15, Jesus calls Beelzebul "ruler of demons" is compared with the Jewish traditions in 1QM 17:5–6; Jub 10:8; 48:15; T. Dan 5:6 (cf. John 14:30; 16:11; Eph 2:2). In Matthew, Satan is not distinguished from the devil, hence in Matt 4:10 the devil is called Satan (cf. Rev 12:9). In other words, it seems likely that in Matthew the distinction between Satan (Matt 4:10; 12:26; 16:23) and the devil (Matt 4:1, 5, 8, 11; 13:39; 25:41) and Beelzebul (Matt 10:25; 12:24, 27) cannot be made successfully. The demons are the agencies of Satan or Beelzebul. The Jesus of Q seems to consider that demons are possessed of unclean spirits (Q 11:20–26). In Q, thus, the demons with the unclean spirits are called evil spirits (Q 11:26) and later a demoniac is a person who is possessed by a demon (John 7:20; 8:48, 52; 10:20; Dialogue with Tripho 69).

What are the purposes of the demons with unclean spirits? Q testifies that their purposes are (1) to tempt (Q 4:2) and (2) to make worse the state of person than the first (Q 11:26). In other words, in Q, the devil is the one who tempts (Q 4:1) and the ruler of the demons (Q 11:25, Beelzebul), while the demons are "the strong one" (Q 11:21), "the one who is not with Jesus and is against him" (Q 11:23), and "the one who makes a person worse than at first" (Q 11:26). These are not worthwhile in the kingdom of God. Hence Jesus teaches us that when these demons with the unclean spirits are cast out by the finger of God, then the kingdom of God has come upon us (Q 11:20).

With this conclusion, the exorcism and the miracle stories of Jesus throughout Q cannot be understood at the level of the activity of exorcism and the miracles, but in the dimension of the mission of the kingdom of God.[14] For example, in the story

---

13. Havener, *Q*, 87.

14. Jeremias, *New Testament Theology*, 153–54. He regards this pericope [Matt 12:43–45 // Luke 11:24–26] is related to unclean spirits as a parable of the kingdom of God in the view of anti-exorcism. Cf. Jeremias, *Parable of Jesus*, 197–98.

of casting out a dumb demon, the dumb person speaks and the crowds are amazed (Q 11:14). In this story, I want to identify the speaking of the dumb demon in the preaching of the kingdom of God by the Q community. In my opinion, therefore, that the story that Jesus healed the dumb demon can be related to the mission of the kingdom of God in Q, is supported by the following story: The Beelzebul controversy. It should be note that without doubt, the Beelzebul controversy is deeply associated with the mission of the kingdom of God (Q 11:20).[15] The sayings of the spirit, which is to be discussed in the next chapter, is focused on the mission of the kingdom of God that the earthly Jesus was fundamentally interested in, for the kingdom of God has the central place among the teachings of Jesus.

Spirit

"Spirit" in Q is *ruach* in Hebrew, which means "wind" or "breath," and in Greek *pneuma*. When Jesus is baptized by John, the heaven is opened and the spirit comes upon him (Q 3:21–22). At this moment, the sonship of Jesus is announced.[16] After this event, Jesus is led by the spirit into the wilderness to be tempted by the devil and eats nothing for forty days, hence he is hungry (Q 4:1–2). These two events at the beginning of the ministry of the earthly Jesus happened primarily by means of the spirit from heaven. Who is the spirit descending from heaven? Does this spirit mean the spirit of God? If that is the spirit of God, does God announce the sonship of Jesus after the act of baptism and does God watch out for him throughout the temptations and hunger in the wilderness?

In order to confirm whether the spirit in Q is the spirit of God, first of all, we must pay attention to the following expressions: "the spirit of God" in Matt 12:28 and "the finger of God" in Luke 11:20. Before determining which reading the Q text originally took, to note in judging between "the finger of God" and "the spirit of God," it is very important to note that this passage is a central key to understanding the reality of the spirit in Q. Unfortunately, scholarly opinions are equally divided determining between "the finger of God" and "the spirit of God."

Criticizing the possibility of "the finger of God" in the original Q text, James D. G. Dunn suggests that Matthew just follows the expression of "the spirit of God" in Q. For the reason for this, pointing out the conflicts between Jesus and the enthusiasts in Matt 7:22–23, he concludes that "that Matthew replacing 'finger' with 'Spirit' is hardly as cogent since the motif of the Spirit is less prominent in Matthew"[17] unlike Luke, although the enthusiasts oppose Jesus overvaluing their charismatic powers. When we think carefully about the expression "the finger of God" written in Exod 8:19, we

---

15. Jacobson, *First Gospel*, 65, 233. He insists that the miracles in Q are related to the kingdom of God (Q 11:20; 10:8–9. cf. Q 10:23–24).

16. Segundo, *Historical Jesus of the Synoptics*, 86–103.

17. Dunn, *Jesus and the Spirit*, 45.

can find that Matthew regards Jesus as a New Moses and the Sermon on the Mount as a new law. Hence it is hardly likely that Matthew would change "finger" to "spirit" in Q and Matthew could not miss in the book of Exodus the expression of the "finger." In other words, Dunn concludes that Matthew accepts the tradition of "the spirit of God" without any correction since the "spirit" is originally transmitted in Q.[18] This conclusion of Dunn, however, is faced by a serious challenge, because this passage cannot be dealt with as a simple story of an exorcism or miracle[19] and Matthew alters Q's "finger" to "spirit" on the basis of the possibility of a Matthean redaction.

In Matt 12:8–12, Jesus heals the man with a shriveled hand on the Sabbath, in Matt 12:15, Jesus heals all the sick, and in Matt 12:16–21, Jesus approves his activity of the healing quoting the passages of Isa 42:1–3 and Isa 61:1. After that, he heals the dumb demon (Matt 12:22), and then there is the controversy of Beelzebul (Matt 12:23–29). Here we must explain the relationship between "my spirit" in Matt 12:18 and "the spirit of God" in Matt 12:28. Quoting the passages of Isaiah, Matthew seems to be persuaded by "my spirit," "the spirit of God" in Matt 12:16–21. When Matthew quotes the story of a dumb demon in Q 11:14 and the Beelzebul controversy in Q 11:15–22, it is likely that Matthew distinguishes the power of God from that of the demon on the basis of the theme of "power" and he alters "the finger of God" in Q 11:20[20] to "the spirit of God" in Matt 12:28, in order to harmonize in the theme of "spirit" compared to Matt 12:18.

In contrast, Luke faithfully preserves "the spirit of God" from the original Q text. Accepting the Q tradition of the story of the dumb demon in Luke 11:14 and the Beelzebul controversy in Luke 11:15–22, Luke uses a typically redactional expression, "the Holy Spirit" in Luke 11:13. Hence in this context "the finger of God" in Luke 11:20 might not be altered to "the spirit of God." Nevertheless, it is quite possible that Luke accepts the tradition of "the finger of God" without alteration and preserves it on the basis of the Q text.

As mentioned above, Dunn's suggestion of "the spirit of God" for the reconstruction of Q is hardly likely. The most important thing, however, is a question whether there is any difference in meaning between "the finger of God" in Q and "the spirit of God" in Matthew. When we consider the tradition of the Old Testament, we are sure that the expression of "the finger of God" means primarily "the hand of God" (Exod 3:20; 8:19). According to Dunn, it is likely that all the expressions can be understood as "the power of God," in disregarding the problem of whether Matthew alters "the finger of God" in Q to "the spirit of God" on the basis of the Matthean context, and whether Luke preserves the expression of Q without any Lukan context.[21] In the Old Testament, "the spirit" and "the hand of the Lord" (or "the hand of God") are syn-

18. Ibid., 45.
19. Ibid., 44–53. He discusses this passage on the basis of "the power of exorcism."
20. Allison, *Jesus Tradition*, 124.
21. Dunn, *Jesus and the Spirit*, 46, 374.

onyms (Ezek 3:14; 8:1–3; 37:1; Ps 8:3; 33:6; 1 Kgs 18:12; 2 Kgs 2:16; 1 Chron 28:12, 19; Isa 8:11).[22] In the case of these passages, "the spirit of God" or "the hand of God" connotes activities of the power of God. In other words, the spirit of God has been understood in the miracle power of God or the miracle itself.[23] Hence the spirit of God, the finger of God, the hand of God, and the power of God is the same as the expression of the Hebrews who wanted to portray the great activity of God.[24] Q, Matthew, and Luke show that the exorcism is due to the great power of God. That God stood at the back of exorcism, therefore, is a basic point of faith in Q.

It is likely that in the Q community the spirit is the spirit of God, the finger of God is a synonym of the spirit of God, and all the expressions are concepts representing the power of God. When we regard the spirit as the spirit of God, we can understand that the spirit announced Jesus as the son of God and descended from heaven at the time of Jesus' baptism. The Q community also describes that when Jesus is tempted by the devil in the wilderness, God is with him in the background of the event. In other words, the Q community regards the baptism and the temptations of Jesus as connected to the mission of the kingdom of God prepared thoroughly by the spirit of God.

We can understand that the Q community is based on the mission of the kingdom of God provided by the spirit, the spirit of God. In other words, that the teaching of Jesus is that when the demons with the unclean spirits are cast out the kingdom of God has come upon them, and that the earthly Jesus begins his public mission after the baptism and the temptation led by the spirit, all this would encourage the Q community in being devoted to the kingdom of God and that it all is designed by the spirit of God.

The Holy Spirit

The Q community would interpret spirit clearly as the Holy Spirit since it understands the spirit in the perspective of the kingdom of God, although in Q the term "the Holy Spirit" is only used twice in the sermon of John the Baptist (Q 3:16) and the preaching of Jesus (Q 12:10). Ivan Havener concludes that these sayings are to be understood in an apocalyptic perspective,[25] while many scholars insist that they can be understood as the Holy Spirit in eschatological aspect and that such a perspective affected the writers

---

22. Conzelmann, *Outline of the Theology*, 38. He argues that "in the connection with Judaism, the first mention is of the spirit of God, but then there follows mention of the spirit of Christ, or of the Lord." Cf. Dunn, *Jesus and the Spirit*, 46, 373.

23. Conzelmann, *Outline of the Theology*, 182–84.

24. For this understanding, Alan Richardson suggests that Christ is not identified with the spirit of God as he is with the wisdom of God, the word of God, and the power of God, although in the Old Testament the spirit is a personification of the divine activity of the same order as the wisdom, the word, and the power. Cf. Richardson, *Introduction to the Theology*, 121.

25. Havener, *Q*, 87–88.

of the New Testament.[26] One can probably say that in Q the spirit is characterized by an apocalyptic figure, since the spirit is a figure descending from heaven and such a figure identifies with the Jewish apocalyptic one. In Q 3:16, however, John the Baptist says that he baptizes with water but "the coming one" will baptize with "the Holy Spirit" and "fire." Here we can find that John identifies "the coming one" with Jesus. We must pay attention to the relationship between Jesus and the Holy Spirit. We cannot identify the spirit of God with Jesus in that the spirit or the Holy Spirit can be identified with the spirit of God or the power of God. Rather comparing water and the Holy Spirit/fire, John the Baptist regards Jesus as a judgmental figure of the end time in an eschatological perspective.[27] Nevertheless, the Spirit and fire are not the Judge itself who is coming in the end time. Rather, John the Baptist says that Jesus is coming after him, Jesus is stronger than he, and Jesus will baptize with the Holy Spirit and fire. According to the sermon of John, therefore, Jesus is "the coming one."

"The coming one" is presented three times in the Q text (Q 3:16; 7:18; 13:35). This designation is a kind of a christological title[28] and is addressed through the mouth of Jesus himself, John the Baptist, and his disciples. In connection with John, Q 3:16 is his sermon pointing out Jesus as "the coming one" and Q 7:18 is his question sending his disciples to Jesus as to whether he is truly "the coming one." Here the content of both focus on the sermon in the wilderness and the question of prison do not match. Hence we must feel a kind of an eschatological insight that the Q community would face in its contemporary time: John, his disciples, and even the Q community seem to expect "the coming one" as the Judge. He will judge with the Holy Spirit and fire. Q 13:34–35 can be interpreted in that the Q community has an eschatological expectation, waiting for the coming one in the name of the Lord and worrying about the imminent destruction of Jerusalem. Here we can make sure that "the coming one" has in the context of the Lament over Jerusalem come to refer to "an eschatological figure,"[29] in the eschatological sense Jesus should indicate who he himself is, although we cannot find any term "Messiah" in Q.

EPILOGUE

This eschatological insight is presented in the relationship between the Holy Spirit and Jesus within the Q community, when it is related to the word against the Son of Man and the one who blasphemes against the Holy Spirit in Q 12:10. Here we must pay attention

---

26. Richardson, *Introduction to the Theology*, 106–7. He argues that the thoroughly eschatological conception of the Holy Spirit is found everywhere in the New Testament and the early church considers herself to be living in the latter days, the age of the fulfillment of the prophecies concerning the pouring forth of God's Spirit upon all flesh (Acts 2:16–18; 10:45; Rom 5:5; Gal 4:6; Titus 3:6; etc.).

27. Jacobson, *First Gospel*, 84–85. He insists that both the spirit and fire are agents of judgment. Here one thing is important: according to him, the spirit is not "the Holy Spirit," but simply "wind."

28. Robinson, "Sayings Gospel Q," 362.

29. Ibid., 363.

to the designation of the "Son of Man." The "Son of Man" is a kind of a circumlocution and a third person in its expression that Jesus calls himself (Q 6:22; 7:34; 9:58; 11:30; 12:10; 17:24, 26, 30). In Q 12:10, Jesus is just called a normal person, hence whoever says a word against the Son of Man will be forgiven. But whoever blasphemes against the Holy Spirit will not be forgiven, since the Holy Spirit is coming from heaven, God, and thus it is divine. Here it is quite possible that the Holy Spirit is thoroughly recognized in the divine, while Jesus is merely recognized in a person. We must pay attention to this saying from the mouth of Jesus, since this saying presents not only the humility of Jesus, but also the relationship between Jesus and the Holy Spirit.

In Q 12:10, Jesus teaches the Q community not to blaspheme against the Holy Spirit, since it is sanctified by God and the Holy Spirit is the spirit of God and it brings to man the will of God. In this passage, Jesus identifies the will of God as the will of the Holy Spirit and teaches us not to go against the will of both. We can learn Jesus' intention in acquainting one with true commitment to God in this passage.[30] In Q, this passage is located between the woe sayings against the Pharisees (Q 11:42–52) and the negative saying against the Gentiles (Q 12:30). In this context, the Q community is spoken of as a true believing community, as a Christian community and obeying the will of the Holy Spirit. Since this passage presupposes knowledge of the sin of blasphemy against the Holy Spirit, we can interpret that the Q community understands this saying in an eschatological sense.

---

30. Jonnes, *Study of Spirituality*, 65.

XII

The Eschatology of the Q Community

PROLOGUE

THIS CHAPTER SEEKS TO understand the eschatology of the Sayings Gospel Q in relation to the Q community. I do not view the eschatology of the Q community in an apocalyptic perspective, since there is no apocalyptic world view in the eschatology of Q and I cannot find any apocalyptic figures in Q. Rather, the Q text has an eschatological tendency due to the influence of the idea of imminent judgment affected by Jesus. Under the milieu of persecution, the Q community as a Christian group retrospects the sayings of Jesus regarding the imminent judgment. Hence the Q community outwardly pronounces the judgment of God against the Pharisees, and at the same time they inwardly search the identity of the Q community in order to build up the inner solidarity of their community. However, when the Q community has to face the delay of the parousia of the Son of Man, they have been affected by this eschatological motif on the basis of a non-apocalyptic view of the earthly Jesus. This non-apocalyptic eschatology in the Q community also affects the eschatology of the Gospel of Matthew and the Gospel of Luke. I would like to interpret the sayings of Q 10:9 and 16:16 in an eschatological perspective, not from an apocalyptic view, since the phrasing suggests an understanding of eschatological history on the basis of a non-apocalyptic understanding of history and the kingdom of God. I would conclude that the characteristics of the eschatology in Q are non-apocalyptic eschatological and that the eschatology of the Q community has the dual meaning of the present and futuristic aspects. Whereas the futuristic eschatology in Q announces judgment against the Jews and comforts the Q community with a message of hope, the present eschatology encourages the Q community to live in responsibility to the realized kingdom of God.

PART 2: THEOLOGY OF Q AND THE GOSPELS

The Q Community and Eschatology

Howard C. Kee insists that the whole of the Q tradition is eschatologically oriented."[1] He refers to Lukan materials and classifies them relating to the eschatology of Q as follows:

Discipleship: Its Privileges and Trials

Luke 6:20–49; 9:57–62; 10:2–20; 10:21–23; 11:2–13; 12:51–53; 14:16–24; 14:26–27; 16:13; 17:3–6

The Prophet as God's Messenger

Luke 3:7–9, 16–17; 11:49–51; 12:2–3; 12:4–10, 11–12, 42–46; 13:34–35; 16:16–17

Repentance or Judgment

Luke 11:33–36; 11:39–48, 52; 12:54–59; 13:14–29; 17:23–30, 35, 37; 19:12–13, 15–26

Jesus as Revealer and Agent of God's Rule

Luke 4:2b–12; 7:18–35; 10:24; 11:14–22; 13:20–21; 15:4–7; 22:28–30[2]

Unfortunately, these passages referring to the Q material excessively exaggerate the eschatology of Q. In fact, the International Q Project excluded many Q passages that he suggested for the Q reconstruction.[3]

This chapter wants to understand the eschatology of Q in relation to the Q community. When the Q text was transmitted, the Q community residing in the upper Galilee was interested in collecting the sayings of Jesus rather than the narratives of the traditions regarding the passion, death, resurrection, and ascension of Jesus because the earliest believing community witnessed those traditions concerning Jesus.

Furthermore, (1) Since the Q community as the believing community started on the basis of the facts of the resurrection of Jesus has already witnessed and experienced the events of cross and resurrection of Jesus, it presupposed everything of the death and resurrection of Jesus in its present faith and life.[4] (2) Since the traditions such as the passion narrative, the resurrection narrative, the miracle source, the parables, the birth narrative, the apocalyptic discourses, etc. had already been transmitted when the Q text was collected, the Q community initially collected the in-danger-of-

---

1. Kee, *Christian Origins*, 135. On the basis of the eschatology of Q, he regards Jesus as "an eschatological prophet" (106, 135) or "the charismatic leader" (135).

2. For more information, see the above book, 106, 133–43.

3. For the reconstructed Q text, see *Journal of Biblical Literature* 111 (1992) 500–508; *JBL* 112 (1993) 500–506; *JBL* 113 (1994) 495–99; *JBL* 114 (1995) 475–85; *JBL* 116 (1997) 521–25.

4. Cf. Laufen, *Die Doppelüberlieferungen*, 386: He concludes that the characteristics of the Q text are transmitting the traditions of Jesus after Good Friday presupposes the theological insights of the death and resurrection of Jesus.

getting-lost sayings traditions of Jesus, rather than represent those known traditions. (3) Since the disciples who were the eyewitnesses were passing away one by one and unfortunately the tradents of the Jesus sayings were disappearing, the Q community independently brought into being as a collection the sayings gospel of Jesus in the literary wisdom sayings tradition. (4) Because the collections of the Jesus sayings were insufficient for a biographical witness to Jesus, the Q community finally elaborated a biographical cast"[5] collecting the temptation story (Q 4:1–13) of Jesus.

Likewise, the eschatology of Q is also related to the milieu of the Q community. We should not try to understand the eschatology of Q in an apocalyptic perspective, since the eschatology of Q does not reflect in itself an apocalyptic world view and many apocalyptic figures are not represented in it.[6] Rather, Q is affected by the eschatological tendency because of the influence of the idea of the imminent judgment derived from John the Baptist and Jesus. Remembering the sermon of the imminent judgment under the milieu of persecution, the Q community was building up a firm foundation for a believing community, and was announcing the judgment of God against the external attacks of the Pharisees, and was finding inwardly the inner identity of the Q community. But the change of situation caused by the delay of the *parousia* offered the Q community an eschatological motif. Hence the Q community would have a chance to develop strongly such eschatology.[7] This eschatology of Q affected the Gospel of Matthew and the Gospel of Luke. Q 16:16 shows that the Q community understands history in an eschatological perspective, rather than an apocalyptic one, and that in the teaching the law and the prophets . . . until John. From then the kingdom of God has suffered violence and the violent take it by force, the Q community suggests an eschatological understanding of history in relation to the reign of God and its expansion on the non-apocalyptic understanding of history.

In relation to the saying of Q 16:16, Matthew 11:13 implies that the law and the prophets have a prophetic function, inserting the verb *propheteumein*; likewise, Luke 16:16 shows a missionary concern by using the verb *euaggelizesthai* on the basis of an eschatological consciousness of history.[8]

---

5. Robinson, "Jesus from Easter," 22.

6. Jacobson, "Apocalyptic and Q," 412, 418–19. Although he advocates the non-apocalyptic background of Q, he insists that the "Son of Man" designation of Q 12:8–9 can be understood in an apocalyptic setting. In my opinion, however, it can be understood in an eschatological setting because it encourages the Q community on the basis of an eschatological dimension and teaches us to follow Jesus instead of denying him.

7. Mattill, *Luke and the Last Things*, 13. Specifically, Mattill understands the saying of Luke 16:16 in the concept of De-Apocalypticizing of Luke-Acts. For more study in detail, see his book, 13–25.

8. So, "Sabbath Controversy of Jesus," 20–21.

Imminent Judgment

In the eschatology of Q, first of all, the idea of imminent judgment offers the Q community an eschatological motif. Unlike what is exhibited here, the judgment idea of apocalyptic means the great catastrophe of human history and the great reversal of human order. The judgment idea of Q has two faces of a coin and it is as follows:

(1) It sends Jews a message of warning and requests repentance.

(2) It sends the Q community a message of hope and encourages it.

Hence the judgment idea of Q can be understood in an eschatological perspective because it has a message of warning and hope.

The eschatology of the Q text begins with the message of imminent judgment. Q 3:9, "Even now the ax is laid to the root of the trees," presupposes that judgment does not take place in the future, but is already at hand in an eschatological sense. Q 3:16b–17 says that the one coming after John the Baptist is stronger than Jesus, Jesus' winnowing fork is in his hand, and he will clear his threshing floor and gather the wheat into his granary, but the chaff he will burn with unquenchable fire. This expresses a strictly serious aspect of judgment.[9] Here the "coming one" clearly indicates an eschatological figure.[10] In Q 12:51–59 Jesus says that he has not come to bring peace but a sword and has come to separate family members (Q 12:51, 53) and judgment has already been taking place (Q 12:56, 58). Hence one should recognize the *kairos* of the judgment of God (Q 12:56) and prepare in order not to be judged (Q 12:58). The reason why this eschatological judgment is announced is only to encourage the audience to repent their sins (Q 3:8; 10:13–15). Q 13:28 talks about the Jews who lose their chance of repentance and weep and gnash their teeth in the judgment court, and gives an eschatological message of warning.

Here the question whether the hour of the eschatological judgment can be suggested is raised and the response is that Jesus teaches us that the Son of Man is coming at an hour you do not expect" (Q 12:40; cf. 12:46). Although the judgment is at hand, the hour at which it is coming is as if a thief was coming (Q 12:39). The imminent judgment is like the days of Noah (Q 17:26–27). Here "the day of the Son of Man" (Q 17:24, 26, 30)[11] retains something of the symbol of the days of Noah, i.e., the days are at hand but nobody recognizes them. Thus the reason that Jesus is speaking of the imminent judgment is to prepare the audience for it.

Although the judgment is imminent, it does not matter to the Q community because although the message of judgment comes as a warning against the Jews and

---

9. Arnal, "Redactional Fabrication," 170.

10. Ibid., 171–74. The passages of the coming one in Q (3:16; 7:18–23; 13:34–35) are related to Mal 3:1–2.

11. Luke uses the expressions "one day" or "one of the days of the Son of Man" (Luke 5:17; 8:22; 17:22; 20:1), these are reflected Semantic expressions. Cf. Black, "Aramaic Dimension," 243; Jeremias, *Sprache des Lukasevangeliums*, 267.

the people of "this age" however it comes as a hope and comfort for the Q community. Q 17:34–35 is a saying about the reality of the two dimensions at the time of judgment, i.e., one is taken and one is left. This teaches the Q community in relation to an eschatological judgment and the meaning of salvation. This passage is placed into an apocalyptic setting in Matt 24:41 and the context of Q just shows an eschatological setting regarding to an eschatological judgment in the idea of selection or discard.

Furthermore, the Jesus of Q often mentions eschatological realities in different dimensions. (1) Three cities in Galilee have been judged because they have not repented (Q 10:13, 15). Tyre and Sidon shall be tolerable in the judgment (Q 10:13–14). (2) The faithful and wise servant does not worry about the delay of his Lord (Q 12:42). The faithless servant shall be judged on a day when his Lord returns (Q 12:45–46). (3) Enter through the narrow door for many will seek to enter (Q 23:23). Few will find the door (Q 13:24). (4) The evil doers shall be rejected (Q 13:25–27, 28b). Many shall come from the east and the west and recline with Abraham and Isaac and Jacob in the kingdom of God (Q 13:29, 28a).

These different realities are based on the idea of imminent judgment. These could be interpreted to mean hope and comfort for the Q community because they criticize the Jews, protect the Q community, and encourage its identity.

Delay of Parousia

The eschatology of Q faced a new challenge in the context of the delay of Jesus' *parousia*. Although the eschatology of Q begins with an imminent expectation of the end, in a context of the *parousia*'s delay, as long as with the passing of time, people are asked to prepare a delayed *parousia*. Q 12:39–40, 42–46 and Q 17:23–24, 37, 26–27, 30, 34–35 attest to the strong eschatological faith of the Q community.[12] The day of *parousia* in Q cannot be understood in an apocalyptic setting because the world view of apocalypse expects an apocalyptic end beyond history in disconnection with human history. But Q regards the day of *parousia* as an eschatological event of Jesus and understands that it shall take place in human history. Many scholars argue that those passages talk about the milieu of the *parousia*'s delay, not the idea of imminent judgment.[13] These passages have a common source in that the Son of Man will come on a day when nobody expects it in the milieu of the *parousia*'s delay (Q 12:40; 17:24, 26, 30). Hence Paul Hoffmann often says there is a connection between the *parousia*'s delay (*Parusieverzgerung*) and the imminent expectation (*Naherwartung*).[14]

---

12. Tuckett, Q, 155–60.
13. Lührmann, *Redaktion der Logienquelle*, 69–71; Schulz, Q, 50, 268–322; Hoffmann, *Studien*, 37–50; Catchpole, *Quest for Q*, 214–17; Tuckett, Q, 156.
14. Hoffmann, *Studien*, 13–50.

Now we are going to talk about the Greek word *xronizo*[15] of Q 12:45 in the direct milieu of the *parousia*'s delay. In the parable of the faithful servant and the faithless servant Jesus teaches us that the servant says in his heart, my Lord is delayed, and begins to beat the servants and eats and drinks and gets drunk. This faithless servant is compared to the people of this generation, who does not prepare for the coming of the Son of Man. The meaning of only one use of the word *xronizo* in Q is disclosed by the abrupt hopeless actions of the faithless servant who behaved, seemingly, to give up all hope of the coming of his Lord.[16] For the faithless servant the milieu of the *parousia*'s delay just does not mean delay, but the forsaking of all hope. Hence the parable of Jesus asks one to not give up the hope of the coming of the Lord, but prepare wisely his coming (Q 12:46). John S. Kloppenborg suggests that the saying of "my Lord is delayed" (Q 12:45) cannot be anything other than an allusion to the delay of the "day" of the Son of Man.[17]

The consciousness of the *parousia*'s delay could be placed into the eschatology of the Q community as its most fundamental motive.[18] Comparing the days of Noah in Q 17:26–27 to the days of Lot in Luke 17:28–29, scholars used to study these twin sayings as pericopes of God's judgment.[19] When the Q text is reconstructed by the IQP, however, Luke 17:28–29 is excluded from the Q text because the days of Noah in Q 17:26–27 is understood as a symbol of the Son of Man. Of course, the word for the *parousia*'s delay is not used in Q 17:26–27. But people ate, drank,[20] married, and were given in marriage in the days of Noah. This motive is the same as in the story that the servant does not know the time of the coming of the Son of Man, and that he eats, drinks, gets drunk, in Q 12:45. In these two passages, the days of the Son of Man and the days of Noah have an imminent eschatological motive. Hence the two passages hold the consciousness of the *parousia*'s delay as a basic motive because they presuppose that judgment does not take place right now and that it has been delayed for a while. Q 17:26, therefore, says that the days of the Son of Man are the same as the ones of Noah, remembering the sayings of Q 12:40, 46 that the day of the Son of Man is delayed but it will come on an unexpected day. For this reason, the *parousia* of the Son of Man is compared with the coming of the thief (Q 12:39) and the coming of the flood (Q 17:27).[21]

---

15. This word is used in LXX Exod 32:1 for the first time in the Old Testament. Deut 23:21; Hab 2:3; Tobit 10:4 also uses it. Hab 2:3 is used in Heb 10:37 of the New Testament again.

16. Catchpole, *Quest for Q*, 215–16: The behavior described in Q 12:45b is not that of someone who expects the coming to occur, even though that occurrence has been delayed: it is the conduct of someone who regards the delay as so great that the coming is no longer envisaged at all."

17. Kloppenborg, "Jesus and the Parables of Jesus in Q," 293.

18. Hoffmann, *Studien*, 44–45.

19. Lührmann, *Redaktion der Logienquelle*, 75–83; Catchpole, *Quest for Q*, 248.

20. The image of eating and drinking is usually negative in Q (7:33–34; 12:45; 13:26; 17:27).

21. Hoffmann, *Studien*, 47.

In Q 19:12–26, Jesus refers to the parable of the Minas (or Talents) about the coming of the master (Q 19:15, 23). And here the coming of the master is related to the *parousia* of the Son of Man. If so, we can infer that Jesus presupposes an unexpected circumstance facing the servants in this parable. Paul Hoffmann suggests that the parable of the talents is composed by circulative motifs such as the imminent expectation, the judgment, and the Judge Lord.[22] The imminent expectation reminds one that the Q community as the audience of the parable must follow the life of Jesus and prepare thoroughly for the day of the *parousia* when the Judge, Lord, comes and judges the servants according to their works.

In Q, thus "the days of the Son of Man" indicates the days of the *parousia* of the Son of Man. The Q community in an imminent expectation of the *parousia* is waiting for a new milieu of hope and comfort, and prepares wisely for the imminent coming of "the days." This motive must later on influence the Matthean community and the Lukan community.[23] Matt 24:36–44 // Luke 12:35–40; Matt 24:45–51 // Luke 12:42–46; Matt 25:14–30 // Luke 19:12–27 have the motive of the delay of the *parousia* and teach their own communities to prepare for the *parousia* of the Lord which comes on an unexpected day. Dieter Lührmann's evaluation is that Matt 25:1–13 // Luke 12:35–38; Matt 7:13–14, 22–23; 25:31–46 // Luke 13:24–27 are to be attributed to the Q text and suggests a new interpretation of the eschatology in Q on the basis of the delay of the *parousia*.[24] In this sense, Matt 24:27, 37, 38–39 // Luke 17:24, 26–27, 30 teach the Q community to make a thorough preparation in spite of all the delays of the *parousia*.[25] Hence Q 12:39–46 becomes the basic source for the eschatological discourse in Luke 12:35–48,[26] and Q 17:23–24, 37, 26–27, 30, 34–35 becomes also the basic source for the core passages, verses 22–37, of the eschatological motive in Luke 17:20—18:8.[27]

Present or Future?

When the eschatology of Q begins with an idea of imminent expectation and encounters the milieu of the delay of the *parousia*, it encourages the Q community to remember and prepare thoroughly for the *parousia* of the Son of Man. Here is a confusing matter: Is the eschatology of Q (1) futuristic or (2) present?

In relation to the futuristic eschatology of Q, the saying of Q 12:8–9 is often discussed by scholars. The saying about those who acknowledge or deny Jesus, that

---

22. Ibid., 42.
23. Grässer, *Problem*, 218–20, 268–322; Hoffmann, *Studien*, 43.
24. Lührmann, *Redaktion der Logienquelle*, 69–71.
25. Ibid., 75, 86–89. He guesses that the milieu of the delay of the *parousia* is in between 50 and 60 AD, though people have an imminent expectation for it.
26. Carroll, *Response*, 53–60.
27. Ibid., 71–96; Schnackenburg, "Eschatologische Abschnitt," 213–34.

they will acknowledge and deny, reflects implicitly a futuristic expectation.[28] In Q 13:23–30, the sayings that (1) many will seek to enter the narrow door but few will find it (v. 24), that (2) someone begins to knock but the householder will answer her/him (v. 25), I do not know you (vv. 25, 27), that (3) many shall come from the east and the west (v. 29), and that (4) people will be thrown out and they will weep and gnash their teeth (v. 28), etc. are about futuristic eschatology: "The decisive moment is clearly thought of as coming soon."[29] When Jesus also tells the parable of a mustard seed (Q 13:18–19) or the parable of leaven (Q 13:20–21), he does not simply speak of a change of nature or natural growth.[30] Rather, Jesus speaks about the reign of the almighty God in order to explain the eschatological future of the kingdom of God. We can find an eschatological future in the parable a mustard seed of Jesus (Q 13:18–19) in that now the kingdom of God is small but later on it grows and becomes a splendid cedar of Lebanon (Ezek 17:22–23). Likewise, the teachings of the coming of the Son of Man in Q 12:39–40; 17:24, 26–27, 30 go beyond the dimension in which the *parousia* simply means the hope of the Q community and has the further dimension of a futuristic characteristic of eschatology.[31] Q 11:31–32 and 22:30 also mention the judgment of the Jews and the Q people sitting on thrones in order to judge the Jews in a futuristic eschatological perspective.

Nevertheless, we must not ignore a present aspect of Q's eschatology because that present-oriented material consistently precedes the futuristic eschatological material in Q. The sayings of Q 12:51, 53 (cf. 14:26) are not of some future apocalyptic travail but have a present eschatological implication.[32] The coming of Jesus shall shake the human order and the world view of people because he challenges the present life of people. Q 10:2–12 mentions the sending of laborers of the harvest (Q 10:2) in order to preach the present and/or realized kingdom of God (Q 10:9): The kingdom of God has come near to you. Here the verb *eggizo* is used, which includes the meaning of the adverb *eggus*,[33] and suggests a present meaning of the eschatology of Q. Of course, *eggika* of Q 10:9 is a form of perfect tense, although the term is debated among current scholars, whether it is understood as having a meaning of "come near," but it usually seems to be understood as having a meaning of suggesting a realized eschatology

---

28. Tuckett, *Q*, 144.
29. Ibid., 145.
30. Kloppenborg, *Symbolic Eschatology*, 297; Mack, *Lost Gospel*, 124.
31. Jacobson, "Apocalyptic and Q," 415; Tuckett, *Q*, 156. David Seeley also insists that "the evidence directs us toward seeing futuristic eschatology as a late development within the trajectories of the group behind Q." Seeley, "Futuristic Eschatology," 152.
32. Jacobson, "Apocalyptic and Q," 415.
33. This adverb is used 32 times in the New Testament (Matt 24:32, 33; 26:18; Mark 6:36; 13:28, 29; Luke 19:11; 21:30, 31; John 2:13; 3:23; 6:4, 19, 23; 7:2; 11:18, 54, 55; 19:20, 42; Acts 1:12; 9:38; 27:8; Rom 10:8; 13:11; Eph 2:13, 17; Phil 4:5; Heb 6:8; 8:13; Rev 1:3; 22:10). Specifically, *eggizo* and *eggika* in Luke-Acts seem to be exchangeable in meaning for each other for our understanding of present eschatology. Luke-Acts uses the verb *eggizo* as favorite terms 24 times, but the verb is used only 10 times outside Luke-Acts.

because Q 11:20 says that if by "the finger of God"[34] Jesus casts out demons, then the kingdom of God has come. In Q Jesus has already healed the centurion's boy (Q 7:1–10) and cast out the dumb demon (Q 11:14a), through this miracle power Jesus preaches here to the crowds (Q 11:14b), the Beelzebul controversy and the sermon of the kingdom of God (Q 11:20). The demons are still acting, but Jesus speaks of the realized kingdom of God.

Another term used in Q 11:20 is *phthano*. This term has a close meaning of *eggizo* in a sense of the present kingdom of God. Although Paul the Apostle uses *phthano* in the meanings of "precede" (1 Thess 4:15), "come to someone" (2 Cor 10:14), or "attain" (Rom 9:31; Phil 3:16; 1 Thess 2:16), *phthano* in Matt 12:28 and Luke 11:20 are derived from Q which is used in the same meaning as in the Old Testament (LXX Jud 20:34, 42; LXX Dan 4:28; LXX Eccl 8:14).[35]

EPILOGUE

Q 16:16 shows the present eschatology of Q in that "the law and the prophets . . . until John. From then the kingdom of God has suffered violence and the violent take it by force." Here Jesus disagrees with the apocalyptic understanding of history which demands an interruption of human history, that has an eschatological understanding of history which demands a continuity of human history under the sovereignty of God, and says that the kingdom of God, which is already inaugurated (or/and realized), and has suffered violence through Jesus in succession to the law and the prophets.

In Q, therefore, present eschatology and futuristic eschatology seem to be two faces of a coin. As the demons were cast out, the realized eschatology is like the present. Nevertheless, the kingdom of God will still be fulfilled in a future time[36] since the demons are acting though the kingdom of God has already been realized.

---

34. The finger of God is identified with the expressions the hands of God, the power of God, or the spirit of God in the interrelationship of the Hebrew concepts (Ezek 3:14; 8:1–3; 37:1; Ps 8:3; 33:6; 1 Kgs 18:12; 2 Kgs 2:16; 1 Chr 28:12, 19; Isa 8:11).

35. Mattill, *Luke and the Last Things*, 168–76.

36. Schweizer, "Significance of Eschatology," 3.

XIII

A Tradition-History Development of the Meals

PROLOGUE

A SUSPICION FREQUENTLY ENTERTAINED in scholarship is that the issues of most significance in early conflicts between Christians and various forms of Judaism were questions related to meal practice. Meals were apparently very important occasions. The main references are: Christ cult ritual (1 Cor 11:23–26; 10:14–22; Mark 14:22–25; cf. Acts 2:43–47); miracle chains (Mark 6:30–44; 8:1–10; cf. John 6); pronouncement stories (Mark 2:15–17; 2:18–22; 2:23–28; 7:1–23; 14:3–9); the issue between Paul and the pillars (Gal 2:11–21); other signs of conflict over meals (1 Cor 8:1–13; 11:27–34; Acts 10:9–16; 11:1–10; 15:29; Col 2:21); and the meal ritual in the Didache (Did 9; 10).[1]

This chapter is to examine the Lord's Supper in Mark's literary style and strategy, and to evaluate it in the context of the interpretation of Mark, especially, the failure of the disciples to understand Jesus. Therefore, this chapter will show the feather of the Lord's Supper in the Markan narrative. And this chapter will consider the content and function of the Eucharistic prayers presented by the Didache; it will show that the thanksgiving prayers in Didache 9 and 10 are either actual Eucharistic prayers or liturgical scripts. At the same time, it will be necessary to compare the Lord's Supper in Mark with the pre-Pauline supper tradition, 1 Cor 11:23–25, and the prayers of an early Christian community, the Didache 9 and 10. Therefore, this chapter is in connection with a study of a tradition-history development of the meals.

The Lord's Supper and Discipleship in Mark 14:12–25

It is necessary to turn to discipleship in Mark closely connected with the Lord's Supper. Many scholars have noted the function of discipleship in Mark.[2]

---

1. Mack, *Myth of Innocence*, 80.
2. For examples, see Weeden, *Mark*; Kelber, *Kingdom*; Kelber, *Passion*; Tannehill, "Disciples in

A Tradition-History Development of the Meals

The theme of the failure of discipleship has generated considerable speculation about the relationship between disciples portrayed in Mark's gospel and disciples in Mark's community. The text of Mark's gospel will be used to trace briefly the theme of failure of discipleship. Vernon K. Robbins[3] connects the disciples' misunderstanding of the feeding stories and connects this with the Last Supper. However, he does not develop all of the connections between discipleship and food, but just links the Christian meal with Jesus' suffering and death and resurrection into heaven.

The Eucharistic dramatization portrayed by Mark 14:12–25 reflects Markan theology.[4] The preparation (14:12–16) forecasts Passover Day as the period of time in which the meal, arrest, trial, and crucifixion occur; the meal (14:17–21) delineates betrayal as the act of a disciple who fulfills scripture but evokes the judgment of God; and the bread and cup (14:22–25) interpret the death of Jesus and anticipate his return. Above each scene is in Mark's literary compositional techniques.

Mark 14:12–16 is initiated by the disciples as they ask. These verses hark back to the first feeding story (6:30–44) in Mark. When the disciples ask Jesus if they should go away to prepare the Passover, they are mimicking their action in the feeding of the 4,000 when they asked Jesus if they should go away to food for the crowd (6:37). Verses 13–16 also compares with the parallel to preparation for Jesus' entry into Jerusalem (11:1–6). For Mark the instruction to the disciples for the preparation of the Passover (14:13–16) has the same introductory function for the passion as 11:1–10 has for the Jerusalem entry of Jesus. For Mark, therefore, Passover presents a general framework for the last meal, but direct interest in Passover traditions is lacking.

After the preparation, a meal is expected. However, Mark inserts Jesus' betrayer (14:18–21) in a story about a special meal Jesus eats with his disciples (14:22–25). Therefore, we must ask why Mark inserts this betrayer. Markan redaction within 14:17–21 suggests that Mark wove the scriptural wording into the scene. Mark composes 14:17 as a transition from the preparation to the meal. Since two disciples had already been sent into the city for preparation, technically only ten would accompany Jesus in the evening. But Mark brings "the twelve," an important concept within his theology, into the meal scene through v. 17, and he adds "one of the twelve" to the saying in 14:20. Robbins considers "twelve" to be redactional in every instance in Mark except 3:16. The first part of 14:18 is traditional except for the clause "and eating," but the last clause, "he who eats with me," appears to be a redundant insertion by Mark. The opening words in 14:19 are redactional, but the last part comes from the traditional scene. Therefore, Mark himself appears to introduce the allusion to Ps 41:9, "he who eats with me," as he depicts the conflict arising within the inner circle. The formula, "as it is written," continues the idea of scriptural fulfillment in 14:21. Moreover, it provides the rationale for the specific identification of one of the twelve as the betrayer. Mark composes 14:21a

---

Mark," 386–405.

3. See "Last Meal," 21–40.

4. I mainly owe this suggestion to Mack and Robbins, *Patterns of Persuasion*, 21–40.

to link the woe-oracle (14:21b, c) with the eating scene that defines the betrayer on the basis of Ps 41:9. The purpose of the Markan adaptation of the woe-oracle is to intensify the scriptural necessity for the betrayer to be one who "shared table" with Jesus.

Mark 14:22–25 portrays Jesus' taking bread and blessing it, then passing a cup from which all drink. The descriptive words in the first verse (14:22) are amazingly close to the narration of Jesus' acts with the bread and fish in the feeding stories (6:41, 8:6–7). In the feeding stories, Jesus discovers that the disciples do not understand the meaning of the bread (8:17–21). Instead of explaining the bread to them, he begins to teach them about the suffering, death, and resurrection of the Son of Man (8:31). In the Lord's Supper, Jesus abruptly interprets the meaning of the bread and adds a new feature by introducing a cup and interpreting its meaning. He interprets the bread as the body which has been prepared for burial (14:8, 22), and with the cup he invokes the Son of Man Christology which points to his absence until his return in a future, cosmic scenario. For Mark, therefore, the bread links with the body of Jesus which undergoes death. Drinking the cup represents the emphatically Markan emphasis, for this activity unites the believer with the fate of Jesus, and it evokes anticipation of the coming of the Son of Man. The cup gives meaning to the absence of Jesus: he will not drink again until he drinks anew in the kingdom of God.

The Lord's Supper represents a narrative climax of the Markan gospel, for at it table fellowship, discipleship and betrayal all come together. In terms of table fellowship, it is the last meal and the only meal with Jesus and the twelve together by themselves. In terms of discipleship, it is here that the disciples' final failure to understand and to follow Jesus is revealed. And in terms of betrayal, immediately before Jesus hands over to his disciples the bread which is his body, the identity of the one who is to hand him over to the chief priests and scribes is exposed.

The Eucharistic Prayers in the Didache 9 and 10

More recently there are scholars interested in the prayers of Did 9 and 10.[5] When discussing the prayers in Did 9 and 10, the work of textual criticism comes first. The second step in analyzing the prayers in Did 9 and 10 is to ascertain the literary sources, if any, that provided forms for the prayers. The third step in discussing the prayers in Did 9 and 10 is to discuss the context of the prayers. The prayers in Did 9 and 10 are kinds of the thanksgiving prayers.

The thanksgiving prayer varies in content, depending on the stage of development of Christology. At first it probably contained a simple thanksgiving for creation and redemption through Christ. As Edward J. Kilmartin, SJ, says, "With the development of Wisdom Christology, one might expect the prayer to reflect the interpretation of the Lord's Supper as fulfillment of the banquet of Wisdom."[6] As will be seen, Did 9 and

---

5. Riggs, "From Gracious Table," 83–101.
6. Kilmartin, "Eucharistic Prayer," 119.

10 provides an example of this. Moreover, in the opinion of most scholars, the prayers of thanksgiving in Did 9 and 10 is associated with the agape preceding the Eucharist alluded in Did 10:6. Nevertheless, this pericope shows signs of having undergone a development. The initial prayer over the cup which introduces the meal (9:2) does not correspond to the order reflected in 9:5 (eating and drinking of the Eucharist) and 10:3b (spiritual food and drink). This leads to the inference that it was transferred from the prayer over the final cup of the meal. Did 10:3a, giving thanks for food and drink created by God, is not at home in the passage. It breaks the christological train of thought between 10:2 and 10:3a. Also the new address of God found here, *despota pantokpator*, differing from the original *pater hemon* (9:2, 3) and *pater hagie* (10:2), indicates a later Hellenistic influence on the verse. The insertion of 10:3a is explainable on the basis that it was called for when the prayer was linked to a meal of satiation.

These observations lead to the conclusion that the original order of the prayers was: 9:3–5; 10:2, 3b–5. It is a prayer used for the Lord's Supper and expresses the Eucharistic event in the Hebrew Bible categories. This is the conclusion of Johannes Betz in his new study of Did 9 and 10.[7] The Eucharist reflected in the original prayer had the form: (1) breaking of bread with prayer of praise-thanksgiving and petition for the church (9:3–4); (2) exclusion formula (9:5); (3) meal (10:1); (4) prayer of praise-thanksgiving over the cup and petition for the church (9:2; 10:2, 3b–5). As Kilmartin, who is dependent on J. Betz, concludes, "The prayers over the bread and cup have a parallel structure and resemble the Jewish grace-at-meals which contains the elements of praise (rite of the bread), praise-thanksgiving and petition (rite of the cup). The addition of a prayer of thanksgiving and petition for the church in the rite of the bread, found in Didache, is undoubtedly due to the significance of the Eucharistic bread."[8]

The thanksgiving for "life and knowledge" revealed through Jesus (9:3), in a meal context, points to the banquet of wisdom. In the late Hebrew Bible period, wisdom is identified with the Torah (Sir 24:23) or personified as revealer (Wis 7–9). It is described as seeking and finding a dwelling place in Israel (Sir 24:8). In keeping with this motif, wisdom is portrayed as food and drink (Sir 24:19–21). Wisdom, as host of the meal, gives the bread of knowledge and the water of insight (Sir 15:3). With this tradition in mind, the Didache community saw its Eucharist as an anticipated eschatological meal, providing the gifts of the primordial epoch. This community, persuaded that the end-time had broken in with the coming of Jesus, correspondingly interpreted its Eucharistic food and drink as the gifts of paradise. The prayer of petition of Did 10:5, as 9:4, focus on the future fulfillment. But the eschatological world is seen as already at work in the present. This allows the food to be qualified as "spiritual" (10:3b) and so ordered to this sphere where the resurrected live (1 Cor 15:45). Hence it is no surprise when eternal life is ascribed as effect of the food (10:3).

---

7. Betz, "Eucharistie in der Didache," 10–39.
8. Kilmartin, "Eucharistic Prayer," 127.

John W. Riggs proposes a Jewish traditional-historical approach to these prayers which concentrate on their formation in three stages. At the first stage, the Christian community prayed using a *Birkat Ha-Mazon* as a model, but the prayer was restructured to reflect the response to the good news of God's reign ushered in through God's servant (*pais*) Jesus. At this stage disciples of Jesus continued the eschatological table-fellowship which was central to his ministry. The second stage marks the first explicit Christology. Prayers (10:2–3) were modeled on *berakoth* for the wine and bread at Sabbath *Kiddush*, and these prayers were placed together at the beginning of the meal. Did 9:4 was designed to parallel 10:5 and had the tenth benediction of the 'Amidah as its model. During these stage, Christian phrases from Did 9 were added to Did 10 to make the christological references explicit. The third stage shows a later development in how bread and cup prayers, as well as a thanksgiving prayer, occur before the cultic event. The meal has dropped out, and the elements themselves have become something sacred. This parallels the Markan account in which the meal context, already beginning to be lost at Corinth, has become lost entirely. The cultic event has the two moments of consuming the sacramental elements.

This understanding of the Didache 9 and 10 shows that it is either an actual Eucharistic prayer or the elements of an earlier one.[9] While none of the New Testament texts provides a liturgical "script," the Didache 9 and 10 provides an example of a text that does. As many scholars confirm, the Didache 9 and 10 is a liturgical script which is the completion of a long history. To be sure, the Didache 9 and 10 is a liturgical script and not a narrative.

A Tradition-History Development of the Meals

Although earlier scholars, most notably Joachim Jeremias, have argued for the priority of the Markan text,[10] Willi Marxsen has carefully analyzed the similarities and differences between the Pauline and Markan Eucharistic texts and persuasively argued for the priority of the Pauline text.[11] Although the direct dependence of Mark on Paul cannot be maintained, comparison of the ritual meal is of the Hellenistic Christ cult.

Gathering for meals was a common social custom during the Hellenistic period. Business and pleasure and such repartee as the group could command were poured into the common bowl of what amounted to a middle-class symposium. Jesus community must have met to talk about their common interests. Since the only model at hand for free association was the gathering for a meal, which must have been what they did. Simple invitations by a patron or householder would have sufficed. But, quite soon in some movements, fully organized congregations appeared that looked very much like Hellenistic associations. The Pauline communities, for instance, can

---

9. Kilmartin, "Sacrificium Laudis," 276.
10. Jeremias, *Eucharistic Words*.
11. Marxsen, *Lord's Supper*.

A Tradition-History Development of the Meals

be described as associations in the name of Christ. The social practices within the Jesus movements are less visible, and, judging from their views of Jesus, they did not develop in the direction of cults. But meeting for meals to talk about Jesus and the kingdom would still have been the common practice.

However, the focus of the pre-Pauline supper tradition is not on the meal itself, but on the elements of bread and cup. Its text embodies an etiological legend. Interpreting bread and a cup of wine in terms of Jesus' death gave expression to the Christ cult's mythology: the death of Jesus was a founding event for the community. And the text roots the supper in the life of Jesus. This is seen in the effort to situate the supper on the night Jesus was handed over. At the same time, the concern to describe Jesus' actions suggests that the common meal has become ritualized.

With a comparison of the Markan and Pauline text Willi Marxsen argues for a raditional-historical development of the Lord's Supper.[12] Marxsen analyzes the accounts of the supper in 1 Cor 11:23–25 and Mark 14:22–24 and argues that the pre-Pauline account embedded in 1 Corinthians is the earlier account. The two most important arguments for the priority of the Pauline version are these: (1) Within the pre-Pauline version there is clear reference to a meal situation during which the bread blessing at the beginning of the meal and the cup blessing at the end of the meal were not two special moments of the sacrament but parts of the meal itself. In contrast, the Markan version presents two moments, one placed after the other, giving the impression of a celebration encompassing only these two moments. The pre-Pauline formula would reflect the more ancient Palestinian meal tradition for the supper. (2) In the "word of interpretation" there are considerable differences between the formulas that have been transmitted by Paul and Mark. The pre-Pauline version shows the situation of bread = body and cup = covenant, modified by "blood." In the Markan version, on the other hand, this stylistic incongruence has become a parallelism where body = bread and cup = blood, modified by "covenant." Precisely this observation raises the suspicion that in Markan formula the incongruence of the Pauline version has been harmonized.

Marxsen then points out that more than liturgical development can be seen here. A development in the supper itself can be traced through the pre-Pauline, Pauline, and Markan stages. In the pre-Pauline account there is no mention of distributing or eating the bread. Distributing and eating the bread certainly happened, but the emphasis is on breaking and blessing the bread. This emphasis can hardly be accidental. What is being interpreted is not the bread itself but the action of breaking and blessing the bread. When the cup is blessed, there is no mention of the contents of the cup. What is blessed is the cup to be shared, which is described as the New Covenant, and the word "blood" then serves to modify the word "covenant." The eschatological community of the New Covenant is actualized in the sharing of the cup whose basis is the death of Jesus.

Marxsen returns now to Paul, who takes the development one step further. Paul presents a stage intermediate between this pre-Pauline stage and the situation that can

12. Ibid., 4–33.

be seen in Mark. It can be shown that it is he who for the first time speaks expressly of eating and drinking. In 1 Cor 10:21, for example, he speaks of "drinking the cup of the Lord," and in 11:26–27, where he paraphrases the action at the celebration of the Lord's Supper, once again it is Paul who makes explicit mention of eating the bread and drinking the cup, points on which the formula itself is silent. This means that Paul now expressly includes what was indeed implicit in the formula but had not yet been stated or even emphasized, namely, eating and drinking. It seems, however, that Paul thinks not so much about the bread and wine, but that in the partaking together the covenant is actualized; "what is at issue is the partaking which is actualized at the eating."[13] To take the food together in the context of love is the important matter.

According to Marxsen, in Mark's version we see a further development of the idea of consuming the elements. Words have been added to the bread saying, "he gave it to them," as well as the command, "Take!" Moreover, words have been added to the cup saying, "He gave it to them, and they drank of it." What is referred to in the cup saying is not the cup but the contents of the cup, which naturally can no longer be described as a "covenant." The contents of the cup are the "blood" which then is modified by the word "covenant." The harmonization of the pre-Pauline "word of interpretation" is more than just stylistic because something different is being interpreted in the Markan formula than in the pre-Pauline formula: the contents of the cup rather than the cup which is shared.

Within New Testament scholarship, John W. Riggs argues for a traditional-historical development of the Lord's Supper that parallels the development of the Didache 9 and 10. He analyzes the accounts of the supper in 1 Cor 11:23–25, Mark 14:22–24 and the Didache 9 and 10. Below is a table that Riggs presents the developments in the Didache 9 and 10, and in 1 Cor 11:23–25 and Mark 14:22–24 as Marxsen analyzes the passages.

Did 9 and 10	
STAGE I	
	1 Cor 11:23–25; Mk 14:22–24
Christianized berakah without christological references (Did 10:2–5).	
Eschatological table sharing that continues Jesus' witness.	
	Pre-Pauline
	Bread and cup sayings with christological references at beginning and end of meal.
No explicit reference to eating the bread or drinking the cup.	Bread broken and cup shared.

---

13. Ibid., 14.

STAGE II	
	Paul
Christological cup and bread prayers placed together and start meal (Did 9:2–4).	Christological bread and cup sayings placed together and end meal.
Thanksgiving prayer after the Meal (Did 10:2–5 with a phrases added).	Meal still retained.
Instructions in 9:1, 2, 3; 10:1.	Paul makes explicit partaking the bread and cup with context of love.

STAGE III	
	Mark
Bread and cup prayers and Thanksgiving prayer prior to cultic event.	Bread and wine sayings from cultic event stand together.
Table is fenced, elements are sacred, eat-drink order (9:5).	Elements themselves are sacramental.
Eucharist to follow (10:6).	Eucharist without meal.

EPILOGUE

This chapter has examined the Lord's Supper in Mark. The significance of the Lord's Supper sums up all of the significant Markan themes: Discipleship, misunderstanding, betrayal, denial and suffering. A great deal of effort has taken place to explain the role of the failure of discipleship in Mark. Certainly, recognition of the relationship between the failure of discipleship and the Lord's Supper brings a new consideration to this discussion. The Lord's Supper represents a narrative climax of the Markan gospel. And this chapter has undertaken the examination of the prayers in the Didache 9 and 10. The analysis of the Did 9 and 10 has recognized them as the thanksgiving prayers, depending on the stage of development of Christology as an actual Eucharistic prayer or a liturgical script and not a narrative. Finally, this chapter has shown that the comparison of the Lord's Supper (1 Cor 11:23–25; Mark 14:22–24) and the thanksgiving prayers (Did 9 and 10) leads to a tradition-history development of the meals. As a result, this chapter has traced a tradition-history development of the meals in pre-Pauline, Pauline, Markan version, and the Didache 9 and 10.

XIV

The Narrative of the Raising of the Widow's Son from Nain

PROLOGUE

THE NARRATIVE TELLS US of a lot of people who were dead but were raised by the speaking of God's Word: the widow's son with whom Elijah stayed, the young man of Nain, Jairus' daughter and Lazarus. But there is one person who rose without any help. Jesus did. By rising from the dead on His own, Jesus demonstrates that He is the One who is able to raise others from death.

Jesus entered Nain with a large crowd following him. They met another procession leaving the town. The crowd with Jesus was full of joy and hope; the other crowd was a sorrowful and despairing funeral procession. The dead person was the only son of a widow. Jesus' heart went out to her. He said, "Don't cry." Jesus is the compassionate shepherd who knows our sorrows and gives us his heart. Jesus spoke to the young man in the coffin and life came into his body. He sat up and began to talk. Jesus' word gives life. Only the Creator God can give life to the dead. The people praised God and said, "God has come to help his people." Jesus is the living God who turns our despair into hope and our sorrow into joy.

This chapter offers a few examples to illustrate the value of the various literatures surveyed for the narrative of the raising of the widow's son from Nain in Luke 7:11–17. This chapter does not represent attempts to deal with all of the questions that the interpreter is expected normally to address. The point here will be simply to show how non-canonical writings at times significantly contribute to the intertextual task. The narrative of the widow's son exemplifies Jesus' Elijah/Elisha-like ministry introduced earlier in the Nazareth sermon. The story of the famine and Elijah's assistance given to the widow of Zarephath is alluded to 1 Kgs 17:1–16. Many of the stories in detail are surely intended to parallel the stories of Elijah and Elisha raising the widow's son in 1 Kgs 17:17–24 and 2 Kgs 4:32–37.

The Narrative of the Raising of the Widow's Son from Nain

Relation to the Narrative of Elijah and Elisha

This narrative is only in Luke's Gospel. In this narrative Jesus raises from the dead the son of a widow, manifesting the kind of powers similar to those of Elijah and Elisha (1 Kgs 17:1-24, esp. in vv. 17-24; 2 Kgs 4:18-37, esp. in vv. 32-37). According to C. A. Evans, this narrative "exemplifies Jesus' Elijah/Elisha-like ministry introduced earlier in the Nazareth sermon (4:25-27)."[1] In Luke 4:25, Luke reflects the story of "many widows in Israel in the days of Elijah," of "the drought for three years and six months," and of "a great famine over all the land." And in Luke 4:26, Luke reflects also that "Elijah was sent to none of them but only to Zarephath, in the land of Sidon, to a woman who was a widow." In Luke 4:25-26, thus, the story of the famine and Elijah's assistance given to the widow of Zarephath is alluded to 1 Kgs 17:1-16. "Arise, get to Zarephath, which belongs to Zidon, and dwell there." This might be a trial of the prophet's faith, to be sent to dwell in a place belonging to the Zidonians, among whom Jezebel had an interest, being the daughter of their king, in 1 Kgs 16:31 the place is so called, to distinguish it from another Zarephath, in Obadiah 1:20, near to Zidon, yet not as belonging to it, but of the land of Israel; though it rather seems to be a Gentile city; it is called, in Luke 4:26 Sarepta of Sidon.

According to 1 Kings, Elijah departed for Zarephath after telling Ahab of the coming drought. Although we are not explicitly told, Elijah probably left Israel to avoid persecution, even death. This is hinted at 1 Kgs 17:3 ("hide yourself"), while the element of persecution is clearly seen elsewhere. According to 1 Kgs 18:4, Queen Jezebel had murdered many of Israel's prophets. Having defeated the prophets of Baal (1 Kgs 18:17-40), Elijah fled after being threatened by Jezebel (1 Kgs 19:2-3). Thus it was while fleeing was when Elijah ministered to (and was ministered to by) a Gentile family; Elijah turned to the Gentiles because of rejection and persecution at home. Jesus too is unwelcome among his own (Luke 4:24) and, like Elijah, turns to outsiders and outcasts. Although this theme is only implied here, a major justification for turning to Gentiles later in Acts is Jewish rejection and persecution (Acts 13:46; 18:6; 28:28).

When Jesus preached in the synagogues of Nazareth he touched off an outburst that nearly resulted in his being cast down a cliff, possibly as a prelude to stoning (Luke 4:16-30). Commentators have often wondered what it was that angered the audience so much. The suggestion was that it was the realization that Jesus was Joseph's son (v. 22) and therefore, as the son of a humble carpenter, he had no right to make great claims for himself is probably not the reason. The audience's recognition that it was indeed Jesus who stood before them should be interpreted as a joyful and expectant discovery. The proverb that Jesus quotes in the next verse and the interpretation that he gives confirm this. The real turning point in the sermon comes when Jesus cites the examples of Elijah and Elisha and by doing so suggests that the blessings and benefits of his Messianic ministry will be shared with Israel's traditional enemies.

---

1. Evans, "Function of the Elijah/Elish," 76.

The reason for the audience's angry reaction may have been clarified through the discovery and publication of 11QMelchizedek. In this Dead Sea Scroll, portions of Isa 61:1–2, the very passage with which Jesus began his Nazareth sermon (cf. Luke 4:18–19), are cited and linked with Isa 52:7 in order to expound upon the meaning of Lev 25:13, a passage understood to promise the coming of an eschatological era of jubilee. Indeed, 4Q521, a passage that makes explicit reference to God's Messiah, alludes to words and phases from Isa 61:1–2 and related passages. It is therefore very probable that many Jews of Jesus' time understood Isaiah 61 as not only eschatological but also Messianic.[2]

If Qumran's understanding of Isa 61:1–2 approximated the understanding of audience of Nazareth synagogue, we are able to appreciate much better the dynamics at work. When Jesus quoted Isa 61:1–2 and announced that it was fulfilled, he and his audience would have drawn two opposing conclusions. For Jesus the eschatological jubilee meant forgiveness and mercy for all, but for his kinsmen and longtime friends it meant blessings for them and judgment for their enemies. Jesus' omission of the line, "and the day of vengeance of our God," might have initially slipped by unnoticed. But when he illustrated his understanding of prophetic passage by appealing to the examples of mercy Elijah and Elisha showed Israel's enemies, his audience clearly understood his position and they did not like it. They viewed Jesus' interpretation as a betrayal of their Messianic hopes.

Relation to the Widow's Son in 1 Kings 17:17–24 and 2 Kings 4:32–37

Many of the stories in detail are surely intended to parallel the stories of Elijah and Elisha raising the widow's son in 1 Kgs 17:17–24 and 2 Kgs 4:32–37. This narrative begins with movement in opposite directions: Jesus is approaching the town with his train of followers while the funeral procession in coming out. Jesus' initiative prevents the two groups from simply passing by each other. The mercy Jesus shows the mother in both word and deed (vv. 13, 15b, each time with Jesus as subject) frames the central event: Jesus' gesture and his words spoken to the dead man, followed by the latter reaction and demonstration of the miracle (vv. 14, 15a). The result is depicted through the fear of the people and their praise of what God has done in Jesus (v. 16) as well as through the spread of Jesus' fame (v. 17).

Several parallels immediately suggest themselves:

---

2. In understanding Isa 61:1–2 in an eschatological sense the author of 11QMelchizedek agrees with Jesus, who had proclaimed to his audience: "Today this scripture has been fulfilled in your hearing" (Luke 4:21). But in emphasizing the judgmental nature of the passage the author of 11QMelchizedek moves in a completely different direction. The very line that Jesus had omitted from his quotation, "and the day of vengeance of our God" (cf. Isa 61:2), seems to hold the key to Qumran's understanding, not only of the jubilee of Lev 25:13, but even of the "good news" passages, Isa 52:7. The Hebrew text, which consists of consonants, not vowels, has been revitalized, so that it not only promises "peace" to the faithful, but "retribution" to Qumran's enemies.

The Narrative of the Raising of the Widow's Son from Nain

1) "Nain" (Luke 7:11) is a town in southern Galilee (modern Nein), which is mentioned here in the Bible. Nain may allude (rightly or wrongly) to the ancient city of Shunem where the woman of Elisha's miracle lived (2 Kgs 4:8). This name (from the Hebrew Na'im ["pleasant"] and/or Latin Naim) may represent an abbreviation of Shunem. In any case, Nain was situated in the proximity of the ancient site.

2) Both stories involve widows (Luke 7:12; 1 Kgs 17:9, 17). The sadness of the bereavement, thus accentuated, is further emphasized by the additional comment that the mother was a mother. The fact that the mother was a widow is reminiscent of 1 Kgs 17:9, 17. The attendance of a crowd at the funeral is in keeping with Jewish custom, since it ranked as a work of love. Therefore, Grundmann's suggestion, that the death of husband and son was a judgment of God upon some especial sin of the widow,[3] has no basis in the text.

3) Both stories involve the death of an only son (Luke 7:12; 1 Kgs 17:17; 2 Kgs 4:32). Luke describes as an only son, a detail found editorially elsewhere in Luke (μονογενής, 8:42 and 9:38). There is no proof that it did not belong to the original form of the story here. In Luke, μονογενής means "only," using it in the sense of "one of a kind" (monos + genos). It stresses the straits in which the widowed mother has been put by the death of her only child, and incidentally her only means of support.

4) Jesus meets the grieving widow at the "gate of the city" (Luke 7:12), as Elijah had met the widow (1 Kgs 17:10). When Elijah arrived at the city gate, he met a widow engaged in gathering wood. To discover whether it was to her that the Lord had sent him, he asked her for something to drink and for a morsel of bread to eat; whereupon she assured him, with an oath by Jehovah, that she had nothing baked (מעוג equals עגה, ἐγκρυφίας, a cake baked in hot ashes), but only a handful of meal in the כד (a pail or small vessel in which meal was kept) and a little oil in the pitcher, and that she was just gathering wood to dress this remnant for herself and her son, that they might eat it, and then die. From this statement of the widow it is evident, on the one hand, that the drought and famine had spread across the Phoenician frontier, as indeed Menander of Ephesus attests.[4]

This case was unique in its misery—the only son of a widow was being carried in the coffin. First she had lost her husband, and now she had lost her only son. The Jesus' compassion was also unique in his loving sympathy. He volunteered, in his tender mercy, his power of resurrection to raise the widow's son from death, without being asked to do so. This indicates his unique commission, coming to save lost sinners (19:10), and shows the high standard of his morality,

---

3. Grundmann, *Evangelium nach Lukas*, 159–60.
4. Josephus gives this statement from his Phoenician history: ἀβροχία τε ἐπ᾽ αὐτοῦ (Ἰθοβάλου) ἐγένετο ἀπὸ τοῦ Ὑπερβερεταίου μηνὸς ἕως τοῦ ἐρχομένου ἔτους Ὑπερβερεταίου (Ant. viii. 13, 2).

as a Savior, in saving sinners. In his compassion, the Savior spoke to the widow and touched the coffin. He was not asked to do these things. But seeing the situation, he initiated the action that caused the dead son to be raised up. To the great surprise of those present, Jesus initiated this action according to his human virtue. What caused him to be moved with compassion? The cause of this was his human virtue. Then in his human virtue His divine attributes were expressed by raising the young man from the dead. Again we see that Jesus is full of the human virtues and of the divine attributes. In his raising up the dead son and giving him to his mother, we see the expression of the Savior's divine attributes in his human virtues. When Jesus touched the coffin, he showed his sympathy, affection, and love.

5) Both passages describe the speaking or crying out of the resuscitated son (Luke 7:15; 1 Kgs 17:22). And the soul, נפש, of the child came into him again, על קרבו, into the midst of him; and he revived, ויח, and he became alive. Did he not become alive from the circumstance of the immaterial principle coming again into him? Although רוח is sometimes put for the breath, yet נפש generally means the immortal spirit, and where it seems to refer to animal life alone, it is only such a life as is the immediate and necessary effect of the presence of the immortal spirit. The words and mode of expression here appear to me as a strong proof, not only of the existence of an immortal and immaterial spirit in man, but also that spirit can and does exist in a separate state from the body. It is here represented as being in the midst of the child, like a spring in the center of a machine, which gives motion to every part, and without which the whole would stand still.

6) The clause, "He gave him to his mother" (Luke 7:15), follows 1 Kgs 17:23 LXX verbatim. This clause agrees word for word within both passages (identical wording): Luke 7:15 and 1 Kgs 17:23 LXX καὶ ἔδωκεν αὐτὸν τῇ μητρὶ αὐτοῦ. This clause that Jesus gave him to his mother serves to remind the readers of the Elijah typology and also to indicate Jesus' concern for the widow.

In 1 Kgs 17:21–24 (LXX) Elijah prayed: "Oh Lord my God, please let the life of this child return to him." It happened as [he had prayed], and the child cried out. [Elijah] led him down from the upper room into the house and gave him to his mother, and said, "See, your son lives" (ζῇ ὁ υἱός σου). The woman said to Elijah, "Behold, I have known (ἔγνωκα) that you are a man of God and the word of the Lord is true (ἀληθινόν) in your mouth."

In John 4:50, Jesus said to him: "Go, your son lives. (ὁ υἱός σου ζῇ)" The man believed the word that Jesus said to him and began going.

...ὁ παῖς αὐτοῦ ζῇ (4:51)

...ὁ υἱός σου ζῇ (4:53)

The Narrative of the Raising of the Widow's Son from Nain

In John, repetition and final sayings are often keys to the meaning of stories. "Your son lives" is Jesus' final saying in this pericope, and it is recorded three times. Jesus' saying reminds us of John's theme of Jesus as the source of life, found in almost every pericope in John. As with the rest of the "signs" in John, the healing of the nobleman's son is designed primarily to reveal something about Jesus' identity.

"Your son lives" also seems designed to draw the readers' attention to Elijah's famous healing of the widow's son at Zarephath. The phrase is distinctive; it is not found elsewhere in the New Testament or LXX. It also functions as an allusion in that the phrase causes the reader to notice other connections between the two miracle accounts. In both cases, the miracle results in the parent's belief that the healer is genuinely from God and speaks for God. The nobleman believed when he heard Jesus (4:50), and then he believed when he heard news of his son's healing (4:53). The widow's response to the healing affirms her belief in Elijah in terms that could be comfortably applied to Jesus in the gospel of John. The use of the perfect ἔγνωκα to intensify or solemnize a statement of belief is well-known in John (6:69; 11:27; cf. 1:34; 1:41; 1:45; 4:42). Elijah, like Jesus, is a "man of God" who speaks the word of God. John may have even been drawn to this passage because of his interest in "truth" (ἀληθινόν).[5] Although many books in the LXX use ἀληθινόν, in the NT, it is primarily a Johannine term, and usually applies to Jesus or his message (23 of its 28 occurrences in the NT are in John, 1 John, or Revelation). John's theology of signs is very similar to the theology of Elisha's miracle: both produce faith in God's representative and his message.

If John 4:7 contains an allusion to 1 Kgs 17:10 (argued above), then John 4 contains two successive allusions to two successive passages in the Elijah narrative. In intertextual studies, repeated allusions to the same text or nearby texts is one of the criteria for verifying the genuineness and strength of an allusion. The second allusion confirms the suspicion in the reader that the first allusion was intentional. Combined, the allusions suggest that John wanted to show a Jesus who was like Elijah.

John is not the only New Testament author to allude to Elijah's raising of the widow's son. Luke's account of the raising of the widow's son at Nain contains the allusive phrase "and he gave him to his mother" (καὶ ἔδωκεν αὐτὸν τῇ μητρὶ αὐτοῦ, Luke 7:15 / 1 Kgs 17:23).[6] Luke's allusion is stronger than John's, since it has more details in common (the raising of a dead widow's son by touch rather than the healing of a nobleman's son at a distance). This suggests that John's appropriation of Elijah imagery for Jesus is not unique to John.

---

5. Similarly, John's ἡ ἄμπελος ἡ ἀληθινή (John 15:1) is an allusion to Jeremiah's ἄμπελον ... ἀληθινήν (Jer 2:21).

6. A similar allusion can be found in Acts 20:7–10 / 2 Kgs 4:32–37. Paul raised Eutychus from the dead by laying down on top of him, as Elisha did to raise the son of the Shunammite woman.

7) Although the exclamation of the astonished crowd in Nain (Luke 7:16, "A great prophet has arisen among us") approximates the widow's exclamation (1 Kgs 17:24, "Behold, I know that you are a man of God"), it may not be a true parallel. But there is an allusion to the story of 1 Kgs 17. Here astonishment or fear (cf. Luke 1:12; 5:26) is the natural reaction of men to a demonstration of unearthly power. From a painful experience often great beauty comes. Elijah lived at a widow's home when her son suddenly died. In the agony of that hour, Elijah prayed, and God raised the boy back to life (1 Kgs 17:24). From this experience, the widow learned much about Elijah and more about God.

This narrative has the typical form of a miracle story; it was affected by Luke's special source material, since there is no reason to suppose that it stood in Q, and has been included here because of its obvious relevance to the general theme of the section. Bultmann claimed that it was created in Hellenistic Jewish Christian circles. In favor of this suggestion is the fact that several parallels can be cited from Hellenistic miracle stories.[7] Pliny, NH 26:15, relates how Asclepiads met the funeral cortege of a man unknown to him, had removed from the pyre, and saved his life. Philostratus, Vita Apollonius 4:45,[8] about 200 CE, tells how a young bride was thought to have died on the day of her wedding; the prophet met the funeral procession, touched the dead girl, said something secretly to her, and awakened her from her apparent death. In this case Philostratus was skeptical whether a miracle had really taken place.[9] In fact, however, the story as a whole finds its closest parallels in the Hebrew Bible, and the only feature that cannot be paralleled is the funeral procession setting, which is surely integral to the story. D. Schürmann's conclusion that the story belongs to the preaching of the Palestinian Jewish church is much more plausible than that of Bultmann.[10]

Relation to Others: Ruth 1:6, Sir 48:1–14, and Lives of the Prophets

Relation to Ruth 1:6

Let's return to the story of Luke 7:11–17. In this narrative, I could not find any direct quotations except v. 16 which would be ascribed to Ruth 1:6. Look at this parallel:

---

7. Bultmann, *Geschichte der synoptischen Tradition*, 230. Weinreich, *Antike Heilungswunder*, 171–73.

8. Here a pagan miracle worker of the first century CE is compared to Hercules: "A girl appeared to be dead at the hour of her marriage. The bridegroom was following the bier, lamenting.... Now when Apollonius arrived just at the time of the misfortune, he said, 'Set the bier down.' ... But he merely touched her and said something under his breath and thus aroused the girl from her supposed death. The virgin made a sound, and returned to house of her father."

9. For other parallels, see Artemidorous 4:82; Apuleius, Florida 19; IG IV 952:27–29. These parallels prove, or rather disprove, nothing as regards the historicity of the present story, since the motif of raising the dead is a familiar and widespread one.

10. Schürmann, *Lukasevangelium I*, 403–5.

The Narrative of the Raising of the Widow's Son from Nain

Ruth 1:6	Ruth 1:6
‏. . . ומע תא הוהי דקפ יכ. . .	. . . ὅτι ἐπέσκεπται Κύριος τὸν λαὸν αὐτοῦ . . .
. . . how that the Lord had visited His people . . .	. . . that the Lord had visited His people . . .

Luke 1:68	Luke 7:16
. . . ὅτι ἐπεσκέψατο καὶ ἐποίησε λύτρωσιν τῷ λαῷ αὐτοῦ . . . καὶ ὅτι ἐπεσκέψατο ὁ Θεὸς τὸν λαὸν αὐτοῦ.	
. . . for He has visited and redeemed His people.	. . . and that God has visited His people.

In Ruth 1:6 (LXX), ἐπέσκεπται denotes God's gracious visitation of his people, bringing them deliverance of various sorts (cf. Exod 4:31; Pss 80:14; 106:4).[11] Lord's visitation is associated with "salvation" in Pss 106:4, whereas here it is specifically related to his raising of "the horn of salvation." In Luke 7:16 God's visitation certainly echoes a motif sounded in the infancy narrative. God's compassionate and gracious visitation of his people is seen in the manifestation of Jesus' miraculous power. The collocation of visitation and death may echo from Gen 50:24–25, where the patriarch Joseph relates his town to a visitation.[12]

Relation to Sir 48:1–14

The work of Ben Sira[13] (Wisdom of Jesus the Son of Sirach)[14] was transmitted to us only through Jewish Sages and should be underlined with rabbinic traditions. In Ben

---

11. This religious sense of the verb, apparently unattested in extra-biblical Greek, renders the Hebrew דקפ.

12. This use of ἐπέσκεπται should be compared with the use of Hebrew דקפ in the Qumran Damascus Document (CD 1:7–11, where God is said to have raised up a Teacher of Righteousness in a similar "visitation").

13. I. Gruenwald claims that Sir 3:21–22 and 49:8 presuppose an existing esoteric tradition which is substantially identical with that of the apocalyptic literature. With his views, contrast von Rad's observation on the attitude of the wisdom tradition to those areas of knowledge lying beyond its realm of discourse. Gruenwald's case as regards Ben Sira and consequent early dating of the apocalyptic tradition is strengthened by early date of the first and third parts of 1 Enoch. Cf. Gruenwald, *Apocalyptic and Merkavah Mysticism*, 16–19.

14. Ben Sira's name is Yeshua, Jesus (Prologue 7; 50:27; 51:30), whose father was Eleazar, a Jerusalemite (50:27). Following the classical tradition of Hebrew poetry, Ben Sira often makes use of parallelism in a verse. And he seems only to have written in couplets.

Sira[15] God rewards the righteous and punishes the wicked, a theme characteristic of Deuteronomized wisdom (cf. Baruch and Wisdom of Solomon 3–4).

Wisdom uses the history of Israel as the basis of its reflections, and builds its vision of history much more organically than Sir 44–49 into its exposition.[16] It is in Sir 44–49, however, that ben Sira appears as the most ancient representative in Israel of a type of literature found later to some extent in 1 Macc 2:51-64 and Wis 10. Further, he does not praise so much of God's action in them and through worth propounding and imitating by the Sages. There is no doubt that depraved characters are among them, of whom he speaks frankly, like the Bible itself. Some examples are not to be followed, like that of Solomon. No other thread can be seen to run through this historical retrospect. The covenant is not used to justify the choice of the people spoken of. At most, one could note some insistence on Aaron and Phinehas, that is, on the sacerdotal tradition; but Ezra is not mentioned. In fact, the survey simply follows the historical sequence of patriarchs, prophets, kings and so on.[17] This is because, except for some special cases, all are worthy of the admiration of the Sages.

Sir 48:1-14 is a part of the "Praises of Famous Men" (44:1—49:16).[18] When Ben Sira reviews the heroes of the past, he says the longest with Aaron, describing with relish the magnificence of his liturgical trappings, and the eternal covenant made with his descendants (45:6-22). Ben Sira often speaks of the world, but more often of history and humanity. The "Praises of Famous Men" (44–49) are preceded by a passage on nature (42:15—43:33), where Ben Sira praises the Lord for his created works.[19] These are enumerated on the ancient catalogue system (Gen 2:19-20; 1 Kgs 5:13; Job 38–39), but he uses it to disclose in them the glory of their creator, in which their mystery cannot hide from the Sages.

Relation to the Lives of the Prophets with Luke and Matthew

The Lives of the Prophets is an account of the Hebrew prophets, each of whom is portrayed as telling where he was born, to what tribe he belonged, and where he was

---

15. Wisdom is well-planned and homogeneous exposition, much different from Ben Sira, where text seems to have been strung together with no such order. Cf. Stone, *Jewish Writings*, 310.

16. Stone, *Jewish Writings*, 311.

17. Sir 44–49 includes Genesis (44:16-23; 49:14-16), Exodus and Leviticus (45:1-15), Numbers (45:15-24; 46:7), Joshua (46:1-10). Judges (46:11-12), Samuel (45:25; 46:13—47:8; 47:11), Kings (47:12—48:9; 48:11-23; 49:1-6), Isaiah (48:24-25), Jeremiah (49:6-7), Ezekiel (49:8-9), the Twelve Minor Prophets (49:10), Haggai (49:11), Malachi (48:10), Psalms and Proverbs (44:4-5; 47:8, 14-17), Ezra-Nehemiah (49:11-13), and Chronicles (47:9-10). Cf. Mulder, *Mikra*, 46.

18. Maertens, Siebeneck, Jacobson, Mack, Murphy, and Carm has been studied it as the "Praises of the Fathers." Cf. Kraft and Nickelsburg, *Early Judaism*, 376.

19. These are the "Praises of Famous Men," which gives a survey of the great heroes of the Bible. The main thing which strikes one in these chapters is that Ben Sira while following the chronological order of these persons (down to Nehemiah, though with Adam to close the series), seems to rely on the Bible as an established canon. Thus, the twelve prophets are mentioned as 49:10.

buried. The biblical materials about the prophet's life are not repeated but supplemented. Many legendary stories have been added. This holds true in the geographies of Isaiah, Jeremiah, Ezekiel, Daniel, Jonah, and Habakkuk, while those of other prophets are short and as a rule contain extra-biblical material.

The Lives of the Prophets is an ancient apocryphal account of the lives of the prophets from the Hebrew Bible. It is not regarded as scripture by any Jewish or Christian denomination. The work may have been known by the author of some of the Pauline Epistles, as there are similarities in the descriptions of the fates of the prophets, although without naming the individuals concerned.

The work survives only in Christian manuscripts. There are two groups of Greek manuscripts: the first group includes many versions, well known in the past centuries, with heavy Christian's additions. Some of these versions were attributed to Epiphanius of Salamis, others to Dorotheus of Tyre. The other group of Greek manuscripts is more stable and free from the interpolations found in the previous group: the best codex is a sixth-century CE manuscript usually referred to as Q or as anonymous recession. There is also a Latin version with a text near to Q used by Isidore of Seville (before 636 CE). There are also versions in Syriac, Armenian, and Arabic.

There is not a consensus among scholars about the original language. Torrey proposed Hebrew, other authors proposed Aramaic. The preferred use of quotations from the Septuagint suggests a Greek original with Semitic coloring. Authenticating the dating is highly problematic due to the Christian transmission and presumed expansions. Most scholars consider this work to be of Jewish origin dating the first century CE. Torrey[20] suggests a date before 106 CE. Hare[21] the first quarter of the first century CE. Satran[22] proposes an early Byzantine origin in the fourth-fifth century on previous materials.

The following contents show how the Lives of the Prophets are similar to filial language from the texts in its account of Jesus with Luke and Matthew:

> The Spirit of God will come down upon you and this thing is the proof that this child is the awaited Christ who will rule forever (Luke 1:32–33, 35).
>
> If you are truly the Messiah of the Most High God, command these stones to become bread (Luke 4:3).
>
> Afterward, the Devil took Him to Jerusalem and stood Him on the edge of the House of God. If you are truly the Messiah of God, throw yourself down from up here (Luke 4:9).
>
> Just as God is merciful, be merciful to people (Luke 6:36).

---

20. Torrey, *Lives of the Prophets*.
21. Hare, "Lives of the Prophets," 379–400.
22. Satran, *Biblical Prophets*, 121–28.

Oh . . . oh . . . Jesus . . . oh Messiah of the most high God . . . what do you want from me? I beg of you, don't torture me (Luke 8:28).

Anyone who comes with me must deny himself and bear persecution for my sake (Luke 9:23–24).

Whoever is ashamed of me and my teachings, the Son of Man will be ashamed of him on the day on judgment when He comes in His glory and in the glory of God and of the pure angels (Luke 9:26).

They heard a voice from heaven saying: This is the beloved Messiah whom I have sent, so listen to him and obey him (Luke 9:35).

When you pray, say: Our loving, heavenly Lord (Luke 11:2).

If you being evil know how to give your children good gifts, then how much more is it true of the Lord of the world who gives his Holy Spirit to the people who ask him? (Luke 11:13).

You who were patient with me in my trials, I will give you the right to sit and eat and drink at the table in the kingdom that God the praised and most high has bestowed upon me (Luke 22:28–30).

Oh Lord . . . If it's your will, take this effort or sufferance away from me. But, oh Lord, by your will and not my will (Luke 22:42).

Then you are the Messiah of God? (Luke 22:70).

Oh Lord, forgive them. They don't know what they are doing (Luke 23:34).

Oh Lord . . . oh Lord, I surrender my Spirit into Your hands (Luke 23:46).

. . . and I will send the Holy Spirit to you, so remain here until this strength from heaven comes to you according to God's promise (Luke 24:49).

God has given me all authority in heaven and on earth, so go and tell the people from all the nations about the message of salvation so that they may be my followers . . . and baptize them with water in the name of God and his Messiah and the Holy Spirit. And teach them to do all that I commanded you to do. And be sure that I am with you all the days until the end time (Matt 28:18–20).

EPILOGUE

This chapter examined a few examples to illustrate the value of the various literatures surveyed for the narrative of the raising of the widow's son from Nain in Luke 7:11–17. This chapter did not represent attempts to deal with all of the questions that the interpreter is expected normally to address. The point here in this chapter simply showed how non-canonical writings at times significantly contribute to the intertextual task. The narrative of the widow's son exemplified Jesus' Elijah/Elisha-like ministry introduced earlier in the Nazareth sermon. The story of the famine and Elijah's assistance given to the widow of Zarephath was alluded to 1 Kgs 17:1–16. Many of the stories in detail are surely intended to parallel the stories of Elijah and Elisha raising the widow's son in 1 Kgs 17:17–24 and 2 Kgs 4:32–37. For this reason, this chapter compared the narrative of the raising of the widow's son from Nain in Luke 7:11–17 with the parallels of the stories in the narrative of Elijah and Elisha (1 Kgs 17:1–24, especially in vv. 17–24; 2 Kgs 4:18–37), Ruth 1:6, Sir 48:1–14, and the Lives of the Prophets.

XV

Korean Recent Trends in the Study of the Gospels

PROLOGUE

RECENTLY THE RESULTS OF the study of the Gospels in Korea have been playing a role in international New Testament scholarship and are receiving attention from many foreign scholars. In the past 132 years since foreign missionaries gave Koreans the gospel,[1] Korean Christians have dramatically developed churches in a manner that is difficult to find elsewhere. As a result of this growth, many Korean New Testament scholars have played a role in domestic and foreign academic fields. The number of New Testament scholars with a doctoral degree is growing rapidly and has reached about four hundred. The quantity of dissertations, articles, and books is increasing in proportion to the number of New Testament scholars. Their fields of study are becoming diverse and specialized. Some scholars reach an international level in certain areas.

In 1787, Johann Philipp Gabler gave his inaugural lecture at the University of Altdorf, entitled "*De iusto discrimine theologiae bibilcae et dogmaticae regundisque recte utriusque finibus*,"[2] in which he first introduced the concept of biblical theology. Many years after Gabler suggested the necessity of distinguishing biblical studies from dogmatic theology, this way of studying the New Testament has finally begun receiving attention in Korea, too. After confirming the trajectory of New Testament study in an independent Korean biblical theology, this chapter will examine further the recent trend of studying the Gospels and various outcomes of such study. Unfortunately, this chapter cannot cover all the history and outcomes of New Testament study that

---

1. In 1884, Koreans received the gospel from two American missionaries, Underwood and Appenzeller.

2. His lecture is on the suggestion of right distinction between biblical theology and systematic theology regarding proper decision of their field. The Latin words mean "On the proper distinction between biblical and dogmatic theology and the specific objectives of each." Cf. Merk, *Biblische Theologie*.

Korean biblical theologians have produced during the past years. Rather, while referring to the background history of Korean New Testament studies, this chapter will introduce recent views of the Gospels, reflected in various fields of the New Testament that Korean biblical theologians have raised directly.[3]

New Testament Studies in the Early Korean Church

In Korea, New Testament studies have for a long time been carried out without acknowledging their independence as an academic field—in contrast to the way it has been done around the world. In 1884, Koreans received the gospel from foreign missionaries; in 1901, Samuel Moffet established Presbyterian Seminary.[4] Theological education, however, was based on the conservative and pious movement that foreign missionaries gave to Koreans, and thus was carried out in a pre-critical manner. Hence, the Korean church remained on a level where Korean Christians understood simply the contents of the Bible, as explained by Western missionaries. In the early Korean church, "New Testament studies could not be called a 'science' because of passing through the pre-critical era."[5] This evaluation is proper because in that era there was no critical study of the New Testament. Pastoral and missionary works were occasionally published; but the authors were the Western missionaries, and the Korean writers were only translators for "their" missionary. Korean New Testament studies, therefore, was solely dependent upon the works of foreign missionaries or scholars, pietistic and evangelistic. The field showed great concern for Jesus' life and thought.

In 1920, however, Erdmann, a missionary, wrote the paper, "High Criticism." Thus at that time there were some attempts to apply a historical-critical approach to the Bible. In contrast to the application of methods like high criticism, early Korean missionaries only tried to understand the Bible on the basis of linguistic, grammatical, and historical methods. This early Korean criticism could not employ historical criticism of the Bible because it was limited by the school of salvation history and evangelism. *The Interpreter's Bible* (Abingdon) was published for the fifty-ninth

---

3. In 2001, Korea Association of Christian Studies gathered together to sum up the Korean theology in celebrating the thirtieth anniversary. At that time Park Soo Am presented a paper in which he outlined the history and trend of Korean New Testament studies, entitled "Retrospect and Prospect," 119–42. In 2002, thirteen scholars have also published an introductory study of the New Testament, *Introduction to the New Testament*. I, first of all, am indebted to those papers. I am also indebted to the paper, "History of the New Testament Society of Korea," 143–71.

4. Missionary Moffett began teaching Chong-Sub Kim and Ki-Chang Pang at his home in Pyongyang in 1901. And in 1903, the Presbyterian Council decided to officially start the theological education in Korea. In the beginning, missionaries from each Presbyterian synod went to Pyongyang to teach a course which was designed to give three months of study and nine months of ministry in a five year span. In June of 1907, the first class of seven students graduated from the theological course, and among them were the first ordained pastors of Korea: Sun-Joo Kil, Suk-Jin Han, and Ki-Pung Lee.

5. Park, "Retrospect and Prospect," 127. Park Soo Am argues that this pre-critical era was up to 1950.

anniversary of the Korean mission, but the Presbyterian Church of Korea prohibited its use. In fact, many translators of the commentary faced opposition and were called "liberal" for their theological stance. At this time the Korean church was divided into 3 groups: (1) Park Hyung Rong (1897–1978), who argued the theory of complete biblical inspiration, (2) Jung Kyung Ok (1903–1945), who understood the Bible in a liberal and existential way through historical study, and (3) Kim Jae Jun (1901–1987), who argued a liberal and historical understanding of the Bible.[6]

Meanwhile, even as the Korean churches suffered many divisions, biblical scholars began to apply historical criticism to the New Testament. As a result, M. Dibelius' *Jesus* was translated in 1957; Kim Jung Jun wrote *A Portrait of Jesus* in 1951–1955. In 1958 Chun Kyung Yun, Chi Dong Sik, Kim Chul Son, and Kim Yong Ok worked together to publish *Introduction to the New Testament*, the first New Testament Introductory text written by Korean scholars. It introduced historical-critical methodology, which had existed theoretically in the eighteenth and nineteenth centuries, to its first practical use in Korean biblical studies. It made the existential approach, as source criticism, form criticism, and redaction criticism appear as methodologies of biblical interpretation, and proceeded in a moderate way.

Broad acceptance of this academic theological methodology, which resulted in the division of various seminaries, also gave a scientific character to the entire field of theology. Several young scholars, who came back from foreign countries after acquiring their academic degrees on the basis of historical-critical methodology, accelerated this trend. All historical methodologies were fully applied to all areas of New Testament studies. Young scholars also showed great concern for hermeneutical issues, the historical Jesus problem, the Synoptic problems, New Testament theology, and inter-religious issues. This could be called "the dawn of historical criticism,"[7] in which Korean scholars applied historical criticism to their New Testament studies, introduced it to their students, and published their writings using it.

The New Testament Society of Korea

The New Testament Society of Korea, which added energy to these academic developments, was founded in May 29, 1961. The eleven founding members were Chun Kyung Yun (Han Shin University), Chi Dong Sik (Yon Sei University), Park Chang Hwan (Presbyterian University and Theological Seminary), You Dong Sik (Yon Sei University), You Si Wook, Koo Doo In (St. Michael's College), Kim Yong Ok (Methodist Theological University), Moon Sang Hee (Yon Sei University), Lee Yeo Jin (Han Shin University), Lee Sang Ho (Yon Sei University), and Kim Chul Son (Methodist Theological University). Chun Kyung Yun was appointed the first president. The New Testament Society of Korea invited James M. Robinson, Edward Schweitzer, Richard

6. Joo, *Theological History of Korean Christianity*, 174–220.
7. Park, "Retrospect and Prospect," 141.

Hays, and other distinguished foreign scholars in order to provide an opportunity for Korean scholars to establish an academic relationship with them. At this time each area of historical criticism became related to other fields of science, bringing contextualization and interdisciplinarity to biblical interpretation. Some scholars accepted not only historical-critical, but also sociological and literary-critical methodology. Scholars showed great concern for New Testament theology. They also paid attention to the historical and diachronic approaches, acknowledging the diversity of New Testament writers.

The activity of the New Testament Society of Korea during the 1970s and 1980s was faced with the national crisis under the regime of military dictatorship. At the same time, Korean churches were rapidly growing. The government restricted public gatherings; nevertheless, thousands of Koreans enrolled in churches, increasing the number of seminary students. Thus the members of the New Testament Society of Korea spent much of their time educating more seminarians. (Many of these students had a chance to study abroad in Germany, England, and the USA, and Korean churches by the 1990s and 2000s had produced many young scholars in all areas of New Testament studies.) The national crisis of the 1970s and 1980s motivated *Min Jung*[8] theology. New Testament scholars became interested in the political context, and addressed questions raised by Korean society rather than the text. Several papers were illuminated by the context of the relationship between the church and the state. Because the church in Korea could not force itself to submit under the military power of dictatorship, many papers by New Testament scholars discussed power and the state. In this confrontational situation, the Korean church began to exert effort in the social participation movement. The development of Korean theology during this period, particularly *Min Jung* theology among Korean liberal theologians, was very exciting and significant.[9]

The 1970s also saw the publication of several papers in which New Testament scholars reevaluated trends in Korean New Testament study. These included Ahn Byung Moo's "The Historical Jesus and the Kerugmatik Christ: A Modern Trend of New Testament Studies" (1971); Hwang Sung Kyu's "A Recent Trend of New Testament Studies" (1975); and Kim Yong Ok's "A Current Trend of New Testament Studies" (1976).

This attempt to establish an identity for the Korean church and for New Testament scholarship led to a *contextualization* theology, directed toward the Korean theological *context*. Kim Yong Ok published his paper, "World Church and Korean Church" (1971), suggesting that New Testament scholars must reinterpret and reevaluate the issues of the world church in a Korean context in order to establish a Korean theology regarding contextualization.[10] He published many papers that argued along similar lines, such as "Korean Theology in Asian Theology" (1971), "Korean Issues

8. *Min Jung* means "people" or "crowd" in Korean.
9. Kang, "Theological Trends," 171.
10. Kim, "World Church and Korean Church," 68–71.

of Theological Education" (1973), and "Christianity and Nationalism: Focusing on the Jesus and Paul" (1976). Kim also suggested a discussion of Bultmann's concept of presupposition in order to build up Korean theological formation.[11]

In 1977 Ahn Byung Moo published his paper, "The Understanding of Jesus in Korean Church." Criticizing radical Biblicism based on a literary dictation theory of the Bible, he also classified the various understandings of Jesus among the leaders and scholars in the Korean church:

"Ideal Human Jesus" (Park Hyung Rung, Lee Yong Do)

"Revolutionary Jesus" (You Kyung Sang)

"Jesus of History" (Kim Jae Jun)

"Human Jesus" (You Dong Sik, Hong Hyun Sul)

"Liberator Jesus" (Moon Dong Hwan, Park Hyung Kyu)

"Jesus, Friend of Min Jung" (Suh Nam Dong).[12]

According to Ahn, the Korean church needed to solve the problems caused by various views on the historical Jesus and Jesus of history, views which were confusing Korean New Testament scholars at that time.

The Dawn of Tong Chun[13] Theology

As already mentioned above, the Korean church generally divided into liberal and conservative positions over the question of whether New Testament scholars should accept historical-critical methodology in studying the Bible; the results of biblical criticism challenged the Korean church's authoritative understanding of the Bible as the word of God and the book of the church.

Interestingly, acceptance of Rudolph Bultmann and his hermeneutical method seemed to form a standard for distinguishing the positions of liberal versus conservative. Heu Hyuk of E-Hwa Women's University translated many of Bultmann's writings into Korean, with introductory comments and critiques. The Korean church was divided, as was the Western church, on whether or not to accept Bultmann's hermeneutical method. For example, Han Shin University created a new liberal denomination called *"Ki Chang"* after accepting Bultmann's biblical criticism. Then Chong Shin University created a new conservative denomination called *"Hap Dong,"* which did not acknowledge the membership of WCC. Park Soo Am took the moderate ground (*Tong Hap*) between the two sides. He too evaluates theological positions by the standard of acceptance of Bultmann's theology:

---

11. For more information, see also Kim, "Several Tries Toward Korean Theological Formation," 110–20; Kim, "Sum-Up of Korean Theology," 61–67.

12. Ahn, "Understanding of Jesus in Korean Church," 65–79.

13. *Tong Chun* means "wholeness" in Korean.

The biblical theology of Presbyterian University and Theological Seminary chooses the moderate position of historical, soteriological, and historical-critical study, following the stream of evangelical pietism after the reformation. Its position was neither the line of the only evangelical pietism like Ko Shin University, nor the one of corrective Bultmannian work like Methodist Theological University, nor yet the one of radical Bultmannian work like Han Shin University. Its position was moderate; therefore, it did not bend either to the right or left side. It was biblical, reformed, evangelical, and conservative.[14]

This evaluation is a good example of the holistic perspective of *Tong Chun* theology,[15] followed by Koreans who want to study biblical studies in the center. The theology of Rhee Jong Sung is called to the holistic theology. On the one hand, he did not success his holistic theology, even though he published 40 great volumes of his systematic theology. In spite of its incompleteness, this book presupposes that the holistic theology of Rhee Jong Sung is based on the foundation of the biblical theology and evaluates his theologies that he enterprised during his whole life of almost ninety years: co-relational studies of various fields, a biblical understanding, Trinity theory, science and theology and literature, an acceptance of interreligious and interdisciplinary dialogue, and eschatology etc. As a result of this evaluation, on the other, this book evaluates the *ohn* theology of Myung Yong Kim,[16] which is based on the Rhee's holistic theology that "united" various theological aspects, because Kim thinks that his *ohn* theology further contains the concepts of no one side or more holistic view.

From this perspective, Korean New Testament studies of the past depended on partial interpretations, but scholars gradually moved toward understanding the New Testament as a whole—*Tong Chun* theology. *Tong Chun* means "holistic" or "whole," as a totality which also acknowledges the individual parts; it does not disregard individuality. Hence, *Tong Chun* theology acknowledges each individual perspective while seeking the complete. It is concretive and comprehensive, individual and total.

What are the constructive principles of the *Tong Chun* theology that he thought? He understood other civilizations (even science and religion) as "the preliminary process for the Christianity" or "the one toward the Gospel." And how the Christian world view can understand the other religious world view through the holistic theology and lead the other different civilizations into the Christian civilization? Those questions are the major tasks that must be solved by the scholars who success the holistic theology.

---

14. Park, "Yesterday, Today," 41.

15. Lhee, who was dean of the Presbyterian University and Theological Seminary, suggested "*Tong Chun*" Theology ("holistic" theology) in his great theological books, *Lhee Jong Sung's Great Works*, 40 vols.

16. Kim, *Ohn Theology*.

Markan Studies

The single largest area of scholarly work by the Korean New Testament Society is the Synoptics.[17] The Gospel of Mark drew particular attention, as it did among Western New Testament scholars. The concerns of Markan study were motivated by the approaches of *Min Jung* theology which Ahn Byung Moo suggested. Ahn wanted to search for the historical Jesus in the Gospel of Mark and to confirm the reality of the suffering and alienated *Min Jung* in the *ochlos* that followed Jesus.[18] Unfortunately, when the study of the Gospel of Mark was regarded as the *Min Jung*'s hermeneutics, the majority of New Testament scholars were not persuaded; they chose the historical meaning of the Markan texts rather than the contemporary meaning of the *Min Jung*.

Since the 1980s, Kim Deuk Jung and Park Soo Am have been emphasizing the study of the Gospel of Mark on the basis of historical criticism. Kim Deuk Joong published *The Theologies of the Evangelists* (1985) and *The Studies on the Gospel of Mark* (1989) in order to reconstruct the historical Jesus and the evangelists' communities on the basis of redaction criticism. Park Soo Am recommended reading the Gospel of Mark in the light of Mark 13 in his book, *Mark 13 and the Gospel of Mark* (1993). Park used redaction criticism to argue that Mark 13 is a crucial chapter which Mark composed as a warning for his community based on Jesus' tradition.

Suh Joong Suk also investigated the community behind the Gospels in his book, *Interpreting the Four Gospels* (1991). Using the study of the sociology of knowledge,[19] Suh reconstructed Jesus' community as an alternative community like the Markan community and Matthean community. According to Suh, the Markan community reflects an alternative disciple group with a struggling relationship with "the twelve," whose central figure is Peter. In the Gospel of Mark, the alternative disciples can be implied in images like the blind (Mark 10:46–52), the children (Mark 9:33–37; 10:13–16), and the women (Mark 7:24; 16:1–8, etc.). Suh also suggests that the Matthean community consisted of two groups in tension at the boundaries of the gospel mission and of the interpretation of the law.

---

17. According to the investigation of Kim Deuk Joong, the ratio of the classification in New Testament papers during the 1970s has been shown as follows:

40 %	the Synoptics
5 %	the Gospel of John
3 %	the Acts of the Apostle
8 %	the major Pauline Letters
2 %	the letters written in prison
0 %	the Pastoral Letters
0.8 %	the Letter to the Hebrews
2 %	the General Letters
0.8 %	the Revelation
37 %	others

For more information, see Kim, "New Testament Studies in 1970s," 41.

18. Ahn, "Jesus and *Min Jung*," 3–18; Ahn, "*Min Jung* theology," 504–36.

19. Berger and Luckmann, *Social Construction of Reality*.

The Society of Korean Q Studies

Korean Synoptic studies raised the issue of Q for understanding the historical Jesus during the 1990s. Prior to this time, the study of Q was limited to the "two-document theory" that Korean New Testament scholars used to explain the relationship of the Synoptic texts as the basis for source criticism. In the mid-1990s, however, young scholars who had studied in Europe and particularly in the United States were newly interested in the theory of Q as the earliest Gospel and in the discussion of the Q community. They accepted the hypothesis of Q as the source of the traditional strata common to the Gospel of Matthew and Luke. Recently, Korean New Testament scholars are also concerned with the work of reconstructing Q, "the lost gospel."[20]

In 1992 Sung Jong Hyun summarized the history of European Q studies in his paper, "Recent Study of Jesus' Logia (Q Source)." Cho Tae Yeun also introduced the recent trend of Q in his serial study "A Holy Quest for the Jesus Movement" (1995), printed in *Christian Thought*. After the serial print, it was published in 1996: *The Jesus Movement—A Quest of Christian Origins*.

Ky-Chun So, who studied at Claremont Graduate University and was a student of James M. Robinson, started the most important study of Q. He explored the transition of early Christianity from the Q community to the Matthean community, based on Robinson's theory. His books, *Trajectories through the Sayings of Jesus* (2000) and *An Introduction to the Sayings Gospel Q* (2004), attempt to reconstruct the social world of early Christian communities. Specifically, Ky-Chun So introduced Koreans for the first time to the Greek Q text reconstructed by *IQP*. He also reconstructs the theological outcomes of the Q community in several papers:

"The Sayings Gospel Q Started as Logio Sophon" (1999)

"The Sayings Gospel Q: An Introduction, the Korean Translation, and Notes" (1999)

"The Gentile Mission and Sabbath Controversy" (1999)

"Jesus and the God of the Q Community" (1999)

"The Redaction and Christology in Q" (1999)

"The Eschatology of the Q Community" (1999)

"Jesus' Understanding of the Spirit and the Milieu of the Q Community" (2000)

"The Respect of Life in Jesus' Sayings" (2000)

"A Study of the Relationship of Jesus and the John the Baptist" (2001)

---

20. For the reconstruction of Q, see *Critical Edition of Q*. For the explanation of the International Q Project and its study outcomes, see *JBL* 109 (1990) 499–501; *JBL* 110 (1991) 494–99; *JBL* 113 (1994) 495–99; *JBL* 111 (1992) 500–508; *JBL* 112 (1993) 500–506; *JBL* 113 (1994) 495–99; *JBL* 114 (1995) 475–85; *JBL* 116 (1997) 521–25; So, *Trajectories through the Sayings of Jesus*; So, *Introduction to the Sayings Gospel Q*.

"The Influences of Jesus' Sayings: From the Sayings Gospel to the Gospel of Matthew" (2002)

"The Tradition of Jesus' Sayings to the Power of State Transmitted in Edessa" (2002)

"Co-relationship with Jewish Mission and the Gentile Mission in the New Testament" (2003)

"Dating Q Regarding the Community Rules in Jesus' Inaugural Sermon" (2003)

In his papers, So examines the theological identity of the Q Community behind the Q text.

Interesting theological perspectives have emerged from the Korean study of Q. On the one hand, Kim Myung Soo has been studying the Q text since the 1990s from the perspective of *Min Jung* theology. Kim published *the Study of Jesus in Primitive Christianity* (1999), binding all of the papers that he had printed in several magazines. In his new book, *Christianity and Postmodernism* (2000), he also regards the Q text as the tradition which best preserved the aspect of the historical Jesus and contained the point of contact with *Min Jung* theology. On the other hand, Kim Hyung Dong suggests a new insight into the theology of God's kingdom on the basis of the apocalyptic eschatology which some scholars identify as a central motif of Q. Kim published several papers: "A Study of Q Beatitudes (Q 6:20–23) and Q Woes (Q/Luke 6:24–26: Q 11): The Vantage Point of the Kingdom of God and Prophets in Their Formation" (1999), "Two Texts Related to the Spread of the Gospel and the Violence of the Violent (Luke 16:16/Mk 11:12): The Understanding of Q 16:16 from the Perspective of the Kingdom of God" (2001), and "The Importance of the Kingdom of God in Q Mission Discourse (Q 10:2–16)" (2002). Finally, Joseph Ra published his book, *the First Text Q about Jesus* (2002), dividing the four redactional layers. Here Ra concretely examines the theology of the Q Community and the change of its social world. Ra also recently published *The Origin and Formation of the Gospel* (Wipf & Stock, 2015) on Q.

The Society of Korean Q Studies, which added energy to these Q developments, was founded in June 15, 2013, at Presbyterian University and Theological Seminary. The twenty founding members were Kim Myung Soo (Kyung Sung University), Ky-Chun So (Presbyterian University and Theological Seminary), Duck Ki Kim (Tae Jun Theological University), Pan Im Kim (Sejong University), Joseph Ra (My Lord), Hyung Dong Kim (Pusan Jangshin University), Byung Gu Moon (Seoul Theological University), Kyung Mi Park (E-Hwa Women's University), In Hee Park (E-Hwa Women's University), Jae Hyun Kim (Kye Myung University), Hyo Sim Yeun (Presbyterian University and Theological Seminary), Byung Soo Choi (Hanshin University), Jae Hyung Cho (Claremont Graduate University), Yang Mook Lee (Presbyterian University and Theological Seminary), Jae Chun Koo (Seoul Theological University), Seung Yeup Lee (Presbyterian University and Theological Seminary), Jin Suk Ro Lee (Presbyterian University and Theological Seminary), Eun Hye (Grace) So (UC Berkeley/Graduate

Theological Union), Ye Ji Park (Princeton Theological Seminary), and Esther Park (Presbyterian University and Theological Seminary). Kim Myung Soo was appointed the first president; Ky-Chun So is now the second president.

The Society of Korean Q Studies invited James M. Robinson, John S. Kloppenborg, Dennis McDonald, and other distinguished foreign scholars in order to provide an opportunity for Korean scholars to establish an academic relationship with them. The Society of Korean Q Studies gathers together twice per year and publishes its academic journal, *Journal of Q Studies* (ISSN 2288-324X) as follows:

Vol. 1 (June 2013)

James M. Robinson (Claremont Graduate University), "From the Apostles' Creed to Jesus' Own Trust in God," 1–14.

Kim Myung Soo (Kyung Sung University), "A Comparative Study on Image of Jesus by Korean Thinker Yoo, Yung-Mo and Q Community in Early Christianity," 15–28.

Ky-Chun So and Yang Mook Lee (Presbyterian University and Theological Seminary), "A Study of Old Testament Tradition Motives towards Joshua Typology and Double Structure of ἡ βασιλεία τοῦ θεοῦ in the Sayings Gospel Q," 29–48.

In Hee Park (Ewha Women's University), "The Metaphoric Use of 'Slave' in Q," 49–65.

Joseph Ra (My Lord), "A Theological Study of the Historical Jesus in Q," 66–79.

Hyo Sim Yeun (Presbyterian University and Theological Seminary), "A Study on Messianic Representation of Son of Man in Q," 80–99.

Duck Ki Kim (TaeJun Theological University), "Trajectory of Twisted Fusion of Apocalyptic and Wisdom Traditions Manifested in Q's Interpretation of Death of Jesus," 100–121.

Hyung Dong Kim (Pusan Jangshin University), "Q: Contra-cultural Rhetoric/Culture of the 'Hidden Transcript,'" 122–40.

Jae Hyun Kim (Kye Myung University), "Labor Discourses of Q Gospel," 141–56.

Vol. 2 (Festschrift for Myung Soo Kim, November 2013)

Kim Myung Soo (Kyung Sung University), "Jesus Humanism and My Academic Journey," 3–21.

Jae Hyun Kim (Kye Myung University), "The Study on the Q Gospel by Dr. Myung-Soo Kim," 22–39.

Ky-Chun So (Presbyterian University and Theological Seminary), "A Study of Jesus' Sayings of the Poor in Q and the Gospel of Luke," 40–61.

Dennis R. MacDonald (Claremont School of Theology), "Alternative Q, the Sinful Woman, and the Son of Man," 62–77.

Jung Hoo Bae (Presbyterian University and Theological Seminary), "A Study of 'this generation' (genea.au[th) in Jesus' Sayings," 78–93.

Jung Chang Kyu (Dae Jun Theological University), "The Jesus Sayings in Acts (Acts 20:35)," 94–116.

Part 2: Theology of Q and the Gospels

Vol. 3 (James M. Robinson's Special Occasion at His 90th Birthday, June 2014)

Ky-Chun So (Presbyterian University and Theological Seminary), "Dr. Professor James M. Robinson's Visitations to Korea: For Robinson's Special Occasion at His 90th Birthday," 1–17.

Joseph Ra (My Lord), "Jesus Who Gave a Dagger Instead of Peace—An Exegesis on Q 12:49–53," 18–37.

In Hee Park (Ewha Women's University), "Narratological Reading of Q: The Domestic Image of the Kingdom of God," 38–58.

Duck Ki Kim (Dae Jun Theological University), "Postmodern Hermeneutics of Q and Gospel of Thomas in the Context of Rome: Towards New Paradigm of 21 Cent. Postmodern Theology," 59–88.

Byung Soo Choi (Hanshin University), "A Study of Thomas 21:5, Q Matt 24:43–44/Luke 12:39–40: Q of the Gospel of Thomas, Written or Oral?," 89–104.

Kim Myung Soo (Kyung Sung University), "Mammon and God," 105–9.

Vol. 4 (November 2014)

James M. Robinson (Claremont Graduate University), "The Nag Hammadi Scriptures," 1–10.

In Hee Park (Ewha Women's University), "The Concept of ἡ βασιλεία in Q Gospel," 11–20.

Ky-Chun So (Presbyterian University and Theological Seminary), "A Study of the Apostolic Integrity of Mary of Magdala in the Early Christian Literatures," 21–40.

Byung Soo Choi (Hanshin University), "The Androgenic Unite with God in the Religious Movements of the Early Christianity: The Gospel of Thomas 114:3 and Q 17:20–21, Matt 23:26," 41–54.

Eun Hye (Grace) So (UC Berkeley / Graduate Theological Union), "A Study of the Centurion Story in Q," 55–70.

Anne Moore (Calgary University), "The Metaphor 'God Is King' within the Hebrew Bible," 71–91.

Vol. 5 (June 2015)

Joseph Ra (My Lord), "A Study of the Etiological Role regarding the Relationship between Male and Female in Q," 1–18.

Kim Myung Soo (Emeritus, Kyung Sung University), "The Social Vision of Q in the Perspective of Publicity Ethic by Dong-Hak Movement in Korea," 19–33.

Ky-Chun So (Presbyterian University and Theological Seminary), "Docetism and Gnosticism Viewed in the Nag Hammadi Library," 34–53.

In Hee Park (Ewha Women's University), "A Study of the Q Community Ethics of the Parable of Builders in Q 6:46–49," 54–67.

In Hee Park (Ewha Women's University), "Q, the Proto-Gospel," 68–78.

Ji Sun Park (Presbyterian University and Theological Seminary), "The Gospel of Thomas," 79–114. Book Review.

Yoseop Ra, *The Origin and Formation of the Gospel* (Wipf & Stock, 2015), 115–18.

Vol. 6 (November 2015)

Hyung Gi Lee (Emeritus, Presbyterian University and Theological Seminary), "A Study of the Public-Theological Aspects of the Sayings of Jesus as Presented in the Narratives of the Gospels: With a Comparison between Hans Frei's Narrative Theology and Moltmann's Theology," 1–51.
Duck Ki Kim (Dae Jun Theological University), "Reinterpretation of Jesus Saying Tradition of Divorce Prohibition in light of Celibacy Issues between Stoicism and Cynicism: Focused upon Q 16:18 (Matt. 5:32) and I Cor. 7:10–11 (Matt. 19:4 = Mark 10:6)," 52–81.
Hyun Nung Kim (Seoul Janshin University), "The Relationship between Mark and Q in the View of Oral Tradition," 82–107.
Jae Hyun Kim (Kye Myung University), "Erich Fromm and Q," 108–15.

Vol. 7 (July 2016, This Journal in Memory of James M. Robinson [1924–2016] is sponsored by Kyung Chun Church)

James M. Robinson (1924–2016), "Curriculum Vitae," 1–8.
James M. Robinson, "Sermon," 9–16.
James M. Robinson, "Documenta Q," 17–23.
Dennis MacDonald, "Which Q? What Kind of Book?," 24–48.
Dennis MacDonald, "Οἱ Λόγοι τοῦ Ἰησοῦ," 49–62.
Yoseop Ra, "The Edenic Kingdom of God in Q," 63–89.
In Hee Park, "The Orality of Q," 90–111.
Byung Soo Choi, "Illuminating the Son of Man with the Gnostic Understanding of the Historical Jesus: Q 9:58 (Matt 8:20) and the Gospel of Thomas 86," 112–32.
Pannel Discussion, Presiding Eun Hye Grace So (UC Berkely / GTU); panelists, Dennis MacDonald, Duck Ki Kim, Yoseop Ra, In Hee Park, and Byung Soo Choi, Journal of Q Studies (ISSN 2288-324X), 133–35.

Studies of the Historical Jesus

The most interesting topic of recent Korean New Testament studies is the historical Jesus, as indicated by the trend mentioned above. Korean scholars regard the historical Jesus as the real Jesus in history, differing from the Jesus of the Gospels—a picture that was colored by the Christ of faith as the Lord of the church.

The many different scholarly perspectives on this historical Jesus can be differentiated into three types. First, since Albert Schweitzer, New Testament scholars have paid attention to the eschatological Jesus of hope, who expected a new world based on Jewish apocalypticism. Second, the members of the Jesus Seminar are portraying the sapient Jesus. Here one can imagine the wandering charismatics on the basis of the wisdom tradition. Third, some scholars are interested in the Jesus of social reform, who violates social norms, as the ideal figure for an equal society.

Ahn Byung Moo, who studied the historical Jesus and belonged to the third type, reconstructed the liberator Jesus. He published *The Testimony of History* (1972), *The*

Part 2: Theology of Q and the Gospels

Liberator Jesus (1975), *The Jesus of History* (1983), and *Jesus of Galilee* (1990). He portrays the figure of Jesus who would suggest the kingdom of God in a political perspective, in order to give hope for *Min Jung* in this real society. Similarly, Kim Myung Soo reconstructs the historical Jesus in the structure of *Min Jung* theology, concluding that Jesus' death is the result of a sectarian praxis for the marginal *Min Jung* and its collision with the Israeli upper class.[21] Kim Chang Rak stands in a different line with regard to *Min Jung* theology; he emphasizes the apocalyptic eschatological characteristics of the kingdom of God that Jesus proclaimed,[22] as Albert Schweitzer suggested.[23]

Choi Gap Jong reconstructed the historical Jesus in his book *Nazareth Jesus* (1996), but he merely accepted the traditional figure of the church. Unfortunately, he did not lose the tension between the Christ of faith and the historical Jesus, because he regarded the event and proclamation of Jesus as both theological and objective history. Hence, he accepted Jesus in the Gospels as the very Jesus in history. Cha Jung Sik, on the other hand, differentiated the texts of the Gospels as several genres in his book *The Heavens of Apocalypse and the Earth of Wisdom: Criticism to the Jesus Theology* (2001). He suggested a subjective reading of the historical Jesus which differed from the apocalyptic characteristic of Jesus, addressing the sapient Jesus based on the ground of wisdom. As a result, his position of the historical Jesus agrees with that of the Jesus Seminar.[24]

21. Kim, *Christianity and Postmodernism*.

22. Kim, "Kingdom of God."

23. Historical investigation of the Jesus tradition untrammeled by theological agendas is the product of the 18th-century Enlightenment. One of the first to undertake such an investigation was the orientalist Reimarus (1694–1768), with whose work Schweitzer begins his classic work, *Quest of the Historical Jesus*. Reimarus saw in Jesus of Nazareth a Jewish messianic revolutionary whose failure led his followers to steal his body and create a new story of Jesus based on aspects of Jewish messianism. The Christian religion did not grow out of the teaching of Jesus; it is a new creation, which gradually unfolded out of a series of failed expectations. The story of the "Quest of the Historical Jesus," as told by Schweitzer, includes not only rationalist attempts at discrediting traditional Christian teaching, but also attempts by Christian theologians to fend off such critiques by creating an edifice of critical theological scholarship by which a believable "real Jesus" might emerge to view. The result, often enough, was a "modernized" Jesus, one whose ethical genius and message of a "spiritual kingdom" brought him close to the liberal ideas of 19th-century German Protestantism. Schweitzer's own position on the historical Jesus, present from beginning to end in his famous book but developed especially at the end, is represented by what he calls "thoroughgoing eschatology." This is Schweitzer's lasting contribution to scholarship; even though his own reconstruction of Jesus' short career is open to considerable criticism.

24. In March of 1985 Funk, a well-known New Testament scholar, presided over the first meeting of a group of scholars that he had convened, dubbed the "Jesus Seminar." Meeting on the campus of the Pacific School of Religion in Berkeley, California, the group embarked on an unprecedented project, to examine the available sources, canonical and non-canonical, in quest of "the voice of Jesus," i.e., "what he really said." The procedure would be as follows: the group would meet biennially, each meeting focusing on a particular set of sayings attributed to Jesus with discussion of previously circulated position papers, with the view to achieving a consensus on the authenticity or non-authenticity of each of the sayings. After discussion and debate a vote would be taken, with each participant casting a colored bead into a box. There would be four colors: *red*, indicating that Jesus undoubtedly said this, or something very close; *pink*, indicating that Jesus probably said something like this; *gray*, indicating that Jesus did not say this, though the idea(s) contained in it may reflect something of Jesus' own; and *black*, indicating that Jesus did not say anything like it, the saying in question reflecting a different

Among other subjects, Korean New Testament scholars are particularly interested in the Jesus movement as an area for studying the historical Jesus. The concept of the Jesus movement is based on a hypothesis of an early faith community composed of Jesus' followers from Galilee, reflected in the early church of the Gospels. This study searches for the community life and ideas of those who preserved intimately the teachings of the historical Jesus, differing from the Christ of faith. Following the *Min Jung* theology of Ahn Byung Moo, Hwang Sung Kyu wrote his book, *The Jesus Movement and Galilee*, in order to reconstruct the history of primitive Christianity and illuminate the meaning of the Jesus movement for the Galilean people.

Helmut Koester, well known as a New Testament scholar but unfortunately little known in Korea as a historian of the primitive church, argued that the early church did not develop as one single community, but various communities through different kinds of trajectories.[25] Following this theory, Cho Tae Yeun wrote regarding the Jesus movement as the followers of Jesus who existed in Palestine and Syria during the last forty years from dating the death of Jesus (30 CE) to dating the Gospel of Mark (70 CE). If the Hellenistic Christians (of whom Paul is typical example) were based on the kerugmatik faith in the Christ of death and resurrection, they also followed the ethos and pathos of the historical Jesus by practicing the teachings and actions of Jesus (based on the Jesus tradition). Korean New Testament scholars also assume that such a Jesus movement was similar to the ministry and teachings of the historical Jesus.

In several studies, scholars examined the historical Jesus by illuminating one part of his ministry, proclamation, and teachings. Kim Jie Chul regarded Jesus' healing ministry as the completeness of the kingdom of God in the human recovery of the whole personality in his paper, "The Healing of Jesus" (*Church and Theology* 28, 1996). Kim Kwang Soo interpreted Jesus' exorcism and healing on the level of social ideology. According to him, Jesus' exorcism ministry meant a protest against the social-political system that unjustly oppressed possessed people. It also meant raising the possessed from dehumanization, and bringing the righteous judgment of God against such a system.[26] He also understood the healing ministry of Jesus in a similar social-political perspective.[27]

Studies of Jesus' Parables

The recorded parables are close to Jesus' real teachings, because of their uniqueness among the characteristics of the historical Jesus that Korean New Testament scholars

---

or later tradition. Each color would be assigned a rating (red = 3; pink = 2; gray = 1; black = 0). The tabulated votes would be reflected in the published results, in which sayings attributed to Jesus would be color-coded, in a kind of "red-letter edition" of the gospels. For more information, see Pearson, "Gospel according to the Jesus Seminar," 1–48.

25. Koester, "*Gnomai Diaphoroi*," 143–56.

26. Kim, "Social Political Understanding," 15–84. He also published several papers in the same title in the following journal, *Gospel and Practice* 19 (1996), 23 (1999), 25 (2000).

27. Kim, "Social Cultural Background," 35–64.

have suggested. The study of Jesus' parables began with the classical theory of Adolf Jülicher, who argued that the parables of Jesus have a simple single story without any allegorical element. Chun Kyung Yun published his book *The Parables of Jesus* (1962), following Jülicher's simplicity theory of in order to suggest the interpretation of the parables. Heu Hyuk also translated *The Parable of Jesus* of Joachim Jeremias into Korean in 1974. His translation was widely used as a textbook in Korea.

There were many studies of Jesus' parables because Korean New Testament scholars understood the purpose and message of the parables in terms of the ministry and teachings of the historical Jesus. In his book *The Parables of the Gospels* (1988), Kim Deuk Jung suggests that the parables of Jesus were a rhetorical tool to allow the audience to stand firmly on eschatological hope, because the parables result from the conflicts and controversy with Jesus' opponents. Choi Gap Jong, agreeing with Kim Deuk Jung, argues in his book *The Study of the Parables of Jesus* (1993), that the purpose of the parables was based on the structure of conflict and eschatological optimism. Following them, Roman Catholic Jung Tae Hyun, in his book *An Amazing Discovery* (1996), suggests the unique skill of persuasion by which the parables of Jesus gave the audience hope. Kim Chang Rak therefore paid attention to the relationship between the speaker and the audience in his book *The World of the Parables You Hear* (1999), trying to create a point of contact with the audience in order to illuminate the parables in the context of the movement of the kingdom of God that the historical Jesus activated.

Later on, in Korea, the study of the parables appeared across a broad spectrum, from the objective quest to reconstruct the proclamation and teachings of the historical Jesus to the subjective quest to let modern readers respond to and participate in the historical reconstruction. Specifically, the so-called "literary-historical criticism" in Korea tended to disregard the question of the historical Jesus in the interpretation of the parables. For example, Oh Duk Ho suggests literary-historical criticism as a tool for the study of the Gospels in his book *What Is the Literary Historical Criticism?* (2002), and focuses on the interpretation of the parables for the position of the authorial reader which the final text of the Bible intended. Here, in contrast with Jülicher, the allegorical expositions that the evangelists added into the parables of the Gospels can be regarded as the important parts. Cho Tae Yeun's interpretation of Jesus' parables is interested in the social-economic structure of Galilean agricultural villages, the milieu of the historical Jesus, but he concentrates on the complete narrative rather than each parable, extending the scope of the parables to the scenes before and after them in the Gospel texts. The narrative of the parables can be "triggered," so to speak, into the time of the historical Jesus and added into a structure in relationship with the parables, which are reconstructed in the setting of interpreters' thinking. Cho called his methodology "a hermeneutical dialogue to develop the interpretation of the parables in the setting of oriental thinking."[28]

---

28. Cho, "Study of the Synoptic Gospels," 537.

Korean Recent Trends in the Study of the Gospels

Recent trend in Korean study of the historical Jesus is the attempt to apply Jesus' teachings to Christian life. Kim Jie Chul, on the one hand, published many monographs and textbooks studying the New Testament from a homiletic perspective, hosted many public lectures for pastors and laypeople, and continued to help Bible teachers and preachers at practical levels. The *Word*, a magazine published by Tyrannous in Seoul, on the other hand, continued to study the Bible for preachers. These and other interdisciplinary studies connected the New Testament and teachings of Jesus to other academic areas. For example, Ky-Chun So suggested the love of God as a missiological principle in the teachings of Jesus in his book *The Love of God and World Mission* (2001); he dealt with the Jewish and Gentile missions of Jesus from a missiological perspective.

EPILOGUE

Tong Chun theology, mentioned above, has led to new missiological concepts. In the past, the concept of *missio Dei* was understood only in christological perspective on the basis of Western thought. Such a concept lacked a fully Trinitarian understanding, emphasizing the mission of human more than the mission of God. It eventually drew criticism because Western theology determined the identity of *missio Dei*.[29] Hence Kim Yong Dong suggests that one must keep in mind christological levels and a Spiritual level to the *missio Dei*. When the concept of *missio Dei* is understood from both christological and Spiritual perspectives, one can reach the Trinitarian *Tong Chun* theology of *missio Dei*.

This example indicates how *Tong Chun* theology must lead Korean New Testament studies to develop in breadth (of spirit), depth (of inner maturity), height (of quality or morality), expanse (of external relationship with the world church), and length (until the *parousia* of Jesus Christ, not temporal growth or mature).[30]

One hundred thirty-two years have passed since Protestantism set foot in Korea in 1884. A number of changes have taken place in the field of New Testament studies in Korea during the past years. Now Korean New Testament studies must play a leading role in international New Testament studies, and be ready to reevaluate Western theology in light of Korean contexts. Specifically, studies of the historical Jesus that can move the spirits of Korean people with subjectivity and independence are based on many theological contents. I will conclude briefly as following:

Regarding the studies of the historical Jesus in Korea, there was *Min Jung* theology in the past, but now there is *Tong Chun* theology.

Broadly speaking, *Min Jung* theology interpreted Jesus as an alienated friend of *Min Jung*, and *Tong Chun* theology suggests Jesus in the midst of wholeness.

---

29. Kim, *Theology Activating Church*, 131–65. He also specifically criticized the Western concept of *missio Dei* in 145–49, 163.

30. Suh, *Church and Mission*, 64–66.

PART 3

Jewish Influences and Christological Insights

XVI

A Theological and Anthropological Understanding of Creation

PROLOGUE

CREATION IN GEN 1–2 cannot be separated from Israelite appreciation of God and particularly from God's action as savior in their midst. Therefore, it is more appropriate to focus upon the "Creator" than "creation," upon the personality and motivation of the Creator than upon the origin and form of the created world.[1] This emphasis upon the Creator brings up another important distinction. The word "Creator" in Hebrew is a participle, literally "the one [who is] creating." Also God the Creator in the sense of the Hebrew Bible is present in the other action. The Hebrew word "Creator," therefore, deals primarily with the present moment and its promise for the future, and the past is merely secondary. Because the Creator is acting now within the contemporary world, the Hebrew Bible will not normally attend to creatio ex nihilo as a single, unique event of the past. The closest that the Hebrew Bible gets to the idea of "nothing" is the "chaos" out of which the Creator brings life, good order, balance, harmony, and security.

Over the centuries the traditions about creation in Gen 1–2 have been understood and explained in many ways. One can presume that Ancient Israel shared many of the cosmological perceptions of neighboring people. However, the framework and content of the accounts about creation may reflect the primary theological focus,[2] not cosmological. Also one must remember that these accounts are narrative symbols for anthropological realities and are not to be understood literally. This means that the narratives in Gen 1–2 are not only served as a statement of their theological understanding, but characterized as a statement of their anthropological understanding.

---

1. Westermann, "Reden von Schoepfer," 105.
2. Von Rad, "Theological Problem," 131–33.

The creation narratives found within Gen 1–2 are examples of Priestly and Yahwistic theology respectively. Each is a product of a different period of Israelite history. Each has its own specific concerns and needs.

Genesis 2

This account is the literary and theological product of a much earlier generation. It reflects the concerns of the united kingdom of David and his successor Solomon.[3] This tradition reveals biblical Israel's appropriation of royal ideology and its development as a national entity. The traditions of the founding of the Israelite describe the gradual integration of a federation of loosely knit tribes. The threats from a common enemy convinced them that centralization was their only hope for survival. Such a position was judged by some apostasy. Had not their God protected them in the past? Had they lost all hope for continued protection in the future? Besides, royal ideology itself was sacrilegious. In it the sovereign was presumed divine, with power over both heaven and earth.[4] No loyal worshipper of the God of the tribes of Israel could entertain such a view.

The theology that emerged from tenth-century Israel contains a refashioning of royal ideology that both legitimized the monarchy and at the same time held it accountable to the Mosaic law and the Deuteronomistic law. The creation narratives found within these traditions are an anthropological and theological rather than a cosmological statement.

The narrative in the Yahwist consists of various distinct related primordial themes. Apparent inconsistencies and presence of doubts are evidence of this. There are two descriptions of the earth. First, in 2:5–6 the earth is arid, with only a mist coming up from the ground. Second, in 2:8–10 the earth contains a garden with trees and a river that branches out in four directions. Twice the Lord God places the human creature[5] in the garden; twice the man names the woman (2:23; 3:29); twice he is driven from the garden (3:23, 24). Surely, this was not meant to provide an explanation of the origin of the world.

Here the man is brought into a world depicted as a wilderness. Without rain and human toil the earth cannot bring forth vegetation (2:5). The Yahwist proposes a terrestrial, not a celestial. "In the day that the Lord God made the earth and heavens" (2:4b) is followed by an explanation for the barrenness of that earth.

---

3. Gottwald, *Hebrew Bible*, 137. According to him, this account was composed ca. 960–930 BCE.

4. Anderson, *Understanding the Old Testament*, 211. He concludes that the Yahwist's interpretation was based on the faith of covenant community and in the covenant faith; Yahweh is the sovereign Lord upon whose grace and goodness, manifested in the great events of the past, Israel was utterly dependent.

5. Trible, *God and the Rhetoric of Sexuality*, 80. She contends that sexual differentiation did not appear until the creation of the woman.

The desolation of the land is due to the lack of rain and the absence of a human being to serve the ground. Rain, so necessary for life, is supplied by God alone. It seems, however, the earth is incomplete without someone to work the land and thereby enable the herb of the field to sprout forth. The verb that expresses this working is *'abad*, which also means "to serve," and which implies a certain kind of relationship. This server of the ground is not its servant but is serving it for another. The selection of this world highlights the Yahwist's anthropological understanding. The human serves God by serving the ground.

Verse 7 is often called the *locus classicus* of ancient Israelite anthropology. After God caused the mist coming up from the earth and give drink to the ground, God took some of the dust from the ground and formed a human creature as a potter would form an object. In the Yahwist tradition the word used to describe this creation is *yasar*, a verb that denotes the activity of a potter.[6] The human creature is formed or fashioned as a piece of pottery is fashioned. Likewise, as pottery is molded from clay material, so this creature is molded from clay of the ground. *'Apar* (dust) denotes the dry surface of the ground. It also refers to the ground of the grave and thus has the added nuance of commonness or worthlessness.

The relationship between this creature of the ground and the ground itself can be seen from the account of the creative act (being formed), from the material employed therein (dust from the ground), and from the play on words between *'adam* (man or humankind) and *adama* (ground). The human creature who has been taken from the ground will in turn work the ground that has now been watered by God. Thus the herbs of the field will be able to sprout forth.

This human creature is not yet a *nepesh hayya* (a living being). Only by means of a second creative act is this accomplished. It is when God breathes the breath of life into the nostrils that the creature comes alive. One must remember that these accounts are narrative symbols for anthropological realities and are not to be understood literally. The author has set out to show both the affinity between human beings and other earth-creatures and the special character of the former in respect to the latter. The author chose this way of accomplishing that twofold goal.

In the present narrative, no life existed before the human creature, and this creature did not live before receiving the breath of life from God. God is the source of life, but life comes to the earth through human agency. Such a theology has profound implications for the people Israel struggling to incorporate elements of royal ideology into their theological view. It can be seen as a polemic against those who would cast the human ruler in the role of divine benefactor. At the same time, it leaves no doubt about the indispensability of human instrumentality.

The reason given for the creation of the animals is that the human creation is not alone (2:18). However, these animals are unfit to serve as (helpers) for this unique being. The word *'ezer* appears in other biblical passages where the context is usually

---

6. Cf. Isa 29:16; 41:25; 43:1, 7; 45:9, 18; Jer 18:4, 6.

one of blessing after deliverance, and where the *'ezer*, or mediator of blessing, is God.[7] In this creation account, since no animal was found fit to serve as a source of blessing, God made the woman. The word "alone" comes from the verb *badad* and means "to separate" or "to divide" and, therefore, carries the meaning "incomplete" rather than "by oneself." It is not good that the man remains incomplete, and so God will make someone like this man who will act as a mediator of blessing for him.

It is in the woman that the man finds a helper. She is like the man because since taken from him, she is made of the same substance. Her origin is from him as his origin is from the ground. The play on words *'ish* (man) / *'ishsa* (woman) and *'adama* (ground) / *'adam* (man) illustrate this. Here the Yahwist has retained the link between the woman and the man in the view of the woman of the rib of the man.

Verse 23 is an obvious poetic construction. The word pair "bone and flesh" are of the type that is characteristically coupled.[8] While this expression probably originated in the ancient idea of the family or kinship, its use in the Hebrew tradition is not limited to this context.[9] The bond is deeper than a merely physical tie. There is a conventional implication.[10] This nuance carries the added connotation of loyalty and responsibility stemming from choice. The very words "bone" and "flesh" have psychological as well as physiological meanings. The first has the root meaning of "power," while the second refers to "weakness." When coupled, they embrace the two extremes and everything between. This antithetical construction is a comprehensive expression and is used to speak of a person's total range of interaction with another. The man recognizes that the woman is one with whom he can interact in his totality: he is no longer incomplete.

Genesis 1

The exile was a devastating experience for Israel both politically and theologically.[11] The priestly writer has a version of earlier ancient Near Eastern myth, *Enuma Elish*.[12] However, this account reshaped the creation in such a way as to portray the God of Israel establishing the cosmos in an orderly fashion for the elect people Israel in Genesis 1. The rekindling of confidence in this God rather than the reporting of the history of primordial times was the intent of this narrative. Theology and anthropology, not cosmology, underlie the account.

---

7. Cf. Exod 18:4; Deut 33:7, 26, 29; Isa 30:5; Ezek 12:14; Pss 20:3, 33:20; 70:6; 115:9; 121:1, 2; 124:8; 146:5.

8. Gevirtz, *Patterns in Early Poetry of Israel*, 140–61.

9. Cf. Gen 29:14; Judg 9:2; 2 Sam 5:1; 19:13.

10. The following ideas are found in Brueggemann, "Of the Same Flesh," 532–42.

11. Gottwald, *Hebrew Bible*, 139. According to him, this account was composed ca. 550–450 BCE.

12. For more information, see Anderson, *Understanding the Old Testament*, 427; Anderson, *Creation versus Chaos*, 11–42; Coote and Ord, *In the Beginning*, 5–18.

From a careful look at the tradition I am sure that this is not an account of *creatio ex nihilo* nor is it a summary of some evolutionary process.[13] The text itself illustrates this. Light appears on the first day (1:3–5). From whence does it emanate? There are no luminaries until the fourth day (1:14–19). On the second day God made the firmament to separate the waters (1:6–8). There has been no mention of the creation of these waters. Instead, they seem to have been present before the creative activity began (1:2). On the third day God gathered the waters, and thus the dry land appeared (1:9–10). This cannot mean that the earth was created then, for the earth had already been in existence, but void and without form before the light appeared (1:2). These few examples show that the intent of the account was not cosmological. Rather, its purpose was to remind the people of God's ability to bring order out of disorder and to establish the regularity and harmony of the universe. This may be represented as follows:

first day	Light	=	fourth day	Luminaries
second day	Sky	=	fifth day	Birds and fish
third day	Land	=	sixth day	Animals and Men
	(Plants)			(Plants for food)
	↘			↙
	Seventh day			Sabbath

Dramatically this structure has two poles finishing with a close-up on Sabbath.[14]

It also served as a statement of their anthropological understanding. The structure of the document has carefully been arranged in order to set forth the Priestly teaching about the restoration of Israel. The sequence of the acts of creation seems to proceed from what is farthest from God to what is closest, beginning with chaos and continuing to the appearance of humankind.[15] The anthropological passage is Gen 1:26–28. A simple analysis of the structure of vv. 20–28 enables one to see the place of humanity within the entire plan of creation:

narrative description	v. 20	"and God said..."
of creation of water	v. 21	"and God created..."
animals	v. 22	"and God blessed..."
narrative description	v. 24	"and God said..."

13. According to von Rad, the verb *bara'* contains "the idea of complete effortlessness and *creatio ex nihilo*, since it is never connected with any statement of the material." Cf. Von Rad, *Genesis*, 49.

14. Cf. Wenham, *Genesis 1–15*, 7. For more information of Sabbath in relation to the Priestly teaching, see Coote and Ord, *In the Beginning*, 77–93. Also for more information of the creation order, see ibid., 117–33. Specifically, Coote and Ord apply the issue of the creation in the Hebrew Bible not only to the Priestly account in the New Testament but also to creation in our present time.

15. Schmidt, *Schoepfungsgeschichte*, 188.

of creation of land	v. 25	"and God made..."
narrative description	v. 26	"and God said..."
of creation of humans	v. 27	"and God created..."
	v. 28	"and God blessed.

Verses 20–28 described three different acts of God. All of these actions are directed toward the *nepesh hayya* (living beings) of the waters and the birds of the air. Verses 24–25 pertain in the same way to the *nepesh hayya* of the earth. One would expect v. 26 to relate the blessing of the land animals, but it does not. The pattern is resumed in vv. 26–28. Whether this pattern was original with the writer or was a reworking of an older creation account, the fact remains that the final form contains the pattern, and it is this form that has been handed down as Priestly teaching.

A significant point to note is the expression used to refer to the entire group of animals. That designation (*nepesh hayya*) is not applied directly to humans (v. 26). Since the blessing that completes the pattern (vv. 22, 29) is missing after v. 25, the account of the creation of the land animals either has been cut short by the account of human creation or has been extended to include it. My concern is that the pattern has been adjusted in order that humankind is included with the *nepesh hayya* of the land, thereby indicating the existence of a bond between them. Humans are a kind of beings of the earth.

Further, the *nepesh hayya* of the waters and birds are created "according to their kind" (v. 21). The *nepesh hayya* of the earth, further classified as cattle, creeping things, and living things of the earth, are also made "according to their kind" (v. 25).[16] This phrase is absent in the account of human creation. In its place we read that humankind is created in God's image and according to God's likeness. In keeping with the rest of the interpretation of Genesis 1, this point should also be understood as an anthropological rather than a biological statement. While acknowledging human affinity with the creatures of the earth, the early Israelites recognized that there was a dimension to this earth creature that transcended the purely material.

The blessing of the *nepesh hayya* of the waters and birds is "increase and multiply and fill the waters... and the earth" (v. 22). The blessing that one might associate with the *nepesh hayya* of the earth is found in the blessing of the humans along with the commission to "should it [the earth] and dominate the fish of the sea and the birds of the heavens and all the living, the creeping things of the earth" (v. 28). By incorporating the blessing of the land animals with that of the humans the author has linked the two species. At the same time and in the same verse the commission to subdue and to dominate has bestowed upon the humans the distinction of rulers over the land and animals, thereby indicating human superiority.[17]

---

16. The exact meaning of this phrase is not clear from the text. Perhaps it has to do with creation of a species rather than an individual member of the species.

17. Schmidt, *Schoepfungsgeschichte*, 187.

A Theological and Anthropological Understanding of Creation

The use of the technical creation verb *bara'* is another indication of the uniqueness of the human creature. The verb denotes extraordinary divine activity and contains the notion of newness and of awesome or epochal production.[18] The word indicates God's creation activity through the Word.[19]

Verses 26–27 also speaks of creation in God's image and according to God's likeness. Immediately after the mention of this image and likeness the commission is stated. It would seem that there is a relationship between the image and likeness and ability to bring the earth into submission and to rule over the animals. *Zelem* is the word used to refer to molten images, painted pictures, or some kind of physical representation cut out of material.[20] *demut* is less concrete in meaning and denotes a likeness or similarity in exterior appearance.[21] It would seem that the priestly writer found the connotations of *zelem* too physical in meaning to express their anthropology, and so they coupled it with a word having a less concrete nuance. This does not mean that the image/likeness of God is restricted to a spiritual entity. Rather, it transcends the physical/spiritual alternative without denying either. Hebrew thought seldom separated the physical and spiritual but considered the human in its entirety.

More attention is given to the purpose of the image/likeness of God. It appears that Israel, like its neighbors, understood image/likeness in relational terms. The primary significance of this notion was divine relationship, not the possession of a divine element. This image/likeness explains not only the human relationship with God but also their relationship with the animals and the land.

If the people in exile understood their national humiliation and spiritual desolation as due punishment for their infidelity to the solemn covenant with God and for their prostitution of the land that had been given to them as a gift, then this anthropological interpretation might serve several purposes. It could reinforce Israel's faith in God's ability to bring order and life out of chaos, even a chaos such as they were experiencing. It could remind them of their fundamental but violated relationships and forgotten responsibilities. And it could instill in them a hope that the creative power God would once again form them into faithful people, assuming responsibility for the rest of the created world. These ideas converged in forming the theology of the Priestly account of creation. Creation has been interpreted in the light of God's covenant with Israel and the promise of Land; thus, creation theology is found close to the heart of Israel's religion.

---

18. Koehler, *Old Testament Theology*, 136, 144.
19. Westermann, *Genesis*, 52–57.
20. Brown et al., *Hebrew and English Lexicon*, 853–54.
21. Ibid., 198.

EPILOGUE

The first account of creation in Genesis 1 was attributed to the Priestly tradition; the second account in Genesis 2 to the Yahwist tradition. Each drew upon ancient myths, not to repeat the myth or to copy the mythological religion. Rather, each offered insights into the central, "inside" theological synthesis that Yahwist chose Israel and remained faithful to divine covenant with Israel. The Priestly account in Genesis 1 reached its final form during the exile, or immediately afterward, and served to strengthen the faith of Israel in the re-creation of their land, thoroughly destroyed and reduced to chaos by the Babylonian conquerors in 587 BCE. The Yahwist account of creation in Genesis 2 reached its final form much earlier and was intended to support and direct the concept of royalty within Israel. Israel's king was never to be considered divinely equal to Yahweh, but the king was God's instrument for securing unity, stability, and fertility in the land and among its people. The king symbolized God's continuous presence as Creator and preserver of life.

It is clear from this brief look at the traditions of biblical Israel that the sacred authors were well acquainted with the myths of ancient Near Eastern world. Imbued with faith in their own God and occupied with national as well as theological matters, they refashioned these myths so as to address their own particular concerns. Political, sociological, biological, physiological, and cosmological references are discernible, but they serve the theological and anthropological interests of the covenant between God and Israel and should be appreciated as such.

XVII

A Rhetorical Aspect in the Wisdom of Solomon

PROLOGUE

THIS CHAPTER DEALS WITH a brief introduction to the text of the Wisdom of Solomon: author, date, contents, provenance, genre, etc. In literary analysis, two forms of arguments will be presented: flashbacks or the fragment repetition of significant ideas in similar phrasing, and themes sustained throughout the Wisdom of Solomon. This chapter will show a rhetorical aspect in chapter 10 of the Wisdom of Solomon: The Hebrew epic profile, relationship with the Wis 9:18, and genealogical relation to form an epoch and combination to the Wisdom and apocalyptic traditions of Israel.

Biblical scholarship has attempted to apply secular literary criticism to biblical texts for more than two decades. The trend of part of biblical scholarship has moved from historical-theological approaches to literary techniques in biblical texts. In any case, there has been an attempt to understand biblical texts as secular literature by employing contemporary literary criticism.

The goals of this chapter are as follow: (1) to give a brief introduction to the text of the Wisdom of Solomon: date, provenance, authorship, genre, intertextual relations or place in the literary traditions of the time, etc.; (2) to read chapter 10 of the Wisdom of Solomon using the literary devices, i.e., rhetoric, narrative structures, etc.; (3) to work through the existing index (or indices) of biblical references, list these references, verify these references by encoding with *sigla*, "AL" means "allusion"; (4) to work through the text and a list of epic references that occur in addition to those just noted as textual references; and (5) to analyze the rhetorical function of the epic references to the argument, point, or purpose of the composition as a whole. Thus this chapter is a case study or a tentative attempt.

I am deeply indebted especially to David Winston, James M. Reese, and Burton L. Mack, for setting up the primary routines and devices for this topic. In this chapter,

I will not seek to create either new routines or devices *ex nihilo*. Rather, I will attempt to utilize appropriately their ready-made ideas to meet the goals of this chapter.

General Information

Author, Date, Contents and Provenance

The Wisdom of Solomon is an exhortatory discourse written in Greek by a learned and thoroughly Hellenized Jew of Alexandria,[1] perhaps active in the second half of the first century BCE. Therefore, James M. Reese concluded that "the author is evidently a teacher in one of the Jewish centers of learning in Alexandria, well acquainted with contemporary culture and committed to demonstrating the relevance of the principles of Judaism to the future intellectual leaders of his people."[2] The Wisdom of Solomon is divided into three closely related and interlocking parts: the book of eschatology, the book of wisdom, and the book of history.[3]

> 1:1—6:21. The book of eschatology. An exhortation to the rulers of the world;
>
> 6:22—9:18. The book of wisdom. Solomon's prayers for wisdom and wisdom as the savior of the Just;
>
> 10–19. The book of history. God dispenses justice towards the Israelites and Egyptians during the exodus.

The composition combines the refinement of a Hellenistic rhetoric and the acumen of a biblical exegete, and serves as an excellent illustration for the use and influence of both biblical and Hellenistic literary traditions.[4]

Genre

The literary genre employed by the author of the Wisdom of Solomon is the *logos protreptikos* or exhortatory discourse.[5] In the Hellenistic world of the first century BCE a literary genre that comprised the smaller literary forms discovered to be present in Wisdom of Solomon. Such a form not only did exist but was in common use, namely, the protreptic or *logos protreptikos*, a didactic exhortation.[6] The Wisdom of Solomon is an exhortation to pursue wisdom and thereby to live the righteous life that issues in immortality. In order to accomplish his purpose the author employs the popular Hellenistic genre of the protreptic, a treatise that made "an appeal to follow a meaningful

---

1. Winston, *Wisdom of Solomon*, 3.
2. Reese, *Hellenistic Influence*, 151.
3. Nickelsburg, *Jewish Literature*, 175.
4. Dimant, "Use and Interpretation of Mikra," 410.
5. Winston, *Wisdom of Solomon*, 18.
6. Reese, *Hellenistic Influence*, 117.

philosophy as a way of life."[7] Working with this literary form and its typical rhetorical devices and modes of expression and structuring his material with consummate artistry, the sage combines the wisdom and apocalyptic traditions of Israel, synthesizing them with an elective use of Greek philosophy and religious thought. In assuming the identity of King Solomon he specifies wisdom as his chief topic, roots that wisdom in the religious tradition of Israel, and claims authority for his address to the kings and rulers of the earth.[8]

Literary Analysis[9]

Burton L. Mack noted that "the unity of the Wisdom of Solomon has found strong support in Reese's analysis of its composition and that its intention, setting, and mode of argumentation have been clarified to some extent by his analysis of its rhetorical genre."[10]

According to Reese, two forms of arguments will be presented for the unity of the Wisdom of Solomon: (1) the frequent repetition of significant ideas in similar phrasing; for convenience these are called "flashbacks." The term "flashback" simply implies an interaction between the two passages. Whether the sage was anticipating the later development or simply recalling a previous passage, it does not affect the argument that this phenomenon is a sign of unity. In reality, the book probably grew over an extended period of time during which the sage added to and modified his work. (2) Themes sustained throughout the book.

Flashbacks

Flashback will mean a short repetition of a significant word or a group of words or a distinctive idea in two different parts of the Wisdom of Solomon. The tendency of the Wisdom of Solomon is to concentrate upon one detail or aspect of a concept at a time and then to complete the concept by an allusion later in a different context. This stylistic tendency has produced the "flashbacks." Reese concluded that "flashbacks will be treated as a literary feature to give the book unity, to maintain a consistent approach in dealing with diverse material."[11] The large number of vocabulary repetitions and the use of identical phrases and examples to describe disparate situations cannot be considered as either the work of chance or the result of imitation. They reveal a consistent scholarly effort to construct an elaborate exhortation calculated to appeal to the audience envisioned by the sage.

7. Ibid., 117–21. See the genre of Wis. as a whole.
8. Nickelsburg, *Jewish Literature*, 175.
9. I owe mainly this suggestion to Reese, 122–45.
10. Mack et al., "Wisdom Literature," 381.
11. Reese, *Hellenistic Influence*, 124.

Themes

Wis. has many themes that are maintained throughout the passage convey to its readers the author's theological positions. Reese suggested five themes: religious knowledge of God, theological use of the concept of "seeing," interaction of malice and ignorance, man's immortality and related themes, and didactic use of history.

Wisdom Myth and the Quest for Logic[12]

Burton L. Mack attempted to work out a typology of the mythological configurations of wisdom (hidden-transcendent; near-immanent; once near-now retreated) which functioned as theological categories. Mack suggested that, in wisdom, the dialectic of wisdom as immanent and transcendent, together with the identification of wisdom and *pneuma*, enabled a new theology of revelation. He argued also that the pattern of destiny for the *dikaios* (Wis 1–5), "Solomon" (6–9), the series of Patriarchs (10), and Israel as *laos* (11–19) could be understood as developments of wisdom mythology and theology that has focused on the problem of the nature and destiny of Israel.[13]

Mack concluded that "all subsequent wisdom mythology can be understood in just this way, as junctures explored in the interest of working out the problem of fragmentation. But the mythic episodes themselves do not relate how the gaps actually are to be bridged. They cannot do this until three conditions are met: (1) a full narrative logic must be discovered that can relate together again all of the orders now apart; (2) the orders must be conceptualized structurally, systematically, and in such a way that they can be combined in a single complex system; and (3) a new social order must be actualized and rationalized in accordance with the wisdom myth."[14]

A Rhetorical Aspect in the Chapter 10 of the Wisdom of Solomon

To build up Hebrew epic, wisdom's saving and punishing power is here illustrated by the enumeration of seven righteous heroes and their wicked counterparts, although the contrast is not consistently carried out. The chapter 10 of the Wisdom of Solomon has Adam-Cain; Noah-generation of the flood; Abraham-the nations confounded in their wickedness; Lot-Sodomites; Jacob-Esau; Joseph-his critics; Israel under Moses-the Egyptian oppressors under Pharaoh. Now I can outline the righteous ones in chapter 10 of the Wisdom of Solomon as follows:

---

12. I owe mainly this suggestion to Mack, *Wisdom and the Hebrew*, 139–51. Special note should be made of the work of Mack on the relation of Wis 6–9 and the Isis aretalogies. Mack has applied his study to illustrate the way in which the wisdom tradition contained to be open to these sources for its metaphors in Isis mythology. Cf. *Early Judaism*, 382–84; Mack, *Logos und Sophia*, 63–107.

13. Mack, "Wisdom of Solomon," 384.

14. Mack, *Wisdom and the Hebrew Epic*, 149–50.

A Rhetorical Aspect in the Wisdom of Solomon

The Hebrew Epic Profile in Chapter 10 of the Wisdom of Solomon
("AL" means "allusion")

Text	Reference	Type	Epoch	Place	Figure	Code	Theme	Flash-backs
10:1	Gen 2:7	AL	Creation	Eden	Adam	Genealogies	Creation	
4	Gen 6–9	AL	Flood	Flood	Noah	Genealogies	Sin	
5	Gen 12	AL	Election	Election	Abraham	Promises	Obedience	
6	Gen 19	AL	Election	Election	Lot	Honor	Judgment	Wis 4:4–6
10	Gen 27	AL	Election	Shrines	Jacob	Blessings	Rescue	Wis 5:
13	Gen 37	AL	Captivity	Egypt	Joseph	Blessings	Deliverance	Wis 2:18
15	Exo 6	AL	Exodus	Egypt	Moses	Blessings	Deliverance	
21	Exo 4:10	AL	Exodus	Egypt	Moses	Blessings	Deliverance	

Relationship with Wis 9:18

Many scholars insist that Wis 9:18 sums up the prayer and introduces the historical sketch in chapter 10. The first appearance of *esothesan* becomes a basic theme in the following section (10.4; 14.4–5; 16.7, 11; 18.5).[15] In the first nine chapters wisdom remained faithful to man until he found salvation. Now, in the second half of the book, salvation becomes the key word; especially in the account of the heroes of the sacred history in chapter 10.[16]

Genealogical relation to form an "epoch"

The wisdom is here presented by the seven righteous heroes that counterparted by their wicked. The sage composes genealogical relation to form an "epoch," as follows:

The names of the seven great figures		A singular typology	
Wis	10:1 Adam	Gen	2:7
	4 Noah		6–9

---

15. Wiston, *Wisdom of Solomon*, 209. "The word *esothesan* which occurs here for the first time in this work announces the theme for the rest of the book."

16. Clarke, *Wisdom of Solomon*, 65.

PART 3: JEWISH INFLUENCES AND CHRISTOLOGICAL INSIGHTS

The names of the seven great figures		A singular typology
5	Abraham	12
6	Lot	19
10	Jacob	27
13	Joseph	37
15	Moses	Exod 6

Here Adam only is not called *dikaios*, but we are sure all the seven heroes have saving and punishing power against the wicked counterparts. As above mentioned, we outline the chains like Adam-Cain, Noah-flood, Abraham-wicked nations, Lot-Sodomites, Jacob-Essau, Joseph-his opponents, Moses-Egyptian oppressors.

Combination to the Wisdom and apocalyptic traditions of Israel

Seven times it happens that "the righteous one" is "saved" by wisdom. The epic history in Genesis was obviously understood to be an account of the primeval age.[17] The sage combines the wisdom and apocalyptic traditions of Israel, as follows:

	e.g. "the righteous one"(7x)	"saved"(7x)
Wis	10:1	10:1
	5	4
	6	6
	10	9
	13(2x)	12
	20	13
		15

Certainly, ancient people considered that numbers had some mystical significance. Consequently, numerology is to be found in both apocalyptic and non-apocalyptic writings. Thus it is averred that apocalypticism is characterized by numerology. In chapter 10 of the Wisdom of Solomon, the sage obviously has the apocalyptic imagination, and combines the wisdom and apocalyptic traditions of Israel.

---

17. Mack, *Wisdom and the Hebrew Epic*, 186.

In order to show evidence of apocalyptic in the Wisdom of Solomon, it must be recognized that "the identification of the Serpent of Gen 3 with the Satan was inevitable, especially in view of the Dragon Myth. It is first made in Wis 2:24."[18]

EPILOGUE

I would like to briefly summarize the outcomes from this case study. The Wisdom of Solomon is exhortatory discourse or *logos protreptikos* written in Greek by a learned and thoroughly Hellenized Jew of Alexandria, perhaps active in the second half of the first century BCE. In literary analysis, there are two forms of arguments for the unity of the Wisdom of Solomon: flashbacks and themes. Also, I suggested working out a typology of the mythological configurations of wisdom which functioned as theological categories.

To show a rhetorical aspect in chapter 10 of the Wisdom of Solomon, I figured out the Hebrew epic profile, relationship with Wis 9:18, combination to the wisdom and apocalyptic traditions of Israel. The seven righteous ones are similar to the seven figures enumerated in Adam, Enoch, Noah, Abraham, Isaac, Jacob (18:13) and completed with the addition of Moses (17:4).

The Wisdom of Solomon describes the providential ordering of Israel's history through wisdom's generation-by-generation election of holy servants. Hence, in the Wisdom of Solomon the old salvation history with its idea of miraculous divine eruption in history is reinterpreted.

18. Frost, *Old Testament Apocalyptic*, 26.

XVIII

Thomas Christianity

PROLOGUE

STEPHEN J. PATTERSON, IN his book *The Gospel of Thomas and Jesus*, asks the question of how Thomas Christianity might fit into the overall development of ancient Christianity. This question is still not satisfactorily answered in his book. Nevertheless, his book is an attempt to draw the trajectory between Thomas Christianity and the literary development of the Jesus tradition like Q, and between Thomas Christianity and the historical development of early Christianity like the Q Community.

Patterson poses the question of the place of Thomas Christianity in the literary development of the Jesus tradition, and focuses specially on the Thomas tradition in relation to the Synoptic Gospels. His strong argument is: In the case of the parallels between Thomas and the Synoptic traditions, both share a saying each inherited from an older tradition or an oral tradition.[1] Therefore, according to him, Thomas presents its sayings in a sequence that is almost entirely divorced from the Synoptic texts.[2] He concludes that one finds little to suggest that the Gospel of Thomas was aware of the Synoptic texts. Specifically, according to him, there are three groups of sayings affording comparison with the Synoptic tradition: "Synoptic twins" who have very close parallels, "Synoptic siblings" which have loose parallels, and "Synoptic cousins" which is almost removed from the Synoptic tradition. According to him, even if Synoptic twins seem to be dependent upon the Synoptic Gospels, there is little evidence to suggest that the Gospel of Thomas is literally dependent upon the Synoptic Gospels.

Patterson searches for a place for Thomas within the social-historical development of that tradition. Of first priority, of course, there are the issues of Thomas's date and provenance. He suggests a date for the Gospel of Thomas (NHC II,2; P. Oxy.

---

1. However, Sean Freyne argues that some common sayings in the Synoptics were subsequently developed by GTh. For more information, see Freyne, *Galilee and Gospel*, 210.

2. Patterson, *Gospel of Thomas and Jesus*, 3.

1,654; 655; Hippolytus, *Refutation of All Heresies*) as in the vicinity of 70–80 CE.[3] He is also sure the provenance for Thomas as at eastern Syria, where the popularity of Thomas is well attested. Here once more the question of Thomas relationship to the Synoptic Gospels is worked out; it is argued that Thomas Christianity tends to perpetuate the tradition of social radicalism. Their itinerant mode existing in the world represents the Thomas Christians' radical protest against the world. Such a view, in fact, is originally drawn from Gerd Theissen's theory. Theissen's thesis is that "characteristic of the persons who first collected and transmitted the sayings of Jesus was a particular style of living, which placed a premium on leaving behind house and home, family and profession to take up the life of the wandering preacher."[4] However, those Thomas Christians who continued the tradition of itinerant social radicalism hardens their commitment to a Gnostic view of the world. At the same time, they believe in the path of salvation that is laid in the interpretation of Jesus' secret sayings.[5]

Patterson asks the last question of how Thomas Christianity might contribute to a better understanding of the historical figure of Jesus himself.[6] By playing Thomas and the Synoptic tradition off the one against the other, he argues that it is possible to arrive at a very early stratum in the sayings tradition, which stands the best chance of preserving some continuity with the sayings of Jesus. Within that common tradition are a number of wisdom sayings which may be described roughly as social radicalism. Concluding his book, Patterson states a firm claim: "No new quest of the historical Jesus can proceed now without giving due attention to the Thomas tradition."[7]

Gnostic or None-Gnostic?

How Gnostic is the Gospel of Thomas (GTh)? Grobel says, "Certainly not 'in toto'!"[8] However, I want to try arguing that GTh is found among a large corpus of clearly

---

3. Koester recently attests that the Gospel of Thomas must be dated to the end (as early as the second half) of the first century CE. Cf. Koester, *From Jesus to the Gospels*, 14, 25.

4. Theissen, "Itinerant Radicalism," 86. It was a radical form of existence. Theissen thus calls it "wandering radicalism." Thomas Christianity's radical divorce from the world becomes a new set with religious rules. And Patterson argues further that the social radicalism of Thomas Christianity finds its theological correlatio in the anti-cosmic stance of Gnosticism. Therefore, Patterson attempts to show how the social radicalism of Thomas Christianity is related to the anti-Gnosticism.

5. Patterson, *Gospel of Thomas and Jesus* 4.

6. However, many scholars doubt the historical value of GTh. For more information, see Evans, *Jesus and His Contemporaries*, 29–30

7. Patterson, *Gospel of Thomas and Jesus* 241. This is the book I have been looking for several years. I have been waiting for a response to some of the subject of many studies and controversies on Thomas' independence of Jesus' sayings as they appear in the Thomas tradition. Patterson describes carefully their relationships to the Synoptic Gospels in this book. Besides he presents a plausible thesis about the social and religious world of the Thomas disciples who preserved these sayings of Jesus.

8. Grobel, "How Gnostic," 373.

Gnostic works. I can confirm that the Gnosticizing trend is throughout the sayings in GTh 4; 8; 11:4; 21; 22:4–5; 28; 29; 56; 61:5; 72:3; 80; 83; 84; 87; 106; 107; 112; and 114.

However, this is not the end of the case. The question of how Gnostic is GTh is challenged for me because of the relationship to Jewish wisdom literature. As Steven Patterson points out that wisdom literature of late Judaism is the larger literary context for GTh.[9]

In my opinion, however, GTh is somewhat different from Jewish wisdom literature (see Excursus 1–3). While Jewish wisdom literature indicates wisdom sayings like Proverbs and Ecclesistes, GTh speaks of somewhat different wisdom sayings, which are hidden and secret. In GTh those wisdom sayings can only be revealed to definite persons who have "Gnosis." So to speak, on the one hand, GTh has a relationship to Jewish wisdom literature, but somewhat different from it because GTh has secret wisdom sayings; on the other hand, GTh stands within Gnostic works which are different from Jewish literature. How do I solve this kind of confrontation?

Here is a suggestion to solve that problem. According to James M. Robinson, GTh indicates "the Gnosticizing distortion of sayings."[10] This means that GTh has a Gnosticizing proclivity. Therefore, one cannot reject the relationship to Jewish wisdom literature and Gnostic literature in GTh. In short, one can see the trajectory through Jewish wisdom sayings to Gnostic sayings in GTh, which is indicated as follows:

Jewish Wisdom Sayings   +   Gnostic Sayings

GTh

After examining GTh 69, I find that Thomas Christianity is not dependent on the Synoptic traditions and also that Q is not derived from GTh. In GTh, logion 69 is found within part of the sermon traditions (GTh 26, 34, 45, 54, 68, 69, 95), which are apparently independent from the Synoptic traditions.[11] If GTh is not dependent on the Synoptic Gospels, I can say that GTh 69:2 is not dependent on Luke 6:22, nor is GTh 69:1 dependent on Matt 5:11, as I agree with Gregg's opinion.[12] Koester also attests that Matt 11:27 and Luke 10:22 are not dependent on John 8:19, John 14:7–10, GTh 69, or Dialogue of the Savior III, 5:134, 14–15.[13] Rather both Thomas and the Synoptic evangelists share each saying derived from the oral traditions. This means that the Q

---

9. Patterson, "Gospel of Thomas," 93. Agreeing with Patterson, Marvin Meyer attests that "the Gospel of Thomas is a wisdom gospel. "For more information, see Meyer, "Gospel of Thomas," 43.

10. Robinson, "Logoi Sophon," 112–13.

11. However, Meyer argues that "the Gospel of Thomas has attracted a great deal of popular interest and was portrayed as a significant and suppressed collection of sayings of Jesus in the film *Stigmata*." (Meyer, "Gospel of Thomas," 44).

12. Gregg, *Historical Jesus*, 159.

13. Koester, *From Jesus to the Gospels*, 188.

version is not derived from the Thomas version and Q receives its versions from the oral traditions, as well.

Stephen J. Patterson argues that Thomas does not have anything corresponding to the verb (in Matt 5:10 and Luke 6:21) ascribed to Q.[14] According to him, this serves to confirm that Thomas is "unaware of the Synoptic texts themselves, it seems to be independent of their source, Q, as well."[15] If in GTh one cannot find anything corresponding to the Synoptic texts, then Q is also independent on GTh.

In GTh 69, there are differences between the Thomas and Synoptic versions:

GTh 69	Luke 6:21 (Q)	Matt 5:10 (Q)
Jesus said, "Blessed are those who are persecuted In their hearts They are the ones Who have truly come to know the Father."		"Blessed are those who are persecuted for righteousness' sake, for theirs is the reign of heaven."
"Blessed are the hungry the hungry that the stomach of the on in what may be filled."	"Blessed are you that hunger now for you shall be filled."	

GTh is not dependent on the Synoptic texts, and rather are simply "the result of Thomas own process of remembering the oral Synoptic tradition,"[16] which Thomas shares with the Synoptic texts. This means that the order within the cluster of Thomas logia was already determined at an oral stage in the tradition, before the sayings had been written down in GTh. Thus, the words show that the sayings in GTh were collected independently.[17] Furthermore, nothing of Matthew's redactional hand ("righteousness") or Luke's hand ("now") is to be found in GTh.[18] Thus, Thomas derivation from the Synoptic traditions certainly cannot be assumed, because GTh shows characteristics of Christianity in Edessa.[19] This means that Thomas independently manages his sayings' tradition in order to produce his own sayings. This difference between the Synoptic versions and Thomas' provides the strongest argument for Thomas' independence from the Synoptic tradition and also Q's independence from Thomas.

The Odes (Songs) of Solomon (Odes) perhaps reflect a form of Thomas Christianity.[20] There are so many parallels between GTh and Odes. However, now I want to examine the relationship to them on the basis of "baptism."

14. Patterson, *Gospel of Thomas*, 52.
15. Ibid.
16. Ibid., 102.
17. Ibid.
18. Ibid., 53.
19. Klijn, "Christianity in Edessa," 70–77.
20. Odes are one of the great wisdom poetry anthologies of antiquity and constitute a second-century Gnostic hymnbook. Cf. Barnstone and Meyer, *Gnostic Bible*, 357.

GTh	Odes
4	3
13	4
21	15
22	25
36	30
37	33
53	35

GTh has a lot of allusion to ritual, especially for "baptism." GTh 21 and 37 indicate the stripping aspect of Baptism.[21] J. Z. Smith's study is the most detailed study of possible aspects of ritual reflected in GTh 37. The Odes have a lot of clothing imagery. This includes not only the metaphor of the garment for the body that covers the soul, but the talk of "stripping" and "clothing" in relation to the spirit, corruption and incorruption, and putting on Christ.

In addition, there are parallels to the Bridal Chamber between GTh and Odes.

GTh	Odes
75	42
104	

The Odes come to a close with reference to the Bridal Chamber in GTh. Indeed, all of Ode 42 could be allusion to ritual in GTh.

Both the Bridal Chamber and baptism may have been ritualized by the community of the Gospel of Thomas (GTh, NHC II,2), the Gospel of Philip (Gphil, NHC II,3) and the Acts of Thomas (Ath). The ritual of the Bridal Chamber replaces conception by the physical acts between female and male in GTh 114. Physical act of lust is replaced by the spiritual marriage of the male and female initiates. In the Bridal Chamber, both the soul and its image make children. In Ath 12–13, creating children is strongly discouraged. There the children are deeds of righteousness. The presence in Ath of the Bridal Chamber narrative, when the information of the Bridal Chamber motif in GTh 104 and Gphil 53, provides one with an interesting starting point in discussion of ritual in the acts. According to Gphil 60, there are five rituals: baptism, chrism, Eucharist, redemption, and Bridal Chamber.

GTh 27, 37, and 87 are clearly portrayed by baptism. Cultic nudity was present within the Greco-Roman world and was also very common in late Judaism. Even in early Christianity there seems to have been an association of baptism with nakedness since it seems to be a symbol of sinfulness and "ultimate insecurity and nothingness"

---

21. See for more information, Smith, "Garment of Shame."

(Gphil 101). Thus, it seems that baptism in these contexts is symbolic of sacramental rebirth.

The idea of sacrament is found in Gphil. Gphil 22, 37, 45, 51, 60, 67–68, 78–79, 83–84, 86, 92 are mentioned about baptism. Chrism and anointing with oil appears in Gphil 22, 41, 58–60, 67, 72, 80, 83–84, 94, 106. The Eucharist is in Gphil 21, 24, 46, 60, 84, 86, 91.

The Book of Thomas the Contender (NHC II,7) should be considered regarding the relevance of two points. On the one hand, the material of Bth displays striking parallels to some obscure passages of the Gospel of John (John) 3. Bth 138:21–36 contains parallels to John 3:12 and 3:21 (plus 1 John 1:6). Bth 140:5–18 throws light on John 3:11. One the other hand, the dialogue framework of Bth as a whole proves to be attractive for Johannine scholarship since Bth and John are obviously linked by the phenomenon that the Savior's dialogue partner(s) frequently misunderstand him.[22]

The genre of Bth is a Gnostic revelation dialogue, typically occurring between the resurrected savior and a trusted apostle(s) during the period between his resurrection and ascension. Bth thus fits into a natural interpretive development of the genre of sayings of Jesus-beginning perhaps with relatively unadulterated individual sayings, which were gradually collected and expended by means of new interpretive material as in GTh. Bth presents a tradition about the apostle Judas Thomas as Jesus' twin and the recipient of his most secret teaching. Bth is redactionally composed from two sources: a dialogue between Thomas and the savior. The first composition is 138:4—142:21(26), which is perhaps entitled the Book of Thomas the Contender writing to the Perfect. The second one is 142:26—145:16, which is a collection of the savior's sayings.[23]

The Acts of Thomas in Tradition[24]

In the Acts of Thomas (Ath) I can meet numerous allusions to passages in the New Testament. I may suppose that Ath knew all the books of the New Testament, even if direct quotations from the New Testament are few. Ath also seems to know GTh; hence, Ath belongs to a group of ancient Christian apocryphal Acts of the Apostles: Paul, John, Andrew and Peter.[25]

In Ath 1, Matt 10:2–4 is quoted in agreement with the names of the text. The list of apostles at the beginning of Ath tallies exactly with that of Matt 10.

It is impossible to prove that Thomas visited India. The traditions referring to this tradition were based on Ath only. Before the composition of Ath, no traditions are available according to which Thomas went to India.

22. Cf. Schenke, "Book of Thomas," 232–40.
23. Turner, "Book of Thomas," 237.
24. I have indebted this report by Klijn, *Acts of Thomas*.
25. Riley, "Thomas Tradition," 533–42.

It seems that Ath is its present form tend to show that the apostle visited India. Such is evident from Ath 3, 4 and 62, according to which goes aboard a ship to go to India. It is, however, not quite clear what is meant by "India."

In Ath 2, Judas is sold as a slave. This remains a leading theme in Ath. In such a way, he is equal to Jesus who was a slave to liberate many people. In accordance with this picture, I can see a parallel with Christ being a slave (John 13:1–17 and Phil 2:5–11). This also appears from Ath 143 in which is said about Christ: this, the freeborn, and king's son, who became a slave and a poor. And Ath 30 also appears to Thomas: freeborn, who became a slave to bring many to freedom through his obedience. In Ath 142 and 167, a slave (of Christ) means actually freedom.

Ath shows the theme of baptism and Eucharist. In the prayer before baptism, according to Ath 48, Thomas shows the things done by Jesus for humanity. The main theme is that Jesus gave life to all people. In Ath 49, baptism is described; after baptism, the Eucharist is prepared like Ath 50. It shows remarkable agreement with the one in Ath 27. Let's go back to Ath 27.

In Ath 27, I can find the anointing before baptism with water in order. The background is found in the liturgical practice of the early church: Those who are not yet baptized are able to hear the voice, but are not able to see. A parallel is available in Acts 9:7 (but contrary to Acts 22:9). Relations are there as follows:

Between being baptized and seeing.

Between hearers and those being able to see.

The course of events in Ath 27, 49, 121, 132 and 157 is quite clear: Anointing with oil is first placed before baptism with water. Relations between the Acts of Thomas (Ath) and the Acts of Peter (Apt):

Ath 2: "I, Jesus, the son of Joseph the carpenter, from the village of Bethlehem, which is in Judaism."

APt 14: "and I will convict you of having believed in a (mere) man, a Jew and the son of a carpenter." (61:28–29)

APt 23: "You presume to talk of Jesus the Nazarene, the son of a carpenter and a Carpenter himself." (71:24–25)

Dependency cannot be proved. The passages above appear that I can point out some agreement between Ath and APt. It is, however, not quite possible to decide the matter of dependency:

Ath 27: "then, appeared unto them a youth holding a lighted torch-. Thy light, O Lord, is not to be contained by us."

APt 5: "And it came to pass that at the same place where Theon was baptized, there appeared a young man shining with splendor, saying to them 'Peace (be) with you.'" (50:33—51:2).

The idea of light appearing at baptism is often found in ancient Christian literature. It is striking that in both cases a youth appears. If I have to suppose a dependency it seems that Ath is secondary to APt. In APt the voice is connected with the appearance; in Ath the voice is heard sometime before the appearance.

The conclusion of this survey is that sometimes the same ideas in Ath are met in the New Testament and APt. Whether these ideas go back to a mutual dependency or to a common background are difficult to say. In most cases I am dealing with a common tradition available also in early churches, with standard phrases and examples taken from the kerygma of the church. If a dependency is available, Ath seems to be dependent on APt. Ath show the closest relation with APt. If this means that Ath are dependent on APt, Ath were written in the beginning of the third century CE.

Ascetic Movements

The so-called "asceticism" pursues a denial of physical desires as an affirmation of spiritual morality. Thus ascetic behavior decreases the power of the Demiurge and demonstrates Gnostic contempt for Moses' law.

In the Hebrew Bible, there is an evidence of asceticism. Two groups are represented: the Nazirites and the Rechabites: (1) the Nazirites (Num 6:2–21; Judg 13:5; Amos 2:11), (2) the Rechabites (Num 10:29–32; Judg 1:16; 2 Kgs 10:15, 23; 1 Chron 2:55). The usual ascetic practice mentioned in the Hebrew Bible is fasting. Fasting is instituted on special occasions to aid prayer, rather than as a religious experience in and of itself.

In Thomas Christianity, asceticism is most propounded. In the Book of Thomas the Contender, the most ascetic behavior is found:

> Everyone who seeks the truth from the truly wise one will make himself wings so as to fly, fleeing the lust that scorches the spirits of man (NHC II, 7:140, 1–4).
>
> Woe to you who hope in the flesh (NHC II, 7:143, 10–11).
>
> Woe to you who love intimacy with woman and polluted intercourse with her (NHC II, 7:144, 8–10).
>
> Woe to you who beguile your limbs with the fire (NHC II, 144, 14).

According to J. D. Turner, the anthropology of the Book of Thomas the Contender is ascetic and anti-*hylic*.[26] "The moral teaching of Thomas the Contender . . . (is predicated upon its ascetic character."[27] Turner's interpretation of section 139, 2–6 suggests that Thomas condemned the eating of meat.[28]

In the Acts of Thomas, sexual abstinence is more propounded:

26. Turner, *Book of Thomas the Contender*, 226–27.
27. Ibid., 232.
28. Ibid., 131–36 and 232.

> Remember my children . . . If you abstain from this filthy intercourse, you become holy temples . . . If you obey, and keep your souls pure for God, you shall have living children (First Act, 12).

> I have not had intercourse . . . the end of which is lust and bitterness of soul (First Act, 14).

> Men and woman, boys and girls, youths and maids, vigorous and aged, whether you are slaves or free, abstain from fornication and avarice and the service of the belly (Second Act, 28).

The Gospel of Thomas is the earliest Thomas piece of literature and thus the least ascetic. Nevertheless, in this gospel several sayings center on the rejection of the sexual life as well as on the rejection of the world: GTh 27, 112, 114.

In his dissertation, "Doubting Thomas: Controversy over the Resurrection in Early Christianity,"[29] Gregory J. Riley focuses on the concept of the body and resurrection in a foundational aspect of Thomas Christianity. Riley deals with his topic by tracing the background of such ideas in the Semitic and Greco-Roman world, specifically in the Gospel of Thomas and its related literatures: the Book of Thomas and the Acts of Thomas. But his main focus is "the controversy between the two closely related Christian communities of Thomas and John, between the Gospel of Thomas and the Gospel of John, on the issue of resurrection, expressed in John most clearly in the story of Doubting Thomas."[30]

Thomas tradition is the heir of the long development in the eastern Mediterranean of Greek and eastern philosophy and religion so that Riley shows huge materials afforded for the interpretation of the resurrection of Jesus in categories which excluded a physical body because of the substantive nature of the soul, and its ability postmortem to participate in all embodied human experiences.[31]

---

29. His dissertation is not easy to read because Riley shows the background of the concept of the body and resurrection in various *religionsgeschichtlich* materials: Semitic, Greco-Roman, Johannine and Thomas'. Main point of this book was the controversy between the two closely related Christian communities of Thomas and John on the issue of resurrection. Riley has not presumed to deals with the theological issues of resurrection in all their nuances in early Christianity, but he has described the background of resurrection sufficiently well to indicate where popular support in related materials stood. For example, in traditional circles, the pericope of Doubting Thomas (John 20:24–29) has been theologically interpreted for "the proof of the resurrection," "the proof of the deity of Christ," or "the recommendation of belief without seeing." However, Riley sees a homiletic extension in that pericope. According to him, Thomas is clearly the vehicle for doubt; he carries the doubt of all the disciples, and by homiletically extension, every believer's doubt." So to speak, by homiletic extension, the same blessing of that pericope has been delivered to Christians in other communities and times. Such a homiletic interpretation by Riley is nothing new to me, but the selective exegesis of that pericope and the message communicated to the Thomas community is quite useful.

30. Ibid., 2.

31. Ibid., 6–73.

According to the Gospel of John, the name "Thomas" appears in John 11:16; 14:5; 20:24, 26, 27, 28; 21:2.[32] But John 21:2 is left out of Riley's discussion, as Thomas is mentioned in the verse as means of linking John 21 to the conclusion of John 20. According to Riley, the figure of Doubting Thomas is a character created by John.[33]

Unlike R. E. Brown,[34] Riley argues that the Gospel of John is in no way the original source from which the Thomas tradition was formed. According to him, therefore, it was written in part as a reaction against, and a correction of, the earlier Thomas tradition, which held steadfastly to the "original," that is culturally prior, conception concerning the body and after-life, and had its own independent and culturally prior mode of spirituality and relationship with the divine.

Riley presents that the picture of Doubting Thomas in John is shown to correspond well with the Thomas literatures: the Book of Thomas and the Acts of Thomas. The Book of Thomas shows woe upon, and assigns to eternal punishment, those who hold future hope for the body. Nevertheless, the Acts of Thomas pronounces a like picture, and closes with a scene similar to that in the Gospel Easter stories, while containing many "orthodox" interpolations and revisions. The Acts of Thomas describes that the body of the twin brother of Jesus remains in the grave, whereas his soul ascends to heaven.

Riley's opinion is also an exceedingly useful adjunct to the study of the methodological controversies related to the Thomas Christianity. Riley's starting point is that the Gospel of Thomas and the Gospel of John stand in a somewhat similar and parallel position relative to the Synoptic material. He does not argue that the Gospel of Thomas is a work later than the Gospel of John, as R. E. Brown does. According to Riley, each expresses its own distinctive and at times opposing theology in part by manipulating this common inheritance, yet the two are much closer to each other in spirit than either is to the Synoptics. In addition, the two Gospels share material which is not found in the Synoptics, or interpret material in a common manner but distinct from the Synoptics. Therefore, he correctly recognizes that the reason for the prominence of Thomas in the Gospel of John is the contact of the two communities of John and Thomas.[35] The picture of Thomas in John, therefore, is an attempt to influence a Thomas Christianity already in existence.

---

32. Ibid., 4. Such portrayal of Thomas is countered in the pericope cohere well with the pericopes in the Gospel of Thomas. The Gospel of Thomas contains evidence of reciprocal debates with the community of John, although in a form that predates the Gospel.

33. Ibid., 84–137. Thomas is shown to be wrong, and wrong in the specific context of body and resurrection. This observation by him, hence, is important for understanding not only the meaning of the Doubting Thomas pericope, but also the tradition of body and resurrection.

34. For more information, see Brown, "Gospel of Thomas," 155–77.

35. Riley, "Doubting Thomas," 3.

PART 3: JEWISH INFLUENCES AND CHRISTOLOGICAL INSIGHTS

EPILOGUE

The above three Thomas's writings mentioned embrace ascetic themes in varying degrees. Thus I can conclude that ascetic ethics become more prominent in the movement of Thomas Christianity during the first, second, and third centuries. The problem of the relation of Gnosticism to Thomas Christianity is not sufficient. Hence, in this chapter I did not trace effectively the course of the trajectory from historical Jesus to Gnosticism because of overestimation of Thomas' independence on Synoptic Gospels.

Even though Thomas Christianity is not dependent on Jesus' sayings of the New Testament, I have traced the trajectory from Jesus' sayings to Thomas Christianity because Thomas' sayings were formally colored by some characteristics of ascetic movements. Such a trajectory would be very important to know whether Gnosticism was present in Thomas Christianity.

Excursus 1. The Sayings Gospel (Q)-Thomas Parallels

No	Q	Thomas	Type of Saying	Title/Beginning
1	11:9	2:1	Wisdom saying	Seek...
2	12:2	5:2	Prophetic saying	Hidden and revealed
3	[11:1–4]	6:1	Prayer	Lord's prayer
4	6:31	6:2	Proverb	Golden rule
5	12:2	6:5–6	Wisdom saying	Hidden and revealed
6	12:49	10	Prophetic saying	Fire upon the earth
7	[16:17]	11:1	Undecided	Law
8	10:8–9	14:4	Wisdom saying	Go into any country
9	12:51–53	16:1–4	Prophetic saying	Peace on the earth
10	[10:23–24]	17	Wisdom saying	What eye has not seen
11	12:39	12:5	Prophetic saying	A thief is coming
12	[12:35]	12:6	Wisdom saying	Guard against world
13	6:41–42	26:1–2	Proverb	Speak in brother's eye
14	12:3	33:1	Wisdom saying	Preach from housetops
15	11:33	33:2–3	Prophetic saying	Lamp under a bushel
16	6:39	34	Proverb	Blind leading the blind
17	12:22–30	36	Wisdom saying	On cares
18	[10:23–24]	38:1	Wisdom saying	Eye-witness
19	11:52	39:1–2	Prophetic saying	Keys of knowledge
20	19:26	41:1–2	Undecided	Who has will be given
21	6:43–44a	43:3	Proverb	Love tree, hate fruit
22	12:10	44:1–3	Prophetic saying	Blasphemy against spirit

No	Q	Thomas	Type of Saying	Title/Beginning
23	6:44b	45:1	Proverb	No figs from thorns
24	6:45a	45:2	Wisdom saying	Good and evil
25	6:45b	45:4	Wisdom saying	Out of heart
26	7:28	46:1	Prophetic saying	Superior to John
27	16:13	47:2	Proverb	Serving two masters
28	17:6	48	Community rule	"Tree" move away
29	6:20b	54	Wisdom saying	Blessed are the poor
30	14:26	55:1	Wisdom saying	Hate his father
31	14:27	55:2	Wisdom saying	Take up his cross
32	6:22	58	Wisdom saying	Blessed when hated
33	17:34	61:1	Prophetic saying	Two will rest on a bed
34	10:22a	61:2–3	Wisdom saying	Given from the Father
35	12:16–21	63	Wisdom saying	Rich fool
36	14:15–24	64:1–12	Prophetic saying	Great banquet
37	6:22	68	Wisdom saying	Blessed when hated
38	Mt 5:10	69:1	Prophetic saying	Blessed are the persecuted
39	6:21	69:2	Wisdom saying	Blessed are the hungry
40	10:2	72	Wisdom saying	The harvest is great
41	12:13–14	73	Wisdom saying	Divided the possessions
42	12:33	76:3	Wisdom saying	Treasure in heaven
43	7:24–26	78:1–3	Prophetic saying	Why come into the desert
44	9:58	86:1–2	Wisdom saying	Foxes have holes
45	11:39–40	89:1–2	Prophetic saying	Wash outside of the cup
46	12:56	91	Prophetic saying	Read face of sky & earth
47	11:9	92	Wisdom saying	Seek . . .
48	11:10	94	Wisdom saying	Whoever seeks finds
49	6:34–35a	95:1–2	Wisdom saying	Lending at interest
50	13:20–21	96:1–2	Parable	Leaven
51	14:26–27	101:1–3	Wisdom saying	Being my disciples
52	12:39	103	Prophetic saying	Householder & thief
53	15:3–7	107:1–3	Parable	Lost sheep
54	17:20–21	113	Undecided	Kingdom is among you

PART 3: JEWISH INFLUENCES AND CHRISTOLOGICAL INSIGHTS

Excursus 2. Thomas-the Special Source of Matt (SM) Parallels

NO	Thomas	SM	Type of Saying	Title/Beginning
1	8	13:47–50	Parable	The fisher
2	23:1–2	22:14	Proverb	I shall choose you
3	30:1–2	18:20	Wisdom saying	I am with that one
4	32	5:14b	Wisdom saying	A city on a hill
5	39:3	10:16b	Wisdom saying	Snakes and doves
6	40:1–2	15:13	Wisdom saying	Plant
8	48	18:19; 17:2	Parable	Move from there
9	51:2	17:11–12	Wisdom saying	You don't know it
10	57	13:24–30	Parable	Good seed & weeds
11	62:2	6:3	Wisdom saying	On almsgiving
12	76	13:45–46	Parable	The pearl
13	90	11:28–30	Wisdom saying	Come unto me
14	93	7:6	Wisdom saying	On profaning the holy
15	109	13:44	Parable	The treasure

Excursus 3. Thomas-the Special Source of Luke (SL) Parallels

NO	Thomas	SM	Type of Saying	Title/Beginning
1	3	17:21b	Wisdom saying	Kingdom
2	50:2	16:8	Parable	Children of ...
3	63	12:16–21	Parable	rich farmer

XIX

Jewish Gnosticism in the Apocalypse of Adam

PROLOGUE

THE BACKGROUND OF THIS chapter will be demonstrated by examining a Gnostic text, the Apocalypse of Adam, which may be derived from Jewish traditions. Of course scholars,[1] who think that several of the earliest Gnostic texts show Jewish influences, are faced with the disagreement among other scholars,[2] who think that Gnosticism is not derived from such Jewish traditions, but from Christian traditions. Between both opinions, I recognize that there has been a history of argumentation that some Gnostic ideas came from the Hebrew Bible and the Jewish elements. That was a kind of change toward the study of Gnosticism in the Apocalypse of Adam under Jewish influences. Therefore, this chapter wants to show that Jewish influences in the Apocalypse of Adam are not only with regard to images which are derived from the Hebrew Bible, but also with regard to traditional Jewish themes. The purpose of this chapter is to show the Jewish elements in one of the earliest Gnostic texts, the Apocalypse of Adam, in that this type of Gnosticism can be considered as a Jewish heretical movement.

A Pre-Christian Text

It is not easy to suggest a definition of Gnosticism.[3] T. P. van Baaren ever suggested "a short definition" of Gnosticism, listing sixteen characteristics of Gnosticism.[4] Such definitions, however, are based on the broad sense within a radical dualism between

---

1. For examples, Böhlig and Labib, *Koptisch-gnostische Apocalypsen*.

2. For examples, Tuckett, *Nag Hammadi*; Hedrick, *Apocalypse of Adam*.

3. For a recent study of Gnosticism, see Logan, *Gnostic Truth*; Markschies, *Gnosis*; King, *What Is Gnosticism*.

4. See Van Baaren, "Toward a Definition of Gnosticism," 178–80. Also Yamauchi summarized the definitions in his book. See for more detail, Yamauchi, *Pre-Christian Gnosticism*, 14–15.

233

the demiurge[5] and human beings. This radical dualism implies an anti-cosmic enmity against the material world and its creator demiurge. Hence, G. MacGregor recognizes that the short definition of Gnosticism is impossible and criticizes those sixteen definitions briefly with general contentions within Christianity.[6] However, when we examine the Apocalypse of Adam, we can recognize the characteristic of non-Christian Gnosticism, i.e., an esoteric Jewish Gnosis, which was later incorporated into Gnosticism. Jewish Gnosis in the Apocalypse of Adam refers to cosmological speculations based on an esoteric exegesis of Genesis. Examining the characteristics of Gnosticism in a narrower sense, I am interested in heretical movements within Jewish tradition.

Greek noun *hairesis* originally means 1) sect and party (Acts 5:17–18; 15:5; 26:5), or 2) separation, division and faction (1 Cor 11:18–19; Gal 5:20). Here it is sure that "heresy" was designed for categorizing a false sect or division to destroy the unity of traditional Christian churches. In the early Christian church, "heresy" is a sect, which was distinguished from the orthodox group or faith.[7] Likewise, Jewish Gnosticism has some characteristics, which can be distinguished from traditional Jewish faith. Here we can recognize that Jewish heresy means departure from traditional Judaism, and it is with Jewish Gnosticism as a heresy that this chapter is concerned. At this point, therefore, it is reasonable to characterize Jewish heresy as departure from traditional Jewish belief. This understanding stands on the negative or heretical side to understand Jewish Gnosticism. This is useful because this negative side can show the Jewish elements, which Gnosticism relies on in the Apocalypse of Adam. In addition to the negative power of heresy, however, it is also important to sense the positive side of it. Heresy presupposes orthodoxy.[8] Likewise, as a Jewish heresy, Gnosticism presupposes traditional Jewish elements in the Apocalypse of Adam. It means that we can also recognize the origin of Jewish Gnosticism in the Apocalypse of Adam.

After the discovery of Nag Hammadi Library, Jean Daniélou opted for a Jewish influence of Gnosticism:

> It will have become clear by now that gnosis in this sense [the knowledge of eschatological realities] cannot be regarded as once it was, as the result of Hellenistic influence, but must have been a characteristic of later Judaism.[9]

---

5. In the Apocalypse of Adam, the demiurge is called "god," who was lower than his creatures Adam and Eve (64:16–17) is called "god," like "the eternal God." In fact, Seth is the only son of Adam mentioned in the Apocalypse of Adam: Abel is absent, and Cain, Eve's first son, was begotten by the demiurge *Sakla* (66:25–28).

6. Cf. MacGregor, *Gnosis*, 38–48. "By examining in some detail so long a list of alleged characteristics of the Gnostic outlook, I hope I have shown that it does almost nothing to specify anything more than what is either common to religion in general or else is not radically if at all alien to widely accepted features of Christian spirituality" (ibid., 48).

7. Christie-Murray, *History of Heresy*, 1.

8. For more information, see Bauer, *Rechtgläubigkeit und Ketzerei*; Ehrman, *Lost Christianities*.

9. Daniélou, *Theology of Jewish Christianity*, 1:69–70. And see also n34 and n69.

I would like to accept this position. Such a hypothesis is a good way of understanding the Jewish influences of the Apocalypse of Adam.

Further, Hans Jonas argues, on the one hand, that "the Jewish strain in Gnosticism is as little the orthodox Jewish as the Babylonian is the orthodox Babylonian, the Iranian the orthodox Iranian, and so on."[10] If Jewish Gnosticism stemmed from Judaism through a Gnostic stream, the Jewish Gnosticism is actually syncretistic. Gnosticism in the Apocalypse of Adam not only stems from Jewish tradition, but quite apart from the traditional Judaism in syncretistic aspects. For this reason, Gnosticism in the Apocalypse of Adam is quite syncretistic. A. Böhlig, on the other hand, argues that the Apocalypse of Adam is a pre-Christian text stemming from Jewish-Iranian Gnosticism. He makes a case for a specifically Iranian origin for some of the mythological elements in the Apocalypse of Adam. He finds clear reference to the god *Mithras* in the combination of Jewish and Iranian legends.[11] The Iranian legend of the great king of the end time, of which *Mithras* is the typical representative, is the best parallel to explain the literary framework reflected in the individual explanations, i.e., the threefold structure consisting of birth, rearing and the assumption of power. Iranian legend mentioned a six thousand–year fight between the good god and the evil god, until the appearance of *Mithras*. In the Apocalypse of Adam a history is similarly characterized in the fight between the Pantokrator and Seth. The illuminator came during the third period to separate the righteous from the evil ones in a final struggle. Hence, the Apocalypse of Adam could be best understood as Jewish and Iranian by Böhlig, not as Christian.

To show the characteristic of Jewish Gnosticism through reading of the Apocalypse of Adam, this chapter suggests that Gnosticism in the Apocalypse of Adam, which can be criticized as a Jewish heretical movement, is apart from the traditional Judaism. According to W. Schmithals, even "Jewish Gnosticism existed alongside the proper 'orthodox' Judaism."[12] His term helps me to understand that Jewish Gnosticism in the Apocalypse of Adam is a heretical movement, which came after the traditional Judaism of the Hebrew Bible. However, the term "'orthodox' Judaism" by Schmithals can be criticized because in the era of the Apocalypse of Adam there were only several competing sects (Sadducees, Pharisees, etc.), instead of Jewish orthodoxy. Here though I cannot give an exact definition of Gnosticism, Gnosticism in the Apocalypse of Adam can be characterized as a Jewish heretical movement, which is deviate from the traditional Judaism. With no doubt, such a Gnosticism in the Apocalypse of Adam has been influenced by traditional Jewish elements.

---

10. Jonas, *Gnostic Religion*, 34. "Gnostic systems compounded everything-oriental mythologies, astrological doctrines, Iranian, theology, elements of Jewish tradition, whether biblical, rabbinical, or occult, Christian salvation-eschatology, Platonic terms and concepts. Syncretism attained in this period its greatest efficacy" (ibid., 25).

11. Böhlig, "Jüdische und iranisches," 155–56.

12. Schmithals, *Gnosticism in Corinth*, 293.

Jewish Gnostic Apocalypse

The Apocalypse of Adam is taken as a non-Christian text, especially because of many characteristics of Jewish Gnostic apocalypse. A. Böhlig also claimed that "the text [the Apocalypse of Adam] stems from pre-Christian Gnostic."[13] Böhlig claims that the Apocalypse of Adam does not have any contact with Christianity. Later on in the discussion of the issue, Edwin M. Yamauchi evaluates in his review of Böhlig's edition that "the extraordinary importance of this document [the Apocalypse of Adam] lies in the claim of the editor Böhlig that here we have a non-Christian and a pre-Christian presentation of a redeemer figure."[14] And Yamauchi points out that, Rudolph in his review agrees with Böhlig's estimation, and writes: "The importance of this document [the Apocalypse of Adam] resides especially in the fact that it is obviously a non-Christian, indeed probably a pre-Christian product."[15]

In view of these considerations, I recognize the Apocalypse of Adam as a pre-Christian text or a non-Christian text. Its non-Christian nature is usually asserted by appealing to the absence of Christian motifs.

There are some characteristics in the Apocalypse of Adam, which may be regarded as echoes of Christian traditions. On the one hand, C. W. Hedrick agrees that three motifs in the Apocalypse of Adam have been described as Christian: "the illuminator suffers in his flesh, his converts are called 'fruit-bearing trees,' and the illuminator performs 'signs and wonders.'"[16] It is striking that Hedrick argues that the three motifs are indirect references to Jesus. However, the motifs cannot be considered as Christian because the name of Jesus is not mentioned in the Apocalypse of Adam and the main characteristic of the motifs is not attested to the Christian tradition only. On the other hand, we must also consider Simone Pétrement's interpretation concerning explicit references to Christianity if the Apocalypse of Adam has influenced by Christianity. According to Pétrement,

> Christianity appears not only in the passage concerning the Illuminator but in the final invocation. In 83:14, for example, one reads that the elect of the Illuminator will shine, "in such a way that they will enlighten the whole age."

---

13. Here "pre-Christian" in German "vorchristlich" means "before the contact with Christianity," rather than "before the existence of Christianity." See for more details, Böhlig and Labib, *Koptisch-gnostische Apocalypsen*, 95.

14. Yamauchi, *Pre-Christian Gnosticism*, 108. In addition, Yamauchi quotes some from Böhlig's book: "The text [the Apocalypse of Adam] is undoubtedly Gnostic and also a Sethian writing. It must however strongly be doubted, whether it has been created only by Sethians in the strict sense; it points moreover to a pre-Christian origin out of Jewish-Iranian Gnosticism." Cf. Böhlig, *Koptische-gnostische Apocalypsen*, 149.

15. Böhlig, "Jüdische und iranisches," 109 and n36. Cf. See more information, Rudolph, "Review of Böhlig," 361.

16. Hedrick, *Apocalypse of Adam*, 154–60. He has examined the motifs in an attempt to isolate their sources underlying the present form of the texts.

In the Epistle to the Philippians (2:15) Paul says to the Christians at Philippi: "You shine as lights in the world."[17]

After the suggestion of the relationship with Christianity in the Apocalypse of Adam, Pétrement concludes that the text "is not only a pre-Christian work, which is now generally acknowledged, but that it is also not a work of non-Christian provenance."[18] This conclusion has some persuasive points, which argue for the Apocalypse of Adam as a kind of Christian text.

With regard to Synoptic traditions in the Apocalypse of Adam, however, there is the reference in 76:15 to "fruit-bearing trees." At the first sight, this seems to be reminiscent of Matt 7:16. This striking characteristics shared in the Gnostic writings have great variety. Christopher M. Tuckett suggests that "This appears to be alluded to in a number of texts"[19] in the Gnostic texts. There are number of features of the allusions noted in the Nag Hammadi Library to the "fruit-bearing trees."[20] However, the "fruit-bearing trees" phrase in the Nag Hammadi Library is not quoted from the Synoptic Gospels. Rather, those ideas have some overlap with common imagery.[21]

The "illuminator" in the Apocalypse of Adam is described as redeeming the souls of the "fruit-bearing trees" (76:15–17) and as performing "signs and wonders"[22] (77:1–3). Here the concept of redeeming the individual soul at the time of death appears. The exegetical interpretation of the statement regarding salvation (76:17–27) leaves little question about its meaning.[23] The "fruit-bearing trees" were formally "creatures of the dead earth," which were therefore under the authority of death. However, because they now have gnosis in their heart, they will not perish, but will be redeemed. Enlightenment brings with it a spirit different from the unenlightened inhabitants of a dead earth destined for death. In the Apocalypse of Adam, therefore, the phrase "fruit-bearing trees" applies to the saved remnant of the "seed"[24] of Adam, not to the people with the Christian traditions. Therefore, we should recognize the Apocalypse of Adam as a non-Christian text, and as Jewish tradition.[25]

17. Pétrement, *Dieu séparé*, 434.

18. Ibid., 436.

19. Tuckett, *Nag Hammadi Library*, 152.

20. Ibid., 152–53. He suggests many references related to this striking feature as follows: the Tripartite Tractate 118:23–24; the Gospel of Truth 33:30, 38–39; the Apocalypse of Peter 75:7–9; the Testimony of Truth 31:21f; A Valentinian Exposition 36:32–34; perhaps also the Apocalypse of Adam 76:15.

21. The motifs of "fruit-bearing trees" as demonstration of religious dedication are too common in antiquity to allow one to regard it as unique to any one religious movement.

22. The exact nature of the "signs and wonder" that disturbed the ruler of the powers is not specified in the Apocalypse of Adam. Probably the phrase is not really intended to refer to any specific act as such, but is simply a traditional phrase serving to authenticate the work of the illuminator (cf. 77:4–7).

23. This exegetical interpretation in 76:17–27 has a sermon-like character. It is an explanation that clarifies the reason is the illuminator must save the souls of the Gnostics and how he saves them. Further, it states why the illuminator must redeem the Gnostics, explaining the statement in 76:15–16.

24. 65:8; 66:4; 68:12; 71:5; 72:24; 73:14, 25, 28; 74:11, 17; 76:7, 12; 83:4; 85:22, 29.

25. We can find various passages for the "fruit-bearing trees" in the Hebrew Bible: Ps 1:3; Prov

The Apocalypse of Adam is a revelation of Adam to his son, Seth.[26] According to G. W. MacRae, "the Apocalypse of Adam is a Sethian work in the sense that Seth and his posterity are the tradents of the saving knowledge."[27] The revelation or knowledge explains the salvation of Noah from the flood and the salvation of Seth's seed from destruction by fire.

Adam received the revelation from three men who are heavenly figures when Adam was in a dream "from the sleep of death" (66:2–3). Through the sayings of the Apocalypse of Adam, Adam explains his experiences with their god, the judgment affairs of god to destroy human beings with flood and fire and final judgment. These revelations concern the future history of Adam's descendants. He foretells flood and fire and final judgment. But the Apocalypse of Adam shows the first, second, third salvation figures that are represented as the "illuminators." Thus Adam finally foretells the coming of the savior. The third illuminator will redeem people from the dominion of death.

Here important to me is the figure of the Gnostic redeemer myth. The redeemer myth is the root for the Gnostic doctrine of redemption or soteriology.[28] Its doctrine is based on the idea of the heavenly journey of the soul. According to Pheme Perkins,

> The heavenly revealer descends to bring his knowledge that will enable the "seed" to return to its heavenly origins. Descent of the revealer belongs to the Gnostic myth because it is a requirement for communicating with those in the lower world.[29]

Here Perkins tries to explain that the illuminator in the Apocalypse of Adam is the heavenly figure who descends from heaven, as 82:23–28 mentioned as follows: "He caused knowledge of the undefiled one of truth to come to be in him. He said, 'Out of a foreign air, from a great illuminator came forth.'"

Those scholars who regard the Apocalypse of Adam as a veiled statement of Christian Gnosticism may also see the Christ-Seth identification in the figure of the illuminator of Gnosis who comes into the world "for the third time" (76:8–11). However, I prefer not to see a reference to Christ in the passage though it is quite probable that the figure in question is meant to be a docetic incarnation of Seth. It could be assumed that Christian "Sethian" Gnostics who traced their descendant from Seth, was merely an earthly counterpart of a heavenly Seth and would interpret Christ the

---

11:30; Jer 11:19; 17:7–10; 21:14; Hos 10:1. The author of the Apocalypse of Adam would be familiar with these passages.

26. More accurately, the Apocalypse of Adam is a "revelation, which Adam taught his son, Seth, in the seven hundredth years" (64:2–4). In effect it is therefore an apocalypse revealed by Seth. The role of Seth as recipient of secret revelations or knowledge is again emphasized at the conclusion of the work, which is also a double conclusion: "These are the revelations, which Adam made known to Seth his son. And his son taught his seed about them. This is hidden knowledge of Adam, which he gave to Seth . . ." (85:19–24).

27. MacRae, "Nag Hammadi," 152.

28. Rudolph, *Gnosis*, 58.

29. Perkins, *Gnosticism*, 101–2.

Savior as Seth incarnate. However, it is better assumed that such a link with Christ is a secondary development in the history of the tradition. In that case the idea of a saving intervention of Seth in history would be quite consistent with legends and speculation about Seth already current. Because of the lack of Christianizing features in the Apocalypse of Adam, the "illuminator" who is represented as the Gnostic redeemer is not Jesus Christ but Seth. In the Apocalypse of Adam Seth appears in various manifestations for the salvation of his "seed."[30] The illuminator in 76:8–15 is indeed the Great Seth, as a parallel passage reveals in the Gospel of Egerton 63:4–8:

> He [the Great Seth] passed through the three parousias, which I mentioned before: the flood, and the conflagration, and the judgment of the archons and the powers and the authorities.

The third coming was thus the final one; it brought the Gnostics everlasting salvation by destroying the kingdom of the demiurge. This characteristic of the third illuminator's coming is a major feature of Gnostic salvation in the Apocalypse of Adam. Although the demiurge sent a flood to destroy the righteous seed of Seth with all flesh, the third illuminator saved the Gnostics. After the flood, the demiurge tried once more to kill the Gnostics, in what is clearly an inverted interpretation of the catastrophe which befell Sodom and Gomorrah:[31] "Then fire and sulphur and asphalt will be cast upon those men" (75:9–11). But the people escaped his wicked schemes again: "great clouds of light" (75:17) came down from "the great aeons" (17:21), bring those people from "the fire and the wrath" (17:25) and taking them away of "the rulers of the powers [of death]" (17:27).

From this perspective, Birger A. Pearson concludes that the passages of the Apocalypse of Adam "can be interpreted without recourse to the New Testament or Christian tradition."[32] Even though the Apocalypse of Adam had interpreted in relation to Christianity by some scholars, Pearson understands the text as "the original themes of Sethian gnosis, based on Jewish traditions."[33] G. E. MacRae has contributed a number of studies indicating how the Gnostic Sophia is derived from Jewish wisdom literature. For example, he links the traditions of wisdom and creation by attributing the fall of Sophia to Jewish traditions of the fall of celestial beings.[34] For him, "Gnosticism arose as a revolutionary reaction in Hellenized Jewish wisdom and apocalyptic circles."[35] On the other hand, G. Quispel not only supports MacRae in

---

30. Pearson, "Problem of 'Jewish Gnostic' Literature," 31. According to him, "The imperishable illuminators who came from the holy seed: Yesseus, Mazareus, Yessedekeus" (85:28–31) may represent 'the three avatars of Seth at each of his comings' ... The names are therefore mystical names of Seth. The last one, 'Yessedekeus,' could have been modeled on the name *iosedek* in Jer 23:8 (LXX)." Cf. Pearson, "Problem of 'Jewish Gnostic' Literature," 31n94.

31. For the allusion to Sodom and Gomorrah in the Apocalypse of Adam, see Wilson, *Gnosis*, 135.

32. Pearson, "Problem of 'Jewish Gnostic' Literature," 31.

33. Ibid., 33.

34. MacRae, "Jewish Background," 98 and 100.

35. MacRae, "Nag Hammadi," 150.

principle, but also further suggests that Jews were "among the first to develop the Gnostic conception of a demiurge."[36] Quispel suggests Alexandria as the location where these views were formulated for the first time. Thus I would like to accept the Apocalypse of Adam as the text of Jewish influences on Gnosticism.

Jewish Influences

To support the hypothesis that the Apocalypse of Adam is a non-Christian text and has Jewish influences, it will be shown that some characteristics of the Gnostic texts emerged from Jewish traditions in the Apocalypse of Adam. The outcomes of this consideration will show that only Jews who were familiar with their Jewish traditions could have known such Jewish elements in the Apocalypse of Adam. Actually, in the Apocalypse of Adam, Jewish context exists in Judaism independent of Christian influence. Without acquaintance with the Jewish tradition, can the Apocalypse of Adam cite frequently the passages of Genesis of the Hebrew Bible? The answer is "Certainly not." If the Apocalypse of Adam cites some passages from Genesis of the Hebrew Bible, it means that the text was written by a Jewish that was influenced by Jewish traditions. Only Jews would have had access to such Jewish traditions.

In the Apocalypse of Adam, Genesis is not directly quoted even though some passages are almost citations. For example, "And I breathed into you a spirit of life as a living soul" (66:21–23) reflects "and breathed into his nostrils the breath of life, and the man became a living being" (Gen 2:7). And "Therefore the days of our life became few" (67:10–11) should be compared with "his days will be a hundred and twenty years" (Gen 6:3). This statement echoes that God limited human beings' lives to 120 years as a punishment for their corruption. This reference should be compared with the allusion of 83:14–17, "They shall live forever because they have not been corrupted by their 'desire,' along with the angels." Here interesting to me is the expression of the "desire" of human beings. The shortening of human life and the appearance of death are explicitly said to be due to human beings' "desire." In 67:2–4, the Apocalypse of Adam obviously represents human beings' desire. Such a sweet desire would be felt by Adam for Eve.[37] The appearance of human beings' "desire" is implicitly presented as consequent to the intercourse of the demiurge with Eve. Anyway, this interpretation in the Apocalypse of Adam can be understood as a dependency of the traditional midrashic methods on the Hebrew Bible.

The role of the illuminator as the suffering revealer-redeemer in the Apocalypse of Adam can be interpreted as a Gnostic midrash in the Deutero-Isaiah servant songs. G. E. MacRae argues that the story in the Apocalypse of Adam, like Gen 2:7 and 6:3, is based on the midrashic methods and the apocalyptic tradition, and that justifies

---

36. Quispel, "Origins of the Gnostic Demiurge," 218.

37. The sweet desire in the Gospel of Thomas Contender is also related to the intercourse of the flesh. Cf. 140:20–25.

the fact which is used by Jews who were educated about the midrashic methods. As a result, MacRae regards the Jews as most likely urban dwellers.[38] This argumentation supports that only Jews can have such knowledge of the Jewish elements in the Apocalypse of Adam, and points out that Jews were the most likely mediators of the Jewish tradition. Therefore, MacRae's suggestion, which traces the origin of the apocalypse too late due to "Jewish sectarian influences,"[39] can be supported interpreting the Jewish elements in the Apocalypse of Adam.

Several studies have traced the role of Seth and the Sethians in the Apocalypse of Adam.[40] These studies are surprising to me because several texts of the Nag Hammadi Library are identified as Sethian.[41] According to A. F. J. Klijn, even the church fathers knew such tractates.[42] In order to examine the origin of the Jewish elements in the Apocalypse of Adam, this chapter will not deal with the church fathers. More than any others, regarding the Apocalypse of Adam as the text of "the steles of Seth," A. Böhlig suggested that Gnosticism in the Apocalypse of Adam depends on Jewish background.[43] Later in Böhlig's argumentation, Klijn discusses the relation between Sethian Gnosticism and Judaism, and concludes that "almost all the Gnostic ideas about Seth can be found in Jewish writings."[44] He asserts that such Sethian origins can be traced by Jewish exegetical traditions.

Stroumsa develops the idea that Seth was "another seed." Interpreting the Apocalypse of Adam 69:11–18, Stroumsa suggests that:

> This passage refers to the offspring of Seth, a figure named "by the name of that man who is the seed of the great generation" (65:7–8), and who remained a stranger to the powers of the demiurge unlike his parents (65:18–19). Seth was thus described as the forefather of the Gnostics. These Gnostics would be saved from the flood by "great angels" who "would come on high clouds" in order to bring them "into the place where the spirit of life dwells" (69:23–24), i.e., to their proper land, where the Great Seth "will build for them a holy place" (72:4–6). It is noteworthy that since Noah was evil, the ark could in no way be a vessel of salvation for the Gnostics.[45]

---

38. For more information, see MacRae, "Coptic Gnostic Apocalypse," 27–35.

39. MacRae, "Apocalypse of Adam," 575.

40. Pearson, "Egyptian Seth," 25–44; Klijn, *Seth in Jewish*; Stroumsa, *Another Seed*; Martin, "Genealogy and Sociology," 25–36.

41. For more detail, see Stroumsa, *Another Seed*, 13n33. He suggests that the Nag Hammadi tractates are identified to Sethian as follows: The Apocryphon of John, the Hypostasis of the Archons, the Gospel of the Egyptians, the Apocalypse of Adam, the Three Steles of Seth, Zostrianos, Melchizedek, the Thought of Norea, Marsanes, Allogenes, Trimorphic Protennoia, the Paraphrase of Shem, etc.

42. See their names, Klijn, *Seth in Jewish*, 82–90.

43. Böhlig, "Jüdische und judenchristliche Hintergrund," 128.

44. Klijn, *Seth in Jewish*, 116.

45. Stroumsa, *Another Seed*, 83.

Part 3: Jewish Influences and Christological Insights

The common denominator of almost all Gnostic works in which Seth has a prominent role is the notion that the Gnostics themselves are the race or posterity, "the seed," of Seth. This is no doubt the fixed point of what may be called Sethian Gnosticism. It is not useful here to list all occurrences of the expression, but the range and contexts of some of them deserve notice. The revelation, which Adam gives to his son, Seth, in the Apocalypse of Adam is essentially the story of the history of the seed of Seth from its origin, through flood and fire, to its final vindication before the confession and bewilderment of the hostile cosmos and its powers. This subject is a main topic of study regarding Sethian Gnosticism in the Apocalypse of Adam. According to Gen 4:25, Sethians are the biological descendants or heirs of Seth. In the Apocalypse of Adam, such developments of Sethian mythology are impossible without ineptness to Jews. This suggests that Sethian Gnosticism, namely that the origin of Sethian Gnosticism, is indebted to Jewish traditions. That's why the Apocalypse of Adam is familiar with Jewish traditions. Only Jews were responsible for the tradition from Jewish to Gnostic apocalyptic. Thus the Apocalypse of Adam "probably reacted against a previous Gnostic stand"[46] and might have been found in some trends of Jewish exegesis. His interpretation is based on the absence of Christian elements. Such an argumentation by Stroumsa not only lights on the Jewish background of Gnosticism in the Apocalypse of Adam, but also roots from Gnosticism in the first century CE.[47] From this perspective, the Apocalypse of Adam is frequently cited as evidence for first-century CE Gnosticism.[48] The Apocalypse of Adam relates a revelation received by Adam and passed on to his son, Seth. The text is dependent on the Genesis story. Thus, according to D. Parrott, "its close dependence on Jewish apocalyptic traditions suggests that it may represent a transitional stage in an evolution from Jewish to Gnostic apocalyptic."[49] In the Apocalypse of Adam, the apocalypse mentions Adam, Eve, Noah, flood, Noah's sons, Ham, Japheth and Shem. All these characters and events suggest that the author of the Apocalypse of Adam was familiar with Jewish traditions.

A. Segal's analysis of the links between Jewish influences and Gnosticism in the Apocalypse of Adam emphasizes its characteristics:

> It appears that the myth of the arrogance of the demiurge was created to make Gnostic sense of particular scriptural references, especially those from

---

46. Ibid., 84. In Stroumsa's opinion, the Apocalypse of Adam must be rooted in Jewish exegetical traditions about Genesis.

47. Stroumsa dated the Jewish tradition identifying Seth's sister with the maiden Naamah as in place by the first century CE and postulates Jewish Hellenistic influences.

48. For evidence of a pre-Christian or non-Christian origin and first-century CE composition, see Kasser, "Bibliothéque gnostique V," 316–33; Böhlig, "Jüdisches und iranisches," 149–61; Robinson, "Johannine Trajectory," 234 and n4; MacRae, "Coptic Gnostic Apocalypse," 27–35; MacRae, "Apocalypse of Adam," 573–77.

49. Parrott, *Nag Hammadi Codices V*, 2–5, 152.

Genesis. But the Gnostic interpretation appears to have been transmitted in elements ... rather than as a single exegetical interpretation.[50]

Here Segal gives special attention to Philo in this development. He comments that Philo speculated on the same passages in the Hebrew Bible as the heretics who were opposed by the rabbis. Moreover, Philo discusses the concept of a second deity (a *deuteros theos*) and is indebted to mystical and apocalyptic traditions concerning the divine name of God as a separate hypostasis. The concept of "two divine powers in heaven"[51] was therefore known in Alexandria in the middle of the first century CE. Thus, Gnostic midrashes of the second god, the demiurge, may have emerged from Alexandria for, according to Segal, "there is nothing specifically Christian about [them] ... rather [they] depend on Jewish exegesis of Genesis."[52] Segal's analysis of the links between Jewish influences and Gnosticism in the Apocalypse of Adam points to Jews revolting against traditional Judaism. He emphasizes the fact that Gnostic evolution is developmental and that the patterns of Gnostic mythology began to evolve in the first century CE and are indebted to Jewish exegesis. Thus, Segal's analysis, like those of Stroumsa, associates Gnosticism with intellectually heretical Jews who had knowledge of traditional Judaism. The Jews were non-Palestinian,[53] felt alienated and advocated segregation from other Jewish sects like Pharisees and Sadducees.

EPILOGUE

This chapter has not mentioned that Gnosticism is a Jewish heresy, but has examined the relation between Jewish tradition and the origin of Gnosticism. It has been discussed that in the Apocalypse of Adam, Gnosticism is regarded as a Jewish heretical movement. The main point is that traditional Judaism in the Apocalypse of Adam was altered in Gnosticism. In the Apocalypse of Adam, thus, I have studied Jewish influences on Gnosticism. Jewish Gnosticism can be identified with a heretical movement because of its characteristics. In this chapter, Jewish Gnosticism can have a hypothetical meaning of a Jewish sect or faction because it stemmed from Jewish tradition. Hence, we can say that the author of the Apocalypse of Adam rebelled against traditional Jewish themes and established a Jewish Gnostic sectarian stream, which contributed somewhat to the development of the Gnostic Redeemer myth.

50. Segal, "Rabbinic Polemic," 28.

51. Segal has examined the relationship between Judaism and the origins of Gnosticism. He does not address the historical connections between the rabbis and their opponents but rather chooses to examine the rabbinic evidence for two powers in heaven. According to him, the "two powers in heaven" heresy refers to an interpretation of "scripture to say that a principal angelic of hypostatic manifestation in heaven was equivalent to god." See his *Two Powers in Heaven*, x.

52. Segal, "Rabbinic Polemic," 28.

53. As postulated by Quispel, the Apocalypse of Adam and the Apocryphon of John may have been produced in the first century CE by Alexandrian Jews. See his "Demiurge in the Apocryphon of John," 22.

XX

PssSol and Q in the Christological Insights

EPILOGUE

MANY THEOLOGICAL CATEGORIES IN Christology return back to the Bible, especially to the historical Jesus.[1] Christology is based on the relationship between the Bible and the interpretation of it by those of us involved in the study of the first-century churches as well as early Judaism. I will study PssSol for rooting the announcement of Jesus in early Judaism because I understand PssSol in early Judaism as a prerequisite for understanding the appearances of Jesus. Furthermore, because of the connections with the wisdom books of the Old Testament, I can probably relate PssSol with Q.

Four possible motifs may be put forward to account for a comparative study of the christological insights in both PssSol, which is a collection of psalms written around 50 BCE, and Q, which is a document composed in the period between 30 CE and 50 CE. The following four similar insights in PssSol are also found in Q, though the terminologies are sometimes different.

> The Poor. PssSol recognizes a merciful God, who is the refuge of the poor and the needy (PssSol 5:1–2, 11–12; 10:6; 15:1; 18:2; or about poverty, 16:13–15). PssSol restricts the poor to the righteous as the true Israel or "the children of God" (17:27). The individual Israelite is also the righteous man or "a beloved son" (13:8). Q also has a concrete concept of a merciful God (Q 6:36); Q has God siding with the poor (Q 6:20; 7:22; 14:21). In Q the poor are the lost personal groups—the poor, the hungry and mourning, the sick and the sinners.
>
> The Kingdom of God. In PssSol I can find many similarities, both in form and content, with Wisdom books contained in the Bible; however, my concern is also based on the expression of the kingdom of God in PssSol 5:18 and 17:3. Without doubt, such a kingdom is a Davidic messianic kingdom. In Q I find that the

---

1. Cf. Schnackenburg says that the theology asks back to the Bible, especially to Jesus, namely his message and his behavior. For more information, see his "Befreiung in der Blickweise Jesu."

kingdom of God appears frequently in several thematic sections of the document (Q 6:20; 7:28; 10:9, 11; 11:2, 20; 12:31; 13:18, 20, 29; 16:16). However, in Q, the kingdom is an eschatological kingdom.

The Judgment Announcement. The theme of judgment is very closely related to the theme of punishment and condemnation. In PssSol I can easily find the theme for judgment (PssSol 2:10, 15–18, 32–33; 3:3; 4:8, 1l, 24; 5:1, 4; 8;3, 8, 23–26, 32; 9:2, 5:10:5; 15:8, 12; 18:3). In Q the announcement of judgment is related to the imminent anticipations (Q 3:9, 17; 11:51b; 12:51–53, 54–56) and to the grounds for judgment and condemnation (Q 7:31—35:11:19–20, 24–26, 29–32, 33–36, 49–51; 12:57–59).

Christological Insights. I can hear the voices of eschatological expectations in PssSol 8, 11, 17 and 18. A major theme may be included in an anticipation of fulfillment of promises (12:7), namely, the coming of a messianic king (17:21—18:9), who would rule by the power of God (11:37). The righteous king will be the Lord Messiah (17:32) and will be characterized by wisdom (17:35). PssSol has two remarkable titles: "the son of David" (17:21) and "the Lord Messiah" (17:32; 18:7). In short, the hope of a Davidic Messiah is strong in PssSol, a document of pre-Christian Judaism. In Q Jesus is also implicitly a messenger of wisdom (Q 7:31–35; 11:29–32, 47–51; 13:34–35). I can easily find that Jesus refers to himself as the Son of man (Q 6:22; 7:34; 9:57; 11:30; 12:8, 10, 40; 17:22, 24, 26, 30). Jesus may sit on thrones judging the twelve tribes of Israel with those who have persevered with him (22:28–30). Q mentions the coming one, which depends upon Q 3:16; 7:18; 11:22; 13:35. The Son of God in Q is the subject of explicit treatment of the christological title (Q 3:22; 4:3, 9; 10:22).

These four motifs are probably mutually exclusive. A comparison of these motifs which are found in PssSol with parallel ideas in Q raises fascinating and fundamental problems of higher criticism relating to the christological insights.

To be sure, this comparative study between PssSol and Q will make for a clearer understanding of the biblical thinking on the christological insights. Although there are no actual agreements in both documents because the similarity lies not simply in the terminology, they have pretty much the same insights. This means that Q somewhat may have depended on PssSol for its insights.

The Insights in PssSol

PssSol is a collection of eighteen Hebrew psalms (or hymns) written around 50 BCE, probably in response to the Roman takeover a few years earlier. PssSol is preserved in eleven Greek manuscripts dating from the tenth to the sixteenth century and Syriac versions made from the Greek.[2]

It is certain that Pharisaic circles stand behind PssSol[3] and these psalms constitute an outstanding source for the mood within Palestinian Judaism just before the birth of Jesus. "Because of the concentration on Jerusalem and Temple, the place of its origin is very probably Jerusalem or some place in Judea."[4]

PssSol does not directly describe historical events, but it reflects them. Here the psalms contain some observations about the events of 63 BCE that could be taken as the impetus for the formation of the group. PssSol is clearly against the Hasmoneans, who did not discharge their priestly duties in a proper way (1:8; 8:11–13, 22) and usurped the high priesthood (8:1) as well as royal authority (17:5f). For the majority of scholars, therefore the events of 63 BCE are clearly reflected in PssSol 8, which describes Pompey's entry into Jerusalem, together with the events leading up to and following it (comp. 17:7–14). The Party of Hyrcanus opens Jerusalem to the conqueror, Pompey (8:16–20). When he finally breaks through the walls of Jerusalem, killing of many people at once happens as a result (8:21–23, 28). Additionally, the family of Aristobulos is taken captive to Rome (8:24).

I want to set forth my opinion that PssSol is rooting the announcement of Jesus in early Judaism: PssSol is a prerequisite of the appearance of Jesus. For comparing the christological insights it is important to note that PssSol has the "Messianological"[5] message.

The Poor

Matthew has specified the poor as "the poor in spirit" (Matt 5:3). Though PssSol does not show this supplement, PssSol refers to the poor in other qualified terms.

PssSol understands God as a merciful God, who is the refuge of the poor and the needy (5:1–2, 11–12; 10:6; 15:1; 18:2; or about poverty, 16:13–15). In PssSol God is clearly represented as "the defender of the pious poor (5:2, 11; 15:2; 18:2)."[6] Who

---

2. According to the majority of scholars, the PssSol was composed in Hebrew—there are no Hebrew manuscripts extant—and very soon afterward translated into Greek, and after some time into Syriac. For more information, see O'Leary, *Syriac Church and Fathers*.

3. According to Mack, PssSol is "a precious record of a Palestinian sect of Hasidim." Even if it is controversial whether "purists of the Qumran variety" and "Pharisees of the lawyer type" stand behind PssSol, they "produced these psalms experienced together the history of Jerusalem from a certain point of view throughout most of the first century BCE." Mack, *Myth of Innocence*, 49.

4. De Jonge, *Outside the Old Testament*, 161.

5. For "Messianology," see the *Princeton Seminary Bulletin* 6 (1985) 98–115. Messianology is a neologism created by James H. Charlesworth: "In order to clarify and simplify a comparison of Jewish beliefs in a Messiah and Christian contentions that Jesus is the long-waited Messiah; or succinctly to juxtapose and compare Messianology and Christology." Cf. Charlesworth, "From Jewish Messianology to Christian Christology," 255n1.

6. Oseik, *Rich and Poor*, 20.

are the poor? Undoubtedly, the poor are the pious in PssSol. Especially, PssSol has the special members focused for the poor. They are the Israelites or Israel herself. The pious poor, therefore, as Israelites who suffer martyr-like in this age, wait expectantly on God for their deliverance in the coming age.

In PssSol 10:6, I encounter the idea of salvation for the poor: And the devout shall give thanks in the assembly of the people, and God will be merciful to the poor for the joy of Israel. It must be pointed out that PssSol 10:6 does not necessarily imply an equivalence of meaning between *ptokoi* and *hosioi*. However, it clearly does show knowledge of the idea that the poor are the heirs of Israel's salvation:

> Just and kind (hosios) is our Lord in His judgments forever, and Israel shall praise the name of the Lord in gladness, and the pious (hosioi) shall give thanks in assembly of the people. And to the poor (ptokous) shall God have mercy in the gladness of Israel. For good and merciful are God forever and the assemblies of Israel shell glorifying the name of the Lord? The salvation of the Lord is upon the house of Israel unto everlasting gladness.[7]

In PssSol 10:6 the pious and the poor are in parallel not because the terms are synonymous or closely related, but because, having suffered the affliction of conquest and having bared their backs to chastisement, the pious have become "poor and needy" and thus specially qualified to receive God's help.

In PssSol *euphrosyne* has also become almost a technical term for Israel's salvation (10:5–6, 8; 11:3; 14:10; cf. 17:35). In PssSol 16:13–15 it is also seen as a chastisement for the righteous which can only be borne with the strength of God. Hence, it is possible that PssSol identifies salvation of the poor with the salvation of Israel. At this point PssSol 13:9 recognizes one of the pious in Israel as the son of God: "For he will admonish the righteous as a beloved son and his discipline is as for a firstborn."

PssSol also restricts the poor to the pious, viewing its own community as the true Israel because of their piety, and as the poor because of the chastening they have willingly accepted (10:1–3). Nevertheless, it is Israel's salvation which is the focus of PssSol's attention (2:22; 7:8, 10; 8:26–28, 34; 9:11; 11:1–3; 12:6; 14:5; 17:2l–22, 45). And this is coterminous with the salvation of the poor. Also PssSol 18:1–5 probably be understood this way. In short, as the poor Israelites are called "children of God" (11:27) and the individual Israelite is the righteous man or "a beloved son" (13:8).

The Kingdom of God

The leading theological category of PssSol is the proclamation of the kingdom of God. Unlike the apocalyptic kingdom of Dan 7–12 which could be brought about by angels, PssSol has the more traditional messianic kingdom. The attributes of God which are most stressed in PssSol are precisely those which pertain to his ceaseless surveillance

---

7. Percy, *Botschaft Jesu*, 64–65.

of human life. Although implacably wrathful against hardened sinners, he is otherwise merciful and forgiving and especially tender in his love for Israel (5:9–11; 7:4–5; 9:6–7; 18:1–4).

According to Nickelsburg, "God's kingly power is also the central concept and underlying theme that runs like a thread through this PssSol."[8] God is the king over all the earth (2:30, 32; 5:18–19; 8:24; 17:1, 3). What does the kingdom mean exactly in PssSol? PssSol has only two passages of "*basileia*."

> Those who fear the Lord are happy with good things. In your kingdom your goodness (is) upon Israel. (5:18)
>
> But we hope God our savior, for the strength of our God is forever with mercy. And the kingdom of our God is forever over the nations in judgment. (17:3)

In Odo Camponovo's analysis, the kingdom, which is now named exactly in "your" or "our" God's reign, here is the key word for the future salvation. This kingdom strengthens also the hope of "*Betenden*," God's kingdom for salvation in future. Here the kingdom also does not mean God's realm as the state of salvation, but God's effective kingly reign.[9] This is a very important discovery. Certainly this would lend further support to my suggestion about Q's awareness of the idea of the kingdom in PssSol.

As the majority of scholarship confirm, the concept of the kingdom of God in PssSol is mostly fully laid out in 17. Here an affirmation of the eternal royal rule of God is absolutely clear.

In PssSol 17, after an initial declaration that "Lord, You are our king forevermore"—God is Israel's king forever—(1) and that "the kingdom of our God is forever over the nations in judgment," (3) PssSol recalls how God chose David as king (4)-his kingdom extends forever over the Gentiles. God chose David and his descendants to be the human agents exercising that reign (5). The Hasmoneans usurped the privilege of this monarchy (6–8). The Romans have deposed them (8–20). Thus PssSol prays, "See, Lord, and raise up for them their king, the son of David, to rule over your servant Israel in the time known to you, o God" (21).

PssSol expects a Davidic messianic kingdom. Hence, the kingdom ruled by this messiah is essentially the restoration of a national Jewish kingdom:

> Undergrade him with the strength to destroy the unrighteous rulers, to purge Jerusalem from gentiles who trample her to destruction; in wisdom and in righteousness to drive out the sinners from the inheritance; to smash the arrogance of sinners like a potter's jar. (22–23)

I know how the history of Israel continued: first of all, the rebuilding of the temple in Jerusalem, namely, a national strengthening, then again the dependence on the Seleucids in the Hellenistic time and under the Syriac king Antiochus IV. Who

---

8. Nickelsburg, *Jewish Literature*, 207.
9. Cf. Camponovo, *Königtum, Königsherrschaft*, 217–18, 221–22.

violated the temple again? The great rebellion was brought about by the Maccabeus and their followers, namely, Hasmoneans. But this time of national independence between 164 BCE and 63 BCE fulfilled by no means the hopes for a good and peaceful life. Pompeius conquered Jerusalem in 63 BCE again, and Israel remained under foreign rule, Roman domination. In PssSol the thought of a reign of justice and peace continued in the poor, namely the pious people, as it corresponded to the will and the promises of God. Hence, I can easily find the thinking of the future expectations or the longing with the similar beatitudes in PssSol:

> Blessed are those born in those days to see the good fortune of Israel which God will bring to pass in the assembly of the tribes (17:44).
>
> Blessed are those born in those days to see the good things of the Lord which he will do for the coming generation (18:6).

At this point, the kingdom of God in PssSol is always the hope of the future or the future expectations by God.

The Judgment Announcement

In PssSol, the theme of an eschatological judgment runs right through the whole collection. Of course, this judgment announcement for the Jewish opponents—"the sinners"—who were like the Hasmonian Sadducees, parallels the concept of salvation for the righteous—"the pious"—which was characteristic of Pharisees[10] in PssSol. For this reason, George W. E. Nickelsburg confirms "two groups, their relationships to God, their deeds, and their fates at the hand of divine judge."[11] In PssSol the pious are called the righteous (of the Lord), those who fear the Lord, and those who love the Lord; the sinners are also called the transgressors, those who are lawless, and those who are wicked.

According to R. B. Wright, therefore, PssSol is a kind of "a literature of crisis. But it is more than the crisis of an alien army invading the homeland; it is one of harsh reality invading a traditional theology." As Wright said, here one can find a theme of great theological importance: Theodicy is a theme to which PssSol returns repeatedly (2:1, 15–18; 3:3–5; 4:8; 8:3, 23–26; 9:2). Theocracy is also represented by the expression of "the Lord is King" (2:30, 32; 5:18, 19; 17:1, 34, 36).[12] Hence, PssSol is characterized by affirmations of need to praise "the righteousness of God"[13] as a standard of

---

10. The identity of the pious has a controversial problem. Although traditionally the pious have been identified with the Pharisees, some scholars like Eissfeldt, Dupont-Sommer, Ryle and James identified with the Essenes as the pious. However, Wright suggests that the pious are Pharisees and Essenes under an examination of the theology and theodicy of the PssSol.

11. Nickelsburg, *Jewish Literature*, 207. For him two groups are clearly Pharisees and Essenes.

12. Wright, "Psalms of Solomon," 643. Cf. ibid., 642.

13. For nouns, 2:15; 4:24; 5:17; 8:24f, 26; 9:2, 4, 5; 17:23, 26, 29, 37, 40; 18:7. For verbs, 2:15; 3:5; 4:8; 8:7, 23, 26; 9:2. For adjectives, 2:10, 18, 32; 5:1; 8:8; 9:2; 10:5; 17:32. Cf. Schupphaus, *Psalmen Salomos*, 83.

judgment (2:18; 8:32; 9:2, 4; 17:22). Here one can find that the righteousness of God is obviously related to the concept of judgment upon the sinners.

Therefore, PssSol reflects one of the typical insights that God helps the pious continually (5:7; 6:3–5; 7:6:15:1; 16:3–4; 17:3) and destroys the sinners (3:13–15; 13:10; 14:4–6; 15:7, 9–15; 16:5). And running throughout is the conviction that the pious are honored and raised to life (esp. 2:31; 3:12), that Israel is united with God by a covenant (esp. 9:16–19; 10:5; 17:7), and that the sinners are destroyed (esp. 2:31, 34; 15:12). For this reason, the judgment announcement is considered in the heart of the prophetic message. In PssSol, in a negative sense, the prophetic form of the judgment announcement is based on the primacy of the judgment motif. Since repentance by Hasmoneans is no longer anticipated, there remains only the judgment for them. Therefore, the judgment announcement is closely related to the warning statement which I will consider here in the same basic category. And there are warnings which assume a future judgment. The theme of PssSol is the righteousness of God and his help in difficulties.

As it has already been suggested above, such arguments can be applied to figure out the christological insights related with the judgment announcement in this chapter.

God will do justice; the righteous will prosper and the wicked will be punished. This prosperity and punishment are visible signs of God's favor and displeasure. The end-time is at hand. Here, following a review of Israel's immediate history up to his time, PssSol concludes that the only solution lies in the immediate intervention of God in history. This is called of the day of God's "supervision" or "overseeing" of Israel (10:4; 11:6; 15:12). According to this idea, at the time of the day, God takes a direct control of Israel's destiny. Thus, PssSol not only speaks with approval of God's deliverance from suffering but also explicates how this suffering serves as punishment for sinners.

Christological Insights

PssSol preserves one of the most detailed messianic expectations in the immediate pre-Christian century. As well known, PssSol 17 and 18 are very important for the understanding of Jewish "Christology"; they concern the kingship and judicial functions of the eagerly awaited Davidic Messiah.[14]

Wisdom

Arguing a critique of the apocalyptic hypothesis to the origins of Christology, Burton L. Mack suggests that "wisdom as an intellectual tradition may have contributed far more too early Christian thinking than has normally been considered."[15] Therefore,

---

14. In his book De Jonge suggests a translation and comment of PssSol 17 and 18 for its expectation of "a new king," "the son of David" and "the anointed of the Lord." Cf. De Jonge, *Outside the Old Testament*, 168–77.

15. Mack, "Christ and Jewish Wisdom," 194. For him the understanding of the apocalyptic

he argued that "several of the imageries of major importance for early Christian mythmaking can and should be traced to the provenance of Jewish wisdom thought in general, rather than to Jewish apocalyptic in particular" (195). According to him:

> Several early "Christologies" will be discussed in relation to their use of wisdom idiom. It will be argued . . . that the formation of these Christologies can be understood as mythmaking on the model of the intellectual activity of the wisdom scribes (authors), and that the function of these myths of origins was similar to that of the ideal figures produced by wisdom thinkers (197).

One should read wisdom poetry in relation to its social circumstance. In PssSol the messianic king who rules by wisdom plays significant roles.[16] Three descriptions of the term "wisdom" are given in PssSol 17 and 18:

> He will judge peoples and nations in the wisdom of his righteousness. (17:29)
>
> He will strike the earth with the word of his mouth forever; he will bless the Lord's people with wisdom and happiness. (17:35)
>
> (He will be) under the rod of discipline of the Lord Messiah, in the fear of his God, in wisdom of spirit. (18:7)

Obviously in these verses the nationalistic messianic hope of Israel is expressed. The king will be characterized by wisdom. Thus in PssSol, wisdom is for the messianic king. It is important to note here that the messianic king will judge by the wisdom or in wisdom of spirit, and rule by the word of his mouth forever. Here charismatic traits are attributed to this messianic king: He has the wisdom of his righteousness and he is endowed with a spirit. In PssSol wisdom is presented as an aspect qualifying character and effectiveness of this messianic king.

According to Burton L. Mack, "The notion of wisdom employed here is, mythologically conceived, that of her universal reign. This reign can be imagined as her own. Or it can be imagined as that of the king she blesses and exalts (cf. the Wisdom of Sol. 7–9)."[17] "It is not yet said in the psalms that Israel's wisdom is its law and that its law is the basis for an institution of the people without a king. It is not yet seen that the new and sufficient authority could be that of the teacher and sage alone." (41) It is not yet said that wisdom herself becomes someone like Jesus or her messenger in such a special status, as Q mentions.

---

hypothesis is that "Jesus proclaimed the imminence of the kingdom of God, a reign or domain ultimately imaginable only in apocalyptic term. Early Christians somehow associated Jesus himself with the kingdom of God he announced (thinking of him as the king of the kingdom) and thus proclaimed him to be the Messiah" (ibid., 192).

16. Mack summarizes that three images created by wisdom thinkers plays significant roles in the process of studied reflection upon the nature and destiny of Israel: (1) the figure of wisdom personified, (2) the king who rules by wisdom, and (3) the righteous one rescued from troubled by wisdom. For details see ibid., 199–204.

17. Mack, "Wisdom Makes a Difference," 41.

Part 3: Jewish Influences and Christological Insights

The Lord Messiah

Pharisaic beliefs and hopes are important for our purposes: they cherished very definite ideas about the restoration of the Israelite at a time not too remote from their own day and within the borders of their own land. According to T. W. Manson,

> The nature of the ends to be realized determines the main outlines of the messianic picture, in so far as the messiah is brought in as a necessary agent for the fulfillment of God's plan and the establishment of God's kingdom.[18]

Therefore, for answering the question of how the average godly and patriotic Jew of the period imagined the Messiah, he does not think we can have a better view than that given in PssSol 17 and 18.

The description of the Lord Messiah is given in PssSol 17 and 18 is one of the classical messianic texts.

> And he will be a righteous king over them, taught by God. There will be no unrighteousness among them in his days, for all shall be holy, and their king shall be the Lord Messiah (17:32).

> May God cleanse Israel for the day of mercy in blessing, for the appointed day when his Messiah will reign (18:5).

> Blessed are those born in those days, to see the good things of the Lord which he will do for the coming generation; (which will be) under the rod of discipline of the Lord Messiah (18:6–7a).

The messianic figure described in these verses is clearly the Messiah. Here his functions are clarified by the active verbs: "to be a righteous king," "to be holy," "to cleanse his people," "to reign for the appointed day."

Elaborating the example given of a sectarian interpretation of PssSol, Burton L. Mack evaluates that "Christian scholars have always taken this psalms (PssSol 17–18) to be an apocalyptic vision of the messianic hope of Judaism, a percussive desire fulfilled in Jesus as Christ."[19] Obviously PssSol 17 and 18 call the king of the future, a descendant of David, the Messiah.

According to R. B. Wright,

> The title "Messiah," which in the old Testament commonly referred to any legitimately appointed priest or king, and which in later Jewish writings become the repository of all those ideal hopes which were unrealized in the present, is given shape and dimension in these psalms as they describe the person of Messiah and the character of his government in the age to come. There is more substance to the ideas concerning the Messiah in PssSol than in any other extant Jewish writing. The Messiah is here identified as a son of David who

---

18. Manson, *Servant-Messiah*, 23–24.
19. Mack, "Wisdom Makes a Difference," 49.

will come to establish an everlasting kingdom of God.... These psalms link for the first time the concepts of Messiah and Lordship into a new construct which the Gospel of Luke later seizes as a title for Jesus (Luke 2:1), and the New Testament develops into the concept of "Christ the Lord," a concept that played an important part in the development of New Testament Christology.[20]

PssSol has influence on the New Testament. A major theme may include an anticipation of fulfillment of promises (12:7), the coming of a messianic king (17:21–18:9), who would rule by the power of God (17:37).

How are the royal rule of God and the royal rule of the Messiah related? PssSol has solved this question quite elegantly, by subordinating the Messiah to the Lord. According to James H. Charlesworth, "Nowhere else in early Jewish literature are the functions of the Messiah so well delineated? The Messiah, however, is totally subservient to God."[21] Hence, the Messiah acts only according to God's will. At this point, it is clear that only God himself will finish successfully the functions of the Messiah (17:45–46). He should really govern the people of Israel: "The Lord himself is his king, the hope of one who has a strong hope in God" (34). PssSol 17:21-33 emphasizes that the Messiah will not rely on a sword, horse, or other military weapons.[22] He will conquer not with a weapon in his hand but with what streams forth from his mouth, the word (esp. 22–24, 33). This means that the Messiah will establish a peaceful kingdom under righteousness. In the place where righteousness appears in PssSol 17, therefore, "it is associated with justice (19), power to expel sinners from the inheritance (23), strong leadership (26, 29, 37), and faithfulness as shepherd of Israel (40)."[23]

The Coming King

In PssSol, of course, the title "the coming one" like Q or "the coming king" is not presented. Most important here is the hope for a Davidic or royal Messiah (17:32, 18:5–6). The designation "the king of Israel" occurs in PssSol 17:42. Talk of an expected coming of the Messiah would have been meaningful to the Jews of PssSol and represented a major strand of Jewish eschatological expectations. It is important to note that PssSol projects an ideal future figure.

Among the collections, which are especially relevant to our inquiry, the most instructive is PssSol 8:27–30, 17 and 18, for they give the leading ideas of the collection in the simplest and clearest form: corruption within Israel, punishment of the Israel by God at the hands of the Gentiles, restoration of the Israelites by God at the hand of his Messiah. These are perennial themes; in PssSol the corruption and punishment have

---

20. Wright, "Psalms of Solomon," 643.
21. Charlesworth, "From Jewish Messianology to Christian Christology," 236.
22. In PssSol, the Messiah is a political figure, but not a military figure. Obviously, PssSol was written against the belief that the Messiah will be a military warrior.
23. Davenport, "Anointed of the Lord," 76.

their special exemplification in the misconduct of the later Hasmonean priest kings and the destruction of the national independence by Pompey. PssSol returns again and again to describe the wickedness of the Sadducee aristocracy and the blasphemous presumption of the Roman invader; however, restoration of Israel is of deliverance to come.

> O God, turn your mercy upon us and be companionate to us. Bring together the dispersed of Israel with mercy and goodness, for your faithfulness is with us.... Do not neglect us, our God, lest the gentiles devour us as if there were no redeemer. (8:27–28, 30)

The meaning of "redeemer" here is made clear by PssSol 18:11.
They stole from the sanctuary of God as if there were no redeeming heir.

Here the Hasmonean priest-kings are described as plundering the holy things as if there were no "redeeming heir." The Hasmoneans in assuming the royal dignity were taking the place of the rightful heir of the Davidic dynasty, destined by God to deliver Israel. This Davidic king is the agent of national redemption, and, what is more, the only legitimate agent.

In the beginning of PssSol 17:

> Lord, you are our king forevermore, for in you, o God, does our soul take pride.... Lord, you chose David to be a king over Israel, and swore to him about his descendants forever, that his kingdom should not fail before you. (1, 4)

It begins with the assertion of the sole sovereignty of God and a confession of Israel's faith in him alone. In the end of PssSol 17:

> May God dispatch his mercy to Israel; may he deliver us from the pollution of profane enemies; The Lord Himself is our king forevermore. (45–46)

Here it is also noted that the restoration of the dispersed of Israel to their land is a principle element in the description of the coming deliverance. It is also the theme of PssSol 11 and it appears in PssSol 17:31 and 44.[24] Numerous functions are attributed to the Davidic messianic king: He will judge the wicked, destroy them, deliver God's people and reign in a blessed kingdom.

As has already been suggested above, the dominant emphasis is on the restoration of a national kingdom where the kingship of God is mediated by a Davidic Messiah as v. 32 says:

> And he will be a righteous king over them, taught by God. There will be no unrighteousness among them in his days, for all shall be holy, and their king shall be the Lord Messiah.

---

24. It is already present in Isa 66:18–20.

What is problematic here is the literary connection with the messianic king. Hopeful messianic prospects are offered again and again with obvious traces of utopianism alongside important allusions to the history of the period.

The Davidic royal king is truly the coming king so that he may be raised over "the house of Israel to discipline it" (17:42). This is certainly a striking imagery. To be sure, in this present passage I can read the apparent promise of a future ideal figure.

The Son of David

It is important to remember that Isaiah 11 has exercised a considerable influence on Jewish expectation concerning the Messiah and the coming royal Son of David. A very conspicuous example in PssSol 17 and 18 often referred to as a typical example of the earthly and nationalistic messianic expectation. Probably composed briefly after Pompey's conquest of Jerusalem (63 BCE), PssSol draw heavily upon biblical passages to portray the promised Son of David as the ideal king and the Messiah, in explicit contrast to the illegitimate and corrupt Hasmoneans. Obviously PssSol favored the hope for the restoration of the Davidic kingdom and a Davidic Messiah.

PssSol goes on to say that, under God and by God's appointment, there is a single legitimate royal dynasty in Israel—the house of David. But the monarchy has been usurped by another line—the Hasmonean. God has overthrown these upstarts by the hand of the Roman Pompey whose momentary triumph must be regarded as the just judgment of God on the unrighteousness rampant in Israel. At the same time the Gentile instrument of the wrath of God, just because he was a Gentile and ignorant of the true religion, "acted arrogantly and his heart (was) alien to our God" (17:13). But the punishment of Israel's sins, the overthrow of the Hasmonean usurpers, and the miserable end of the Roman oppressor, cannot be the last word. These things are but the preliminaries to the unfolding of God's purpose of good for Israel. This purpose is to be achieved, under God, by the rightful redeemer, the Davidic King-Messiah, whose accession to the throne of his fathers is now eagerly expected.

Although inheriting the throne as the son of David (17:21), he will be chosen by God and will rule in his name and authority. It is important to note that the Son of David is presented as a standard messianic title in PssSol (17:21–35; cf. 18:5–9), and can trace a pattern which leads to the emergence of a Son of David as Messiah, as he draws upon traditions within Judaism. In 17:46 God himself is the eternal King of Israel. Therefore, the Son of David is a vice-regent, not the supreme sovereign. In PssSol there is no suggestion of his supernatural birth or preexistence,[25] and he appears throughout as a divinely-appointed man. Yet PssSol seems to regard him as something more than human. The Son of David conquers without earthly weapons, but with

---

25. For the return and the preexistence of the Messiah, Charlesworth suggests many passages such as 2 Baruch 30:1; 1 Enoch 46:1–2; 48:2–3, 6; 62:7; 4 Ezra 7:28–29; 12:31–34; 13:25–26. Charlesworth, "From Messianology to Christology," 29–30.

wisdom (17:35). He is pure from sin, all wise and all powerful (17:36–39). His peculiar vocation is to destroy the dominion of the Gentiles, and to set up in its stead a kingdom of Israel, which he will govern in perfect accordance with, and be qualified, above all, by the attributes of ethical majesty. His power, therefore, will be founded on holiness, justice, and wisdom. He will set his hope solely upon God and will tolerate the presence of no iniquity. As his kingdom will be one of righteousness, so that all its individual members will be holy—all of them "children of their God" (17:21, 31).

While relating to the preexistence of the Messiah in paradise in the early Judaism literatures, James H. Chalesworth suggests that PssSol seems to refer to the return of the Messiah to the earth with glory. This idea seems to be found in the Greek text of PssSol 18:5. In 18:5, according to him,

> The Greek verb (anaksei) can mean "lift up," but here it probably means "to bring back." The author was referring either to the return of an anointed one like David or, as seems more probably, to the return of the Messiah, who is like the wonderful King David.[26]

He convinces without doubt that some Jews conceived an eschatological christological belief like the return of the Messiah. This is a very important discovery:

> If some Jews held a belief in the return of the Messiah, then we have an important foundation for the Christian belief in the parousia of Jesus. At this point Messianology flows into Christology.[27]

His suggestion makes clear that some early Jews contemplated the return of the Messiah. It is important to note that the belief of the return of the Davidic messianic king is probably compared with that of the coming one in Q.

The Insights in the Sayings Gospel Q

The name "Q" delivered from Johannes Weiss who was the first person to use "Q" to designate the sayings source used by Matthew and Luke. Hence, Q comes from the earliest Christian periods and it is prior to the composition of the Synoptic Gospels. Thus the author is a Christian community which is found in the historical ministry of Jesus with his call to repentance and acceptance of the kingdom of God. Q is a written source of sayings and discourses attributed to Jesus used commonly by Matthew and Luke. Q points out the Sayings Gospel of Jesus as a document which "was compiled and composed in Greek."[28]

---

26. Ibid., 30.
27. Ibid.
28. Kloppenborg, *Formation of Q*, 64.

Q is "normally dated sometime in the period between 50 CE and 70 CE."[29] Thus Q reflects the previous circumstances of certain historical events, namely the Jewish war (66–70 CE) and the fall of Jerusalem (70 CE). However, I attested that the earliest redaction of Q is probably dated between 30 and 40 CE and the secondary redaction of Q is sometime before 50 CE in chapter 7. The place of Q's origin is very probably Galilee.

For a different view on Q, it is helpful to ask the question, "How does Q relate with the christological insights in PssSol?" Thinking of Q's leading theological debates, in general, most of Q scholars are not interested in these christological insights.

The Poor

The wisdom tradition of the Old Testament is carried on in the sapiential writings of the intertestamental period. Thus, on the one hand, there is a high estimate of wealth and praise for the rich, with accompanying harsh words for the poor. On the other hand, there is also a polemic uttered against the exploitation, greed and deceit of the rich. Like PssSol, therefore, Q may have been influenced in a positive fashion: "Blessed are you poor. For yours is the kingdom of God" (Q 6:20). The blessing of the poor is much closer to PssSol.

According to Paul Hoffmann,[30] the poor and the sinners were victims of political-economical development. Jesus delivers his message about the present action of the salvation of God, especially for the lost personal groups—the poor, the hungry and mourning, the sick and the sinners—in his contemporary society. They are worthy of God's special attention in his perspective.

Q has a concrete concept of God in mercy (Q 6:36); Q has God for the poor (Q 6:20; 7:22; 14:21). Q's material on the poor and possessions is found not to be the expression of a single theme. In Q, God has promised to save the poor and set them high, and with the appearance of Jesus these promises are being fulfilled. Jesus proclaims the end of the age of wickedness and the coming of the kingdom of God which will mean for the poor, the end of all need and the dawning of peace, joy, freedom, plenty and laughter.

In the Beatitudes of the poor (Q 6:20–21), the dawn of divine liberation action is introduced to the captives and the mourning people with the announcement of salvation on the poor (compare Luke 4:18–19; cf. Isa 61:1–2). The blessing of the poor fits well within Jesus' own time appears to be early in the transmission of Jesus' sayings and may very well derive ultimately from him. Though poverty is synonymous with hunger and lamentation in Q (Q 6:20), these "poor" are not necessarily beggars in the strict sense, that is, persons who economically are completely dependent on help from others.[31] The most likely function of Q 6:20a, then, is to indicate Q's view that

---

29. Kloppenborg, *Q-Thomas Reader*, 5.
30. Hoffmann, *Erbe Jesu und die Macht*, 23–24.
31. Schottroff and Stegmann, *Jesus and the Hope of the Poor*, 16.

the salvation which Jesus declares openly to all Israel will ultimately rest only upon his disciples. The inheritance of the poor, therefore, is finally fallen to the disciples of Jesus. Because the rest will not follow Jesus, preferring the present order to the salvation Jesus proclaims, they are characterized as rich and satisfied and laughing, though in socio-economic terms they may not have been wealthy. If I turn to Q's version I notice that it is the disciples who are addressed (Q 6:20), Q also regards them as the Q community of his time.

Who are the poor in Q? Some see the poor as the pious, and some as a particular social group. Some see them as those who have voluntarily abandoned their possessions, and others emphasize the condition of those afflicted with literal poverty. But still Q sees the poor in the light of PssSol, as the designated heirs of salvation. Therefore, this chapter tends to group the poor with the tax collectors, the hungry and mourning, and sinners because they call for special attention in Q. And Jesus proclaims salvation for these people. And in Q there are members focused on the poor: the disciples of Jesus. In Q 9:2–6 Jesus says to his disciples to take nothing for their journey, such as a staff, or knapsack, or bread, or silver, or two tunics. Jesus, however, tells his disciples to become financially poor or to make people poor; he exhorts them to share possessions with the poor.

Certainly, Q emerges as a reflection and development upon the wisdom tradition recorded in PssSol. When Q makes reference to the mercy for the poor, Q shows an awareness of PssSol tradition. This awareness supports my suggestion about Q's knowledge of PssSol tradition.

The Kingdom of God

The leading theological category of Q is the proclamation of the kingdom of God. As Ivan Havener suggests, the term "kingdom of God" refers to God's sovereignty or reign at the end time, when Satan's control over the kingdoms of the world is overcome forever. According to him, Q speaks of the kingdom of God in a twofold manner, for it claims on the one hand that God's reign was already present and manifest in Jesus' life and ministry, and on the other hand, that the kingdom's advent is still a future event associated with God's judgment at the end of time. Both of these ways of speaking of God's reign are treated in some depth by Q.[32]

Q suggests definitely one of the earliest thoughts for the meaning of God's kingdom among the primitive Christian congregations. As compared to PssSol, Q has also the form "your kingdom" (Q 11:2) in the expression of the Lord's Prayer.

In Q one can find that the kingdom of God appears in various thematic sections (Q 6:20; 7:28; 10:9, 11; 11:2, 20; 12:31; 13:18, 20, 29; 16:16). In some sections, the kingdom of God in Q is closely connected with a transcendent power, which can be recognized in exorcisms. That is the important thing. Like the eternal rule of God in

32. Havener, Q, 50.

PssSol. Q remains the transcendent power of God. At this point, PssSol and Q share the common idea of the kingdom, which means not God's realm as the state of salvation, but God's effective kingly reign. Certainly this would lend further support to my suggestion about Q's awareness of the idea of the kingdom in PssSol.

As Jacobson noted, "Exorcism is linked directly to the kingdom."[33] But the context does not permit this saying to refer exclusively to Jesus' exorcisms. Rather, the coming of the kingdom is the presupposition for all exorcisms. According to Jacobson, other scholars have emphasized that while Jesus and the Jewish exorcists both exorcise through the power of God, only Jesus' exorcisms had eschatological significance (163).

The connection of the kingdom of God with exorcism is especially clear in the Beelzebul controversy (Q 11:14–23, 24–26):

> And if I exorcise demons by Beelzebul, by whom do your sons exorcise? Therefore, they shall be your judges. But if it is by the finger of God that I exorcise demons, then the kingdom of God has come upon you. (Q 11:19–20)

The Beelzebul section has a two sided kingdom of God and Satan. What is manifested in exorcism, however, is not the kingdom of Satan but the kingdom of God. Therefore, now the kingdom of God can be experienced in exorcisms (cf. Q 10:9).

When I think of the kingdom of God in the christological insights, it intersects the course of human history and experience. Life within the kingdom—the living performance issuing from the interaction of the transcendent kingdom and historical existence—suggests liberation and obedience. Israelites that refuse to repent at Jesus' proclamation of the kingdom are characterized as the rich because they betray themselves as being satisfied and happy with their lot in this age. Thus Q warns not to treat the good things of this age, but to reach out for the kingdom to come to Jesus, suffering for a while if it is needed, but ultimately to inherit the new age. Because Jesus is the one who brings the kingdom, the final result of living for Jesus, and his kingdom will be a glorious reception into the new age and an eschatological kingdom. In short, in Q the kingdom of God means liberation for the new age. At this point, the kingdom of God in Q is somewhat present.

The Judgment Announcement

In Q one can find a number of prophetic sayings or "*Drohworte*" (threats),[34] of which R. Bultmann suggested there are 15 such sayings. His opinion about such sayings was that Q has twelve threats among fifteen (Q 12:8–9; 10:13–15; 11:31–32; 11:43, 46, 52, 42, <39>, 44, 47; 11:49–51; 13:34–35; 12:54–56; 13:28–29; 6:46; 13:26–27; 17:26–27,

---

33. Jacobson, *First Gospel*, 70. The kingdom of God linked to exorcism was already stressed by Bultmann. Cf. Bultmann, *History of the Synoptic Tradition*, 14.

34. Bultmann, *History of the Synoptic Tradition*, 111–18.

<28–29>, 34–35; 3:7–9). At this point, this judgment announcement is a literature of *Drohworte* (threats).

Such a return to Bultmann's attribution of such threat sayings is reminiscent of other advocates of attributing more sayings in the Q tradition to the historical Jesus: Arland D. Jacobson and John S. Kloppenborg. According to Jacobson, these sayings mentioned above point out that most of such sayings present judgment announcement "in view of impenitence or failure to respond to a divine appeal."[35] This then raises the concern as to the deviation of Q from the theme of judgment. Kloppenborg wrote in his book:

> The call to repentance, the threat of apocalyptic judgment and the censure of "this generation" for its recalcitrance are prominent in several clusters of Q sayings. In fact, they are the formative and unifying themes for John's preaching (3:7–9, 16–17), the healing of the centurion's servant and the sayings about John (7:1–10, 18–35), the large block of material beginning with the Beelzebul accusation and ending with the woes against the Pharisees (11:14–52) and the two section of Q dealing with the parousia (12:39–59 and 17:23–37).[36]

These five complexes of Q sayings account for the preaching of judgment, judgment announcement in Q: the imminent anticipations (Q 3:9, 17; 11:51b; 12:51–53, 54–56) and the grounds for judgment and condemnation (Q 7:31–35; 11:19–20, 24–26, 29–32, 33–36, 49–51; 12:57–59). According to John S. Kloppenborg, this theme pervading these materials is the announcement of judgment and is often expressed in the deuteronomistic language of reproach for unfaithfulness to God's covenant[37] (cf. 105, 112, 143, 166–68). Like PssSol, therefore, theocracy is a theme to which Q returns repeatedly. Theocracy is also represented by the expression of "By the finger of God that I exorcise demons" (Q 11:20).

For this reason, the judgment sayings are considered in the heart of the prophetic message. Unfortunately, in a negative sense of Q, the prophetic form of the judgment announcement is based on the primacy of the judgment motif. Kloppenborg rightly says that repentance by Israel is no longer anticipated in this preaching of judgment and there remains only the judgment (148). Therefore, judgment sayings are closely related to the warning statement which I will consider here in the same basic category (Q 3:7; 10:12, 13–15; 11:31–32). And there are warnings which assume a future judgment (Q 11:49–52; 12:2–4, 8–9, 59; 13:27–29; 17:35, 37). In summary, like PssSol, Q has here the prophetic sayings, no repentance by the opposite, relation to a warning statement, and future judgment. These, therefore, raise the concern as to the deviation of Q from the theme of judgment in PssSol.

In addition, God will judge Israel, who rejects the repentance and does not respond to God's appeal. This judgment is a kind of visible sign of the divine reproach

---

35. Jacobson, *First Gospel*, 64.
36. Kloppenborg, *Formation of Q*, 102.
37. Of course, the term "covenant" of God does not appear in Q.

for the unfaithfulness to God's covenant in the deuteronomistic language. At the same time, however, God will save the people who repent directly from unfaithfulness. Therefore, whereas the scribal or Pharisaic opposition remains in the murder of the prophets and hence in opposition to God's actions in history (Q 11:47–48), the Q community who accepts their mission will be delivered from suffering.

Christological Insights

WISDOM

In Q there are the so-called wisdom pericopes (Q 7:31–35; 10:21–22; 11:29–32; 11:49–51; 13:34–35). But among them wisdom plays an important role in these references. Jesus is implicitly a messenger of wisdom except Q 10:21–22. The fact to be tested is that these remarkable references to Jesus as wisdom are introduced as part of a larger redactional effort by Q.

As the position taken in his article, Burton L. Mack concludes that

> Wisdom as a mode of thinking was pervasive throughout early Judaism and Christianity. The connections between Jewish wisdom mythology and early Christian Christology are therefore indirect. There may be no straight-line developments or "identifications" of Jesus with a particular image or myth of Jewish wisdom or of "wisdom's child."[38]

This means that Q has somewhat borrowed the implication of idea or concept and transmitted from Jewish tradition like PssSol.

James M. Robinson summarizes the present state of research on the Sophia (wisdom) in Q:

> The identification of the apocalyptic son of man with Jesus applied not only to the future but already to his public ministry. This called for some theological category for comprehending his public ministry as a positive category in its own right. The final emissary of Sophia becomes this category.... The association of this final emissary of Sophia with the unique apocalyptic son of man made it easy to heighten the Christology in the wisdom sayings of Q by according to the son Sophia's unique relation to the Father, in effect identifying Jesus with Sophia itself. This Sophia Christology was then further developed in Matthew, and in the first half of the second century become common, in the Gospel of the Hebrews, the Gospel of Thomas, Justin Martyr, and so on, and thus became a permanent if minor ingredient in all subsequent Christology.[39]

---

38. Mack, "Christ and Jewish Wisdom," 194–95.
39. Robinson, "Jesus as Sophos and Sophia," 14–15.

Robinson proposed, "The relation between Jesus and personified wisdom, Sophia" (1), in his article which sketches the wisdom trajectory through Jewish and primitive Christian traditions, especially Q. Thus, Sophia is identified with Jesus.

Above all, in Q 7:31–35 the wisdom pericope comes in the form of a parable. According to Jacobson, wisdom in Q 7:35 is personified: she has children: Since the "children" of 7:35 are presumably opposite to the "children" of 7:32, they must be those who respond to John and Jesus and who, by doing so, vindicate wisdom.[40] This means that John and Jesus in some sense represent wisdom, presumably as bearers of her message, so that wisdom is vindicated when people respond affirmatively to her messages, John and Jesus. "The only characters in the pericope who can be regarded as wisdom's children are, therefore, Jesus and John."[41] Jesus and John are, as the logion implies, wisdom's representatives, agents or envoys.

This may also be implicit in the "Son" of 10:21–22. The exclusive reciprocal knowledge of Father and Son can best be explained on the basis of wisdom tradition. What is most important for our purpose is that here "Jesus is not simply cast in the role of one of Sophia's spokesman, even the culminating one, but rather is described with predications that are reserved for Sophia herself" (9). Quoting from the treatment of Q by Siegfried Schulz, *Q: Die Spruchquelle der Evangelisten*, James M. Robinson concludes that "the exclusivity of is attributed to the son, who is identified with Jesus" (10) in question about the exclusive reciprocal relation of Father and Son.

In addition, in Q 11:29–32 we can also detect the influence of the wisdom tradition. Here it is important to note that in Q 11:31–32 wisdom has taken the place of God as the sender of prophets like Q 11:49–51.[42] In Q 11:49–51 I can find "personified wisdom, Sophia."[43] Here wisdom relates sending of prophets and apostles and speaks of their rejection by persecution. And in Q 13:34–35 even though the word "wisdom" are not used, its contents are closed to Q 11:49–51. And here the messenger sent by wisdom is also called prophets. Obviously, Q seems to presuppose the idea that Jesus is wisdom's and at the same time he becomes wisdom herself in such a special status, in which he sends his disciples to the world in the mission charge periscopes (Q 10:2–16).

The Son of Man

Unlike PssSol, the title "the Messiah" (Christ) does not appear in Q at all; Q never calls Jesus "the Christ." In Q, the Son of man is used almost exclusively in the words of Jesus—Jesus refers to himself as the Son of man (Q 6:22; 7:34; 9:58; 11:30; 12:8,

---

40. Jacobson, *First Gospel*, 124–25. Here wisdom's children vindicate her by affirming both John and Jesus.
41. Suggs, *Wisdom, Christology*, 35.
42. For the idea that wisdom sends prophets, see ibid., 38–48.
43. Robinson, "*Logoi Sophon*," 71.

10,[44] 40; 17:22, 24, 26, 39). However, unlike the apocalyptic appearance of "one like a son of man" in Dan 7, the Son of Man should no longer be understood as a title for a well-known apocalyptic figure. Arland D. Jacobson indicates that "the Q community does not understand the title 'son of man' as a reference to an apocalyptic figure of judgment."[45] Unfortunately, in early Christian circles the vision of Dan 7:13 was the primary source for the conception of the Son of man figure. But, even in Dan 7:13 "son of man" is descriptive, namely that "one like a son of man," It means that "son of man" in there is not titular. The Gospel's Son of man sayings derived from utterances which made use of the Aramaic phrase *bar (a) nash (a)*[46] as a way of referring to the speaker. Especially, Q also did not use *bar (a) nash (a)* as a title.

In Q 6:22 the Son of man is embedded in the context of material which is clearly rooted in the tradition of the suffering of the righteous who are "oriented toward the specific situation of persecution of the Christian community."[47] It is clear that Q recognizes the Son of man as a self-designation of Jesus. However, his disciples didn't hear Jesus referring to himself as the Son of man.

Q 7:34 is placed in Jesus' public ministry as well as Q 6:22; 9:58; 11:30.[48] Here Jesus who calls himself the Son of Man presented as a glutton and a drunkard, a friend of tax collectors and sinners. Such a reputation of Jesus should be true because he came from the poor comparable to the sage at that time.

---

44. According to Kloppenborg, Q 12:10 is usually seen as contradicting Q 12:8–9 (see the *Formation of Q*, 211–12). In its present context, the Son of man in Q 12:10 can only be the heavenly Son of man mentioned by Q 12:8. In neither instance is this Son of man identified with Jesus.

45. Jacobson, *First Gospel*, 101. The current studies of non-apocalyptic figure for the origin of the Son of man of the Gospels are made by many scholars, of who but I will mention here two scholars, Leivestad and Hare. Cf. See Leivestad, "Exit the Apocalyptic Son of Man," 234–67, and Hare, *Son of Man Tradition*. For attempting to confirm the non-apocalyptic view, Leivestad suggested a series of strong reasons for refuting the hypothesis of an apocalyptic Son of man title. He argued that in the comparison with the postulated apocalyptic Son of man connected with supernatural power and glory in the Gospels "the Son of man is only used as a self-designation" (ibid., 264). Answering the ultimate question, what Jesus meant by designating himself as the Son of man, he concluded that "the Son of man is not a pretentious designation but a humble one, denoting solidarity and identification with the sons of man? The son of man is he who is a friend of sinners. The Son of man is he who came to serve and give his life. The self-designation is an evidence of his self-dedication to men" (ibid., 267). When I consider this conclusion, this interpretation is proven not for Q because it is related with the Markan humble servant (Mark 10:45). After all, Leivestad' analysis of the Son of man is based on Mark rather than Q in character. Hare's suggestion would bring closure to the argument of the non-apocalyptic view.

46. For this phrase, and much of the following theoretical reflections, I am dependent on the seminar with Robinson at *IAC* (Fall, 1993).

47. Kloppenborg, *Formation of Q*, 173. Here Kloppenborg placed this saying in the layer of the sapiential speeches (Q^2), but it should be Q^1 picture which is a prophetic saying.

48. Robinson, "Son of Man," 27 ix 93, 1. Also he argued that Q 7:34; 9:58 are thought to be authentic Son of Man sayings and Q 12:8, 10, 40; 17:24, 26, 30 are references to the coming Son of Man. "The preeminence of Jesus in the Q tradition is derived conceptually from the identification of Jesus with the coming son of man who will determine mankind's fate at the last judgment" ("Jesus as Sophos and Sophia," 6).

In Q 9:58 the Son of man has no connotative force, only denotative effect. This saying is related with discipleship, namely, that the Son of Man encourages the life style for Christian discipleship. "As Jesus on earth was rejected by his people and wandered homeless, so must the disciples expect to be."[49] Obviously, that kind of life style must be shared by those who follow Jesus.

According to James M. Robinson, Q 11:30 has sometime been classified as an instance of the future apocalyptic titular usage. . . . But here it is the Ninevites and this generation who are to be present at this Day of Judgment, without any reference to a presence at the judgment of Jonah and Jesus. Rather the point has to do with Jesus' public ministry: "Something greater than Jonah is here."[50] Here the future tense "will be" (ἔσται) is far more ambiguous. Ἔσται "would seem to be gnomic, not apocalyptic" (7). Furthermore, Jacobson argues that, assuming Luke 11:30 to be more original than Matt 12:40, the next question concerns the identity of the Son of man. The presence of the future 'will be' (ἔσται), could require that the Son of Man be an agent of apocalyptic judgment; however, this "will be" merely answers to the "shall be given" (*hoothesetai*) in the previous verse. Further, if Son of man designates an agent of apocalyptic judgment, then comparison with Jonah becomes difficult. How could an apocalyptic judge to "this generation" what Jonah was to the Ninevites? In what sense is the apocalyptic Son of man a "sign"? The difficulties with this interpretation have led a number of scholars to argue that Son of man cannot refer to an apocalyptic judge.[51] Therefore, Q may understand this saying to refer to Jesus' prophetic ministry in Jerusalem. One of the interesting things I think is this: It is possible that an earlier form of this logion was uttered by Jesus as a statement about his prophetic ministry. Hence, this saying says that the sign which the Son of man will give to this generation will be the sign of Jonah. Of course, here the Son of man idiom was chosen by himself for the sake of a self-designation of Jesus.

In Q 12:8 the Son of man functions as "I." This saying is quite similar to that of Mark 8:38, but in Q Jesus does not use the Son of man idiom as a way of referring to his future heavenly glory. What I am convinced is this: Here Mark 8:38 and Luke 12:8 juxtapose the first personal pronoun with the term Son of man in the third person. I do not know that in Q this saying shows whether a role of a judgment and a heavenly witness, or not. But according to James M. Robinson, it was Vielhauer who broke from the standard Bultmannian solution still represented by Tödt, by arguing that even the apocalyptic Son of man sayings is inauthentic. He argued forcefully for the inauthenticity of Q 12:8–9, on the grounds that this saying presupposed judicial processes against Christians, which would hardly, have taken place during the public ministry (13; see also n54). Therefore, the Son of man in Q 12:8 is "not the judge of the Day of Judgment, nor is he anywhere so portrayed in Q. Rather he is a character witness, to the effect that his followers have kept his word (Q 6:47–49)" (14).

49. Higgins, *Jesus and the Son of Man*, 126.
50. Robinson, "Son of Man," 7.
51. Jacobson, *First Gospel*, 165–66.

Q 12:10 has the parallel in Mark 3:28-29. Mark changed this generic expression to its plural equivalent, "the sons of men," while the Q tradition altered the structure of the clause so as to make "the Son of man" the object of the slander rather than the recipient of forgiveness. In Q this saying is provided to understand the Son of man as a way of referring to Jesus, but "as the designation of a heavenly figure whose role Jesus would fulfill."[52] So to speak, in its present context the Son of man in Q 12:10 not be the heavenly Son of man as well as in Q 12:8. In both instances is this Son of man identified with Jesus.

Q 12:40 is attached to Q 12:39, though many scholars have noted Q 12:39-40" "a secondary composition."[53] Undoubtedly, the following materials are associated with the statement "Nobody knows the time the Son of man is coming" (see also Q 12:46). Probably in connection with the sudden coming of the thief, the Son of man saying is a secondary interpretation of the parable. This saying, however, speaks not of the advent of a heavenly figure but of the return of Jesus. Hence this saying also must be avoided from an apocalyptic picture.

Like Q 12:40, in Q 17:24, 26, 30 the coming Son of man is the focus of final layers of Sayings Gospel (Q 17:23-24, 26-30, 34-35, 37). John S. Kloppenborg calls them "the logia apocalypse"[54] which is given the opponents, so to speak, "those who live oblivious to the imminent catastrophe of the coming of the Son of man (Q 12:54-56)" (ibid., 167). Therefore, Kloppenborg recognized these sayings as "an adaptation of a current apocalyptic slogan" (ibid., 160) providing the terms of the Son of man eschatology. For this reason, according to Kloppenborg, "the Son of man will come as a heavenly figure" (ibid., 161).

Certainly, however, there is a scholarly opinion opposing the interpretation in comparison with the apocalyptic. Here Robinson talked about a consensus of scholarly opinion: "Vielhauer opposed Tödt's interpretation in analogy to the apocalyptic comparisons in Q 17:24, 26-27, and 30."[55] Now Robinson suggested that this saying has nothing pointing to an apocalyptic Son of man, but is comparable to the apocalyptic instances of the correlative.[56] For Q the Son of man is not an apocalyptic title but a name for the earthly Jesus that can be also used of the returning Jesus.

It seems probably that the Q community retains present Son of man sayings in order to present "Jesus in his life time" (earthly Jesus) as the Son of man.

---

52. Hare, *Son of Man Tradition*, 64. Here in this way Hare perceives Luke's intention in placing (or retaining) the saying in the context.

53. Kloppenborg, *Formation of Q*, 149. See also n203. Such a secondary is proven by Robinson, "Son of Man," 14.

54. Kloppenborg, *Formation of Q*, 154. For more detail explanations, see 154-66. But Conzelmann termed aptly them "the logia apocalypse" for the first time. See Kloppenborg, *Formation of Q*, 154n225. Cf. Conzelmann, *Outline of the Theology*, 135.

55. Robinson, "Son of Man," 15.

56. Ibid., 16. According to him, Crossan also has designated it as "apocalyptic correlative." See n66.

PART 3: JEWISH INFLUENCES AND CHRISTOLOGICAL INSIGHTS

THE COMING ONE

Q mentions another christological title, the coming one which depends upon Q 3:16;7:19; 11:22; 13:35. In Q the leading notion of the kingdom focuses on the realized eschatology which is supported by C. H. Dodd, though Tödt[57] said the kerugma of Q centered in the identification of Jesus with the Son of Man announced by Jesus as yet to come and assumed at least the sayings about the Son of man as a future figure, not one who "has come." The dominant scholarly view of the last twenty-five years is that the coming one saying in Q has an eschatological figure.

According to James M. Robinson,[58] the Christianizing of Q 3:16, by identifying Jesus with the one who, though coming after John, is stronger than he, and whose sandals John is not even worthy to remove, has the effect of a sharp reversal of values. This saying about the coming one stronger than John is obviously breaking up the sequence of Q 3:7–9 and 3:17 in order to identify Jesus with the coming one after John because Q 3:16 is Christianized.

In Q 7:19 the title of the coming one is clearly a reference back to the preaching of John. Thus, in Q the title can be understood in no other way than as a reference to the figure announced by John—the end time judge. However, Arland D. Jacobson here didn't regard Jesus as the apocalyptic figure of judgment announced by John. Here this is true whether "the coming one" is interpreted messianically or as a reference to the "eschatological prophet."[59] To be sure, the coming one is an eschatological figure announced by John to Jesus. As in Q 3:16, therefore, this identification is presupposed. At earlier stage of the Christianizing[60] the coming one may be identified with Jesus.

Q 13:35 comes together in the context of the Lament over Jerusalem (Q 13:34). Here the coming one also refers to an eschatological figure, as in the case of Q 3:16. That christological development consisted in the claim that this eschatological figure will be, since it already is, Jesus. Here Jesus is engaged in such eschatological figure. Despite its utterance to the prophets in Q 13:34, Q 13:35 is usually described as an oracle of wisdom.[61] The purpose of wisdom is to gather "children together as a hen gathers her own brood under her wings" (Q 13:34b). Jesus as the coming one can do such gathering.

Jesus is truly the coming one so that he may sit on his throne judging the twelve tribes of Israel with those who have preserved with him (Q 22:28–30). To be sure, in this present passage I can read the apparent promise of a future reward.

---

57. Tödt, *Son of Man in the Synoptic Tradition*.
58. Robinson, "Sayings Gospel Q," 362.
59. Cf. Cullmann, *Christology of the New Testament*, 26.
60. Jacobson suggested that "at a later stage in the Q tradition the identification of Jesus with the figure announced by John (and designated 'coming one') was made." See his *First Gospel*, 113. However, Robinson insisted that "perhaps this is indicative of the earliness of Q traditions, when such things were still in the formative stage." See his "Sayings Gospel Q," 363.
61. Suggs, *Wisdom, Christology*, 63–70.

The Son of God

The Son of God in Q is the subject of explicit treatment of the christological title (Q 3:22; 4:3, 9; 10:22). The title "Son of God," however, is rare in Q, and occurs only in Q 4:3, 9.

Though R. Bultmann thinks that Q had no account of baptism of Jesus,[62] current Q scholars are sure that Q had a baptism account. As Kloppenborg argues, "The Son of God Christology presupposed by the temptation account demands the existence of a baptismal account."[63] Thus the temptation account (Q 4:1–13) presupposes the baptism account.

In Q 3:21–22, Q seems to presuppose Jesus as the Son of God. Q 3:22 just has "son" in his baptism account, as Q's version of the voice from heaven shows, "You are my son." It is important to note that Q 10:22 is a claim to be the exclusive source for the revelation of God, whereas Q 10:21 is a thanksgiving. Though Q 10:21 and 22 are originally independent sayings, the two sayings share common vocabularies, "father" and "son." In Q 10:21f. the relation of Jesus to God is disclosed. It must be said that "son" refers to Jesus as the Son of God. Only this passage uses the "Son" designation in a unique sense and it appears on the lips of Jesus himself . . . This passage proclaims that Jesus is God's son that only by accepting the Son as the revealer of God the Father can God be known.[64] Therefore, that the Son of God Christology is presupposed by Q 3:22 and Q 10:22 is obvious.

Q 4:1–13 containing this motif has unique examples for the title "Son of God." What is said about the sonship of Jesus in the baptism account is repeated here in the temptation account, where the devil calls Jesus the Son of God (Q 4:3, 9): "If you are the son of God." According to Burton L. Mack, the story of the temptation of Jesus introduces three themes characteristic of Q^3. They are the mythology of Jesus as the son of God, the relationship of Jesus as the son of God to the temple at Jerusalem, and the authority of scriptures.[65] He says that upgrading the mythology of Jesus from children of wisdom in Q^2 to the Son of God in Q^3 may seem to be a small step, but note the consequences (ibid., 173). Anyway, in Q^3 the Son of God becomes a high Christology, to which I can trace its trajectory from children of wisdom through the Son of man and the coming one to the Son of God in the Christology of Q.

In Q^3, according to Joon Ho Chang, "Jesus, the Son of God, as a sort of the Hellenistic divine man is asked to perform a miracle of turning stones into loaves."[66] He says that in Q 4:3 the Son of God has an active power in his miraculous ministry, while

---

62. Bultmann, *History of the Synoptic Tradition*, 251.

63. Kloppenborg, *Formation of Q*, 84.

64. Havener, *Q*, 71. In addition, Havener comments that "this is the very heart of Q's understanding of the way of salvation. Jesus himself is the very means of salvation, but it is not through his redeeming death, which is nowhere mentioned in Q, rather, in his revealing of God's reign and of the way to share in that kingdom" (ibid.).

65. Mack, *Lost Gospel*, 173.

66. Chang, "In Memory of Him," 17.

in Q 4:9 the son of God is described as a passive figure who is the Son not the Father (ibid., 17–18).

In the temptation account, however, Jesus does not accept the temptation asked to prove himself as a Son of God. Rather, Jesus teaches the life in obedience to God, quoting the deuteronomistic references (Deut 8:3b LXX; 6:16 LXX). Thus Q³ clearly recognizes Jesus as "the obedient Son of God."[67] To be sure, in Q³ the devil wants to find out through the temptations whether or not Jesus is truly the Son of God because the human nature of Jesus is the veil which deceives the devil.

In addition, in the Sermon on the Plain Q 6:35c says that those who obey Jesus also become "sons of the Most High." Like in this sense of Q 10:21–22, Jesus "reveals the Father to others, and those, to whom the Son chooses to reveal the Father, also know the Father like the son. In this sense they become real 'sons of God' themselves."[68] To be sure, Jesus as the Son of God shares his sonship with his people who listens him.

A Comparison of the Similar and Christological Insights

The similarity lies not simply in the terminology that is common to PssSol and Q, but especially in the thought-content common to both. While Q makes no direct quotations from PssSol, Q is closely related to PssSol in the christological insights. Here the correspondences between PssSol and Q will be investigated by paying attention to the christological insights in which agreements may be observed. Therefore, this chapter has a step of a comparative examination for the christological insights in PssSol and Q. First of all, a brief comparison of these correspondences will be presented.

While the descriptions may look somewhat similar at first glance, I don't think the actual agreements were similar. However, if PssSol and Q have pretty much the same insights, certainly Q intentionally focused on the christological insights that were received from PssSol. But Q also quite clearly eliminated the style of psalms and the Pharisaic traditions in PssSol. One way to answer the question would be to suggest that the christological insights were in fact the same, but that Q chose to focus on a different formation, namely the narrative or the Gospel.

It is necessary to keep in mind that there is one more important thing. Even if there are some actual agreements in the terminology in both PssSol and Q, this chapter must find the contrasts between them. For these contrasts I will design the category of "difference/ similarity."

---

67. Luz, *Matthew 1–7*, 188.

68. Havener, *Q*, 71. "On the other hand, those who reject Jesus are, in effect, also rejecting the Father who sent him" (cf. Q 10:16).

Chart I: A Comparison in the Similar Insights

Classification	PssSol	Q	Difference(D)/ Similarity(S)
Background			
Date	Around 50 BCE	Between 50 CE and 70 CE	(D)
Language in versions	Hebrew (not extant) Greek Syriac	Greek	(S)
Place of origin	Jerusalem or some place in Judea	Galilee	(D)
Author	Pharisaic circles	Christian(Q) community	(D)
Historical Event	After Pompey's entry into Jerusalem (63 BCE)	Before the fall of Jerusalem (70 CE)	(S)
Historical situation	Crisis	Crisis	(S)
Message	Messianological message	Christological message	(S)
The poor Who are the poor	The Pious	Tax collector, the hungry and mourning, the sick, and the sinners	(D)
Focused members	Israelites/Israel	Disciples of Jesus/Q community	(S)
God	The refuge of the poor	In mercy & for the poor	(S)
Characteristic	Salvation for the poor	Salvation for the poor	
The kingdom of God Topic	Davidic messianic kingdom	Eschatological kingdom	(D)
	God's kingly power	God's sovereignty	(S)
	God's reign	God's reign	(S)
Characteristic	The eternal rule of God	The transcendent power of God	(S)
	The hope of the future	God's kingdom is present	(D)
	A restoration of a Jewish kingdom	A liberation for the new age	(D)
The Judgment Announcement			
The Pious	Pharisees	Q community or disciples of Jesus	(D)
The sinners	Hasmonian Sadducees	Israel	(D)
Opposition	Against Hasmoneans	Against scribal or Pharisaic circles	(D)
Approval	For Pharisees	For Christians	(D)
A great theological theme	Theodicy/theocracy	Theocracy	(S)

Part 3: Jewish Influences and Christological Insights

Classification	PssSol	Q	Difference(D)/ Similarity(S)
Characteristic	A literature of crisis	A literature of Drohworte	(S)
	Prophetic message	Prophetic message	(S)
	No repentance by the opposite (Hasmoneans)	No repentance by the opposite (Israel)	(S)
	Relation to a warning statement	Relation to a warning statement	(S)
	Future judgment	Future judgment	(S)
	God's righteousness	Rejection of the repentance	(D)
A standard			

Chart II. A Comparison in the Christological Insights

Classification	PssSol	Q	Difference(D)/ Similarity(S)
Wisdom		Wisdom	
Word:	Wisdom	Wisdom	(S)
	Characteristic trait	Characteristic trait	(S)
Characteristic	Wisdom carrier→King	Wisdom's Messengers/ children → Jesus and John	(S)
	King has the wisdom	Wisdom is idenrified with Jesus	(D)
The Lord Messiah		The Son of man	
Title	The messiah	The Son of Man: Non-titular in Q	(D)
	Title "the Messiah"	Title "the Christ" : Not in Q	(D)
	Messianic picture→Davidic Messiah	Human picture →"I"(Jesus)	(D)
	Agent for God's Plan	Earthly Jesus	(D)
Characteristic	A righteous King	A glutton and a drunkard, a friend of tax collectors and sinners	(D)
	Non-present figure	Present figure	(D)
	Future Messiah	Present Son of man	(D)
	The definite idea about the restoration of Israel	A certain designation of a way of referring to the speaker	(D)
	The messiah is subservient to God	Jesus refers to himself as the Son of Man	(D)

PssSol and Q in the Christological Insights

Classification	PssSol	Q	Difference(D)/ Similarity(S)
The coming king			
Title:	"The king of Israel"	"The coming one"	(D)
Concept	The coming king	The coming one	(S)
Characteristic	Messianic expectation	Non-messianic expectation	(D)
	The hope for a Davidic royal king	The hope for an eschatological figure	(S)
	Apocalyptic future	Eschatological future	(D)
	Apocalyptic future→Redeemer	Non-apocalyptic Judge → Eschatological Judge	(D)
Purpose	Restoration of Israel	To gather his people	(D)
The future Judge	He may be raised over the house of Israel to discipline it	He may sit on thrones to judge the twelve tribes of Israel	(S)
The Son of David			
Title:	The Son of David		
Characteristic	Davidic Messiah	Divine son	(D)
	The relationship of David	The relationship of Jesus as the Son of God the Father	(D)
	The promised Son of David	The revealer of God	(D)
	A positive figure→An ideal king will rule over the Hasmoneans	A passive figure → Jesus is not God Jesus is the obedient son of God	(D)
Purpose	Restoration of a Davidic kingdom and a Davidic Messiah	Revealing God the Father to the people	(D)
Christology:	High Messianology	High Christology	(S)

In the above survey the correspondences are limited to what appear to be close associations or allusions. This brief comparison of PssSol and Q has been examined in order to illustrate the correspondences and similarities, or contrasts. Now my attention will be devoted to those correspondences that are seen to exist between PssSol and Q. The intention is to show the high number of relationships between the documents involved and to draw some conclusions from these relationships.

I want to set PssSol forth to prove that the announcement of Jesus is rooted in early Judaism. Hence, I understand PssSol as a prerequisite to the appearance of Jesus. Whereas PssSol has the events of 63 BCE (Pompeii's entry into Jerusalem), Q anticipated the fall of Jerusalem, 70 CE. At those similar historical situations, PssSol responds to the Roman takeover a few years later, but Q is earlier to the takeover. Therefore, both documents use the messianological (PssSol) or christological (Q) message to liberate the oppressed in the new reflection of their socio-historical situations, crisis.

Whereas Matthew has specified the poor as "the poor in spirit," PssSol and Q do not show this development. They both, however, refer to "the poor" in another way of qualified terms. Who are the poor? In PssSol, they are the pious; in Q, tax collectors, and the hungry and mourning, the sick, and the sinners. Members especially focused upon are the Israelites or Israel (PssSol) and the disciples of Jesus or the Q community (Q). At this point, Q lies closer to PssSol tradition of simply "the poor." In both cases, the poor are contrasted to the rich. In PssSol, God is the refuge of the poor; in Q, God is merciful and stands for the poor. Therefore, in both cases, salvation is for the poor. Certainly Q emerges as a reflection and development upon the wisdom tradition recorded in PssSol. When Q makes reference to mercy for the poor, Q shows an awareness of PssSol tradition. This awareness supports my suggestion about Q's knowledge of PssSol tradition.

The leading theological category of both PssSol and Q is the proclamation of the kingdom of God. While PssSol names the kingdom as "your" or "our" God's reign, this is the key word for that stands for the future salvation, Q refers to the kingdom of God which means God's sovereignty or reign at the end time. Like the eternal rule of God in PssSol, Q retains the transcendent power of God. At this point, PssSol and Q share the common idea of the kingdom, which does not mean God's realm as the state of salvation, but God's effective kingly reign. Certainly this would lend further support to my suggestion about Q's awareness of the idea of the kingdom in PssSol. There are, however, some actual differences between them. Whereas PssSol expects a Davidic messianic kingdom and a restoration of a Jewish kingdom, Q has an eschatological kingdom and liberation for the new age. Even if the kingdom of God is always hoped for in the future in PssSol, in Q, God's kingdom is somewhat present.

In comparing the relationship between PssSol and Q, the judgment announcement must be kept in mind. Too often a formal identity for the judgment announcement is made between both of them. In both documents God will judge the people who do not respond to God's appeal, though both suggest a different standard for the judgment—God's righteousness in PssSol and rejection of the repentance in Q. Thus, in both, this judgment announcement is a kind of visible sign of God; God will save the people who repent directly from unfaithfulness. At this point I can suggest theodicy or theocracy for a great theological theme in both documents. For the similarities both of them have a prophetic message, no repentance by the opposite (in PssSol Hasmoneans, in Q Israel, especially scribal or Pharisaic circles), relation to a warning statement, and future judgment. These then raise the concern as to the deviation of Q from the theme of judgment in PssSol. In some cases of the contrasts, hence, I can easily find many correspondences between PssSol and Q. The differences precisely reflect the historical political situations. It means that the application of both documents is almost the same if their concrete *Sitz im Leben* is taken away. For this reason, it is important to note that the Pious in PssSol are Pharisees, instead of the Q community or the disciples of Jesus in Q; the sinners are Hasmonian Sadducees in PssSol, but scribes or Pharisees in Q. These situations indicate that PssSol is against the Hasmoneans and for the Pharisees, and at the same time Q is against scribal or Pharisaic circles and for Christians.

Wisdom as a mode of thinking was pervasive in PssSol and Q, though the connections between Jewish wisdom mythology and early Christian Christology are not direct. Even if there may be no straight-line developments or "identifications" of Jesus with a particular image or myth of Jewish wisdom, Q has somewhat of an implication of an idea or concept borrowed from Jewish wisdom tradition like PssSol. Wisdom as an intellectual tradition certainly that has contributed to early Christian thinking, especially Q. A charismatic trait is attributed to the messianic king in PssSol, and to Jesus and John in Q. In PssSol wisdom as a charismatic trait is presented as an aspect qualifying character and the effectiveness of this messianic king; in Q wisdom is identified with Jesus as wisdom's child. For a contrary, therefore, it is not yet said in PssSol that wisdom herself becomes someone like Jesus of her messenger in such a special status, as Q mentions. In other words, whereas PssSol suggests that the king has the wisdom of his righteousness and is endowed with a spirit, Q implies that Jesus is implicitly a messenger of wisdom and wisdom's representative, agent, envoy or wisdom. Thus, in PssSol wisdom is carried by the king; in Q by Jesus.

This chapter is precisely considered as the difference emphasized in contrasting PssSol and Q. So far, as I examine for this designation, Q didn't receive the tradition of PssSol. Pharisaic beliefs and hopes have definite ideas about the restoration of the Israelite. The messiah is brought in as a necessary agent for the fulfillment of God's plan and the establishment of God's kingdom. However, as an apocalyptic figure, the Messiah is totally subservient to God. Hence the Messiah acts only according to God's will. In contrast, the Q community does not understand the title "Son of man" as a reference to an apocalyptic figure like the Messiah of PssSol. Whereas PssSol calls the Lord, Messiah, and a righteous king, in Q, Jesus calls himself the Son of man presented as a glutton and a drunkard, or a friend of tax collectors and sinners. At this point, in Q, the Son of man functions as "I." For PssSol the Messiah is a title, but in Q, the Son of man is a certain designation of a way of referring to the speaker. It seems probably that the Q community leaves Son of man sayings, in order to present "Jesus in his life time" (earthly Jesus) as the Son of man.

PssSol preserves one of the most detailed messianic expectations in the immediate pre-Christian centuries. In PssSol, of course, the title "the coming one" like Q or "the coming king" is not presented. Most important in PssSol is the hope for a Davidic or royal Messiah. The designation "the king of Israel" occurs just once. Talk of an expected coming of the Messiah would have been meaningful to the Jews of PssSol and represented a major strand of Jewish messianic expectations. As if the kingship of the eagerly awaited Davidic Messiah of PssSol is understood in the view of Jewish

"Christology," the apocalyptic future figure, in Q, an idea of a future figure who comes to realize the eschatological reversal can be understood in the same way. Q concerns the identification of Jesus with the Son of man announced by Jesus as a future figure, not one who "has come." Unlike PssSol, however, in Q the coming one is in non-messianic expectation. The coming one is an eschatological figure announced by John to Jesus. It is also noted that in PssSol, the restoration of the dispersed of Israel to their own land is a principle element in the description of the coming deliverance, instead of Q's motif of the gathering his people by the coming one. Jesus as the coming one can do such gathering. The most important thing in both documents is that in PssSol, the coming king may be raised over the house of Israel to discipline it and in Q the coming one may sit on a throne to judge the twelve tribes of Israel.

Q implies a traditional idea from Jewish messianological tradition like PssSol. PssSol draws heavily upon biblical passages to portray the promised son of David as the ideal king and the Messiah, in explicit contrast to the illegitimate and corrupt Hasmoneans. Obviously PssSol favors the hope for the restoration of the Davidic kingdom and a Davidic Messiah who is a positive figure: the Son of David as an ideal king will rule over the Hasmoneans. Unlike PssSol, the title "the Messiah" (Christ) does not appear in Q at all; Q never calls Jesus "the Christ." Nevertheless, the Son of God in Q is the subject of explicit treatment of the christological title. Q seems to presuppose Jesus as the Son of God. Q explains the relationship of Jesus to the Son of God by accepting the Son as the revealer of God the Father. In Q, however, the Son of God is described as a passive figure who is the Son, not the Father. It is important to note that PssSol designates the Son of David for the restoration of a Davidic kingdom or a Davidic Messiah and Q designates the Son of God for revealing the God the Father to the people. If the Messiah as the Son of David in PssSol is presented in a high Messianology, the Son of God in Q is considered a high Christology.

When I think of the christological titles—the Son of God and the coming one— in Q, I can recognize that such titles are probably affected by the "christological" ideas in early Jewish documents like PssSol. For this reason, such titles in Q are clearly rooted in early Judaism.

EPILOGUE

I have already mentioned above, PssSol has the two messianic titles, "the Son of David" and "the Lord Messiah" in addition to wisdom and the coming king. There is a close relation between Messiah, the Son of David, wisdom and the coming king. Especially, the Son of David is the final, apocalyptic king, who, in possession of the full range of idealized royal virtues, will accomplish all the chores left unfulfilled by lesser sons of David. "Lord Messiah," the title used by Luke and a base for the theology of the New Testament, combines categories of all God's anointed agents—from priest to prophet to king—with the lordship to be exercised on earth by God's vizier. It is God who rules—the psalms are clear on that—but his agent is the Lord Messiah.[69] When I consider these messianic titles in the christological insights, I can find that "Messiah is a kingly figure, a scion of the house of David. Messiah is distinctly a royal and, one might say, a political figure" (ibid., 645).

As the manifestation of God's kingship over Israel and the World, Messiah overthrows the gentile occupiers, ejects all aliens and sinners, and gathers together a purified nation which he leads in righteousness, justice, and holy wisdom (17:23–25). The dispersed of Israel will return to their homeland (17:31; 11; 8:28); the land will be distributed according to the ancient tribal system (17:28); Jerusalem and the temple will be re-sanctified (17:30–31). As affirmed assuredly in PssSol 17:21–23, Messiah will gather a holy people. Therefore, this aspect of the messianic king is given equal emphasis as his deliverance of them from the Gentile oppressor.

When I talk about these four christological titles like wisdom, the Son of man, the coming one, and the Son of God etc.[70] in Q, such four titles are explicitly characterized by the christological insights. Jesus is child of wisdom or wisdom itself, though Jesus preaches wisdom, he never calls himself as "wisdom." Instead, in Q Jesus refers to himself as the Son of man. But Jesus is clearly referred to in Q as the coming one and the Son of God. Jesus, however, was never identified as the Christ (Messiah) in PssSol.

In brief summary again, from this investigation it is clear that Q shows a number of close associations with PssSol tradition in the christological insights. Although there are no actual agreements in both documents, because the similarity lies not simply in the terminology, they have pretty much the same insights. This means that Q somewhat focused on the christological insights that might be received from PssSol. This awareness would support my suggestion about Q's knowledge of PssSol tradition.

---

69. Cf. Wright, "Psalms of Solomon," 646.

70. The other title that Q applies to Jesus is "Lord." According to Havener, "The passages that clearly use 'Lord' for Jesus and which certainly belongs to Q use this designation as a direct address. This always in dialogue (or feigned dialogue) with Jesus and not in the outer framework of sayings. . . . By itself, this vocative form of address is simply a polite way of speaking, the equivalent of 'Sir' in English. As such, it has no special Christological significance" (ibid., 83–84). For this designation of "Lord (meaning 'sir')," see Q 6:46, 7:6 and 9:59. In Q 10:2 and 13:35, however, "Lord" is certainly to God, though "the parables of Q in which Jesus makes use of the 'Lord' designation is equally difficult to evaluate" (ibid., 85). For these examples, see Q 12:42–48, 13:27 and 19:12–26 (ibid., 85–86).

XXI

Religion and Science

PROLOGUE

IT IS COMMONLY ASSERTED that religion and science arose from the fear of danger, particularly natural dangers, such as particulate matter, El Niño, lightning, snows, floods, earthquakes, volcanic eruptions, and hurricanes. These dangers have threatened human beings throughout the ages. Ancient people, ignorant of the workings of nature, could not understand the causes of these natural forces. Terrified at the threat they presented, they began to search for answers. This quest precipitated an interest in the nature that surrounded people, and a desire to find some solutions to their problems.

This awareness of dangers is the common origin of both religion and science. The desire for security was the motivating force for the birth of religion and science. Together with the fear of dangers arose a sense of wonder at the marvels of nature, which led to the desire to know its truths. This was no idle curiosity: human beings were forced to find out about nature in order to address the dangers which threatened them. Thus the aspiration to be free of dangers, which was based on fear, indirectly led to the desire to know nature's truths, which gave birth to religion and science. Religion was born from the desire to escape dangers, and science was born from the desire to know nature's truths.

Does there truly exist an insuperable contradiction between religion and science? Can religion be superseded by science? The answers to these questions have, for centuries, given rise to considerable dispute and, indeed, bitter fighting. Yet, in my own mind there can be no doubt that in both cases a dispassionate consideration can only lead to a negative answer. What complicates the solution, however, is the fact that while most people readily agree on what is meant by science, they are likely to differ on the meaning of religion. This study is based on the following aspects.

Science is accessible to those who are capable of understanding it, the thinkers. Its essence is preserved through verifiable truths and valid methods of experimentation.

Science thus preserves and propagates its truths through wisdom, or, more specifically, the scientific method. Religion seeks to convey an all-embracing, absolute truth, an answer which addresses an immediate need. It might be more accurate to say that the answer thus provided is what becomes known as religion, rather than that religion provides the answer. There is no institution of religion, as such, which comes up with these answers. It is rather that the answers proposed by humanity have become institutionalized as religion.

This chapter compares the following four disciplines, using the fundamental questions of nature as a measuring stick, in this way: Science: is still in the process of verification and observation and is yet to come up with an answer. Philosophy: attempts to give an answer pending verification by using reasoned analysis. Process theology: has become one of the major theological options. Religion: provides an absolute answer which needs no verification.

Both science and philosophy appeared after religion, and both science and religion attempt to give clearer answers. However, both of them fail to give answers that are satisfactory and fulfilling for everyday life and that is why religion still exists and answers a need through faith.

John F. Haught

Is religion opposed to science?[1] To solve this question, John F. Haught has been teaching classes on science and religion at Georgetown University for twenty-five years.[2] During that time the world view has drastically shifted. For this reason, he has written his book in order to set forth some responses to the change. In fact, the encounter of religion with science is a very complex subject. However, he brings us his book as an introduction for non-experts to the central issues in science and religion today so that I can also easily follow him. He said, "I have tried to draft it in a way that would be accessible to scientists, theologians, students and any others who may be interested."[3]

1. Religion is "an enemy of science and inquiry," writes atheist Hitchens (*God Is Not Great*). The logic behind this accusation runs like this: religion hates science, because religion is about power. Once people learn how nature really works, they won't need God anymore and they won't need churches or church leaders to tell them what to do.

2. Evolution makes good scientific sense. The question is whether it makes good theological sense as well. Christians who find evolution contrary to faith often do so because they focus solely on the issues of the world's design and the notion of the gradual descent of all life from a common ancestry. But that point of view overlooks the significance of the dramatic narrative going on beneath the surface. What evolution is has become more important than what it means. Haught suggests that, rather than necessarily contradicting one another, theologians and Darwinian scientists actually share an appreciation of the underlying meaning and awe-inspiring mystery of evolution. He argues for a focus on evolution as an ongoing drama and suggests that we simply cannot—indeed need not—make complete sense of it until it has fully played out. Ultimately, when situated carefully within a biblical vision of the world as open to a God who makes all things new, evolution makes sense scientifically and theologically. Cf. Haught, *Making Sense of Evolution*.

3. Haught, *Science and Religion*, 1.

Haught takes up the so-called "problem" of science and religion. According to him, the questions of science and religion seem "no closer to resolution than ever; yet they remain very much alive and continue to evoke an interesting range of responses."[4]

Before moving on to the author's main argumentation, I have to say that I am interested in a concept of "religion" considered by the author. "When I speak of 'religion' in his book, I am thinking primarily of theistic belief in the 'personal' God associated with the so-called 'prophetic' faiths: Judaism, Christianity and Islam. Also, under the category of 'religion' I mean to include the kind of reflection on religious faith commonly known as 'theology.'"[5] Here he considers "religion" as a "theistic belief."[6] As a result, the author wants to avoid "the specific theological emphases of each tradition" of the God-religions.[7]

According to Haught, there are at least four principal ways in which religion and science are related to each other: conflict, contrast, contract, and confirmation. The first holds that religion is utterly opposed to science or that science invalidates religion. The reason is that "religion apparently cannot demonstrate the truth of its ideas in a straightforward way, whereas science can. Religion tries to sneak by without providing any concrete evidence of God's existence. Science, on the other hand, is willing to test all of its hypotheses and theories against 'experience.'"[8] In addition, "religion is based, skeptics often claim, on *a priori* assumptions, or 'faith', whereas science takes nothing for granted."[9]

The second position—in contrast—holds that religion and science are clearly different from each other, and that religion and science are both valid but rigorously separable. The main reason for drawing this conclusion is that science is concerned with "how" / "causes" / "working" questions of nature, but religion with "why" / "meaning" / "ground" questions of it.[10] According to Haught, "The impression that religion conflicts with science is almost always rooted in a previous confusion, or 'conflation', of science with either a religious or a secular belief system."[11] Thus, he argues that "the method of contrast prohibits the conflation of scientific method with

---

4. Ibid., 2. To set forth the most important of the questions of science and religion, he examines methodologically four different principal ways which express the understanding of the relationship of religion to science: conflict, contrast, contact and confirmation.

5. Ibid., 4–5.

6. Ibid., 6. Examining this consideration of religion, I am sure that the author was oriented by the "God-religion" of Christianity. He, however, has presented his topic from the much wider perspective of what the "God-religions" have in common.

7. Ibid., 5.

8. Ibid., 10.

9. Ibid., 11. "Religion relies heavily on untamed imagination, whereas science sticks to observable facts. And religion is highly emotional, passionate and subjective, whereas science strives to remain disinterested, dispassionate and objective."

10. Ibid., 15. This approach emphasizes that science and religion have "separate containers."

11. Ibid., 13. Here he defines simply "conflation" as the collapsing of distinct items in such a way that their differences are apparently lost.

any belief system."[12] Therefore, the contrast approach suggests that one "must first avoid conflating science and belief into an undifferentiated smudge."[13] In short, the contrast approach sees the differences as a reason for sharply "segregating" the two. Both are independent.

According to Haught, therefore, "the contact approach is concerned that theology always remain positively 'consonant' with cosmology. This position tries to make a dialogue, interaction, and possible 'consonance' between science and religion. Theology cannot rely too heavily on science, but it must pay attention to what is going on in the world of scientists."[14]

Confirmation, the last way of looking at the relationship, emphasizes the subtle but significant ways in which religion positively supports the scientific adventure of discovery. This position holds that "religion is in a very deep way supportive of the entire scientific enterprise."[15] In addition, the confirmation approach is further described as follows:

> This is not to argue that religion provides scientists with any information about the universe of the sort that science can gather all by itself. Religion has no special insights to dish out about particle physics or the genetic code. Its confirmation of science in no way involves any conflation or fusion with particular scientific hypotheses and theories. Rather, its support of science goes much deeper.[16]

Haught simply provides these approaches as a kind of prologue to meaningful conversation in science and religion. I believe that those positions can rightly respond to the fascinating questions that science is rising for religion today as follows: (1) How to define "religion" in a non-theistic fashion unlike Haught? (2) Which approach is favorite?

Charles Darwin

Neal C. Gillespie presents us with a well-studied essay on Charles Darwin.[17] His book is an attempt to answer the question in which creation was a problem for Dar-

---

12. Ibid., 17.

13. Ibid., 13. Some argue that although religion and science are distinct, science always has implications for religion and *vice versa*. Science and religion inevitably interact, and so religion and theology must not ignore new developments in science.

14. Ibid., 18. As a result, this position "looks for an open-ended conversation between scientists and theologians."

15. Ibid., 21. Haught calls this approach "confirmation," a term equivalent to "strengthening" or "supporting," because "it holds that religion, when carefully purged of idolatrous implications, fully endorses and even undergirds the scientific effort to make sense of the universe."

16. Ibid., 22.

17. Darwin's book, *Origin of Species*, was a scientific bombshell in its day and remains a much-discussed work 160 years later. Darwin was the official naturalist aboard the British ship Beagle during its world voyage of 1831–1836. His observations during the journey led him to develop a theory of

win.[18] Like many others, Gillespie became curious as to why Darwin spent so much time attacking the idea of divine creation.

Positivism saw the purpose of creation to be the history of laws that reflected the operation of purely natural or "secondary" causes. Many of these positivists were theists or even good Christians. Yet, contrary to creationists, they did not reflect upon God in their scientific pursuits. For them science developed a completely natural world system, one that was neither logically nor theoretically obligated to theology. So there was a "willingness of so many scientists, even pious ones, to dispense with the God hypothesis as a part of the presuppositions of scientific work."[19]

The main struggle, however, was not between science and religion but between two systems of science, the one in which theology still dictated the ways of looking at science and the other that was understood as being self-sufficient. The author claims that "Darwin's hostile preoccupation with the belief that God has separately and individually created each of the animal and plant species in the world is one of the most intriguing but neglected features of the *Origins of Species*."[20] When Darwin attacked special creation, he was not assaulting a moribund theology but a living and powerful idea. For instance, Charles Lyell, Louis Aggassiz, George Cuvier, and Adam Sedgwick still believed in miraculous creation when the *Origins of Species* appeared in 1859. But for Darwin special creation was a dead end since it asserted causes beyond conceptualization. He wanted intellectual autonomy of science from other influences, such as religion. When he wrote his book, Darwin did not set out to prove evolution, but he introduced evolution as a hypothesis, "based on plausibly ordered evidence and heuristic in purpose."[21]

It was not so easy for Darwin to break with the Bible as the source of scientific truth. For example, he was preoccupied with design throughout his life, and he was quite often ambivalent about it. It was a nagging doubt that never left his mind and he found it difficult to build a model to test the argument for design within a world

---

evolution: the notion that species evolve as the fittest members survive and pass their traits on to future generations. Darwin announced his initial ideas of natural selection in 1858, and in 1859 he formally published *Origin of Species*. His book was both popular and controversial: although Darwin was a religious man himself and once considered a career in the church, his theory of evolution was attacked by those who felt it was contrary to the teachings of the Bible.

18. Gillespie, *Charles Darwin*. In his book, Gillespie tries to show that a huge part of the conflict into which Darwin was drawn arose from two major epitomes in natural history, positivism and creationism.

19. Ibid., 13. There was a gradual movement in the 19th century from the conception of a law of nature as divine will to a law as no more than observed regularity of behavior. This shift is reflected in Darwin's continuing frustration over defining the relationship of the creator to the world. This shift of episteme (from creationism to positivism) can be observed in Darwin's own work. He also wants to show that many theists were never entirely easy within the fold of the new positive science.

20. Ibid., 19. Darwin's eventual rejection of a special creation can be seen as part of the transformation of biology into a positive science. Since creationism had run into increasing difficulties, Darwin wanted to resolve the crisis by prompting the restructuring of biology along positivist lines.

21. Ibid., 63.

understood in positive terms. While Gillespie states that "it took [Asa] Gray years to begin to appreciate the real threat to design contained in natural selection," he introduces Charles Hodge as "one of the most astute writers on the theological implication of Darwin's work."[22] Darwin was not to see God reduced to a capricious or even immoral force as natural selection might sometimes indicate. Gillespie rightly asserts:

> The Origins was the work of Darwin the theist as well as Darwin the positivist, and the intermingling of positivism and theology in that great work is one of its most fascinating features.... During the twenty years or so in which he worked on his theory and even during the aGnostic period of his later life made so familiar by his autobiography, elements of the creationist and positivist epitomes coexisted in Darwin's mind in a loose, paradoxical, and curiously antagonistic way.[23]

Similarly, Darwin thought that God had impressed some general laws upon nature in a creative act. Yet he was unwilling to endorse spontaneous creation publicly. Not the least of his reasons was that he could not resolve how God could be omnipotent and omniscient and at the same be irrational and even immoral in introducing superfluous laws of nature and waste of life. So "Darwin found God's relation to the world inexplicable."[24]

Darwin's belief in orthodox Christianity vanished slowly, not to a small degree, because of the shortcomings of Biblicism in science. But Darwin did not throw out belief in God altogether. He was not interested in a thoroughgoing atheistic philosophical or metaphysical materialism, and he was still a theist when he wrote the *Origins of Species*. Although the dominant tone of his *Autobiography* is agnostic, he still acknowledged in 1879 that his religious beliefs were constantly shifting and he confessed to Gray in 1860 and to Joseph D. Hooker in 1870 his "hopelessly muddled theology."[25]

Gillespie concludes that "Darwin's own approach to evolution fell short of complete positivism."[26] Yet there was a general acceptance of positivism as a tool for his

---

22. Ibid., 112. Darwin admitted that the ultimate causes of variability were unknown, thereby not invoking some unknown design but acknowledging the ignorance of what he assumed to be natural causes. Of course, this unknown factor of the cause of variations still threatened the whole idea of natural selection. But Darwin felt there were enough data to support the idea of random variation.

23. Ibid., 124–25. Very early Darwin rejected the idea that God would have created the world in such a way as to make it appear that it had evolved. While for Darwin God was not directly involved in the transformation of the species, still in the 1850s he thought of some sort of initial creation to explain the origin of life.

24. Ibid., 133.

25. Ibid., 142.

26. Ibid., 146. Darwin continued to speculate about the creation of the first form of life and could not abandon the universe to complete meaninglessness, as a total positivistic view of the cosmos entailed.

work and as a world view. Gillespie sums up his investigation by saying that Darwin's "life is a model of how one episteme displaces another."[27]

Was Darwin ever a practicing Christian who was gradually edged out of his orthodoxy through his scientific observations? Or did he already come from a nominally Christian background? I witness the immense struggle in him to maintain meaningful life and still accept the facts of science as natural phenomena. Although Gillespie continually refers to other leading naturalists of his time, he does not emphasize that many of them did not become as skeptical or helpless in relating religion and science.

It is true that during Darwin's time a gradual shift from creationism to positivism did take place. But the question must be asked whether this was really a replacement of one by the other or whether positivism became the dominant stream while creationism was largely submerged. The issues with which Darwin wrestled—omniscience and foreknowledge or chance and necessity—are still with us today.

John B. Cobb Jr and David Ray Griffin

The book *Process Theology*[28] was written by two authors (chs. 1–4 and appendix A were written by Griffin[29] and chs. 5–9 by Cobb),[30] but each has revised the work of the other, as the authors said. They have not called this book "an introduction to process theology" but "an introductory exposition" because they did not want to survey the basic ideas represented within the process movement. For this reason, they have, "besides explicating some of Whitehead's basic ideas, simply spelled out our own views."[31] "This book is an introductory exposition of the theological movement that has been strongly influenced by the philosophies of Alfred North Whitehead and Charles Hartshorne."[32]

His book begins the discussion with the basic concepts of process philosophy, showing that Whiteheadian process thought gives primacy to process philosophy. Probably the concept of "process" can be taken as a key. Introducing Whitehead's view

---

27. Ibid., 156. In his careful study Gillespie convincingly shows that Darwin's approach to the relationship of science and religion is much more complex than I often assume. However, unfortunately I do not hear anything about Darwin's faith.

28. Cobb and Griffin, *Process Theology*.

29. Griffin, *God and Religion*. Also published in Korean (Seoul: Cho Myung, 1995; trans. Kang), Persian (Tehran: 2002; trans. and ed. Ayatollahy), and Chinese (Beijing: Central Compilation & Translation, 2003; trans. Sun).

30. Cobb (born February 9, 1925) is an American United Methodist theologian who played a crucial role in the development of process theology. He integrated Alfred North Whitehead's metaphysics into Christianity, and applied it to issues of social justice.

31. Ibid., 10.

32. Ibid., 7. This sentence might be taken as a keynote, making the entrance of process thinkers into this realm through the eleven chapters (including two appendices) arranged in this volume. This book is divided into three parts, dealing with process thought: foreword, nine chapters and two appendices. The mode of writing on Christian theology is really philosophical, rather than theological.

of process that "the temporal process is a 'transition' from one actual entity to another,"[33] Griffin explains "the process of transition from occasion to occasion which constitutes temporality."[34] This Whiteheadian emphasis on the process of transition and the process of concrescence opens the door for the introductory exposition of a number of theological ideas like "enjoyment," "essential relatedness," "incarnation," "creative self-determination," "creative self-expression," "novelty" and "God-relatedness."

Dealing with the significance of the recognition of the experience for Christian doctrine, Griffin challenges the ability of process thought to speak to this issue. The four subsections are based on (1) the desirability that doctrines conform with prethematized experience, (2) the inevitability of selective emphasis introduced by doctrine (3) the implication of these ideas for the grounds for belief, and (4) the relation of Christian doctrine to history.

Griffin addresses God as creative-responsive love, as the foreword states that "process theology speaks about God."[35] Distinguishing between the "Primordial Nature of God" and the "Consequent Nature," Whitehead conceives a divine bipolarity: one is abstract, but the other is actual and thus called "God's concrete actuality" by him. The term "consequent" makes the same point as "relative," that God as fully actual is responsive to and receptive of the worldly actualizations.

Griffin deals with three aspects of a theology of nature. The discussion sketches (1) an interpretation of the evolutionary development of the world as rooted in the divine creative activity, (2) the issues of how process theology deals with the problem of theodicy, and (3) an ecological attitude.

Griffin deals with the issues of human existence, which one can learn as well from Heidegger as from Whitehead. Both agree that human existence is "a being-in-the-world" which means that "the world belongs to it as it belongs to the world."[36] Though four points are noted for the differences between them, the contrasting view of human historicity is very distinguished! Bultmann stresses that human existence is historical in the sense of *geschichtlich*. Whitehead can agree with what is said of human existence as *geschichtlich*, but for him "the human existence we know emerged through several stages from pre-human animal forms of existence."[37]

33. Ibid., 14.

34. Ibid., 15. Besides the temporal process, there is another type of process called "concrescence," which means becoming concrete. In the process of concrescence, "the real individual occasions of which the temporal process is made are themselves processes. They are simply the processes of their own momentary becoming."

35. Ibid., 18. Here the process dipolar notion of deity, in contrast to traditional theism with its doctrine of divine simplicity, is introduced by the author. Whereas the traditional theism regards God as "Controlling Power," the process theism regards God as "Cosmic Moralist."

36. Ibid., 81. However, from the beginning there were tensions between them. For example, Heidegger regards human existence as "being-toward-death," but Whitehead regards it as "a sequence of moments."

37. Ibid., 84. So to speak, the "evolutionary-historical" character of human existence is regarded by Whitehead.

Griffin begins with a summary of Whitehead's direct contributions to the reflection about Jesus and about incarnation. It proceeds with an explanation of Christ as creative transformation and of the relation of Jesus to Christ. It concludes with brief comments on the church as the Body of Christ and the Trinity. In this chapter, the church is described christologically as the Body of Christ and extension of the incarnation. The church is seen as a voluntary community of "Peace." Peace is "a mark of the church as the extension of the incarnation and the eschatological community."[38]

Griffin begins with the relation of the extant churches to the church as with the shaping of ideal images of the church. The churches must be creatively transformed through their openness to Christ. Openness to Christ as creative transformation is rightly feared as a threat to the extant churches. "The work of Christ they find outside themselves truly threatens them to the extent to which they have resisted Christ and thereby creative transformation."[39] And the encounter with Buddhism seems to assist Whiteheadians in answering some questions. "One example of the illumination that Buddhism may bring to process theology is through its doctrines of emptiness. The ideal for the Buddhist is the nothingness of perfect emptiness. In Whiteheadian terms the individual actual occasion is to realize itself as a void that interposes nothing to the many that would constitute it as one."[40]

Griffin serves to summarize process theology as well as to apply it to the global crisis. Four categories are discussed in this chapter: "the spatiotemporal scale," "the human and the natural," "ecological sensitivity," and "responsibility and hope."[41]

In recent years, process theology has become one of the major theological options. One of the strengths of process theology is its unified cosmological scheme in terms of which both God and the natural world are described by using the same philosophical categories. For this reason, this book is very attractive to those persons who seek to integrate science and religion and overcome the fragmentation of modern culture.

However, I would like to criticize Whiteheadian process theology by challenging the religious and philosophical adequacy of its conception of God. First of all, I would like to argue that the distinction drawn between God and creativity in process theology is both philosophically and religiously inadequate. I prefer an ontological theory of creation *ex nihilo*. In my perspective, God is the creator of everything determinate, creator of things actual as well as of things possible. God exercises ontological creativity

---

38. Ibid., 127. Peace characterizes "Christian existence as that reflects the creative-responsive love of God."

39. Ibid., 131. Then ch. 8 turns to the issues of women's liberation, as a challenge to Christianity arising in the orbit of its own influence. The liberation of women is the long-delayed realization of the meaning of the Christian truth that in Christ there is neither male nor female.

40. Ibid., 141.

41. Appendix A gives a short definition of process theology in that process theology is a philosophical theology. This appendix introduces of their religious importance. Here Whitehead's philosophy is characterized in both cosmological and theistic. Appendix B is very useful because the important bibliographies are available.

which is not shared by his creatures or explained by created categories. Consequently, I reject the process position that both God and the world may be subsumed under the same philosophical categories. I want to challenge the religious adequacy of process theism as well. Whereas Cobb's book, for example, accounts for evil as a product of human freedom which limits God's power, I believe that God is the creator of both darkness and light. I am sensitive to the terror of God as well as God's love and care. So to speak, my evaluation of the philosophical adequacy or inadequacy of process thought is integrally related to my religious experience and sensitivity. My perspective is informed by the experience of God as total presence in all things sacred and profane.

Scientific Creationism

The book titled *Scientific Creationism*[42] originally has two volumes prepared by the Institute of Creation Research. The public school edition deals with all aspects of the creation-evolution question from a strictly scientific point of view, attempting to evaluate the physical evidence from the relevant scientific fields without reference to the Bible. However, the general edition has the addition of a comprehensive chapter that places the scientific evidence in its proper biblical and theological context.[43] The book, therefore, is to show the fact that this world is not a product of an evolutionary process but, rather, is special creation of God and that most Christian schools are committed to biblical creationism as a basic premise in their philosophy of evolution.[44]

First of all, his book outlines the issues between the evolution model and the creation model to help restore confidence in special creation as the true explanation of the origin and meaning of the world. Generally, one recognizes that evolution is scientific, whereas creationism is religious. According to his book, however, this is not a true concept. Neither creation, nor evolution, can be proved.[45] According to the book, therefore, it is clear that neither evolution nor creation is either a scientific theory or a scientific hypothesis.[46]

In a comparison of these two models, his book summarizes that the evolution model is naturalistic, self-contained, non-purposive, directional, irreversible, universal, and continuing. Diametrically opposed to the evolution model, according to

---

42. Morris, *Scientific Creationism*.

43. Ibid., iv. Morris edited these volumes because he thought that the Bible and theistic religion have been effectively banned from curricula, and a nontheistic religion of secular evolutionary humanism has become, for all practical purposes, the official state religion promoted in the public schools, in the name of modern science and of church-state separation.

44. Ibid., iii.

45. Ibid., 5. In a comparison of these two models, the book argues that neither evolution nor creation can be either confirmed or falsified scientifically. This is because neither can be tested. A valid scientific hypothesis must be capable of being formulated experimentally, such that the experimental results either confirm or reject its validity.

46. Ibid., 9.

the book, is the creation model, which involves a process of special creation—super naturalistic, externally directed, purposive, completed, universal, and irreversibly directional—but its direction is downward toward lower levels of complexity rather than upward toward higher levels.[47]

Even if two basic models of origins are given the same weight, in the rest of the first chapter, however, the book insists that most private Christian schools have to teach creation as the true doctrine of origins.[48]

Another section, "Creation According to Scripture," contains a thorough exposition of the Genesis records of creation, the flood and other important events of early history. It also includes the various "theories" that have been proposed (unsuccessfully) for harmonizing the Bible with the evolutionary framework of history. In this chapter, first of all, I can easily find many examples edited by Morris:

> The basic facts of science today fit the special creation model much better than they do the evolution model";[49] "It [evolution] implicitly, if not explicitly, denies God as Creator, Redeemer and Judge";[50] "This is what all liberal theologians have done long ago, and what increasing numbers of evangelicals are doing today";[51] "It must be unequivocally rejected and opposed by Bible-believing Christians.[52]

Now his book turns to various theories to align the Genesis record with the assumed evolutionary history of the earth and man. However, Morris' intention is that each of these various compromising theories will be shown as unacceptable on biblical, theological and scientific grounds. According to his book, neither the theistic theory, the day-age theory, the gap theory, nor any other theory, is capable of reconciling itself with Genesis.[53]

Theistic evolution, on the one hand, involves one consistent process, always the same, established by God at the beginning and maintained continually thereafter. Progressive creation, on the other hand, implies that God's creative forethought was not adequate for the entire evolutionary process at the beginning. Theistic evolution is

---

47. Ibid., 11.

48. Ibid., 14. This is unfair because his suggestion is based on the view of fundamentalists.

49. Ibid., 203.

50. Ibid., 215. In the exposition of the Genesis record, the book summarizes that the biblical model of earth history centers around three great worldwide events: (1) a period of six days of special creation and formation of all things, the completion and permanence of which are now manifest in the law of conservation of energy; (2) the rebellion of man and the resultant curse of God on all man's dominion, formalized now in the law of increasing entropy; and (3) the world-destroying flood in the days of Noah, leaving the new world largely under the domain of natural uniformity.

51. Ibid., 243.

52. Ibid., 247.

53. Ibid., 255. First of all, his book summarizes theistic evolution in comparison with progressive creation. According to the book, theistic evolution seems less unreasonable and inconsistent with God than progressive creation.

creation by continuous evolutionary processes initiated by God. Progressive creation is creation by discontinuous evolutionary process initiated by God, but having to be shored up by sporadic injections of non-evolutionary process.[54]

Many Bible expositors, according to his book, have felt that the most obvious way of attempting "the day-age theory" is to interpret the Genesis record of creation in such a way that the ages of geology correspond to the history of creation.[55] Hence, the "days" must correspond more to the geological "ages."[56] The main argument for the day-age theory is based on the exposition that the Hebrew word *yom* does not have to mean a literal day, but could be interpreted as "a very long time." Also specific biblical warrant for such an interpretation is presumably found in 2 Pet 3:8, "one day is with the Lord as a thousand years."[57]

The gap theory, according to the book, places the geologic ages in a supposed gap between Gen 1:1 and Gen 1:2. The gap theory, in its usual form, assumes primeval creation as stated in Gen 1:1. In Gen 1:1, the creation, coming direct from the creative hand of God, is supposed to have been complete and beautiful in every respect.[58] According to the gap theory, the geological ages are placed in the interval after the primeval creation in Gen 1:1 and before the ruined condition of the earth described in v. 2.[59]

The framework hypothesis of Gen 1–11 views these chapters as essentially a rhetorical framework within which are developed the grand spiritual themes of "creation" (the divine source and meaning of reality), of man's "fall" (man's ever-recurring experience of spiritual and moral inadequacy), and of "reconciliation" (the broad currents in history through which man is seeking to understand and appropriate spiritual meaning in life).

On the bases of all these theories, his book summarizes that the genealogical lists in Genesis 5 give the age of each man in the line from Adam to Abraham at the birth of the son who is next in the line. When these are added, they give a total of 1656 years from Adam to the flood. A similar list for the patriarchs in Gen 11 gives 368 years. For the reason of the incapability of reconciling these theories with the Genesis record, however, the geological ages must be rejected altogether.

The above mention is very apologetic and fundamentalistic. Sometimes I could not understand several points when Morris often mentioned dogmatically some points against evolution in order to blindly follow the biblical creationism. One of the intentions

---

54. Ibid., 221.

55. Since the latter is given in terms of six "days" of creative work by God, the creation week must somehow be expanded to incorporate all of earth history from its primeval beginning up to and including man's arrival.

56. Ibid., 222.

57. Ibid., 223.

58. In Gen 1:2, it is then said to describe a different condition of the earth, many aeons after the primeval creation.

59. Ibid., 231. Then, God proceeded to "re-create" or "re-make" the earth in the six literal days described in Gen 1:3–31.

of this book was to oppose the evolution theory suggested by C. Darwin. If so, why his book did not directly mention the voices from C. Darwin? As his book indicated, it had a purpose to teach creation as the true doctrine of origins. Does this mean that the students in private Christian schools should not be instructed concerning evolution?

EPILOGUE

Science deals with the outside world, which is measured by the five senses of human beings. Here religion differs yet again. It not only looks at the outside world, but also the human being, the one who is observing. While science concerns itself solely with the objects of observation, religion concerns itself with the observer, the one who is using five senses. Thus, religion is not confined to data observable through the five senses, but is directly related to the level of development of each individual. The way religion is perceived is directly related to the level of mental development of the perceiver, which gives it an added level of complexity.

In any case, as far as religion goes, even though it lays emphasis on the human being, it does so only insofar as the human being is experiencing a problem and that problem need to be dealt with. When looking for the causes of that problem, however, most religions look, like science, to the external environment. In this respect, most religions are similar to science: they look to the external natural world as the source of problems or suffering.

Religion's search for truth is in order to solve the human problem, while science's search for truth is in order to satisfy the thirst for knowledge. For most religions, which are compelled to have ready answers, the causes of problems, whether internal or external, are seen as existing behind that natural world, in the form of spirits, deities, gods or other supernatural forces. For external disturbances, such as lightning, earthquakes and so on, sacrifices and prayers are prescribed. For internal disturbances, such as sickness, mental disease or hysteria, mediums or spirit healers perform mystic ceremonies. Meanwhile science, not being compelled to find any immediate remedies, slowly and systematically goes about its search for data.

XXII

Robinson's Impacts on the Scholarship of the New Testament and Q

PROLOGUE

THIS CHAPTER WANTS TO show James M. Robinson's history,[1] language, theology, and hermeneutics to the New Testament and the Sayings Gospel Q. Reviewing many spectacular works done by James M. Robinson, I specifically went over his intellectual biography, his theological insights that came after Karl Barth and Rudolf Bultmann, and his impact on scholarly improvements in New Testament scholarship.

I was his student when I studied biblical studies as his PhD student at the Claremont Graduate University in California. The first encounter with Robinson took place just before I finished my MDiv program in 1984. At that time, I was attending my last year at the Presbyterian University and Theological Seminary in Korea. Although it was my first encounter, it was not an encounter with the real person but with a book entitled *A New Quest of the Historical Jesus* (1959). In the fall of that year, I wrote my MDiv project paper at the seminary in Seoul, Korea.[2] I gave my highest praise in my review of his second book among the other three volumes because I finished my MDiv project paper relating to that book a lot.

---

1. Robinson was the former director of the *Institute for Antiquity and Christianity* and professor emeritus at the Claremont Graduate University. He was honored as a Fulbright scholar, American Council of Learned Societies fellow and American Association of Theological Schools fellow at the University of Heidelberg. The editor of *Sayings Gospel Q in Greek and English* (2002), *Critical Edition of Q* (2000), and author of *Trajectories Through Early Christianity* (1971, with Helmut Koester) and *New Quest of the Historical Jesus* (1959), he is best known for his work on the Nag Hammadi Codices and as the general editor of *Nag Hammadi Library in English* (1977).

2. For my project paper, I was told to review his books *Later Heidegger and Theology* (1963), *New Hermeneutic* (1964), and *Theology as History* (1967) entitled *New Frontiers in Theology*, with three volumes in all, respectively featuring Heinrich Ott, Ernst Fuchs and Gerhard Ebeling, and Wolfhart Pannenberg.

PART 3: JEWISH INFLUENCES AND CHRISTOLOGICAL INSIGHTS

A Hermeneutical Understanding of Biblical Language: On the Focus of Ernst Fuchs and Gerhard Ebeling (1985), was awarded on the first honor roll at the commencement ceremony which was the beginning point leading to the endless adventures that was waiting for me in the future. Although I lived in a totally different country than that of my professor Robinson, I was able to try and understand who he was and what his theological insights were and grew fond of his works by researching his marvelous books available at the library.

Academic Autobiography

Robinson was strictly raised as a Presbyterian by "the very sheltered existence of faculty housing" at the Columbia Theological Seminary in the suburban area in Atlanta, Georgia, where his father was "an orthodox Calvinist" and a professor of church history for over forty years.[3] He recalls his Sunday school life giving nickels as offerings every Sunday for constructing seminary buildings at the Pyong Yang Presbyterian Seminar in North Korea, which had been already collapsed by the Korea War and was the former seminary of the Presbyterian University and Theological Seminary.

Robinson's father spent his sabbatical period just before World War II studying under Karl Barth at the University of Basel, Switzerland. At that period, there was a great debate between Karl Barth and Emil Brunner. Brunner argued that humans have an innate capacity to hear God's word, which Barth had repudiated as "works righteousness," in his famous pamphlet entitled simply "Nein!"[4] Robinson's father took Barth's side of the argument then that of Brunner and, as a result, sent his two sons to Basel to study under Barth in 1947.

However, all things had been changed somehow over the years, war had been raging. German students studying in Basel smuggled into Marburg, New Testament theology of Rudolf Bultmann; existentialism and demythologizing. Hence Robinson had moved from Basel to Germany for the winter semester of 1950–1951 to attend Bultmann class in Marburg just before he retired.[5]

Robinson moved from the Barthian stream to the Bultmannian to be the most exciting Bultmannian. But he in fact became a "post-Bultmannian" before he actually became a "Bultmannian." In effect, his theological trajectories over fifty years have moved step by step from Bultmann to Post Bultmann. Ernst Käsemann provided a crucial early transition, once it had become clear to Robinson that Oscar Cullmann, his house-father at the Alumneum in Basel, was a leading scholar for making his salvation theology in a conservative aspect but Robinson felt that it did not meet up to

---

3. Robinson, "Theological Autobiography," 3.

4. Robinson, *Language, Hermeneutic, and History*, ix.

5. There, he wrote his dissertation relating to the bifurcation of dialectic theology into Barthian and Bultmannian alternatives in 1952 entitled "*Problem des Heiligen Geistes bei Wilhelm Hermann*," even though Hermann had very little to say about the Holy Spirit.

his expectations. For Robinson's whole academic career was not focused on church dogmatic but on New Testament studies.

After the years, Robinson returned again to Princeton Theological Seminary, where he had finally finished his doctorate dissertation in the department of the New Testament in 1955 entitled "The Problem of History in Mark." Robinson's dissertation on the understanding of history in the Gospel of Mark dealt with the problem of the famous term "messianic secret" which William Wrede found and announced to the world of New Testament scholarship in the beginning of the twentieth century.[6]

Robinson attempted to intellectually trace his academic trajectory from his doctor father Karl Barth's *Theology of the Word* and Rudolf Bultmann's kerygmatic *Theology of the New Testament*, to Robinson's own projects,[7] and recently he has been writing more books for the general audience such as *The Gospel of Jesus*, *The Gospel of Judas*, and *Jesus*.

Hermeneutics and Theology

Robinson's study of hermeneutics and theology has broad interests,[8] which includes but not limited to, philological, historical, literary, sociological, feminists, postcolonial, post-modernistic, and especially theological approaches.[9]

Robinson's *Language, Hermeneutic, and History*[10] has an introduction, abbreviations, three chapters, three bibliographies, and indexes of names, scripture, key foreign words and phrases. The works of Martin Heidegger, Heinrich Ott, Rudolf Bultmann, Ernst Fuchs and Gerhard Ebeling, and Wolfhart Pannenberg are all referenced and brought into fruitful conversation.

The historical relevance of the Later Heidegger will be familiar to readers with a background in existential philosophy and ontological theology. If there are any surprises, however, it is the amount of attention given to the smaller works of Heidegger.[11]

---

6. Koester, "Intellectual Biography of James M. Robinson," xiv.

7. *Das Problem des Heiligen Geistes bei Wilhelm Hermann, Das Geschichtsverständnis des Markus-Evangeliums, A New Quest of the Historical Jesus, the Nag Hammadi Library, Database Q, the Sayings Gospel Q*, etc.

8. It was also my interest. For more information, see So, "Hermeneutical Understanding of Biblical Language."

9. The following explanation is based on the book review by So, "Language, Hermeneutic," 12–14.

10. This slim edition incorporates seminal introductions from the New Frontiers in Theology series: vol. 1, *The Later Heidegger and Theology* (1963), vol. 2, *The New Hermeneutic* (1964), and vol. 3, *Theology as History* (1967). Cobb says there are no other volumes where the impetus and import of Continental theology is so meticulously and thoughtfully presented. In each work, Robinson has an extensive essay that points to a new hermeneutical direction: "The German Discussion of the Later Heidegger," "Hermeneutic since Barth," and "Revelation as Word and as History."

11. *Being and Time, Existence and Being, Der Feldweg, Die Frage nach der Technik, Gelassenheit, Holzwege, An Introduction to Metaphysics, Kant und das Problem der Metapyisik*, etc.

Paul J. Achtemeier descriptively notes the full range of Robinson's encompassing encyclopedic knowledge and his mastery of theological issues. I highly recommend this chapter for anyone interested in the development of German theology and philosophy.

Regarding Heidegger's philosophy, Robinson sees *Dasein* being relatively grounded in the Supreme Being, which is the uncaused cause (*causa sui*). The investigation of this problem has been the traditional task of ontology since this Supreme Being is often conceived by metaphysics as God. Heidegger speaks of "the onto-theo-logical nature of metaphysics."[12] In this context, Heidegger understands modern science and technology as the outcome of metaphysics. Robinson perceives that the end result of this metaphysics is modern technology.[13]

Ott is seen as the first theologian to attempt a programmatic way of using the Later Heidegger for theological purposes. Ott finds a correspondence between the biblical faith in God the Creator and the philosopher's basic questions.[14] Robinson argues that the Heideggerian understanding of being makes it possible to see the two basic objections that led Barth to reject the *analogia entis* and still affirm the being of God. "*Wesen* is not static *essentia*, but rather a 'taking-place'; truth is not a static correlation, but an unveiling; *physis* is not a static nature, but the being of beings as it comes forward shows itself. (The Greek verb *physein* means to put forth shoots, engender, and grow.) Being is itself not a static 'is-ness' (*Seiendheit*), but an unveiling."[15]

Even the ontological difference between being and the beings is not a fixed separation, but it itself is the unveiling of being. According to Robinson, the outcome of this transformation of categories is that the word "event" is given a deeper significance in Heidegger's philosophy. The correlation of *Being and Time* with respect to theology is of course worked out by Bultmann and his pupils. Indeed, the Bultmannian School was the first to take up the discussion of the relevance of the Later Heidegger for New Testament theology.

Robinson makes a brief methodological point: "It is a central recognition of the new hermeneutic that language itself says what is invisibly taking place in the life of a culture. An instance of this would be the sudden re-emergence of the term *hermeneutik* within post-Bultmannian German theology."[16] Robinson offers a comparison between Bultmann and his pupils Fuchs and Ebeling. The differences are striking. For Bultmann, his approach was based on existential interpretation and demythologiz-

---

12. Robinson, *Language, Hermeneutic*, 15.

13. Under technology, Heidegger understands not only the machines of production, but also the materialized nature, engineered culture, professional politics, superimposed ideals, and the whole artificial stance of modern man toward being a whole.

14. He describes this as the philosopher's encounter with "secularized Christianity." Hence, the attempt to work out a correlation between the Christian concept of God and Heidegger's philosophy consisted in a correlation between the believer's numinous awareness of the world as creation and the philosopher's amazement at the being of beings.

15. Ibid., 47.

16. Ibid., 103.

ing. In the project of Fuchs and Ebeling, existential philosophy is relegated to the periphery. It is none other than language, the basis of the Later Heidegger that takes center stage.

For Heidegger, the term language does not merely designate audible or verbal articulation. It is more of the conveying of meaning. Fuchs' understanding of language is well summarized in a passage where the form illustrates the central role of language in hermeneutic. In this sense, the "saving event" is a "language event" since language is God's saving word. Ebeling arrives at a new hermeneutic that embraced the doctrine of the word of God which became the focus of his theological position. Robinson argues that New Hermeneutic is a new theology, just like dialectic theology and Ritschlianism that preceded it. Ebeling's conviction is that theology itself is hermeneutic since it consists of translating what the words of the Bible have to say for us today. So Heidegger's contribution to New Hermeneutic provides a new understanding for the nature of the theological task while furthering it in the context of the academy.[17]

Robinson notes that it is not surprising that the Barthian wing of dialectic theology gradually moved toward salvation history—re-translating Paul's statement "Christ is the end of the law" as "Christ is the end of history." Salvation history, however, was soon replaced by Bultmann's "saving event," and the nascent philosophy of history that gave way to existentialism's historicness of existence. On the Old Testament theology side, Gerhard von Rad began working out theology as an interpretation of history. Of course, the Later Barthian movement moved closer to the view of revelatory history, which is seen as the genesis of the Pannenberg movement.

Robinson has argued that the situation in which Pannenberg's theology emerged is not simply history being eliminated in favor of existentialism, but a different understanding of history resulting in its various implications for the structuring of theology. In several instances, Robinson summarizes succinctly that Pannenberg speaks directly of "history" as "reality in its totality." It is not the case that Pannenberg's purpose was to produce a Christian narration of history, what he calls a "total concept of history," i.e., "a conception of the whole course of history in terms of revelational history," which would indeed limit both the freedom of God and man and the contingency of history. Rather, he wished to achieve a "total view of reality as history directed by promises toward fulfillment."[18] Robinson argues that Pannenberg traced the development of this understanding of reality as history from ancient Israel to the present.

According to Robinson, Pannenberg's understanding of historical occurrence can only be grasped in terms of the total sweep of history.[19] Robinson says that the

17. The hermeneutical principle for theological exegesis in New Hermeneutices exponentially by even asking what is meant by the term God. If New Hermeneutic seriously proposes to bridge the gulf between historical and systematic theology, in terms of a recurrent event of language that moves from Jesus' word to that of a preacher, then New Hermeneutic becomes a fascinating new mode for the theological task.

18. Ibid., 168.

19. Robinson argues that Pannenberg's universal scope may not be permitted to weaken the

historiographical execution of this program must take into account Pannenberg's understanding of universal history, one which cannot be derived from smaller segments of history, but only from the total sweep of history; one which is visible only in the end of history: "Yet the role of Jesus' resurrection as the proleptic anticipation of that end of history to some extent removes it from the category of just a particular and makes of it the key for attaining a universal grasp of history before the end comes."[20] Thus, the historical proof of the resurrection ("absolute metaphor") can serve as a materially decisive model for Pannenberg, an alternative to Bultmann.

The style of Robinson's presentation on hermeneutics and theology will benefit the educated public as well as the scholar. The author does not force a hermeneutical conclusion but guides the reader through several options. I see the logic and usefulness to lifting the three introductions of the three volumes and reprinting here, together, as an entry point for Continental philosophy, language, hermeneutic, history, and theology.

The Nag Hammadi Library and International Q Project

Robinson's studies of the Nag Hammadi Library are remarkable in two aspects. First, he possessed good photographs of all the Nag Hammadi codices, and to this extent was in a position to break the monopoly. But then he had no publication rights. He was lucky to have access to the texts at the Coptic Museum in Cairo because he was working for the Arab Republic of Egypt and UNESCO as a Representative of the USA and was the Permanent Secretary of the International Committee for the Nag Hammadi codices (1970–1984). Using the contract at UNESCO, Robinson was able to bypass the exhibition of obscurantism, and eventually the monopoly of the Nag Hammadi documents was completely broken.[21]

Second, when Robinson had completed the bulk of his Nag Hammadi responsibilities at his age of sixty, he decided to return to his new beginning that was aborted with the Sayings Gospel Q. His return to New Testament scholarship thus took the form of organizing the International Q Project in 1985 to reconstruct a critical text of the Sayings Gospel Q which is a written Greek collection of a couple of hundred sayings ascribed to the historical Jesus as the *ipsissima verba* used by the Gospels of Matthew and Luke, who are in the process "improving" the wording of Q to make it

---

recognition of the contingency of history. Hence, universality may not be conceived in terms of an evolutionary or morphological pattern to which histories conform.

20. Ibid., 171.

21. As a result, the 13 codices were published by Brill entitled *Facsimile Edition of the Nag Hammadi Codices* with 17 volumes since 1972 just seven years after he had seen the originals in Cairo, Egypt. At the same time he published one volume that was an English translation entitled *The Nag Hammadi Library in English* (1977), which has subsequently sold over 100,000 copies. Above all, the 14-vol. critical edition entitled *Nag Hammadi Codex* was completed and the last volume was published by Brill in 1995.

clearly reflect their own understanding of Jesus' sayings. He led the project with two subsidiary centers created in Toronto, Canada and Bamberg, Germany. Robinson and the leaders of those two centers like Paul Hoffmann and John S. Kloppenborg had become general editors of *The Critical Edition of Q*[22] and *Documenta Q*.[23] In addition to this *Critical Edition of Q*, the database of citations from scholarly document of the past 180 years, on the basis of which the final decisions for each variation unit had been determined, is being published in a series estimated to comprise thirty-one volumes entitled *Documenta Q*.

According to Robinson, the Q archetype behind Matthew and Luke is based on a written Greek text for this saying; here we surely have the oldest attestation for written sayings of Jesus, even older than the copy of Q shared by Matthew and Luke.[24] Furthermore, the Q people, that is to say, the few who still identified themselves with Jesus in Galilee, have largely been lost from sight, as has always been the case since Luke almost completely bypassed Galilee in Acts 1:8: "You shall be my witnesses in Jerusalem and in all Judea and Samaria and to the end of the earth." A Galilean church is only mentioned once in passing, in a generalized statement (Acts 9:21): "So the church throughout all Judea and Galilee and Samaria had peace and was built up."

> The Jesus movement had its center apparently in Galilee, to judge by the specific place names where this tradition says it carried on a mission, Chorazin, Bethsaida, and Capernaum (Q 10:13-15), though it should not be overlooked that this demographic information includes the point that these locations rejected the message. Q mentions neither James nor Peter (both of whom had left Galilee), nor any of the twelve, nor the concept of the twelve, nor that of apostles . . . , nor the names of any disciples.[25]

Nor does the book of Acts reveal a Jesus movement where re-proclaiming his sayings was the dominant variety of religious experience. Thus *The Critical Edition of Q* renders much more accessible not only the text of Q itself, but also the pre-Q collections, the *Sitz im Leben* of the Q materials, and sayings going back to Jesus.

---

22. *Critical Edition of Q*.

23. The outcome of this project was a one-volume synopsis of the critical text of Q entitled *Critical Edition of Q* reconstructed by the Matthean and Lukan texts. It should become a standard tool in the discipline, much as the Nestle-Aland's *Novum Testamentum Graece*, or Aland's *Synopsis Quattuor Evangeliorum*, or Baur's *Greek-English Lexicon*, which are assumed to be on the desk of anyone, involved in serious work in his/her discipline.

24. Robinson and Heil, *Zeugnisse eines schriftlichen*, 30-44; Robinson, "Pre-Q Text," 143-80; Robinson, "Written Greek Sayings," 61-78; and Robinson, "Excursus on the Scribal Error," in Robinson et al., *Critical Edition of Q*, xcviii-c. See also the photographs of the relevant passages from Codex Sinaiticus and P. Oxy. 655 in the Endpapers of that volume. Concerning Schröter, "Vorsynoptische Überlieferung," 265-72.

25. See Robinson's brief comments in *Judaism, Hellenism*, 241-50, esp. 244. The location of the Q movement remains quite conjectural. The hypothesis of a Galilean location, which could have also involved a Syrian dispersion due to the war with Rome, is really based to a large extent on the absence from Q of traits of polity and Christology associated with the Jerusalem church.

Now it is possible to trace the board lines of the Jesus movement, as it has come to be called, from Jesus through the Q community to the Gospel of Matthew, thus into the main stream of early Christianity of which we are heirs. Robinson and Helmut Koester were convinced that the entire enterprise of a fresh and very unconventional interpretation of early Christian texts and of the diversity of early Christian beginnings had to be stated programmatically once more.[26]

James M. Robinson in Korea

James M. Robinson visited Korean twice. On the first time, he visited Korea himself in 1965 via Japan because he was on the tour heading Jerusalem from the East to the West. At that time, he presented his lectures over the Historical Jesus, "The Debate between Bultmann and His Pupils," translated by Kyung Yun Chun, and the New Hermeneutic, "Hermeneutics since Barth," translated by Yong Ok Kim. He recalls that Korean theologians were very polite and their relationship seemed intimate, even though the seminaries vary in Seoul.

In 2006 Robinson was invited again with his wife, Anne Moore.[27] He presented papers on Q at that time: "The Gospel of Jesus" and "The Sayings Gospel Q" at the Presbyterian University and Theological Seminary. When he visited Korea, the National Geographic magazine published the Gospel of Judas that many Christians were embarrassed about because the magazine insisted that Judas was a helper of Jesus' death instead of his betrayal. With regard to the Gospel of Judas, Robinson interviewed with a reporter of the *Dong-A Daily*, which is one of the majors in Korea, that Jesus was crucified on the cross by his own will, as opposing to the Gospel of Judas that looked back to the Gnostic tradition which was standing at the heretic side.

---

26. Their outcome was the publication of *Trajectories through Early Christianity* (1971). Unwritten is the history of the Jesus movement whose variety of religious experience was primarily the re-proclamation of the sayings of Jesus, which is not a variety attested in Acts, until ultimately the Galilean Q movement became the Matthean community of Antioch.

27. Her research has been concentrated on the origins of Christianity examining the development of the religion as it emerged from within the context of Second Temple Judaism through to the establishment of various diverse Christian communities within the context of the Greco-Roman Empire. Her approach incorporates both "canonical process criticism" and sociological theories. This approach has resulted in the rejection of the canon and creed as boundaries or perimeters for analyzing the Origins of Christianity. The full range of "scriptural" literature is taken into account in reconstructing the socio-historical matrix including texts from the Dead Sea Scrolls, Gnostic Gospels, Hebrew Bible Pseudepigrapha, New Testament Apocrypha and the Magical Papyri and the diverse scope of the Greco-Roman Empire is also assumed including its mystery religions, philosophies and arcane mundi. Currently, her research interests include the development of Christian communities between the period of 100–800 CE especially the evolution of Christian doctrine, self-identity and role of women in the churches. This research includes reexamining the methods used in the study of church history with the idea of introducing a more interdisciplinary approach that would include insights from archaeology, art, folk literature and sociology. This research dovetails with additional research in the relationship between religion and culture with a focus on the popular mediums of film and television.

Robinson's revisit of 2006 was the most important event for Korean scholars because he gave a couple thousand copies on Q that he possessed in the Q room at the Institute for Antiquity and Christianity in Claremont Graduate University. In order to allow many people in Korea use the materials, he organized the Korean Q institute called "*Jesus Sayings Hub*" with its web site, "www.jesussayings.net" and is the permanent honorary director of the institute.

For the first project of the *Jesus Sayings Hub*, I translated his book entitled *A New Quest of the Historical Jesus and other Essays* into Korean in May 2008 with the assistant of Il Seo Park, who was my MDiv and ThM student at Presbyterian University and Theological Seminary and is now a PhD student of the Claremont School of Theology. Robinson sent his preface for the Korean version.[28] The volume translated into Korean begins with a small book Robinson wrote soon after World War II. That was the time when German New Testament scholarship, led by Ernst Käsemann and Günther Bornkamm, returned to the study of Jesus, after a generation of scholarship in which Jesus himself had been ignored in favor of the kerygma, the church's message, to the neglect of Jesus' own message. The "new question of the historical Jesus" recognized that we have to establish historically what can be known about Jesus, since otherwise Jesus would seem not to be fully human, which would be the modern equivalent to what in the early church was called the heresy of "Docetism." *A New Quest of the Historical Jesus and other Essays* also includes an essay on the apocalyptic interpretation of Jesus advocated a century ago by Albert Schweitzer in his famous book *The Quest of the Historical Jesus*. Robinson had been invited to write an introduction to both the German and the English reprints of that classic work.[29] But then in the second half of the twentieth century the renewal of the quest of the historical Jesus became possible, when scholarship took a new look at Jesus' teaching. It is this focus on "Jesus' parables as God Happening" that comes to expression in the final essay of that volume.

For the second project of the *Jesus Sayings Hub*, Yil Song, who was my MDiv student at Presbyterian University and Theological Seminary and already graduated with

---

28. I am delighted that my former student Dr. Ky-Chun So has translated this volume containing my early research on how to understand Jesus. For the doctoral dissertation of Dr. Ky-Chun So, under my guidance at the Claremont Graduate University, was part of the final phase of my lifelong study of Jesus. Indeed, he became a member of the International Q Project that I organized. This project reconstructed the collection of Jesus' sayings used by Matthew and Luke, but then lost from sight over the centuries, until rediscovered, still embedded in Matthew and Luke. Indeed, his dissertation was part of that reconstruction itself: "Sabbath Controversy of Jesus; between Jewish Law and the Gentile Mission." It was a high privilege for me to be able to be Prof. Ky-Chun So's guest in Korea for a week of lectures at his seminary, Presbyterian University and Theological Seminary, and church, Dong-An Presbyterian Church, two years ago in May 2006 . . . I hope that readers of this small book will find in it a way to experience God happening in your life today.

29. In his introduction he showed how Schweitzer slanted the history of the quest of the historical Jesus that had taken place during the nineteenth century in such a way as to give the misleading impression that his own apocalyptic view of Jesus was the only logical outcome. It was Schweitzer's fanatical Jesus that had led German scholarship during the first half of the twentieth century to abandon Jesus in favor of the more familiar and acceptable Pauline Gospel.

a PhD degree from the Claremont Graduate University, and he and I also translated *The Gospel of Jesus: In Search of the Original Good News* into Korean in September, 2009. Robinson also sent his preface for the Korean version.[30] He has spent the last seventy years (he was born in 1924) studying Jesus in various ways, trying to get into a position where he could really hear him speaking, and know what he was trying to say, both to the people back then in Galilee, and still today to people around the world. In addition to the four Narrative Gospels with which we are more familiar from the New Testament, Matthew, Mark, Luke, and John, there are two Sayings Gospels that have come to light in more recent times.[31] The authors of the Gospels of Matthew and Luke wrote their Gospels with the help of two written sources.[32] In Matthew and Luke, Jesus' sayings from Q are also imbedded, indeed almost "hidden," among the stories from Mark with which we are more familiar. Robinson organized a team of international scholars that has tried to reconstruct this Sayings Source Q, word for word. Robinson began by detecting the fingerprints of Matthew and Luke as they edited this sayings collection, and then moving behind their improvements to the older wording that more nearly goes back to Jesus.[33] Actually, the church over the centuries has built its Gospel more upon the Easter faith and Paul's theology, so what Jesus himself had to say in his ministry in Galilee has often been lost from sight. It has been rediscovered over the centuries from time to time, tried to see what Jesus' message really meant in the down-to-earth situations of their own day and age. Each generation, and each culture, needs to do that over and over again.

The *Jesus Sayings Hub* has three dimensional tasks to practice Jesus teaching into our lives: Evangelizing, counseling/healing, and disciple training.[34]

---

30. I am delighted that my book the *Gospel of Jesus* has been translated into Korean by Yil Song. He has studied at the Presbyterian University and Theological Seminary under the guidance of Dr. Ky-Chun So, who did his doctorate with me at Claremont Graduate University. Hence it is highly appropriate for Yil Song to translate my book on the *Gospel of Jesus* into Korean for me . . . It is my hope that my book on the *Gospel of Jesus* will inspire the good people of Korea to seek to hear afresh Jesus' Gospel, and listen to it for themselves and their neighbors in the situation of Korea today.

31. One is the Gospel of Thomas, a collection of 114 sayings attributed to Jesus, which is the most valuable text in the 13 books that have been discovered in Egypt near Nag Hammadi in 1945. The other is a collection of Jesus' sayings lying behind Matthew and Luke, hidden in the New Testament itself.

32. One is the Gospel of Mark with which we are familiar from the New Testament. The other is a collection of sayings that scholars nicknamed Q, the first letter of the German word for source, *Quelle*, meaning the second "source" used by Matthew and Luke, in addition to Mark. So all the sayings that are in "Q" are already in the New Testament, though with the updating and adaptations that Matthew and Luke, each in his way, thought appropriate.

33. Robinson published in 2000 a massive, 688-page book with the reconstructed text of Q, which was the result of that team research over the preceding generation. This reconstructed collection of sayings ascribed to Jesus is presented in ch. 2 of *The Gospel of Jesus*, since it is primarily in this Sayings Source that Jesus' own Gospel is best preserved.

34. For the third project of the *Jesus Sayings Hub*, on the one hand the Korean Q Institute directed a prayer school and narrative Bible study: Praying and Practicing with a Clean Spirituality in 2009, on the other hand will launch the program of a theory and practice of the school of the Sprit-filled at the

In relation to the influence of Robinson's Q studies, the concern of Q regarding the historical Jesus in Korea was raised in the study of the Synoptic Gospels during 1990s. In relations to the *Jesus Sayings Hub* in Korea, Robinson thinks that Jesus sayings should be accorded at least in equal status with the gospel that has only slowly gained ground among Christians.[35]

EPILOGUE

For Robinson, Jesus was a real idealist, a committed radical, in any case a profound person who had come up with a solution to the human dilemma that was at least worth listening to. The way Jesus reached a basic understanding of the human dilemma and proposed a solution was of course couched in the language and potions of his cultural situation. But the dilemma he confronted is still our dilemma.[36] The human dilemma in large relates to the part that people are each other's fate, the tool of evil that ruins the other person, as people look out for number one, having wised up with regard to any youthful idealism people might once have cherished. Robinson states the cultural responsibilities of Christians as follows:

> But if I would basically cease and desist from pushing you down to keep myself up, and you for your part would do the same, then the vicious circle would be broken. Society would become mutually supportive, rather than self-destructive. Count on God to look out for you, to provide people that will care for you, and listen to him when he calls on you to provide for them. This radical trust in and responsiveness to God is what makes society function as God's society. This what, for Jesus, faith and discipleship were all about. Nothing else has a right to claim any functional relationship to him.[37]

Robinson trusts that God is looking out for him and for that reason he feels that it is also his duty to reach out to those that are in need. The openness to hear God when he sends one to help the neighbor or enemy in deed—and conversely, the humility to receive what one needs from others as a gift from God—is kind of trust Jesus exemplified. The "doing" is harder than "believing."[38] The hardest saying of Jesus is: "Why do you call me, Master, Master! and do not do what I say?" Robinson thinks that people do not do what he says, not simply because of the shift in cultural conditions, for which an adequate hermeneutic might provide a solution, but ultimately, because people do not trust God as Jesus did.

Presbyterian University and Theological Seminary, coming March, 2010.

35. Like Francis of Assisi, Tolstoy, Mahatma Gandhi, Yohan So (my grand father), Albert Schweitzer, and Martin Luther King Jr., etc.

36. Robinson, *Gospel of Jesus*, xiii.

37. Robinson, "Theological Autobiography," 32.

38. Robinson, "What I Believe."

Scholars rediscovered Jesus' word imbedded in a collection of his sayings, which had been brought together in Greek translation by the Jewish Christian branch of the church. One discovered that the focus of Jesus' message was on God reigning, the kingdom of God taking place now, happening here and there. The focus of the study of Jesus then turned quite naturally to the parables of Jesus. It turned out that they were not intended as coded theological doctrines, as they had traditionally been understood. Rather Jesus understood them as God happening, just as he understood his healings and exorcisms.

Conclusion

THE TEXTS IN THE Sayings Gospel Q have been reconstructed by the International Q Project since 1995 at the annual meeting of the Society of Biblical Literature. This book investigated a trajectory through the sayings of Jesus from the Synoptics to second-century Christian literatures.[1] For a relatively simple solution to the problem, this book examined the influence of the sayings of Jesus on the biblical texts of first-and second-century Christian literatures: the Hebrew Bible, the Synoptics, Acts, Pauline letters, some of the Catholic letters, the earliest Christian writings (1 Clement, the Didache, Barnabas, the letters of Ignatius of Antioch), the later Christian writings (2 Clement, Polycarp, Apocalypses, Nag Hammadi Library), Apologists (Aristides, Justin Martyr, Tatian), the Jewish philosophers (Philo, Josephus), and the apocryphal writings (the Wisdom of Solomon, the Psalms of Solomon, the Gospel of Thomas, the Dead Sea Scrolls, and the Apocalypse of Adam).

This book explained the influence of the sayings of Jesus and established the biblical texts of the freedom in the use of the oral and written tradition. Therefore, the use of the Synoptics can be demonstrated; the similarities with the gospel texts are explained by the survival of oral tradition or written gospels. The question of the Jewish influence of the sayings of Jesus from early church to second-century church on biblical texts is central to an understanding of the trajectory through the Sayings Gospel Q. Such a study of biblical texts is also closely related to a study of early Christianity. Hence this book concludes in favor of the Jewish prevalent influence of the sayings of Jesus in early Christian literatures.

Those subjects mentioned above have had renewed attention, especially in the last seven decades. Just as the discovery of the Dead Sea Scrolls in 1947–1956 reopened the question of the Hebrew Bible, so too has the seventieth discovery of the Nag Hammadi Library since 1945[2] stimulated interest in the study of the Hebrew Bible and the New

---

1. For early Christian traditions, see Labahn and Schmidt, *Jesus, Mark and Q*; Warren et al., *Early Christian Voices*; Zetterbolm, *Formation of Christianity in Antioch*; Wedderburn, *History of the First Christians*; Stanton, *Jesus and Gospel*.

2. Robinson, *Nag Hammadi Library*; Elliott, *Apocryphal New Testament*; Barnstone and Meyer, *Gnostic Bible*.

Testament. Walter Bauer, Edgar Hennecke, Montague Rhodes James, Fans Neirynck, James M. Robinson, and Helmut Koester have built substantially upon the work of the Coptic Library, in part at least by focusing attention on the sayings of Jesus of the canon and of the extracanonical Christian literatures. Also the diversity of biblical texts within early Christianity has been made more evident, and even within the texts of the canonical New Testament itself and the discussion of this diversity of biblical texts within the earliest church has been found its way into basic trajectories toward texts.

Texts are literary ways of conveying or transmitting meaning and content. They are used in making languages or pictures, signs or symbols, and even rudimentary scratches. Interestingly enough, making careful observations into details of a particular composition can also help trace to their origin which gives a basic idea of who perfected and brought the texts into existence. Writers as well as artists all have their distinct characteristic traits making them easy to attach their personal intuition and style to their respective work. Thus texts are generally referred to writing in books and manuscripts within a narrow range of all the types of records drawn or described by humans, as well as illustrated or created pieces such as in paintings and inscriptions within a broad range of records expressed by the intellectual or artistic like storytellers, poets, drawers, speakers, writers, painters, narrators, scribers, etc.

Texts are original languages written in a type of "message" that is to communicate in various ways. They convey or transmit ideas or themes, and could also have an array of "signs" which points to entities or concepts,[3] and "total meaning or content of a discourse" in communication.[4] Not all elements of the meaning in given languages can be expressed by interpretation and translation. Such a work is impossible and also not quite necessary. To convey or transmit the content of message within languages, interpreters or translators produce and/or reproduce the meaning of the texts. Hence texts are coherent to written messages referred independently through traditions, situations, circumstances, or environments in which they were created or illustrated. For example, in many perspectives, Bible interpreters and translators stand on all systems of communication which even takes account for stories that are passed down orally.

A lot of these communication systems are based on each Gospel traditions, situations, circumstances, or environments and relating to texts can influence and shape their interpretations or translations that comes in multiple "organizational frames" involving structure and culture in terms of legends, epics, tales, myths, rituals, proverbs, oracles, pronouncements, and sacred sermons in the New Testament.[5] Culture within texts can be expressed in which a certain group of early church experiences their identity in relation to the reality of their traditions, situations, circumstances, or environments involving Jesus' sayings. Not only religions, social structures and arts, but also texts in the Jesus' sayings of Gospels are part of a culture in a Jew or Gentile.

3. Wilt, "Translation and Communication," 27–80.
4. Nida and Taber, *Theory and Practice of Translation*.
5. Bantz, *Understanding Organizations*.

Conclusion

Interpreters or translators must consider this and recognize that the texts reflect the Jewish or Gentile culture of the group.

Biblical texts in the Gospels depend on the culture of Jewish or Gentile people. Biblical texts are identifiable in terms of traditions, situations, circumstances, or environments like "settings (time, place, and physical circumstances) and scenes (psychological setting; cultural definition of a particular occasion)" in Jewish or Gentile culture. Speech situation in relation to texts is known as Jewish or Gentile "communication situation."[6] In this matter, biblical texts' situation is related to language situation in Jewish or Gentile cultural frames. Participants of texts (i.e., speaker, or sender; addresser; hearer, receiver, or audience; addressee) have long been used to the idea that words and their referents are matters negotiated by speakers within a given "cultural frames."[7]

These cultural frames are giving "form and meaning" to texts that interpreters or translators interpret or translate.[8] Texts are form and meaning of languages appearing in letters like the so-called idiomatic expressions and thus every text has its own form of expressing meaning. Interpreters or translators must also need to recognize this aspect when they interpret or translate texts from one language into another. Interpreters or translators at this point must take into account both the source text, the text from which they interpret or translate, and the receptor text, the text into which they interpret or translate. If interpreters or translators interpret or translate too literally, they focus too much on forms and expressions in the source text and may not do adequate justice to the receptor text. The text gives expression to something, but the fact that it does so is in the last analysis contributed by the interpreter or translator.

Texts involving the Sayings Gospel Q of Jesus are employed through common tradition and brought forward (re-presented) by the speakers to bear upon the community to which they were spoken in the early church's antiquity. Contexts within texts are the historical, cultural, social, political, economic, national, and international context situations to which the speakers applied the ancient texts. Hermeneutics is known as the ancient theological mode, as well as a literary technique, by which that application was made by the speakers. Whether true or false—hermeneutics is dependent on how the texts are read how they are related context-wise with others.[9] Hermeneutics in the Sayings Gospel of Q is full of texts and contexts. Texts, contexts, and hermeneutics may indicate their interdependence and interrelationship seen within the Christian Q community behind the Sayings Gospel Q. The evangelists of Matthew and Luke all belonged in their respective communities at the time of their existence and within the Sayings Gospel Q. Texts came into being as well as the Q community which formed through the common texts within Matthew and Luke.

---

6. Hymes, *Foundations in Sociolinguistics*.
7. Katan, *Translating Cultures*.
8. De Blois, "From and Meaning of the Text," 409–16.
9. Sanders, *Canon and Community*.

Like a pyramid each came along one another each closely defendant and knitted tightly together. Texts and circumstances of their discovery deserve a story or full-scale account in order to tell about their thrilling and sometimes obscure background. Texts have many more stories to tell if you listen closely to the sounds of the details the preserves for today's world. Texts aim to describe how human acts of communication succeed in mediating sense. This communication sense through texts is adequately described only to the extent when one examines the whole communicative act in which the written text functions, that is to say text production and text reception. This is so because all relations of meaning which are ordered in the texts remain pure possibilities until the time they are received and thus actualized. The relation of meanings in the texts has accordingly the character of directives which can in each case be implemented by the recipient.[10] Texts are a carrier of sense or meaning. The text sense is accordingly always more than the sum of single meanings. The text sense designates the potential communicative role of texts as manifold of directives, and the text directive signifies the realized, informative, communicative relevance of the texts as implemented by the communicating partners, in the interplay of communicative acts.

Biblical texts mediate author-reader or author-audience interaction. Texts in the Gospels involve both author and reader; they are the very interaction of these two that results in a given context, and the interaction of author and audience. In a very real sense, then, transmission and composition converge in texts. Transmission refers precisely to the construction or re-construction and verbalization or re-verbalization of what already exists within memory.[11] Biblical texts do not compose tradition *de novo* but retell it from memories of author and reader interaction in the shadow of Gospel tradition's performative history in the early church. Hence tradition consists of information existing in memory. It is in memory most of the time, and only now and then are those parts recalled which the needs of the moment require. Tradition is not composed *ex nihilo*, as it were, in text; rather, tradition, which lacks a fixed textual form outside of context, is embodied in the performative act.

Historically, for nearly a century and in varying degrees, critical scholarship has attempted to account for the historical near-certainty of oral Gospel traditions in its readings of written Gospel texts. New Testament scholarship, in a rare consensus, recognizes that people were telling stories of Jesus before, during, and even after, they were writing Jesus sayings in the Sayings Gospel Q. While a significant portion of that scholarship has implicitly assumed that the evangelists were not individuals with considerable experience performing these traditions, this book considered the probability that evangelists were tradents of the oral Jesus traditions and that their texts relate to the history of their performative experiences.[12] The Gospel texts represent performances, of a sort, relating to the tradition of Jesus. Hence this book emphasized here

---

10. Weinrich, *Sprache in Texten*.
11. Kelber, *Oral and the Written Gospel*.
12. Bauckham, *Jesus and the Eyewitnesses*.

CONCLUSION

that the authors of the Gospel traditions were also performers of the Jesus tradition. They were not merely writers composing in a traditional idiom; they were performers speaking and living (as well as writing) within the idiom.

I owe a debt of gratitude to the members of the New Testament Seminar Group for their critical reading of this study at various stages. I am especially indebted to Linden Youngquist, who read this book. The Claremont School of Theology and the Claremont Graduate University has also supported me in this endeavor by granting me full tuition scholarships and fellowships. I am grateful for their commitment to promoting excellence through this scholarship.

Thanks are due to Rolf P. Knierim, Burton L. Mack and Karen Torjesen, whose seminars helped in understanding the Hebrew Bible, the New Testament, various Christian origins, and the early Christianity. Special thanks are due to Jon Asgeirsson, Stanley Anderson, Milton Moreland, Christoph Heil, Thomas Hieke, Saw Lah Shein and Steven Johnson, whose friendship and advice helped in completing the International Q Project sponsored by the Institute for Antiquity and Christianity and the Society of Biblical Literature. John O. Najarian, Robert Kelley, Stephan Lee, and Moana Vercoe of the Claremont Presbyterian Church have edited this book with their insightful comments. I am also grateful to Karl Pagenkemper and Minoru Nakano, who provided me with considerable comment at the beginning of my journey toward the Sabbath controversy in the New Testament Seminar at the Institute for Antiquity and Christianity. They all provided me the opportunity for frank, honest, and humorous dialogues with my colleagues.

I am particularly grateful to my parents, Dong Wook So (1928–2014) and Rae Chang, and my parents-in-law, Jae Ku Hong (1935–2013) and Ki Jung Park, for their regular and substantial support. Along with their financial support, Sun Hee Kwak of So-Mang Presbyterian Church in Seoul and Young Soo Lim and Hee Min Park of Young-Nak Presbyterian Church in Seoul and Los Angeles has encouraged me in this research with their prayers and love. Thanks also are due to my students, Hyung Ju Yang, Hye Sung Kim, and Hyo Jin Kim, whose typing helped me to finish this book at the Presbyterian University and Theological Seminary.

Finally, I wish to express my appreciation and admiration for my wife, Jin Ju Hong, my son Samuel, my daughter Grace Eun Hye, and my son Joseph for putting up with this enterprise, through their constant support and love. Without their patience, understanding and encouragement this work could never have been completed.

Soli Deo Gloria

Bibliography

Ådna, Jostein, and Hans Kvalbein, eds. *The Mission of the Early Church to Jews and Gentiles.* Wissenschaftliche Untersuchungen zum Neuen Testament 127. Tübingen: Mohr Siebeck, 2000.

Ahn, Byung Moo. "The Understanding of Jesus in Korean Church." *Christian Thought* 21 (1977) 65–79.

———. "Jesus and *Min Jung*: On the Focus of the Gospel of Mark." *Presence* 106 (1979) 3–18.

———. "The *Min Jung* Theology: On the Focus of the Gospel of Mark." *Theological Thought* 34 (1981) 504–36.

Albright, William F. "The Date and Personality of the Chronicler." *JBL* 39 (1920) 104–24.

Allen, L. C. *Ezekiel 20–48.* WBC 29. Dallas: Word, 1990.

Allison, Dale C., Jr. *The Jesus Tradition in Q.* Harrisburg: Trinity International, 1997.

———. *The New Moses: A Matthean Typology.* Minneapolis: Fortress, 1993.

Anderson, B. W. *Creation versus Chaos: The Reinterpretation of Mythical Symbolism in the Bible.* New York: Association, 1967.

———. *Understanding the Old Testament.* Englewood Cliffs, NJ: Prentice-Hall, 1975.

Anderson, Stanley D. *Documenta Q: Reconstructions of Q through Two Centuries of Gospel Research Excerpted, Sorted and Evaluated; Q 11:2b–4.* Leuven: Peeters, 1996.

Andreasen, Niels-Erik. *The Old Testament Sabbath: A Tradition-Historical Investigation.* SBL Dissertation Series 7. Missoula: University of Montana Press, 1972.

Arnal, William E. *Jesus and the Village Scribes: Galilean Conflicts and the Setting of Q.* Minneapolis: Fortress, 2001.

———. "Redactional Fabrication and Group Legitimation: The Baptist's Preaching in Q 3:7–9, 16–17." In *Conflict and Invention: Literary, Rhetorical, and Social Studies on the Sayings Gospel Q*, edited by John S. Kloppenborg, 165–80. Valley Forge: Trinity International, 1995.

Attridge, Harold W. "Josephus and His Works." In *The Literature of the Jewish People in the Period of the Second Temple and the Talmud*, vol. 2, *Jewish Writings of the Second Temple Period*, edited by Michael E. Stone, 185–232. Compendia rerum Iudaicarum ad Novum Testamentum 2/2. Assen, Netherlands: Van Gorcum, 1984.

Augustine. *City of God.* Vol. 1. Translated by W. H. Green. Cambridge: Harvard University Press, 1963.

Aune, David Edward. *Prophecy in Early Christianity and the Ancient Mediterranean World.* Grand Rapids: Eerdmans, 1983.

Avemarie, Friedrich and Hermann Lichtenberger, eds. *Bund und Tora: Zur theologischen Begriffsgeschichte in alttestamentlicher, frühjüdischer und urchristlicher Tradition.* Tübingen: Mohr, 1996.

Bacchiocchi, Samuele. *From Sabbath to Sunday: A Historical Investigation of the Rise of Sunday Observance in Early Christianity.* Rome: Pontifical Gregorian University, 1977.

———. *The Sabbath in the New Testament.* Berrien Springs, MI: Biblical Perspectives, 1990.

Balch, David L. *Social History of the Matthean Community: Cross-Disciplinary Approaches.* Minneapolis: Fortress, 1991.

Banks, Robert. *Jesus and the Law in the Synoptic Tradition.* Cambridge: Cambridge University Press, 1975.

Bantz, C. *Understanding Organizations: Interpreting Organizational Communications Cultures.* Columbia: University of South Carolina Press, 1993.

Barrett, Charles Kingsley. "The Gentile Mission as an Eschatological Phenomenon." In *Eschatology and the New Testament: Essays in Honor of George R. Beasley-Murray*, edited by W. Hulitt Gloer, 65–76. Peabody: Hendrickson, 1988.

Barth, Gerhard. "Matthew's Understanding of the Law." In *Tradition and Interpretation in Matthew*, edited by G. Bornkamm, et al., translated by Percy Scott, 58–164. New Testament Library. London: SCM, 1963.

Barth, Karl. "Die Theologie und die Mission in der Gegenwart." In *Theologisch Fragen und Antworten*, 3:100–26. Zollikon: Evangelischer, 1957.

———. "An Exegetical Study in Matthew 28:16–20." In *Landmark Essays in Mission and World Christianity*, edited by Robert L. Gallagher and Paul Hertig, 17–30. Maryknoll: Orbis, 2009.

Bartlett, John R. *Jews in the Hellenistic World: Josephus.* Cambridge: Cambridge University Press, 1985.

Bauckham, R. *Jesus and the Eyewitnesses: The Gospels as Eyewitness Testimony.* Grand Rapids: Eerdmans, 2006.

———. "Sabbath and Sunday in the Post-Apostolic Church." In Carson, *From Sabbath to Lord's Day*, 198–251.

Bauer, Walter. "Jesus der Galiläer." In *Festgabe für Adolf Jülicher zum 70. Geburtstag, 26. Januar 1927*, 16–34. Tübingen: Mohr, 1927.

———. *Rechtgläubigkeit und Ketzerei im ältesten Christentum.* Tübingen: Mohr, 1934. English translation: *Orthodoxy and Heresy in Earliest Christianity.* Translated by a team from the Philadelphia Seminar on Christian Origins. Philadelphia: Fortress, 1971.

Baumgartner, W. "Die literarischen Gattungen in der Weisheit des Jesus Sirach." *ZAW 34* (1914) 161–98.

Beare, Francis W. "The Mission of the Disciples and the Mission Charge: Matthew 10 and Parallels." *JBL* 89 (1970) 1–13.

———. "The Sabbath Was Made for Man?" *JBL* 79 (1960) 130–36.

Beckwith, R. T., and W. Stott. *This Is the Day: The Biblical Doctrine of the Christian Sunday in Its Jewish and Early Church Setting.* London: Marshall, Morgan & Scott, 1978.

Beernaert, Pierre Mourlon. "Jésus controversé: Structure et théologie de Mark 2,1—3,6." *Nouvelle Revue Theologique* 105 (1973) 129–49.

Belkin, Samuel. *Philo and the Law: The Philonic Interpretation of Biblical Law in Relation to the Palestinian Halakah.* Cambridge: Harvard University Press, 1940.

Benko, Stephen. *Pagan Rome and the Early Christians.* Bloomington: Indiana University Press, 1984.

Berger, Klaus. *Die Gesetzesauslegung Jesu: Ihr historischer Hintergrund im Judentum und im Alten Testament.* Teil 1, *Markus und Parallelen.* Wissenschaftliche Monographien zum Alten und Neuen Testament 40. Hamburg: Neukirchener, 1972.

Berger, Klaus, and Carsten Colpe. *Religionsgeschichtliches Textbuch zum Neue Testament.* Texte zum Neuen Testament 1. Göttingen: Vandenhoeck & Ruprecht, 1987.

Betz, Johannes. "Die Eucharistie in der Didache." *ArchivLiturgWiss* 11 (1969) 10-39.

Beyer, Klaus. *Semitische Syntax im Neuen Testament.* Studien zur Umwelt des Neuen Testaments 1. Göttingen: Vandenhoeck & Ruprecht, 1962.

Bilde, Per. *Flavius Josephus between Jerusalem and Rome.* Journal for the Study of the Pseudepigrapha Supplement Series 2. Sheffield: Sheffield Academic, 1988.

Bishai, Wilson B. "Sabbath Observance from Coptic Sources." *Andrews University Seminary Studies* 1 (1963) 25-43.

Bishop, K. M. "St. Matthew and the Gentiles." *Expository Times* 59 (1947-1948) 249.

Black, M. *An Aramaic Approach to the Gospels and Acts.* Appendix on the Son of Man by Geza Vermes. Oxford: Westminster, 1946; 2nd ed., 1954; 3rd ed., 1967.

———. "The Aramaic Dimension in Q with Notes on Luke 17:22 and Matthew 24:26 (Luke 17:23)." In *The Historical Reader: A Sheffield Reader,* edited by Craig A. Evans and Stanly E. Porter, 33-41. Sheffield: Sheffield Academic, 1995.

———. "The Aramaic Spoken by Christ and Luke 14,5." *JTS* 1 (1950) 60-62.

Blair, Edward P. "Paul's Call to the Gentile Mission." *Biblical Research* 10 (1965) 19-33.

Blenkinsopp, Joseph. *Wisdom and Law in the Old Testament: The Ordering of Life in Israel and Early Judaism.* Oxford: Oxford University Press, 1995.

Bloch, P. *The Biblical and Historical Background of the Jewish Holy Days.* New York: KTAV, 1978.

Blomberg, Craig L. "The Law in Luke-Acts." *JSNT* 22 (1984) 53-80. Reprinted in *The Synoptic Gospels: A Sheffield Reader,* edited by Craig A. Evans and Stanley E. Porter, 240-67. Sheffield: Sheffield Academic, 1995.

Böhlig, A. "Der Jüdische und judenchristliche Hintergrund in gnostischen Texten von Nag Hammadi." In *Le Origini Dello Gnosticismo,* 109-40. Leiden: Brill, 1967.

———. "Jüdische und iranisches in der Adamapokalypse des Codex V von Nag Hammadi." In *Mysterion und Wahrheit: Gesammelte Beiträge zur spätantiken Religionsgeschichte,* 149-61. Leiden: Brill, 1968.

Böhlig, A., and P. Labib. *Koptisch-gnostische Apocalypsen aus Codex V von Nag Hammadi im Koptischen Museum zu Alt-Kairo.* Berlin: Halle-Wittenberg, 1962.

Boismard, M.-É., and Par P. Benoit. *Synopse des quatre évangiles en français.* Vol. 2. Paris: Éditions de Cerf, 1972.

Borg, Marcus J. *Conflict, Holiness & Politics in the Teachings of Jesus.* Studies in the Bible and Early Christianity 5. New York: Mellen, 1984.

Borgen, Peder. "Philo of Alexandria." In *The Literature of the Jewish People in the Period of the Second Temple and the Talmud,* vol. 2, *Jewish Writings of the Second Temple Period,* edited by Michael E. Stone, 232-82. Compendia rerum Iudaicarum ad Novum Testamentum 2/2. Assen, Netherlands: Van Gorcum, 1984.

Boring, M. Eugene. *The Gospel of Matthew.* New Interpreter's Bible Commentary 8. Nashville: Abingdon, 1995.

Bosch, David. *Die Heidenmission in der Zukunftsschau Jesu: Eine Untersuchung zur Eschatoligie der synoptischen Evangelien.* Zürich: Zwingli-Verlag, 1959.

———. *Transforming Mission: Paradigm Shifts in Theology of Mission*. Maryknoll: Orbis, 1991.
Botterweck, G. Johannes. "Der Sabbat im Alten Testament." *Theologische Quartalschrift* 134 (1954) 134, 147, 448–57.
Bovon, François. *Das Evangelium nach Lukas: Lk 9,51—14,35*. Evangelisch-Katholischer Kommentar zum Neuen Testament 3/2, vol. 2. Zürich: Benziger, 1996.
———. "The God of Luke." In *New Testament Traditions and Apocryphal Narratives*, 67–80. PTMS 36. Allison Park, PA: Pickwick, 1995.
———. "The Knowledge and Experience of God according to the New Testament." In *New Testament Traditions and Apocryphal Narratives*, 105–18. PTMS 36. Allison Park, PA: Pickwick, 1995.
———. *Luke the Theologian: Thirty-Three Years of Research (1950-1983)*. Translated by Ken McKinney. Allison Park, PA: Pickwick, 1987.
———. "Tracing the Trajectory of Luke 13,22-30 Back to Q." In *From Quest to Q: Festschrift James M. Robinson*, edited by J. M. Asgeirsson et al., 285–94. Leuven: Leuven University Press, 2000.
Branscomb, Bennett Harvie. *Jesus and the Law of Moses*. London: Hodder & Stoughton, 1930.
Braulik, G. "Menuchah: Die Ruhe Gottes und des Volkes im Lande." *Bik* 23 (1968) 75–78.
Braun, Willi. *Feasting and Social Rhetoric in Luke 14*. Society for New Testament Studies Monograph Series 85. Cambridge: Cambridge University Press, 1995.
Bright, J. *Jeremiah*. AB 21. New York: Doubleday, 1965.
Brin, Gershon. *Studies in Biblical Law: From the Hebrew Bible to the Dead Sea Scrolls*. JSOT Supplement Series 176. Sheffield: Sheffield Academic, 1994.
Brooks, Stephenson H. *Matthew's Community: The Evidence of His Special Sayings Material*. JSNT Supplement Series 16. Sheffield: Sheffield Academic, 1987.
Brown, Francis, et al., eds. *A Hebrew and English Lexicon of the Old Testament*. Oxford: Clarendon, 1907.
Brown, John Pairman. "The Form of 'Q' Known to Matthew." *NTS* 8 (1961–1962) 27–42.
Brown, Raymond E. *Antioch and Rome*. New York: Paulist, 1983.
———. "The Gospel of Thomas and St John's Gospel." *NTS* 9 (1962) 155–77.
———. "The Matthean Community and the Gentile Mission." *Novum Testamentum* 22 (1980) 193–221.
———. "The Mission to Israel in Matthew's Central Section." *Zeitschrift für die Neutestamentliche Wissenschaft* 69 (1978) 73–90.
———. "Not Jewish Christianity and Gentile Christianity but Types of Jewish/Gentile Christianity." *Catholic Biblical Quarterly* 45 (1983) 74–79.
Brown, S. "The Two-Fold Representation of the Mission in Matthew's Gospel." *Studia Theologica* 31 (1977) 21–32.
Bruce, Alexander B. *The Expositor's Greek Testament: The Synoptic Gospels*. Vol. 1. 6th ed. London: Hodder & Stoughton, 1910. Originally 1897.
Brueggemann, W. "Of the Same Flesh and Bone (Gn 2:23a)." *CBQ* 32 (1970) 532–42.
Bultmann, Rudolf. *Die Geschichte der synoptischen Tradition*. Forschungen zur Religion und Literatur des Alten und Neuen Testaments 29. Göttingen: Vandenhoeck & Ruprecht, 1921; 2nd rev. ed., 1931; 4th ed., 1958. Trans., John Marsh, *The History of the Synoptic Tradition*. Oxford: Blackwell; New York: Harper; rev. ed., 1968.
Burkert, Walter. *Ancient Mystery Cults*. Cambridge: Harvard University Press, 1987.

Burkitt, Francis Crawford. *The Gospel History and Its Transmission.* Edinburgh: T. & T. Clark, 1906; 5th ed., 1925.

Busse, Urlich. *Die Wunder des Propheten Jesus.* Forschung zur Bibel 24. Stuttgart: Katholisches Bibelwerk, 1977.

Bussmann, Wilhelm. *Synoptische Studien.* Vol. 2. Halle: Buchhandlung des Waisenhauses, 1929.

Cadbury, Henry J. *The Style and Literary Method of Luke.* Harvard Theological Studies 6. Cambridge: Harvard University Press, 1920. Repr., New York: Kraus, 1969.

Camponovo, Odo. *Königtum, Königsherrschaft und Reigh Gottes in den Frühjudischen Schriften.* Göttingen: Vandenhoeck & Ruprecht, 1984.

Carr, David McLain. *From D to Q: A Study of Early Jewish Interpretations of Solomon's Dream at Gibeon.* SBL Monograph Series 44. Atlanta: Scholars, 1991.

Carroll, John T. *Response to the End of History: Eschatology and Situation in Luke-Acts.* SBL Dissertation Series 92. Atlanta: Scholars, 1988.

Carroll, R. P. *Jeremiah 1–25.* OTL. London: SCM, 1986.

Carruth, Shawn. "Persuasion in Q: A Rhetorical Critical Study of Q 6:20–49." PhD diss., Claremont Graduate University, 1992.

Carson, D. A., ed. *From Sabbath to Lord's Day: A Biblical, Historical, and Theological Investigation.* Grand Rapids: Zondervan, 1982.

———. "Jesus and the Sabbath in the Four Gospels." In Carson, *From Sabbath to Lord's Day,* 57–97.

Casey, Maurice. "Culture and Historicity: The Plucking of the Grain (Mark 2.23–28)." *NTS* 34 (1988) 1–23.

Cassuto, U. *A Commentary on the Book of Exodus.* Jerusalem: Magnus, 1961.

Castor, George DeWitt. *Matthew's Sayings of Jesus: The Non-Marcan Common Source of Matthew and Luke.* Chicago: University of Chicago Press, 1912.

Catchpole, David. "Q and 'the Friend at Midnight' (Luke 11,5–8/9)." *JTS* 34 (1983) 407–24.

———. *The Quest for Q.* Edinburgh: T. & T. Clark, 1993.

Chang, Joon Ho. "In Memory of Him: Allusions to the Founder of the Q School in the Latest Stages of Q." New Testament seminar paper, Claremont Graduate School, spring 1993.

Charlesworth, James H. *The Dead Sea Scrolls: Hebrew, Aramaic, and Greek Texts with English Translations.* Vol. 1, *Rule of the Community and Related Documents.* Louisville: Westminster John Knox, 1994.

———. "From Jewish Messianology to Christian Christology: Some Caveats and Perspectives." In *Judaisms and Their Messiahs at the Turn of the Christian Era,* edited by Jacob Neusner et al., 225–64. Cambridge: Cambridge University Press, 1987.

———. "From Messianology to Christology: Problems and Prospects." In *The Messiah: Developments in Earliest Judaism and Christianity,* 3–35. Minneapolis: Fortress, 1992.

———. *Jesus' Jewishness: Exploring the Place of Jesus within Early Judaism.* Philadelphia: American Interfaith Institute, 1991.

———. *The Old Testament Pseudepigrapha.* 2 vols. Garden City: Doubleday, 1983–1985.

Childs, B. S. *The Book of Exodus.* Philadelphia: Fortress, 1974.

———. *Introduction to the Old Testament as Scripture.* OTL. London: SCM, 1979.

Chilton, Bruce, and Craig Evans, eds. *The Missions of James, Peter, and Paul: Tensions in Early Christianity.* Supplements to Novum Testamentum 115. Leiden: Brill, 2005.

Cho, Tae Yeun. "The Study of the Synoptic Gospels." In *New Testament Introduction: A Recent Study for Koreans*, Ky-Chun So et al., 538–42. Seoul: Christian Literature Society of Korea, 2002.

Christie-Murray, D. *A History of Heresy*. Oxford: Oxford University Press, 1987.

Clark, Kenneth W. "The Gentile Bias in Matthew." *Journal Biblical Literature* 66 (1947) 165–72. Reprinted in *The Gentile Bias and Other Essays*, 1–8. Leiden: Brill, 1980.

Clarke, Ernest G. *The Wisdom of Solomon*. Cambridge: Cambridge University Press, 1973.

Clines, D. J. A. *Ezra, Nehemiah, Esther*. NCB. London: Marshall, Morgan & Scott, 1984.

Cobb, John B., and David Ray Griffin. *Process Theology: An Introductory Exposition*. Philadelphia: Westminster, 1976.

Cohen, Boaz. "The Rabbinic Law Presupposed by Matthew 12.1 and Luke 6.1." *Harvard Theological Review* 23 (1930) 91–92.

Cohn-Sherbok, D. M. "An Analysis of Jesus' Arguments concerning the Plucking of Grain on the Sabbath." *Journal of the Study of the New Testament* 2 (1979) 31–41. Reprinted in *The Historical Jesus: A Sheffield Reader*, edited by Craig A. Evans and S. E. Porter, 83–130. Sheffield: Sheffield Academic, 1995.

Conzelmann, Hans. *History of Primitive Christianity*. Translated by John E. Steely. Nashville: Abingdon, 1973.

———. *An Outline of the Theology of the New Testament*. Translated by John Bowden. London: SCM, 1969.

Conzelmann, Hans, and Andreas Lindemann. *Interpreting the New Testament: An Introduction to the Principles and Methods of N.T. Exegesis*. Translated by Siegfried S. Schatzmann. Peabody: Hendrickson, 1988.

Coote, Robert B., and David R. Ord. *In the Beginning: Creation and the Priestly History*. Minneapolis: Fortress, 1991.

Creed, John Martin. *The Gospel according to St. Luke: The Greek Text with Introduction, Notes and Indices*. London: Macmillan, 1930; repr., 1953; 2nd ed., 1965.

Crossan, John Dominic. *Four Other Gospels: Thomas, Egerton, Secret Mark, Peter*. Sonoma: Polebridge, 1985; repr., 1992.

———. *In Fragments: The Aphorisms of Jesus*. San Francisco: Harper & Row, 1983.

Crossan, John Dominic, and Jonathan L. Reed. *In Search of Paul: How Jesus' Apostle Opposed Rome's Empire with God's Kingdom; A New Vision of Paul's Words and World*. San Francisco: HarperSanFrancisco, 2004.

Crum, J. M. C. *The Original Jerusalem Gospel: Being Essays on the Document Q*. New York: Macmillan, 1927.

Cullmann, Oscar. *The Christology of the New Testament*. Translated by S. C. Guthrie and C. A. M. Hall. London: SCM, 1963.

———. "Sabbat und Sonntag nach dem Johannesevangelium: *heos erti* (Joh. 5,17)." In *Memoriam Ernst Lohmeyer*, edited by Werner Schmauch, 127–31. Stuttgart: Evangelischesswerk, 1951.

Culpepper, R. Alan. *The Johannine School: An Evaluation of the Johannine School Hypothesis Based on the Investigation of the Nature of Ancient Schools*. SBL Dissertation Series 26. Missoula: Scholars, 1975.

Danby, Herbert, trans. *The Mishnah: Translated from the Hebrew with Introduction and Brief Explanatory Notes*. Oxford: Oxford University Press, 1933.

BIBLIOGRAPHY

Daniélou, Jean. "Le Ve Esdras et le judéo-christianisme Latin au second siècle." In *Ex Orbe Religionum: Studia Geo Widengren*, 162–71. Studies in the History of Religion 21. Leiden: Brill, 1972.

———. *Théologie du judéo-christianisme*. English translation by J. A. Baker, *The Theology of Jewish Christianity*. London: Darton, Longman & Todd, 1964.

Davenport, Gene L. "The 'Anointed of the Lord' in Psalms of Solomon." In *Ideal Figures in Ancient Judaism: Profiles and Paradigms*, edited by Nickelsburg et al., 67–92. Chico: Scholars, 1980.

Davies, Philip R. *The Damascus Covenant*. JSOT Supplement Series 25. Sheffield: Sheffield Academic, 1982.

Davies, William David. *The Setting of the Sermon on the Mount*. Cambridge: Cambridge University Press, 1966.

Davies, William David, and Dale C. Allison Jr. *A Critical and Exegetical Commentary on the Gospel according to Saint Matthew*. 3 vols. International Critical Commentary. Edinburgh: T. & T. Clark, 1988–1997.

Dawsey, James M. *The Lukan Voice: Confusion and Irony in the Gospel of Luke*. Macon, GA: Mercer University Press, 1986.

De Blois, Kees F. "From and Meaning of the Text: Expressing One Meaning by Means of Different Forms." In *Discover the Bible: A Manual for Biblical Studies*, edited by R. Omanson, 409–16. Columbia: American Bible Society, 2001.

Derrett, John Ducan. *Law in the New Testament*. London: Darton, Longman & Todd, 1970.

Dewey, Joanna. "The Literary Structure of the Controversy Stories in Mark 2:1—3:6." *JBL* 92 (1973) 394–401.

Dibelius, Martin. *Die Formgeschichte des Evangeliums*. English translation by B. L. Woolf, *From Tradition to Gospel*. New York: Scribner, 1935, 1965.

Dieterich, Albrecht. *Eine Mithrasliturgie. Wissenschaftliche Buchgesellschaft*. Leipzig: Teubner, 1903.

Dietzfelbinger, C. "Vom Sinn der Sabbatheilungen Jesu." *Evangelische Theologie* 38 (1978) 281–98.

Donaldson, Terence L. *Paul and the Gentiles: Remapping the Apostle's Convictional World*. Minneapolis: Fortress, 1997.

Doyle, B. Rod. "A Concern of the Evangelist: Pharisees in Matthew 12." *Australian Biblical Review* 34 (1986) 17–34.

Dressler, H. H. P. "The Sabbath in the Old Testament." In Carson, *From Sabbath to Lord's Day*, 21–41.

Dunderberg, Ismo, et al., eds. *Fair Play: Diversity and Conflicts in Early Christianity; Essays in Honor of Heikki Räisänen*. Supplements to Novum Testamentum 103. Leiden: Brill, 2002.

Dunn, James D. G. "Jesus and the Constraint of Law." *JSNT* 17 (1983) 10–18.

———. *Jesus and the Spirit: A Study of the Religious and Charismatic Experience of Jesus and the First Christians as Reflected in the New Testament*. New Testament Library. London: SCM, 1975.

———. *Jesus, Paul and the Law: Studies in Mark and Galatians*. Louisville: Westminster John Knox, 1990.

———. "Mark 2.1–3.6: A Bridge between Jesus and Paul on the Question of the Law." *NTS* 30 (1984) 395–415.

Dupont-Sommer, Andre. *The Essene Writings from Qumran*. Oxford: Blackwell, 1961.

---. *The Jewish Sect of Qumran and the Essenes: New Studies on the Dead Sea Scrolls.* London: Vallentine, 1954.

Easton, Burton Scott. "First Evangelic Tradition." *JBL* 50 (1931) 148–55.

---. *The Gospel according to St. Luke: A Critical and Exegetical Commentary.* New York: Scribner, 1926.

Edwards, Richard A. *The Sign of Jonah in the Theology of the Evangelists and Q.* London: SCM, 1971.

---. *A Theology of Q.* Philadelphia: Fortress, 1976.

Ehrman, Bart D. *Lost Christianities: The Battles for Scripture and the Faiths We Never Knew.* Oxford: Oxford University Press, 2003.

Eichrodt, W. "Der Sabbat bei Hesekiel: Ein Beitrag zur Nach Geschichte des Prohetentextes." In *Lex tua Varitas: Festschrift für Huberth Junker,* edited by H. Gross and F. Mussner, 65–74. Trier, Germany: Paulinus-Verlag, 1961.

---. *Ezekiel.* OTL. London: SCM, 1970.

Eisenmann, Robert H., and Michael Wise, eds. *The Dead Sea Scrolls Uncovered: The First Complete Translation and Interpretation of 50 Key Documents Withheld for over 35 Years.* Shaftesbury: Element, 1992.

Eissfeldt, Otto. *The Old Testament: An Introduction.* New York: Harper & Row, 1965.

Epiphanius. *The Panarion of Epiphanius of Salamis.* Translated by Frank Williams. 2 vols. Nag Hammadi Studies 35. Leiden: Brill, 1987.

Epstein, I., trans. *The Babylonian Talmud.* 35 vols. London: Soncino, 1935–1952.

Ernst, Josef. *Das Evangelium nach Lukas.* Regensburger Neues Testament 3. Regensburg: Friedrich Pustet, 1977.

---. "Gastmahlgespräche: Lk 14,1–24." In *Die Kirche des Anfangs,* edited by Rudolf Schackenburg et al., 57–77. Erfurter theologische Studien 38. Leipzig: St. Benno, 1979.

Eskenazi, Tamara Cohn, and Daniel J. Harrington, eds. *The Sabbath in Jewish and Christian Traditions.* New York: Crossroad, 1991.

Esler, Philip Francis. *Community and Gospel in Luke-Acts.* Cambridge: Cambridge University Press, 1987.

Evans, Craig A. "The Function of the Elijah/Elisha Narrative in Luke's Ethic of Election." In *Luke and Scripture: The Function of Sacred Tradition in Luke-Acts* C. A. Evans and J. A. Sanders. Minneapolis, 1993.

---. *Jesus and His Contemporaries: Comparative Studies.* Boston: Brill Academic, 2001.

Evans, Craig A., and James A. Sanders. *Luke and Scripture: The Function of Sacred Tradition in Luke-Acts.* Minneapolis: Fortress, 1993.

Evans, C. F. *Saint Luke.* Philadelphia: Trinity International, 1990.

Feldmann, Louis H. *Jew and Gentile in the Ancient World: Attitudes and Interpretations from Alexander to Justinian.* Princeton: Princeton University Press, 1993.

Fischel, H. A. "Martyr and Prophet: A Study in Jewish Literature." *JQR* 37 (1946/1947) 265–80, 363–86.

Fitzmyer, Josef A. *The Gospel according to Luke.* Vol. 2. Anchor Bible 28A. Garden City: Doubleday, 1985.

---. "The Role of the Spirit in Luke-Acts." In *The Unity of Luke-Acts,* edited by J. Verheyden, 165–83. Leuven: Leuven University Press, 1999.

Flusser, David. *Die rabbinischen Gleichnisse und der Gleichniserzähler Jesus.* Das Wesen der Gleichnisse 1. Bern: Lang, 1981.

---. *Judaism and the Origins of Christianity.* Jerusalem: Magnes, 1988.

Fohrer, Georg. *Die Hauptprobleme des Buches Ezechiel*. BZAW 72. Berlin: Töpelmann, 1952.

Fohrer, Georg, and Kurt Galling. *Ezechiel*. Handbuch zum Alten Testament 13. Tübingen: Mohr, 1955.

Forbes, Greg W. *The God of Old: The Role of the Lukan Parables in the Purpose of Luke's Gospel*. JSNT Supplement Series 198. Sheffield: Sheffield Academic, 2002.

Fox, Robin Lane. *Pagans and Christians*. New York: Knopf, 1987.

France, R. T. *Jesus and the Old Testament: His Application of Old Testament Passages to Himself and His Mission*. London: Tyndale, 1971.

France, R. T., and D. Wenham, eds. *Gospel Perspectives: Studies in Midrash and Historiography*. Vol. 3. Sheffield: JSOT, 1983.

Frend, W. H. C. *Martyrdom and Persecution in the Early Church: A Study of Conflict from the Maccabees to Donatus*. Oxford: Blackwell, 1965.

Freyne, Sean. *Galilee and Gospel*. Boston: Brill Acedemic, 2002.

Frost, Stanley Brice. *Old Testament Apocalyptic*. London: Epworth, 1952.

Frotinus. *Strategemata*. In *The Strategemata and the Aqueducts of Rome*. Cambridge: Harvard University Press, 1980.

Funk, Franciscus Xaverius, ed. *Didascalia et Constitutiones apostolorum*. 2 vols. Torino: Botegga D'Erasmo, 1964.

Gagnon, Robert A. J. "Luke's Motives for Redaction in the Account of the Double Delegation in Luke 7:1–10." *Novum Testamentum* 36 (1994) 122–45.

Gammie, John J. "Paraenetic Literature: Toward the Morphology of a Secondary Genre." *Semeia* 50 (1990) 41–77.

Gese, Hartmut. "Das Gesetz." In *Zur biblischen Theologie: alttestamentliche Vortrage*, 55–84. Beiträge zur evangelischen Theologie 78. Münich: Kaiser, 1977.

Gevirtz, S. *Patterns in Early Poetry of Israel*. Chicago: University of Chicago Press, 1963.

Giem, Paul. "Sabbaton in Col 2:16." *Andrews University Seminary Studies* 19 (1981) 195–210.

Gillespie, Neal C. *Charles Darwin and the Problem of Creation*. Chicago: University of Chicago Press, 1979.

Gils, Félix. "Le Sabbat a été fait pour l'homme et non l'homme pour le Sabbat (Mc, 2, 27)." *Revue Biblique* 69 (1962) 506–23.

Goldberg, A. "The Mishna—A Study Book of Halakah." In *The Literature of the Jewish People in the Period of the Second Temple and the Talmud*, vol. 3, *The Literature of the Sages: Midrash, Mishna, Talmud*, part. 1, edited by Shmuel Safrai, 211–62. Compendia rerum Iudaicarum ad Novum Testamentum 2/3. Assen: Van Gorcum, 1987.

Goldenberg, Robert. "The Jewish Sabbath in the Roman World up to the Time of Constantine the Great." In *Aufstieg und Niedergang der Römischen Welt* II.19.1, 411–47. Berlin: Gruyter, 1979.

———. *The Sabbath-Law of Rabbi Meir*. Brown Judaic Studies 6. Missoula: Scholars, 1978.

Goodenough, Erwin R. "Philo's Exposition of the Law and His De Vita Mosis." *HTR* 26 (1933) 109–25.

———. *The Theology of Justin Martyr*. Jena: Frommannsche Buchhandlung, 1923.

Goppelt, Leonhard. *Theology of the New Testament*. 2 vols. Grand Rapids: Eerdmans, 1981.

Gottwald, Norman K. *The Hebrew Bible: A Socio-Literary Introduction*. Philadelphia: Fortress, 1985.

Goulder, M. D. *Luke: A New Paradigm*. Vol. 1–2. JSNT Supplement Series 20. Sheffield: JSOP, 1989.

———. *Midrash and Lection in Matthew: Speaker's Lectures in Biblical Studies*. London: SPCK, 1974.

Grant, Frederick C. *Ancient Judaism and the New Testament*. Edinburgh: Oliver & Boyd, 1960.

Gray, J. *1 and 2 Kings*. OTL. London: SCM, 1977.

Green, Michael. *Evangelism in the Early Church*. Grand Rapids: Eerdmans, 1970.

Greeven, von Heinrich. "Wer unter Euch . . . ?" In *Gleichnisse Jesu: Positionen der Auslegung von Adolf Jülicher bis zur Formgeschichte*, edited by Wolfgang Harnisch, 238–55. Wege der Gorschung 366. Darmstadt: Wissenschaftliche Buchgesellschaft, 1952; repr., 1982.

Gregg, Brian Han. *The Historical Jesus and the Final Judgment Sayings in Q*. Tübingen: Mohr Siebeck, 2006.

Griesbach, Johann Jakob. *Novum Testamentum Graece*. Cantabrigiae: Nov-Anglorum, 1809.

Griffin, David Ray. *God and Religion in the Postmodern World*. Albany: State University of New York Press, 1989. Also published in Korean (Seoul: Cho Myung, 1995; trans. Sung Do Kang), Persian (Tehran, 2002; trans. and ed. Hamidreza Ayatollahy), and Chinese (Beijing: Central Compilation & Translation, 2003; trans. Mutian Sun).

Gruenwald, I. *Apocalyptic and Merkavah Mysticism*. Leiden: Brill, 1980.

Grundmann, Walter. *Das Evangelium nach Lukas*. Theologischer Handkommentar zum Neuen Testament 3. Berlin: Evangelischesanstalt, 1961.

———. *Das Evangelium nach Matthäus*. Theologischer Handkommentar zum Neuen Testament 1. Berlin: Evangelischesanstalt, 1968; 9th ed., 1981.

Gundry, Robert H. *Matthew: A Commentary on His Literary and Theological Art*. Grand Rapids: Eerdmans, 1982.

Haenchen, Ernst. *Der Weg Jesu*. Sammlung Töpelmann 2/6. Berlin: Töpelmann, 1966.

———. *Die Apostelgeschichte*. Kritisch-expectischer Kommnetar über das Neue Testament 3. Göttingen: Vandenhoeck & Ruprecht, 1965.

Hagner, Donald A. *The Jewish Reclamation of Jesus: An Analysis & Critique of the Modern Jewish Study of Jesus*. Eugene, OR: Wipe & Stock, 1997.

Hahn, Ferdinand. *Das Verständnis der Mission im Neuen Testament*. English translation by F. Clarke, *Mission in the New Testament*. Naperville, IL: Allenson, 1963, 1965.

Halivni, David Weiss. *Midrash, Mishnah, and Gemara: The Jewish Predilection for Justified Law*. Cambridge: Harvard University Press, 1986.

Halliday, William Reginald. *The Pagan Background of Early Christianity: The Ancient World*. London: University of Liverpool Press, 1925.

Hamm, M. Dennis. "The Freeing of the Bent Woman and the Restoration of Israel: Luke 13,10–17 as Narrative Theology." *JSNT* 31 (1987) 23–44.

Han, Kyu Sam. *Jerusalem and the Early Jesus Movement: The Q Community's Attitude toward the Temple*. JSNT Supplement Series 207. Sheffield: Sheffield Academic, 2002.

Hare, Douglas R. A. "The Lives of the Prophets." In *The Old Testament Pseudepigrapha*, vol. 2, *Expansions of the "Old Testament" and Legends, Wisdom and Philosophical Literature, Prayers, Psalms and Odes, Fragments of Lost Judeo-Hellenistic Works*, edited by James Charlesworth, 379–400. New Havens: Yale University Press, 1983.

———. *The Son of Man Tradition*. Minneapolis: Fortress, 1990.

Hare, Douglas R. A., and Daniel J. Harington. "Make Disciples of All the Gentiles (Mt 28,19)." *Catholic Biblical Quaterly* 37 (1975) 359–69.

Harnack, Adolf von. *Die Mission und Ausbreitung des Christentums.* English translation by J. M. Moffatt, *The Mission and Expansion of Christianity in the First Three Centuries.* 2 vols. New York: Williams & Norgate, 1902.

———. *Judentum und Judenchristentum in Justins Dialog mit Trypho.* Leipzig, 1913.

———. *Sprüche und Reden Jesu.* Beiträge zur Einleitung in das Neue Testament II. Leipzig: Hinrichs'sche Buchhandlung. English translation by J. R. Wilkinson, *The Sayings of Jesus.* New York: Putnam, 1907; London: Williams & Norgate, 1908.

Harrington, Daniel J. "Matthean Studies since Joachim Rohde." *HeyJ* 16 (1975) 375–88.

———. "Sabbath Tensions: Matthew 12.1-14 and Other New Testament Texts." In *The Sabbath in Jewish and Christian Traditions,* edited by T. C. Eskenazi et al., 45–56. New York: Crossroad, 1991.

Haught, John F. *Making Sense of Evolution: Darwin, God, and the Drama of Life.* Louisville: Westminster John Knox, 2010.

———. *Science and Religion: From Conflict to Conversation.* New York: Paulist, 1995.

Haupt, Walther. *Worte Jesu und Gemeindeüberlieferung: Eine Untersuchung zur Quellengeschichte der Synopse.* Untersuchungen zum Neuen Testament 3. Leipzig: Hinrichs'sche Buchhandlung, 1913.

Havener, Ivan. *Q: The Sayings of Jesus.* Wilmington, DE: Glazier, 1987.

Hawkins, John C. "Probabilities as to the So-Called Double Tradition of St. Matthew and St. Luke." In *Oxford Studies in the Synoptic Problem,* edited by W. Sanday, 95–140. Oxford: Clarendon, 1911.

Hedrick, Charles W. *The Apocalypse of Adam.* SBL Dissertation Series 46. Chico: Scholars, 1980.

Heidel, Alexander. *The Babylonian Genesis: The Story of Creation.* Chicago: University of Chicago Press, 1951.

Heil, Christoph. "Beobachtungen zur theologischen Dimension: der Gleichnisrede Jesu in Q." In *The Sayings Source Q and the Historical Jesus,* 649–59. BEThL 158. Leuven: Leuven University Press, 2001.

Henderson, Ian H. *Jesus, Rhetoric and Law.* Biblical Interpretation Series 20. Leiden: Brill, 1996.

Hengel, Martin. *The Charismatic Leader and His Followers.* New York: Crossroad, 1981.

———. "Die Ursprünge der Christlichen Mission." *NTS* 18 (1972) 15–38.

Hicks, J. M. "The Sabbath Controversy in Matthew: An Exegesis of Matthew 12.1-14." *Restoration Quarterly* 27 (1984) 79–91.

Higgins, A. J. B. *Jesus and the Son of Man.* Philadelphia: Fortress, 1964.

Hinz, C. "Jesus und der Sabbat." *Kerygma und Dogma* 19 (1973) 91–108.

Hirsch, E. *Frühgeschichte des Evangeliums: Die Vorlagen des Lukas und das Sondergut des Matthäus.* Vol. 2. Tübingen: Mohr Siebeck, 1941.

Hirschfeld, H. "Remarks on the Etymology of Sabbath." *Journal of the Royal Asiatic Society of Great Britain and Ireland* 53 (1896) 353–59.

Hoenig, S. B. "The Designated Number of Kinds of Labor Prohibited on the Sabbath." *Jewish Quarterly Review* 68 (1977) 193–208.

Hoffmann, Paul. *Das Erbe Jesu und die Macht in der Kirche: Ruckbesinnung auf das Neue Testament.* Mainz: Mathias-Grunewald, 1991.

———. *Studien zur Theologie der Logienquelle.* Münster: Aschendorff, 1972.

———. *Tradition und Situation: Studien zur Jesusüberlieferung in der Logienquelle und den synoptischen Evangelien.* Münster: Aschendorff, 1995.

Hubbard, Benjamin J. *The Matthean Redaction of a Primitive Apostolic Commissioning: An Exegesis of Matthew 28:16–20.* SBL Dissertation Series 19. Missoula: University of Montana Press, 1974.

Hübner, H. *Das Gesetz in der synoptischen Tradition: Studien zu einer progressiven Qumranisierung und Judaisierung innerhalb der synoptischen Tradition.* Witten: Luther, 1973.

Hulst, A. R. "Bemerkungen zum Sabbatgebot." In *Studia Biblica et Semitica*, edited by T. C. Vriezen, 152–64. Wageningen: Veenman, 1966.

Hultgren, Arland J. "The Formation of the Sabbath Pericope in Mark 2:23–28." *JBL* 91 (1972) 38–43.

Hyldahl, Niels. *Philosophie und Christentum. Eine Interpretation der Einleitung zum Dialog Justins.* Copenhagen: Munksgaard, 1966.

Hymes, D. *Foundations in Sociolinguistics: An Ethnographic Approach.* Philadelphia: University of Pennsylvania Press, 1974.

Jacobson, Arland D. "Divided Families and Christian Origins." In *The Gospel behind the Gospels: Current Studies on Q*, edited by Ronald A. Piper, 361–80. Leiden: Brill, 1995.

———. *The First Gospel: An Introduction to Q.* Sonoma, CA: Polebridge, 1992.

———. "The Literary Unity of Q." *JBL* 101 (1982) 171–89. Reprinted in *The Shape of Q: Signal Essays on the Sayings Gospel*, edited by John S. Kloppenborg, 98–115. Minneapolis: Fortress, 1994.

Jaubert, A. "Le Calendrier des Jubilé et le jours liturgiques de la semaine." *VT* 7 (1957) 35–61.

———. "Jésus et le calendrier de Qumrân." *NTS* 7 (1960–1961) 1–30.

Jenni, Ernst. *Die theologische Begründung des Sabbatgebotes im Alten Testament.* Theologische Studien 46. Zollikon-Zürich: Evangelischer, 1956.

Jeremias, Joachim. *Die Gleichnisse Jesu.* Translated by S. H. Hooke, *The Parable of Jesus.* New York: Scribner, 1963; 6th ed., 1972.

———. *Die Sprache des Lukasevangeliums: Redaktion und Tradition im Nicht-Markusstoff des dritten Evangeliums.* Göttingen: Vandenhoeck & Ruprecht, 1980.

———. *The Eucharistic Words of Jesus.* Philadelphia: Fortress, 1977.

———. *Jesu Verheissung für die Völker.* English translation by S. H. Hooke, *Jesus' Promise to the Nations.* Studies in Biblical Theology 24. Naperville, IL: Allenson, 1956, 1958.

———. *New Testament Theology.* Translated by John Bowden. London: SCM, 1971.

Jervell, Jacob. "Das gespaltene Israel und die Heidenvölker." *Studia Theologica* 19 (1965) 76–77, 83.

———. *Luke and the People of God: A New Look at Luke-Acts.* Minneapolis: Fortress, 1972.

Jocz, Jakob. "Jesus and the Law." *Judaica* 26 (1970) 105–24.

Johnston, Robert M. "The Eschatological Sabbath in John's Apocalyse: A Reconstruction." *Andrews University Seminary Studies* 25 (1987) 39–50.

Jonas, Hans *The Gnostic Religion: The Message of the Alien God and the Beginnings of Christianity.* Boston: Beacon, 1958.

Jones, D. R. *Jeremiah.* NCB. London: Pickering, 1992.

Jones, G. H. *1 and 2 Kings.* NCB. London: Marshall, Morgan & Scott, 1984.

Jonge, M. de. *Outside the Old Testament.* Cambridge: Cambridge University Press, 1985.

Jonnes, Cheslyn, et al., eds. *The Study of Spirituality.* Oxford: Oxford University Press, 1986.

Joo, Jae Yong. *A Theological History of Korean Christianity.* Seoul: Christian Literature Society of Korea, 1998.

Justinus. *Historiae Philippicae.* In *Justin Cornelius and Eutropius*, translated by J. S. Watson. London: Bell, 1902.

Kang, Keun Whan. "Theological Trends Developed through the Historical Stream of the Protestant Church in Korea." *Korea Journal of Christian Studies* 22 (2001) 143–71.

Käsemann, Ernst. *New Testament Questions.* Translated by W. I. Montague. New Testament Library. London: SCM, 1969.

Kasser, R. "Bibliothèque gnostique V: Apocalypse d'Adam." *RTP* 17 (1967) 316–33.

Katan, D. *Translating Cultures: An Introduction for Translators, Interpreters and Mediators.* Manchester: St. Jerome, 1999.

Katz, Steven T. "Issues in the Separation of Judaism and Christianity after 70 CE: A Reconsideration." *JBL* 103 (1984) 43–76.

Kee, Howard C. *Christian Origins in Social Perspective.* London: SCM, 1980.

Kelber, Werner H. *The Kingdom in Mark.* Philadelphia: Fortress, 1974.

———. *The Oral and the Written Gospel: The Hermeneutics of Speaking and Writing in the Synoptic Tradition, Mark, Paul, and Q.* Philadelphia: Fortress, 1977; 2nd ed., 1983.

———, ed. *The Passion in Mark: Studies on Mark 14–16.* Philadelphia: Fortress, 1976.

Keresztes, Paul. *Imperial Rome and the Christians: From Herod the Great to about 200 AD.* Vol. 1. Lanham: University of America, 1989.

———. *Imperial Rome and the Christians: From the Severi to Constantine the Great.* Vol. 2. Lanham: University of America, 1989.

Kilian, Rudolf. *Literakritische und formgechichtliche Untersuchung des Heiligkeitsgesetzes.* Bonn: Hansten, 1963.

Kilmartin, Edward J. "The Eucharistic Prayer: Content and Function of Some Early Eucharistic Prayers." In *The Word in the World*, edited by Richard J. Clifford and George W. MacRae. Cambridge, MA: Weston College Press, 1973.

———. "Sacrificium Laudis: Content and function of Early Eucharistic Prayers." *Theological Studies* 35 (1974) 268–87.

Kilpatrick, George Dunbar. *The Origins of the Gospel according to St. Matthew.* Oxford: Westminster, 1946.

Kim, Chang Rak. "The Kingdom of God: A History of Its Origin and Interpretation." In *The Kingdom of God: Its Interpretation and Practice.* Seoul: Korea Theological Study Institution, 2000.

Kim, Deuk Joong. "New Testament Studies in 1970s." *Theological Thought* 36 (1982) 37–57.

Kim, Kwang Soo. "The Social Cultural Background of Jesus' Healing Ministry." *Gospel and Practice* 27 (2000) 35–64.

———. "A Social Political Understanding of Jesus' Demoniac Exorcism Ministry." *Bible and Theology* 23 (1988) 15–84.

Kim, Myng Yong. *Ohn Theology.* Seoul: PCTS, 2015.

Kim, Myung Soo. *Christianity and Postmodernism.* Seoul: Christian Literature Society of Korea, 2000.

Kim, Yong Dong. *Theology Activating Church.* Seoul: PCTS, 2003.

Kim, Yong Ok. "Several Tries toward Korean Theological Formation." *Christian Thought* 15 (1971) 110–20.

———. "A Sum-Up of Korean Theology: Today and Tomorrow in Korean Theology." *Theological Thought* 1 (1973) 61–67.

———. "World Church and Korean Church." *Christian Thought* 15 (1971) 68–71.

Kimbrough, S. T., Jr. "The Concept of Sabbath at Qumran." *Revue de Qumran* 5 (1966) 483–502.

King, Karen L. *What Is Gnosticism?* Cambridge: Harvard University Press, 2003.

King, M. A. "Notes on the Bodmer Manuscript of Luke." *Bibliotheca Sacra* 122 (1965) 234–40.

Kingsbury, Jack Dean. "The Composition and Christology of Matt 28:16–20." *JBL* 93 (1974) 573–84.

Kitchen, K. A. "Basic Literary Forms and Firmulations of Ancient Instructional Writings in Egypt and Western Asia." In *Studien zu Altägyptischen Lebenslehren*, edited by Erik Hornung and Othmar Keel, 235–82. Freiburg: Universitaets Verlag, 1979.

Klauser, Theodor, et al., eds. *Rellexikon für Antike und Christentum: Sachwörtebuch zur Auseinandersetzung des Christentums mit der antiken Welt*. 16 vols. and supplement. Stuttgart: Hiersemann, 1950–1994.

Klijn, A. F. J. *The Acts of Thomas*. Leiden: Brill, 1962.

———. *Seth in Jewish, Christian and Gnostic Literature*. Leiden: Brill, 1977.

Klijn, A. F. J., and G. J. Reinink. *Patristic Evidence for Jewish-Christian Sects*. Novum Testamentum Supplement 36. Leiden: Brill, 1973.

Kline, M. G. *The Structure of Biblical Authority*. Grand Rapids: Eerdmans, 1972.

Klinghardt, Matthias. *Gesetz und Volk Gottes*. Wissenschaftliche Untersuchungen zum Neuen Testament 2/32. Tübingen: Mohr, 1989.

Kloppenborg, John S. *The Formation of Q: Trajectories in Ancient Wisdom Collections*. Philadelphia: Fortress, 1987.

———. "Nomos and Ethos in Q." In *Gospel Origins & Christian Beginnings: In Honor of James M. Robinson*, edited by James E. Goehring et al., 35–48. Sonoma, CA: Polebridge, 1990.

———. *Q Parallels*. Sonoma, CA: Polebridge, 1988.

———. *Q-Thomas Reader*. Sonoma, CA: Polebridge, 1990.

Kloppenborg Verbin, John S. *Excavating Q: The History and Setting of the Sayings Gospel*. Minneapolis: Fortress, 2000.

Klostermann, Erich. *Das Lukasevangelium*. Handbuch zum Neuen Testament 5. Tübingen: Mohr Siebeck, 1929.

Klumbies, Paul-Gerhard. "Die Sabbatheilungen Jesu nach Markus und Lukas." In *Jesu Rede von Gott und ihre Nachgeschichte im frühen Christentum: Beiträge zur Verkündigung Jesu und zum Kerygma der Kirche*, edited by Dietrich-Alex Koch et al., 165–78. Gütersloh: Gütersloherhaus, 1989.

Koester, Helmut. *Ancient Christian Gospels: Their History and Development*. Philadelphia: Trinity International, 1992.

———. "Gnomai Diaphoroi: The Origin and Nature of Diversification in the History of Early Christianity." *Harvard Theological Review* 58 (1965) 279–318. Reprinted in *Trajectories through Early Christianity*, edited by James M. Robinson and Helmut Koester, 114–57. Philadelphia: Fortress, 1971.

———. "An Intellectual Biography of James M. Robinson: Speech at the Occasion of His Retirement." In *From Quest to Q: Festschrift James M. Robinson*, edited by Jon Ma Asgeisson et al. Leuven: Leuven University Press, 2000.

Kosch, David. *Die eschatologische Tora des Menschensohnes: Untersuchungen zur Rezeption der Stellung Jesu zur Tora in Q*. Göttingen: Vandenhoeck & Ruprecht, 1989.

Kraft, Robert A. "Ezra's Materials in Judaism and Christianity." *Aufstieg und Niedergang der Römischen Welt* 2.19.1 (1979) 119–36.

---. "Some Notes on Sabbath Observance in Early Christianity." *Andrews University Seminary Studies* 3 (1965) 18-33.
Kraft, Robert A., and George W. E. Nickelsburg, eds. *Early Judaism and Its Modern Interpreters*. The Bible and Its Modern Interpreters. Philadelphia: Fortress, 1986.
Kremer, Jacob. *Lukasevangelium*. Die Neue Echter Bibel 3. Würzburg: Echter, 1988.
Kruijf, T. de. "Go Therefore and Make Disciples of All Nations." *Bijdragen* 54 (1993) 19-29.
Kümmel, Werner Georg. *Introduction to the New Testament*. Nashville: Abingdon, 1973.
---. "Jesus und der jüdische Traditionsgedanke." In *Heilsgeschehen und Geschichte*, 15-35. Marburg: Elwert, 1965.
Küng, Hans, and David Tracy, eds. *Das Neue Paradigma von Theologie*. English translation by M. Köhl, *Paradigm Change in Theology*. New York: Crossroad, 1984, 1989.
Kuthirakkattel, Scaria. *The Beginning of Jesus' Ministry according to Mark's Gospel (1,14—3,6): A Redaction Critical Study*. Analecta biblica 123. Rome: Editrice Ponticicio Istituto Biblico, 1990.
Kutsch, Ernst. "Sabbat." In *Die Religion in Geschichte und Gegenwart*, vol. 5, edited by Kurt Galling, 1258-60. Tübingen: Mohr, 1958.
Labahn, Michael, and Andreas Schmidt, eds. *Jesus, Mark and Q: The Teaching of Jesus and Its Earliest Records*. JSNT Supplement Series 214. Sheffield: Sheffield Academic, 2001.
Lacey, D. R. de. "The Sabbath/Sunday Question and the Law in the Pauline Corpus." In Carson, *From Sabbath to Lord's Day*, 159-95.
Lagrange, Marie-Joseph. *Évangile selon saint Luc*. Etudes bibliques. Paris: Librairie Lecoffre, 1941.
Lake, Kirsopp, ed. *Apostolic Fathers*. 2 vols. Loeb Series. London: Heinemann, 1912-1913.
Lampe, Peter. *Die stadtrömischen Christen in den ersten beiden Jahrhunderten: Untersuchungen zur Sozialgeschichte*. English translation by M. Steinahuser and M. D. Johnson, *From Paul to Vallentinus: Christians at Rome in the First Two Centuries*. Minneapolis: Fortress, 2003.
Lategan, B. C. "Structural Interrelations in Matthew 11-12." *Neotestamentica* 11 (1977) 115-29.
Laufen, Rudolf. *Die Doppelüberlieferung der Logienquelle und des Markusevangeliums*. Bonner biblische Beiträge 54. Bonn: Hanstein, 1980.
LaVerdiere, Eugene, and W. G. Thompson. "New Testament Communities in Transition: A Study of Matthew and Luke." *Theological Studies* 37 (1976) 567-97.
Layton, Bentley. *The Gnostic Scriptures: A New Translation*. Garden City: Doubleday, 1987.
Leitch, James W. "Lord also of the Sabbath." *Scottish Journal of Theology* 19 (1966) 426-33.
Leivestad, Ragnar. "Exit the Apocalyptic Son of Man." *NTS* 18 (1971-1972) 234-67.
---. *Jesus in His Own Perspective: An Examination of His Sayings, Actions, and Eschatological Titles*. Minneapolis: Augsburg, 1987.
Lennart, Persson. "The Gentile Mission in the Markan Interpolation (Mark 7:1—8:26)." *Bangalore Theological Forum* 12 (1980) 44-49.
Leslie, Elmer A. *Jeremiah: Chronologically Arranged, Translated, and Interpreted*. Nashville: Abingdon, 1953.
Levine, Amy-Jill. *The Social and Ethnic Dimensions of Matthew's Salvation History: "Go Nowhere among the Gentiles . . ." (Matt. 10:5b)*. Lampeter: Mellen, 1988.
Levine, Etan. "The Sabbath Controversy according to Matthew." *NTS* 22 (1976) 480-83.
Lhee, Jong Song. *Lhee Jong Sung's Great Works*. 40 vols. Seoul: Korea Institute of Advanced Christian Studies, 2001.

Liese, H. "Dominus ad cenam invitatus die Sabbati." *Verbum Domini* 11 (1931) 257–61.
Lieu, Judith M. *Christian Identity in the Jewish and Graeco-Roman World*. Oxford: Oxford University Press, 2004.
Lincoln, A. T. "From Sabbath to Lord's Day: A Biblical and Theological Perspective." In Carson, *From Sabbath to Lord's Day*, 343–412.
———. "Sabbath, Rest, and Eschatology in the New Testament." In Carson, *From Sabbath to Lord's Day*, 197–220.
Lindemann, A. "Der Sabbat ist um des Menschen willen geworden . . ." *Wort und Dienst* 15 (1979) 79–105.
Lipmann, Eugene J. *The Mishnah: Oral Teaching of Judaism*. New York: Norton, 1970.
Loader, William R. G. *Jesus' Attitude towards the Law: A Study of Gospels*. Tübingen: Mohr Siebeck, 1997.
Logan, Alastair H. B. *Gnostic Truth and Christian Heresy: A Study in the History of Gnosticism*. Peabody: Hendrickson, 1996.
Lohmeyer, Ernst. "'Mir ist gegeben alle Gewalt!': Eine Exegese von Mt. 28, 16–20." In *In Memoriam Ernst Lohmeyer*, edited by Werner Schmauch, 22–54. Stuttgart: Evangelischesswerk, 1951.
Lohse, Eduard. *Die Texte aus Qumran*. Munich: Kosel, 1964.
———. "Jesu Worte über den Sabbat." In *Judentum, Urchristentum, Kirche: Festschrift für Joachim Jeremias*, edited by Walther Eltester, 79–89. Berlin: Töpelmann, 1960.
———. "*Sabbaton*." In *Theological Dictionary of the New Testament*, translated and edited by Geoffrey W. Bromiley, 7:1–35. Grand Rapids: Eerdmans, 1964, 1971.
Loisy, Alfred Firmin. *Les évangiles synoptiques*. 2 vols. Ceffonds: Près Monteier-en-Der, 1908.
———. *L'Évangile selon Luc*. Paris: Nourry, 1924.
Long, O. *The Problem of Etiological Narrative in the Old Testament*. BZAW 108. Berlin: de Gruyter, 1968.
Ludemann, Gerd. *The Successors of Pre-70 Jerusalem Christianity*. Philadelphia: Fortress, 1980.
Lührmann, Dieter. *Die Redaktion der Logienquelle*. Wissenschaftliche Monographien zum Alten und Neuen Testament 33. Neukirchen-Vluyn: Neukirchener, 1969.
———. "Liebet euer Feinde (Lk 6:27–36 / Mt 5:39–48)." *Zeitschrift für Thelogie und Kirche* 69 (1972) 412–38.
Luz, Ulrich. *Mt 1–7*. Vol. 1 of *Das Evangelium nach Matthäus*. Zürich: Benzinger, 1985. English translation by Wilhelm C. Linss, *Matthew 1–7*. Minneapolis: Augsburg, 1989.
———. *Mt 8–17*. Vol. 2 of *Das Evangelium nach Matthäus*. Zürich: Benzinger, 1990.
Maccoby, Hyam. *Early Rabbinic Writings*. Cambridge: Cambridge University Press, 1988.
MacDonald, Dennis R. "Alternative Q, the Sinful Woman, and the Son of Man." *Journal of Q Studies* 2 (2013) 62–77.
MacGregor, G. *Gnosis: A Renaissance in Christian Thought*. Wheaton, IL: Theosophical, 1979.
Mack, Burton L. "The Christ and Jewish Wisdom." In *The Messiah: Developments in Earliest Judaism and Christianity*, 192–22. Minneapolis: Fortress, 1987.
———. "Elaboration of the Chreia in the Hellenistic School." In *Patterns of Persuasion in the Gospels*, 31–67. Sonoma: Polebridge, 1989.
———. *A Myth of Innocence: Mark and Christian Origins*. Philadelphia: Fortress, 1988.
———. *Rhetoric and the New Testament*. Minneapolis: Fortress, 1990.

———. "Wisdom Makes a Difference: Alternatives to 'Messianic' Configurations." In *Judaisms and Their Messiahs at the Turn of the Christian Era*, edited by Jacob Neusner et al., 15–48. Cambridge: Cambridge University Press, 1987.

Mack, Burton L., and Vernon K. Robbins. *Patterns of Persuasion in the Gospels*. Sonoma, CA: Polebridge, 1989.

Mack, Burton L., et al. "Wisdom Literature." In *Early Judaism and Its Modern Interpreters*, edited by R. A. Kraft and G. W. E. Nickelsburg, 371–410. Philadelphia: Fortress, 1986.

MacMullen, Ramsay. *Changes in the Roman Empire: Essays in the Ordinary*. Princeton: Princeton University Press, 1990.

———. *Christianizing the Roman Empire: AD 100–400*. New Haven: Yale University Press, 1984.

———. *Paganism in the Roman Empire*. New Haven: Yale University Press, 1981.

MacRae, George E. "Coptic Gnostic Apocalypse." *HeyJ* 6 (1965) 27–35.

MacRae, George W. "The Apocalypse of Adam (V, 5:64,1–85,32)." In *Nag Hammadi Codices*, edited by Douglas M. Parrott. Leiden: Brill, 1979.

Manson, Thomas W. "Mark 2,27–28." In *Coniectanea neotestamentica*, 11:138–46. Lund: Gleerup, 1947.

———. *The Sayings of Jesus as Recorded in the Gospels according to St. Matthew and St. Luke Arranged with Introduction and Commentary*. London: SCM, 1957.

———. *The Servant-Messiah*. Cambridge: Cambridge University Press, 1956.

———. *The Teaching of Jesus: Studies of Its Form and Content*. Cambridge: Cambridge University Press, 1935.

Manson, W. "Mission and Eschatology." *International Review of Missions* 42 (1953) 390–97.

Marcus, Ralph. *Law in the Apocrypha*. Columbia University Oriental Studies 26. New York: Columbia University Press, 1927.

Markschies, Christoph. *Die Gnosis*. English translation by John Bowden, *Gnosis: An Introduction*. New York: T. & T. Clark, 2003.

Marshall, I. Howard. *The Gospel of Luke: A Commentary on the Greek Text*. New International Greek Testament Commentary. Grand Rapids: Paternoster, 1978.

Martin, Luther H. "Genealogy and Sociology in the Apocalypse of Adam." In *Gnoticism & the Early Christianity World: In Honor of James M. Robinson*, edited by James F. Goehring et al., 25–36. Sonoma: Fortress, 1990.

———. *Hellenistic Religions: An Introduction*. Oxford: Oxford University Press, 1987.

Martinez, F. G., ed. *The Dead Sea Scrolls Translated: The Qumran Texts in English*. Leiden: Brill, 1992.

Marxsen, Willi. *The Lord's Supper as a Christological Problem*. Philadelphia: Fortress, 1970.

März, C. P. "Zur Q-Rezeption in Lk 12,35—13,35 (14,1–24): Die Q-Hypothese und ihre Bedeutung für die Interpretation des Lukanischen Reiseberichtes." In *The Synoptic Gospels: Source Criticism and the Literary Criticism*, edited by Camille Focant, 177–208. Leuven: Leuven University Press, 1993.

Massaux, Édouard. *Influence de l'évangile de saint Matthieu sur la littérature chrétienne avant saint Irénée*. English translation by Norman Belval and Suzanne Hecht, *The Influence of the Gospel of Saint Matthew on Christian Literature before Saint Iranaeus*. New Gospel Studies 5. 3 vols. Macon: Mercer University Press, 1950–1985, 1990–1993.

Matthey, Jacques. "The Great Commission according to Matthew." *International Review of Missions* 69 (1980) 160–73.

Mattill, A. J., Jr. *Luke and the Last Things: A Perspective for the Understanding of Lukan Thought*. Dillsboro: Western North Carolina Press, 1979.

Mays, J. L. *Amos*. OTL. London: SCM, 1969.

McCarthy, D. J. *Old Testament Covenant*. Oxford: Blackwell, 1972.

McConnell, R. S. *Law and Prophesy in Matthew's Gospel: The Authority and Use of the Old Testament in the Gospel of St. Matthew*. Basel: Kommissionsverlag, 1969.

McKane, William. *A Critical and Exegetical Commentary on Jeremiah*. ICC 1. Edinburgh: T. & T. Clark, 1986.

McKay, Heather A. *Sabbath and Synagogue: The Question of Sabbath Worship in Ancient Judaism*. Religions in the Graeco-Roman World 122. Leiden: Brill, 1994.

Meeks, Wayne A. "Breaking Away: There New Testament Pictures of Christianity's Separation from the Jewish Communities." In *To See Ourselves as Others See Us: Christians, Jews, "Others" in Late Antiquity*, edited by Jacob Neusner and Ernest S. Freichs. Chico: Scholars, 1985.

Meier, John P. *A Marginal Jew: Rethinking the Historical Jesus*. New York: Doubleday, 1991.

———. "Nations or Gentiles in Matthew 28.19?" *Catholic Biblical Quaterly* 39 (1977) 94–102.

———. "Salvation-History in Matthew: In Search of a Starting Point." *Catholic Biblical Quaterly* 37 (1975) 203–15.

———. "Two Disputed Questions in Matt 28:16–20." *JBL* 96 (1977) 407–24.

Meinhold, J. *Sabbat und Sonntag*. Leipzig: Quelle & Meyer, 1909.

Mendelson, Alan. *Philo's Jewish Identity*. Atlanta: Scholars, 1988.

Merk, Otto Biblische. *Theologie des Neuen Testaments in ihrer Anfangszeit: Ihre methodischen Probleme bei Johann Philipp Gabler und Georg Lorenz Bauer und deren Nachwirkungen*. Marburger tehologische Studien 9. Marburg: Elwert, 1972.

Metz, Johann Baptist. *Die Theologie der Befreiung: Hoffnung Oder Gefähr für die Kirche?* Düsseldorf: Patmos, 1986.

Meyer, Ben F. *The Early Christians: Their World Mission and Self-Discovery*. Wilmington, DE: Glazier, 1986.

Meyer, Marvin. "The Gospel of Thomas." In *The Gnostic Bible*, edited by Willis Barnstone and Marvin Meyer. Boston: New Seeds, 2006.

Meyer, Paul D. "The Community of Q." PhD diss., University of Iowa, 1967.

———. "The Gentile Mission in Q." *JBL* 89 (1970) 405–17.

Michael, J. H. "The Jewish Sabbath in the Latin Classical Writers." *AJSL* 40 (1924) 120.

Michaelis, Wilhelm. *Das Evangelium nach Matthäus*. Zürich: Zwingli, 1949.

Millgram, Abraham E. *Sabbath: The Day of Delight*. Philadelphia: Jewish Publishing Society of America, 1944.

Moo, Douglas J. "Jesus and the Authority of the Mosaic Law." *JSNT* 20 (1984) 3–49. Reprinted in *The Historical Jesus: A Sheffield Reader*, edited by C. A. Evans and S. E. Porter, 83–130. Sheffield: Sheffield Academic, 1984.

Moore, George Foot. *Judaism in the First Centuries of the Christian Era: The Age of the Tannaim*. 3 vols. Cambridge: Harvard University Press, 1927–1930. Repr., Peabody: Hendrickson, 1997.

Morris, Henry M., ed. *Scientific Creationism*. Green Forest, AR: Master, 1974, 1985, 2000.

Mowinckel, S. *Zur Komposition des Buches Jeremia*. Kristiania: Dybwad, 1914.

Muilenburg, James. "Introduction and Exegesis to Isaiah 40–66." In *The Interpreter's Bible*, vol. 5, edited by George A. Burttrick, 381–773. New York: Abingdon, 1956.

Mulder, Martin Jan, ed. *Mikra: Text, Translation, Reading and Interpretation of the Hebrew Bible in Ancient Judaism and Early Christianity*. Philadelphia: Fortress, 1988.

Müller, G. H. *Zur Synopse: Untersuchung über die Arbeitsweise des Lk und Mt und ihre Quellen*. Forschungen zur Religion und Literatur des Alten und Neuen Testaments 11. Göttingen: Vandenhoeck & Ruprecht, 1908.

Munck, Johannes. "Israel and the Gentiles in the New Testament." *Studiorum Novi Testamenti Societas Bulletin* 1 (1950) 26–38.

———. *Paulus und die Heilsgeschichte*. English translation by Frank Clarke, *Paul and the Salvation of Mankind*. Richmond: John Knox, 1954, 1959.

Murray, Michele. *Playing a Jewish Game: Gentile Christian Judaizing in the First and Second Centuries CE*. Studies in Christianity and Judaism 13. Waterloo: Wilfrid Laurier University Press, 2004.

Neirynck, Frans. "Jesus and the Sabbath: Some Observations on Mark 2,27." In *Jésus aux origines de la christologie*, edited by Jacques Dupont, 227–70. Leuven: Leuven University Press, 1975.

———. "Luke 14,1–6: Lukan Composition and Q-Saying." In *Der Treue Gottes trauen: Beiträge zum Werk des Lukas: FS für Gerhard Schneider*, edited by Claus Bussmann and Walter Radl, 243–63. Wien: Herder, 1991.

———. *The Minor Agreements of Matthew and Luke against Mark with a Cumulative List*. Leuven: Leuven University Press, 1974.

———. *Q-Synopsis: The Double Tradition Passages in Greek*. Leuven: Leuven University Press, 1988.

———. "Recent Developments in the Study of Q." In *Logia: The Sayings of Jesus*, edited by Joel Delobel, 29–75. Bibliotheca Ephemeridum Theologicarum Lovaniensium. Leuven: Leuven University Press, 1982.

Neusner, Jacob. *Ancient Judaism and Modern Category-Formation: "Judaism," "Midrash," "Messianism," and Canon in the Past Quarter-Century*. Lanham: University of America, 1986.

———. "'First Cleanse the Inside': Halakhic Background of a Controversy Saying." *New Testament Studies* 22 (1976) 486–95.

———. *Judaism: The Evidence of the Mishnah*. Chicago: University of Chicago Press, 1981.

———. *The Mishnah: A New Translation*. New Haven: Yale University Press, 1988.

———. *The Rabbinic Traditions about the Pharisees before 70*. 3 vols. Leiden: Brill, 1971.

Neusner, Jacob., et al., eds. *The Tosefta*. 6 vols. New York: KTAV, 1977–1986.

Neyrey, Jerome H. "The Thematic Use of Isaiah 42.1–4 in Matthew 12." *Biblica* 63 (1982) 457–73.

Nickelsburg, George W. E. *Jewish Literature between the Bible and the Messiah*. Philadelphia: Fortress, 1981.

Nida, E., and C. Taber. *The Theory and Practice of Translation*. Leiden: Brill, 1969.

Nock, Arthur Darby. *Conversion: The Old and the New in Religion from Alexander the Great to Augustine of Hippo*. Oxford: Oxford University Press, 1933.

———. *Early Gentile Christianity and Its Hellenictic Background*. London: Longmans Green, 1928. Repr., New York: Harper & Row, 1964.

North, R. "The Derivation of Sabbath." *Biblica* 36 (1955) 182–201.

Noth, M. *Exodus*. OTL. London: SCM, 1962.

———. *Numbers*. OTL. London: SCM, 1968.

Novak, Ralph Martin. *Christianity and the Roman Empire: Background Texts*. Harrisburg: Trinity International, 2001.

O'Leary, De Lacy. *The Syriac Church and Fathers*. London: Society for Promoting Christian Knowledge, 1909. Repr., Piscataway: Gorgias, 2002.

Oseik, Carolyn. *Rich and Poor in the Shepherd of Hermas: An Exegetical-Social Investigation*. Washington, DC: Catholic Biblical Association of America, 1983.

O'Toole, Robert F. "Some Exegetical Reflections on Luke 13,10–17." *Biblica* 73 (1992) 84–107.

Overmann, J. Andrew. *Matthew's Gospel and Formative Judaism: The Social World of the Matthean Community*. Minneapolis: Fortress, 1990.

Park, Soo Am. "Retrospect and Prospect on Korean New Testament Studies of the Twentieth Century." *Korea Journal of Christian Studies* 22 (2001) 119–42.

———. "Yesterday, Today, and Tomorrow of the Biblical Studies of Presbyterian College and Theological Seminary." *Church and Theology* 40 (2001) 41.

Parrott, D. *Nag Hammadi Codices V, 2–5 and VI with Papyrus Berolinensis 8502, 1 and 4*. Nag Hammadi Studies 11. Leiden: Brill, 1979.

Patterson, Stephen J. *The God of Jesus: The Historical Jesus & the Search for Meaning*. Harrisburg: Trinity International, 1998.

———. *The Gospel of Thomas and Jesus*. Sonoma: Polebridge, 1993.

Patton, Carl S. *Sources of the Synoptic Gospels*. London: Macmillan, 1915.

Pearson, Birger A. "Egyptian Seth and Gnostic Seth." In *1977 Seminar Papers*, edited by Paul J. Achtemeier, 25–44. Society of Biblical Literature. Missoula: Scholars: 1977.

———. *The Future of Early Christianity: Essays in Honor of Helmut Koester*. Minneapolis: Fortress, 1991.

Percy, E. *Die Botschaft Jesu: Eine traditionaskritische und exegetische Untersuchhung*. Lunds Universitets Arsskrift 49/5. Lund, 1953.

Perdue, L. G. "The Wisdom Sayings of Jesus." *Forum* 2 (1986) 3–35.

Perkins, P. *Gnosticism and the New Testament*. Minneapolis: Fortress, 1993.

Perrin, Norman. *Jesus and the Language of the Kingdom: Symbol and Metaphor in New Testament Interpretation*. Philadelphia: Fortress, 1976.

———. *Rediscovering the Teaching of Jesus*. New York: Harper & Row, 1976.

Pétrement, Simone. *Le Dieu séparé: les origines du Gnosticisme*. English translation by Carol Harrison, *A Separate God: The Christian Origins of Gnosticism*. San Francisco: HarperSanFrancisco, 1984.

Philo. *Philo*. 10 vols. Translated by Francis Henry Colson and G. H. Whitaker. London: Heinemann, 1929–1962.

Piper, Ronald Allen. *The Gospel behind the Gospels: Current Studies on Q*. Leiden: Brill, 1995.

———. *Wisdom in the Q-Tradition*. Monograph Series Society for the New Testament 61. Cambridge: Cambridge University Press, 1988.

Polag, Athanasius. *Die Christologie der Logienquelle*. Wissenschaftliche Monographien zum Alten und Neuen Testament 45. Neukirchen-Vluyn: Neukirchener, 1968.

———. *Fragmenta Q: Textheft zur Logienquelle*. Neukirchen-Vluyn: Neukirchner, 1979.

Porton, Gary G. *Goyim: Gentiles and Israelites in Mishnah-Tosefta*. Brown Judaic Studies 155. Atlanta: Scholars, 1988.

———. *The Stranger within Your Gates: Converts and Conversion in Rabbinic Literature*. Chicago: University of Chicago Press, 1994.

Quispel, Gilles. *Gnostic Studies I*. Istanbul: Nederlands Historisch-Archaeologisch Institute, 1974.

———. "The Gospel of Thomas Revisited." In *Collogue international sur les textes de Nag Hammadi*, edited by Bernard Barc, 218–66. Bibliothèque copte de Nag Hammadi Section Édudes 1. Louvain: Peeters, 1981.

Rabin, C. *The Zadokite Documents: I. The Admonition. II. The Law.* Edited, with a translation and notes. Oxford: Oxford University Press, 1958.

Reed, Jonathan L. "Places in Early Christianity: Galilee, Archaeology, Urbanization, and Q." PhD diss., Claremont Graduate University, 1994.

Reese, James M. *Hellenistic Influence on the Book of Wisdom and Its Consequence*. Rome: Biblical Institute, 1970.

Reitzenstein, Richard. *Hellenistic Mystery-Religions: Their Basic Ideas and Significance* [Die hellenistischen Mysterienreligionen nach ihren]. Translated by John E. Steely. PTMS 18. 1927. Repr., Pittsburgh: Pickwick, 1978.

———. *Poimandres: Studien zur Griechisch-ägyptischen und frühchristlichen Literatur*. Leizig: Druck, 1904.

Richard, Earl. "The Divine Purpose: The Jews and the Gentile Mission (Acts 15)." In *SBL Seminar Papers*, edited by Paul J. Achtemeier, 267–82. Chico: Scholars, 1980.

Richardson, Alan. *An Introduction to the Theology of the New Testament*. London: SCM, 1958.

Richardson, Cyril, et al., eds. and trans. *Early Christian Fathers*. New York: Macmillan, 1953.

Richter, Wolfgang. *Recht und Ethos: Versuch einer Ortung des weisheitlichen Mahnspruches*. Munich: Kösel, 1966.

Riesenfeld, Harold. *The Gospel Tradition*. Philadelphia: Fortress, 1970.

Riggs, John W. "From Gracious Table to Sacramental Element: The Tradition-History of Didache 9 and 10." *Second Century* 4 (1984) 83–101.

Riley, Gregory J. "Doubting Thomas: Controversy over the Resurrection in Early Christianity." PhD dissertation, Harvard University, 1992.

———. *One Jesus, Many Christs: How Jesus Inspired Not One True Christianity, but Many*. San Francisco: HarperCollins, 1997.

———. "Thomas Tradition and the *Acts of Thomas*." In *SBL Seminar Papers 30*, edited by Eugene Lovering, 533–42. Atlanta: Scholars, 1991.

Roberts, Alexander, et al., trans. *The Ante-Nicene Fathers*. 10 vols. Grand Rapids: Eerdmans, 1885–1887; repr., 1973.

Robinson, G. "The Idea of Rest in the Old Testament and the Search for the Basic Character of Sabbath." *Zeitschrift für die Alttestamentliche Wissenschaft* 92 (1980) 32–42.

Robinson, James M. "Building Blocks in the Social History of Q." In *Reimagining Christian Origins: A Colloquium Honoring Burton L. Mack*, edited by Elizabeth A. Castelli and Hal Taussig, 87–112. Valley Forge: Trinity International, 1996.

———. "Die Hodajot-Formel in Gebet und Hymnus des Frühchristentums." In *Apophoreta: Festschrift für Ernst Haenchen*, edited by W. Eltester, 194–235. BZNW 30. Berlin: Alfred Töpelmann, 1964.

———. "A Down-to-Earth Jesus." In *Jesus and His World: An Archaeological Cultural Dictionary*, John J. Rousseau, xiii–xviii. Minneapolis: Fortress, 1995.

———. *The Future of Our Religious Past: Essays in Honour of Rudolf Bultmann*. New York: Harper & Row, 1971.

———. *The Gospel of Jesus: A Historical Search for the Original Good News*. San Francisco: HarperSanFrancisco, 2005.

———. *Jesus according to the Earliest Witness*. Minneapolis: Fortress, 2007.

———. "Jesus as Sophos and Sophia: Wisdom Tradition and the Gospels." In *Aspects of Wisdom in Judaism and Early Christianity*, edited by Robert L. Wilken, 1–16. London: University of Notre Dame, 1975.

———. "The Jesus of Q." Claremont Graduate University, spring 1992.

———. "Jesus' Theology in the Sayings Gospel Q." In *Early Christian Writings Inside and Out: F. Bovon Festschrift*, edited by David H. Warren et al. Leiden: Brill, 2003.

———. "Judaism, Hellenism, and Christianity. Jesus' Followers in Galilee until 70 CE." In *Ebraismo Ellenismo Christianesimo*, edited by Mathieu Vittorio. Archivio di Filosofia. Padova: Cedam, 1985.

———. *Language, Hermeneutic, and History: Theology after Barth and Bultmann*. Eugene, OR: Cascade, 2008.

———. "Logoi Sophon: On the Gattung of Q." In *Zeit und Geschichte: Dankesgabe an Rudolf Bultmann zum 80 Geburstag*, edited by E. Dinkler, 77–96. Tübingen: Mohr, 1964. Reprint, *Trajectories through Early Christianity*, edited by James M. Robinson and Helmut Koester, 71–113. Philadelphia: Fortress, 1971.

———. "The Matthean Trajectory from Q to Mark." In *The Bible and Culture: Ancient and Modern Perspectives*, edited by Adela Yarbro Collins. Atlanta: Scholars, 1998.

———. *A New Quest of the Historical Jesus*. London: SCM, 1959.

———. "The Pre-Q Text of the (Ravens and) Lilies." *MThSt* 50 (1999) 143–80.

———. "The Q Trajectory: Between John and Matthew via Jesus." In *The Future of Early Christianity: Essays in Honor of Helmut Koester*, edited by Birger A. Pearson, 173–94. Minneapolis: Fortress, 1991.

———. "The Real Jesus of the Sayings Gospel Q." *Princeton Seminary Bulletin* 28 (1997) 135–51.

———. "The Sayings Gospel Q." In *The Four Gospels: Festschrift F. Neirynck*, vol. 1, edited by F. Van Segbroeck et al., 361–88. Leuven: Leuven University Press, 1992.

———. *The Sayings Gospel Q in Greek and English with Parallels from the Gospels of Mark and Thomas*. Minneapolis: Fortress, 2002.

———. "The Sayings of Jesus: Q." *Drew Gateway* 54 (1983) 26–38.

———. "The Sequence of Q: The Lament over Jerusalem." In *Von Jesus zum Christus: Christologische Studien Festgabe für Paul Hoffmann zum 65. Geburtstag*, edited by Rudolf Hoppe and Ulrich Bussee, 225–60. New York: de Gruyter, 1998.

———. "The Son of Man in the Sayings Gospel Q." In *Tradition und Translation*, edited by C. Elsas, 315–35. Berlin: de Gruyter, 1994.

———. "Theological Autobiography." In *The Sayings Gospel Q*, 3–24. Leuven: Leuven University Press, 2005.

———. "A Written Greek Sayings Cluster Older Than Q." *HTR* 92 (1999) 61–78.

Robinson, James M., and Christoph Heil. "Zeugnisse eines schriftlichen, griechischen vorkanonischen Textes. Mt 6,28b a*, P.Oxy. 655 I,1–17 (EvTh 36) und Q 12,27." In *ZNW* 89 (1998) 30–44.

Robinson, James M., et al. *The Critical Edition of Q: A Synopsis Including the Gospels of Matthew and Luke, Mark and Thomas with English, German and French Translation of Q and Thomas*. Minneapolis: Fortress, 2000.

Rordorf, Willy. *Der Sonntag: Geschichte der Ruhe-und Gottesdiensttages im ältesten Christentum*. Abhandlungen zur Theologie des Alten und Neuen Testaments 43. Zürich: Zwingli, 1962. English translation by A. A. K. Graham, *Sunday: The History of the Day of Rest and Worship in the Earliest Centuries of the Christian Church*. Philadelphia: Westminster, 1968.

———. *Sabbat und Sontag in der Alten Kirche*. Zürich: Theologischer, 1972.

Rosenthal, Judah. "The Sabbath Laws of the Qumranites or the Damascus Covenanters." *Biblical Research* 6 (1961) 10-17.

Rowland, C. "A Summary of Sabbath Observance in Judaism at the Beginning of the Christian Era." In Carson, *From Sabbath to Lord's Day*, 43-55.

Rudolph, K. *Gnosis: The Nature & History of Gnosticism*. San Francisco: HarperSanFrancisco, 1987.

Rudolph, W. *Jeremiah*. HAT. Tübingen: Mohr, 1958.

Rushdoony, R. J. *The Institutes of Biblical Law*. Nutley: Craig, 1973.

Safrai, S., and M. Stern, eds. *The Jewish People in the First Century: Historical Geography, Political History, Social, Cultural and Religious Life and Institutions*. 2 vols. Philadelphia: Fortress, 1974.

Saldarini, Anthony J. *Matthew's Christian-Jewish Community*. Chicago: University of Chicago Press, 1994.

———. *Pharisees, Scribes and Sadducees in Palestinian Society*. Edinburgh: T. & T. Clark, 1988.

Sand, Alexander. *Das Gesetz und die Propheten: Untersuchungen zur Theologie des Evangeliums nach Matthäus*. Biblische Untersuchungen 11. Regensburg: Friedrich Pustet, 1974.

Sanders, E. P., ed. *Jesus and Judaism*. London: SCM, 1985.

———. *Jewish and Christian Self-definition*. 3 vols. Philadelphia: Fortress, 1980-1981.

———. *Jewish Law from Jesus to the Mishnah: Five Gospels*. Philadelphia: Trinity International, 1990.

Sanders, Frank, and Charles F. Kent, eds. *Messages of the Bible*. Vol. 3 of *The Messages of Israel's Lawgivers*. New York: Scribner, 1902.

Sanders, Jack T. *The Jews in Luke-Acts*. London: SCM, 1987.

Sanders, James A. *Canon and Community: A Guide to Canonical Criticism*. Philadelphia: Fortress, 1984.

Satran, D. *Biblical Prophets in Byzantine Palestine: Reassessing the Lives of the Prophets*. SVTP 11. Leiden, 1995.

Sato, Migaku. *Q und Prophetie: Studien zur Gattungs-und Traditiongeshichte der Quelle Q*. Tübingen: Mohr Siebeck, 1988.

Sauer, Jürgen. "Traditionsgeschichtliche Überlegungen zu Mk 3,1-6." *Zeitschrift für die Neutestamentliche Wissenschaft* 73 (1982) 183-203.

Schaff, P., et al., trans. *The Nicene and Post-Nicene Fathers*. 28 vols. Grand Rapids: Eerdmans, 1886-1888; repr., 1956.

Scharvit, B. "The Sabbath of the Judean Desert Sect." *Immanuel* 9 (1979) 42-48.

Schenk, Wolfgang. *Die Sprache des Matthäus: Die Text-Konstituenten in ihren makro-und mikrostrukturellen Relationen*. Göttingen: Vandenhoeck & Ruprecht, 1987.

———. *Synopse zur Redenquelle der Evangelien: Q-Synopse und Rekonstruktion in deutscher Übersetzung mit kurzen Erläuterungen*. Düsseldorf: Patmos, 1981.

Schenke, Hans-Martin. "The Book of Thomas: Introduction." In *New Testament Apocrypha*, edited by W. Schneemelcher, 232-47. English translation edited by R. McL.Wilson. Lousville: James Clarke & Westminster John Knox, 1990.

Schlatter, Adolf. *Das Evangelium des Lukas*. Stuttgart: Calver, 1960.

Schmid, Josef. *Matthäus und Lukas: Eine Untersuchung des Verhältnisses ihrer Evangelien.* Biblische Studien 28. Freiburg: Herder & Herder, 1930.

Schmidt, Daryl. "The LXX *Gattung* 'Prophetic Correlative.'" *JBL* 96 (1977) 517–22.

Schmidt, Werner. *Die Schoepfungsgeschichte der Priesterschrift.* Neukirchener-Vlyun: Neukirchener, 1964.

Schmithals, Walter. *Das Evangelium nach Lukas.* Züricher Bibelkommentare. Neues Testament 3/1. Regensburg: Pustet, 1960.

———. *Einleitung in die drei ersten Evangelien.* Berlin: de Gruyter, 1985.

———. *Gnosticism in Corinth.* Translated by J. E. Steely. Nashville: Abingdon, 1971.

Schnackenburg, Rudolf. "Befreiung in der Blickweise Jesu und der Urkirche." In *Die Theologie der Befreiung: Hoffnung Oder Gefähr für die Kirche?*, edited by Johann Baptist Metz. Düsseldorf: Patmos, 1986.

———. "Der eschatologische Abschnitt Lk 17,29–37." In *Mélanges Bibliques*, edited by A. Descamps, 213–34. Gembloux: Duculot, 1970.

Schneemelcher, W., ed. *New Testament Apocrypha.* 2 vols. Louisville: Westminster John Knox, 1991.

Schneider, Gerhard. *Das Evangelium nach Lukas.* Vol. 2. Ökumenischer Taschenbuchkommentar zum Neuen Testament 3. Gütersloh: Gerd Mohn, 1977; 2nd ed., 1984.

Schniewind, Julius. *Das Evangelium nach Mattäus.* Das Neue Testament deutsch neues Göttinger Bibelwerk 2. Göttingen: Vandenhoeck & Ruprecht, 1956.

Schoeps, Hans Joachim. "Jésus et la loi juive." *Revue d'histoire et de philosophie religieuses* 33 (1953) 1–20.

Schottroff, Luise, and Wolfgang Stegmann. *Jesus and the Hope of the Poor.* Translated by Matthew J. O'Connell. New York: Orbis, 1986.

Schröter, Jens. "Vorsynoptische Überlieferung auf P. Oxy. 655? Kritische Bemerkungen zu einer erneuerten These." In *ZNW* 90 (1999) 265–72.

Schuepphaus, Joachim. *Die Psalmen Salomos.* Leiden: Brill, 1977.

Schulz, Siegfried. *Q: Die Spruchquelle der Evangelisten.* Zürich: Theologischer, 1972.

Schürer, Emil. *Geschichte des Jüdischen Volkes im Zeitalter Jesu Christ.* 4 vols. 4th ed. Leipzig, 1901–1911.

———. *The History of the Jewish People in the Age of Jesus Christ (175 BC–AD 135).* 3 vols. Revised and edited by Geza Vermes and Fergus Millar. Edinburgh: T. & T. Clark, 1973–1987.

———. *The Literature of the Jewish People in the Time of Jesus.* New York: Schocken, 1972.

Schürmann, E. *Das Lukasevangelium I.* Herders theologischer Kommentar zum NT 403–5. Freiburg: Herders, 1969.

Schürmann, Heinz. "Proto Lukanische Spracheigentümlichkeiten?" *Biblische Zeitschrift neue Folge* 5 (1961) 266–86. Reprinted in *Traditionsgeschichtliche Untersuchungen zu den synoptischen Evangelien*, 209–27. KBANT. Düsseldorf: Patmos, 1968.

———. "Sprachliche Reminiszenzen an abgeänderte oder ausgelassene Bestandteile der Spruchsammlung im Lukas-und Matthausevangelium." *NTS* 6 (1960) 193–210.

———. "Zur Kompositionsgeschichte der Redenquelle: Beobachtungen an der Lukanischen Q Vorlage." In *Der treue Gottes trauen: Beiträge zum Werk des Lukas; Festschrift G. Schneider*, edited by C. Bussmann and W. Radle, 325–42. Wien: Herder, 1991.

Schweitzer, Albert. *Von Reimarus zu Wrede: Eine Geschichte der Leben-Jesu-Forschung.* English translation by W. Montgomery, *The Quest of the Historical Jesus: A Critical Study of Its Progress from Reimarus to Wrede*. New York: Macmillan, 1906; repr., 1954; New York: Macmillan, 1968 (introduction by James M. Robinson); London: SCM, 1981.

Schweizer, Eduard. *Das Evangelium nach Lukas*. Göttingen: Vandenhoeck & Ruprecht, 1982.

———. *Das Evangelium nach Matthäus*. Göttingen: Vandenhoeck & Ruprecht, 1973; 4th ed., 1986. English translation by David E. Green, *The Good News according to Matthew*. Atlanta: John Knox, 1975.

———. "Matthäus 12.1–8: Der Sabbat—Gebot und Geschenk. Der Weg vom Text zur Predigt." *Glaube und Gerechtigkeit: Im Memoriam Rafael Gyllenberg*, edited by J. Kilunen, et al., 169–80. Helsinki: Schriften der Finnischen Exegetischen Gesellschaft, 1983.

———. "Observance of the Law and Charismatic Activity in Matthew." *NTS* 16 (1970) 213–30.

———. "The Significance of Eschatology in the Teaching of Jesus." In *Eschatology and the New Testament: Essays in Honor of George Raymond Beasley-Murray*, edited by W. Hulitt Gloer. Peabody: Hendrickson, 1988.

Seeley, David. "Futuristic Eschatology and Social Formation of Q." In *Reimagining Christian Origins: A Colloqium Honoring Burton L. Mack*, edited by Elizabeth A. Castelli and Hal Taussig, 144–53. Valley Forge: Trinity International, 1996.

Segal, Alan F. "Matthew's Jewish Voice." In *Social History of the Matthean Community*, edited by David Balch, 3–27. Minneapolis: Fortress, 1991.

Segundo, Juan Luis. *The Historical Jesus of the Synoptics*. Jesus of Nazareth Yesterday and Today 2. New York: Orbis, 1985.

Shea, W. H. "The Sabbath in the Epistle of Barnabas." *Andrews University Seminary Studies* 4 (1966) 149–75.

Sigal, Phillip. *The Halakah of Jesus of Nazareth according to the Gospel of Matthew*. Lanham: University of America, 1986.

Silberling, Kathryn J. "Text and Tradition in Matthew: A Case for Literary Stratigraphy in the Gospel of Matthew." PhD diss., Claremont Graduate University, 1997.

Simon, Ulrich. *Heaven in the Christian Tradition*. New York: Harper, 1958.

Smart, J. D. *History and Theology in Second Isaiah: A Commentary on Isaiah 35, 40–66*. London: Epworth, 1967.

Smith, Jonathan Z. "The Garment of Shame." *History of Religion* 5 (1966) 217–38.

Snodgrass, K. "Matthew and the Law." In *Treasures New and Old*, edited by David R. Bauer et al., 99–127. Atlanta: Scholars, 1996.

———. "Matthew's Understanding of the Law." *Interpretation* 46 (1992) 368–78.

So, Ky-Chun. "A Hermeneutical Understanding of Biblical Language: On the Focus of Ernst Fuchs and Gerhard Ebeling." MDiv project paper, Presbyterian University and Theological Seminary, 1985.

———. *An Introduction to the Sayings Gospel Q*. Seoul: Christian Literature Society of Korea, 2004.

———. "*Language, Hermeneutic, and History: Theology after Barth and Bultmann.* By James M. Robinson. Eugene, OR: Cascade." *Horizons in Biblical Theology* 31 (2008) 12–14.

———. "Recent Trends in the Study of the Historical Jesus in Korea." In *The Historical Jesus around the World*, edited by Chrystian Boyer, 99–127. Montreal: FIDES, 2009.

———. "Religion and Science: 4 Different Ways to Solve Its Relationship." *Journal of Asian and Asian American Theology* 11 (2013) 118–39.

———. "The Sabbath Controversy of Jesus: Between Jewish Law and the Gentile Mission." PhD diss., Claremont Graduate University, 1998.

———. *Trajectories through the Sayings of Jesus.* Seoul: Christian Literature Society of Korea, 2000.
So, Ky-Chun, et al. *New Testament Introduction: A Recent Study for Koreans.* Seoul: Christian Literature Society of Korea, 2002.
Sparks, H. F. D., ed. *The Apocryphal Old Testament.* Oxford: Oxford University Press, 1984.
Spier, E. *Der Sabbat.* Das Judentum 1. Berlin: Institut Kirche und Judentum, 1992.
Stanton, Graham N. "Aspects of Early Christian-Jewish Polemic and Apologetic." *NTS* 31 (1985) 377–92.
———. "The Communities of Matthew." *Interpretation* 66 (1992) 379–91.
———. "5 Ezra and Matthean Christianity in the Second Century." *JTS* 28 (1977) 67–83.
———. *A Gospel for a New People: Studies in Matthew.* Louisville: Westminster John Knox, 1992.
———. *The Gospels and Jesus.* Oxford Bible Series. Oxford: Oxford University Press, 1989.
———. *The Interpretation of Matthew.* Edinburgh: T. & T. Clark, 1983; 2nd ed., 1995.
———. *Jesus and Gospel.* Cambridge: Cambridge University Press, 2004.
Steck, Odil Hannes. *Israel und das gewaltsame Geschick der Propheten: Untersuchungen zur Überlieferung des deuteronomistischen Geschichtsbildes im Alten Testament, Spätjudentum und Urchristentum.* Wissenschaftliche Monographien zum Alten und Neuen Testament 23. Neukirchen-Vluyn: Neukirchener, 1967.
Steinhauser, Michael. *Doppelbildworte in den synoptischen Evangelien.* FB 44. Würzburg: Echter, 1981.
Stendahl, Krister. *The School of St. Matthew and Its Use of the Old Testament.* Ramsey: Sigler, 1968, 1990.
Stephenson, T. "The Overlapping of Sources in Matthew and Luke." *JTS* 21 (1920) 127–45.
Stern, Menahem, ed. and trans. *Greek and Latin Authors on Jews and Jerusalem.* 3 vols. Jerusalem: Israel Academy of Sciences and Humanities, 1974–1984.
Stern, Sacha. *Jewish Identity in Early Rabbinic Writings.* Arbeiten zur Geschichte des antiken Judentums und des Urchristentums 23. Leiden: Brill, 1994.
Stone, Michael E., ed. *Jewish Writings of the Second Temple Period: Apocrypha, Pseudepigrapha, Qumran Sectarian Writings, Philo, Josephus.* Philadelphia: Fortress, 1984.
Stone, Michael E., and David Safran, eds. *Emerging Judaism: Studies on the Fourth & Third Centuries BCE.* Minneapolis: Fortress, 1989.
Strack, H. L., and P. Billerbeck. *Das Evangelium nach Markus, Lukas und Johannes und die Apostelgeschichte.* Kommentar zum Neuen Testament aus Talmud und Midrasch 2. München: Beck'sche, 1924.
———. *Das Evangelium nach Matthäus.* Kommentar zum Neuen Testament aus Talmud und Midrasch 1. München: Beck'sche, 1922.
Strack, H. L., and G. Stemberger. *Introduction to the Talmud and Midrash.* Translated by M. N. A. Bockmuehl. Edinburgh: T. & T. Clark, 1991.
Strand, K. A. "Some Notes on the Sabbath Fast in Early Christianity." *Andrews University Seminary Studies* 3 (1965) 167–74.
Strecker, Georg. *Der Weg der Gerechtigkeit: Untersuchung zur Theologie des Matthäus.* Forschungen zur Religion und Literatur des Alten und Neuen Testaments 82. Göttingen: Vandenhoeck & Ruprecht, 1971.
Streeter, Burnet Hillmann. *The Four Gospels: A Study of Origins Treating of the Manuscript Tradition, Sources, Authorship, & Dates.* London: Macmillan, 1924; repr., 1951.

———. "The Original Extent of Q." In *Oxford Studies in the Synoptic Problem*, 185–208. Oxford: Westminster, 1911.
Stroker, William D. *Extracanonical Sayings of Jesus*. Atlanta: Scholars, 1989.
Stroumsa, Gedaliahu A. G. *Another Seed: Studies in Gnostic Mythology*. Nag Hammadi Studies 24. Leiden: Brill, 1984.
Stylianopoulos, Theodore. *Justin Martyr and the Mosaic Law*. SBL Dissertation Series 20. Missoula: Scholars, 1975.
Suggs, M. Jack. *Wisdom, Christology, and Law in Matthew's Gospel*. Cambridge: Harvard University Press, 1970.
Suh, Jung Woon. *Church and Mission*. Seoul: Tyrannous, 1990.
Tacitus. *Historiae*. In *Tacitus in Five Volumes*, vol. 3, translated by C. H. Moore and J. Jackson. Cambridge: Harvard University Press, 1969.
Talbert, Charles H. *Literary Patterns, Theological Themes, and the Genre of Luke-Acts*. SBL Monograph Series 20. Missoula: Scholars, 1974.
Tannehill, Robert C. "The Disciples in Mark: The Function of a Narrative Role." *JR* 57 (1977) 386–405.
Tashjian, Jirair S. "The Social Setting of the Mission Charge in Q." PhD diss., Claremont Graduate University, 1987.
Taylor, Vincent. *Behind the Third Gospel: A Study of the Proto-Luke Hypothesis*. Oxford: Clarendon, 1926.
———. *Formation of the Gospel Tradition*. London: Macmillan, 1953.
———. *The Gospels: A Short Introduction*. London: Epworth, 1930/1950.
Thackeray, H. St. J., et al., eds. *Josephus*. 10 vols. London: Heinemann, 1926–1965.
Theissen, Gerd. *Biblical Faith: An Evolutionary Approach*. Philadelphia: Fortress, 1985.
———. *The Gospels in Context: Social and Political History in the Synoptic Tradition*. Translated by Linda M. Maloney, *Lokalkolorit und Zeitgeschichte in den Evangelien*. Minneapolis: Fortress, 1991.
———. "Itinerant Radicalism: The Tradition of Jesus Sayings from the Perspective of the the Sociology of Literature." Translated by A. Wire. *Radical Religion* 2 (1976).
Thompson, J. A. *The Book of Jeremiah*. NICOT. Grand Rapids: Eerdmans, 1980.
Tischendorf, C. *Novum Testamentum Graece*. Leipzig: Giesecke & Devrient, 1869.
Tödt, Heinz Eduard. *Der Menschensohn in der synoptischen Überlieferung*. English translation by Dorothea M. Barton, *The Son of Man in the Synoptic Tradition*. Philadelphia: Westminster, 1963, 1965.
Tomson, Peter J. *Paul and the Jewish Law: Halakha in the Letters of the Apostle to the Gentiles*. Philadelphia: Fortress, 1990.
Tomson, Peter J., and Doris Lambers-Petry, eds. *The Image of the Judaeo-Christians in Ancient Jewish and Christian Literature*. Wissenschaftliche Untersuchungen zum Neuen Testamentum 158. Tübingen: Morh Siebeck, 2003.
Torrey, C. C. *The Lives of the Prophets*. SBLMS 1. Philadelphia: Society of Biblical Literature and Exegesis, 1946.
Trautmann, Maria. *Zeichenhafte Handlungen Jesu: Ein Beitrag zur Frage nach dem geschichtlichen Jesus*. Forschung zur Bible 37. Würzburg: Echter, 1980.
Trible, P. *God and the Rhetoric of Sexuality*. Philadelphia: Fortress, 1978.
Tuckett, Christopher M. "The Christology of Luke-Acts." In *The Unity of Luke-Acts*, edited by J. Verheyden, 133–64. Leuven: Leuven University Press, 1999.

———. *Nag Hammadi and the Gospel tradition: Synoptic Tradition in the Nag Hammadi Library*. Edinburgh: T. & T. Clark, 1986.

———. *Q and the History of Early Christianity: Studies on Q*. Edinburgh: T. & T. Clark, 1996.

———. "Q, the Law and Judaism." In *Law and Religion: Essays on the Place of the Law in Israel and Early Christianity by Members of the Ehrhardt Seminar of Manchester University*, edited by Barnabas Lindars, 90–101. Cambridge: James Clarke, 1988.

———. *The Revival of the Griesbach Hypothesis: An Analysis and Appraisal*. Cambridge: Cambridge University Press, 1983.

———. "Synoptic Tradition in the Didache." In *The New Testament in Early Christianity / La réception des écrits néo-testamentaires dans le chritianisme primitive*, edited by Jean-Marie Sevrin, 197–230. Bibliotheca Ephemeridum theologicarum Lovaniensium 86. Leuven: Leuven University Press, 1989.

Turner, John D. "The Book of Thomas." In *The Nag Hammadi Scriptures*, edited by Marvin Meyer. New York: Harper Collins, 2007.

———. *The Book of Thomas the Contender*. SBLDS 23. Missoula: Scholars, 1970.

Turner, Max M. B. "The Sabbath, Sunday, and the Law in Luke/Acts." In Carson, *From Sabbath to Lord's Day*, 99–158.

Tyson, J. B. "The Gentile Mission and the Authority of Scripture in Acts." *NTS* 33 (1987) 619–31.

———. "Scripture, Torah, and Sabbath in Luke-Acts." In *Jesus, the Gospels, and the Church: Essays in Honor of William R. Farmer*, edited by E. P. Sanders, 89–104. Macon: Mercer University Press, 1987.

Urbach, Ephraim E. "Self-Isolation or Self-Affirmation in Judaism in the First Three Centuries: Theory and Practice." In *Jewish and Christian Self-Definition*, vol. 2, *Aspects of Judaism in the Graeco-Roman Period*, edited by E. P. Sanders et al., 269–98. Philadelphia: Fortress, 1981.

Uro, Risto. *Sheep among the Wolves: A Study on the Mission Instructions of Q*. Helsinki: Suomalainen Tiedeakatemia, 1987.

Vaage, Leif E. "Composite Texts and Oral Myths: The Case of the 'Sermon' (6:20b-49)." *SBL Seminar Chapters 28*, edited by David J. Lull, 424–39. Atlanta: Scholars, 1989.

———. "Ethics: 'Love Your Enemies'-Strategies of Resistance (6:27–34)." In *Galilean Upstarts: Jesus' First Followers according to Q*, 40–54. Pennsylvania: Trinity International, 1994.

———. "Q: The Ethos and Ethic of an Itinerant Intelligence." PhD diss., Claremont University, 1987.

VanderKam, J. C. "The Book of Jubilees." In *Outside the Old Testament*, edited by M. de Jonge. Cambridge: Cambridge University Press, 1985.

———. *Textual and Historical Studies in the Book of Jubilees*. Missoula: Scholars, 1977.

Van Goudoever. J. *Biblical Worship in the Earliest Centuries of the Christian Church*. Philadelphia: Westminster, 1968.

Varneda, Père Villalba I. *The Historical Method of Flavius Josepus*. Leiden: Brill, 1986.

Vassiliadis, Petros. "The Nature and Extent of the Q Document." *Novum Testamentum* 20 (1978) 49–73. Reprinted in ΛΟΓΟΙ ΙΗΣΟΥ: *Studies in Q*, 39–59. Atlanta: Scholars, 1999.

Vermes, Geza. *The Dead Sea Scrolls: Qumran in Perspective*. Philadelphia: Fortress, 1981.

———. *The Dead Sea Scrolls in English*. Sheffield: Sheffield Academic, 1987.

———. *Jesus the Jew*. London: SCM, 1983.

———. *The Religion of Jesus the Jew*. Minneapolis: Fortress, 1993.

Verseput, D. J. "Paul's Mission to the Gentiles Is Confirmed by the Jewish Church: Gal 2.1–10." *NTS* 39 (1993) 44–58.

Vögtle, A. "Die Einladung zum grossen Gastmahl und zum königlichen Hochzeitsmahl." In *Das Evangelium und die Evangelien*, 171–218. Düsseldorf: Patmos, 1971.

Von Rad, Gerhard. *Genesis*. OTL. Translated by J. H. Marks and J. Bowden. London: SCM, 1972.

———. "There Remains Still a Rest for the People of God." In *The Problem of the Hexateuch and Other Essays*. New York: McGraw-Hill, 1966.

Voss, B. R. *Der Dialog in der fr€uhchristlichen Literatur*. Munich: Fink, 1970.

Vouga, François. *Jésus et la loi: Selon la tradition synoptique*. Genève: Labor et Fides, 1988.

Warren, David H., et al., eds. *Early Christian Voices: In Texts, Traditions, and Symbols; Essays in Honor of François Bovon*. Biblical Interpretation 66. Leiden: Brill, 2003.

Watson, Alan. *Jesus and the Law*. Athens: University of Georgia Press, 1996.

Watson, Francis. *Paul, Judaism and the Gentiles: A Sociology Approach*. Cambridge: Cambridge University Press, 1986.

Watts, J. D. W. *Isaiah 1–33*. WBC 24. Waco, TX: Word, 1972.

Weaver, Dorothy Jean. *Matthew's Missionary Discourse: A Literacy Critical Analysis*. JSNT Supplement Series 38. Sheffield: Sheffield Academic, 1990.

Wedderburn, Alexander J. M. *A History of the First Christians*. New York: T. & T. Clark International, 2004.

Weeden, Theodore J. *Mark: Traditions in Conflicts*. Philadelphia: Fortress, 1971.

Wefald, Eric K. "The Separate Gentile Mission in Mark: A Narrative Explanation of Markan Geography, the Two Feeding Accounts and Exorcisms." *JSNT* 60 (1995) 3–26.

Wegner, Uwe. *Der Hauptmann von Kafarnaum (Mt 7,28a; 8,5–10.13 par Lk 7,1–10): Ein Beitrag zur Q-Forschung*. Tübingen: Mohr Siebeck, 1985.

Weiss, Bernard. *Das Matthäus-Evangelium*. Göttingen: Vandenhoeck und Ruprecht, 1898.

———. *Das Matthäusevangelium und seine Lucas-Parallelen*. Halle: Waisenhaus, 1876.

———. *Die Evangelien des Markus und Lukas*. Göttingen: Vandenhoeck und Ruprecht, 1901.

———. *Die Quellen der synoptischen Überlieferung*. Leipzig: Hingischs'sche Buchhandlung, 1908.

———. *Die Quellen des Lukasevangelium*. Stuttgart und Berlin: Cotta'sche Buchhandlung Nachfolger, 1907.

Weiss, Herald. "The Sabbath in the Synoptic Gospel." *JSNT* 38 (1990) 13–27.

Weinrich, Harald. *Sprache in Texten*. Stuttgart: Kohlhammer, 1976.

Weinreich, O. *Antike Heilungswunder*. Giessen, 1909.

Welch, Adam C. *The Book of Jeremiah*. London: National Adult School Union, 1928.

Wellhausen, Julius. *Das Evangelium Lucae*. Berlin: Reimer, 1904.

———. *Einleitung in drei ersten Evangelien*. Berlin: Reimer, 1911.

Wenham, G. *The Book of Leviticus*. NICOT. Grand Rapids: Eerdmans, 1979.

———. *Genesis 1–15*. Word Biblical Commentary 1. Waco: Word, 1987.

Wernle, Paul. *Die synoptische Frage*. Tübingen: Mohr Siebeck, 1899.

Westcott, B. F., and F. J. A. Hort. "Notes on Select Readings." Appendix 1 in *The New Testament in the Original Greek*, 1–140. New York: Harper, 1882.

Westerholm, Stephen. *Jesus and Scribal Authority*. Coniectanea Biblica New Testament Series 10. Lund: Gleerup, 1978.

Westermann, Clause. *Das Buch Jessaja: Kapitel 40–66*. ATD 19. Göttingen: Vandenhoeck & Ruprecht, 1966.

———. *Genesis 1–11*. BK 1. Neukirchen-Vluyn: Neukirchener, 1966.

Wilken, Robert L. *Aspects of Wisdom in Judaism and Early Christianity*. Notre Dame: University of Notre Dame Press, 1975.

———. *The Christians as the Romans Saw Them*. New Haven: Yale University Press, 1984.

Wilkinson, John. "The Case of the Bent Woman in Luke 13:10–17." *English Quarterly* 49 (1977) 195–205.

Williamson, H. G. M. *Ezra, Nehemiah*. WBC 16. Waco, TX: Word, 1985.

Williamson, Ronald. *Jews in the Hellenistic World: Philo*. Cambridge Commentaries on Writings of the Jewish and Christian World 200 BC to AD 200. Cambridge: Cambridge University Press, 1989.

Wilson, R. McL. *Gnosis and the New Testament*. Philadelphia: Fortress, 1968.

Wilson, Stephen G. *The Gentiles and the Gentile Mission in Luke-Acts*. Cambridge: Cambridge University Press, 1973.

———. *Luke and the Law*. Cambridge: Cambridge University Press, 1983.

———. *Related Strangers: Jews and Christians 70–170 CE*. Minneapolis: Fortress, 1995.

Wilt, Timothy. "Translation and Communication." In *Bible Translation: Frames of Reference*, edited by T. Wilt, 27–80. Manchester: St. Jerome, 2003.

Winston, David. *The Wisdom of Solomon*. New York: Doubleday, 1979.

Wintermute, O. S. "Jubilees." In *The Old Testament Pseudepigrapha*, vol. 2, edited by J. H. Charlesworth. London: Darton, Longman & Todd, 1985.

Wise, Michael, et al., eds. *Dead Sea Scrolls: A New Translation*. San Francisco: HarperSanFrancisco, 1996.

Wolfson, Harry Austryn. *Philo: Foundations of Religious Philosophy in Judaism, Christianity, and Islam*. 2 vols. Cambridge: Harvard University Press, 1947; repr., 1962.

Wong, Kun-Chun. "The Matthean Understanding of the Sabbath: A Response to Graham N. Stanton." *JSNT* 44 (1991) 3–18.

Woods, Edward J. *The "Finger of God" and Pneumatology in Luke-Acts*. JSNTSS 205. Sheffield: Sheffield Academic, 2001.

Wright, R. B. "Psalms of Solomon: A New Tradition and Introduction." In *The Old Testament Pseudepigrapha*, edited by James M. Charlesworth, vol. 2. New York: Doubleday, 1985.

Yamauchi, Edwin M. *Pre-Christian Gnosticism: A Survey of the Proposed Evidences*. Grand Rapids: Eerdmans, 1973.

Yang, Yong-Eui. *Jesus and the Sabbath in Matthew's Gospel*. JSNT Supplement Series 139. Sheffield: Sheffield Academic, 1997.

Yonge, C. D., trans. *The Works of Philo: Complete and Unabridged New Updated Version*. Peabody: Hendrickson, 1993.

Zahavy, Tzvee. "The Sabbath Code of Damascus Document X, 14–XI, 18: Form Analytical and Redaction Critical Observations." *Revue de Qumran* 40 (1981) 589–91.

Zeitlin, S. "The Book of Jubilees: Its Character and Its Significance." *Jewish Quarterly Review* 30 (1939).

Zeller, Dieter. "Das Logion Mt 8,11f/Lk 13,28f und das Motiv der 'Völkerwallfahrt.'" *Biblische Zeitschrift* 15 (1971) 222–37; 16 (1972) 84–93.

———. *Kommentar zur Logienquelle*. Stuttgart: Katholisches Bibelwerk, 1984.

Zetterbolm, Magnus. *The Formation of Christianity in Antioch: A Social-Scientific Approach to the Separation between Judaism and Christianity*. New York: Routledge, 2003.

Zimmerli, W. *Ezechiel*. BK 13. Neukirchen-Vluyn: Neukirchener, 1969.